MARRIAGES AND FAMILIES

MARRIAGES AND FAMILIES
Diversity and Change

MARY ANN SCHWARTZ
Northeastern Illinois University

BARBARA MARLIENE SCOTT
Northeastern Illinois University

PRENTICE HALL, Englewood Cliffs, New Jersey 07632

Library of Congress Cataloging-in-Publication Data

SCHWARTZ, MARY ANN.
   Marriages and families: diversity and change/Mary Ann Schwartz,
BarBara Marliene Scott.
     p. cm.
   Includes bibliographical references and index.
   ISBN 0-13-818550-6
   1. Marriage—United States.   2. Family—United States. I. Scott,
BarBara Marliene. II. Title.
HQ536.S39 1994
306.8'0973—dc20

93-5383
CIP

Acquisitions editor: Nancy Roberts
Development editor: Robert Weiss
Cover and interior design: Jerry Votta
Art director: Anne Bonanno
Marketing manager: Maria DiVencenzo
Copy editor: Carole Brown
Production coordinator: Mary Ann Gloriande
Associate editor: Sharon Chambliss
Editorial assistant: Pat Naturale
Photo researcher: Ilene Cherna Bellovin
Photo editor: Lori Morris-Nantz
Cover art: (Collage of modern families—clockwise from top): Elyse Lewin/The Image Bank;
   Elaine Sulle/The Image Bank; Art Kane/The Image Bank; Ann Purcell/Photo Researchers;
   Stephen Marks/The Image Bank; (Background montage on front and back covers): Garry Gay/
   The Image Bank.
Editorial/production supervision and electronic page makeup: Rob DeGeorge

©1994 by Prentice-Hall, Inc.
A Paramount Communications Company
Englewood Cliffs, New Jersey 07632

Printed in the United States of America

10 9 8 7 6 5 4 3 2 1

ISBN 0-13-818550-6

PRENTICE-HALL INTERNATIONAL (UK) LIMITED, *London*
PRENTICE-HALL OF AUSTRALIA PTY. LIMITED, *Sydney*
PRENTICE-HALL CANADA INC., *Toronto*
PRENTICE-HALL HISPANOAMERICANA, S.A., *Mexico*
PRENTICE-HALL OF INDIA PRIVATE LIMITED, *New Delhi*
PRENTICE-HALL OF JAPAN, INC., *Tokyo*
SIMON & SCHUSTER ASIA PTE. LTD., *Singapore*
EDITORA PRENTICE-HALL DO BRASIL, Ltda., *Rio de Janeiro*

We dedicate this book to our marital partners, our families, friends, students, and teachers, whose collective wisdom, love, and, most of all, good humor made this book possible.

BRIEF CONTENTS

CONTENTS

Chapter 10

Childbearing and Parenting   265

Chapter 11

Evolving Work and Family Structures   295

Chapter 12

Violence and Abuse   321

Chapter 13

The Process of Uncoupling: Divorce in the United States   347

Chapter 14

Remarriage and Remarried Families   375

BOXES

APPLYING THE SOCIOLOGICAL IMAGINATION

CRITICAL ISSUES

GLOBAL PERSPECTIVES

FOR YOUR INFORMATION

PERSONAL REFLECTION

PREFACE

Our decision to write this text originated from our discussions of student reactions to our courses on marriage and family life. Repeatedly we found that although students are keenly interested in how marriages and families function, they often have little knowledge of marriages and families in earlier periods of U.S. history. Without a historical perspective, students have difficulty interpreting the changes that are occurring around them in marriages and families. Additionally, much of the information students have acquired regarding marriage and family life reflects a white, middle-class orientation. Consequently, they often view marriages and families in a monolithic and idealized form. Thus, the plural usage in the title of this book, *Marriages and Families*, is deliberate and is intended to dispel the popular notion that there exists a single and correct family form. The inclusion of historical, cross-racial, cross-cultural, and feminist perspectives throughout the text is aimed at helping students understand how the structured relationships of race, class, and gender affect the many ways in which people experience marriage and family life.

Our objectives in writing this book are fourfold: (1) to help students recognize and understand the dynamic nature of marriages, families, and intimate relationships; (2) to enable students to recognize, con-

front, and dispel prominent myths about marriages, families, and intimate relationships; (3) to help students see the interactive relationships of race, class, and gender; and (4) to encourage an informed openness in student attitudes that will empower them to make informed choices and decisions in their own marriage, family, and intimate relationships. To accomplish these goals we have emphasized two key themes throughout the text: change and diversity.

CHANGE

Although many of us quietly accept the fact that societies undergo technological changes over time, we often have difficulty acknowledging that marriages and families are also subject to change and always have been. For example, over the last several decades the number of people living in family households, particularly in "traditional" nuclear families, has declined; high divorce and remarriage rates have led to changes in family forms, increasing the numbers of single parents and stepfamilies; different fertility rates and patterns of immigration have increased the proportion of families of color in the total population.

Marriages and families are heavily affected by the organizational demands and arrangements of the larger society. Economic and political forces have always created an array of both problems and opportunities for U.S. families. In each historical period, the nature and structure of family life have reflected the impact of these forces on individuals and groups. How we respond to these forces in the present will have far-reaching consequences for the organization and structure of marriages and families in the future.

New communication technologies rapidly disseminate information about marriages and families, making us far more aware of changes than previous generations were. Yet although we are increasingly aware (often from our own personal experiences) that families are somehow different today than in the past, we are not always sure exactly how, when, and why these changes have occurred, nor are we necessarily pleased with all of the ways in which families have changed. We hear conflicting messages about these changes. Some people interpret these changes as a decline in family values, indeed, in the family itself. Other people reject this line of thought, seeing the changes as simply the diversification of families. Frequently, these changes are viewed ahistorically and within frameworks that reflect widespread myths about an idealized family form.

In addition, issues germane to marriages and families are now debated in public arenas, including the highest U.S. courts. The politicization of issues such as abortion and the reproductive rights of women; the high separation and divorce rates; the increasing numbers of children born outside legal marriages, particularly to teenagers; lesbian and gay unions; family violence; the feminization of poverty; AIDS; and homelessness has generated numerous social-policy initiatives, many of which are discussed in this text. Although there are no simple resolutions to these issues, it is important that we engage in a critical evaluation of the policies proposed for dealing with them.

DIVERSITY

Changes in the racial and ethnic composition of the U.S. population have focused our nation's attention on diversity. Although some dimensions of this issue are new, a historical review quickly shows that throughout U.S. history marriages and families have taken many diverse forms. A focus on structured relationships such as race, class, and gender allows us to see how marriages and families are experienced differently by different categories of people. In this text we have made a special effort to treat this diversity in an integrative manner. Thus, we have no separate chapters on class or families of color. Instead, when marriage and family experiences are differentiated by race, class, or gender, these differences are integrated into the discussion of specific experiences. Two examples will illustrate this point. First, although the vast majority of all Americans will eventually marry, the marriage rate is lower for some groups than for others. White females are more likely to marry than black females, who are confronted with an increasing shortage of black men of comparable age and education. Second, although both women and men suffer from the dissolution of their marriages through divorce or death, gender also differentiates those experiences in important ways. The most striking difference is an economic one: The standard of living improves for men but declines for women.

It is not always easy to discuss diversity, partly because our thinking about diversity is itself diverse. One of the first issues we face in discussing diversity is language: What are the appropriate designations to use to refer to different groups at this point in time? Names are often controversial and reflect a power struggle over who has the right or authority to name. Not surprisingly, those in positions of power historically have assumed that right and authority. As the "named" groups themselves become more powerful and vocal, however, they often challenge the naming process and insist on designations they believe more clearly express their sense of their own identity. For example, people with mixed ancestry are currently striving to achieve official recognition of a biracial or multiracial category on U.S. Census and other government forms.

Although there is no unanimity on these matters even among members of the same group, some terms have emerged as preferred terms. Thus, for example, *Latino* is preferred to *Hispanic*, *Native American* is preferred to *American Indian*, *lesbian* and *gay* are preferred to *homosexual*, and *African American* is preferred to *black*. Throughout this text we try to be consistent in using the preferred terms. When we make specific comparisons by race, however, we use the terms *black* and *white* for ease of presentation. In addition, we have consciously avoided using the term *minority group* to refer to racial and ethnic groups in our society. Instead, we use the term *people of color*. Although this term is not problem-free, it avoids an implicit assumption in the term *minority* that groups so designated are not part of the dominant culture in terms of shared values and aspirations.

PEDAGOGY: READER INVOLVEMENT

Marriages and Families: Diversity and Change is intended as a text that challenges students to become involved in a direct way in examining their personal belief systems as well as societal views of the many forms that marriages and families have taken in the past and are taking in the present. Based on over 40 years of combined teaching experience, we have found that a course on the sociology of marriages and families almost always invokes concern and interest among students regarding how the general principles and descriptions of marriages and families in a given textbook apply to and are similar to or different from their own personal experiences. Thus, throughout the process of writing this book we have utilized an innovative, sensitive, and inclusive approach to writing about and understanding marriages and families. We use a sociological and feminist/womanist perspective, encouraging the application of the sociological imagination to everyday life. In this context we focus on the link between social structure and our personal experiences of marriages, families, and intimate relationships. That is, we examine how cultural values; historical context; economic and political changes; and structured relationships of race, class, gender, sexual orientation, and age interact and affect individuals and groups as they create, sustain, and change their various intimate relationships. There are many benefits to using a sociological approach to study marriages and families. Most important, such an approach enables us to understand the constraints and opportunities that affect our lives and those of other people, thereby positioning us to make more discriminating and successful decisions and exercise greater control over our lives.

Several pedagogical strategies have been included to facilitate students' involvement in understanding marriages and families and to empower them to make intelligent lifestyle decisions.

CHAPTER OPENER

Each chapter begins with a brief vignette of a real-life or hypothetical situation. These vignettes invite the readers to think about the issues to be covered in that chapter along with their own values, expectations, and experiences relevant to that situation. For example, in Chapter 13 we introduce Bill and Terry, whose friends and families regarded them as an ideal couple. Yet 2 months before their fifteenth wedding anniversary they were divorced. Students are asked to consider what went wrong in Bill and Terry's relationship and in so many others today.

KEY TERMS

The important terms and concepts that help us understand and analyze marriages and families are boldfaced and defined in the text. The key terms are also listed at the end of each chapter and defined in the glossary at the end of the book as a way of facilitating the study and review process.

CHAPTER QUESTIONS

Throughout the text students will find a shaded question mark that asks them to apply the material in the chapter to their own experiences and to evaluate critically aspects of interpersonal relationships.

CONTENT BOXES

In each chapter students will find boxed inserts to enrich their study of marriages and families. Five different types of boxes are located throughout the text.

APPLYING THE SOCIOLOGICAL IMAGINATION The content of these boxes challenges students to use a sociological perspective in analyzing aspects of marriages and families. It requires students to see the relationship between personal behavior and how society is organized and structured. For example, in Chapter 1 students are asked to identify an aspect of their own biography (race, class, gender, age, or marital status) and to transport themselves to an earlier period of history to see what their life would have been like had they lived during that period. Other boxes in this category examine contemporary marriage and family situations.

CRITICAL ISSUES   These boxes illustrate the complexity of many unresolved social issues concerning marriage and family life. For example, Chapter 9 focuses on reproduction and the parenting decision. A critical issue has arisen in this regard about who should have custody over a couple's stored frozen embryos should the couple divorce. Many of the new reproductive technologies raise questions about the meaning of parenthood. Critical Issues boxes contain a series of critical-thinking questions that require students to evaluate their own feeling about these issues.

PERSONAL REFLECTIONS   The Personal Reflection boxes offer students an opportunity to assess their own feelings and beliefs regarding interpersonal relationships and related behaviors. For example, in Chapter 4 students have an opportunity to discover their own style of loving and to compare it with other styles. On the basis of this self-knowledge, they may be satisfied with their present style, or they may decide to alter it.

GLOBAL PERSPECTIVE   Because we are so immersed in our own culture, we sometime assume that our way of doing things is the "natural" or "right" way. The Global Perspective boxes challenge this assumption and offer insight into the diverse structures and functions found in marriages and families around the globe. For example, in Chapter 10, we compare some of the differences between U.S. and Japanese parenting styles.

FOR YOUR INFORMATION (FYI)   FYI boxes are intended to provide students with additional information on key topics. For example, in Chapter 14 we provide information on the Stepfamily Association of America, a support group for stepfamilies.

END-OF-CHAPTER STUDY AIDES

At the end of each chapter students will find a summary of the chapter's main points, a list of key terms, a set of questions for study and discussion, and suggestions for further reading. The chapter summary and key terms are designed to facilitate a quick review of the material in the text. The study questions and suggested readings are to help students stretch their understanding of marriages and families beyond the contents of this textbook.

APPENDICES

The appendices included at the back of the book supplement the text's sociological discussion of key aspects of relationships by providing technical information on sexual anatomy (Appendix A), sexually transmitted diseases (Appendix B), conception and pregnancy (Appendix C), abortion techniques (Appendix D), methods of birth control (Appendix E), and state marriage and divorce laws (Appendix F).

KEEPING A JOURNAL

It has been our experience in teaching that when students keep a journal in which they react to the material in the text, two positive things are likely to happen. First, they retain the information for longer periods of time. Second, they become more adept at applying sociological insights to their own experiences. Thus, we encourage all users to write regularly in a journal. They may simply want to record their reactions to what they are reading, or they may want to respond directly to the questions developed throughout the text and at the end of each chapter. The final chapter provides structured exercises to assist students in making their own life choices and in writing their own marital or relationship script.

SUPPLEMENTS

Instructors who use our textbook have access to a number of materials specially designed to complement the classroom lectures and activities and enhance the students' learning experiences. The major supplements are described below.

INSTRUCTOR'S RESOURCE MANUAL   This manual provides learning objectives, chapter outlines, teaching tips, suggestions for classroom activities, questions for class discussion or written assignments, an integrative supplements guide, and lists of audiovisual and software resources. It also provides a guide to the use of the ABC News/Prentice Hall Video Library.

TEST ITEM FILE This test bank contains approximately 1600 multiple-choice, true–false, and essay questions. Questions are page-referenced to the text.

PRENTICE HALL TEST MANAGER For use on either IBM or Macintosh computers, this computerized test item file streamlines the test-design process, allowing instructors to create customized exams easily.

 ABC NEWS/PRENTICE HALL VIDEO LIBRARY: MARRIAGES AND FAMILIES, SERIES I AND II This collection of video segments from such award-winning ABC News programs as "Nightline," "20/20," and "American Agenda" brings chapter concepts to life by demonstrating their application to significant issues of current interest. Suggestions for relating specific segments to particular chapters and topics are offered in the Instructor's Resource Manual.

 NEW YORK TIMES SUPPLEMENT *The New York Times* and Prentice Hall are sponsoring *Themes of the Times*: a program designed to enhance student access to current information of relevance in the classroom.

Through this program, the core subject matter provided in the text is supplemented by a collection of time-sensitive articles from one of the world's most distinguished newspapers, *The New York Times*. These articles demonstrate the vital, ongoing connection between what is learned in the classroom and what is happening in the world around us.

To enjoy the wealth of information of *The New York Times* daily, a reduced subscription rate is available. For information, call toll-free: 1-800-631-1222.

Prentice Hall and *The New York Times* are proud to co-sponsor *Themes of the Times*. We hope it will make the reading of both textbooks and newspapers a more dynamic, involving process.

TRANSPARENCY MASTERS Taken from tables, graphs, and charts in the text and from other sources as well, these transparency masters offer an effective means of amplifying lecture topics.

STUDY GUIDE This student guide offers chapter outlines and summaries, definitions of key concepts, self-tests, and applied exercises for each chapter.

ACKNOWLEDGMENTS

Although we refer to this book as ours, we recognize that such an endeavor can never singularly be attributed to the authors. As with any such project, its success required the assistance of many people from many different parts of our lives. Our interaction with students both within and outside the classroom has obviously contributed to this book in significant ways. Many of the pedagogical aids such as the boxes and some of the examples grew out of student questions, responses, and presentations in our classrooms as well as out of applied exercises that we have found to be most useful in presenting marriage and family issues and concerns.

We received invaluable support and assistance from copy editors, proofreaders, and other staff at Prentice Hall. We owe a particular debt of gratitude and thanks to Nancy Roberts, our acquisitions editor, for sharing our vision of the type of marriage and family text that we have written and having the faith in us to entrust us with the responsibility and opportunity to actualize that vision. Mere words cannot express our gratitude to Robert Weiss, our development editor, whose professionalism, patience, and endurance was a major factor in our completing this project. He taught us many things about the elements necessary to produce the quality textbook that we desired. Rob DeGeorge, our production editor, skillfully guided the book into print. His encouragement throughout the process made our task easier. Jerry Votta, our designer, is largely responsible for the attractive and accessible appearance of the book. We also thank Lori Morris-Nantz and Ilene Cherna Bellovin for an outstanding job of photo selection.

The timely, thoughtful, and extensive reactions to, suggestions for, and critical review of our prospectus and of each chapter of the book are greatly appreciated and have certainly helped us avoid major mistakes and weaknesses while enhancing our ability to draw on the strengths of the book. These reviewers are Barbara Arrighi-Merz, Northern Kentucky University; Diane Beeson, California State University–Hayward; Paul Brezina, County College at Morris; Jerry Clavner, Cuyahoga Community College; John M. Deaton,

Northland Pioneer College; Henry Fischer, Millersville University; Margaret Gittis, Youngstown State University; Elizabeth Grauerholz, Purdue University; Stephen Hall, Appalachian State University; Richard Higgenbotham, Northeastern Illinois University; Robert R. Higgins, Oakland Community College; Ross Klein, Memorial University; Dan Klenow, North Dakota State University; Phyllis Kuehnl, University of Dayton; Elise S. Lake, University of Mississippi; Joseph J. Leon, California State Polytechnic University–Pomona; Linda Lindsey, Maryville College–St. Louis; Doug Loisel, Citrus College; Jerry B. Michel, Memphis State University; Richard B. Miller, Missouri Southern State College; Brenda Phillips, Texas Woman's University; Phil Piket, Joliet Junior College; Margaret E. Preble, Thomas Nelson Community College; Gerald Scott, Southeast Missouri State University; Edward J. Silva, El Paso Community College; K. S. Thompson, Northern Michigan University; D. Lloyd Thomas, Central Texas College; and Patsy Whitson, Morehead State University.

We also received support and encouragement from the administration at Northeastern Illinois University. During the course of writing this book we both received sabbatical leaves that enabled us to devote the time and care necessary to research and write this book. We are especially appreciative of the strong support provided by our colleagues in the sociology department and for the diligent efforts of our work-study students—Rudolph C. Collum, Jr.; James Lalinde; and Maheen Siddiqui—who assisted in the preparation of the bibliography and glossary.

We wish to acknowledge and thank our marriages and families (nuclear, extended, blended, and fictive) for their love, understanding, and support throughout all of those days when our time, attention, and behavior were dedicated to this book at the expense of our time, attention, and activities with them. Now that we have finished they are as proud as we are, and rightfully so. This book is as much theirs as ours; its completion is due in large part to their understanding and the sacrifices they made to facilitate our writing this book. We thank our parents, Helen and Charles Schwartz, and Lillian and Robert Johnson, for their loving support throughout our lives. Our partners, Richard and Roger, gave us their unconditional support and contributed to partnerships that were critical to our meeting our various demands and deadlines. In addition, we acknowledge our children Jason; Roger, Jr.; Dionne; and granddaughter Courtney for their unwavering love, patience, and understanding when our work forced us to miss family gatherings. We thank them all especially for providing us with continuing opportunities for the exploration and understanding of marriage and family life.

Last, but certainly not least, we wish to acknowledge and thank each other. This book has been a joint effort in every sense of the word. Although either of us individually could have written a marriage and family text, neither of us could have written this textbook alone. We have always valued each other's skills, perspective, and experiences, but this collaborative effort has given us a new appreciation and respect for each other. We also learned much, firsthand, about diversity and the impact of race on various intimate relationships. In the process, we learned a great deal about a particular type of intimate relationship, one based on love, respect, commitment, understanding, tolerance, and compassion: namely, friendship.

ABOUT
THE
AUTHORS

Dr. Mary Ann Schwartz is professor of sociology and women's studies at Northeastern Illinois University. Her research and teaching interests focus on marriages and families; socialization; nonmarital lifestyles; work; aging; and the structured relationships of race, class, and gender.

Dr. BarBara M. Scott is assistant professor of sociology and women's studies at Northeastern Illinois University. Her research and teaching interests focus on marriages and families, particularly African-American families; race, class, and gender; institutionalized racism and inequality; images and the social construction of knowledge in the mass media; and African-American women.

MARRIAGES AND FAMILIES

Chapter 1

MARRIAGES AND FAMILIES OVER TIME

Becky is a cheerful, outgoing 6-year-old who lives with her mother, June, and her mother's boyfriend, Bill. Becky's parents were divorced when she was a baby, and she rarely sees her biological father, who has remarried and lives in another state. Her mother alone cared for her until about 3 years ago, when they moved in with Bill, also divorced. He and June met at work and saw each other socially for about a year before they decided to live together. They worked out a mutually satisfying agreement for sharing expenses, housework, and child care. Neither is eager to remarry at this point, as both went through emotionally difficult divorces, and the idea of another marriage is frightening to them both.

Because Bill has the more flexible work schedule, he took Becky to school the first day and came by to pick her up. He was surprised to find that she had little to say on the way home. When he asked her about what happened at school, she started to cry and ran away from him. When June calmed Becky down, she discovered that a neighbor's child had told Becky that she came from a broken home, that Bill was not her Dad, and that she didn't live in a real family.

Why was Becky so upset by this teasing? If you were June or Bill, how would you handle this situation? What would you tell Becky about the meaning of family? Would you bring the situation to the attention of Becky's teacher? Your neighbor?

Marriage and family are among the oldest human social institutions. An **institution** refers to patterns of behavior that are built around basic needs of individuals and society and that tend to persist over time. Institutions represent the organized aspects of human social existence that are established and reinforced over time by the various norms and values of a particular group or society. The family, and marriage as a process that generates it, exists in some form in all societies. Families are created by human beings in an attempt to meet certain basic individual and social needs such as survival and growth. Although historically marriage and family have been considered the most important institutions in human society, we have created many other important institutions: education, government, economic, religious, and legal.

CONTEMPORARY DEFINITIONS OF MARRIAGES AND FAMILIES

Because all of us belong to some sort of family and have observed marriages (including our parents' and maybe our own), we probably think we know exactly what the terms *marriage* and *family* mean. Although *marriage* and *family* go hand in hand, they are not one and the same. You might ask, then, exactly what are they? Take a few minutes to jot down your perceptions, definitions, and ideas about each of these institutions. How did you define them? Not surprisingly, many of your definitions and images of mar-

riages and families are based on the myth of the white middle-class family of husband, wife, and 2.2 children that is relentlessly portrayed in reruns of 1950s family sitcoms. This pattern is far from typical today, however. More accurate definitions of marriages and families must take into account the many different forms of marriages and families that have existed historically and still exist today, both in the United States and in other countries and cultures.

WHAT IS MARRIAGE?

Marriage has been defined in the United States as a legal contract between a woman and a man who are at or above a specified age and who are not already legally married to someone else. Although some people still regard this definition as adequate, increasing numbers of scholars and laypersons alike consider it too narrow. By focusing on the legal aspect of marriage alone it excludes a variety of relationships such as some heterosexual and homosexual cohabitive relationships that function in much the same way as legally sanctioned marriages, albeit without the same legal protection. Thus, we utilize a more encompassing and reality-based definition of **marriage** as a union between people (whether widely or legally recognized or not) that unites partners sexually, socially, and economically; that is relatively consistent over time; and that accords each member certain agreed-upon rights.

TYPES OF MARRIAGES Marriages across cultures generally have been either monogamous or polygamous. **Monogamy** involves one person married to a person of the other sex. Although legally monogamy refers to heterosexual relationships, any couple can be monogamous if they are committed exclusively to each other sexually and otherwise during the course of the relationship. Monogamy is the legally recognized marriage structure in the United States. In fact, however, over half of all marriages in this country end in divorce, and over three-fourths of divorced people remarry (Martin and Bumpass, 1989). Thus, the U.S. marriage pattern is more accurately classified as **serial monogamy**. Individuals may marry as many times as they like as long as each prior marriage was ended by death or divorce.

In some societies, polygamy is the accepted marriage structure. **Polygamy** is a broad category that refers generally to one person of one sex married to several people of the other sex. It can take one of two forms: **polygyny**, in which one male has two or more wives, and **polyandry**, in which one female has two or more husbands. Although both forms of polygamy are illegal in the United States, some religious groups here routinely practice polygyny. For example, among a dissident Mormon sect in Colorado City, Arizona, the typical household consists of a husband and three or more wives.

A third form of marriage is **cenogamy**, or **group marriage**, in which all of the women and men in a group are simultaneously married to one another. Like polygamy, this form of marriage is also illegal in this country. In the mid 1800s, however, the Oneida Community, a communal group living in New York, practiced cenogamy until they were forced to disband.

WHAT IS A FAMILY?

Like marriage, family, has been defined historically in rigid and restrictive language. For example, the U.S. Bureau of the Census defines a family as two or more persons living together and related by blood, marriage, or adoption. As with the popular definition of marriage, this definition of family is limiting in that it does not take into consideration the considerable diversity found in families. Thus, we define **family** as any relatively stable group of people who are related to one another through blood, marriage, or adoption, or who simply live together, and who provide one another with economic and emotional support. In addition, a family can be a group of people who simply define themselves as family based on feelings of love, respect, commitment, and responsibility to and identification with one another. This concept of family has a subjective element in that it takes into account people's feelings of belonging to a particular group. Thus, communes as well as cohabiting individuals, either of the same or other sex, who identify themselves as a family meet these criteria and can be considered families.

Most Americans, it seems, agree with this broader definition. For example, only 22 percent of those polled in 1989 defined a family exclusively in terms of blood, marriage, or adoption. The overwhelming majority, 74 percent, defined a family as any group of people who love and care for one another (Coontz, 1992).

TYPES OF FAMILIES As with marriages, several types of families are worth noting. The **family of orientation** is the family into which a person is born and raised. This includes, for example, you, your parents, and your siblings, if any. In contrast, when we marry or have an intimate relationship with someone, or have children we create what sociologists call the **family of procreation**. Some of us were born into a **nuclear family** consisting of a mother, father, and siblings. Others were born into an **extended family** consisting of one or both of our parents, our siblings, if any, and other relatives, including grandparents. In both urban and rural areas of the United States a form of the traditional extended family is often evident. That is, in many neighborhoods, especially those with ethnic or poor and working-class groups, a variety of relatives live, not necessarily in the same household, but in very close proximity to one another (upstairs, next-door, down the block, around the corner), interact on a frequent basis, and provide emotional and economic support to one another. Some sociologists have labeled this family form the **modified extended family**.

As you read this book, you will discover that the family mosaic in the United States is not limited to nuclear and extended families. As our definition implies, there is a wide variety of families and, thus, a wide variety of terms to identify them. For example, *voluntarily child-free families* consist of couples who make a conscious decision not to have children. *Single-parent families* consist of one parent and her or his children. Sometimes these families are specifically described as *female-* or *male-headed families*. In either case, legal marriage is not a criterion for family status, as the parent may or may not have been legally married. *Reconstituted, blended,* or *stepfamilies* are formed when a widowed or divorced person remarries, creating a new family that includes the children of one or both spouses. *Lesbian* and *gay families* are composed of individuals of the same sex who live together and identify themselves as a family; these relationships may or may not include natural-born or adopted children.* Traditionally, families in the United States have had a patriarchal structure. A **patriarchal family** is a family in which the male (husband or father) is the head of the family and exercises authority and decision-making power over his wife and children.

RACE, CLASS, AND GENDER

Race, class, and gender are three of the most important social categories of experience for individuals and families in the United States, primarily because they also represent significant and comprehensive systems of oppression. At a very elementary level, we can say that family experiences are shaped by the choices that individual members make. However, the options that families have available to them and, thus, the choices they make are shaped (limited or expanded) by the ways in which race, class, and gender are organized. To fully understand families and how they function we must therefore examine race, class, and gender and explore how these factors have

shaped and continue to shape the experiences of families throughout the United States.

Race, class, and gender are interrelated categories of social experience that affect all aspects of human life, shaping all social institutions and systems of meaning including the institutions of marriage and family, and family values. By "interrelated" we mean that families are not separately affected because of the racial composition of their members, to which is added the influence of their economic situation, after which comes the impact of the gender of their members. Rather, as sociologists Margaret Andersen and Patricia Hill Collins have observed (1992), race, class, and gender are part of the total fabric of experience for *all* families. Although these categories are different aspects of social structure, individual families experience them simultaneously.

Understanding race, class, and gender in this way also allows us to see the interrelationship of other important categories of social experiences such as ethnicity, sexual orientation, age, religion, geographic location, historical context, and physical and mental abilities. Later in this chapter we will see how many of these categories of experience have been interwoven in family form and functioning throughout U.S. history.

FAMILY FUNCTIONS AND THE DEBATE OVER FAMILY VALUES

Historians and the lay public alike have often discussed families in terms of the vital social functions they serve for individuals and the society at large. These functions have included regulation of sexual behavior, reproduction, social placement, socialization, economic cooperation, and the provision of care, protection, and intimacy for family members.

SOCIAL FUNCTIONS OF FAMILIES

REGULATION OF SEXUAL BEHAVIOR Every society is concerned about the sexual behavior of its members. In most societies sexual behavior is regulated and enforced within the context of families. There is no known society where people are free to have sexual relations with whomever they please. Although the **norms**—cultural guidelines or rules of conduct

*We use the terms *lesbian* and *gay* throughout this book to refer individually to homosexual women and men. The term *homosexual* refers to both women and men whose primary emotional and sexual orientation is toward members of their own sex. A large number of homosexual men and women object to being referred to as "homosexuals," feeling that the term, including the cultural attitudes and feelings it invokes, overemphasizes the sexual aspect of their lifestyle. They prefer the terms *lesbian* and *gay*, which encompass all aspects of their individual identity rather than simply their sexual orientation. Although some people commonly refer to both female and male homosexuals as gay, lesbians increasingly reject this term, believing that it more appropriately describes men's experiences and political activities. These women want to reclaim their separate identity and history. Thus, they refer to themselves as lesbians and not gay.

The Todas are a pastoral, polyandrous Indian tribe numbering between 500 and 600 members and living in small villages scattered across the plateau of the Nilgiri Hills in southern India. Toda culture flourished at the end of the nineteenth and the beginning of the twentieth centuries. At that time anthropologists found a classic and durable example of *fraternal polyandry*. A Toda woman married one man and simultaneously became the wife of his brothers. If other brothers were born subsequently, they also shared equally in marital rights. This practice caused little friction or sexual jealousy. When all the members lived in one household and one of the brothers was with the wife, he put his cloak and staff outside the hut as a warning to the rest not to disturb him.

This family form was *patrilocal* (the bride and groom live in the household or community of the husband's family) and extended in the sense that brothers usually did not leave their families of orientation to marry. Instead, the wife came to live with her husband's family. It was common for two or more generations to live together.

When children were born, establishing biological fatherhood was not an issue. Instead "social" or "legal" fatherhood was established through a ceremony held about the seventh month of pregnancy. One brother, usually the eldest, was chosen to give a cere-monial bow and arrow to the wife. By this gesture, performed in front of relatives, he was recognized as the "legal" father of the unborn child. After two or three children had been born, another brother gave the wife the bow, and he then became the father of all subsequent children.

The origins of this family form are not completely understood. However, like many other groups throughout history, the Todas practiced female infanticide, the killing of female infants. Thus, among the Todas there was a surplus of males over females. Once there was a surplus of males, the cultural innovation of fraternal polyandry made it possible for most male Todas to marry.

Source: Selected excerpt from *The Family in Various Cultures* by Stuart A. Queen et al. Copyright © 1985 by Harper & Row, Publishers, Inc. Reprinted by permission of HarperCollins, Publishers, Inc.

that direct people to behave in particular ways—governing sexual behavior may vary among societies, all societies define and regulate who may have sex with whom. For example, all societies prohibit sexual relations between blood or close relatives; this is known as *the incest taboo*. Forcing people to have sexual relations outside the family unit promotes alliances between families, reinforces their social independence, and prevents or minimizes sexual jealousies and conflicts within families. The set of relatives subject to the taboo varies across societies, however. Thus, for example, whereas in most societies parents and siblings are subject to the incest taboo, in ancient Egyptian and Hawaiian societies siblings in the royal families were expected to mate with and marry one another. This system enabled the royal family to maintain its power and property and prevented the splintering of its estate through inheritance.

Moreover, in most societies sexual relations are linked with marriage. Even in those societies where it is not, their members' sexual behavior is nonetheless regulated so that it reinforces the social order. For example, among the Masai (a polygynous pastoral group in Africa), where men dominate in the family, young wives of older men are allowed discreetly to take lovers from the unmarried warrior class. If the wife becomes pregnant from such a relationship, family stability is not disrupted. The children from these unions simply belong to the husband and further increase his wealth and prestige.

REPRODUCTION To perpetuate itself a society must produce new members to replace those who die or move away. In most societies families are given the primary responsibility for reproducing the species. The reproductive function of families is considered to be so important that many societies employ a variety of practices to motivate married couples to have children. For example, in the United States, couples typically receive tax exemptions and other tax breaks for each child they produce. Couples who cannot have children are penalized by tax laws and are sometimes stigmatized by society's members. In addition, sexual intercourse that occurs outside of marriage or that will not produce children, such as lesbian or gay sexual relations is highly stigmatized and discouraged.

In contrast, in certain societies the concern with reproduction translates primarily into a concern with population control. Families are motivated not only to reproduce but also to keep society manageable through population control. For example, in China, material incentives such as work bonuses, free medical care, and other privileges for the child are given to married couples who agree to limit their reproduction to one child (see Chapter 9).

SOCIAL PLACEMENT   When new members are born into society they must be placed within the social structure with a minimum of confusion and in a way that preserves order and stability. The **social structure** of society refers to the recurrent, patterned ways that people relate to one another. It consists of an intricate web of social **statuses** (a position in a group or society) and **roles** (a set of behaviors associated with a particular status). Members of society must be placed within these statuses and motivated to play the appropriate roles. One of the ways in which families function is to assign social status to individuals on the basis of their membership within a particular family. The status placement function of families occurs at a number of levels. On one level, families confer statuses that orient members to a variety of interpersonal relationships including those involving parents, siblings, and a variety of relatives. In addition, simply by being born into or raised in a particular family we automatically inherit membership in, and the status of, certain basic groups, including racial, ethnic, religious, class, and national. Social status influences almost every aspect of our lives. It influences the way we see the world as well as how the world sees us. Much of what we think of as our unique values and preferences are really the results of our assignment to certain statuses through our families.

SOCIALIZATION   Human babies are not born with the knowledge of the norms, values, and role expectations of their society. However, they soon learn what their society considers to be appropriate ways of acting, thinking, and feeling. Children's social development as well as the continuation of society depends on the **socialization** process, a lifetime of social interaction through which people learn those elements of culture that are essential for effective participation in social life. Today as in the past, families are the primary transmitters of culture to each new generation of the young. Many people in our society believe that because parents are more likely than others to be deeply committed to their own offspring, they are thus the best or most appropriate socializing agents. Compulsory education, however, has placed a significant amount of the socialization function in the hands of the state and schools. In addition, the increasing need for mothers to work outside the home has placed part of this function in the hands of child-care workers, and the mass media, especially television, have become important agents of socialization.

ECONOMIC COOPERATION   Children have physical and economic needs as well as social needs. They must be fed, clothed, and sheltered. Providing for these needs is the basis of the economic function of families. Families are responsible for the physical and economic well-being not only of children but of all members of the family. In the past, families consumed primarily goods that they produced. Although this is no longer true, families are still productive economic units. The value of what they produce is less recognized today, however. The goods and services families produce today are those delivered primarily by women (for example, child care and housework). Because men have moved outside the home to work and receive wages and women's work inside families is unpaid, the productive and essential nature of families through the work that women do has been overlooked, downplayed, and often trivialized. Nevertheless, families continue to divide essential tasks among their members and cooperate economically to meet the physical, social, and economic needs of their members. Each member's economic fate is tied to that of the family as a whole.

CARE, PROTECTION, AND INTIMACY A large amount of sociological and psychological research indicates that in addition to the necessities of life, human infants also need warmth and affection. In addition, during infancy and early childhood humans cannot take care of themselves and thus are totally dependent on their caretakers. Furthermore, even as adults humans need intimacy and often need other human beings for care and protection during periods of illness, disability, or other dependencies. Ideally, families function to provide an intimate atmosphere and an economic unit in which these needs can be met. As the center of emotional life, families can provide love, caring, and emotional support that cannot easily be obtained outside the family context. For many of us, throughout our lives, our families will be our most important source of comfort and emotional support.

Any given family may or may not perform any or all of these functions. The family as an institution is so diverse that not all families fulfill all of these functions, and some families who do, do not always fulfill them well. That we live in a time of transition and change is unquestionable. Thus, many of the activities previously identified by social scientists as family functions have been taken over by or are shared with other societal institutions such as schools, religious organizations, mass media, and government agencies. The socialization of children and stabilization for adult family members, however, remain the primary functions of families.

THE PESSIMISTIC VIEW OF FAMILIES

Some people see this loss of function as a contributing factor to a variety of social ills that beset modern families. A proponent of this point of view, social scientist Christopher Lasch (1977, 1978), contends that the encroachment of outside institutions, especially the state, has left modern families with too few functions to perform. Even the socialization function, which had been a primary function of families, has been largely taken over by an educational system that increasingly communicates a set of values and behaviors that may conflict with the realities of some families. Thus, the function of modern families has been reduced to a small number of specialized functions such as affection and companionship. Lasch, along with a number of

other people, including a long line of politicians, believes that families are in grave danger today, perhaps even in a state of crisis and moral decay.

Some people have seen evidence of this moral decay of families in the behavior of women like television's fictional "Murphy Brown," a divorced career woman who spent a night with her ex-husband, became pregnant, and had the child out of wedlock. In 1992, Vice President Dan Quayle criticized television's depiction of this behavior, fueling the ongoing debate and concern about the state of modern families.

Today, many people perceive that the tradition of human family life is being replaced by an alien and destructive set of relationships that is tearing at the very heart of U.S. society. Families are perceived as increasingly violent. Individuals are seen as more sexually promiscuous, as evidenced by the increase in sexual activity among nonmarried people and the growing rate of teenage pregnancy. Family values and morals

Sometimes media portrayals of family life can take on a reality of their own, as was the case when Vice President Dan Quayle criticized the fictional character Murphy Brown's decision to become a single parent.

are said to be collapsing, as evidenced in the visibility of lesbian and gay lifestyles, the high rate of welfare dependency, the high divorce rate, and the increasing number of children experiencing poverty and neglect. Certain trends, such as the tendency to delay marriage, the growth in the number of people not marrying at all, and the apparent popularity of extramarital relationships, are interpreted as signs of a general disregard for marriage. Consequently, the pessimists lament the state of today's families and long for the "good old days" when families were "real" families.

Some political candidates have embraced such themes, calling for a "return to family values." The implications are that something virtuous and stable called "the family" once existed and that it is desirable and even possible to return to this state of familial harmony. How many times have you heard your parents or some other adult say, "Things weren't like this when I was young." "The family had values in those days." "In those days families stuck together." Those who take this point of view frequently suggest that the answer for today's familial problems is to return to the traditional family structure and set of values that characterized the lives of our parents, grandparents, and great-grandparents.

THE OPTIMISTIC VIEW OF FAMILIES

On the other side of the debate are those who are less pessimistic, though equally concerned, about the problems of modern families. They concede that marriages and families may perform fewer direct functions for individual members than they did in the past and that there are serious problems associated with marriage and family life today. They argue, however, that marriage and family life are still extremely important to most people in the United States. They cite census data that indicate that the United States has perhaps the highest marriage rate in the world. Although young people may delay marriage, almost everyone gets married—at least once. In 1990, 95 percent of women and 94 percent of men ages 45 to 54 either were currently or had been married (Ahlburg and DeVita, 1992:12). And although the United States has one of the highest divorce rates in the world, the overwhelming majority of divorced people remarry.

Furthermore, those who view families in a more optimistic way cite survey results that report that most people in the United States hold the family in high regard and report high levels of satisfaction with their own family life. The optimists refute the pessimists' idealized version of families of the past, and give us instead a picture of a traditional family that was often rigid and oppressive. They remind us that traditional families were often based on a clear division of labor along age and gender lines that often resulted in a very restrictive life, especially for women and children. They also question the premise that family values and traditional family structure are one and the same and that both are synonymous with stability. What, they ask, are family values? What have they been historically? Are they fundamentally different today than in the past? Who is to say which family values are correct?

 Who is to be believed, the pessimists or the optimists? Which image of family life past or present is accurate? Were families of yesterday really the way we perceive them to be? Were the "good old days" really that good? Was family life in the past significantly better than it is today? Were traditional families "real" families that were self-sufficient, stable, supportive, and devoid of such problems as violence and teenage pregnancy? Or is much of our thinking about past families no more than wishful thinking?

DEBUNKING MYTHS ABOUT MARRIAGES AND FAMILIES

Take another few minutes to think about the "traditional family." Again, if you are like most people, your vision of the traditional family is similar to or the same as your more general view of families. Therefore, you likely described the traditional family in terms of some combination of the following traits:

- Members loved and respected one another and worked together for the good of the family.
- Grandparents were an integral and respected part of the family.
- Mothers stayed home and were happy, nurturant, and always available to their children.
- Fathers worked and brought home the paycheck.
- Children were seen and not heard, mischievous but not "bad," and were responsible and learned a work ethic.

Indicate which of the following statements are true and which are false.

1. Families in early America were private, self-sufficient units. Unlike many of today's families, they did not receive any outside assistance, nor did they have to endure any government intrusion in their lives.
2. From the beginning of U.S. history the predominant pattern of mate selection was one of free choice based on notions of romantic love.
3. In the past most people lived in extended families with three generations living together.
4. Until relatively recently the characteristic pattern in the United States was for people to marry at early ages—in their teens and early twenties.
5. The high rate of female-headed households among African Americans today is a direct result of the experience of slavery.

6. Compared to the European settlers, Native-American peoples had a less developed family system.
7. Because of the high infant mortality rate, colonial parents had an indifferent attitude toward their children.
8. Children in early America were far more fortunate than today's children. Because divorce was less common than today, only a few children lived in single-parent households.

If you answered false to all of these questions, give yourself a pat on the back. You know your family history. If you missed any of the questions, you are not alone. Most people miss some of them. This is probably due to our preoccupation with current family issues and a tendency to idealize the past. Throughout this book we point out some of the popular misconceptions about family life in the United States.

These images of past family life, which are still widely held, have a powerful influence on people's perceptions and evaluations of today's families. The problem, however, is that these are mostly mythical images of the past based on many different kinds of marriages and families that never coexisted in the same time and place.

A leading authority on U.S. family history, Stephanie Coontz (1992), argues in her book *The Way We Never Were* that much of today's political and social debate about family values and the "real" family is based on an idealized vision of a past that never actually existed.* Coontz further argues that this idealized and selective set of remembrances of families of yesteryear in turn determines much of our contemporary view of traditional family life. A look at some statistics and facts from our historical past supports her argument.

- We bemoan the increasingly violent nature of families (and rightfully so). As you will find in Chapter 12, however, the United States has a long and brutal history of child and woman abuse. Therefore, we cannot blame domestic violence on recent changes in family life or on the disappearance of family values and morals.

- We think that contemporary high school dropout rates are shockingly high. As late as the 1940s, however, less than one-half of all young people entering high school managed to finish, producing a dropout rate that was much higher than today's.

- Violence in all aspects of society is reaching new highs today, but before the Civil War New York City was already considered the most dangerous place in the world to live. As a matter of fact, the United States has had the highest homicide rates in the industrial world for almost 150 years.

- Although alcohol and drug abuse are at alarmingly high rates today, they were widespread well before modern rearrangements of gender roles and family life. In 1820, for example, alcohol consumption was three times higher than today, and there was a major epidemic of opium and cocaine addiction in the late nineteenth century.

*The rest of our discussion concerning the myths and realities of family life, past and present, owes much to the work of Stephanie Coontz. Coontz has written profusely on the social origins and history of U.S. families from the 1600s forward. She has also lectured extensively in Europe and the United States on family history and sociology. She places contemporary family crises in the context of history and exposes many of the myths that surround and cloud contemporary discussions and debates about family values and the way U.S. families actually were.

As these facts show, our memory of past family life is often clouded by myths. A **myth** is a false, fictitious, imaginary or exaggerated belief about someone or something. Myths are generally assumed to be true and often provide the justification or rationale for social behaviors, beliefs, and institutions. And, in fact, most myths do contain some elements of truth. As we will see, however, different myths contain different degrees of truth.

Some family myths have a positive effect in the sense that individual family members are often bonded together in familial solidarity by shared stories (myths) and rituals. When they create unrealistic expectations about what families can or should be and do, however, myths can be dangerous. Many of the myths that most Americans hold today about traditional families or families of the past are white middle-class myths. This is true because the mass media, controlled primarily by white middle-class men, tend to project a primarily white middle-class experience as a universal trend or fact. Such myths, then, distort the diverse experiences of other familial groups in this country, both presently and in the past, and they do not even describe most white middle-class families accurately. We now take a closer look at five of the most popular myths and stereotypes about the family that are directly applicable to current debates about family life and gender roles: (1) the "self-reliant" traditional family, (2) the "naturalness" of the separate spheres for wives and husbands, (3) the private and autonomous family, (4) the unstable African-American family, and (5) the idealized nuclear family of the 1950s.

MYTH 1: THE SELF-RELIANT TRADITIONAL FAMILY

The myth of the self-reliant family assumes that in the past families were held together by hard work, family loyalty, and a fierce determination not to be beholden to anyone, especially the state. It is popularly believed that such families never asked for handouts; rather, they stood on their own feet even in times of crisis. Unlike some families today, who watch the mail for their government checks, families of yesteryear did not accept or expect "charity." Any help they may have received came from other family members.

This tendency to overestimate the self-reliance of earlier families ignores the fact that external support for families has been the rule and not the exception in U.S. family history. Although public assistance has become less local and more impersonal over the past 2 centuries, U.S. families have always depended to some degree on other institutions. For example, colonial families made extensive use of the collective work of others such as African-American slaves and Native Americans, whose husbandry and collective land use provided for the abundant game, plants, and berries that colonial families consumed to survive. Early families were also dependent on a large network of neighbors, churches, courts, government officials, and legislative bodies for their sustenance. For example, the elderly, ill, and orphaned dependents were often taken care of by people who were not family members, and public officials often gave money to facilitate such care. Immigrant, African-American, and native-born white workers could not have survived in the past without sharing and receiving assistance beyond family networks. Moreover, middle-class as well as working-class families were dependent on fraternal and mutual aid organizations to assist them in times of need.

MYTH 2: THE "NATURALNESS" OF DIFFERENT SPHERES FOR WIVES AND HUSBANDS

This myth dates to the nineteenth century, when economic changes led to the development of separate spheres for women and men. Wives and mothers became the caregivers and moral guardians of the family, while husbands and fathers provided economic support and protection and represented their families to the outside world. Thereafter, this arrangement was viewed as natural, and alternative forms were believed to be destructive of family harmony. Thus, today's family problems are seen as stemming from a self-defeating attempt to equalize women's and men's roles in the family. It is assumed that the move away from a traditional gendered division of labor to a more egalitarian ideal denies women's and men's differing needs and abilities and thus destabilizes family relations. Those who hold to this myth advocate a return to traditional gender roles in the family and a clear and firm boundary between the family and the outside world. As we shall see later on, however, the notions of separate spheres and ideal family form are far from natural and have not always existed.

MYTH 3: THE PRIVATE AND AUTONOMOUS FAMILY

The myth of the private, autonomous family revolves around the notion of the family's right to privacy and nonintervention from outside forces. It holds that at some time in the past "a man's home was his castle." Families were private and autonomous units, whereas today that sovereignty has been eroded as a result of an expanding state role. Consequently, modern families have lost much of their authority to courts and public officials. Those who espouse this myth contend that the answer to the problems facing today's families is to get the state out of family matters and give families back their autonomy and privacy.

Contrary to this widespread belief, the family has never been exempt from public intervention. As far back as colonial times, public bodies routinely regulated many phases of family life, including such matters as whether couples could separate and who was eligible for government assistance based on an official definition of family.

MYTH 4: THE UNSTABLE AFRICAN-AMERICAN FAMILY

Although pessimists perceive that the collapse of the family affects all racial and ethnic groups, they frequently single out African-American families as the least stable and functional. The myth of the collapse of the African-American family is fueled by racist stereotypes and media exaggerations and distortions that overlook the diversity of African-American family life. No more is there one black family type than there is one white family type.

Nonetheless, this myth draws on some very real trends that affect a segment of the African-American community. In the 1960s, social historian Andrew Billingsley (1968) called attention to the division of the African-American community along class lines and demonstrated the importance of social class in any analysis of African-American families. According to Billingsley, three distinct classes were visible in the

African-American community: (1) a small upper class (approximately 10 percent) that stressed family and was politically conservative; (2) a middle class (approximately 40 percent) concerned with family, respectability, and individual and family achievement; and (3) a lower class (approximately 50 percent) made up of stable working-class families and both stable and multiproblem poor families. It is generally from the multiproblem poor families within the lower class (which some contemporary sociologists refer to as an "underclass") that stereotypes and generalizations about all African-American families are made.

This segment of African-American families experiences a pattern of chronic and persistent poverty. Some of the most visible manifestations of this pattern are high levels of unemployment, welfare dependency, low marriage rates, high rates of teenage pregnancy, mother-focused families composed of a mother and her dependent children, an increasing number of crack-addicted babies, and an escalating level of violence. For example, although nonmarital childbearing is no longer unusual among most groups in the United States, for African Americans it has become majority behavior. By the end of the last decade almost two-thirds of African-American babies were born to unmarried couples. This trend is especially evident among lower-income and less educated African-Americans. In addition, there has been a major increase in the number of African-American one-parent families.

Based on middle-class standards, these trends seem to support the myth of an unstable, disorganized family structure in the African-American community. And indeed, among some individuals and families, long-term and concentrated poverty and despair, racism, social contempt, police brutality, and political neglect have taken their toll and are often manifested in the behaviors just described. To generalize these behaviors to the entire African-American community, however, is inaccurate and misleading. Moreover, to attribute these behaviors, when they do occur, to a deteriorating, immoral family lifestyle and a lack of middle-class family values ignores historical, social, and political factors such as **institutional racism**, the systematic discrimination against a racial group by the institutions within society. In addition, such claims serve to perpetuate the myth that one particular family arrangement is a workable model for all families in modern society.

As it happens, most of the common knowledge whites have about the nature of black families is not true. Many of the current "facts" they cite are half-truths that seriously impede responsible discussion of the dilemmas facing African-American families today. Without much doubt, not only the black underclass but also many black families across class differ from the white middle-class ideal primarily because their circumstances are and have been different. Nevertheless, these differences have often been exaggerated, and where they occur among African-American families they frequently have been sources of strength rather than weakness. According to Coontz, many of the variations found in African-American families have produced healthy individuals with a strong group consciousness that has helped them cope with widespread racism, violence, and poverty and often to rise above these limitations. (These variations are examined in later chapters of this text.) This view is supported, in part, by statistics that show that an increasing number of African Americans are graduating from high school, attending college, and experiencing some advances in economic and material well-being. Many sociologists today take the position that there is no one family type; African-American families, like other families, should be viewed as unique and essential subcultural family forms and not simply as deviant departures from white middle-class family forms.

MYTH 5: THE IDEALIZED NUCLEAR FAMILY OF THE 1950s

During the 1950s, millions of Americans came to accept an image of the family as a middle-class institution consisting of (1) a wise father who worked outside the home; (2) a mother whose major responsibility was to take care of her husband, children, and home; and (3) children who were well behaved and

In the 1950s few people questioned the idealized image of the family that was reflected in programs like "Ozzie and Harriet." Today there is some attempt to portray more realistically the diversity in families, such as the male single parent in "Blossom."

obedient. This image, depicted in a number of 1950s family sitcoms such as "Leave It to Beaver," "Father Knows Best," and "Ozzie and Harriet," is said to represent the epitome of traditional family structure and values. Many critics today see the movement away from this model as evidence of the decline in the viability of the family, as well as a source of many family problems.

It is true that compared to the 1990s, the 1950s were characterized by younger ages at marriage, higher birthrates, and lower divorce and premarital pregnancy rates. To present the 1950s as representing "typical" or "normal" family patterns, however, is misleading. In fact, the marriage rates of the 1950s represented an all-time high for the United States, and people married earlier than they had at any time during the twentieth century. Although some people worry that young people today are delaying marriage to unusually late ages, Figure 1.1 shows that the median age at first marriage today, 24.1 for women

and 26.3 for men, more closely approximates that of the 1890s than it does the 1950s average of 20.3 for women and 22.8 for men. The earlier age at marriage in the 1950s was a reaction to the hardships and sacrifices brought about by the depression and World War II. Thus, marriage and family life became synonymous with the "good life." Furthermore, images of the good life were now broadcast into living rooms across the country via the powerful new medium of television. Even then, however, there were signs that all was not well. Public opinion polls taken during the 1950s suggested that approximately 20 percent of all couples considered themselves unhappy in marriage, and another 20 percent reported only "medium happiness" (quoted in Mintz and Kellogg, 1988:194).

This discussion of mythical versus real families underscores the fact that not all families are the same; there is not now and never has been a single

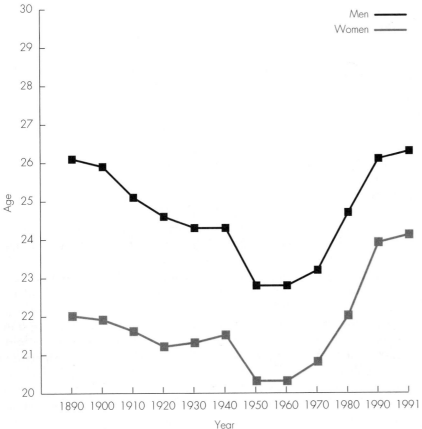

FIGURE 1.1 Median Age at First Marriage, by Sex: 1890–1991

Source: Adapted from U.S. Bureau of the Census, 1992a, *Current Population Reports*, Series P-20, No. 461, "Marital Status and Living Arrangements: March 1991" (Washington, DC: U.S. Government Printing Office): Table C, p. 5.

model of the family. Families and their experiences are indeed different; however, difference does not connote better or worse. The experiences of a poor family are certainly not the same as those of a rich family; the experiences of a young family with young children are little like those of either a child-free family or an older family whose children have "left the nest." Even within families the experiences of older members are different from those of younger members, and the experiences of females and males are different. Certainly the experiences of Latino, Native-American, Asian-American, and black families are not the same as those of white families, regardless of class. Nor are lesbian and gay family experiences the same as heterosexual family experiences. Families are products of their historical context, and at any given historical period families occupy different territories and have varied experiences given the differential influence of the society's race, class, and gender systems.

FAMILIES IN EARLY AMERICA

When the first English and Dutch settlers arrived on the eastern seaboard of North America in the early seventeenth century, there were already between 1 and 2 million people living here, composing more than 240 distinct groups, each with its own history, culture, family, and **kinship** (people who are related by blood, marriage, adoption or who consider one another family) patterns (Mintz and Kellogg, 1988). By the end of that century, a variety of immigrants, primarily from Scotland, Ireland, Germany, and France, had arrived in North America. In addition, large numbers of Africans were forcibly brought to the colonies and sold into slavery. Thus, from the very beginning, the United States was economically, racially, ethnically, religiously, and familially diverse. Consequently, any attempt to describe families of the past must take this diversity into account. One chapter in a textbook cannot possibly convey how all these different groups struggled to adapt to a new and often hostile environment and at the same time to create and maintain a stable family structure. Thus, our depiction of family life in the seventeenth and eighteenth centuries is limited to three groups: white colonial families, African-American families, and Native-American families. A great deal of

African-American family history was connected with slavery. Because slavery ended only after the Civil War, our discussion of African-American families contains references to the nineteenth century as well.

COLONIAL FAMILIES

Our knowledge of family life among the first immigrants to this country comes primarily from three sources: (1) surviving physical objects such as furniture, tools, and utensils; (2) personal diaries, letters, sermons, literary works, and wills, which contain references to the relationships that existed among different family and community members; and (3) census data and other public records. Given that these materials represent only fragmentary remains of that period, our understanding of family life in colonial America is somewhat impressionistic. We do know, however, that there was considerable variation in family organization among the colonists, reflecting the differences in cultural backgrounds that they brought with them as well as differences in the local conditions they encountered in the areas in which they settled. Limitations of space prevent a full discussion of this diversity; hence, our discussion focuses primarily on family life in the northern colonies and incorporates some examples from the other colonies.

HOUSEHOLD COMPOSITION A popular belief about colonial America is that most people lived in extended families. Research, however, shows that the opposite was true. Early colonial families, with few exceptions, were nuclear families, consisting of wife, husband, and children (Greven, 1970; Laslett, 1971). Immediately after marriage the couple was expected to establish their own household. About the only exception to this pattern was when elderly parents were unable to care for themselves and, out of necessity, had to live with their adult children. Nevertheless, colonial families differed in at least three major respects from the modern nuclear family. First, non-kin such as orphans, apprentices, hired laborers, unmarried individuals, and children from other families could and often did join colonial households. These "servants," as they were referred to, lived and worked as regular members of the household. Additionally, at times local authorities would place criminals and poor people with families. These people were to provide service to the household in return for care and rehabilitation.

Second, the family formed the basic economic unit of colonial society. Women, men, and children combined their labor to meet the subsistence needs of the family. Until approximately the middle of the eighteenth century, relatively little was produced to sell. Calling this pattern the "family-based economy," social historians Louise Tilly and Joan Scott (1978:12) observed, "Production and family life were inseparably intertwined, and the household was the center around which resources, labor, and consumption were balanced." Hence, as the basic economic unit of life, the family was synonymous with whoever lived and worked within the household rather than strictly defined by blood and marital ties. As the third difference makes clear, however, this pattern of production did not mean that families were self-sufficient.

Finally, unlike today, the functions of the colonial family and the larger community were deeply intertwined. In his book *A Little Commonwealth*, historian John Demos (1970:183–84) describes how the family in Plymouth colony functioned as a "business," a "school," a "vocational institute," a "church," a "house of corrections," and at times a "hospital," an "orphanage," and a "poorhouse." Although the family was involved in these tasks, public authorities determined how the tasks were to be met. Social life was highly regulated. Individuals were told where to live, how to dress, what strangers to take in and for how long. Unlike today there was little privacy within or among households. Sexual matters, for example, were discussed openly. Because much of daily living took place in common rooms, children were not sheltered from knowledge of sexual matters. Public documents from that period show that neighbors often reported violations of sexual norms and that punishment for such violations was carried out in public. For example, a woman could be flogged if she refused to name the father of a child born out of wedlock. If marriage followed a premarital pregnancy, however, little concern was expressed. This was not uncommon, as is evidenced by the fact that in seventeenth century Maryland, one-third of the immigrant women whose marriages are recorded were pregnant before the ceremonies (cited in Coontz, 1988:89).

MARITAL ROLES The colonial family was a patriarchy. Fathers were regarded as the head of the family, and they exercised authority over wives, children, and servants. Men represented their households in the public sphere and held positions of leadership in the community. However, not all fathers were in this position. Those without property themselves came under the rule of the propertied class. The ownership of property gave men considerable power in their families, and their decisions to distribute property to their offspring had a profound effect on their children's choice of careers and on when and whom their children married. This practice often kept children economically dependent on their parents for much of their adult lives.

Legally a father had the right to determine who could court his daughters, and it was up to him to give or withhold consent from a child's marriage. His decision was based largely on whether the marriage would maintain or enhance the economic and political status of the family. Although romantic love may have existed between courting couples, marriage was viewed first and foremost as an economic arrangement; with the assumption that affection would develop after marriage (Mintz and Kellogg, 1988). Evidence of this attitude and its subsequent change comes from an examination of divorce records. It was only after 1770 that divorce records named loss of affection as a reason for terminating the marriage.

Under these patriarchal arrangements, wives were expected to be submissive and obedient to their husbands. Although unmarried women had the right to own property, enter into contracts, and represent themselves in court; after marriage the English concept of *coverture* was evoked, whereby the wife's legal identity was subsumed in her husband's, giving him the authority to make decisions for her. This doctrine was often ignored in practice, however. Records show that some colonial women, especially widows, entered into contracts and operated stores; ran taverns; and worked as millers, tanners, blacksmiths, silversmiths, shoemakers, and printers—occupations usually held by men.

Although both wives and husbands contributed their skills and resources to the household, the actual division of labor was based on sex. For the most part husbands did the planting, harvesting, bookkeeping, and supervisory tasks. Wives were responsible for cooking, sewing, milking, cleaning, and gardening.

In addition, they produced many products for home consumption and traded surplus goods with other families. A wife sometimes served as a "deputy husband," assuming her husband's responsibilities when he was away on business or military duty. Thus, women often performed traditional male tasks. Men, however, only infrequently reciprocated by performing women's domestic chores (Riley, 1987:13). Today our culture views child rearing as predominantly women's work. Yet according to historian Carl Degler (1980), child rearing in the colonial period was mainly the task of fathers. Fathers were responsible for transmitting religious values and for instilling discipline in their offspring. As we shall see, economic changes in the nineteenth century brought about a major shift in family roles.

CHILDHOOD The social experiences of colonial children differed in several major ways from those of children today. First, survival to adulthood was less likely. Death rates among children were higher than among other age groups. In the more prosperous and healthier communities in seventeenth-century New England, one out of ten children died in infancy; in less healthy communities, the rate was one out of three (Mintz and Kellogg, 1988:14). Initial interpretations of these high death rates suggested that parents protected themselves emotionally by developing an indifference toward young children. Historical documents belie this viewpoint, however, revealing the immense sorrow parents experienced at the death of a child.

Second, child rearing did not occupy the same place it does today. For example, well-to-do families often employed wet nurses to breast-feed and care for infants so that mothers could concentrate their attention on household duties. Children were not viewed as "innocent beings"; rather, they were seen as possessing original sin and stubborn willfulness. Thus, child-rearing practices were designed to break down a child's willful nature. Religious instruction, threats, and even physical beatings were frequently used to discipline wayward children. There were even "stubborn child" laws in early New England that prescribed the death penalty for persistent disobedience to parents. Although there is no record that such sanctions were ever invoked, their very existence symbolized society's concern for domestic tranquility (Powers, 1966).

Third, childhood itself was quite short. Around the ages of 6 or 7 both girls and boys assumed productive roles. Girls were taught domestic skills such as sewing, spinning, and caring for domestic animals. Like their mothers, they also assisted their fathers in the fields or in the shops. Young boys worked small looms, weeded fields, and were taught a craft. Finally, around the age of 14, many colonial children from all social classes were "put out" to other families to learn a trade, to work as servants, or to receive the proper discipline their natural parents could not be expected to deliver (Mintz and Kellogg, 1988).

There was, however, at least one aspect of colonial childhood that is similar to today. Many children in colonial families spent part of their life in a single-parent family. For example, parental death rates in late-seventeenth-century Virginia were so high that most children were reared by just one parent and more than one-third lost both parents (Darrett and Rutman, 1979:153). Thus, many colonial children, like millions of children today, lived part of their lives in stepfamilies, a topic we discuss in detail in Chapter 14.

Thus far, the family patterns we have been discussing applied primarily to the white settlers. People of color had very different experiences. In the process of adapting to their environment, they created some distinct patterns of family life.

AFRICAN-AMERICAN FAMILIES UNDER SLAVERY

Billingsley (1968) points out three important elements that distinguish the experience of African Americans from other groups in the United States.

1. Unlike most of their colonial contemporaries, African Americans came to America from Africa and not from Europe.
2. They were uprooted from their cultural and family moorings and brought to the United States as slaves.
3. From the beginning and continuing even today, they were systematically excluded from participation in the major institutions of U.S. society.

Numerous writings have traced the problems of modern African-American families to the experience of slavery. Clearly slavery had a devastating effect on families. The day-to-day stresses of living as a slave, and many specific practices of slaveholders undermined the authority and stability of many of these families. Slaveholders often prohibited legal marriages among slaves, sold family members away from one another, and sexually exploited African-American women. Nonetheless, a growing body of research shows that many slaves established strong marital and family arrangements that endured for long periods of time, even under conditions of separation. Family arrangements followed fairly distinct patterns, beginning with courtship and often marriage, followed by childbearing and child rearing.

The family structures and practices developed by African Americans incorporated many African traditions. For example, in West African cultures, marriages between first cousins were forbidden, a prohibition that resurfaced in the United States. Records show that although first-cousin marriages were common among whites in the South, they were absent among slaves (Gutman, 1976).

SLAVE MARRIAGES Although Southern laws prohibited slaves from contracting legal marriages, some slaveholders granted permission for their slaves to marry, and a few even provided separate living quarters or household goods for the new couple. For many slaves the solemnity of the occasion was marked by a religious ceremony at which either a black or white minister officiated. Between 1841 and 1860, half of the marriages in South Carolina's Episcopal churches were between slaves (Blassingame, 1979:166). Other marriage rituals were used as well, the most common of which was jumping over a broomstick. A former Alabama slave, Penny Anderson, described the ceremony this way. "After supper dey puts de broom on de floor and de couple takes de hands and steps over de broom, den dey am out to bed" (quoted in Gutman, 1976:275). These rituals, however, did not guarantee that a couple could live together. Slave spouses often had different owners and lived on different plantations and, thus, could see each other only when their masters permitted visits or when, risking severe punishment, they went off on their own.

Although many slave marriages were stable, slave couples lived under the constant fear of forced separation. The reality of these fears was expressed in some of the vows these couples took, "Until death or

One of the consequences of slavery was the frequent separation of family members. However, as historians have documented, many slave families were able to maintain intergenerational ties like the five generations pictured here, all of whom were born on a South Carolina plantation.

distance do you part" (quoted in Finkelman, 1989:xii). This fear became a reality for many slave couples, as evidenced by numerous accounts of ex-slaves who referred to earlier marriages terminated by sale to new owners. Some slaves, however, fought back against this separation. Historian Eugene Genovese (1974) found considerable evidence that when couples were separated by their masters, they often ran away in an attempt to be together. Furthermore, one of the first things African Americans did after the Civil War was to seek out lost relatives on other plantations and to legalize marriages made unofficially under slavery.

According to Genovese, slave communities exhibited a high degree of sexual equality. This pattern has been linked to the slaves' African heritage and to the similar work roles they had on the plantations. African-American women worked alongside men in the fields and in the master's house. Although slave parents did not have legal authority over their children, there is considerable evidence to show that both women and men had ongoing involvement with their families and that both sexes participated in child rearing.

CHILDHOOD Despite the abuses of slavery, African Americans succeeded in forming and maintaining families. Nineteenth-century census data show that both before and after slavery, most African Americans lived in two-parent households. According to plantation records examined by social historian Herbert Gutman (1976), slave women frequently bore their first child in their late teens. Because of harsh living conditions, more than one-third of the babies born to slave women died before the age of 10; a rate double that for white infants (Mintz and Kellogg, 1988:72, 73). As soon as they were able, slave children worked in the barnyards or in the master's house and soon followed their parents into the fields. Between the ages of 7 and 10, children had to leave their parents' cabin and move into quarters occupied by other unmarried youth.

Slave parents had to overcome many obstacles to hold their families together. Many succeeded in asserting some small measure of independence by securing additional food for their families by hunting small game and cultivating small gardens. Like other parents, they instructed their children in religious and cultural beliefs and trained them in the various crafts in which they worked. They also developed networks of extended kin that helped family members survive the material privations and harsh treatment under slavery and the chaotic economic conditions that followed them into freedom after the Civil War.

EXTENDED KINSHIP PATTERNS According to Gutman (1976) strong kinship feelings among slaves are evident from the naming practices of slave families. Table 1.1 shows that slave parents frequently named their children after fathers, grandparents, recently deceased relatives, and other kin. Gutman believed that this kin network was especially important in helping slaves adapt to family breakup. When children were sold to neighboring plantations, any blood relative living there took over parental functions. In the absence of such relatives, strangers assumed these responsibilities. Slave children were taught to call all adult slaves "aunt" and "uncle" and younger slaves "sister" and "brother," practices that created a sense of mutual obligations and responsibilities among the broader slave population.

FREE AFRICAN-AMERICAN FAMILIES

Prior to the Civil War there were approximately 250,000 free African Americans in the United States. About 150,000 lived in the South, and the remaining 100,000 lived in the North (Mintz and Kellogg, 1988). Many slaves freed themselves by running

---

TABLE 1.1

Naming Practices Among the Stirling Plantation Slaves, West Feliciana Parish, Louisiana, 1808–65

Date of Birth	Name of Newborn	Name of Parents	Relation of Newborn to Person with Same Name
1808	Leven	Big Judy–Leven	Father
1833	Julius	Dolly–Sidney	Father's father
1836	Ginny	Clarice–John	Mother's mother
1837	Hannah	Liddy–Luke	Mother's sister
1839	Barika	Nelly	Mother's husband (stepfather)
1846	Antoinette	Henrietta	Mother's sister's son (dead)
1846	Hester	Harriet–Sam	Father's sister
1853	Monday	Sophy–Sampson	Father's brother
1865	Duncan	Antoinette–Primus	Dead sibling

Source: Adapted from Herbert G. Gutman, 1976, *The Black Family in Slavery and Freedom, 1750–1925* (New York: Vintage Books): 119–21.

away; others were freed by slaveholders after the American Revolution. A few managed to buy their own freedom. Freedom, however, did not mean full integration into the larger society. In many communities, both in the North and South, free African Americans were not allowed to vote, hold public meetings, purchase liquor, marry whites, or attend white churches and schools. Although some men were able to earn a fair livelihood as carpenters, shoemakers, tailors, and millwrights, most lived in conditions of extreme poverty (Berlin, 1974).

Most free African-American families were structured around two-parent households. Nevertheless, as today, inadequate family income, high levels of unemployment, illness, and early death put considerable strain on these families. One study found, for example, that in Philadelphia during the nineteenth century, between one-quarter and one-third of the city's African Americans lived in female-headed households, a figure two to three times higher than that for other groups in the city. This differential is explained by two factors. First, slaveholders tended to free women rather than men. Employment opportunities were better for women than men in urban areas as whites sought black women to be domestic servants, cooks, nurses, and seamstresses. Many fathers remained slaves and could not migrate with their families. Consequently, free African-American women outnumbered men in urban areas. Second, then as now, life expectancy was lower for African Americans, especially for men, leaving many women widowed by their 40s. When property holdings are held constant, however, the higher incidence of one-parent families among African Americans largely disappears revealing the significant impact of economic factors on family stability (Mintz and Kellogg, 1988:78–79).

NATIVE-AMERICAN FAMILIES

A review of the literature on family life among early Native-American peoples reveals that no one description adequately covers all Native-American families. Prior to the European settlement of North America, Native-American peoples were widely dispersed geographically. As a result, each group developed an economic system, a style of housing, and a kinship system that fit the demands of its particular environment. Even those groups living in the same region of the country were likely to develop different organizational patterns (Mintz and Kellogg, 1988). For example, there were two basic language groups among the Woodland groups living in the Northeast: the Algonquin and the Iroquois. The social and economic unit of the Algonquins was a dome-shaped structure called a *wigwam*, usually occupied by one or two families. In contrast, the basic social unit of the Iroquois was the *longhouse*, a large, rectangular structure containing about ten families.

Among groups living in the Southeast social life centered around the extended family. After marriage the new husband went to live in his wife's family's household. For many tribes living in what is now California, however, that pattern was reversed, and the wife moved in with her husband's family after marriage. The basic economic unit for the Eskimos who inhabited the Arctic regions was either a family composed simply of wife, husband, and children or a household containing two such families.

RULES OF MARRIAGE The rules of marriage also varied from one group to another. Although most Native-American peoples practiced monogamy, some were polygamous. Unhappy marriages were easily dissolved in some groups, with either spouse able to divorce the other. Among some peoples special practices governed widowhood. In the *sororate* a widower married a sister of his deceased wife; in the *levirate* a widow married one of her dead husband's brothers.

Native-American women married early, many between the ages of 12 and 15. Men were usually several years older than women when they married. There was considerable variation in mate selection among different groups. Some permitted free choice, whereas others practiced arranged marriages.

CHILDHOOD Rules of descent also varied among Native-American societies. Some peoples, like the Cheyenne, were **patrilineal**, whereby property and status in the tribe came through one's father. Others, like the Pueblos, were **matrilineal**, whereby membership in the group was determined by the mother. Historical records indicate that Native-American families were generally small. Infant and child mortality were high. Additionally, mothers nursed their children for 2 or more years and refrained from sexual intercourse until the child was weaned.

In contrast to early European families, Native-American parents rarely used physical punishment to discipline their children. Instead, they relied on praise, ridicule, and public rewards to instill desired behavior. Among some groups child care was in the hands of mothers; among others fathers and maternal uncles played a more significant role. From early on children worked alongside their parents and other adults to learn the skills that would be required of them as adults.

CONSEQUENCES OF EUROPEAN CONTACT

One of the first consequences of contact with Europeans was a sharp increase in mortality rates. Native Americans lacked immunity to the diseases carried by white settlers. Consequently, thousands died from influenza, measles, smallpox, and typhoid fever. And, although some of the early contact between the two groups was friendly and character-ized by mutual exchanges of goods and services, the clash of cultural differences soon dominated inter-group contacts. Europeans found it difficult to understand and even harder to appreciate the diverse patterns of family life that existed among Native Americans. *Ethnocentrism*, the belief that one's culture is superior to others, led the Europeans to denigrate the lifestyles of Native Americans and to treat them as subhuman. This inability and unwillingness to accept Native-American culture as valid, combined with the introduction of firearms and alcohol and the ever increasing competition for land, led to violent clashes between the two groups. In the end many Native Americans were displaced from their home-lands and forced onto reservations, where many of their cultural values and practices were systematically undermined. Since that time, many Native-American peoples have struggled to revitalize their culture.

FAMILIES IN THE NINETEENTH CENTURY

Major changes occurred in the United States at the beginning of the nineteenth century, radically trans-forming family life. New technology brought about the creation of the factory system, which required a concentrated supply of labor away from the home. Wages took the place of private family farms or shops as the main means of economic livelihood. The patri-archal preindustrial household no longer functioned as a unit of economic production. Consequently, it grew smaller in size as apprentices and other live-in laborers gradually left to find work in the new facto-ries. Over time the nuclear family of only parents and children became the new family form, a form that has lasted well into the twentieth century. Work and family became separated, leading to the development of a division of family labor that divided the sexes and the generations from each other in new and far-reaching ways. These changes did not affect all fami-lies in the same way, however. There were significant variations across race and class.

EMERGENCE OF THE GOOD PROVIDER ROLE

In the opening stages of industrialization, women and children worked in the factories. After that period, however, men became the predominant workers in the factories, mines, and businesses of the nation. According to sociologist Jesse Bernard (1981), a spe-cialized male role known as the *good provider* role emerged around 1830. The essence of the role was that a man's major contribution to his family is economic, that is, as primary (and often sole) wage earner. Masculinity became identified with being a successful breadwinner (Demos, 1974). To be a success in the breadwinning role men had to concentrate their ener-gies on work, and other roles such as husband, father, and community member became less important. Consequently, husbands and fathers were often emo-tionally as well as physically distant from their families.

Throughout U.S. history, Native-American families have had to struggle to maintain their cultural and family traditions.

More and more, men's status and, therefore, that of their families depended on their occupation. Men's success was measured by whether they could afford to keep their wives and children out of the labor force.

THE CULT OF DOMESTICITY

The movement of production out of the household affected the roles of women, too. Although from the beginning of U.S. history women were encouraged to think of themselves primarily in a domestic role, as industrialization advanced, this ideology became even more prevalent. Now women were expected to stay at home, have children, and be the moral guardians of the family. This *cult of domesticity*, or as historian Barbara Welter (1978) called it, the "cult of true womanhood," was the counterpart to the good provider role. If men were to spend long hours working away from home, then women would offer men emotional support, provide for their daily needs, raise the children, and, in short, create for men a "haven in a heartless world" (Lasch, 1977). Aspects of this domestic role were oppressive and limiting for women, who by and large were excluded from most institutional life outside the family.

CHANGING VIEWS OF CHILDHOOD

The economic transformation that took place in the early nineteenth century altered not only marital roles but also children's roles. Childhood came to be seen as a distinct period, a time of innocence and play without much responsibility. Children no longer had to begin productive work at an early age. Instead, they became economic dependents. During this time, children's birthdays became occasions to celebrate, and the first specialty toy stores for children were opened. For the first time, books written especially for children were published, and other books were targeted for mothers to give them guidance about child rearing.

THE IMPACT OF CLASS AND ETHNICITY

The family lifestyle just described did not apply to all families but primarily to white middle- and upper-class families in which the father made a "family wage" that

enabled him to support his entire family. In contrast, large numbers of African-American, immigrant, and native-born white working-class men found it impossible to support their families on their income alone. Thus, the working-class family did not embrace the ideal of privacy and separate spheres of a nuclear unit to the same degree as did the middle class. Working-class family boundaries were more fluid. Between 1850 and 1880 there was an increase in the number of extended families among the urban, industrial, immigrant working class (Coontz, 1988:306).

Additionally, working-class family life, both for blacks and whites, did not develop in isolation from the community. Alleys, stoops, gangways, and streets functioned as common areas where adults could socialize, exchange information, and observe their children at play. Contrary to many stereotypes of working-class families, there was no simple or rigid gender differentiation in these activities. In fact, "In the 1880s, when the first modern investigations of working-class family life were undertaken by the Massachusetts Bureau of Labor Statistics, one of the findings that most shocked and dismayed the middle-class male investigators was that working-class men would cook, clean, and care for the children while their wives were at work and they were not" (quoted in Coontz, 1988:306).

IMMIGRATION AND FAMILY LIFE

Many working-class families in the nineteenth century were immigrants. Between 1830 and 1930, over 30 million immigrants left their homes to come to the United States. The first wave of immigrants were predominantly from Northern and Western Europe—England, Germany, Ireland, and Scandinavia. Beginning in the early 1880s, emigration patterns shifted to Southern and Eastern Europe—Italy, Greece, Austria–Hungary, and Russia. Historians refer to the Slavs, Italians, Greeks, and Eastern European Jews who came to the United States at this time as the "new" immigrants. Frequently, the decision to emigrate followed economic or political upheavals. At the same time, immigrants were attracted to the United States by the promise of land and jobs.

The manner of emigration varied. Some immigrants, especially the Italians, Poles, and Slavic peoples, came without families, planning to return home after making their fortunes. A Polish folk song conveys the enormity of disruption such families experienced when the father returned after several years. "There my wife was waiting for me. And my children did not know me. For they fled from me, a stranger. My dear children I'm your papa; three long years I have not seen you" (quoted in Daniels, 1990:219). Other unaccompanied immigrants hoped to earn enough to send for their families. Still others came with their families and planned to settle permanently in the United States. To help ease their problems of adjustment, these new arrivals, whether alone or with families, sought out family, friends, or neighbors from their native country who were already settled here.

All immigrant groups faced a common set of problems: language barriers, periodic unemployment, difficulties in finding housing, inadequate income, and often hostility from native-born workers who feared the immigrants would take their jobs and lower the overall wage scale. Each group of immigrants developed distinct family and work patterns in response to these problems. At the same time immigrants shared many common experiences with native-born members of the working class. Among the most serious of these was the need to have more than one breadwinner so that they could make ends meet.

THE ECONOMIC ROLES OF WOMEN AND CHILDREN

Women and children in the working class contributed to the material support of the family in a variety of ways. Overall, a working-class wife did not work outside the home unless her spouse lost his job or was unable to work because of illness or injury. Maintaining a household was a full-time job. Working-class wives grew some of their own food, baked bread, carried water and wood for cooking and heating, managed the family finances, and coordinated the schedules of working members. Additionally, wives often supplemented family income by taking in boarders or by doing laundry or sewing in their homes. Working outside the home was more common among first-generation immigrant women whose husbands earned less than their native-born counterparts. The choice of occupation varied among ethnic groups. For example, Polish women chose domestic work over factory work, whereas the opposite pattern was true for Jewish women (Coontz, 1988).

Working-class children did not experience the luxury of a playful childhood. As the FYI box documents, children were employed in factories by the age of 8. Even though children and women worked as hard and as long as men, often in unhealthy and unsafe environments, they were paid considerably lower wages than men. "Until the end of the nineteenth century, women customarily received about one-third to one-half of the prevailing male wage, a sum seldom sufficient even for a single woman to support herself" (Kessler-Harris, 1981:62).

ETHNIC AND RACIAL FAMILY PATTERNS

Racism and discrimination also made a profound difference in how work and family roles were constructed. For example, although immigrant Chinese males were recruited to build the railroads of America, they were not allowed to build families. The Chinese Exclusion Act of 1882 restricted Chinese immigration and thus restricted Chinese women from joining the men already here. "From 1860 to 1890 the sex ratio fluctuated from 1284 to 2679 Chinese men per 100 Chinese women" (Wong, 1988:235). Faced with this unbalanced sex ratio and prevented by law from marrying whites, single Chinese laborers were destined to remain bachelors if they stayed in the United States. Married Chinese laborers, who were required to leave their families behind, could play the "good provider" role only minimally by sending money home to China. Sociologist Evelyn Nakano Glenn (1983) called this pattern of maintenance the "split-household family system."

With the end of slavery black men, like white men, preferred that their wives remain at home. African-American men had difficulties finding jobs, however, and when they did, the jobs paid very poorly. Thus, these men could not afford to keep their wives and daughters from working. "In 1900 approximately 41 percent of black women were in the labor force, compared with 16 percent

FOR YOUR INFORMATION

FAMILY CONTRACT

During the nineteenth century, it was common for fathers to seek employment for themselves and their children with one employer. They often signed contracts like the one below that specified the wages each member of the family would receive:

Dennis Rier of Newbury Port has this day engaged to come with his family to work in our factory on the following conditions. He is to be here about the 20th of next month and is to have the following wages per week:

Himself	$5.00
His son Robert Rier, 10 years of age	.83
Daughter Mary, 12 years of age	1.25
Son William, 13 years of age	1.50
Son Michael, 16 years of age	2.00
	10.58
His sister, Abigail Smith	2.33
Her daughter Sally, 8 years of age	.75
Son Samuel, 13 years of age	1.50
	4.58

House rent to be from $20 to $30. Wood cut up $2. per cord.

Source: Selected "Family Contract" from *America's Families: A Documentary History* by Donald M. Scott and Bernard Wishy. Copyright © 1982 by Donald M. Scott and Bernard Wishy. Reprinted by permission of HarperCollins, Publishers, Inc.

---

of white women" (quoted in Staples, 1988:307). Sojourner Truth, a former slave, speaking as far back as 1851 at a women's rights convention in Akron, Ohio, eloquently addressed the exclusion of African-American women from the "cult of true womanhood."

"That man over there says that women need to be helped into carriages, and lifted over ditches, and to have the best place everywhere. Nobody ever helps me into carriages, or over mud puddles, or gives me any best place! And ain't I a woman? Look at me! Look at my arm! I have ploughed and planted, and gathered into barns and no man could head me! And ain't I a woman? I could work as much as a man—when I could get it—and bear the lash as well! And ain't I a woman? I have borne thirteen children, and seen them most all sold off to slavery, and when I cried out with my mother's grief, none but Jesus hear me! And ain't I a woman?" (Quoted in Schneir, 1972:94–95)

MEXICAN-AMERICAN FAMILIES

Similarly, Chicanos (Mexican Americans) were rarely able to exercise the good provider or domestic roles exclusively either. After the Mexican-American War in 1848, the United States annexed a considerable amount of Mexico's territory, an area that encompasses present-day Texas, New Mexico, Arizona, and California. The Mexicans who lived within this new region were granted U.S. citizenship and the right to retain ownership of their land by the Treaty of Guadalupe Hidalgo. Through unscrupulous practices of some Anglos, however, many of the original Chicano landowners soon lost their land. The erosion of the Chicano agrarian economic base had a profound impact on Mexican-American family life.

FAMILY AND KINSHIP One of the most distinctive features of the Chicano family was its emphasis

Sojourner Truth was born a slave in Ulster County, New York, and sold four times before she was 30 years old. She obtained her freedom in 1827. An electrifying public speaker, she became a forceful advocate for human rights for all people.

ents, providing discipline, companionship to both parents and godchildren, emotional support, and, when needed, financial aid (Griswold del Castillo, 1984).

MARITAL ROLES Chicano households tended to be large. In part this was due to a high fertility rate, but households also expanded in response to economic privation as kin and unrelated individuals, especially children, were taken in by other families. Households practiced a fairly rigid division of labor based on gender. Wives were expected to stay home and take responsibility for domestic chores and child rearing. They were also expected to be the carriers of cultural traditions and to organize celebrations of important rituals such as baptisms, weddings, saints' days, and funerals.

In contrast, men were expected to protect and control their families and to perform productive work outside the household. This traditional male role is sometimes referred to as *machismo.* Although some writers have called attention to the negative aspects of this role, such as male infidelity and oppression of women (Madsen, 1964), most contemporary social scientists believe that these aspects have been exaggerated. More recent research tends to focus on what has been called a "genuine machismo" characterized by bravery, courage, and generosity (Mirande, 1985).

SIGNS OF CHANGE White settlers bought up large tracts of land in the Southwest and instituted commercial agricultural production. The displaced Chicanos became a source of cheap labor. Much of this work was seasonal, and men experienced periodic unemployment. At times men migrated in search of jobs in the mines or on the railroads. As a result, their wives became heads of families, sometimes on a permanent basis as a result of prolonged separation, divorce, or, more frequently, desertion. Even when men worked full-time, their wages were often insufficient to support their families. Consequently, wives and mothers were drawn into the labor force, most frequently in low-paying domestic or agriculture-related work such as canning and packing-house work. Kinship structures were weakened as entire families left the area to find work. With the entrance of wives into the labor force and the frequent migration of families outside their familiar cultural area,

on familism, "a constellation of values which give overriding importance to the family and the needs of the collective as opposed to individual and personal needs" (Bean et al., 1977:760). Although the primary family unit was nuclear and patriarchal in form, there was heavy reliance on extended kinship networks for emotional and economic support. Another centuries-old source of support was the ritual kinship of *compadrazgo*, which linked two families together. Within this system, *madrinos*, or godmothers, and *padrinos*, or godfathers, were carefully chosen from outside the kinship circle to become members of the extended family, participating in all the major events of their godchildren's lives. In effect, they assumed the role of *compadres* or copar-

the foundation of the patriarchal family structure began to erode. Working wives demanded more power in decision making, and by the twentieth century a new balance in gender relations was already being observed. Like other families before them, the Chicano family was realigning itself.

FAMILIES IN THE EARLY TWENTIETH CENTURY

Although they applied only to certain groups, these idealized images of men as providers and women as homemakers continued to influence popular thought about the family well into the twentieth century. However, economic and political changes were already at work to undermine these roles. Technological innovations led to the mass production of goods and to the development of large-scale corporations. These developments affected almost every aspect of social relationships.

In this new work environment the demand for child labor declined, and schools assumed more of the responsibility for the socialization of children. Young working-class women increasingly left domestic service for better opportunities in industry and in the expanding clerical fields. As a result, social contacts increasingly took place outside the family as women and men worked in proximity to each other. New products such as movies, amusement parks, and the automobile changed family recreation patterns. Young adults dated without chaperons and placed more emphasis on personal and sexual attractiveness. Women, discontented with the restrictions of their domestic role, became activists for women's rights, particularly the right to vote.

THE EMERGENCE OF THE COMPANIONATE FAMILY

These changes gradually led to a shift away from the nineteenth century ideal of the family. In its place emerged the idea of a more personal and companionate model for heterosexual relationships based on mutual affection, sexual fulfillment, and sharing of domestic tasks and child rearing. Personal happiness came to be viewed as the primary goal of marriage. New symbols, for example the observance of

Mother's Day, were created to celebrate family life. Although economic and social inequalities persisted across groups, this new model of the family took hold, and many of the distinct cultural differences among families began to disappear.

Other changes were helping reshape families. Life expectancy had increased. Thus, families were less likely to be disrupted by the premature death of spouses. In the short span of 40 years, from 1900 to 1940, the chances of a marriage lasting 40 or more years increased from one in three to one in two (Mintz and Kellogg, 1988:131). Medical advances reduced the rate of infant mortality. The availability of contraceptives allowed couples to plan their families and to enjoy the pleasures of marital sex without fear of an unwanted pregnancy.

SIGNS OF STRESS   There was another side to these changes in family life, however. As more people came to expect companionship and emotional fulfillment in marriage, they also became more willing to terminate an unhappy relationship. In a manner reminiscent of today's controversy over "family values," people in the 1920s and 1930s disagreed over the significance of these changes. Some saw the increase in the divorce rate, the decline in the birthrate, the increase in the number of married women workers, and the change in sexual behavior as a sign of family disintegration and a breakdown of moral values. Others, however, interpreted these same patterns as signs of greater freedom of choice and as a continuing response to changing economic and social conditions in the larger society.

THE GREAT DEPRESSION

In the 1930s, families were rocked by an economic crisis of staggering proportions. Millions of workers throughout the country were unemployed for periods of 1 to 3 years or longer. The consequences of joblessness were enormous. Some families became homeless and wandered from city to city in hopes of finding food and shelter; other families were forced to share living quarters. Young adults delayed marriage, couples postponed having children, and the number of desertions increased. The Depression affected all members of the family, but in particular it undermined the male breadwinner role. This inability to

Major economic upheavals, like the Depression, disrupted the lives of millions of families. Families, like this one from Texas, were often forced to leave relatives and friends behind as they searched for work.

support their family eroded the self-esteem of many fathers. Growing numbers of women became the major source of family income.

Although all groups suffered economic hardships during the Depression, the elderly; the poor; and those in low-paid, unskilled jobs, predominantly people of color, were hardest hit. Family stability was often a casualty of economic instability. As is the case today, high rates of unemployment, lack of stable jobs, and inadequate wages made it difficult for lower-class men to fulfill a breadwinner role. The severe problems confronting millions of families led to a shift in thinking about the family. No longer could the myth of the self-reliant family be sustained. Clearly, outside support was necessary if families were to weather the economic upheavals. The government responded to the Depression by creating a series of social programs, known collectively as the New Deal, to aid distressed workers and their families.

WORLD WAR II AND ITS AFTERMATH

No sooner was the Depression over than another major upheaval confronted families. World War II brought about numerous changes, primary among

them being the dramatic increase in the marriage rate. Between 1940 and 1946 it is estimated that 3 million more Americans married than would have been expected had rates remained at prewar levels (Bailey, 1978:51). There were many reasons for this upsurge. Some couples had postponed marriage because of the Depression and were now financially able to marry. Others feared that if they didn't marry now, it might prove to be too late later on. Some servicemen, fearing their deaths in battle, asked women to marry them "to give them some happiness before going off to fight." Similarly, there was a dramatic increase in the birthrate as many couples decided to have a child right away.

Millions of families were disrupted by wartime migration to find work and by long-term separations for military service. These disruptions resulted in changes in family roles and functioning. With husbands and fathers off to war, wives, mothers, and teenagers went to work in war-related industries. During the war years 250,000 women worked in plants manufacturing electrical equipment; 100,000 worked in ammunition plants; 300,000 built airplanes; and 150,000 worked as riveters, welders, and crane operators in the nation's shipyards (cited in Mintz and Kellogg, 1988:161). "Rosie the Riveter" became a popular image of the woman factory worker. These changes made conditions difficult for families. Although some preschool children were cared for in government-sponsored day-care centers, many mothers had to find child care on their own. As raw materials were diverted to support the war effort, many families faced shortages in housing and other consumer goods.

Although the majority of families experienced some dislocation during the war years, this experience was most intense for Japanese Americans on the West Coast, who were forcibly relocated from their homes to detention centers in isolated regions of several western states. This massive relocation was inspired by fear, prejudice, and economic jealousy and resulted in depression, deprivation, and often family conflicts among the detainees.

Problems did not end with the cessation of hostilities. Families that had been separated for several years had enormous adjustments to make. Many reunited couples were like strangers to each other. Spouses had

During World War II the image of Rosie the Riveter became popular. However, the ideology of women as men's help-mates had not changed, as evidenced in the language of this poster.

grown in different ways. Wives who had assumed both financial and economic responsibilities for their families had experienced a sense of independence, self-confidence, and self-sufficiency that was often at odds with their husbands' desire to return to a traditional family arrangement. Postwar housing shortages contributed to family strain as newly reunited couples found themselves living with other relatives in overcrowded conditions. Children who spent some of the war years as "latchkey" kids, taking care of themselves while their mothers worked, resented the new imposition of parental discipline. Many families were unable to survive the tensions and hardships created by the war and its aftermath. Divorce rates soared. In 1940, one marriage in six had ended in divorce; by 1946 the figure stood at one in four (cited in Mintz and Kellogg, 1988:171).

CONTEMPORARY PATTERNS IN MARRIAGES AND FAMILIES

Given this review of the history of families in the United States, today's patterns may seem more a continuation of trends rather than startling new phenomena. For example, over the last 100 years there has been a steady increase in the number of mothers of small children who are in the labor force (See Chapter 11) and in the percentage of couples who divorce before their children reach adulthood.

In tracking these changes, the U.S. Bureau of the Census distinguishes between households and families. **Households** are defined as all persons who occupy a housing unit, such as a house, apartment, single room, or other space intended to be living quarters (Ahlburg and DeVita, 1992:5). Figure 1.2 reveals some of the changes in U.S. households between 1970 and 1990. One of the most significant changes is the increase in nonfamily households, which grew from 19 percent of all households in 1970 to 29 percent in 1990. According to the Census Bureau, nonfamily households are made up of elderly individuals living alone; people of the same sex who share living quarters, often for financial reasons; cohabiting couples; adults who delay or forgo marriage; or those who are "between marriages."

We find a similar diversity when we look at family composition. Table 1.2 reveals the changes that occurred between 1970 and 1990. The number of married couples with children declined from almost 50 percent of all families in 1970 to only 37 percent in 1990. Population experts project a further decline by the year 2000. Within that broad category are also distinct family forms: the intact biological family and the remarried or step-family (see Chapter 14). Either of these family forms may include children that are adopted or were conceived through one of the new reproductive technologies discussed in Chapter 9. The number of married couples without children has also increased. Here again there is no one pattern. Some of these couples have not yet had children, others have completed their child rearing, and still others will never have children, either by choice or because of fertility problems.

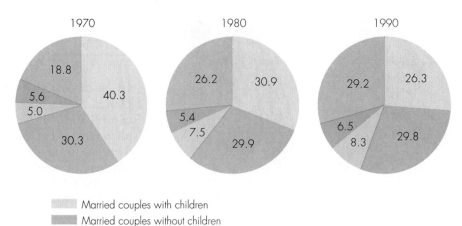

FIGURE 1.2 The Composition of U.S. Households, by Percent, 1970–90

Source: Adapted from U.S. Bureau of the Census, 1990b, *Current Population Reports*, Series P-20, No. 447, "Household and Family Characteristics: March 1990 and 1989" (Washington, DC: U.S. Government Printing Office): 2.

1970

1980

1990

Married couples with children
Married couples without children
Other families with children
Other families without children
Nonfamily households

TABLE 1.2

Family Composition in the United States, 1970–2000

Type of Family	1970	1990	1995	2000
Married couple with children	49.6%	36.9%	36.2%	34.5%
Married couple without children	37.1	41.7	41.8	42.8
Female head with children	5.7	10.2	10.0	9.7
Male head with children	0.7	1.8	2.2	2.7
Other families	6.9	9.4	9.8	10.3

Source: Adapted from Dennis A. Ahlburg and Carol J. DeVita, 1992, "New Realities of the American Family," *Population Bulletin* 47, 2 (Washington, DC: Population Reference Bureau, Inc.) (August): 7.

LESSONS FROM HISTORY

This brief overview of current marriage and family patterns clearly reveals diverse family structures. As we have seen, family diversity is not a new phenomenon in the United States; rather, it is deeply rooted in our nation's past. What lessons then can we draw from this historical review? Five points seem relevant:

1. Although families have changed continuously over time, this change has not been in any single direction.

2. We cannot say with any certainty which changes have been good or bad. Rather, each change brings with it gains and losses. For example, the creation of childhood as a separate and distinct period created many opportunities for children's growth and development, but it also kept them dependent on parents for longer periods of time.

3. Throughout history there has never been a perfect family form that has protected its members from poverty or social disruption, nor has any one structure provided a workable model for how all families might organize their relations in the modern world.

4. Understanding the source of our idealized view of the "traditional" family can lead us to develop a more realistic sense of families both in the past and in the present. Studying families in the past can help us see how they endured and adapted to historical changes. It also helps us realize that many of the changes we observe in contemporary families and that cause us concern, such as the increasing number of children living in poverty and unstable families, are not a result of changing family values per se. Rather, they are more frequently reactions to rapid economic and social transformations taking place on an unprecedented scale. To take one example, within our lifetime we have witnessed the rise of a global economy, which has meant greater competition for the United States. Thus, today's families and the communities in which they live confront powerful forces that are redesigning and redistributing jobs, increasing inequality, and shifting population in and out of cities and regions across the country.

5. Given past history, it is likely that additional changes in family life will continue to occur as families continue to adapt to changing economic, social, and political forces. The more we understand these changes and their impact on families, the more likely that we can develop social policies to assist families in adapting to these changes. We will explore these themes throughout the remainder of the text.

APPLYING THE SOCIOLOGICAL IMAGINATION

In 1959, sociologist C. Wright Mills wrote a book called *The Sociological Imagination*, which has since become a classic in the field. Mills describes how in this age of rapid change ordinary people often feel overwhelmed by the events confronting them, feeling that their private lives are a series of traps over which they have little control. People feel that cherished values are being undermined, and replaced with ambiguity and uncertainty. He believes that part of the reason for this sense of frustration and powerlessness is that our way of looking at the world is limited to the close-up scenes of our jobs, families, and neighborhoods.

Mills argues that individuals can understand their own experiences and gauge their own fate only by locating themselves within their historical period. By this he means that we can understand our own chances in life by becoming aware of those of all individuals in our same circumstances. Thus, he calls on us to develop a "sociological imagination," to

grasp history and biography and the relations between the two within our society. To do this requires asking three questions: (1) What is the structure of a particular society, and how does it differ from other varieties of social order? (2) Where does this society stand in human history, and what are its essential features? (3) What varieties of women and men live in this society and in this period, and what is happening to them?

The sociological imagination allows us to distinguish between what Mills calls "personal troubles of milieu" and the "public issues of social structure." A "trouble" is a private matter, occurring within the character of the individual and within the range of his or her immediate relationship with others. An "issue," however, is a public matter that transcends the local environment of the individual. For example, any couple may experience personal troubles in their marriage, but a U.S. Bureau of the Census (1992) report that 1.2 million divorces occurred in

1990 is an indication of a structural issue having to do with the institutions of marriage and the family and with the other institutions that affect them. Mills argues that many of the things we experience are caused by structural changes. Thus, to understand the changes that affect our personal lives, we must look beyond our private experiences to examine the larger political, social, and economic issues that affect our lives and the lives of others in our society.

Put the sociological imagination to work for you by identifying one or several aspects of your own biography—marital status, age, race, class, or gender. Imaginatively transport yourself to an earlier period of history. What would your life have been like if you had lived during that historical period? In what specific ways would it differ from your life today? Would the quality of your family life have been better or worse than it is today? Explain.

SUMMARY

Marriage and family are among the oldest human social institutions. Each society develops its own patterns of marriage and family life, and these patterns vary considerably across and within cultures. In recent years family values have become a topic for debate in the United States. Such debates are often clouded by mythology about the way families used to be. Myths are false, fictitious, imaginary, or exaggerated beliefs that can create unrealistic expectations about what families can or should be. Five of the most popular myths and stereotypes are directly

applicable to current debates about family life and gender roles are (1) the "self-reliant" traditional family, (2) the "naturalness" of the separate spheres of wives and husbands, (3) the private and autonomous family, (4) the collapse of the African-American family, and (5) the idealized nuclear family of the 1950s.

The discussion of mythical versus real families underscores the fact that not all families are the same; there is not now and never has been a single model of the family. Families are a product of their historical context, and at any given historical period families occupy different territories and have varied experiences. Race, class, and gender are three interlocking categories of social experience that affect all aspects of human life; they shape all social institutions and systems of meaning, including the institutions of marriage and family, and the discussion of family values.

From the very beginning the United States was economically, racially, religiously, and familially diverse. Native Americans, white ethnic settlers, Africans forcibly brought to this country as slaves, and Chicanos whose land was annexed by the United States all struggled to create and maintain a stable family structure in a new and often hostile environment. Over time these and other immigrant groups confronted powerful economic and political forces such as industrialization, depressions, and wars, which led to major transformations in family life.

KEY TERMS

institution	family of orientation	role
marriage	family of procreation	socialization
monogamy	nuclear family	myth
serial monogamy	extended family	institutional racism
polygamy	modified extended family	kinship
polygyny	patriarchal family	patrilineal
polyandry	norms	matrilineal
cenogamy (group marriage)	social structure	households
family	status	

QUESTIONS FOR STUDY AND REFLECTION

1. How is marriage related to family? Is it possible to be married and not be in a family? Is family life possible without the institution of marriage? Do families have to include children? Why or why not?

2. What is meant by the idea that race, class, and gender are interactive systems rather than individual variables? Think about your own family of orientation, and take one particular aspect of your family life as an example. Discuss briefly how race, class, and gender act simultaneously to shape that aspect of your family life.

3. When immigrant families arrived in the United States, they often faced hostility from groups already here. Notices for job openings often read "Dogs and Irish need not apply." Do you see any similarities in attitudes toward the new immigrants to the United States today such as Latinos, Asian Americans, and Caribbean peoples? What is the cause of such attitudes? What can we learn from the earlier patterns of immigration that might help us in dealing with the new immigrants coming to the United States?

4. Trace some of the major changes that have occurred among U.S. families over the last 200 years. Given your understanding of current social and economic trends, what changes if any do you foresee in the composition of families in the twenty-first century? Explain your reasoning.

FURTHER READING

FINKELMAN, PAUL. 1989. *Women and the Family in a Slave Society*, vol. 9. New York: Garland. Contains reprints of key articles that have influenced our understanding of slavery, including important breakthroughs in research and methodology.

GORDON, MICHAEL, ed. 1983. *The American Family in Social–Historical Perspective*, 3d ed. New York: St. Martin's Press. A rich source of articles on family life in the seventeenth, eighteenth, and nineteenth centuries.

MINDEL, CHARLES H., ROBERT W. HABENSTEIN, AND ROOSEVELT WRIGHT, JR., eds. 1988. *Ethnic Families in America*. New York: Elsevier. Provides fascinating data on a large cross section of ethnic groups in the United States and discusses how social class affects family structure and functioning.

WILLIAMS, NORMA. 1990. *The Mexican-American Family*. New York: General Hall. Examines recent changes in the extended and conjugal family arrangements in the Mexican-American working and professional classes.

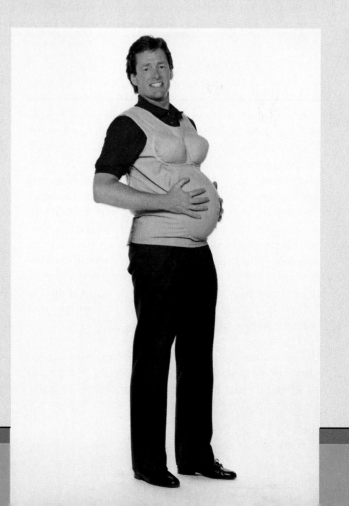

Chapter 2

WAYS OF STUDYING AND EXPLAINING MARRIAGES AND FAMILIES

*W*hat is your reaction to the man in the chapter-opening photo? What is he wearing, and why is he wearing it? Who is this man and what is he thinking? Does he feel his appearance is unusual? Do you? Why is he dressed the way he is? Do you wonder why he is trying to emulate a pregnant woman? Is he trying to make a point? If so, what is his point? Does he think his behavior is normal and acceptable, although others may believe it is strange or perverted? What do we know about men like the one pictured? Perhaps we can begin to understand his behavior by examining the behavior of John in the vignette that follows.

John lives in a midwestern city, where he is a midlevel executive in a small firm. He and his wife, Sarah, the press agent for a local politician, are expecting their first child. John is among a growing number of men labeled by social researchers as nontraditional husbands, who freely share feelings and values with their wives. Before and after their marriage, John and Sarah frequently discussed having children, and both agreed that when the time came the responsibility would fall on both partners rather than solely on Sarah. Both agreed that John would assume a father role that was both active and nurturant.

When Sarah told John that she was pregnant, he was elated to hear that he was going to be a father. He told her that he not only wanted to have a direct role in child rearing but that he would also participate in child-related housework and other domestic responsibilities. As Sarah's pregnancy developed John was very sensitive and responsive to her and the emotional and physical changes she was experiencing. For this reason he decided to use an "empathy belly" that enabled him to simulate pregnancy and experience some of Sarah's experiences, including morning sickness. Although several of John's friends and coworkers ridiculed him, he continued to wear the empathy belly throughout Sarah's pregnancy. After the child was born, John felt that he had developed a special relationship with his daughter that began during the prenatal period, when he shared the pregnancy experience with his wife.

What do you think? Do you think that wearing an empathy belly can be transforming and facilitate a bonding experience with the fetus, or do you think that it is just a lot of hype and simply another infringement by men into the domain of women? If you are a male, would you wear an empathy belly? Why or why not? If you are a female, would you want your husband or partner to wear an empathy belly? Why or why not?

THE SOCIOLOGY OF MARRIAGES AND FAMILIES

It is not unusual to wonder why people act and think the way they do. Why humans behave in the manner that they do is an intriguing question. The sociological perspective and various theories within the discipline provide a unique framework for understanding human behavior. Using John's behavior as an example, how would we go about explaining why he wore an empathy belly even when some of his friends and coworkers ridiculed him? Is his behavior similar to or different from that of other men who work in middle-management jobs? Is there something about John's personality that would make him wear an empathy belly? Or is there something about U.S. society that would lead him to wear an empathy belly?

Traditionally, pregnancy and childbirth have been the domain of women. Men (except for male doctors) were not part of this process and were not expected to know about, understand, or participate in these events. Over the last several decades, women's roles have undergone tremendous change, with a growing number of women deciding to be childless. Traditional norms, however, still define women primarily in terms of their ability to give birth and raise children. Implicit in the traditional view is the idea that pregnancy, childbirth, and mothering are the most important experiences in a woman's life.

In contrast, U.S. men traditionally have not been encouraged to be nurturers and caregivers. Although men are expected to be supportive of pregnant women, they are not typically socialized to think about bonding with children during or after pregnancy, nor are they socialized to understand what women must cope with throughout a pregnancy. Given this reality, how do we explain John's behavior? Do most U.S. men behave in this manner? Only a few? What kind of man wears an empathy belly? What kind of man is John? Is he a "real" man? Your answers to most of these questions would likely explain John's behavior in terms of certain personal characteristics of John himself. The sociological imagination, however, allows us to look beyond John himself (or any individual, for that matter) to the social environment in which he lives so that we can better understand human behavior.

Consider, for example, the dramatic increase over the past few decades in the number of women working outside the home. The mass movement of women into the labor force has affected attitudes toward gender roles and the ways that women and men relate in marriage and family roles. Consequently, a small but growing segment of the population espouses new views of marriages and families that includes sex-role equality and shared roles. For this group, relationships between couples are guided by *androgynous norms*—rules that embody both feminine and masculine traits and capabilities. Thus, doing housework, earning money, and caring for children are thought of as shared responsibilities.

Actual behavior often diverges from these principles, however. Although many men believe in principle in the sharing and interchanging of roles, most spend little time bonding with and nurturing children or doing housework. This fact notwithstanding, at various levels more U.S. men are participating in the pregnancy and birth process than was true in the past.

In essence, then, we cannot look only to the personal character of John or other men who wear empathy bellies: The very structure of marriages and families is in transition. The sociological imagination enables us to identify the link between the personal experiences of people and various structural features of society and to recognize that what is happening to men like John is a point at which their personal lives and larger historical forces intersect.

Some of you might think that because you are already a member of a family, you know all there is to know about marriages and families. In that case you might be asking what sociology can add to what you already know. The answer is that sociologists go beyond individual experiences to study marriages and families in social, historical, political, and cross-cultural contexts. They have conducted thousands of studies on a wide range of marital and family behaviors, relationships, characteristics, and problems. These studies have yielded a tremendous amount of data that have contributed significantly to what we thought we knew about marriages and families.

Furthermore, from their research, sociologists have generated a number of theories that help explain issues like why and how marriages and families emerged, how they are sustained over time, how people involved in these relationships interact with and relate to each other, what significance marriages and families have for U.S. society, and how and why marriages and families change over time. In this chapter we examine the ways in which sociologists discover facts—do research—about marriage and family behaviors and devise theories or explanations of these behaviors. We begin this chapter with a consideration of the link between research and theory.

STUDYING MARRIAGES AND FAMILIES: THE LINK BETWEEN RESEARCH AND THEORY

Sociology involves observing human behavior and society and then making sense out of what we observe. Thus, both research and theory are involved. Research provides us with observations about marriages and families, and various theories and perspectives provide us with basic points of view or frameworks that help us analyze and understand these observations.

What exactly is a theory? A **theory** is an explanation of some phenomenon. Theories relate ideas and observations to each other as well as help explain them. They make certain assumptions about the world, about the nature of society and human behavior. Different assumptions lead to different problems and questions, and therefore, potentially to different answers or explanations about society and human behavior. In addition, most theories include stated or unstated value judgments concerning the topic or issues related to the topic. For example, if we use a theory that assumes that the family is a system held together through a basic harmony of values and interests and that consensus and stability are desirable in the family (a value judgment) because they facilitate this cooperation, then we are most likely to ask questions concerned with order, stability, and balance. Moreover, we are likely to ask questions about how members of families function in an orderly and consensual way to maintain or preserve their families over time. We are less likely to raise questions pertaining to disorder, disagreement, and open hostility in families.

Actually, if you think about it, no theory or perspective on human society and behavior is unbiased or completely value-free. Because they contain assumptions about the nature of human beings and the societies they live in, all such theories implicitly or explicitly suggest that certain arrangements are desirable, good, or better than others. All social theories include these kinds of value judgments.

How do we know, then, if a particular theoretical perspective provides a viable explanation of its subject matter? The answer to this question lies in an understanding of the relationship between theory and scientific research. Theories are important sources of ideas for researchers to test. **Scientific research** provides us with empirical evidence as a basis for knowledge or theories. By **empirical evidence** we mean data or evidence that can be confirmed by the use of one or more of the human senses. Scientific research also allows us to test **hypotheses**, statements of relationships between two or more factors, to determine what is as opposed to what we think should be.

All scientific research is guided by the **scientific method**, a set of procedures intended to ensure accuracy and honesty throughout the research process. The scientific method involves making systematic and objective observations (collecting information), making precise measurements, and reporting the research techniques and results to other interested parties. These procedures permit others to repeat research studies to validate or invalidate previous findings.

Generally speaking, the scientific method refers to the procedures science uses to (1) select or formulate research questions and *operationalize* (state in concrete terms) concepts, (2) select an appropriate research design, (3) collect data, (4) analyze the data, and (5) draw conclusions and report the findings. How these steps are actually carried out is dictated by a number of issues, including the particular research question under study and the researcher's conceptual scheme. Research is also sometimes influenced by practical matters such as the availability of funding, who funds the research, access to subjects, and time constraints. Consequently, biases, compromises, selectivity, and other nonscientific issues often creep into the scientific research process and can have an effect from the beginning to the end of the process.

How exactly are theory and research related? Theory provides insights, often in the form of abstract ideas, into the nature of individuals and soci-

ety, and research provides the objective observations upon which theories are verified. It is a reciprocal, or back-and-forth, relationship. For example, theories that cannot be confirmed by evidence gathered through scientific research mean nothing in and of themselves. Similarly, facts have meaning only when we interpret them and give them meaning based on some theoretical perspective. Contrary to popular belief, facts do not speak for themselves.

METHODOLOGICAL TECHNIQUES IN THE STUDY OF MARRIAGES AND FAMILIES

People today are bombarded with information about marriages and families. We hear, for example, that old-fashioned family moral values have disappeared, that children are having babies, and that entire families are living on the streets. To ascertain what is really happening with marriages and families, we must therefore learn how to separate what is factual from what is not. As previously explained, scientific research enables us to see what is as opposed to what might be, what we want to be, or what we hoped would be. Most research, like theory, begins with the questions why and how. A goal of research is to provide specific answers to questions of why or how by gathering empirical evidence. Ultimately, these answers form explanations or theories about some aspect of human behavior and human society.

A potential problem for all scientific research is objectivity. Researchers constantly have to be aware of how their personal attitudes, expectations, and values might affect their research. It is not possible, even when using the scientific method, to measure or observe social phenomena without committing ourselves to some theoretical perspective. Theory is always implicated in the research process, although it is most often implicit—hidden from view. Therefore, we should be aware that researchers bring theoretical biases into the research process: the problems selected for study, the methods chosen to study those problems, the unique and individual observations made, and general assumptions about the world and about human behavior. The methodological procedures followed have a great effect on the interpretation of the data (Smith, 1981). Although the scientific method minimizes research bias to a great degree, we haven't found a way to eliminate it totally. Therefore, as consumers of massive amounts of research information, we must carefully examine the information we receive and be prepared for the possibility that what is presented as reality is not impartial.

As pointed out earlier, because the study of marriages and families deals with everyday life, we often think we already know all there is to know about these issues. Most people, for example, probably believe that they know all there is to know about welfare and welfare recipients. Most views of welfare include the notion that women who receive welfare have baby after baby as a way to collect higher payments. The findings of scientific research, however, tell us something very different. For example, a recent study of the fertility behavior of women on welfare found that welfare recipients tend to have fewer children than do women in the general population. In addition, the longer a woman receives welfare, the less likely she is to have additional children (Rank, 1989).

In the past, research on families on welfare has reflected a white middle-class bias. Using a mythical model of white middle-class families as a measuring rod, welfare families (often regardless of the empirical evidence) generally have been defined as disorganized and as a system that perpetuates an endless cycle of so-called illegitimate births. Before we accept such viewpoints as factual we must carefully analyze the evidence presented to support such conclusions. This process includes asking questions such as, Are the conclusions actually supported by the empirical evidence? Are the findings presented in such a way that they can be tested by others? What are the biases of the research, and does the researcher state them up front? Basically, we should assess research in terms of its reliability and validity. **Reliability** is the degree to which the research yields the same results when repeated by the same researcher or other researchers. **Validity** is the degree to which the study measures exactly what it claims to be measuring. We should also keep in mind that conclusions are not final but are always open to question and reinvestigation.

In the remainder of this section we examine some of the primary methods used in marriage and family research: surveys, observation, experiments, and case studies. We also address who does and does not get studied by researchers, and why. In this regard, we

pay close attention to issues of ethics and conscious and unconscious biases in the conduct of research on marriages and families.

SURVEYS

One of the quickest ways to find out what we want to know about people is to ask them. **Surveys** do just that: They enable us to gather information by asking people questions. Surveys are particularly useful when what we want to know about people is not easily observable, such as the private lives of married or cohabiting couples. The two basic methods by which researchers ask their questions and receive answers are interviews and questionnaires. The **interview** usually involves one person, the interviewer, asking another person questions, with the interviewer recording the answers. The **questionnaire**, in contrast, usually provides autonomy to the person answering the questions. It is typically a set of printed questions that people read on their own and then record their answers. The survey is the most widely used method of studying marriages and families. It is likely that you or someone you know has participated in a survey regarding some marriage and family issue. You may even have conducted your own survey for a class assignment or some other project. For example, in marriage and family classes students are often asked to survey their parents or grandparents concerning the dating patterns of their youth.

To find out what families actually do in their day-to-day living, sociologists often ask them questions face-to-face in a familiar setting such as the home.

A good example of the use of the survey in marriage and family research is Phillip Blumstein and Pepper Schwartz's (1983) study of U.S. couples. This large-scale survey provided us with important insights into how couples make decisions, what importance sex has in their lives, and how factors such as jobs and money shape their relationships. In terms of couple sexuality, for example, Blumstein and Schwartz found that, in general, the longer people were together, the greater the chance that they would have an outside sexual relationship, a phenomenon that Blumstein and Schwartz described as "nonmonogamy." In their sample, nonmonogamy varied according to the type of relationship a couple shared. For example, married couples were much less likely to be nonmonogamous than were heterosexual cohabiting couples. Lesbians were slightly less likely than cohabiting heterosexual couples to be nonmonogamous, whereas gay couples were the most likely of all to be nonmonogamous.

One of the major advantages of interviews and questionnaires is that they allow researchers to gather large amounts of information at a relatively low cost. On the negative side, the questionnaire method imposes the researcher's point of view on the people being studied by forcing them to respond to questions in terms of preestablished categories of answers. For example, a couple might be given a choice of four categories to describe their relationship when none of these categories is truly appropriate. Another disadvantage is that survey methods must rely on people's ability and willingness to give accurate information, especially when the survey involves information about behavior that is typically considered private, such as sexual relationships. Thus, survey results are sometimes distorted because the respondents say what they think the researcher wants to hear.

OBSERVATION

Surveys are good for telling us what people *say* they do. What people say they do and what they actually do are not always the same, however. An alternative to asking people questions is to observe their behavior systematically. Observational studies are useful when researchers have only a vague idea of the behavior they want to study, when they want to study people or situations that are not accessible to the general public, or when there is no other way to get the information. Researchers may observe behavior in a manner that does not intrude on the situation under study, or they may participate in or become a part of the interaction they are studying. This latter approach is referred to as *participant observation*. Regardless of the approach, observational studies require the researcher to develop a specific set of questions in advance of the study as a way to guide the collection of data.

An interesting example of an observational study in the area of marriages and families is one conducted by researcher Ellen Annandale (1988) at a birthing center operated by midwives. The center's primary objective was the management of woman-directed natural childbirth that avoids such traditional medical practices as the use of drugs and rushing or delaying labor. This philosophy, however, often conflicted with the professional medical model practiced by most obstetricians. In certain cases, for example, more traditional forms of intervention were required to reduce pain or to deal with health risks to the mother or the baby. Thus, the midwives had to compromise their goals, and not all mothers could experience natural childbirth.

A major advantage of observation is that it is, by far, the best method for collecting data on nonverbal behavior. In addition, it allows researchers like Annandale to examine behavior in its natural environment (for example, the birthing center). Although observation is less restrictive or artificial than some other data-collection methods, the presence of the observer makes bias a real possibility. When people are aware that they are being observed, they frequently modify their behavior, either deliberately or subconsciously. This phenomenon, referred to by social scientists as the **Hawthorne effect**, can sometimes be a serious drawback of observational studies. Other problems with observational studies include the following:

- They usually take a long time and thus can be expensive.
- They generally involve only a limited number of subjects.
- They offer the researcher little control over the research situation.

However, the depth of understanding gained through observation research compensates for the disadvantages and has greatly added to our knowledge about marriages and families.

EXPERIMENTS

In an **experiment** the researcher designs a series of steps that enable her or him to examine cause-and-effect relationships among differing phenomena under controlled conditions. Perhaps the greatest advantage of the experimental method is the control it offers the researcher over **variables**—factors that can take on different values in different situations. The classic experimental design is usually conducted in a laboratory setting and involves three basic steps: (1) the *dependent variable*, a variable that is changed or affected by some other variable, is measured; (2) the dependent variable is exposed to the effects of the *independent variable*, a variable that causes change in or affects another variable; and (3) the dependent variable is measured again to see what change, if any, has taken place as a result of exposure to the independent variable.

Very little research is done using the classic experimental design in the area of marriages and families because most marriage and family behaviors and situations cannot readily be replicated in the laboratory. For example, suppose we wanted to examine the strategies families develop to cope with a member who is chronically ill or a substance abuser. Or suppose we wanted to study the type of family interactions and environment that lead some family members to use violence against other members. These situations could hardly be duplicated in a laboratory. When sociologists use experiments, the experiments are usually conducted in the field—the natural environment in which people normally interact—rather than in a laboratory.

Of the methods described in this section, the experiment is the closest to the scientific ideal. It allows the researcher a degree of control that no other method does, and it enables the researcher to study change over time. A disadvantage of experiments is that the experimenter's expectations can affect the results of the experiment. It is always possible that the subjects under study will try to please the researcher and adapt her or his behavior or attitudes accordingly. Perhaps the most important problem with using the experiment is that sufficient control over all variables is impossible in a natural setting, which is where most marriage and family behavior is best studied.

CASE STUDIES

Sociologists who study a particular category of people or a particular situation typically do so as a **case study**. Case studies use newly collected and preexisting data such as those from interviews, participant observation, or existing records for in-depth examination of a particular individual, group, or organization. Researchers Bruce Brown and Tony McCormick's 1988 study of six families in which one family member had suffered a head injury in an accident is an example of the case study method applied to marriage and family issues. These researchers conducted an in-depth study of each family member to uncover the strategies these families developed to cope with the presence of a neurologically disabled family member. Among their many results they found that extended family members and friends initially rallied around the injured person. However, they soon tired of hearing about or being reminded about the problem, and thus they gradually lessened their support. This left immediate or close family members to cope almost exclusively with the disabled member. With lessening support from others, these family members developed a variety of strategies to cope with their family situation.

One of the advantages of a study like Brown and McCormick's is that it provides a great deal of detail about the research subject. In addition, the case study approach offers long-term, in-depth analysis of various aspects of the phenomenon being studied. A disadvantage is that each case study focuses on a very specific case and thus cannot be generalized to the larger population. For example, the Brown and McCormick findings apply to the specific families that they studied and not to all families with a neurologically injured member. Furthermore, as with observation, the presence of the researcher may change how people act or interact. For example, we might ask to what extent Brown and McCormick's presence affected the behaviors of family members. Overall, case studies have provided some significant insights into marriage and family processes. They have helped researchers understand and explain how families create roles, patterns, and rules that various family members follow, very often without even being aware of them.

FEMINIST METHODOLOGY

Over the past few decades feminist scholars have become increasingly concerned with who researchers study and how they study them, how conclusions are drawn, and what evidence those conclusions are based on. They have been particularly concerned with how women have either been omitted from scientific research or have been studied according to male models of attitudes and behavior. Much of their work is a corrective to these problems.

You are probably wondering: What is distinctive about the methods that feminists use? Are their methods fundamentally different from the scientific methods that other researchers use? In fact, no method of research is of itself a feminist method. According to feminist sociologist and researcher Marjorie DeVault (1990), what distinguishes feminist methods is what feminist researchers do—how they use the methodologies available to them. Thus, for example, feminist researchers generally avoid using the more abstract, impersonal methods that characterize **quantitative methods**, those methods designed to study variables that can be measured numerically. Rather, they use **qualitative methods**, those designed to study conditions or processes that are hard to measure numerically. In particular, they utilize field methods such as the in-depth, face-to-face interview, participant observation, and the **ethnography** or *life history*—a study of a particular culture, subculture, or group, most often through the use of participant observation or in-depth interviews. Although other researchers also use these methods, feminist researchers differ in how they define their research goals and how they view their own role as researcher.

A basic goal of feminist research is to present information that had been previously ignored or suppressed so as to make visible both the experiences of the people they study (particularly women) in all their diversity and the **ideologies**, or systems of beliefs, that have kept these experiences invisible. In this respect, gender is at the forefront of analysis, with special attention paid to how race, class, and gender interact and affect the lives of women and men. A major advantage of how feminists do their research is the way they define their role as researcher. As researchers they are conscious of the need to be respectful of the people they are studying, to be personal, collaborative, inclusive, and empowering.

These qualities characterize feminist methods because researchers consciously use techniques of data gathering that allow them to utilize the perspectives of the people they study. Instead of imposing their personal interpretations on the experiences of the people they study, feminist researchers develop theories and explanations that reflect the real-life experiences of their subjects, as reported by the subjects themselves. Ideally, feminist research is inclusive of the experiences of all women and not just a few, and it is empowering to the extent that it seeks to avoid defining women as victims. For example, as we will see in Chapter 12, although women are often victims of violence and abuse, they are also survivors. So feminist researchers view women as actively involved in the world in which they live.

An example of the feminist methodology applied to the people that researchers study can be found in the research on upwardly mobile African-American women that was conducted by one of this text's authors, BarBara Scott. Scott (1988) used the life history method of collecting data about the experiences of these women. Her research showed that race and gender are important factors in upward mobility as well as family socialization. These women's self-reports of the process of mobility as they experienced it have greatly added to our knowledge about mobility, an area of research where previously women and people of color were almost totally excluded.

The choice of the life history method reflected a central assumption of the feminist researcher that behavior can be best understood from the perspective of the persons involved. Scott assumed that her subjects understood their experiences better than other people did, and she respected their way of reporting and interpreting these experiences. Using this method Scott avoided substituting her own interpretations for those of the women she studied. Her methodology was at once personal and collaborative. Scott was both the researcher and the researched in the sense that she, being an upwardly mobile African-American woman, shared many of the experiences of her respondents.

The very features that feminist researchers consider advantageous and confirming have been singled out by critics as an important limitation of this research. Because this research is intentionally personal and collaborative, for example, critics immediately raise the question of objectivity. Many feminist researchers agree that their work is subjective in that it is research on people like themselves—other women. But, they argue, it is also objective in that women's experiences are explained in terms of the forces that shape their lives. Thus, like most research, which to date has been male-centered, feminist research clearly has a point of view and a mission.

A CRITICAL LOOK AT TRADITIONAL RESEARCH ON MARRIAGES AND FAMILIES

Historically, sociology as a discipline has claimed as a major goal the improvement of social life. Today, most sociologists operate from this premise and believe that the purpose of their research is to affect social policy and provide the impetus for social change. Some critics, such as feminist scholars, have argued that in practice sociology has not lived up to this goal. Until the upsurge of the new feminist research and scholarship, women, their experiences, and their consciousness were largely absent from traditional sociological research and the theoretical paradigms that guide sociological thinking (Andersen, 1988). The same can be said of people of color. In addition, sociological researchers historically have failed to recognize groups other than the white middle class. That is, white middle-class marriages and families have been used as the norm against which other families are measured. When lower-class and working-class families differ from the white middle-class model, they are defined as deviant. At the other end of the class continuum, little scientific research has been conducted among the upper classes. Thus, much of what we know is based on a model of the family that represents only a small proportion of today's marriages and families.

WHO DOES AND DOES NOT GET STUDIED

Conventional topics studied by sociologists lead us to ignore issues that would illuminate women's lives. When women have been studied in traditional mar-

riage and family research, for example, it has usually been in terms of a one-dimensional stereotypical model of women as nurturant caregivers and caretakers confined to the home. Most of this research has been conducted by men who use themselves as the standard, and gender is seldom considered to be a significant factor that influences behavior. Evidence of this trend recurs in study after study that draws conclusions about marriage and family life based on investigations in which all the research subjects are male. This approach is particularly evident in research concerning issues of individual and family mobility.

The large-scale study of the U.S. occupational structure conducted by noted social scientists Peter Blau and Otis Duncan (1967), for example, has been the definitive statement in the mobility literature. Blau and Duncan concluded that social mobility was simply a function of education and social origins and that no other conditions affect chances for mobility in the United States. Clearly, this set of conclusions ignores the reality of gender and its differing impact for women and men. In fact, Blau and Duncan's research study was based on a national sample of 20,000 men and no women.

Following this pattern, subsequent mobility research has been primarily male-specific, measuring mobility strictly by comparing men occupationally with their fathers. When women's mobility has been addressed, it has been primarily that of white women and has been measured by comparing the husband's occupational standing with that of the woman's father. In general, women's mobility is seen as a function of male status, that of either a father or a husband. The Blau and Duncan model of social mobility is particularly problematic for some women of color, such as African-American women, who historically have been required to work outside the home to help support their families.

Like feminist scholars, African-American and other scholars of color have long criticized social-science research for the negative and stereotypical ways in which African Americans, various people of color, women, and poor and working-class families have been portrayed. African-American women scholars in particular have been particularly vocal in their critiques concerning many myths and half-truths about African-American women and their role in their families.

The longest lasting of these seems to be the myth of the "black matriarchy." One of the most widely publicized documents on African-American family life, sociologist and government researcher Daniel Moynihan's 1965 study titled *The Negro Family: The Case for National Action*, illustrates dramatically the use of social-science methodology to promote ideas that are based on questionable data and oversimplification. The Moynihan Report, as it is often called, has been widely criticized in the social-science literature. Based on U.S. census data, Moynihan found that almost 25 percent of African-American families were female-headed, a statistic he cited as evidence of a "matriarchy." Moynihan then explained the problems in the African-American community in terms of this alleged structural feature of African-American families. Although Moynihan recognized the historical fact of slavery and its impact on African-American family life, he essentially placed the burden of an alleged family pathology squarely on the shoulders of African-American women. In addition, even if one accepts his notion of a black matriarchy, he failed to explain what is innately problematic or detrimental about matriarchies.

In addition to women and various people of color, other groups are either absent from or overrepresented in marriage and family research. For example, very little research has been done on Native-American families. When they are studied, it is often within erroneous or outdated models of family life that are generalized to a very diverse group of people. For example, Native-American families are often described in terms of an extended family model, although many Native-American peoples never adopted that family form.

Research on African-American families exists, but it focuses primarily on lower- and working-class families. As critics have pointed out, not only are most of the subjects of marriage and family research on African-American families from the lower class, but they are frequently from the most deprived segment of the lower class. Little systematic research exists focusing on middle-class families of color, especially the upper-middle class.

Even less is known about wealthy families across race. Thus, like gender and race, class is an important factor in who gets studied and who doesn't. Across race and gender little research is carried out on upper-class families. Power is an issue here. Because women, people of color, and the lower classes generally lack power, they are either largely ignored by

Do soap operas such as "Dynasty" reflect the real-life experiences of the wealthy? Because so little scientific research on the family life of the upper classes exists, we cannot answer this question for certain.

researchers or they are easily accessible to researchers, many of whom allow their race, sex, and class biases to affect their research. Those individuals and families with considerable wealth and power can control researchers' access to them and thus researchers' ability to use them as subjects. Because there is so little information on the marriage and family lifestyles of the upper classes, Americans, hungry for a glimpse of such lifestyles, are fascinated with media portrayals (for example, "Dynasty," "Dallas," "Lifestyles of the Rich and Famous") of how such families live. Whether these media portrayals reflect the real world of upper-class marriages and families is not readily known because there is so little scientific information against which to compare.

THE NEED FOR A NEW SCHOLARSHIP ON MARRIAGES AND FAMILIES

Unfortunately, shoddy research methodologies, faulty generalizations, and researcher biases, myths, stereotypes, and oversimplifications continue to affect some research on marriages and families. Much of this research continues to be sex-, race-, and class-specific, even though it is generalized as applicable to the largest possible population. Social scientist Marianne Ferber's observation on this subject seems appropriate here: "It is interesting to note…one significant difference between studies concerned with only men as opposed to those investigating women. The latter tend to be unmistakably labeled, while the former have titles which give no hint that they are restricted to men" (1982:293).

Scientific research on marriages and families does not exist in a vacuum. Its theory and practice reflect the structure and values of U.S. society. In a society where massive inequalities in power, wealth, and prestige exist among classes and racial groups, as well as between women and men, scientific research, its methods, content, and conclusions, reflects these inequalities. Given this reality, social research must be evaluated by who is or is not the researcher, who does and does not get studied, which theoretical paradigms and underlying assumptions are accepted, which methods are used and how, and what the research actually says and does not say about the subjects. Given our discussion of marriage and family research, there is little doubt that a new scholarship on marriages and families is needed.

As it turns out, we are already witnessing the emergence and proliferation of such a scholarship. Contemporary family researchers exhibit a growing recognition of race, class, and gender diversity in marriage and family lifestyles. Although no research techniques are specific to people of color, women, or poor and working-class people, some existing methods seem more productive than others. For example, as we have already pointed out, various field methods such as face-to-face interviews, participant observation, and case studies enable the research subjects to tell their stories from their own point of view. This newer scholarship has opened up a new and healthy discourse in the area of marriage and family research. This continuing discourse has greatly enhanced our knowledge of marriages and families.

Now let us turn our attention to the other half of the scientific enterprise, namely, theories pertaining to marriages and families.

THEORETICAL PERSPECTIVES

Try as we may we cannot separate theory from real life. The way we look at and understand society and human behavior depends on our theoretical perspective. In sociology, there is no single theory of marriages and families. Many different perspectives exist. By *perspective* we simply mean a broad explanation of social reality from a particular point of view. These perspectives provide us with a basic image of society and human behavior. They define what we should study, what questions we should ask, how we should ask them, what methods we should use to gather information, and how we should interpret the answers or information we obtain. In addition, theoretical perspectives often generate subtheories or theory models. Social scientist David Cheal (1989) describes a **theory model** as a minitheory, a set of propositions that is intended to account for a limited set of facts.

To understand properly the sociology of contemporary marriages and families, we should know something about the different views that are part of the discipline of marriage and family study. It is therefore worthwhile not only to describe the different theoretical perspectives but also to look at them with a critical eye to weigh their relative advantages and disadvantages as explanation systems.

In the remainder of this chapter we examine and critique some of the major theoretical approaches and perspectives in the field of sociology. In addition, we examine and critique some of the specialized theories (theory models) of marriages and families. As you study the different theories of family life presented in this chapter, pay particular attention to how the choice of a theoretical perspective influences not only the way data are interpreted but also the very nature of the kinds of questions asked. Ask yourself how a different theoretical perspective would lead to a different set of questions and conclusions about marriages and families. Ask yourself, for example, how each of these perspectives might explain the behavior of the men in the chapter-opening photo and vignette.

Sociologists approach the study of human behavior and society with a particular set of theoretical assumptions. As in other disciplines, sociology contains not just one but a number of theoretical perspectives. Although there is some debate over how many sociological perspectives exist, there is general agreement that three basic perspectives form the backbone of what has been called mainstream sociology: structural functionalism, conflict theory, and symbolic interaction. To this we add a fourth, the social-exchange perspective. Although none of these theories applies only to marriages and families, we examine them as they have been used to explain marriage and family life in the United States.

STRUCTURAL FUNCTIONALISM

In the history of the sociology of marriages and families, structural functionalism has been one of the leading theoretical perspectives used to explain how families work and how they relate to the larger society. Basically, **structural functionalism** views society as an organized and stable system, analogous to the human system, that is made up of a variety of interrelated parts or structures. Each structure performs one or several functions or meets vital social needs. These structures, sometimes called *subsystems*, are the major social institutions in society and include the family, economy, government, and religion. Each of these structures has a function for maintaining society. The family, for example, through reproduction, provides society with new members, which ensures that society is ongoing. At least in theory, all institutions in society work in harmony for the good of society and themselves. Thus, a functional analysis examines the ways in which each part of a system (society or any one of its parts) contributes to the functioning of society as a whole. In this analysis, the terms *system* and *structure* refer to the interrelatedness or interaction of the parts. *Function* refers to the consequence or impact of something for itself and other parts of the system as well as the system as a whole.

Many Americans believe in a singular model of the family to which all families must conform. Those families that do not conform are seen as problematic. People who believe that families must be structured in a certain way (for example, two parents) to fulfill important family tasks and who see single-parent or female-headed families, stepfamilies, and the changing role of women in marriages and families as threats to marriage and family life or as indicative of the demise of the family share a common view with structural functionalists. Are you a structural functionalist? Do you share these views?

THE FAMILY FROM A FUNCTIONALIST PERSPECTIVE In analyzing the family, a person using the functionalist perspective would ask general questions such as: What do families contribute to the maintenance of society? How does the structure of society affect families? How do families mesh with other institutions in society? Not only does this perspective view society as a system but it regards families themselves as systems. Therefore, a functional analysis would examine such issues as how families organize themselves for survival and what functions families perform for society and for their individual members.

According to functionalists, family functions historically have been divided along gender and age lines. Women and men must perform different tasks, as must younger and older people. Particularly since the Industrial Revolution, an important family task has been to provide economic support for family members. If the family is to survive, someone has to earn money by working for wages outside the home. At the same time, someone must work inside the home to maintain it for the wage earner as well as for other family members. This division of labor

In contrast to the conventional view of families presented in functional theories, today many men are assuming nurturant and child-care roles.

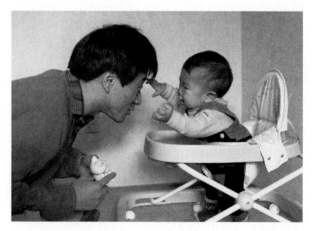

along gender lines is said to make women and men interdependent.

Functionalists are interested not only in the intended, overt, or **manifest functions** of social institutions such as the family but in the unintended, unrecognized, or **latent functions** as well. Thus, a manifest function of having children might be to continue the family lineage or to add to marital satisfaction. Because children can add stress to a relationship, however, the introduction of children in the early years of family life often has the latent function of decreasing marital satisfaction. In addition, not all features of a social system are **functional**—performing a positive service by helping to maintain the system in a balanced state or promoting the achievement of group goals. Some features of the system might actually hamper the achievement of group goals and disrupt the system's balance. Such features are said to be **dysfunctional**. A single feature can be functional and dysfunctional at the same time. For example, the movement of married women into the labor force is functional in that their salaries contribute to the family income but dysfunctional in that their time with their families is limited.

CRITIQUE Probably no other sociological perspective has been the center of as much attention, controversy, and criticism as structural functionalism. Although it was the dominant theory in the field for over 30 years, the changing political consciousness of the 1960s brought about increasing criticism of this perspective. Today, functionalism has greatly declined in importance as a viable frame of reference for understanding society, its institutions, and its members. In fact, some of its strongest supporters during its peak now declare that it is "embarrassing" (Moore, 1978) and "dead," and that it should be abandoned and replaced by more enlightened perspectives (Turner and Maryanski, 1979).

Although functionalism has provided some insights, such as how marriages and families work and presumably why they exist, there are several important problems with this perspective. First, it implies *functional imperatives*, inherent purposes or ends for institutions and commodities. For example, the purpose of a luxury yacht is entertainment and comfort; it is designed and built with that goal in mind. Applying this kind of reasoning to society and its institutions is problematic. Although families

often set goals for members, such as securing and maintaining a particular lifestyle, it is questionable whether any given set of goals preceded the development of marriage and family systems.

Moreover, although functionalism may be a useful framework for identifying a society's structural parts and the alleged functions of these parts, what function a particular structure serves and why is not always clear. For example, what is the function of the division of labor in the family along gender lines? Is it efficiency and survival, as the functionalists maintain, or is it the perpetuation of the social dominance of certain categories of people, namely, men; and the subordination of others, namely, women? A third and equally important criticism is the conservative bias of functional analysis. Critics argue that by assuming that consensus lies at the basis of any social order, functionalists tend to promote and rationalize the status quo and to understate disharmony and conflict. Thus, they do not consider that something might be wrong with the system itself.

CONFLICT THEORY

Since the 1960s, the conflict perspective has become increasingly popular and important in modern sociology and in the works of feminist scholars across academic disciplines. There are several different approaches to conflict theory; however, all of them have their roots in the nineteenth-century pioneering writings of Karl Marx. Thus, our discussion here is of a very general nature and combines various strands of thought on conflict theory today. First, however, we take a brief look at Marxian theory.

KARL MARX Karl Marx (1818–83) was an economist, political agitator, and social theorist who did much to revolutionize social and philosophical thinking about human society. Appalled by the brutal treatment of workers and their families during the nineteenth-century Industrial Revolution in Europe, Marx sought to understand the causes of this condition, in order to change it. Basically, he believed that the problem lay in the social organization of industrial societies. Such societies were capitalistic: The means of production were privately owned and were used to maximize profits.

Karl Marx is perhaps the best known conflict theorist. His insights about the relationship between social structure and conflict continue to influence modern sociologists, some of whom apply his principles to the study and understanding of marriages and families.

For Marx, every aspect of social life is based on economic relationships. For example, he believed that all industrialized societies are characterized by competition and conflict between two main groups: the *capitalists* (owners of the land and factories) and the *proletariat* (workers). These two groups have fundamentally opposing interests, as well as unequal power. Conflict arises because the capitalists can maximize their profit only by exploiting the proletariat. At the same time, it is in the interest of the proletariat to revolt and overthrow the capitalist system and to establish a classless society in which wealth and power would be distributed evenly. Thus, meaningful social change comes about only as a result of the struggle between competing groups. In essence, for Marx, economic power explains the structure of societies and social relationships: Order and balance are always tenuous in capitalist societies. Such societies are held together by the power of capitalists to dominate the worker.

Relative to the fundamental sociological question, What is the relationship between the individual and society? Marxian theory addresses both structure and action. It deals with structural factors in that it stresses the historical circumstances of capitalism as limiting most of the choices open to people. At the same time, it stresses the action element in that it recognizes the capacity of workers to join together as a class-conscious group to change collectively existing economic and social conditions (Light, Keller, and Calhoun, 1989).

THEMES OF CONFLICT THEORY **Conflict theory**, like functionalism, focuses on social structures and institutions in society. The most basic assumption of a conflict perspective, and perhaps the one that most sets it apart from functionalism, however, is the notion that conflict is natural and inevitable in all human interaction, including family systems. Therefore, a complete understanding of society is possible only through a critical examination of competition, coercion, and conflict in society, especially those processes that lead some people to have great power and control and others to have little or no power and control. Thus, of major concern is the inequalities that are built into social structures or systems. Rather than focusing on interdependence, unity, and consensus, conflict theorists focus on society as an arena in which individuals and groups compete over limited resources and fight for power and control. A key assumption here is that certain groups and individuals have much greater power and access to key resources than others do. From this perspective, disorder, disagreement, and open hostility among individuals and groups are viewed as normal, and stability is the condition that requires explanation.

For the purposes of our discussion we can reduce conflict theory to three central themes: (1) Humans have basic interests or things they want and attempt to acquire; (2) power is at the base of all social relationships, and it is always scarce, unequally distributed, and coercive; and (3) values and ideas are weapons used by different groups to advance their own ends rather than to define society's identity and goals (Wallace and Wolf, 1991). Given these assumptions, the conflict perspective leads us to ask questions about the sources of tension among individuals and groups with different amounts of power, the techniques of conflict control in society, and the ways in which those with power perpetuate, maintain, and extend that power. In short, a major underlying question of conflict analysis is, Who benefits from, and who is systematically deprived by, any given social arrangement?

THE FAMILY FROM A CONFLICT PERSPECTIVE

Whereas functionalists focus on the tasks that serve the interests of the family as a whole, conflict theorists see families, like all societal institutions, as a set of social relationships that benefit some members more than others. Thus, a conflict theorist might ask general questions such as: How is social inequality built into the structure of marriages and families? What is the role of a marital partner or family member in promoting family disintegration or change? When conflict occurs in the family, who wins? How is racial and ethnic inequality perpetuated through the operation of the family?

From this perspective, marriages and families can be viewed as smaller versions of the larger class system, where the well-being of one class (men) is the result of the exploitation and oppression of another class (women). The family exploits women specifically by encouraging them to perform unpaid housework and child care so that men can devote their time to capitalist endeavors. Historically, those men who had the power to do so defined marriages and families in such a way that women were the sexual property of men. In consequence, marriage became a legally and socially enforced contract of sexual property. Although women in the United States are no longer legally defined as the property of men, other examples of male domination of women abound. For example, women continue to have major responsibility for and perform the major portion of housework and child rearing, even though most women are now in the paid labor force (Fuchs, 1986).

In essence, then, the basic source of male dominance and women's subordination is the home and family. Although functionalists may view the family as a refuge, for the conflict theorist the question is, What kind of refuge is it, and whom does it benefit? The link between the traditional family and social inequality involves a number of conflicts that are discussed in some detail in later chapters of this book, including violence against women, children, and the elderly; divorce; female-headed families; and the feminization of poverty.

CRITIQUE For many people, especially those who experience oppression, the conflict perspective offers a concrete set of propositions that explain unequal access to resources in terms of institutional structure rather than personal deficiencies. A major strength of this perspective is the way in which it relates social and organizational structure to group interests and the distribution of resources. Furthermore, it provides a historical framework within which to identify social change: the major shifts in the distribution of societal resources and social and political power. By tracing social behavior back to individuals' interests and the purposeful way they pursue them, it suggests a model to explain social and political change. And finally, unlike functionalism, the conflict perspective does not treat norms, values, and ideas as external to, and constraints on, individual behavior. Rather, the conflict perspective views human beings as very much involved in using the system of norms, values, and ideas as much as being used by it. Those who have the power use these systems to further their individual or group interests.

Conflict theory is not without its criticisms. One major criticism is that the underlying assumptions that (1) power is people's main objective and (2) conflict is the major feature of social life are too narrow and limited. Some critics argue, for example, that within the family, societal norms encourage certain behaviors that either prevent conflict or keep it under control. Thus, for example, disagreements among family members usually can be resolved without the use of physical force.

In addition, the conflict perspective is often criticized for explicitly advocating social change, thereby giving up some of its claim to scientific objectivity. Furthermore, conflict theory, like functionalism, raises the issue of value neutrality. Whereas structural functionalists evaluate social patterns in a system in terms of whether they are positive or negative, conflict theorists are purposely critical of society. Both of these positions pose a dilemma for value-free sociology. Most conflict theorists try to separate their value judgments from their analysis of society. However, when they focus on inequalities in society and claim, for example, that a more equitable distribution of tasks and resources between the genders is desirable, the inherent value judgment is quite clear. These problems notwithstanding, the conflict perspective is a useful framework for analyzing how factors such as race, class, gender, age, and ethnicity are linked to the unequal distribution of valuable resources in marriages and families, including power, property, money, prestige, and education.

SYMBOLIC INTERACTIONISM

Functionalism and the conflict perspective both concern themselves with macro (large-scale) patterns that characterize society or groups like families as a whole. In contrast, the **symbolic-interaction** perspective focuses on micro (small-scale) patterns of face-to-face interaction among people in specific settings, such as within marriages and families. This perspective is based on the notion that society is made up of interacting individuals who communicate primarily through the use of shared **symbols**—objects, words, sounds, and events that are given meaning by members of a culture—and construct reality as they go about the business of their daily lives. The most important set of symbols that humans use is language. People interact with one another based on their understandings of the meanings of words and social situations as well as their perceptions of what others expect of them within those situations. Thus, a major emphasis is on individuals and their social relationships, the subjective meanings of human behavior, and the various processes through which people come to construct and agree on various definitions of reality.

THE FAMILY FROM A SYMBOLIC-INTERACTION PERSPECTIVE

A person using the symbolic-interaction perspective as a frame of reference for analyzing marriages and families might ask questions such as: How are marriages and families experienced? How do individual family members interact to create, sustain, and change marriages and families? How do family members attempt to shape the reality perceived by other family members? How do the behaviors of family members change from one situation to another?

According to the late sociologist Ernest Burgess (1926), the family represents a unified set of interacting individuals. That is, unity in family life comes about as a result of interactions among various family members. In this sense, the concern is with marriages and families as social processes rather than with their structure. Thus, a symbolic interactionist would argue that the reality of marriage and family life is not fixed but is *socially constructed* and is constructed differently by various family members with different roles, privileges, and responsibilities. The **social construction of reality** is the process whereby people assign meanings to social phenomena—objects, events, and character-

istics—that almost always cause those who draw upon these meanings to emphasize some aspect of a phenomenon and to ignore others. These assigned meanings have tremendous consequences for the individuals involved, depending on how they interact with each other, what decisions they make, and what actions they take (Ferrante, 1992).

Taking this perspective, sociologist Jessie Bernard (1982) has argued, for example, that men and women are likely to view and experience their marriages differently. Referring to this phenomenon as "his" and "her" marriages, Bernard contends that due to traditionally different sex-role socialization and expectations, women have less power than men in marriages and families. Married women, therefore, must make certain accommodations, some of which may have negative effects on their mental health. In this respect, the psychological costs of marriage are much greater for wives than for husbands, and the benefits are far less.

CRITIQUE The symbolic-interaction perspective brings people back into our analyses. Rather than seeing humans as passive beings who simply respond to society's rules, interactionists give us a view of humans as actively involved in constructing, shaping, sustaining, and changing the social world. It is a useful framework for examining the complexities of relationships and the daily workings of marriages and families, complexities that functionalism and the conflict perspective miss. One of the major advantages of this perspective is that it helps us understand how the roles we play are so important in our social constructions of reality.

Symbolic interactionism also has certain limitations. In focusing attention on the subjective aspects of human experiences and the situations in which they occur, symbolic interactionism ignores the objective realities of inequality, racism, sexism, and the differential distribution of wealth, status, and power among various groups, and it minimizes the impact of these phenomena on families.

SOCIAL-EXCHANGE THEORY

Probably the theoretical perspective most often used in the discipline to study marriages and families is **social-exchange theory**. This theory adopts an economic model of human behavior based on costs, benefits, and the expectation of reciprocity; for this reason it sometimes is referred to as the *rational-choice perspective*. It tends to be very close to the way that many of us see and explain behavior in our everyday lives.

Have you ever wondered why some person you know or heard about remained in an unhappy relationship? Did you try to analyze this behavior by asking what the person might be getting out of the relationship versus whatever makes her or him unhappy (in other words, the pluses or benefits and minuses or costs of the relationship)? Did the person eventually leave the relationship? Did you wonder what finally made her or him end it? Was your answer that the costs finally became too great or outweighed the benefits?

If you have ever engaged in this type of cost–benefit analysis to explain your own or other people's actions and relationships, you were using a basic social-exchange perspective.

Social-exchange theory shares many of the assumptions of symbolic-interaction theory and thus, in broad terms, is an extension of interaction theory. Social-exchange theory is so named because its underlying premise is that social exchange forms the basis of all social interaction. Exchange theorists view social interaction as an exchange of tangible or intangible goods and services, ranging from money or physical labor to social recognition, love, and respect. Humans are thought to be rational beings who, in making decisions, weigh the profits to be gained from a particular action against the costs it will incur. Only when people feel that the gains of their interactions outweigh the costs do they adopt the behavior. People, then, engage in those actions that bring them the greatest benefits at the least cost. They will continue to engage in these actions as long as they perceive them to be profitable.

The two best-known proponents of social-exchange theory are George Homans and Peter Blau. Homans (1961) focused on actual behavior that is rewarded or punished by the behavior of others. According to Homans, humans react to stimuli based on need, reward, and reinforcement. Thus, in the various exchange relationships in which humans engage, the rewards will usually be proportional to the costs. Blau (1964) was more concerned with explaining large-scale social structures. According to

Blau, not all exchange can be explained in terms of actual behavior. Rather, exchange, like other interactions, is a subjective and interpretative process. Blau agrees with Homans that humans want rewards, and in exchange interactions each person receives something perceived as equivalent to that which is given. Blau refers to this as "fair exchange." He contends, however, that our relationship choices and decisions are not made purely on the basis of the perceived rewards but are affected by various social influences such as family and friends.

A good example of this can be seen in terms of various interracial relationships. An interracial couple might find their relationship mutually beneficial and satisfying, with the benefits far outweighing the costs. Social approval of the relationship may be very important to the couple, however. Thus, if family and friends strongly disapprove, the couple might decide to terminate the relationship.

THE FAMILY FROM A SOCIAL-EXCHANGE PERSPECTIVE   Marriage and family literature is filled with examples of social exchange. Most experts agree that marriage and family life are characterized by an exchange of goods and services. Thus, most exchange analyses of marriage and family behavior focus on relations between couples. Typically, a person using an exchange perspective is concerned with questions like those previously asked of you. In the language of exchange theory, for example, we might explain the observation that when women work they gain power in the family (see Chapter 11) by suggesting that in exchange for their economic contribution, working women share more equitably in decision making.

Family sociologists, particularly those concerned with dating, mating, and marital behavior, have long used exchange theory to explain this behavior. As we will see in Chapter 5, many sociologists use an exchange theory to explain how people in the United States choose whom to date and marry. They contend that Americans search for the best possible mate (product) given their own resources (physical attractiveness, intelligence, youth, status, money). People in this situation weigh a range of costs and benefits before choosing a mate.

Recall the man in the photo at the beginning of this chapter or John in the opening vignette. How do you think an exchange perspective would address his behavior? That is, what do you think an explanation in terms of exchange theory would add to what we know about these men's behavior? Guided by the assumption that they are rational beings, we might assume that they considered wearing an empathy belly to be the most effective means of achieving their goals of bonding with their wives and sharing the feelings and emotions associated with pregnancy. In other words, men who use empathy bellies can be seen as rational decisionmakers who, after weighing alternative means to alternative ends, choose this behavior as the most effective course of action. In so doing, they conclude that the rewards (such as spousal appreciation, love, and support; a special relationship with the child) of this behavior outweigh any possible costs (such as ridicule). Throughout this textbook, think about the value of different types of resources and the exchange processes at work in understanding a variety of marriage and family relationships.

CRITIQUE Exchange theory assumes that humans are rational, calculating beings who consciously weigh the costs versus the benefits of their relationships. A major problem with this notion of human behavior is that it cannot be disproved. Almost any behavior can be explained simply by saying that it must have had some value to the person involved, whether or not this is really the case. Furthermore, the notion of rational choice is limiting in that humans do not always act rationally, nor do we always agree on what is or is not ration-al behavior. We do not always choose relationships or interactions simply because the rewards outweigh the costs. In fact, sometimes the reverse is true in our relationships. One way of analyzing the "battered-woman syndrome" (discussed in Chapter 12) is to assume women stay in abusive relationships not because the rewards outweigh the costs but because other factors, such as fear of physical violence if they leave, override all other considerations.

These criticisms notwithstanding, an exchange perspective provides us with a unique framework for explaining many face-to-face relationships. It provides insight into people's values, goals, and perceptions of reality. Exchange theory is probably most valuable for explaining people's actions when we want to know and understand the details of individual behavior.

MICROSTRUCTURALISM

The **microstructural perspective**, as its name implies, combines the symbolic-interactionist and structural–functionalist approaches to explain gendered relationships. That is, it shows how both micro-level factors such as a society's expectations for behavior and structural forces such as a society's institutions and opportunity structure operate to create and maintain gender-specific beliefs and behavior. Advanced by sociologists Barbara Risman and Pepper Schwartz (1989), microstructural theory focuses on how individuals experience their world. It assumes that women and men adapt to ongoing patterns of interaction that are themselves produced by social-structural features of society. Simply put, according to Risman and Schwartz, individuals are not created all at once—at birth or during early socialization, as implied in social-learning and socialization theories. Rather, they are continually re-created during the life cycle by the opportunities available to them and by their interaction with others. This is particularly true of the female and male roles played out in intimate relationships. As applied to marriages and families, microstructuralist theory focuses on how the format of marriages and intimate relationships, the expectations of others, and the available opportunities (such as the opportunity for social mobility through marriage, family, or work) operate to form gender-specific behavior.

THE FAMILY FROM A MICROSTRUCTURAL PERSPECTIVE Taken to its logical extreme, microstructural theory predicts that women and men would behave exactly the same way if they were given identical expectations and positions in society. Using this perspective, we would ask questions such as: How do various social conditions, options, or situations promote particular kinds of marriage and family behavior? How are marital and family relationships affected by the social situation? More specifically, for example, we might ask questions such as: Can men mother? What opportunities to mother exist in marriage and family systems, and are they equally accessible to women and men?

Microstructuralism approaches such questions by examining the ongoing interaction between women and men in marriages and families. According to this viewpoint, the best way to understand differential parenting styles is to focus on the differing expectations, demands, and opportunities for parenting that exist within marriages and families. Thus, although women are currently expected to shoulder primary responsibility for child rearing, if the responsibilities and expectations for mothering were equally applied to and the opportunities to mother were equally available for women and men, then men would be as likely as women to adopt traditional mothering behaviors. In other words, male nurturance will develop when men are held responsible for caring for others.

Given the microstructuralist point of view, can we now better understand John's behavior? Does his wearing an empathy belly seem a little less odd now? Using this perspective we might explain John's behavior by focusing on the increasing expectations in the decade of the 1990s, in some marriages and families, for men to participate in parenting in a meaningful and equitable way. Furthermore, many families now offer greater opportunities for men to participate meaningfully in parenting, and, as a result, a growing number of these men are adopting such behaviors.

This behavior, then, suggests that gender differences during pregnancy and child rearing are based as much on the differential expectations and role requirements females and males face throughout their lives as on internalized personality traits. When men are expected to parent and bond with children, and opportunities to do so are available, they will do so. Some research (for example, Riseman, 1989) indicates that, at least in their own perceptions, unmarried fathers who have custody of their children are competent as primary parents. Given the situational demands of their role, these men, contrary to traditional gender-role socialization, can mother when they have no wives on whom to depend.

CRITIQUE Microstructural theory provides a useful framework for analyzing gender and intimate relationships. It offers a critical framework within which to analyze marriages and intimate relationships and therefore has direct implications for social change. By focusing on the social forces that shape gender and, thus, intimacy rather than on gender-based personality traits, this perspective forces us to go beyond social-learning and socialization theories to examine the impact of adult life experiences on women's and men's self-concept (their sense of identity, who they are) and behavior.

The microstructural perspective also has its critics. One major criticism involves what many people perceive as an overemphasis on the availability of opportunities and institutional support for various kinds of behavior among women and men and a de-emphasis on social learning and learned personality traits. This leaves microstructuralism open, in some sense, to the criticism of *structural determinism*, that is, blaming the system or society for gender inequality while downplaying the role of individuals in creating and maintaining these structured relationships.

An example of this charge of structural determinism can be seen in the suggestion of Risman and Schwartz that social policies should be designed that not only encourage but expect men to perform substantial infant care. This, they claim, could be done with parental leaves and flexible work schedules like those found in countries such as Germany, Sweden, and Switzerland. In reality, however, opportunities and institutional expectations alone are not enough. Making opportunities available to men does not guarantee that men will take advantage of them. Often, men are reluctant to defy traditional expectations and avail themselves of opportunities to engage in activities traditionally defined as feminine.

Take the example of Sweden, where men are provided by law with the opportunity to participate in parenting through paid parental leave. Nevertheless, Swedish women continue to be the primary caretakers of children. Although a high number of Swedish fathers take parental leaves, most do not, because they do not see themselves in this role because of previous social learning. In other words, many Swedish men apparently are not willing to defy traditional rules pertaining to gender-specific behavior even when offered the opportunities to do so.

FEMINIST THEORY

Feminist theory is not a single unified view. There is no single "feminist" theory. Rather, there are many types of feminist theory, just as there are many types of sociological theory. Nonetheless, this single label is often used to represent a diversity of feminist perspectives that contain certain common characteristics or principles. In this regard, feminist theory presents a generalized set of ideas about the basic features of society and human experience from a woman-centered perspective. It is

Liberal feminist theory assumes that at the basis of women's inequality is **sexism**, a set of beliefs about the superiority of men and inferiority of women that justifies prejudice and discrimination against women. Thus, the focus of this perspective is almost entirely on issues of equal opportunity and individual choice to the neglect of questions about how gender inequality emerged or the effects of race and class inequality in women's experiences. Its analysis for change, therefore, is limited to issues of reform relative to equal opportunity and individual choice.

Socialist feminist theory rejects the reform orientation of liberal feminist theory. Rooted in classical Marxism, this perspective maintains that the sexual division of labor is the first form of class conflict. Thus, class and gender hierarchies become the base from which socialist feminist theorists explain systems of oppression such as capitalism, patriarchy, and domination. Of particular concern here are issues of production, reproduction, socialization, and sexuality and how they exhibit and maintain inequalities.

Marxist feminist theory combines the classic Marxian class analysis and the feminist principle of social protest. This perspective begins with the premise that gender oppression is a reflection, first and foremost, of people's class position and only secondarily a reflection of gender itself. In general, women's inequality is explained in terms of class oppression and property inequality, exploited labor, and alienation. Marxist feminists advocate the abolition of capitalism (and thus class and class oppression) through revolutionary action as the solution to gender inequality.

Radical feminist theory contends that oppression is pervasive throughout society. Most radical feminist theories see patriarchy as the basic cause of women's oppression, and in the process they downplay the impact of race and class oppression in women's experiences. A key point in these analyses is the description of patriarchy as physical and psychological violence practiced by men and male-dominated institutions against women.

Lesbian feminist theory maintains that oppression of lesbians,

woman-centered in three ways: (1) The starting point of all its investigations is the situations and experiences of women; (2) it treats women as the main subjects in the research process, that is, it attempts to view the world from the distinctive vantage points of women; and (3) it is critical and activist on behalf of women (Lengermann and Brantley, 1988).

A word of caution: Not all theories that deal with women or gender issues are feminist theories. To be considered feminist, a theory must reflect a feminist consciousness—an awareness rooted in a commitment to activist goals. In addition, it should adopt three basic philosophical approaches: (1) Gender is the central focus, (2) status quo gender relations are viewed as problematic in that women are defined as subordinate to men, and (3) gender relations are viewed as the result of social, not natural, factors (Chafetz, 1988).

Basically, all feminist theory attempts to answer two fundamental questions. The first is, Where are women? The second is, Why is this situation as it is? In addressing these questions, feminist theory typically focuses on the ways in which specific definitions of gender affect the organization of social institutions and patterns of gender inequality. Finally, a major objective of feminist theory is social change. Perhaps more than most theories, feminist theories are explicitly and self-consciously political in their advocacy of social change.

Although feminist theory is interdisciplinary, it is especially compatible with the sociological imagination because it links individual experience to social organization. Like other major sociological categories such as race and class, gender also influences the distribution of wealth, power, and privilege; how much we will learn and earn; how long we and our children will live; and how we are defined by others. As we have stated, there are many types of feminist theory and, as their various names imply, not all of them adopt the same focus. Brief descriptions of several prominent feminist theories are presented in the FYI box. As you will find, we cannot easily distinguish one from another.

like racial, class, and sexual oppression, is important in determining women's inequality. Lesbian feminists focus on the reasons for the dominance of heterosexuality. Adrienne Rich (1980), for example, argues that heterosexuality is political in nature in that it is "compulsory" in patriarchal societies and that lesbianism represents resistance and a threat to patriarchy. Some lesbian theorists have been among the first to explore how some women, themselves oppressed, actively participate in the oppression of other women; for example, white women oppressing women of color, heterosexual women oppressing lesbians. Thus, much of their analyses for change call for the eradication of prejudice and discrimination within the community of women itself. In addition, some lesbian feminists (as well as some nonlesbian feminists) advocate "separatism"—both the sexual separation of women from men and the wider separation of women from male culture and institutions—as a strategy of liberation. There is no common consensus, however, about how much separatism is necessary or how it will function.

Women-of-color feminist theory, like other feminist perspectives, is an umbrella term for a wide range of viewpoints. Taking as a starting point that women of color have typically been omitted from all analyses, including feminist analyses, women-of-color feminists begin their analyses by bringing women of color from the margins to the center of analysis (see, for example, bell hooks, 1984). A basic premise is that there is no common unified female experience. Rather, each individual woman is shaped not only by her experiences of gender and sexuality but also by her particular experiences of the intersection of race, class, and culture. Thus, a major emphasis is on the forms of racism, sexism, and classism and how these factors are interrelated and affect the lives of all women.

The analyses and insights of bell hooks and other women of color have extended the scope of feminist theory and practice. By including the experiences of women of color, they provide new centers for feminist thought and action.

THE FAMILY FROM A FEMINIST PERSPECTIVE

A feminist investigation of marriages and families asks both macro- and micro-level questions. Macro-level questions include, What are the causes of women's inequality in marriages and families? How does the structure of marriages and families maintain gender inequality? How can change toward greater equality in marriages and families be brought about? Micro-level questions include, What social and interpersonal processes occur in families to generate gender differences and inequality? What roles do various family members play in perpetuating gender inequality? What kind of power structures exist within marriages and families, and how do they affect the distribution of tasks and resources in marriages and families?

Taking the position that women's subordination is based in the social relationships within marriages and families, the objective of an analysis of marriages and families is to explain the ways in which gender inequality is reinforced and maintained in these relationships. On a macro level, for example, a vast Marxist-feminist literature asserts that women's oppression is built into and sustained by the patriarchal family structure. On a micro level, a body of feminist theory exists that, by focusing on what these theorists refer to as the "reproduction of gender" in families, explains how gender inequality and oppression are reinforced and maintained (Chodorow, 1978). These theories suggest that gender identity and gender-specific behaviors are produced and reproduced through the socialization process as women expose their offspring to a variety of gender-specific learning experiences during the child-rearing process.

CRITIQUE There are many critiques of feminist theory. That feminist theory is woman-centered is the most frequent criticism, especially from mainstream sociologists. Basically, the criticism is that feminist theory is biased and excludes male experiences and perspectives. Feminist theorists respond to this criticism by asserting that the partiality to women in their work is necessary given the history of devaluation or exclusion of female experiences and perspectives in traditional social theories. They argue that the inclusion of female experiences and perspectives does not exclude men and male perspectives.

In addition, some critiques have come from feminist scholars themselves who differ in their conceptualizations of the causes of women's oppression and the goals of feminist theory. For example, radical feminists criticize the liberal feminist notion that the major political goal for feminists should be equal opportunity for women and men. Critics contend that because this approach does not address such structural issues as class and race inequality, it would help only some women but would not help many others, particularly poor women and women of color. Marxist feminist theory is often criticized for its focus on women's oppression as a reflection of the more fundamental class oppression in society. This single focus on economic production largely ignores the importance of social and cultural factors.

One very important criticism of most feminist theories is that they are biased toward the experiences of white, middle-class, heterosexual women. (See the discussion of women-of-color feminist theory in the FYI box.) In particular, feminist theory is criticized for not including an adequate analysis of race. Even when feminist theory deals with issues of race, class, and heterosexuality, it focuses primarily on the life experiences of the poor or working-class, women of color, or lesbians. Such analyses cloud the fact that all women experience race, class, gender, and sexual orientation, albeit in different ways. In some cases, for example, women are economically disadvantaged and denied access to power and privilege because of their skin color, sexual orientation, or social class. In other cases, these same factors can enhance access to social and economic resources. For example, women with white skin or a heterosexual orientation might enjoy certain privileges, whereas women with black skin or a homosexual orientation can suffer discrimination and be denied basic opportunities.

THEORY MODELS

In this section we move from the broad theoretical perspectives discussed above to an analysis of some of the more prominent theory models developed by sociologists specifically to explain marriages and families and related behaviors. Three major theory models that have shaped much thinking within the discipline of sociology will provide a good illustration of how sociologists have traditionally explained modern U.S. families. These are the nuclear-family model, the modified extended-family model, and the developmental family life-cycle model.

THE NUCLEAR-FAMILY MODEL

Traditionally, family theorists have relied heavily on the assumptions of the structural–functional theoretical perspective to explain marriage and family behavior. Probably the best known theory model in this regard is the *nuclear-family model*. The writings of the late sociologist Talcott Parsons (1955, 1964) provide the basis for this model. Recall from Chapter 1 that as Western societies became industrialized and urbanized, the nuclear family emerged as the dominant family type to meet the needs of an industrial economy. Parsons agreed with the structural functionalists

The U.S. sociologist Talcott Parsons was one of the most influential proponents of modern functionalist theory, and his views on the family are the basis for the nuclear-family theory model.

that the family is an adaptive system that performs essential functions for its individual members as well as for society as a whole. He argued, however, that in modern society the functional importance of the nuclear family has declined as many of its functions have been taken over and performed by other social institutions. This is particularly true in terms of the family's economic function. The modern nuclear family is no longer an economic unit. (This issue is often debated in the literature and will be discussed in more detail in Chapter 11.) According to Parsons, the two major functions of the modern family are now socialization of the young and personality stabilization of adults. Personality stabilization is the process whereby individuals internalize society's values and expectations concerning gender-appropriate behavior to the point where these values and cultural expectations become a consistent part of the individual's identity throughout her or his lifetime.

The nuclear-family model places great emphasis on the isolation of the nuclear family from the extended family. It also emphasizes that a differentiation of gender roles within the family is a functional necessity for the solidarity of the marriage relationship. Parsons described the male role in this regard as instrumental and the female role as expressive. The personality traits needed to carry out these roles are quite different. **Instrumental traits** encourage self-confidence, rationality, competition, and coolness—qualities that facilitate male success in the world of work. In contrast, **expressive traits** encourage nurturance, emotionality, sensitivity, and warmth—qualities that help women succeed in caring for a husband, children, and a home.

CRITIQUE Parsons's nuclear-family theory model is very controversial. Some of the major criticisms of this model are the same as those directed against functionalism generally: The model is specific to a particular time and space, does not utilize a historical context, and does not deal with the diversity of experiences that have always characterized U.S. families. What seemed true about marriages and families in the 1950s is less true today. In the 1990s fewer and fewer families fit the Parsonian nuclear-family model.

In addition, married-couple families often exhibit a diversity of structures and roles that the Parsonian model does not account for. Using this model, for example, how can we explain the growing number of

men today who are nurturant, caring, and sensitive—traits that Parsons describes as exclusively expressive and female?

The nuclear-family model is especially criticized for its rigid, exaggerated, and oversimplified view of marital interaction generally and women's experiences specifically (Cheal, 1989). For example, how does the nuclear family model apply to African-American families under slavery, where legal marriage was prohibited and women's and men's roles were interchanged? Similarly, can it explain the diversity in Native-American families, particularly those in which women exercised economic power in subsistence residential units that were the basis of their tribal economy?

In essence, the nuclear-family model is limiting as an analysis of families in the United States today and is therefore no longer representative of "mainstream" sociological thought on families. However, its impact, especially on the public, can still be detected. Today when people talk about the family they often have in mind this nuclear model. For many people the nuclear family remains the ideal form, even though such families are less prevalent today than they were in the past.

THE MODIFIED EXTENDED-FAMILY MODEL

Another offshoot of functionalist thought and an alternative to the nuclear family model is Eugene Litwak's *modified extended-family model* (1960). In contrast to Parsons's view of the nuclear family as a completely isolated unit, Litwak contends that in modern society, mass-communication technologies and the money economy allow extended family members to overcome the physical barriers of separation and keep up their connections with each other. The motivation to do so stems primarily from the economic, social, and emotional support they can receive from such relationships. Litwak calls this new type of extended family the modified extended family. He distinguishes this modern family type from the classical extended family, where a group of related kin (usually three or more generations) live in the same household or compound.

According to Litwak, the modern nuclear family, being small in size, often has limited resources and therefore cannot always deal with family-related crises. Thus, extended family kin, even if physically separated, can provide needed supplemental resources that the nuclear family may need. In particular, cross-generational interaction and assistance allow families to respond to the different kinds of needs that emerge at various stages of the family's life cycle.

CRITIQUE The modified extended-family model is simply an extension or expansion of the nuclear-family model and thus shares many of the same limitations. In general, both models view family life in terms of order and consensus based on a fixed arrangement of social roles. In this sense, a primary problem with Litwak's model (as with the Parsonian model) is that it minimizes the changing character of families.

THE DEVELOPMENTAL FAMILY LIFE-CYCLE MODEL

In contrast to the nuclear- and the modified extended-family theory models, the *developmental family life-cycle model* pays close attention to changes in families over time and attempts to explain family life in terms of a process that unfolds over the life course of families. Sociologist Paul Glick (Glick and Parke, 1965) was the first to analyze families in terms of a life cycle. According to Glick, families pass through a series of stages: (1) family formation (first marriage), (2) start of childbearing (birth of first child), (3) end of childbearing (birth of last child), (4) "empty nest" (when the last child leaves home), and (5) "family dissolution" (death of one spouse). Other life-cycle models identify similar, although somewhat different, stages.

According to such developmental models, families change over time in terms of both the people who are members of the family and the roles they play. At various stages in the family life cycle, the family has different developmental tasks to perform. Each new stage in the family life cycle is brought on by a change in the composition of the family. These changes, in turn, affect various aspects of the family's well-being, including its economic viability. At each stage of development, the family is confronted with a distinct set of tasks whose completion is considered to be essential both for individual development and success at the next stage. One of the most widely used developmental models in family sociology is an eight-stage model developed by Evelyn Duvall (1977) and presented below.

As you study this model of family development, think about your own family and other families you know. How do these families "fit" into such a model? How do they differ? Have they progressed straight through these stages, or have some stages been omitted? Does that mean that these families are abnormal or dysfunctional? Can you add other stages to this model?

Stage One: *Beginning families.* At this first stage of development the married couple does not have children and is just beginning married life and adjusting to it.

Stage Two: *Childbearing families.* The family is still forming in this stage. The first child is born, and women are deeply involved in childbearing and child rearing.

Stage Three: *Families with preschool children.* The family's oldest child is somewhere between 2½ and 6 years of age. The mother is still deeply involved in child rearing. This stage lasts about 3 to 4 years.

Stage Four: *Families with schoolchildren.* The oldest child (or children) in the family is school-aged. With children in school, the mother is free to pursue other options such as work outside the home.

Stage Five: *Families with teenagers.* In this stage the oldest child is between 13 and 20 years old. The family must adjust to having adolescents in the home and adapt to their growing independence. This stage may last up to 7 years.

Stage Six: *Families as launching centers.* At this stage, the oldest child has been launched into adulthood. Families must develop adult relationships with grown children as they adjust to children leaving the family "nest." This stage lasts until the last child leaves home, usually a period of about 8 years.

Stage Seven: *Families in the middle years.* This stage is sometimes called the "empty-nest" stage. It is a distinct new stage in the developmental cycle of the family and spans the time from when the last child leaves home to retirement or old age.

Stage Eight: *Aging families.* Members of the family who work outside the home have retired at this stage. In this stage families must cope with events related to aging, such as chronic illnesses and the eventual death of one of the spouses. The remaining spouse must then deal with the factors and experiences associated with widowhood.

CRITIQUE Although the developmental family life-cycle model calls attention to the changing nature of family relationships over time, distinguishing a "typical" family life cycle is difficult, if not impossible. As family norms change, the stages of family development also vary. In fact, some scholars believe that the stages of the family life cycle have become increasingly useful as indicators of change rather than as stages that all or even most families can be expected to experience. Although life-cycle models give us important insights into the complexities of family life, a shortcoming is that they assume that most families are nuclear families with children. These models present a "typical" family life cycle descriptive of the "conventional" family. As with other theory models, this model does not incorporate the diversity of family lifestyles prevalent in U.S. society. Where, for example, do families without children, single-parent families, and remarried families fit in these models?

Moreover, families within various racial and ethnic groups develop through stages that are not recognized in these models. For example, due in part to their general disadvantaged economic position, many families of color and poor families take in relatives at some time in the family life cycle. In addition, a growing number of families in all classes are taking in and caring for aging parents. What does the developmental family life-cycle model tell us about these families? Not only does the model omit these arrangements but it generally implies a linear or straight-line progression in family life that few families actually experience. Families, for example, may progress through several of the early stages only to go back and repeat earlier stages, particularly if children are involved.

Furthermore, developmental models such as Duvall's generally assume that developmental tasks, particularly those in the early stages, are gender-specific. Consider, for example, Duvall's first four stages. Each stage is defined entirely in terms of the presence of children and the role of women as caretakers and caregivers. Men and their parenting roles are totally omitted. In the final section of this chapter we briefly examine some of the contemporary literature on men and their roles in marriages and families.

MEN'S STUDIES RELATIVE TO MARRIAGES AND FAMILIES

As we have seen throughout this chapter, there are many critical social and political issues related to explanations of marriage and family life in the United States. Whether or not we accept the feminist claim that their theory and research does not exclude the experiences or perspectives of men, in recent years a parallel movement has developed among some male activists and scholars who are calling for a larger, visible place in feminist analyses, one that pays attention to the oppression that males experience as a result of social conditioning and learning.

In general, this men's studies perspective encompasses a critical examination of the functional and dysfunctional aspects of the traditional male gender role for men, women, children, and society at large. It begins with the basic premise that there is no hierarchy (ranking in a graded series) of oppression. Men, like women, are oppressed by a social conditioning that makes them incapable of developing and expressing a wide range of personality traits or skills and limits their experiences (Franklin, 1988).

As with feminist theory, the network of men's studies consists of not one but several diverse perspectives. In general terms there seems to be a pro-feminism–antifeminism split in men's studies. The profeminists in men's studies agree with feminists that men gain privilege from oppressing women. They maintain, however, that men also suffer great disadvantages from patriarchy and that society as a whole suffers from gender and sex inequality. In contrast, the antifeminist male perspectives agree that traditional masculine gender roles are harmful and destructive to men, but they argue that women benefit greatly from men's enactments of traditional male roles. In addition, they contend that only a small elite group of men enjoy privilege and advantage in U.S. society. The majority, even those who consider themselves successful, lead powerless, subservient lives in the factory or office. Thus, male privilege and advantage is more illusion than fact for most men.

MEN IN FAMILIES

As we have indicated, a new politics of masculinity has emerged that claims that men's oppression is often overlooked in theoretical analyses of marriages and families. Although many impressive analyses have documented the exploitation of women, little if any attention has been given to the massive disruption and destruction that contemporary economic and political institutions have wrought on men.

In recent times, marriages and families across race and class are experiencing a number of crises that

APPLYING THE SOCIOLOGICAL IMAGINATION

DEVELOPING A MINITHEORY

Virtually every practical decision you make and every practical opinion you hold has some theory behind it. Consider any marriage and family behavior or event of interest to you. Develop a "minitheory" to explain the behavior or event. What are some of the major assumptions you make about human beings, society, marriages, families, women, and men? Is your theory a micro- or macro-level explanation? Which one of the theoretical perspectives or theory models does your theory most resemble?

After you have developed your minitheory, consider that you or some researcher wants to test it. What kinds of questions might you ask? Which research methodology would be most appropriate to test your theory? Why?

---

originate both inside and outside marriages and families. According to some social scientists in the men's studies movement, men are a large part of the growing crises in U.S. families. Men are increasingly isolated from their families by the pressures of work and the circumstances of divorce. Historical trends such as industrialization have forced men off the land, out of the family and community, and into the factory and office, making them virtually invisible in the household.

These researchers contend that the male as head of his family has all but disappeared as more and more women either head their families or contribute equally to family income. The changing conditions of work and career and the tragedies of divorce have seriously eroded men's role as primary provider and thus their most critical relationships: those with their children, their wives, their households, and themselves. Men are no longer full partners and participants in the family. Instead of dealing with this loss of independence and isolation from the family, contemporary society has created a false picture of men that recasts the traditional male role into a new image of men as autonomous, efficient, intensely self-interested, and disconnected from family (Kimbrell, 1991).

On some levels, a "new father" has emerged. An increasing number of young husbands have joined their wives in birthing courses, have donned empathy bellies, and have taken part in the actual delivery of their children. There is little evidence, however, that these experiences by themselves produce a strong father–child (or wife–husband) bond or lead to greater participation by fathers with their children. As we shall see in Chapters 11 and 12, few new fathers assume a major role in child care and child rearing. According to the politics-of-masculinity perspective, for most men, no matter how much they would like to be more active in parenting, the demands of outside employment and the continuing definition of men and masculinity in terms of "work" and "family provider" preclude such participation.

CRITIQUE A major criticism of the new politics of masculinity concerns its view of men as primary victims. Some feminist critics, for example, claim that the politics of masculinity is reactionary and sexist, depicting men as innocent victims of conniving and selfish women or of social structures and institutions that in fact they control. Another criticism is that although many of these analyses focus on the structural and institutional nature of men's exploitation and oppression, they have not clearly identified their alleged oppression or oppressors in society. Some feminist scholars argue that these perspectives as well as the men's rights movement generally are simply strategies for reaffirming men's authority in the face of the challenge presented by feminism (Carrigan, Connell, and Lee, 1987). A final criticism is that the new politics of masculinity is far more therapeutic (healing of men's egos) than political or activist.

Although recognizing the pervasive victimization of women, many proponents of masculinity theory nonetheless caution against the view of some feminists that being a male in and of itself and not the systems of social control and production is responsible for the exploitation of women. Although this point is well taken, according to critics it neglects to emphasize that the systems of social control and production in the United States are owned and controlled by men (albeit, white middle- and upper-class men). Thus, the issues of gender and the exercise of power cannot be separated.

In conclusion, we have seen that sociology offers a variety of theories and perspectives. Although each framework is somewhat distinct, the various frameworks are not completely incompatible with each other. Rather, they can and do offer complementary insights. Before moving on to the next chapter, take a moment to reflect about theory and theorizing. Having studied the various theories in this chapter, try to apply the sociological imagination by constructing your own "minitheory," as described in the Applying the Sociological Imagination box.

SUMMARY

Sociology involves observing human behavior and then making sense out of what we observe. Therefore, both research and theory are involved. Theory is an explanation of some phenomenon, and scientific research includes a set of methods that allow us to collect data to test hypotheses and develop theories. The two are linked in that theory provides insights into the nature of human behavior and society, and research provides the empirical observations on which theories are verified. Sociologists studying marriages and families have used a variety of research methodologies: surveys, observation, experiments, and case studies. Each of these methods has both advantages and limitations.

Although sociology as a discipline claims that the improvement of social life is a major goal, some feminist scholars have argued that in practice sociology has not lived up to this goal. A telling sign is who gets studied and how, and who is left out and why. Until recent times, conventional topics studied by sociologists and their theoretical perspectives had either ignored issues relevant to the lives of women, poor people, and people of color or studied them within white and male middle-class models. Given this history, there is a need for a new scholarship on marriages and families that recognizes race, class, and gender diversity in marriages and families.

Just as there is no single method for studying marriages and families, there is no single theory to explain these institutions. There are four mainstream theoretical perspectives that, while not specifically family theories, can be utilized to explain marriages and families. Structural functionalism and conflict theory provide frameworks for analyzing the determinants of large-scale social structure. Symbolic-interaction theory allows us to focus on individuals within marriages and families and the interaction between couples or among family members. Social-exchange theory is guided by the assumption that people are rational and logical, and that they base their actions on what they think is the most effective way to meet their goals.

Microstructuralism, a combination of micro- and macro-level analysis, combines interaction and structural theory to explain gender in intimate relationships. This perspective suggests that gender and intimate behavior is situational and that the equal availability of various opportunities for women and men would eliminate gender inequality in intimate relationships. Feminist theory is not a single unified view; rather, there are many types of feminist theory. A basic premise of all feminist theories is that women are oppressed and their lives are shaped by a number of important experiences such as race, class, gender, and culture. However, different theories pay primary attention to different sets of women's experiences as causing or contributing to their inequality and oppression.

A number of sociological-theory models are also used to analyze marriages and families. The most common are the nuclear-family model, the modified extended-family model, and the developmental family life-cycle model. Each is an extension of the larger, more encompassing functional perspective and thus provides both the advantages and limitations of a functional analysis.

Finally, in recent years, we have witnessed a growing number of male voices advocating a larger and more visible place in feminist analyses, one that pays attention to the oppression that men experience as a result of gender-role socialization. To date, however, very little effort has been made to extend these ideas into a practical agenda for social and political change.

KEY TERMS

theory	experiment	functional
scientific research	variable	dysfunctional
empirical evidence	case study	conflict theory
hypothesis	quantitative methods	symbolic interactionism
scientific method	qualitative methods	symbols
reliability	ethnography	social construction of reality
validity	ideology	social-exchange theory
surveys	theory model	microstructuralism
interview	structural functionalism	sexism
questionnaire	manifest function	instrumental traits
Hawthorne effect	latent function	expressive traits

QUESTIONS FOR STUDY AND REFLECTION

1. Think about the developmental family life-cycle theory model discussed in this chapter. Which stages are applicable to your immediate family? Are certain stages not covered by the model? If so, what are they? What are some of the major responsibilities, roles, and adjustments that have been necessary at each stage of your family's life cycle?

2. Why do sociologists need different theoretical perspectives to explain marriage and family behavior? Why isn't one perspective sufficient?

3. Why are theory and research important to sociologists in studying marriages and families? How do theory and research contribute to our knowledge about marriages and families? How does sociological research on marriages and families benefit individuals, families, and society?

4. Develop an example of an appropriate research topic for each of the methodologies discussed in this chapter. How valuable is sociological research to our understanding of marriages and families?

FURTHER READING

BURR, WESLEY R., RUBIN HILL, FRANCIS I. NYE, AND IRA L. REISS. 1979. *Contemporary Theories About the Family.* New York: Free Press. This book has several chapters that deal with some of the mainstream theoretical perspectives that we have presented in this chapter, including conflict theory, social-exchange theory, and symbolic interactionism.

KATZER, JEFFREY, KENNETH H. COOK, AND WAYNE CROUCH. 1978. *Evaluating Information: A Guide for Users of Social Science Research.* Reading, MA: Addison-Wesley. A very readable book that focuses on some of the basic problems that all of us encounter at one time or another when we try to make sense of scientific research and decide which findings to accept and which to reject.

LaROSSA, RALPH, ed. 1984. *Family Case Studies.* New York: Free Press. The author presents 14 interesting family case studies in a style that encourages the reader to get involved in really understanding the process of family life.

SMITH, DOROTHY E. 1987. *The Everyday World as Problematic: Feminist Sociology.* Boston: Northeastern University Press. Smith presents a feminist critique of sociology and accuses sociology's standards of objectivity and rationality of still expressing the subjective views and experiences of the men who have dominated the discipline. Combining her own personal experiences with various theoretical perspectives, she presents a feminist framework for the study of society.

Chapter 3

GENDER ROLES

Two researchers, Caroline Smith and Barbara Lloyd (1978), asked mothers who had infants of their own to play with another 6-month-old infant for 10 minutes. The mothers were not told the sex of the child. Sometimes the infant was dressed as a boy; at other times the infant was dressed as a girl. Smith and Lloyd observed that based on how the infant was dressed, gender-stereotyped toys were used in play with the infant. When the mothers perceived that the infant was a girl, they gave the infant dolls; when the mothers thought they were playing with a boy, they gave the infant hammers.

Are you surprised by these findings? Have you observed any similar behavior? Have you ever been in a situation where you were unsure of an infant's sex? How did you respond? Were you uncomfortable? How did the parents react? What does this type of research tell us about gender roles in our society?

What are little girls made of?
Sugar and spice
And all that's nice,
That's what little girls are made of.

What are little boys made of?
Snaps and snails
And puppy dogs' tails,
That's what little boys are made of.

—Anonymous nursery rhyme

Who hasn't, at one time or another, smiled on hearing this nursery rhyme? On one level we don't take it seriously, believing it is just a cute and harmless description of differences between girls and boys. Yet on another level it suggests that there are differences between females and males and that girls must therefore be treated differently from boys. On the basis of this belief system, society constructs an elaborate sex–gender system that has serious ramifications for every facet of our lives. This chapter explores the meaning of sex and gender, the process by which we acquire gender identity, and the role gender plays in marital and family relationships.

DISTINGUISHING SEX AND GENDER ROLES

If you were asked, "Who are you?" chances are you would reply by saying: I am a male, female, Latino, African American, Asian American, Native American; or a student, parent, daughter, son, wife, husband, mother, father, friend. Such responses reflect the statuses we have and the roles we play in the social order. Sociologists use the term **role** to refer to a set of expected behaviors associated with a specific **status**, the position we hold in society. These positions, by and large, determine how we are defined and treated by others and also provide us with an organizing framework for how we should relate to others. We are born into some of these statuses—for example, female, male, daughter, son, white, black—and therefore have little control over them. These are called **ascribed statuses**. Others are **achieved statuses**, acquired by virtue of our own efforts. These include spouse, parent, employee, student, teacher. Every status, whether ascribed or achieved, carries with it a set of role expectations for how we are to behave.

Role expectations are defined and structured around the privileges and obligations the status is believed to possess. For example, our society has traditionally expected males, especially fathers, to be strong and independent, and good providers. In return, they expect to be admired, respected, and obeyed. Females, especially mothers, are expected to be nurturing, caring, and self-sacrificing. In return, they deserve to be loved and provided for. Such shared role expectations serve an important function in society. By making our behavior fairly predictable, they make social order possible.

Role expectations can be dysfunctional as well, however. They can be defined so rigidly that behavior and expression are seriously curtailed to the detriment of the individual and the society at large. Rigid role definitions often lead to the development of **stereotypes**, in which certain qualities are assigned to an individual solely on the basis of his or her social category. Stereotyping is used to justify unequal treatment of members of a specific group. For example, in early America, it was widely believed that women and people of color possessed smaller brains than white men and were incapable of rational, scientific thinking. It was also popularly believed that the rigors of study might disturb women's reproductive capacity, resulting in sterility or the birth of unhealthy babies

(Renzetti and Curran, 1992). As a result, women and people of color were denied admission to colleges and universities until well into the nineteenth century.

The status of being female or male in our society affects all aspects of our lives; thus, sociologists regard it as a **master** or **key status**. For this reason it is important to understand the dynamics associated with gender status and to distinguish between the concepts of sex and gender.

Sex refers to the biological aspects of a person—the physiological characteristics that differentiate females from males. These include external genitalia (vulva and penis), gonads (ovaries and testes), sex chromosomes, and hormones. These characteristics are the source of sex-role differences—women menstruate, get pregnant, and lactate; men have erections and ejaculate seminal fluid. In contrast, **gender** refers to the socially learned behaviors, attitudes, and expectations that are associated with being female or male, what we call *femininity* and *masculinity*. Whereas a person's sex is biologically determined, gender behaviors and expectations are culturally constructed categories and, as such, change over time. **Gender identity** is a person's awareness of being female or male. It sounds simple, doesn't it? We are either female (feminine) or male (masculine), are we not? In fact, as we shall see, human development is not as simple as it first appears.

SEXUAL DIFFERENCES

Our biological sex is established at the moment of conception, when each genetic parent contributes 23 chromosomes to the fertilized egg for a total of 46 chromosomes (23 chromosomal pairs). One pair of chromosomes, the sex chromosomes, determines whether a fertilized egg will develop into a female (XX) or male (XY) fetus. Contrary to past belief, the father's genetic contribution determines the child's sex, in that he provides either an X or a Y chromosome, whereas the mother always provides an X chromosome. The process of sexual differentiation does not begin until the sixth week of embryonic development, however. Prior to that time, the XX and XY embryos are anatomically identical, each possessing a set of female ducts and a set of male ducts.

The process of sex differentiation is as yet not completely understood. Scientists believe, however, that the presence of a Y chromosome stimulates the production of proteins that assist in the development of fetal testes, which then begin to synthesize hormones called *androgens*. Androgens, in turn, cause the degeneration of the female duct system and promote the development of the male duct system. During the eighth week, external male genitalia begin to form as a result of the secretion of the hormone *dihydrotestosterone*. Scientists are less clear about female development, but there is some evidence that the XX gonad synthesizes the female hormone *estrogen* around the same time that the XY gonad begins synthesizing testosterone (Fausto-Sterling, 1985).

GENDER DIFFERENCES: THE NATURE–NURTURE DEBATE

Because chromosomes and hormones play a critical role in sexual differentiation, it is logical to ask whether they also play a role in the physical, behavioral, and personality differences that have been observed between women and men. For example, women, on the average, live longer and score higher on tests of verbal ability than men do. Men, on the average, are taller, heavier, more aggressive, and have better spatial skills than women. As Figure 3.1 shows, however, the differences within each sex are often greater than the differences between the two sexes.

FIGURE 3.1
Overlapping Normal Curves

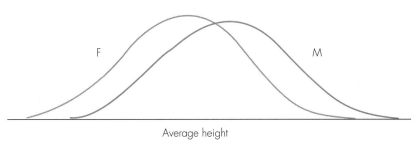

Average height

We are accustomed to thinking of gender as consisting of two categories: female and male. Yet, as sociologists Claire Renzetti and Daniel Curran (1992:52–53) point out, anthropologists have found evidence of multiple genders in other cultures. Renzetti and Curran give several examples of societies with multiple genders, only two of which are presented here. Certain Asian, South Pacific, and North American Indian societies recognized a third gender called the *berdache*, individuals who adopted the gender ascribed to members of the other sex. Although both females and males could become *berdaches*, it was more common for men to do so. Generally, men who chose to become *berdaches* did so at puberty as an alternative to becoming warriors. These individuals lived, worked, and dressed as members of the other sex and were frequently thought to possess supernatural power.

Renzetti and Curran also discuss the Mohave, a Native-American people who lived in California. The Mohave allowed women and men to cross genders. In that society some boys preferred feminine toys and clothing. At puberty they could go through an initiation ceremony and become *alyha*; they would adopt feminine names, perform female tasks, and marry men. Females could pursue a masculine lifestyle by becoming *hwame*, who dressed and lived much like men, hunting and farming rather than performing domestic chores. Although the *hwame* could not aspire to leadership positions or participate in warfare, they could assume parental responsibility for children. In none of these societies were these individuals thought of as abnormal or deviant.

What do these multiple genders suggest about the range of human behavior? Would our culture benefit in any way from having a more fluid view of gender?

Thus, more variation in height occurs within a group of women (or men) than between the average female and the average male. This figure also shows that although most women are shorter than most men, some women are taller than some men. Most of the traits identified as masculine or feminine fit this pattern. The extent of sex differences actually found for most traits is typically quite small.

In the past, a strong tendency has been to assume that all observed differences between females and males must be biologically based (nature). Some scientists, however, suggest that such an approach is too simplistic. For example, studies show that sex differences in math and verbal ability don't manifest themselves much before adolescence and are not found in all societies (Harmatz and Novak, 1983; Fausto-Sterling, 1985). Similarly, other studies have found that when females are rewarded for behaving aggressively, they can become just as aggressive as males (Hyde, 1984). These latter findings suggest that cultural factors (nurture) also play an important role in sex differences. According to developmental biologist Anne Fausto-Sterling (1985), the biological and the cultural are not mutually exclusive categories; rather, they are two essential parts of an interconnected system. An examination of fetal mishaps provides some insight into this interconnectedness.

FETAL MISHAPS

If everything goes right during gestation, the infant is born with clearly identifiable sex characteristics. However, prenatal mishaps occasionally occur, resulting in the birth of infants with biologically mixed or incomplete sex characteristics. We examine three of these conditions: adrenogenital syndrome, androgen insensitivity, and hermaphroditism.

ADRENOGENITAL SYNDROME The first condition, *adrenogenital syndrome* (AGS), causes the adrenal glands of the fetus to malfunction, resulting in a release of excess androgens from the prenatal period onward and causing some masculinizing effects. Girls with AGS have internal female reproductive organs but masculinized external genitalia (an enlarged clitoris that resembles a small penis). The general course of treatment is surgery to feminize the genitals and cortisone therapy to compensate for the adrenal malfunction. Boys with AGS have a normal male appearance but if untreated with cortisone reach puberty years ahead of time. What happens to these AGS children as they mature? Does the presence of this male hormone cause AGS girls to act like boys?

Two studies examined AGS children for signs of masculinization of behavior and personality. In the first study, John Money and Anke Ehrhardt (1972), researchers at the Johns Hopkins University Gender Identity Clinic, interviewed 25 fetally androgenized females (aged 4 to 16) who had received treatment at the clinic. The researchers then compared the responses of these girls to those of a control group of normal girls. The AGS girls were more likely to describe themselves as tomboys, tended to have a higher preference for energetic play, and expressed more interest in a career and less in marriage than did the control group. This finding seems to indicate some support for a biological influence on AGS girls. Critics of this study, however, argue that other factors may have been responsible for the more masculine behavior found among the AGS girls. For example, the social environments of the two groups may have been different. The parents of the AGS girls may have expected their daughters to behave in a more masculine manner and therefore did not discourage such behavior. In fact, many girls with no known history of prenatal or postnatal hormonal abnormalities engage in tomboyish behavior. In one study of heterosexual women, 50 percent of the respondents reported being tomboys as children (cited in Devor, 1989:15). Furthermore, the higher level of activity reported by the AGS girls may have been due to the cortisone treatment they received.

The second study, of 17 AGS females and 10 AGS males, attempted to overcome these criticisms by comparing the AGS children with their unaffected same-sex siblings and parents. Similar patterns were found. AGS girls were more likely to identify themselves as tomboys, prefer boys as playmates, and show low interest in jewelry, makeup, and hairstyles than their sisters or their mothers during childhood. Nevertheless, the AGS girls identified with the female role and did not consider their behavior abnormal. By age 16, about half of the girls had become much more interested in their physical appearance and in dressing attractively (Ehrhardt and Baker, 1974). The only difference found for AGS boys was that they tended to show a higher level of energy expenditure in sports and outdoor activities than did their brothers.

Can we conclude from this study that hormone levels before birth result in specific behaviors? According to Ehrhardt (1985), the likelihood of developing a certain behavior pattern may be great, but whether and how the behavior will be expressed depends on the social context in which the child is raised. Some behaviors may be tolerated and encouraged; others may be forbidden and discouraged.

ANDROGEN-INSENSITIVE INDIVIDUALS Money and Ehrhardt also studied individuals who are *androgen-insensitive*, referred to as "XY females." This is a male chromosomal pattern that because of an inability to use androgen does not result in the development of a male body. These infants are born with the external genitalia of females. Given their female appearance, such infants are typically raised as girls by their parents. Compared with a control group of normal girls of the same age, race, and social class, the androgen-insensitive individuals exhibited similar interest in dolls, dresses, and other feminine behavior. Thus, despite having a male chromosomal pattern, these individuals adopted a female gender role, reflecting the influence of socialization.

HERMAPHRODITISM In yet another condition, known as **hermaphroditism**, the infant's external genitalia are ambiguous in appearance; that is, the baby's sexual anatomy cannot be clearly differentiated. Because sex is generally assigned at birth on the basis of external appearance, studies of hermaphroditism allow us to assess the influence of biology and culture in the development of gender identity. Although few in number, these cases make clear that biological sex alone does not determine gender identity; the sex in which a child is reared plays a crucial role.

Two cases, the first involving a hermaphrodite, illustrate this point. A genetic male (chromosomally XY) was born with a tiny penis (1 centimeter long) and a urinary opening similar to that of a genetic female. The child's sex was surgically reassigned. The parents changed the child's name and reared the child as a girl. By age 3 the child showed "feminine" interests, playing with dolls and other girlish toys.

The power of social learning in gender development was also revealed in the second case, involving a normal male identical twin. At the age of 7 months his penis was burned off while he was being circumcised. After counseling, the parents decided to consider the child to be a female, changing the child's name and rearing the child as a girl. At the age of 17 months the child had reconstructive surgery to feminize the genitals. Follow-up interviews were conducted to see how the two children with the same genetic and prenatal background fared when one was reared as a boy and the other a girl. The boy clearly thought of himself as male, and he participated in masculine activities. More critically, the girl's self-concept was feminine, and she enjoyed playing with dolls and following feminine norms (Money and Ehrhardt, 1972).

Although the nature–nurture debate has been framed as an either–or proposition, these studies suggest that differences between females and males develop out of a complex interaction of biological and cultural factors. Before examining **gender-role socialization**, a process by which people acquire the gender roles that their culture defines as appropriate for them, let us look at the content of these gender roles.

TRADITIONAL MEANINGS OF FEMININITY AND MASCULINITY

 Before reading this section, close your eyes and visualize an individual who is feminine and one who is masculine. What traits do you see them as having? How would you evaluate those traits? Are some positive? Negative? Neutral? How closely does your visualization fit the assumed differences between women and men?

In Chapter 2 we discussed the theory of structural functionalism and the Parsonian dichotomy of expressive (female) and instrumental (male) roles. The assignment of these roles is based on the assumption that (1) females and males are fundamentally different from each other and (2) the content of these roles reflects the biological differences between the sexes. Beginning in the 1960s and continuing to the present day, a number of studies have found a broad

TABLE 3.1

Characteristics Attributed to Women and Men (in percent)

To Women	Total	(Opinions of) Men	(Opinions of) Women
Emotional	81	79	83
Talkative	73	73	74
Sensitive	72	74	71
Affectionate	66	69	64
Patient	64	60	68
Romantic	60	59	61
Moody	58	63	52
Cautious	57	55	59
Creative	54	48	60
Thrifty	52	51	53
Manipulative	51	54	48
Honest	42	44	41
Critical	42	43	41
Happy	39	38	39
Possessive	37	43	32
To Men			
Aggressive	64	68	61
Strong	61	66	57
Proud	59	62	55
Disorganized	56	55	57
Courageous	54	55	53
Confident	54	58	49
Independent	50	58	43
Ambitious	48	51	44
Selfish	47	49	44
Logical	45	53	37
Easygoing	44	48	40
Demanding	43	39	46
Possessive	42	38	45
Funny	40	47	34
Level-headed	39	46	34

Source: Adapted from Linda DeStefano and Diane Colasanto, 1990, "Unlike 1975, Most Americans Think Men Have It Better," *Gallup Poll Monthly* (February): 29.

consensus among different groups of people regarding the existence of different personality traits associated with each sex. Table 3.1 summarizes the results of a Gallup poll in which adults were read a list of 31 personality traits and asked which were more characteristic of women or men. Of the traits describing women, emotional (81 percent), talkative (73 percent), and sensitive (72 percent) led the list. In contrast, men were most often described as aggressive (64 percent), strong (61 percent), and proud (59 percent). Women and men were in general agreement about the assignment of these traits, but members of each sex tend to describe themselves in positive terms and the other sex in more negative terms. The traits used to describe each sex are fairly consistent across cultures. One recent study of 25 countries found that in every country sampled, women were thought to be "sentimental" and "submissive," whereas traits such as "adventurous" and "forceful" were associated with men (Williams and Best, 1990).

TRADITIONAL GENDER ROLES: FEMALE AND MALE

Historically, the female gender role has clustered around family relationships and been patterned after the belief that a woman's place is in the home. Based on this belief, women are expected to marry, have children, and be nurturing, emotional, caring, and attractive. They should not be aggressive, loud, competitive, or independent; rather, they should be passive, submissive, and dependent on their husbands. If women are employed, their work must not interfere with family obligations. To ensure that women can be homemakers, men are to be providers and protectors. Thus, they are expected to be achievement-oriented, competitive, strong, aggressive, logical, and independent. They should not be emotional, expressive, or weak and must be in control at all times.

Now that you have thought about masculinity and femininity in general terms, close your eyes again and think of Latino, African-American, Native-American, and Asian-American women and men. Do you visualize the same characteristics or do you see any differences?

GENDER STEREOTYPES: RACE AND CLASS

Gender stereotypes—the overgeneralized beliefs about the characteristics associated with being female or male—are widely shared within a society.

Concepts of femininity and masculinity change over time. Nevertheless, this 1890s Gibson girl resembles in some ways the contemporary image of femininity.

Nevertheless, they do vary somewhat from one group to another. In the United States, traditional gender roles have routinely been associated with white middle-class heterosexuals. Although there is only a limited amount of research on gender beliefs across race and class lines, from the research available, it does appear that people perceive different stereotypical traits in other groups. For example, one study asked college students to use a list of 23 adjectives to describe the characteristics of black and white middle-class women and black and white working-class women. The results revealed that race and class affect people's perceptions of gender roles. Although all four groups were depicted in ways consistent with the feminine stereotype, the ways in which white women and middle-class women in general were described were most like the traditional views of women. Black women were viewed as less

People often experience stress and anxiety when they don't live up to the gender stereotypes for their sex.
Source: Reprinted by permission: Tribune Media Services.

passive, dependent, status-conscious, emotional, and concerned about their appearance than white women (Landrine, 1985).

Relatively little information is available on gender stereotypes of other racial or ethnic groups. One study, however, suggests that Latinas generally tend to be viewed as more submissive and dependent, hence more feminine, than white women (Vazquez-Nuttall et al., 1987). Similarly, Asian-American women have been described as very feminine and as making desirable brides because "they are cute (as in doll-like), quiet rather than militant, and unassuming rather than assertive. In a word, non-threatening" (Lai, 1992:168).

What are we to make of these findings? As Susan Basow (1992:4–5) points out:

> Gender is not the only variable by which people are stereotyped. Each one of us is situated in sociological space at the intersection of numerous categories—for example, gender, race or ethnicity, class, sexual orientation, and able-bodiedness. These social categories interact with each other in complex ways. A woman who is white, working-class, lesbian, and differently abled will be viewed very differently from a black, middle-class, heterosexual, able-bodied woman.

In sum, humankind is not composed of two homogeneous groupings—one feminine and one masculine. Rather, there is a rich diversity within each gender. To encompass this diversity, Harry Brod (1987), a pioneer in the field of men's studies, has suggested substituting the term *masculinities* for *masculinity*. The same argument could be made regarding the diverse forms of femininity. Although research has shown that Americans tend to adhere to a fairly consistent grouping of gender stereotypes, increasing evidence shows that some people are challenging these stereotypes and creating more flexible gender roles for themselves.

GENDER ROLES IN TRANSITION

Perhaps you find it difficult to identify with the traditional gender roles described in the previous section. Given the many changes that have occurred during your lifetime, that would not be surprising. Of special significance are certain demographic changes: patterns of continuing education for both women and men, the movement of married women into the labor force, delayed marriage and childbearing, high divorce rates, and increased life expectancy, especially for women. These changes, along with the liberation movements of the 1960s and 1970s, have challenged traditional gender roles. Thus, as we shall see throughout this book, there has been a definite shift from traditional to more egalitarian gender roles, at least ideologically if not always behaviorally.

In a 1989 Gallup poll, 57 percent of the adults surveyed preferred a marriage in which housework and child care are shared. In a comparable survey taken in 1977, only 48 percent felt this way. There are, however, generational differences in attitudes. Approximately 73 percent of adults under 30 think shared responsibility in a marriage is more satisfying, whereas 52 percent of adults 50 and older prefer a marriage in which the husband is the only wage earner (DeStefano and Colasanto, 1990:26).

Women today have considerably more options in the workplace, and they are exercising more control over their private lives as well. Men, too, are questioning their roles. For many men this means de-emphasizing their work role and emphasizing their family role. Both women and men feel freer to express a much wider range of personality traits than the traditional gender roles would allow. Because changes in women's roles have been more open to public view than those in men's roles, we are more likely to be aware of assertive and strong women than of gentle and nurturing men. Research commissioned by the American Association of Retired Persons, however, revealed that men spend just as much time as women do at listening, handholding, and expressing concern in familial caregiving situations (Behrens, 1990).

Nevertheless, considerable controversy remains over these changes. Not all people are happy with their direction. Some find them confusing, and others prefer a return to a more traditional world. A 24-year-old truck driver complained, "My girlfriend drives me crazy at times. She wants to be paid the same as a man and to have every opportunity a man does. But she still wants to be treated like a woman. She doesn't believe women should be drafted, and if I don't open the door for her or help her with her coat, she gets upset." A 24-year-old medical student finds that some men feel threatened by changes in gender roles. "Jim and I dated in college. I thought he was a liberated male, but I found out differently when he took me to meet some of his friends. On the way he told me not to tell them I was going to be a doctor. He said he didn't want them to think his girlfriend was smarter than he was."

Other people support the movement to gender equality in theory but have trouble implementing these ideas into their everyday lives. Several factors combine to make change difficult. First, people who hold privileged positions have a vested interest in keeping them. Thus, some men may resist sharing power and authority with women at work and at home, whereas some women may resist sharing with men the aspects they most enjoy about the traditional role, such as nurturing children. Second, existing social arrangements tend to reinforce traditional gender roles. To take just one example, on the average women are still paid less than men. Thus, even if a couple should prefer an arrangement in which the husband is the primary parent and the wife the primary breadwinner, simple household economics might make this impossible. Third, as we will see in the next section, gender identities develop early in life, and much of what we learn from parents and other role models is still based on traditional gender norms.

THEORIES OF GENDER-ROLE SOCIALIZATION

Although socialization is a lifelong process, it is especially significant in our formative years. Psychologists and sociologists have developed several theories to explain the socialization process with respect to the acquisition of gender roles.

PSYCHOANALYTIC/IDENTIFICATION THEORY

One prominent theory, known as **psychoanalytic/identification theory**, originated with Sigmund Freud (1856–1939), the founder of modern psychoanalysis. Freud believed that children learn gender-appropriate behaviors by unconsciously identifying with their same-sex parent and that they pass through a series of stages in their development. During the first two stages, the oral and the anal stages, the experiences and behaviors of girls and boys are similar. Both identify with the mother, who is their primary caretaker. However, in the third stage, the phallic stage, which occurs around the age of 4, the development of girls and boys proceeds in different directions. Freud called the boy's development the *Oedipus complex*, based on the mythical Greek character who unknowingly killed his father and married his mother. According to Freud, the young boy experiences sexual feelings for his mother and sees his father

ROLE OPTIONS IN FAMILIES

Todd and Lynn Hughes have been married for 8 years and have a 6-month-old daughter. Both Todd and Lynn work full-time; Lynn's mother takes care of the baby during the day. Todd is employed by the state as a caseworker for juvenile offenders. He finds the job stressful, but he also feels good about the work he is doing. Last year he earned $30,000. Recently Todd's supervisor told him that he was going to recommend Todd for his position when he retires next year. Todd's new salary would be $45,000. Todd is excited at the prospect of this promotion.

Lynn is a certified public accountant with a prestigious firm. Last year she made $43,000. Yesterday Lynn's boss called her into the office to tell her how pleased the firm is with her work. He offered her the position of manager of the accounting division. One of the requirements of the new job, however, would be to relocate to the firm's Dallas office. Her new salary would be $65,000 plus a stock option plan. Lynn had always dreamed about becoming an executive. Her boss wants her decision next week. Lynn would like to accept the position, but she is concerned about having a stranger take care of the baby. Because Todd is so good with the baby, she suggested he might want to take time off to care for the baby and to go back to school evenings to get his master's degree. Todd mentioned this possibility to his parents when they came for dinner. His mother was supportive, but his father said, "You mean you'd let your wife support you? What kind of man are you?"

Imagine that you are part of the Hughes family. What would you do in their situation? What would your options be? What are the costs and benefits of each option? Do any of the options best meet the needs of the entire family? Would it be easier to reach a decision if Todd had received the Dallas offer?

---

as a rival for her affections. Hence, he wants to get rid of his father. At the same time, however, he becomes aware that he has a penis and that his mother does not. Unconsciously, he fears that if his father were to learn of his feelings for his mother, the father would castrate him. Thus, he resolves the Oedipus complex by identifying with his father (becoming like him) and giving up his desire for his mother. Thus, the boy acquires the appropriate gender role.

The path to feminine identification takes a different turn for girls. Freud called this development the *Electra complex*, after a mythical Greek woman who urged her brother to slay their mother, who had killed their father. According to Freud a girl realizes that boys have something she doesn't—a penis. Because she is missing this organ, she develops a sense of inferiority and jealousy and blames her mother for this deformity, a condition Freud refers to as penis envy. At first she takes her love away from her mother, focusing on her father as her love object. Gradually, however, she realizes she can't have her father, and she reestablishes her identification with her mother, with the goal of one day becoming a mother herself.

CRITIQUES OF FREUDIAN THEORY   What are we to make of Freud's theory? Like Greek mythology, it makes fascinating reading, but because it maintains that the process of identification is unconscious, verifying it empirically is impossible. Other than psychoanalytical reports, which are subject to observer bias, there is little if any scientific evidence of either castration anxiety in boys or penis envy in girls. Furthermore, whether children that age understand the relationships between gender and genitalia is questionable. Finally, Freud's view of women as inadequate or incomplete contains an antifemale bias that later identification theorists sought to modify.

Karen Horney (1967) challenged the notion that women view their bodies as inferior and argued that a girl's psychosexual development centers around her own body rather than that of the male. She also argued that what women envy is not the male penis per se but what it symbolizes—men's higher status, freedom, and power. Erik Erikson (1968) suggested that male dominance is, in part, related to womb envy, the jealousy men have for women because of their unique ability to bear children.

Nancy Chodorow (1978; 1990) sees gender identity (in Western societies) as emerging from the social organization of parenting roles. Women mother; men do not. She sees this "asymmetrical organization of parenting" as the basis for gender inequality and the source of identification problems for boys. Boys must psychologically separate from their mothers and pattern themselves after a parent who is frequently absent. As a result, they form personalities that are more detached from others and in which emotional needs are repressed. Girls, on the other hand, identify with the mother and acquire the capabilities for mothering and attachment behaviors. Implicit in Chodorow's work is the belief that shared parenting between women and men would be beneficial to society. As with Freud's theory, the results of these modifications have yet to be tested and verified.

SOCIAL-LEARNING THEORY

The perspective known as **social-learning theory** has its roots in behaviorism, the theory that human behavior is the result of reaction to objective stimuli or situations. Social-learning theory asserts that gender roles and gender identity are learned directly through a system of positive reinforcement (rewards) and negative reinforcement (punishments) and indirectly through observation and **modeling**, learning through imitation. In direct learning, for example, parents reward their daughters with encouragement and approval for engaging in gender-appropriate behavior such as playing with dolls and dressing up in mother's jewelry and high heels. If boys engage in this same behavior, however, they are punished and told, "Boys don't act that way." Research indicates that at younger ages girls enjoy greater flexibility in engaging in cross-gender behavior than do boys (Lynn, 1966; Martin, 1990). A girl can be a "tomboy," but a boy who engages in cross-gender behavior risks being labeled a "sissy." Sociologist David Lynn suggests that this harsher treatment of boys for acting "girllike" leads boys to develop a dis-

One of the ways children learn what is expected of them as they grow up is through imitating adults as this 5-year-old is doing by dressing up in his father's clothes.

like and contempt for females and femininity, which may explain their later hostility toward females (see Chapter 12).

Social-learning theory maintains that behavior that is regularly followed by a reward is more likely to be repeated, whereas behavior that brings forth punishment is more likely to be discontinued. Thus, children quickly develop an awareness that females and males are different and that separate gender roles are appropriate for each sex.

Children also learn which behaviors are appropriate for their gender by observing and imitating their parents and other adults, their peers, and media personalities. Social-learning theorists believe that children initially model themselves after those who are readily available and perceived as powerful (who control rewards and punishment), warm and friendly (nurturing), and similar to the self (same sex). This modeling of the same-sex is similar to the views of psychoanalytic/identification theorists. However, social-learning theorists do not accept the notion that behavior is fixed according to early learning patterns. Rather, they believe that behavior and attitudes change as situations and expectations in the social environment change. As children grow older, the range of role models expands, and the work of crafting a gender identity continues.

A considerable amount of research supports social-learning theory. Nevertheless, social-learning theory alone cannot fully explain gender-role acquisition. For one, modeling is more complex than the theory suggests. Children do not always model themselves after same-sex individuals. In addition, subcultural differences as well as differences in family structures may affect the variety and choice of available role models. Moreover, learning theory treats children as passive learners. In reality, parent–child interaction is two-directional, in that a child's behavior may have significant influence on parental behavior as well.

COGNITIVE-DEVELOPMENT THEORY

Fundamental to cognitive-development theory is the belief that the child's mind matures through interaction with the surrounding environment. In contrast to social-learning theory, cognitive-development theory asserts that children take an active role in organizing their world. They manage this by creating schemas, or mental categories, that emerge through interaction with their social environment. Subsequently, as new information is encountered, it is processed and assimilated into these categories, or the categories are adjusted to fit the new information. Psychologist Lawrence Kohlberg (1966) adapted cognitive-development theory to explain the emergence of children's gender identities. Early on (about age 2 to 3) children become aware that two sexes exist; they can identify and label themselves and others as girls or boys. This labeling process, however, is based not on anatomical differences but on superficial characteristics such as clothes—girls wear dresses and pastel colors, whereas boys wear pants and bold colors. According to Kohlberg, at this stage children have

not yet developed gender identity. This doesn't develop until children are 6 or 7 and have the mental ability to grasp the concept of constancy or permanency. Prior to this time they are too young to realize that all people can be so classified and that sex is a permanent characteristic that cannot be changed simply by changing clothes.

Cognitive-development theory maintains that once gender identity is developed children are able to organize their behavior around it. That is, they strive to behave in a way that is consistent with their own sex, and they attach value to their behavior. Children come to view gender-appropriate behavior in a positive manner and gender-inappropriate behavior as negative behavior that should be avoided.

A considerable body of research gives support to cognitive-development theory. For example, researchers found evidence that children become more accurate at gender differentiation and labeling as they get older (Coker, 1984). In addition, cognitive-development theory helps explain children's, especially boys', strong preferences for sex-typed toys and for playing with same-sex peers (Zuckerman and Sayre, 1982).

Other researchers have criticized some aspects of cognitive-development theory. John Money and Anke Ehrhardt (1972) question the timing of gender identity. Their research, discussed earlier, implies that an important aspect of gender identity is present as early as 2 years of age; changing a child's sex after that age proves difficult. In a similar vein, other researchers have found that a great deal of sex typing—the degree to which men and women identify with societal definitions of masculinity and femininity (Basow, 1992)—and preference for sex-typed toys occurs before the age attributed to gender permanency (Downs, 1983; Bussey and Bandura, 1984). This apparent discrepancy may simply represent two different phases of gender development. The earlier sex typing may be due to differential reinforcement and imitation, whereas the sex typing that occurs later, after the development of the idea of gender permanency, may be a result of cognitive development (Basow, 1986).

The most serious criticism of cognitive-development theory is that it overemphasizes gender learning as something children do themselves and minimizes the role culture plays in gender socialization. Hence, as psychologist Sandra Bem (1983:609) writes, "The typical American child cannot help observing, for example, that what parents, teachers, and peers consider to be appropriate behavior varies as a function of sex; that toys, clothing, occupations, hobbies, the domestic division of labor—even pronouns—all vary as a function of sex." Bem's point becomes clear as we examine the various **agents of socialization**: individuals, groups, and organizations that help form an individual's attitudes, behaviors, and self-concept.

AGENTS OF SOCIALIZATION

Gender-role socialization begins at birth and continues throughout an individual's lifetime. In our interaction with parents, teachers, and peers, and through books, television and movies, we are constantly taught values, attitudes, and behaviors that our culture sees as appropriate for each sex.

PARENTS

Parents provide children with their first exposure to gender learning and play a key role in helping children develop a sense of themselves as females and males. An extensive body of research indicates that parents treat their daughters and sons differently, even though they frequently are not aware of doing so. When asked by researcher Jeffrey Rubin and his colleagues (1974) to describe their newborns, both mothers and fathers described daughters as delicate, soft, and tiny and sons as strong, alert, and well coordinated, even though the infants did not differ significantly by sex on measures of weight, length, muscle tone, heartbeat, or reflexes. The assessments of fathers were more gender-stereotyped than those of mothers. Later research documented that many expectant parents relate to their fetus on the basis of whether they believe it to be a girl or boy. Perceived female fetuses were thought of as "graceful and gentle," whereas the movements of perceived male fetuses were described as "strong" (Stainton, 1985).

Consistent with these findings, other researchers have found that parents, especially fathers, tend to engage in more rough-and-tumble play with infant and young sons than they do with daughters (MacDonald and Parke, 1986). Studies of father–child interaction show that fathers play more

interactive games with young sons, promoting visual, fine-motor, and locomotor exploration with them, whereas they have more vocal interactions with daughters and appear to encourage closer physical proximity with them. The consequence of this differential play activity may be that boys learn to be more independent and aggressive than girls do (Bronstein, 1988).

Not only do parents play differently with their children, they also communicate differently with them. Stories told to daughters tend to contain more emotion words than do stories told to sons. By the time they are age 2, girls typically use more emotion words than boys do (Goleman, 1988). In contrast, other researchers found that mothers tend to speak to sons more explicitly, ask them more questions, and use more action verbs in conversing with them. Thus, sons seem to receive more of the kind of verbal stimulation that is associated with reasoning skills (Weitzman et al., 1985).

CLOTHING Parents also dress their children differently, initially perhaps to give clues to others so that they can be assured of responding appropriately on the basis of sex. The type of clothing children wear serves other functions as well, however. Frilly dresses are not conducive to rough-and-tumble play. Boys' clothing, by and large, is less restrictive than girls' clothing. Therefore, boys are encouraged to be more active and aggressive in their play than girls are.

TOYS AND GAMES One study of children's rooms revealed another way in which parents affect the gender identities of their children. The decor frequently reflects traditional gender stereotypes—florals and pastels for girls, animals and bold colors for boys (Rheingold and Cook, 1975). More important, however, the rooms contained a marked difference in toys. Boys had a wide range of toys (educational, sports, tools, spatiotemporal objects, large and small vehicles), many of which promote outdoor play, whereas girls' toys were less varied in type (dolls, housekeeping objects, and crafts) and promote mainly indoor activities (Rheingold and Cook, 1975; Pomerleau et al., 1990). In her research on children's toys, sociologist Marsha Liss (1992) found that parents are much more likely to give their children requested gender-typical toys than they are to give gender-atypical ones.

These findings take on greater significance when we consider the way toys function in the learning process. Toys for boys tend to promote exploration, manipulation, construction, invention, and competition. Girls' toys typically encourage creativity, nurturance, and attractiveness. Thus, girls and boys may develop different cognitive and social skills based on play activities, which in turn may lead to very different opportunities as adults.

CHORES   A distinction between inside and outside activities is also apparent in the chores assigned to children. Girls are expected to do inside work (wash dishes and clean the house), whereas boys are given activities outside the home (yard work and emptying the trash). Because girls' chores are daily ones whereas a great deal of what boys do is sporadic, girls spend more time doing chores than boys do. A study by researchers Teresa Mauldin and Carol Meeks (1990) of sex differences in children's time use found that boys spend more time in leisure activities and less time in household and personal care than do girls. From early on, patterns for a division of labor based on sex are formed and will likely carry over into adult marital roles. As we see in Chapter 11, even when women work full-time, they still do the bulk of the housework.

LANGUAGE

One of the first tasks facing a developing child is the mastery of language skills. There is growing agreement among social scientists that children's acquisition of gender identity and their perception of gender roles are strongly influenced by language. As children learn language, they also learn a great deal about how their culture defines females and males. An extensive body of research shows that the English language contains a number of gender biases. For example, the words *man* and *he* can be used to exclude females—"*It's a man's world,*" "*The best man for the job*"—or they can be used generically to refer to both women and men—*mankind.* In fact, the use of male terms frequently serves to exclude females. Think of the words *policeman, fireman, postman, chairman, spokesman, congressman, workman.* Whom do you visualize in these roles? Researchers have found that most people visualize men when such terms are used

(Wilson and Ng, 1988). Other studies show that elementary school children give male-biased responses to story cues that contain the pronoun *he* (Hyde, 1984). When the masculine pronoun is used, as it frequently is in textbooks to refer to doctors, lawyers, and public officials, children tend to associate it with males. Thus, many children may limit their aspirations to what appear to be gender-appropriate occupations. To counter this restrictive influence, many publishers have moved to a more gender-neutral language, using *they, he or she, police officer, firefighter,* and *mail carrier.*

PEERS AND PLAY ACTIVITIES

The games children play and the people with whom they play them also influence socialization into gender identity. At about the age of 3 a process of sex segregation begins. This process accelerates during the school years. Researchers have found that girls and boys both prefer same-sex groups. Psychologists Eleanor Maccoby and Carol Jacklin (1987) explain girls' same-sex preference as stemming from unrewarding mixed-sex play activities. Since boys play more roughly than girls and use physical assertion to resolve differences, they tend to dominate and bully girls in mixed-sex play groups. In contrast, girls enjoy more cooperation and mutuality in same-sex groups.

Boys also prefer same-sex groups, but their motivation is different. Aware of men's higher status, boys attempt to disassociate themselves from girls and anything that suggests femininity (Whiting and Edwards, 1988). Thus, girls and boys grow up in different peer subcultures that reinforce both real and perceived gender differences. Because opportunities for cross-sex interactions are so limited, most gender stereotypes go largely unchallenged. That such behavior exists and is reinforced by social approval is substantiated by a large body of research that shows that from preschool to high school, children who engage in traditional gender-role behavior are more socially acceptable to their peers than are children who engage in nontraditional roles (Martin, 1990). These separate and different spheres, as evidenced in the nature of children's play activities have consequences for later life.

Sociologist Janet Lever (1978) observed and interviewed fifth graders about their activities and found many differences between girls' and boys' activities.

Over the last 20 years efforts have been made to provide more equality for women in sports. Boys and girls now compete together in soccer, Little League, and other sports, although only in small numbers. This Austin, Texas, girl plays on the school football team.

She believes boys' activities better prepare them to succeed in modern industrial societies. Girls' games have only a few rules and frequently involve only a minimum of roles (for example, jumping rope or tag), whereas boys' play groups are larger, have complex rules, and involve a variety of roles. Girls' activities require more cooperation, whereas boys' games are organized around competition. Hence, boys' games provide more training for leadership and complex organizational roles than do girls' games.

Peers may play an even more significant role in the lives of African-American males. Distinct bodily movements; athletic prowess; sexual competence;

and street smarts, including how to fight and defend yourself, are lessons learned in the context of the male African-American peer group (Hale-Benson, 1986).

TEACHERS

Teachers also play a major role in the socialization of children. If you were to ask elementary school teachers whether they treat girls and boys differently, most would probably say no, even though a wide range of research studies reveals differential patterns of interaction between teachers and female and male students.

> *Think back to your elementary and high school days. Were girls and boys in your classes treated in the same way? Who were the class officers? How was playground space allocated? How were sports organized? Did girls and boys do the same classroom chores? Did you have other-sex friends (nondating relationships) in grammar school? In high school?*

Teachers often structure classroom activities along sex-segregated lines, encouraging competition between the sexes—for example, girls against the boys in math or spelling contests. Often playground space is allocated in a gender-specific manner, with boys occupying the large fixed spaces for team sports and the girls having a more limited space for their activities, usually closer to the school building and with adult supervision. This use of space conveys subtle messages, that girls need more protection than boys and that boys are entitled to more space. Teachers may assign different classroom chores to girls (watering the plants and dusting) than to boys (handling equipment and running errands).

Teacher behavior can send other gender messages to students as well. A study of fourth-, sixth-, and eighth-grade classes in the Washington, D.C., and New England areas found that teachers provide more assistance and challenges for boys than for girls (Sadker and Sadker, 1985). Other studies show that boys receive more praise for the intellectual quality of their work, whereas girls receive more praise for being neat (Dweck et al., 1978).

Messages like these are often reinforced by the curricular materials used in the classroom. Researchers Piper Purcell and Lara Stewart (1990), for example,

Below are four nursery rhymes. The first two are the traditional versions, most probably the ones you read when you were a child. The second are revised versions that attempt to be nonsexist.

Humpty Dumpty

Humpty Dumpty sat on a wall, Humpty Dumpty had a great fall;
All the King's horses, and all the King's men cannot put Humpty Dumpty together again.

Jack

Jack be nimble, Jack be quick, Jack jump over the candlestick.

Source: Reprinted by permission of Running Press, Philadelphia, PA. © 1992, *The Miniature Mother Goose*: 59, 29.

Humpty Dumpty

Humpty Dumpty sat on a wall, Humpty Dumpty had a great fall;
All of the horses, the women and men put Humpty Dumpty together again!

Jack and Jill be Nimble

Jack be nimble, Jack be quick, Jack jump over the candlestick!
Jill be nimble, jump it too, if Jack can do it, so can you.

Which nursery rhymes did you prefer? Why? What do you think of efforts to present nonsexist reading materials to children?

Source: Copyright © 1985 by Dr. Douglas W. Larche. Reprinted with permission from the publisher, Advocacy Press: 14, 8.

found many examples of gender stereotyping in children's readers. Although both sexes are depicted in a wider range of activities than had previously been the case, certain basic trends remain. Boys are frequently portrayed as being forced to deny their feelings and demonstrate their manhood; girls often need rescuing by boys. The Zurich Office for the Equality of Men and Women studied primary and secondary school textbooks in use in Zurich, Switzerland, and revealed similar findings. Men and boys are depicted in Swiss texts as much as 10 times more frequently than women and girls are (*Chicago Tribune*, 1992a:1).

Even at the college level researchers have observed differential treatment of females and males. For example, in many classes professors call on male students more often than on female students, they interrupt female students more than they do male students, and they are more likely to refer to female students as "girls" or "gals" while referring to male students as "men." Female students are not always taken as seriously as male students, particularly in fields traditionally dominated by males, such as math and science (Hall and Sandler, 1985). A 22-year-old female student complained of discriminatory treatment by a

math professor. "There were only two other women in the advanced calculus class I was taking. The professor didn't want us there. He made jokes about women not being able to balance their checking accounts, and he always seemed surprised when one of us solved his math challenges. I was going to drop his course because he made me feel like a freak for liking math, but my advisor encouraged me to stay with it."

THE MASS MEDIA

That the mass media play an important part in shaping the values, beliefs, and behaviors of modern societies is difficult to dispute. Let us take television as an example. More than 98 percent of U.S. households have at least one television set, almost 65 percent have videocassette recorders, and 52 percent subscribe to cable television (U.S. Bureau of Census, 1990c). In the average home the television set is on 6 or more hours per day. The average school-aged child watches approximately 27 hours of television every week. By the age of 18, the average U.S. child has spent twice as much time (22,000 hours) watching television as

For Better or For Worse® by Lynn Johnston

By the time children are in their teens, they have internalized images of the ideal body form for their sex.

attending school (11,000 hours) and has seen 350,000 commercials (*Staples and Jones, 1985*; *Tracy, 1990*; Black children and adolescents watch more television than their white peers, and children from blue-collar families spend more time in front of the television set than do children from middle-class families.

What gender messages do these children (and adults) get when they watch television? To answer this question researchers employ a technique called **content analysis**, whereby they examine the actual content of programs. They do this by counting particular items within specific categories, for example, the number of males and females featured in the program. As we shall see, most programming, from children's shows to prime time, casts its major characters in traditional roles.

CHILDREN'S SHOWS   Content analysis reveals that children's shows are predominantly white-male-oriented, featuring more than twice as many male as female roles. This discrepancy implies that boys are more significant than girls, an image that is reinforced by the way in which female and male characters are portrayed. In a major study of commercial children's television programs, researcher Earle Barcus (1983) found that the sexes are presented in a biased and somewhat unrealistic way. Females are more likely to be found in minor roles with little responsibility for the outcome of the story and are rarely shown working outside the home. In con-

trast, male characters are depicted in a variety of occupations to which many boys realistically can aspire.

Little has changed since that study. According to one report, television executives decided to feature only males as dominant characters, with females playing peripheral roles, if any, during fall 1991 Saturday morning programs. This decision was based on a finding that boys will watch shows only with male leads but girls will watch shows with either female or male leads (Carter, 1991). Even in the popular and highly acclaimed "Sesame Street" the major characters often portray a restricted view of female and male behavior. The situation is not much different on prime-time television either.

PRIME-TIME TELEVISION   In 1986, research conducted by the Women's Institute for Freedom of the Press (WIFP) found that despite the introduction of gender-equality issues and specials on problems of sexual assault and family violence, much of prime-time programming continues to portray traditional gender roles. This study analyzed 620 episodes from over 20,000 programs between 1955 and 1985 and found that women characters are outnumbered by men two to one (67 percent to 33 percent). Besides appearing more frequently, male characters are older, more mature, and more authoritative than women characters. Besides being younger, female characters are typically thin and physically attractive. For example, in one study researchers rated 69 percent of the female characters as thin compared with just 17.5 percent of male characters but rated only 5 percent of the female characters as heavy compared with 25.5 percent of male characters (Silverstein et al., 1986). Such findings may help explain recent reports of eating disorders in girls as young as nine. Timothy Brewerton of the Medical University of South Carolina surveyed 3100 fifth-to eighth-grade students. As Table 3.2 shows, although 41.4 percent felt they were too fat, girls were twice as likely to feel that way as boys (54.4 percent to 27.8 percent). More significantly, 42.6 percent of the girls but only 19.7 percent of the boys said they had tried to lose weight by dieting. Furthermore, 32.5 percent of the girls and 13.0 percent of the boys indicated that they had experienced being afraid to eat because they thought they would gain weight. This gender differential reflects patterns observed in teens and adults as well. Of the 8 million people in the U.S. estimated to have eating disorders, 7 million are women (Campbell, 1992).

Although we cannot assume a direct cause-and-effect relationship between television images and behavior such as eating disorders, there is evidence to suggest that such a relationship may exist. For example, an analysis of commercials aimed at children found that the overwhelming majority (86 percent) of commercials advertising products to enhance personal appearance were aimed at girls (Ogletree et al., 1990). The authors of that study suggest that the early differential emphasis on the importance of appearance for the female may play a role in the higher incidence of eating disorders experienced by females.

Other studies have focused on the activities undertaken by female and male characters. Although there are some notable exceptions ("Murphy Brown," "L.A. Law," "Designing Women," and "The Golden Girls"), the vast majority of programs depict women in a limited range of roles; mostly in home or family situations, regardless of whether they are employed. When women characters are employed, their occupations are generally high-status ones, for example, lawyers, doctors, or business executives, a pattern not typical of the majority of working women. Thus, television distorts the reality of the working lives of most women and perhaps gives viewers an erroneous notion that gender barriers have disappeared.

In contrast, male characters are shown as powerful individuals, interacting in a wide variety of settings. Just as in children's readers, males are depicted as the problem solvers, whereas females generally are characterized

TABLE 3.2

Percentage of Children with Eating Disorders, by Sex, 1992

	Total	Females	Males
Do you want to lose weight now?	42.0	55.0	28.5
Have you ever thought you looked fat to other people?	41.4	54.4	27.8
Have you ever been afraid to eat because you thought you would gain weight?	23.0	32.5	13.0
Have you ever tried to lose weight by dieting?	31.4	42.6	19.7

Source: "The Kids' Eating Disorders Survey (KEDS): A Study of Middle School Students," in Ann C. Childress, Timothy D. Brewerton, Elizabeth L. Hodges, and Mark P. Jarrell, *Journal of American Academy of Child and Adolescent Psychiatry* (in press).

as needing male help in solving their problems. There is one notable case in which women out-perform men, however. In contrast to men, women readily express emotions, and they are seven times more likely to use sex or romantic charm to get their way (Condry, 1989). Nonetheless, there is one way in which male portrayals do not fare so well: Male characters are much more likely than female characters to use force or violence to get what they want and to commit crimes.

NEWS PROGRAMS Thus far, the studies we have reported on have been concerned primarily with media representations of fictional characters and situations. Studies suggest, however, that the same trends characterize news reports of real people. Not only are women underrepresented in major news stories, but when they are included, they are often treated differently from men. Stories about women frequently mention their sex ("the female doctor"), their physical appearance ("the attractive brunette"), and marital status or family relationship ("Representative Brown, the mother of three"). Rarely are these details provided in male-centered stories (Foreit et al., 1980; "Study Reports Sex Bias," 1989). Although more women than men graduate with degrees in journalism, women account for less than 2 percent of newspaper corporate management, 5 percent of publishers and general managers, and 13 percent of directing editors ("Women in Media," 1988). Perhaps as more women gain positions of power in the news media, coverage will become more balanced.

In sum, gender stereotypes are presented in various degrees by all the agents of socialization. Even when parents make efforts to treat their daughters and sons equally, other socializing forces may undermine those efforts. As we have seen, rarely are either women or men portrayed in terms of the rich diversity and complexity that constitutes the human condition. Thus, it is not surprising that many children develop a stereotypic gender schema in the process of acquiring their gender identity. However, the socialization process itself does not tell us why one gender role is more highly valued than another. Although a discussion of the causes of gender inequality is outside the scope of this text, the theories discussed in the previous chapter, particularly structural functionalism and conflict theory, give some insight into how existing social arrangements define and support gender inequality. For now let us turn our attention to the many ways in which our lives are affected by the cultural constructions of gender.

CONSEQUENCES OF GENDER STEREOTYPING

 Imagine for a moment that you had to spend the next year of your life as a member of the other sex. How would your life be different? What advantages and disadvantages would you experience as a female? As a male?

Studies show that each gender role has its advantages. Women live longer, can express their emotions more easily, and have closer interpersonal relationships than men do. Men have more power, both economically and socially, and greater freedom, and they experience less sexual discrimination or harassment than women do. These advantages notwithstanding, both women and men perceive the female role as having more disadvantages than the male role. A 1989 Gallup poll survey found that nearly half of all the adults surveyed (49 percent) believe men in the United States have a better life than women. Only 22 percent of the respondents believe that women's lives are better. A similar number of respondents (21 percent) believe women and men have a similar quality of life (DeStefano and Colasanto, 1990). Indeed, the fact that women and men are socialized differently has major consequences for individuals, families, and society at large. This is particularly true when existing social arrangements reinforce these differences, for example, institutionalized patterns of inequities in pay and job opportunities that disregard individual abilities. The scope of this book allows us to consider only a few of these consequences, so we will focus on lifestyle choices, self-esteem, self-confidence, mental illness, female–male interactions, and gendered patterns of communication.

LIFESTYLE CHOICES

Although women have made major advances in a wide range of fields, from construction work to executive business positions, this progress is still more the exception than the norm. Current gender expectations continue to limit women's lifestyle choices. For example, the choice of a single lifestyle by a growing number of women is still viewed as second best. Women who wish to combine career and family often must do so without much societal support. High-profile women who challenge the status quo are often labeled "radical feminists" and are suspected of undermining "family values." During the 1992 presidential campaign, attorney Hillary Clinton became the subject of such criticism.

Men, too, have found their lifestyle choices limited by traditional gender expectations. Not all men can or want to achieve "success" as defined by having a meaningful career or a high-paying job. Yet they are pressured to assume the role of the major breadwinner in the family. As a result, they may experience serious conflict between their work and family roles. In addition, if they are not considered financially successful, they may be viewed as unsuitable marriage prospects.

SELF-ESTEEM

Given that society values traits identified as masculine more highly than those identified as feminine, we might well expect to find gender differences in **self-esteem**, the overall feelings—positive or negative—that a person has about him- or herself (Alpert-

Gillis and Connell, 1989). The research literature generally bears this out. As a category, females have lower self-images than males do. This does not mean, however, that all females have lower self-esteem than all males. At least two factors seem to play a crucial role in the relationship between gender and self-esteem: age and the degree of individual sex typing.

AGE A 1991 study by the American Association of University Women (AAUW) of a national sample of more than 3000 students in grades 4 through 10 found that not only did boys have higher self-esteem in elementary school than girls but that the gap between them widened in high school. In elementary school 60 percent of the girls and 67 percent of the boys agreed with the statement, "I'm happy the way I am." By high school only 20 percent of the girls and 46 percent of the boys felt that way. This finding, documented in other studies as well, is attributed to the conflicting expectations girls encounter when they reach puberty. Girls who were energetic, self-confident, and independent now experience pressure to behave in ways that will make them attractive to and popular with boys, even though this behavior might conflict with their own desires and abilities (Gilligan, 1990). Latinas and white females showed the largest decline in self-esteem. Black females had the smallest decrease, probably because, in contrast to other girls, from early on they are socialized to be more independent and assertive.

SEX TYPING The second factor that helps explain the observed gender differences in self-esteem is sex typing. Over the last several decades, social scientists have asked people to describe themselves using a list of personality traits thought to be characteristic of women and men. Scores are tallied and individuals are then categorized as masculine (high on instrumental traits such as independence, strength, aggressiveness), feminine (high on expressive traits such as understanding, emotion, dependence), or **androgynous** (having both instrumental and expressive traits). Researchers reported that the highest levels of self-esteem are found among both females and males who are high in masculine traits or who are androgynous (the latter's high self-esteem is attributed to the presence of instrumental traits). Conversely, feminine sex-typed individuals have considerably lower levels of self-esteem.

SELF-CONFIDENCE

As with self-esteem, girls and boys differ in levels of self-confidence, and the gap widens with age. In response to the statement "I am good at a lot of things," 45 percent of elementary school females agreed, compared with 55 percent of their male counterparts. In high school, however, only 23 percent of the girls agreed, compared with 42 percent of the boys (AAUW, 1991). At least two patterns are associated with these perceptions. First, females tend to underestimate their abilities, whereas males overestimate theirs. In a small but insightful study, Edward Kain (1990:113) asked his students to grade their own papers. He found an almost perfect correlation between sex and grade estimation: The females gave themselves significantly lower grades, whereas the males gave themselves significantly higher grades. Kain concluded, "By the time students have reached college age, the cultural lessons about gender appear to be strongly internalized."

Second, some activities may be avoided if they are seen as inappropriate for one's sex, regardless of ability. For example, females often see themselves as less competent in fields that have been traditionally defined as masculine (such as math and science) than males who have the same grades. Thus, society may be losing potential mathematicians and scientists simply because of narrowly defined gender roles.

MENTAL ILLNESS

Gender differences in mental illness have long been observed. To take just one example, studies of both clinical populations and the general public consistently find that women have higher rates of depression than men, a ratio of about 2 to 1 (Cleary, 1987). As many as one out of every four women experiences clinical depression sometime during her life (McGrath et al., 1990). There is considerable evidence that gender stereotypes play a pivotal role in these rates. The higher rates of depression found among women may be a result of the fact that women are more likely than men to seek help for their problems (Klerman and Weissman, 1980). This behavior is consistent with traditional gender roles. The traditional feminine role grants women permission to seek help from others, whereas the traditional masculine role requires men to be strong and to "ride out" their problems.

The attitudes and behaviors of mental health professionals are also important in understanding gender differences in mental illness. Historically, the mental health field frequently reflected gender-related stereotypes. In one study, for example, researchers asked a number of clinicians to define a healthy woman, a healthy man, and a healthy, mature adult of no specified sex. Clinicians described a healthy woman as more emotional, more submissive, less independent, less aggressive and competitive, more easily excitable, more easily hurt, and more concerned with her appearance than a healthy male. Significantly, when describing a healthy adult of no specified sex, clinicians listed a number of traits traditionally associated with the male stereotype, such as independence and assertiveness. Thus, women were viewed as possessing characteristics that are less positive and less healthy than those of a typical healthy adult (Broverman et al., 1970). Such an association implied that women who conform to the traditional feminine role don't measure up to the mental health standards of the general adult population.

Clinicians today are more sensitive to gender bias and are unlikely to list different characteristics for healthy adult females and healthy adult males. Nevertheless, some clinicians still hold an adjustment standard of mental health. Thus, women and men who conform to traditional gender roles are likely to be seen as healthier than those who deviate from these roles. Assertive and independent women and gentle and nurturing men may therefore be viewed as maladjusted (Robertson and Fitzgerald, 1990).

Marital status and level of marital power are also related to feelings of depression. Wives who share decision making with their husbands report lower levels of depression than those in unequal relationships (Whisman and Jacobson, 1988). As Susan Basow (1992) observes, women's lives themselves may add to their risk of being depressed. Women are more likely to be unemployed, poor, or in a low-status job. As wives, they feel pressured to make sure that the household runs smoothly and the needs of all family members are satisfied, even when this means that their own needs go unmet.

Although overall men fare better on measures of mental health than women do, some aspects of the traditional masculine role can easily become detrimental. When taken to extremes, dominance and aggression can lead to psychologically and physically destructive behavior. Furthermore, the cultural connection between work and male identity can create considerable psychological stress for unemployed men. Lack of education, inadequate job skills, and discriminatory practices make this particularly problematic for poor men and men of color. Additionally, men's emotional lives are often deficient because of their inability to verbalize their love or show affection. Thus, rigid adherence to traditional gender norms may interfere with the development of good mental health for both women and men. This latter point raises an interesting question. Can both women and men benefit from becoming androgynous, that is, sharing masculine and feminine traits?

Research shows that masculine-oriented individuals (high on instrumental traits), both female and male experience less anxiety, strain, depression, neuroticism, work impairment, achievement conflicts, and dissatisfaction with their lives than do feminine-oriented individuals (Nezu and Nezu, 1987; Long, 1989; Basow, 1992). Similarly, traits traditionally defined as feminine can be beneficial to women and men. The ability to express feelings and show sensitivity to those around you enhances interpersonal adjustment and the ability to form intimate relationships. For example, researchers Lawrence Ganong and Marilyn Coleman (1987) found that androgynous individuals are more expressive in their feelings of love, better able to self-disclose, and more tolerant of faults in their loved ones than are more traditionally oriented people.

FEMALE–MALE INTERACTIONS

A friend of ours, a single parent who lives with her mother and her 9-year-old daughter, told us this story.

> Recently Jane had a male school chum over to the house. The grandmother was home and the mother was at work. The two children went up to Jane's room to play computer games. Upon realizing they went upstairs, the grandmother became excited and sent the boy home, telling her granddaughter that it was inappropriate for him to be there.

What do you think motivated the grandmother's behavior? No doubt you have observed mixed-sex groups of preschool children at play. However, this

NEW ROLES FOR MEN AND WOMEN

Should Men Become Child-Care Workers?

Gender barriers have given way in many fields, but men are still finding it extremely difficult to get positions as babysitters or child-care workers. Over 96 percent of child-care workers are female (U.S. Bureau of Labor Statistics, 1991a). Anthony DeBartolo (1991), a reporter for the *Chicago Tribune*, interviewed a number of child-care professionals and found that men who want to pursue day care as a vocation are still regarded with suspicion by most Americans. Three reasons seem to account for this. First, there is a general awareness that statistics show that men are far more likely to commit sexual abuse than are women. Second, even though fathers are becoming more involved in child rearing, our culture still doesn't think of men in nurturing roles. Finally, there is an assumption that something must be wrong with men who want to be child-care

workers—either they can't survive in the "real world" or they must be gay.

Do you think children could benefit by having men become early-child-care workers? Why or why not? What actions could be taken to overcome the cultural resistance to having men in this field?

Should Women Serve in Combat?

This question became a major issue with the introduction of the all-volunteer service in 1973 and the eventual demise of the separate female units in favor of integration into regular military units. Two recent events ignited an intense congressional debate over women in combat. In 1989, the United States took military action in Panama. A military police company commanded by Captain Linda Bray engaged in a firefight with Panamanian forces. In 1991, 26,000 women served in the Persian Gulf conflict. Twelve

women died, including six from hostile fire, and several women were taken prisoner.

People who favor allowing women to serve in combat maintain that women who are properly trained have proven to be as capable as men. Moreover, serving in combat positions is the way to promotion and higher pay. Therefore, to exclude women from combat roles is discriminatory. The arguments against allowing women to serve in combat can be summarized as follows: Women are emotionally unfit for the rigors of conflict; it's not practical for women and men to serve together for long stretches at sea on combat ships; women may get pregnant when they're that close to men; and women POW's may be sexually abused (Waller, 1992).

Do you support changing U.S. policy to allow women in combat? What advantages and disadvantages would such a policy have for women, men, and the society at large?

---

pattern begins to change in elementary school. Like this grandmother, adults become fearful that mixed-sex friendships can become sexual. Thus, whether consciously or not, from early on society erects barriers to mixed-sex friendships. Some of these barriers are reflected in the organization of elementary schools, with their frequent gender-segregated activities; others are embedded in the belief that women and men have opposite characteristics. Still others may be found in gendered patterns of communication, a topic we consider next. Consequently, women and men develop styles of interacting that exaggerate both the perceived and real differences between them and hinder the formation of cross-sex friendships.

GENDERED PATTERNS OF COMMUNICATION

Linguistic scholars from Robin Lakoff (1975) to Deborah Tannen (1990) report that women and men often speak essentially different languages and have different communication goals, which leads to miscommunication between them. According to Tannen, women speak and hear a language of intimacy and connectedness, whereas men speak and hear a language of status and independence. She calls women's conversational style "rapport talk," the goal of which is to signal support, to confirm solidarity, or to indicate they are following the conver-

As more women and men pursue similar occupations and work together, the possibilities for the development of cross-sex friendships increase. These colleagues share a lunch break together.

Although many jobs are still considered women's or men's work, occupational sex segregation is disappearing in some areas. In contrast to the past, male flight attendants are now working on all major U.S. airlines.

sation. In contrast, Tannen sees men's conversational style as "report talk," intended to preserve independence and to negotiate and maintain status in a hierarchical order. These contrasting styles can be problematic in intimate relationships, especially in the realm of self-disclosure. As we will see in other sections of this text, men often find it difficult to self-disclose, even to their wives.

Another linguist, Jennifer Coates (1986), concluded that women normally use conversation as an opportunity to discuss problems, share experiences, and offer reassurance and advice. Men, however, do not see the discussion of personal issues as a normal component of conversation. If someone discloses to them, they are likely to assume the role of expert and offer advice. Thus, in couple relationships women often complain that men don't express their feelings and men feel burdened by such complaints. Such gender differences may result in stress and conflict in marriage.

CHANGING REALITIES, CHANGING ROLES

Whether we like it or not, the world we inhabit today is quite different from that of our parents and grandparents. Consider two examples that will be discussed in detail in later chapters. (1) More married mothers

are working than ever before, many of them in sexually integrated work settings. (2) Increasing numbers of women (and some men) are finding themselves solely responsible for their family's economic and social welfare. Yet, as we have seen throughout this

The face of the U.S. military is changing. Captain Linda Bray of the 988th Military Police Company from Fort Benning, Georgia, led 30 MPs in a clash with Panamanian Defense Forces during the U.S. invasion of Panama.

chapter, some of the agents of socialization continue to perpetuate traditional views of white middle-class femininity and masculinity, often in ways that have negative consequences for women's and men's development and self-esteem. Many of these patterns of socialization are not sufficient to provide solutions to the psychological and economic strains experienced by many people today. Thus, it is necessary to seek new ways to socialize children, to enable them to make satisfying personal choices and to live full and satisfying human lives.

Psychologist Sandra Bem (1983:613) offers two strategies to meet this goal. First, she encourages parents to teach their children that the only definitive gender differences are anatomical and reproductive. Second, she suggests that parents help children substitute an "individual differences" schema that emphasizes the "remarkable variability of individuals within groups" for the gender schema they currently use for organizing and processing information. Sociologist Hilary Lips (1993:397) sums up the possible benefits of such an approach: "As a society, we may finally come to the realization that the function and qualities stereotypically associated with each gender are valuable and necessary—and much more interchangeable and shareable than we used to think."

SUMMARY

Each of us occupies a number of statuses that carry with them expectations for behavior. Some of these are ascribed statuses, such as sex and race. Others are achieved by our own efforts, for example, becoming a parent or a teacher. Role expectations serve an important function in society in that they make behavior predictable. However, expectations can be defined so rigidly that they become dysfunctional for individuals and for society as a whole.

The status of being female or male in our society affects all aspects of our life. Thus, it is important to distinguish between the concepts of sex (being female or male) and gender (the socially learned behaviors, attitudes, and expectations associated with being female or male). From early on we are taught to behave in gender-appropriate ways by parents, peers, teachers, and the mass media.

Psychoanalytical/identification theory, social-learning theory, and cognitive-development theory have been advanced by social scientists to explain the process by which we acquire our gender identity.

Although there is some empirical support for these theories, they do not explain why women and men are treated unequally. For this answer we must examine existing social arrangements.

The traditional notions of femininity and masculinity are based on white middle-class definitions, and they do not accurately reflect the race and class variations in gender-role perceptions. Traditional gender roles limit the lifestyle options of both females and males.

Gender roles are in transition as a result of new demographic and social patterns. Increasing numbers of individuals can be identified as androgynous, having characteristics of both genders. Research shows that both females and males who are high in instrumental (masculine) traits tend to have higher self-esteem and better mental health than those high on expressive (feminine) traits. Researchers have found that androgynous individuals are more expressive in their feelings of love, better able to self-disclose, and more tolerant of faults in their loved ones than more traditionally oriented individuals are.

KEY TERMS

role	gender	cognitive-development theory
status	gender identity	sex typing
ascribed status	hermaphroditism	agents of socialization
achieved status	gender-role socialization	content analysis
stereotype	psychoanalytic/identification theory	self-esteem
master (key) status	social-learning theory	androgynous
sex	modeling	

QUESTIONS FOR STUDY AND REFLECTION

1. Many people use the concepts of sex and gender interchangeably. How does that interfere with our understandings of what it means to be a female and a male in the United States today? What roles do biology and culture play in the development of gender? What evidence can you offer to support your position?

2. Compare and contrast the three theories advanced by social scientists to explain the process of gender acquisition. Using yourself as an example, which theory do you think explains how you acquired your gender identity? Is any one of these theories, or are all of them combined, sufficient to explain the content of gender roles in our society? Explain your position.

3. Assume that you are entertaining visitors from another culture who are unfamiliar with the patterns of female–male relationships in the United States today and who do not want to make any major mistakes in their interactions during their visit. What would you tell them? What problems might they run into without this knowledge?

4. Assume that you have been asked to serve on a presidential advisory committee to analyze ways in which gender-role socialization could be changed to eliminate some of the negative consequences of gender stereotyping. How would you go about determining where changes have to be made? No doubt you would encounter resistance to some of your proposed changes. How would you try to overcome that resistance? What vision would you want to offer for the future in terms of gender relationships?

FURTHER READING

GILMORE, DAVID G. 1990. *Manhood in the Making: Cultural Concepts of Masculinity.* New Haven, CT: Yale University Press. Presents a cross-cultural view of what it means to "be a man" in different cultures around the world.

KIMMEL, MICHAEL S., and MICHAEL A. MESSNER, EDS. 1992. *Men's Lives.* New York: Macmillan. A collection of essays dealing with men's socialization experiences, sports, work, and friendships.

TAVRIS, CAROL. 1992. *The Mismeasure of Women.* New York: Simon & Schuster. A critical look at the problems involved when female behavior is measured against standards based on male behavior.

ZINN, MAXINE BACA, AND BONNIE THORNTON DILL, EDS. 1991. *Women of Color in American Society.* Philadelphia: Temple University Press. Articles that examine the lives of African American, Latina, Native-American, and Asian-American women.

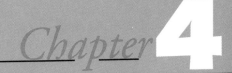

Chapter 4

THE MANY FACES OF LOVE

Courtney is a young urban professional in her late 20s. By some people's definition an independent woman of the 1990s, she has a high-powered and demanding job and earns a six-figure salary. She owns her own luxury home and a brand new sports car, and she invests regularly in the stock market. Courtney has not dated much in her life, nor has she ever married. For the last 3 years, however, she has been exclusively dating Brad, a 24-year-old recent college graduate who is currently an apprentice at a leading advertising agency. Although Brad barely makes ends meet right now, he has the potential to earn an annual salary in excess of $150,000 when he finishes his apprenticeship.

A major issue for this couple is that Brad wants to get married—now. He has told Courtney often enough that he is madly and passionately in love with her and cannot imagine his life without her. Courtney, however, says that she is fond of Brad but has no special feelings toward him. She keeps waiting for her palms to sweat, her knees to buckle, and her heart to skip a beat. To date, none of these things has happened. Because of this she feels that she must not really be "in love" with Brad and therefore cannot make a permanent commitment to him. Thus, she has turned down every one of his proposals.

Although Courtney and Brad's relationship is not the red-hot love affair that Courtney feels it should be, the couple accept and trust each other. Courtney says that although the "passion" is not there, she would never intentionally hurt Brad. In fact, she does not care as much for anyone else and prefers to continue in a dating relationship with him. Courtney and Brad respect each other, confide in each other, and are usually willing to help each other when the need arises.

What is going on in this relationship? Should Courtney end it, or should she marry Brad? Does she love Brad? Is she "in love" with him, or does she simply feel a friendship for him? Is what Brad feels "true love," or is it infatuation? Is it pure and simple passion? Are any of these the same as love? Do you think that Courtney's status and age vis-à-vis Brad's status and age have anything to do with how they feel about each other? What would you do if you were in the shoes of either one of these people? Can you love someone without wanting to marry her or him?

"Love is blind." "Love makes the world go 'round." "Love is a many splendored thing." "True love never dies." "Love at first sight." "Love conquers all." How many sayings like these can you think of? In Western societies, probably more than in any others, love is a central feature of life. It is such a major part of our lives today that most of us cannot imagine life and relationships without love. Most Westerners believe that love gives life meaning, that it is essential to a healthy and satisfying life. Love is referred to or appears as a central theme throughout American popular culture, in the lyrics of all types of music, poems, sonnets, short stories, novels, film, plays, television, and art. Almost everyone at one time or another has been or will be in love. Yet few of us can say exactly what love is.

There are many kinds of love, probably as many as there are types of people who love and are loved. Love encompasses a wide variety of feelings and behaviors ranging from those regarding our parents, friends, siblings, and children to those regarding our spouses or partners. However, the type of love that is dominant in most of our lives, at one time or another, is romantic love. Although a common thread of caring is

woven through all love relationships, the major difference between these feelings of love and romantic love is the element of *eroticism*—concerning or intending to arouse sexual desire. Although each of these types of love is important and merits discussion, our concern in this chapter is with romantic or erotic love.

WHAT IS THIS THING CALLED LOVE?

What is love? How would you respond to that question? If we asked 100 people to define love, we would probably get 100 different responses. Love, it seems, is an elusive emotion. Most of us insist that we experience it at some time in our lives, but we have extreme difficulty explaining it in words. Love is surrounded by myths and metaphors; we dream and hope of finding the love of a lifetime who will love us no matter what and who will transform an otherwise ordinary life into one of bliss.

Because each of us expresses and experiences love differently, there are a variety of definitions and types of love. Some writers, for example, have defined love

There is no single definition of love. Americans of all ages, however, tend to link love with marriage.

Source: Reprinted with special permission of North America Syndicate.

as an emotion that causes us to act irrationally. Other writers have defined it as an emotion that is much more centered on self than on another person; as giving of the heart and soul, the giving of a person's total self; as an ideology that narrows people's perception of the world. Some writers have even argued that love is a male invention used to exploit women. Most definitions of love describe it in terms of any one or several of the following characteristics: deep emotional attachment, openness, self-disclosure, physical attraction, and personal growth.

There is no single definition of love. The most widely cited definition in the scientific literature is probably that of social scientist William Goode (1959:49): "A strong emotional attachment, a cathexis, between adolescents or adults of opposite sexes, with at least the components of sex, desire, and tenderness." We prefer to use a more general and inclusive definition. Therefore, we use the term **romantic love** to refer to, very generally, the intense feelings, emotions, and thoughts coupled with sexual passion and erotic expression that a person directs toward another as well as the **ideology** (set of beliefs) that upholds it.

HOW DOES LOVE DEVELOP IN CONTEMPORARY SOCIETY?

In the United States love develops within the context of a popular culture that inundates us with messages about love: who we should love, how, when, under what conditions, and how we should behave when we're in love. Based on an accumulation of research over the years, the typical developmental sequence of heterosexual love in the twentieth century, particularly in the last half of the century, seems to be: Girl meets boy; they interact; they discover that they have common interests, values, and backgrounds; they find that they like each other; they begin to date; they are physically attracted to each other. Because they like and are physically attracted to each other, they date more frequently and grow more fond of each other. At some point, they define their feelings as *love*. Feeling love for one another, they become engaged and plan to marry. The relationship may or may not include sexual activity, but if it does, sex is probably defined in terms of the couple's love for each other. This sequence is discussed in greater detail in Chapter 5.

Not all love relationships, of course, develop along this sequence. Sometimes the stages are reversed; at other times some of them are omitted. Sometimes, for example, the sequence begins with sexual attraction. In addition, not all love relationships culminate in sex or marriage. In fact, in recent years, several of these stages may not apply to some couples who engage in a series of "involvements" that may or may not lead to marriage. Several social scientists have attempted to explain these newer modifications to the developmental course of love. Later in this chapter we examine some of these theories. First, however, we must understand the history of love and its development in Western society.

LOVE IN WESTERN SOCIETY: A HISTORICAL PERSPECTIVE

As we have indicated, today romantic love is almost always linked to sex and marriage. The moment we think of any one of these concepts, the other two come to mind. For example, we refer to sexual intercourse as "making love" (some people refer to it as "the marriage act"), we marry because we are "in love," marriage is viewed as a "love relationship," and sex is said to be a "natural expression of love." And when we are no longer in love we separate, divorce, or break up. We tend to think that one naturally follows another.

It has not always been this way, however. For much of human history, although marriage and sex were related, there was no conception of love as a necessary part of either of these. The linking of love with sex and marriage is a unique feature of romantic love, a type of love that is relatively new in human social history. It developed in Western societies slowly over many centuries, and its roots can be traced to ancient Greece and Rome.

LOVE IN ANCIENT GREECE Most writers trace contemporary notions of romantic love to Greek society of the fifth-century B.C. and the writings of the philosopher Plato. Plato defined love as the highest expression of human virtue for its ability to inspire people to be kind, honorable, and wise. Plato distinguished several types of love: *Agape* is a selfless love; it is spontaneous and altruistic and requires nothing in return. *Eros* is a selfish love with an emphasis on physical pleasure. It is based on a sexual attraction and can be either homosexual or heterosexual. *Philos* is a deep friendship or brotherly love and includes a love for humanity.

In ancient Greece, love was not associated with marriage. Rather, love had much more to do with the beauty and goodness of a person. Marriages were arranged by families, and men married primarily to reproduce a line of male heirs. The primary role of women was to bear and care for children. Women were considered to be inferior to men and thus were generally uneducated and accorded low social status. Because of this and given that the emphasis of love was on mind and heart and that ancient Greeks believed that high status made people attractive, women were considered unattractive and thus unfit for *agape*. As a

result, ancient Greeks downplayed the significance of heterosexual love. Because only males were considered attractive and good or worthy companions, love often developed between males (especially adult men and young boys). Male homosexual love was considered to be as natural as hetersexual love. Contributing to the prevalence of homosexual love relationships was the fact that men who showed a love for or sexual interest in women were considered to be womanlike or effeminate (Murstein, 1974).

The Greek influence on modern ideas and practices of love can be found throughout our society. For example, we often hear people refer to relationships as "platonic." The idea of platonic love is rooted in the Greek emphasis on love as being of mind and heart, and even today it continues to mean essentially love without sex. The idea of platonic love is most often attributed to Plato; thus, it bears his name. Some contemporary researchers (for example, Solomon, 1981), however, have claimed that this attribution is misleading as some of Plato's writings indicate that he recognized a connection between love and sex.

LOVE IN ANCIENT ROME Female and male relationships in ancient Rome were considerably different from those in ancient Greece. They therefore gave rise to a very different form of love from that described by Plato. Upper-class Roman women were more educated and worldly, and more socially and intellectually equal to Roman men than were their counterparts in Greek society. Thus, in contrast to ancient Greece, Roman love was oriented primarily toward heterosexual love. Love still was not connected to marriage, however. Marriages continued to be arranged by families and took place for the economic, social, and political advantages they accorded.

Love most often occurred in secret, outside these arranged marriages. It consisted primarily of meaningless flirtation and brief encounters between couples. The most important part of love relationships was the seduction of a desirable person. To be desirable, potential lovers, especially women, had to be physically attractive. Love in this context had to be secretive: If exposed, men could be severely fined by the offended husband. Women, however, could lose their lives. The stronger punishments directed toward women reflected a general sexual double standard in terms of female and male behavior in love relationships that is still evidenced today by the fact that we define love relationships differently for each gender, as we will see later in this chapter.

THE EARLY CHRISTIAN IDEA OF LOVE The Roman notion of love was in sharp contrast to early Christian thought and was strongly rejected by Christians. The early Christian idea of love was one of a nonsexual, nonerotic relationship. Even between married couples sexual desire and attraction were frowned upon. As Christianity spread in the Western world, so too did the ideals of celibacy and virginity. From the Christian ideas about love and sexuality grew the notion that priests and nuns should live a celibate way of life, an ideal that is still part of the Roman Catholic faith.

The Christian idea of love emphasized aspects of *agape*, especially the idea of honor and devotion to be directed to the spiritual community rather than to individuals. At the very least, the downplaying of eroticism in Christian love weakened the relationship between married couples, making it relatively easy for people to forsake personal relationships and instead devote themselves to the Christian community (Albas and Albas, 1989).

COURTLY LOVE Not everyone accepted the Christian definition of love. Many among the powerful nobility challenged the Christian notion and espoused a new idea of love—referred to as *courtly love*—that combined two basic ideas of the time period: male chivalry and the idealization of women. Courtly love, which emerged sometime between A.D. 1000 and 1300, is the precursor of contemporary notions of romantic love.

The ideas and messages of courtly love were first heard during this period in the love songs and romantic poetry of French troubadours, men who traveled from one manor to another singing and reciting poetry and sonnets in exchange for food and shelter. The troubadours combined some of the earlier Greek and Roman ideas about love into an idea of courtly love in which the sensual aspect of love was emphasized. Researcher Morton Hunt (1959) indicated that the emergence and development of romantic love was greatly influenced by three general features of heterosexual relations that became widespread during that period: (1) the elevation of women in terms of social status and thus a greater emotional relationship with men, (2) sexual fidelity

to one person, and (3) the notion that love should be reciprocal or mutual.

As in the past, marriages were arranged. Love and romance were not essential elements in marriage and thus were most often found outside of marital relationships. The secrecy of such love relationships was very similar to the early expression of love in ancient Roman society. The main difference between the two types of love is that courtly love was basically nonsexual. Sex was considered to be animalistic, dishonorable, and degrading, so courtly love required that there be no sexual relations between lovers. Couples could, however, and sometimes did, lie nude in bed together and caress each other, but they could not have intercourse (Bell, 1971). Sex was primarily for reproduction and thus was generally reserved for marital relationships.

The idea of love as a reciprocal emotion emerged with the idea of courtly love. For the first time, women were considered to be an important part of the love relationship, worthy of the love and passion of men. Most researchers of the subject contend that a major contribution of courtly love was to raise women's status from despised persons to people worthy of being worshiped and loved. Many women today, however, insist that setting women apart as people to be worshipped and protected by men keep women dependent on men for definitions of self and love and for care and protection. Thus, they criticize the concept and practice of courtly love because it ignores the needs of women, limits women's expression and behavior, and impedes their progress toward gender equality (Cancian, 1991).

Whatever we might think of courtly love, its impact on Western thought and romantic behavior cannot be overstated. In fact, a number of the romantic ideas of courtly love are still apparent in contemporary notions of love. For example, the idea today that you can't love two people at the same time, that love makes your heart beat wildly (palpitations of the heart), and that love can occur at first sight emerged from the period of courtly love.

From these beginnings, romantic love became an institutionalized component of upper-class and then middle-class marriage and family life. Eventually, as Western societies became industrialized and urbanized, romantic love became institutionalized among the lower and working classes.

***THE INSTITUTIONALIZATION OF LOVE IN
MARRIAGE*** As society became more industrialized,
the roles and functions of individuals and societal
institutions changed. For example, work became
institutionalized outside the family, and separate
institutions to educate the young and to provide religious training emerged. As the family lost or passed
on to other institutions many of its old functions,
industrialism created new demands, roles, and
responsibilities for families and their members. The
most relevant of these new responsibilities for the
continued development and spread of romantic love
was the responsibility of the family to provide emotional strength and support to its members.

A major concern of the emerging urban middle
class was with accumulating wealth and with individual family members' needs for an emotional refuge
from the often harsh challenges of a rapidly changing
society. Such needs and concerns encouraged within
the family the development of both economic cooperation and marital love between wives and husbands.
Although strongly influenced by the upper- (or
noble-) class notion of courtly love, the emerging

Most Americans still believe that love is the most important
basis for sex and marriage.

industrial middle class rejected the central idea that
love is to be found outside marriage. What developed
in its place was the notion that love is a part of marriage, an idea that, by the end of the nineteenth century, had become widespread among all classes
(Berger et al., 1975).

With the rise of **capitalism**—an economic system
based on the private ownership of the means of production—and the emphasis on a **Protestant work
ethic**—stressing hard work and frugality—the focus
of life moved from the group (for example, the family) to the individual. This new focus resulted in a
decline in parents' power and authority over their offspring and the loss of their traditional role in choosing their children's mates. Out of this climate
emerged the belief that love should occur *before*, and
not after, marriage.

By the late nineteenth century in the United
States, as the middle classes enjoyed more leisure
time, courtship came to be extended over a longer
period and the idea of love and romance in such relationships began to take hold. By the early twentieth
century, this concept of love was an essential part of
the U.S. courtship process (see Chapter 5). Although
love was now blended with marriage, it was not yet
blended with sex. Romantic love and sex were considered almost polar opposites. For example, romantic love was thought of as tender, warm, and caring,
whereas sex was thought of as crude and vulgar. The
blending of love and sex ultimately grew out of the
sexual revolution of the 1920s, an era that witnessed
a marked increase in premarital sexual behavior, especially among women. In addition, attitudes about sex
changed noticeably as people began to tie it to love,
intimacy, and marriage.

Today, most Americans believe that love is a most
important basis for sex and marriage. Research
conducted among college students, for example,
indicates that love is considered not only to be an
important basis for beginning a marriage but also for
maintaining a marriage (Simpson, Campbell, and
Berscheid, 1986). Furthermore, studies of premarital
sexuality indicate that the majority of females and
males studied report that they find sexual intercourse
acceptable if the couple is engaged (Sprecher, 1989).
The implication of such findings is that many of us
find sexual intimacy before marriage acceptable as
long as the couple is *in love* with each other or committed to a love relationship. Others, however, find

sexual activity recreational and do not need love or commitment as a prerequisite. Such findings highlight the degree to which our ideas about love and marriage have changed over the last 2500 years.

THE IMPORTANCE OF LOVE

Researchers have found that in U.S. society, love is extremely important both in terms of our physical as well as our emotional health and well-being. Various studies, for example, indicate that being in love romantically and being loved are positively related to good physical and emotional health. Moreover, long-term love relationships (even if no longer passionate) appear to have a positive effect on the health of those involved (Kemper and Bolough, 1981). Conversely, being unloved has been shown to be related to heart disease and early death among unmarried people (Lynch, 1977). Not being loved or the loss of love has been linked to depression and can even lead some people to commit suicide (Tennov, 1979; Davis, 1985).

The importance of love in general can also be viewed within the larger context of human social development. Love is essential to the survival of human infants and the social, psychological, and emotional well-being of adults. Various sociological and psychological theories have argued, for example, that from infancy through adulthood, humans have a need for love and attachment with other human beings. Sociological studies of children who have experienced extended isolation from other humans have found that the lack of bonding, attachment, and love with at least one other human being has a detrimental effect on the physical, psychological, and emotional development of the child (Davis, 1940, 1947). Later in their life cycle, these children are often unable to develop intimate love relationships because they did not experience such relationships when they were young. For adults, the experience of extended isolation often causes deep feelings of depression, anxiety, and nervousness (Middlebrook, 1974).

It has been suggested repeatedly in the literature that the ability to feel love, to express it, and to accept it from others are learned behaviors, acquired through our early experiences in infancy and childhood. Infants must be loved so that they can learn how to love. Infants who are held, touched, caressed, and otherwise shown love develop a self-love; that is,

they come to see themselves as important and worthy of love. The experience of self-love seems to be an important prerequisite for loving others (Fromm, 1970). In adulthood, the people most likely to succeed in their intimate relationships are those who have been socialized in childhood to develop their potential to love. It seems, then, that those of us who are most happy with our lives define that happiness in terms of a loving relationship (Swanbrow, 1989), and we typically define a satisfying relationship as one in which there is an intense commitment to love (Hendrick, Hendrick, and Adler, 1988).

HOW DO PEOPLE EXPRESS LOVE?

People express romantic love in a variety of ways. Some focus on commitment; some on passion; and others on caring, respect, or intimacy. Some people focus on a combination of these and other factors associated with love. This diversity in love and loving has inspired some social scientists to attempt to clas-

Throughout history romantic love has been expressed in a variety of ways. During the 1920s, movie idol Rudolph Valentino was the embodiment of the idealized male romantic figure.

sify love in terms of its component parts or in terms of various types and styles of loving.

One social scientist who has focused on love is psychoanalyst Erich Fromm. In his book *The Art of Loving* (1956), Fromm identified four essential components of love: (1) care (we want the best for the people we love), (2) responsibility (we are willingly sensitive and responsive to their needs), (3) respect (we accept them for what they are), and (4) knowledge (we have an awareness of their needs, values, goals, and feelings). When people share these components, they then become a couple or a pair.

Another social scientist, Robert Sternberg (1986), has defined love in terms of a triangle-like relationship among three basic components: commitment, passion, and intimacy (Figure 4.1). That is, each component of love can be represented as one point on a triangle. Commitment refers to a couple's desire to stay together. Passion refers to the romantic feelings, desires, and arousal that partners feel for each other. This desire usually (but not always) includes sexual desire. Intimacy, which rests at the top of the triangle, refers to the bonding and emotional closeness or connectedness that a couple feel for each other. Sternberg goes on to identify a number of types of love in which various components are either present or absent. For example, the absence of all three components represents *nonlove*, whereas the presence of all three components represents *consummate love*. Other types of love identified by Sternberg include

- *Empty love:* a highly committed love with little or no passion or intimacy.
- *Liking:* a highly intimate love with little or no passion or commitment.

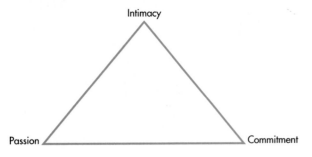

FIGURE 4.1   Robert Sternberg's triangular model of love focuses on the relationship among three components: intimacy, passion, and commitment.

- *Infatuated love:* a highly passionate love with little or no commitment or intimacy.
- *Companionate love:* a highly intimate and committed love with little or no passion.
- *Romantic love:* a highly intimate and passionate love with little or no commitment.
- *Fatuous love:* a highly passionate and committed love with little or no intimacy.

Some other types of love identified throughout the literature include

- *Erotic or passionate love:* a sexually based love that is usually very intense and euphoric.
- *Being love:* a warm and giving love, one that is nonpossessive.
- *Deficiency love:* love based on receiving something that we cannot get or do on our own.
- *Altruistic love:* love based on the emotional satisfaction that a person receives from providing care and affection to another person.
- *Dependent love:* love that develops when one's needs are satisfied by another.

LEE'S SIX STYLES OF LOVING

Whenever the subject of styles of loving comes up in the scientific literature, the person most often referred to is sociologist John Alan Lee. Using data from over 4000 published accounts of love in conjunction with 112 personal interviews, Lee (1974) concluded that there was not one but many types of love relationships. Half of Lee's respondents were females and half were males. All were white, heterosexual, and under the age of 35. Based on findings from this group, Lee proposed six basic styles of loving. Using an analogy of a color wheel, he identified three primary styles of love relationships (analogous to the three primary colors of red, yellow, and blue): *eros*, *ludus*, and *storge*. In the same way that all other colors are a mixture or combination of the three primary colors, Lee contends that all other styles of love represent a combination of these three primary styles. The three most important compounds or mixtures of the three primary styles of love are *mania*, *pragma*, and *agape*.

Although Lee's typology is ideal (in the real world no one's love style match any of the styles perfectly), it nevertheless represents a set of relationships that his respondents reportedly experienced. The six styles of loving are described here.

PRIMARY STYLES OF LOVE Eros is characterized by an immediate, powerful attraction to the physical appearance of another ("love at first sight"). Erotic lovers are often preoccupied with pleasing their lover, and sexual intimacy is strongly desired. In fact, they often engage in sexual relations soon after they meet a partner. Nothing is more problematic for an eros lover than to have a partner that lacks her or his sexual enthusiasm. If the partner is not openly erotic, the relationship will usually be of short duration.

In contrast to eros, *ludus* is playful, nonpossessive, and challenging, without a deep commitment or lasting emotional involvement. Ludus love is carefree and casual; it turns love into a series of challenges and puzzles to be solved. A ludus lover often has several partners simultaneously or encourages her or his partner to have other relationships to prevent the partner from becoming too attached. Unlike with eros, sex is not an integral part of the love relationship. The ludus lover engages in sex simply for the fun of it and not as a means to a deep emotional relationship. Thus, this style of loving seldom leads to marriage.

Storge (pronounced "stór-gay") describes a style of loving that is unexciting and uneventful. An affectionate style of love with an emphasis on companionship, it usually begins as a friendship and gradually develops into love. It is typical of people who grew up together in the same neighborhood. Storge is long-lasting, but it is not passionate. Sexual intimacy occurs late in the relationship. Storge love is similar to the love we might have for our siblings.

DERIVED STYLES OF LOVE Derived loves combine two or more of the primary styles. For example, *mania* combines eros and ludus. Manic love is characterized by obsession. It is a jealous and stressful love that demands constant displays of attention, caring, and affection from the partner. According to Lee, this type of love seldom, if ever, develops into a long-lasting, committed relationship.

In contrast, *pragma*, which combines ludus and storge, is logical, sensible, and practical. A pragmatic lover rationally chooses a partner who shares her or his interests, concerns, and values.

Agape lovers are often likened to Christian saints in that their love is self-giving, self-sacrificing, and altruistic; the happiness of their partner is their most important concern.

Finally, *agape*, a style of love that combines eros and storge, is selfless and giving, expecting nothing in return. It represents the classical Christian idea of love as altruistic, undemanding, and chaste. It is a kind of love that is characteristic of saints. Agape lovers tend to advocate and adhere to sexual abstinence. Lee reports that he did not find a single agape lover in his study.

Although Lee's typology has not been validated by research, it is nonetheless a useful framework. According to Lee, although people generally prefer one particular style of loving, they often express

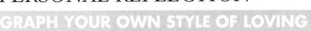
GRAPH YOUR OWN STYLE OF LOVING

Consider each characteristic as it applies to a current relationship that you define as love, or to a previous one if that is more applicable. For each, note whether the trait is *almost always* true (AA), *usually true* (U), *rarely true* (R), or *almost never true* (AN). To diagnose your style of love, look for patterns across characteristics.

	Eros	Ludus	Storge	Mania	Ludic Eros	Storgic Eros	Storgic Ludus	Pragma
1. You consider your childhood less happy than the average of peers	R		AN	U				
2. You were discontent with life (work, etc.) at time your encounter began	R		AN	U	R			
3. You have never been in love before this relationship					U	R	AN	R
4. You want to be in love or have love as security	R	AN		AA		AN	AN	U
5. You have a clearly defined ideal image of your desired partner	AA	AN	AN	AN	U	AN	R	AA
6. You felt a strong gut attraction to your beloved on the first encounter	AA	R	AN	R		AN		
7. You are preoccupied with thoughts about the beloved	AA	AN	AN	AA			R	
8. You believe your partner's interest is at least as great as yours		U	R	AN			R	U
9. You are eager to see your beloved almost every day; this was true from the beginning	AA	AN	R	AA		R	AN	R
10. You soon believed this could become a permanent relationship	AA	AN	R	AN	R	AA	AN	U
11. You see "warning signs" of trouble but ignore them	R	R		AA		AN	R	R
12. You deliberately restrain frequency of contact with partner	AN	AA	R	R	R	R	U	
13. You restrict discussion of your feelings with beloved	R	AA	U	U	R		U	U
14. You restrict display of your feelings with beloved	R	AA	R	U	R		U	U
15. You discuss future plans with beloved	AA	R	R				AN	AA
16. You discuss wide range of topics, experiences with partner	AA	R			U		R	AA

more than one style. This can be true over many different relationships or within one particular relationship. For example, a relationship might begin with an erotic style of loving, but as the relationship matures over time, it might change to a friendship or companionate (storge) style. Lee also observed that the compatibility of styles of loving between two people is important to the success of a love relationship. That is, we have to find a partner who shares the same definition and style of loving as we do if we expect to have a mutually happy and satisfying relationship. The greater the differences between a couple in their style of loving, the harder it is for them to relate to each other.

Were you able to identify your style of loving in one of Lee's six styles? The Personal Reflection box presents a questionnaire developed by Lee to help people identify their own type of loving. The questionnaire is a general guide that can help you see how closely you and your lover match in attitudes. Try taking the test and sharing it with your lover or partner to determine how close or how different your styles of loving are.

	Eros	Ludus	Storge	Mania	Ludic Eros	Storgic Eros	Storgic Ludus	Pragma
17. You try to control relationship, but feel you've lost control	AN	AN	AN	AA	AN	AN		
18. You lose ability to be first to terminate relationship	AN	AN		AA	R	U	R	R
19. You try to force beloved to show more feeling, commitment	AN	AN		AA		AN	R	
20. You analyze the relationship, weigh it in your mind			AN	U		R	R	AA
21. You believe in the sincerity of your partner	AA			U	R	U	AA	
22. You blame partner for difficulties of your relationship	R	U	R	U	R	AN		
23. You are jealous and possessive but not to the point of angry conflict	U	AN	R		R	AN		
24. You are jealous to the point of conflict, scenes, threats, etc.	AN	AN	AN	AA	R	AN	AN	AN
25. Tactile, sensual contact is very important to you	AA		AN		U	AN		R
26. Sexual intimacy was achieved early, rapidly in the relationship	AA		AN	AN	U	R	U	
27. You take the quality of sexual rapport as a test of love	AA	U	AN		U	AN	U	R
28. You are willing to work out sex problems, improve technique	U	R		R	U		R	U
29. You have a continued high rate of sex, tactile contact throughout the relationship	U		R	R	U	R		R
30. You declare your love first, well ahead of partner		AN	R	AA		AA		
31. You consider love life your most important activity, even essential	AA	AN	R	AA		AA	R	R
32. You are prepared to "give all" for love once under way	U	AN	U	AA	R	AA	R	R
33. You are willing to suffer abuse, even ridicule from partner		AN	R	AA			R	AN
34. Your relationship is marked by frequent differences of opinion, anxiety	R	AA	R	AA	R	R		R
35. The relationship ends with lasting bitterness, trauma for you	AN	R	R	AA	R	AN	R	R

Source: John Alan Lee. October, 1974. "The Styles of Loving," *Psychology Today*, Vol. 8, No. 5, p. 51. Reprinted with permission from *Psychology Today* Magazine. Copyright © 1974 (Sussex Publishers, Inc.).

LASSWELL AND LOBSENZ: SIX STYLES OF LOVE

Like John Lee, social scientists Marcia Lasswell and Norman Lobsenz (1980) contend that love can be classified in terms of six general styles of loving, some of which are very similar to those in Lee's typology. For Lasswell and Lobsenz the six styles are best friends, game playing, logical, possessive, romantic, and unselfish. Few of us adhere to only one of these styles. Rather, most of us exhibit a combination of the styles in our intimate relationships, although only

two or three of them will be predominant. Can you find your style of loving from the following?

Best friend's love develops as a result of the feelings of rapport, easiness, or companionship that two people feel with each other. People who adopt this style usually find it difficult to get emotionally involved with someone they do not know or feel comfortable with. In many ways this style of love is similar to the love that occurs between siblings and so resembles Lee's storge love.

Game-playing love views love as a challenge, as a game to be mastered. A game-playing lover does not get too emotionally involved with her or his partner because an objective of the love game is to keep the partner off balance and to avoid commitment. Thus, such a lover makes few demands and does not accept demands from her or his partner. Elements of game-playing love can be found in the ludus style of loving identified by Lee.

Logical love is based on the rational selection of a partner. A logical lover is usually a very practical person who seeks a long-term or permanent relationship and who has a specific idea of whom she or he wants as a partner. This style of lover often has a clear set of criteria by which she or he chooses a partner and is willing to wait until the "right" person comes along. A logical lover is generally unromantic and views love as a practical or logical result of the compatibility between two people. This style of lover is similar to Lee's pragma(tist).

Possessive love, as its name suggests, involves becoming dependent on and obsessed with another person. This style of lover is consumed with the notion of possessing her or his lover and with being possessed in return. A possessive lover is driven by a constant fear of rejection by her or his lover. Thus, such a lover vacillates back and forth between highs (peaks of feeling content, satisfied, and excited about the relationship) and extreme lows (periods of despondency, despair, and fear of not being loved in return and of losing her or his lover). This style of love is characterized by complete devotion on the one hand and extreme jealousy on the other and is reminiscent of the manic lover.

Romantic love is passionate and highly emotional. It is based primarily on the physical attraction of two people to each other and on an ideal image of the lover. A romantic lover desires a total relationship, one that is both intensely physical as well as emotional. The romantic lover corresponds to Lee's eros lover.

Unselfish love is similar to Lee's agape. This style of loving is altruistic, giving, caring, self-sacrificing, and unconditional. An unselfish lover gets satisfaction from giving her or his love unselfishly. This style of love is often expressed by parents (especially mothers) for their children.

As the various typologies demonstrate, regardless of the label we give to styles of lovers, a common set of characteristics appears to describe a small number of styles of loving.

 Given the many types and styles of love that it is possible to experience, how do we know when or if what we feel is truly love? Could what we feel really be close friendship? Is it simply liking? Could it be infatuation? These feelings are often confused with love. How do we confuse them with love? Are they different and independent emotions? If so, how do they differ? How are they similar to love?

LOVE VERSUS FRIENDSHIP, INFATUATION, AND LIKING

How do we know when we're in love? Will we hear bells? Will our heart skip a beat? Will it last, or is it just a passing emotion? Are we old enough to know if it's love? When we were young we were told our feelings of love were not really true love, that they were either "puppy love" or infatuation. Furthermore, we were told not to fret, because we would know when it was true love. Such responses imply that there is a "fake love" or that some other emotion can very easily be confused with love, but that love is some special feeling that we will recognize the minute we experience it. If this is the case, how do we tell the difference? How do we know if what we feel is not simply friendship, infatuation, or liking? And what happens to let us know when the feeling is love?

CLOSE FRIENDSHIP VERSUS LOVE

Over the last several decades a number of researchers have attempted to distinguish love from liking, friendship, and infatuation. In one study, researchers Keith Davis and Michael Todd (1985) compared close friendship and love and found that while the two are alike in many ways, there are crucial differences between them that make love relationships both more rewarding and more volatile. Davis and Todd's prototype of friendship includes the following eight characteristics:

- *Enjoyment:* For the most part, close friends enjoy being in each other's company.
- *Acceptance:* They accept each other for what they are; they don't try to change each other.
- *Trust:* They share the feeling that the other will act in her or his best interest.

It is not easy to distinguish love from close friendship because they are alike in many ways. Couples in love as well as close friends enjoy being in each other"s company.

- *Respect:* Each assumes that the other exercises good judgment in making life choices.
- *Mutual assistance:* They are willing to aid and support each other; they can count on each other when needed.
- *Confiding:* They share feelings and experiences with each other.
- *Understanding:* Each has a sense of what is important to the other and why the other behaves in the manner that she or he does.
- *Spontaneity:* Both feel free to be themselves rather than pretend to be something that they're not.

Love, in contrast, is friendship and more: It is passion and caring. But it is also instability and mutual criticism. Some social scientists (Solomon, 1981; Davis and Todd, 1985; Tennov, 1979) have described romantic love as unstable in that it involves an almost endless series of emotional highs (joys or positive emotions) and lows (despair or negative emotions). It includes all the characteristics of friendship as well as two broad clusters of characteristics not found in friendship: a passion cluster and a caring cluster. The *passion cluster* includes *fascination,* preoccupation with each other and desire to be together all of the time; *exclusiveness,* with top priority given to the love relationship, another such relationship with someone new becomes unthinkable; and *sexual desire,* the desire to be physically intimate with each other. The *caring cluster* consists of *giving the utmost,* caring so much for each other that they give their all to the relationship; and being a *champion* or *advocate,* helping and sup-

porting each other in all types of situations. Figure 4.2 illustrates the similarities between friendship and loving and where the two emotions diverge.

In research conducted by Davis and Todd, a clear difference between love and friendship emerged: Love relationships tend to have a greater influence on both the satisfaction and frustration of the person's basic human needs. That is, compared to friendship, love relationships tend to include much higher levels of positive emotions such as caring, passion, fascination, and exclusiveness. At the same time, love also has the potential for more negative emotions such as distress, ambivalence, conflict, and mutual criticism. In the Davis and Todd study, lovers expressed friendship with their mate at almost the same rate as close friends, and, as the researchers expected, lovers scored overwhelmingly higher than close friends on the passion and caring clusters. An unexpected finding was that close friends perceived their relationships as more stable than did lovers. Davis and Todd attributed this to the possibility of lovers' fears that the relationship might end. This attitude could reflect the fact that love relationships tend to be more exclusive and demanding than friendships.

INFATUATION VERSUS LOVE

That warm and wonderful feeling that we are experiencing, is it love or merely infatuation? How do we begin to know and tell the difference? All too often we confuse these two emotions. **Infatuation** involves a strong attraction to another person based on an idealized picture of that person (Bessell, 1984). It usually focuses on a specific characteristic of the person and has a strong physical (sexual) element. Some social scientists have defined infatuation as passion without commitment. In contrast to love, infatuation is generally superficial and of short duration. It can, however, develop into love. An anonymous writer to an advice column outlined the difference in the following way:

- *Infatuation* leaps into your blood.
- *Love* usually takes root slowly and grows with time.
- *Infatuation* is accompanied by a sense of uncertainty. You are stimulated and thrilled but not really happy. You are miserable when she or he is absent. You can't wait until you see her or him again.

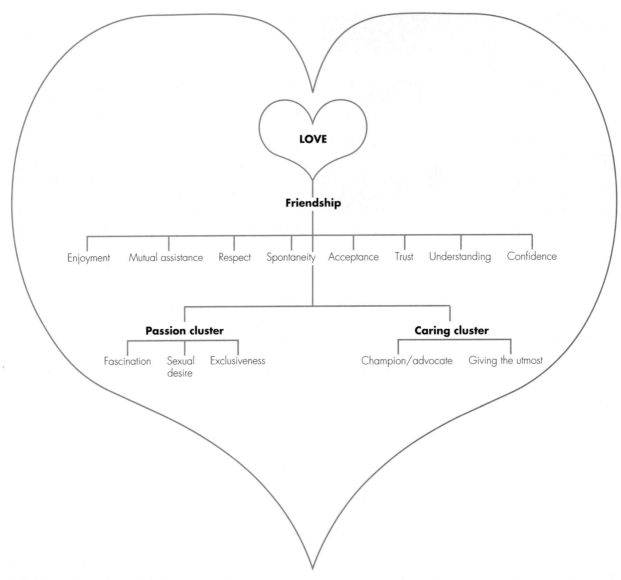

FIGURE 4.2 Love and Friendship

Source: Adapted from Keith Davis, 1985, "Near and Dear: Friendship and Love Compared,"
Psychology Today (February): 24. Reprinted with permission from *Psychology Today* Magazine.
Copyright © 1985 (Sussex Publishers, Inc.).

- *Love* begins with a feeling of security. You are warm with a sense of her or his nearness, even when she or he is away. Miles do not separate you. You want her or him near, but near or far, you know she or he is yours and you can wait.
- *Infatuation* says, "We must get married, right away. I can't risk losing her or him." *Love* says, "Don't rush into anything. You are sure of one another. You can plan your future with confidence."

- *Infatuation* has an element of sexual excitement. If you are honest, you will discover that it is difficult to enjoy one another unless you know it will end in intimacy.
- *Love* is the maturation of friendship. You must be friends before you can be lovers.
- *Infatuation* lacks confidence. When she or he is away, you wonder if she or he is with another woman or man. Sometimes you even check to make sure.

- *Love* means trust. You may fall into infatuation, but you never fall in love.
- *Infatuation* might lead you to do things for which you might be sorry, but *love* never will.
- *Love* leads you up. It makes you look up. It makes you think up. It makes you a better person than you were before.

(*Chicago Sun Times*, 1980: 2)

 What do you think of this writer's assessment of love and infatuation? The author implies that love is a mature emotion whereas infatuation is a very immature emotion. Do you agree or disagree? Does it seem to you to be an overly biased conception of love? How would you define the difference between love and infatuation? Is there really a difference?

LIKING VERSUS LOVE

Liking has been described by some writers as friendship in its most simple form. Liking is generally distinguished from loving as the more logical and rational and the less emotional and possessive of the two emotions. It is believed that liking is the foundation for love. Although liking is closely related to love, however, several researchers have identified some differences.

The most frequently cited research distinguishing liking from loving was conducted by social scientist Zick Rubin (1973, 1974). According to Rubin, both like and love consist of the same basic elements: care, respect, tolerance, need, trust, affection, and attraction. What sets the two apart is their differential emphasis on these components. For example, when we love someone the emphasis is on care, trust, need, and tolerance. In contrast, when we like someone the emphasis is on affection, attraction, and respect. The degree of emphasis we place on the various components of like and love is not absolute. Rather, it will vary in terms of intensity from one time to another, from one relationship to another, and sometimes even within a relationship over time.

Several other researchers have produced findings that are generally consistent with Rubin's conclusions (Dermer and Pyszczynski, 1978; Steck, Levitan, McLane, and Kelly, 1982). However, the difficulty in distinguishing between liking and loving is expressed by researchers Elaine Hatfield and William Walster

(1978), who contend that the only real difference between like and love has to do with the depth of our feelings and the degree to which we are involved with the other person.

SOME THEORIES OF LOVE

In recent decades, the works of several social scientists and researchers have provided us with significant insights into the nature of love. These works have laid the groundwork and become the benchmark for our current theoretical understanding of the topic. Some of the more insightful theories or explanations of love today include the wheel theory of love, limerence theory, and the social-exchange theory.

THE WHEEL THEORY OF LOVE

Generally, when we think about love we think about something unpredictable, sudden, and uncontrollable; something that happens somewhat haphazardly and out of the blue. According to some researchers, however, in reality love is not haphazard, nor is it necessarily sudden. For most of us love does not occur at first sight. Rather, it emerges and develops over time as we interact with the other person. Sociologist Ira Reiss (1960, 1971) has provided a classic theory that focuses on love as a developmental process. That is, stressing our need for intimacy, Reiss focuses on what he sees as the circular progression of love as a couple interact over time. Describing this progression in terms of a wheel—the **wheel theory of love**—Reiss proposes that love involves four major interpersonal processes: rapport, self-revelation, mutual dependence, and need fulfillment. Each of these processes can be thought of as individual spokes on a wheel (see Figure 4.3).

RAPPORT Love can develop only between people who relate to each other. Lovers must develop a sense of *rapport*—feeling at ease or relaxed with one another. A key factor here is social background. In general, we are more at ease and communicate better with people with whom we share a common background and lifestyle. Furthermore, we seem to feel rapport with people with whom we share ideas about social roles. Thus, two people who believe that women's and men's roles are flexible and can thus be interchanged

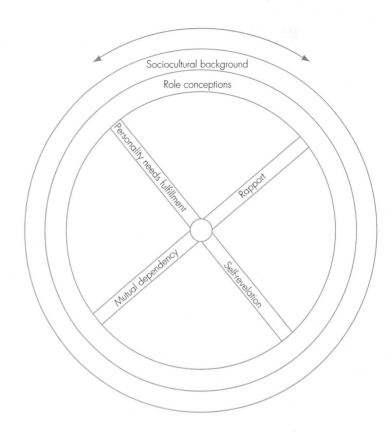

FIGURE 4.3 The Wheel Theory of Love

Source: Adapted from Ira Reiss, 1971, "Toward a Sociology of the Heterosexual Love Relationship," *Marriage and Family Living* 22 (May): 139–45. Reprinted with permission from Abby Press, St. Meinrad, Indiana.

are far more likely to feel rapport than a couple in which only one of the partners feels this way.

Although similarity is important in the development of love, two people who are different are not necessarily precluded from developing a love relationship. Family sociologist Robert Winch and his colleagues (1954), for example, have suggested that people who have different, but complementary, personality characteristics are attracted to each other—the notion that "opposites attract" (see Chapter 5). In addition, love relationships develop between people from different racial, ethnic, religious, and age groups. This fact notwithstanding, some researchers believe that a love relationship can develop only when both partners share certain fundamental values (Murstein, 1971). It seems that if a couple share basic social values, then other differences are not as difficult to overcome.

SELF-REVELATION Ease of communication leads to *self-revelation*, the disclosure of intimate and personal feelings. People who feel at ease are more likely to open up and reveal things about themselves than

they otherwise would be. A couple who feel comfortable with each other want to know more about each other than the kind of superficial information we usually learn about people when we first meet. For example, they want to know what similarities and differences exist between them; how great or how small these similarities and differences are; and how, if at all, they will affect the relationship. As with the development of rapport, a person's background is critical to self-revelation, determining in large part what and how much she or he will reveal about her- or himself. Often, factors like race, ethnicity, social class, gender, and age are important determinants of how willing people are to disclose personal feelings. We often distrust people different from ourselves. Because of this attitude, factors such as race often present initial barriers to the development of trust.

MUTUAL DEPENDENCE As two people develop a sense of rapport and feel comfortable enough with each other to self-disclose, they develop what Reiss describes as a *mutual dependence*—a reliance on each

100 *Chapter 4*

other for fulfillment. At this stage two people become a *couple*. They come to need and depend on each other to share their lives, their happiness, their fears, their hopes and dreams, and their sexual intimacies. They develop interdependent habit systems: ways of acting, thinking, and feeling that are no longer fun or fulfilling when done alone. For example, eating dinner without the other partner may become a lonely experience in that the pleasure of the meal now depends not only on the preparation and taste of the food but on the presence of the other person. The social and cultural background of the couple continues to play an important role in this stage of love. For example, the forms of dependent behaviors that develop between a couple depend on the kinds of behaviors they mutually agree on as acceptable, which, in turn, are influenced by their backgrounds and value systems. Mutual dependence leads to the fourth and final stage in Reiss's wheel theory: the fulfillment of personality needs.

FULFILLMENT OF PERSONALITY NEEDS Reiss defines the *fulfillment of personality needs* as the ability of each partner to satisfy the needs of the other. Reiss describes this stage in terms of a consistent pattern of needs exchange and mutual dependence that develops within a relationship. For example, as the couple satisfies each other's basic needs, their sense of rapport increases, which leads to greater self-disclosure and more mutually dependent behaviors, which, in turn, lead to still greater needs fulfillment.

In his wheel analogy, Reiss captures this circular process of the development of love. All four processes are interdependent. Thus, a reduction in any one of them affects the development or continuation of a love relationship. As long as the wheel moves forward (the processes flow into each other), love develops and increases. However, when the wheel turns in the reverse direction—when there is a reduction in one of the processes—love may not develop, or if it has already developed, it may diminish. For example, if a couple are forced to spend less time with each other and they eventually develop divergent interests, their mutual dependence could weaken, which in turn could lower self-disclosure, which could lead to a reduced sense of rapport.

Reiss's pioneering theory of love as a process has sparked other researchers to extend or modify his the-

ory using other metaphors besides the wheel. For example, social scientist Delores M. Borland (1975) uses the analogy of a clock spring to explain how love develops in a series of windings and unwindings as each new event takes place in the couple's relationship. These windings and unwindings lead toward a closer and more intimate relationship and a greater mutual understanding. Essentially, these theories share with the Reiss model the notions that social background plays an important role in how and if love relationships will develop and that love is basically a matter of social as well as personal definition.

LOVE AS LIMERENCE

Another pioneering theory of love comes to us from the discipline of psychology. Limerence theory, advanced by psychologist Dorothy Tennov (1979), provides important insights into the distinction between being in love and other types of loving. Tennov uses the term **limerence** to refer to a style of love characterized by an extreme attraction, a complete absorption or obsessive preoccupation of one person with another. She defines this emotion as being "in love" as opposed to love, which she defines as caring and concern for another person.

Based on the findings from her study of the love experiences of over 500 people, Tennov concluded that limerence is a state of mind; that its most important features lie in the fantasies and ideas that one person has about another. Thus, the focus of limerence theory is on the experience of falling or being in love rather than on the relationship itself. Although some people never experience limerence, Tennov suggests that the majority do.

Limerence theory underscores the high level of intensity associated with romantic love; it describes and explains the extreme highs and lows that many people experience in their love relationships. Positive limerence can bring an elated feeling, whereas negative limerence can bring feelings of despondency, despair, pain, and depression. Limerence can be characterized by (1) its speed of occurrence at the onset, (2) its intensity, (3) whether or not the feeling is reciprocated, and (4) the length of time it lasts. As these characteristics show, there is no typical limerent experience. Tennov's description of limerent feelings encompasses a wide spectrum including incessant or

Love as limerence or obsession is the theme of the 1988 film "Fatal Attraction," in which actress Glenn Close stalks her married lover, Michael Douglas, and terrorizes his family.

continuous thoughts about the lover, mood swings depending on the lover's actions, being completely closed to the possibility of someone else as a lover, a fear of rejection, a preoccupation or obsession with the lover to the neglect of other interests and concerns, and idealizing the lover.

Tennov's concept of limerence is very similar to that of infatuation. Both stress emotional intensity in romantic relationships, especially in the early stages and particularly for some people. In addition, Tennov's discussion of limerence shares many similarities with Davis and Todd's findings concerning romantic love. In fact, many of the features she identifies with limerence parallel those identified by Davis and Todd as characteristic of the passion cluster.

Do any of these attributes apply to a current or past love relationship in which you have been involved? Most of us can probably identify with one or more of these attributes, especially in the beginning of our romantic love relationships. At that point we won't believe anything negative about our lover; we can't eat, sleep, or enjoy ourselves when we are away from our lover; we daydream about her or him; we feel hurt and dismayed at the thought that she or he may not return our feelings. Does this sound familiar?

Tennov's discussion of limerence calls to mind what could happen when limerence is taken to an unhealthy extreme. The almost obsessive compulsion with another person could develop into a full-fledged obsession that has been immortalized in films, novels, and other aspects of popular culture as a "fatal attraction" and that is all too often a reality. Such full-fledged obsessions in the real world have often had fatal consequences not only for the parties involved but often for intimates involved with the couple as well. Most people's limerence, however, does not go to this extreme. In fact, according to Tennov, if limerence is mutual it can lead to a love affair, a commitment, and ultimately to marriage.

LOVE AS A SOCIAL EXCHANGE

Family sociologist John Scanzoni (1980) describes love in the language of social-exchange theory (recall the discussion of exchange theory in Chapter 2). Basically Scanzoni argues that love, like any other commodity, involves an exchange of rewards between two interested parties. The process of rewarding each other and gratifying each other's needs is continuous and forms the basis on which the relationship is based. As long as the love relationship is mutually rewarding it will continue, but when it ceases to be rewarding it will end. Thus, although people in love clearly care about each other, love is not totally altruistic.

LOVE ACROSS GENDER AND RACE

Romantic love is often considered to be a universal feeling. As we have noted, however, not everyone experiences romantic love. Furthermore, when we do experience such love, a number of other important life experiences come into play, making love different for each of us. Probably the most powerful individual differences that affect how we experience love are gender, sexual orientation, and race.

GENDER DIFFERENCES IN LOVE RELATIONSHIPS

Although both women and men experience love and consider it to be an important experience and relationship, a considerable body of research shows that females and males construct their realities of love in very different terms (Brehm, 1992). Much of this research is based on survey responses of heterosexual couples. In studying the difference between liking and loving, Rubin (1973) found that females distinguish much more sharply between liking and loving than males do. Rubin suggested that this is true because women are much more in tune with their feelings than men are. Given that men are socialized to be task-oriented as opposed to social–emotional, they are often unable to

make the fine distinctions in their feelings that women are. Yet some researchers (Hatfield, 1983) have found that when men are in love, they tend to describe their love in slightly more passionate terms than do women.

In contrast to the popular view of women chasing reluctant men and coyly maneuvering them into an unwanted relationship (the notion of love as a feminine pursuit), it seems that men tend to start a relationship with a much more romantic perspective than females do (Sprecher and Metts, 1989). Men have also been found to fall in love more quickly (Kanin, Davidson, and Scheck, 1970) and to remain in love longer than women (Hill et al., 1976). Once a relationship develops, however, women tend to be more expressive than men (Murstein, 1986) and tend to prefer emotional closeness, whereas men prefer giving instrumental help and sex. In a 1985 survey of college students, researchers Letitia Peplau and Steven Gordon found that male students define sex as more important to them than love, whereas female students define love as more important.

The different emphasis women and men put on love and sex carries over into marriage. For example, researchers have found that wives tend to emphasize emotional expression and talking about their feelings, whereas husbands emphasize physical activities such as providing help to the wife, sharing leisure time, and sexual relations (Stockard and Johnson, 1992). These findings seem consistent with female and male socialization in U.S. society. Females are taught almost from birth to be loving, caring, and nurturant. Men, in contrast, are taught to be detached, independent, and unemotional.

THE FEMINIZATION OF LOVE Discussions and investigations of gender differences in love relationships have led some people, such as Francesca Cancian (1989), to describe this phenomenon in terms of a "feminization of love"—love as a central aspect of the female domain and experience and defined purely in female terms—within U.S. society. That is, love has become feminized in the sense that only women's style of loving is recognized as love, and based on the myth that women both need love more than men do and that women are more skilled at loving than men are, love has become a preoccupation with women.

Basically, Cancian argues that, consistent with their gender roles, women and men prefer different styles of love. At least since the nineteenth century, love has been defined primarily in terms of characteristics reserved for the female, such as emotional expression,

HOW DOES THE MEDIA PORTRAY LOVE?

It is always interesting to examine a culture through the images and messages transmitted by its media. Do a content analysis of U.S. film over the last decade, or compare films made before and after the 1970s, tracing the changes, if any, in the definition of love and the portrayal of love for women and men. If films are not accessible, you might find a content analysis of any of the media such as books, television shows, or popular music equally interesting and revealing.

What types of changes in the portrayal of love did you find? How does the information in this chapter help you account for such changes? Was love portrayed the same way for all groups, or did it vary according to gender, race, class, age, and sexual orientation? Try to categorize the styles of loving presented in the media in terms of either the Lee or the Lasswell and Lobsenz models. Is lesbian or gay love portrayed? If so, how? Does it fit any of the models discussed in this chapter?

---

self-disclosure, and affection. Such a definition typically ignores aspects of love such as providing instrumental help or sharing physical activities. Cancian contends that the feminization of love contributes to male dominance of women because it leads women to focus on interpersonal relationships while encouraging men to achieve independence from women and to specialize in the occupational activities that are more highly regarded in this society. She argues that ideally love should be **androgynous**; that is, it should include a wide range of attitudes and behaviors with no gender-role differentiation. An androgynous view of love validates both feminine and masculine styles of loving and considers both to be necessary parts of a good love relationship.

What do you think? Do you agree with Cancian, or do you think that differentiation along gender lines in terms of love has disappeared? What evidence can you give to support your position? Try applying a sociological analysis to this issue (see the "Applying the Sociological Imagination" box). How close are your findings to what you already knew or have experienced?

LESBIAN AND GAY LOVE RELATIONSHIPS

Love is experienced not only by heterosexual couples but also by lesbian and gay couples. Unlike heterosexual couples, however, lesbian and gay couples often feel compelled to hide their feelings of love because many people do not approve of such relationships. Although Americans tend to prize romantic love, they are generally hostile to love and intimacy between people of the same sex. Because of societal disapproval, gay lovers frequently look to each other to satisfy all their needs. Thus, gay love is often intense and somewhat possessive. In this sense, it is often both highly emotional and highly physical.

Several researchers have identified some basic differences between lesbian and gay styles of loving. A major difference seems to be in the manner in which the love relationship develops and in its duration. For gays, a sexual relationship generally precedes a love relationship. In addition, although some gays maintain long-term love relationships, on average their relationships, no matter how satisfying, are of short duration. On the other hand, lesbian love relationships tend to be more stable and long-lasting, and the love feelings involved are much like those experienced by heterosexual females (Loewenstein, 1985). This does not mean that gays do not maintain mutually committed love relationships over a long period of time; many do. Research simply shows that lesbians usually form more long-lasting love relationships than do gays. In addition, lesbians are more concerned with love as a major ingredient of the relationship.

FEMALE–MALE RELATIONSHIPS AMONG AFRICAN AMERICANS

Over the past several decades, the popular literature has reported a crisis in African-American female–male love relationships. According to several

In the complex and changing world of modern female–male relationships, romantic involvements have often become a one-on-one battle for control.

According to a 1988 article in *Ebony*, in the complex world of modern African-American female–male relationships, romantic entanglements have often become a one-on-one battle for control. African-American men complain that establishing an intimate relationship is increasingly difficult in a climate where some African-American women are more economically independent than some African-American men. In turn, African-American women argue that it is just as difficult for them to develop a committed relationship based on equity because although the roles of women in society have changed, the attitudes of African-American men have not kept pace. Because racism has made achievement of a position of power in the larger society difficult if not impossible for most African-American men, many of these men continue to hold on to the one venue where they have been able to exert power: their intimate relationships with African-American women.

Although little research has been conducted on differences in styles of loving across race in the United States, some evidence suggests that there is a difference in the way blacks and whites view love. This research indicates, for example, that blacks tend to have a more romantic view of love (Mirchandani, 1973). In any case, continuing racism and discrimination in U.S. society, coupled with the changing social roles of women and men, causing conflicting relationships between the sexes, will continue to exert pressure on the development and maintenance of love relationships between African-American women and men.

OBSTACLES TO LOVE AND LOVING RELATIONSHIPS

Few people thrive in an environment of social isolation, so we desire and pursue meaningful love relationships. Unfortunately, a number of individual and cultural factors serve as obstacles to the development and maintenance of love. Some of the most troublesome of these factors are traditional gender-role socialization, patriarchy, lack of trust, and jealousy.

TRADITIONAL GENDER-ROLE SOCIALIZATION

As the discussions in Chapter 3 and throughout this chapter reveal, differential gender-role socialization often creates very different attitudes and behaviors in

popular and scholarly writers on the subject, African-American women and men have experienced considerable difficulty in developing and maintaining meaningful love relationships. This is said to be due, in part, to the suspicions and mistrust generated by years of racism and exploitation, and the pitting of one sex against the other by forces outside their control. The African-American struggle, along with other struggles such as the women's movement, has increased the levels of education and occupational mobility for African-American women (and men) and has added to what some people have claimed to be the traditionally aggressive, assertive, and self-sufficient nature of African-American women. Contrary to all this talk of a crisis, however, African-American females and males tend to fall in love as often and confront the same kinds of obstacles to their relationships as do whites.

females and males. Nowhere is this more evident than in the ways in which the two genders view love relationships. Research has shown that women and men seem to have different priorities when it comes to love relationships. Several researchers have found considerable evidence of an emotional division of labor within heterosexual love relationships, with one partner (usually the woman) more oriented toward the relationship than the other is. That is, the relationship and what it should consist of is more familiar to and central in the life and behavior of one partner than it is in that of the other. Likewise, homosexual couples tend to contain one partner who is more oriented toward the relationship than the other is (Blumstein and Schwartz, 1983).

Researcher Robert Karen (1987) discussed this differential relationship orientation between women and men in terms of who gives and who gets. According to Karen, men get much more out of love relationships than they give. Women, because of the way they have been socialized, are able to be compassionate, to give support, and generally to be there for their partners. Men in contrast require emotional understanding and tenderness but have not been taught to give it. Thus, they often have less access to their feelings than women do. Consequently, it is often the woman who reaches out and makes emotional contact. Feeling this emotional inequality, some women console themselves with the belief that they can rely on their inner strength to make up for what they do not get from their partners. This emotional imbalance between women and men can be an obstacle to either the development or the maintenance of a loving relationship.

PATRIARCHY AS AN OBSTACLE TO LESBIAN LOVE

A number of scholars have identified the patriarchal structure of Western society as an obstacle to same-sex love. Focusing on lesbian love some of these scholars contend that romantic love between women is outlawed and repressed because it is viewed by men as a threat to the patriarchal structure of intimate relationships and to heterosexuality generally. To these scholars heterosexuality includes not only sex between women and men but patriarchal culture, male dominance, and female subordination (Faderman, 1989), all of which benefit men.

Feelings of love are not the exclusive province of heterosexuals. According to some researchers, lesbian love has existed throughout human history.

According to these scholars, the centrality of patriarchy in mate selection is evidenced in the concept of heterosexuality and the notion that women are dependent on men for emotional as well as social and economic well-being. Some of the more common assumptions of patriarchy and heterosexualism are that women's primary love and sexual orientation are naturally directed toward men and that heterosexuality is ordained by nature. Thus, heterosexuals have seldom questioned these assumptions, even though there is ample evidence that lesbian love has existed throughout history and has been accepted at different times by various societies.

From a lesbian perspective, such assumptions not only legitimate heterosexuality as the norm but also denigrate women's romantic relationships with other women, defining these relationships as deviant or pathological. We need only to look at the social sanctions brought against women who love women (as well as men who love men) to understand how, through social control, heterosexuality is maintained as the norm and homosexuality is defined as deviant. For example, society subverts any public expression of homosexual consciousness or behavior, defining it with terms such as *evil, sick, sinful, a crime against nature* (Andersen, 1993). Such ideas and attitudes are detrimental both to lesbian's sense of self-worth and their ability to establish romantic relationships with other women. In addition, the state regulates and controls both heterosexual and homosexual behavior (Freedman and Thorne, 1984). For example, many states have laws outlawing homosexual behavior, even between consenting adults in the privacy of their own homes.

Until women's and men's sexuality is freed from the constraints of patriarchy and heterosexism and society recognizes that there is no one right way to express love, women and men who choose to love people of the same sex will continue to face a wide range of obstacles to the development of romantic love relationships. In the meantime, however, a growing number of lesbians today openly choose other women as love objects even though the patriarchal system continues to define their behavior as deviant and severely restricts their ability to love other women. For many of these women, their selection of a partner is not just a personal choice but rather is a political choice as well.

LACK OF TRUST

Do you trust your partner? Does your partner trust you? Is it important to your relationship that each of you trusts the other? Why? Trust is probably important to your relationship because with it you and your partner can relax; you can feel secure about the relationship and not worry about whether it will continue. Social researchers John Rempel and John Holmes (1986) designed a trust inventory scale to address these questions. According to Rempel and Holmes, **trust**—the degree of confidence a person feels when he or she thinks about a relationship—is one of the most important and necessary aspects of any close or intimate relationship. Because trust can mean something different depending on what aspect of the relationship we are focusing on, Rempel and Holmes identified three basic elements of trust: predictability, dependability, and faith.

Predictability is the ability to foretell our partner's behavior; the knowledge that he or she will consistently act in our best interests. For confidence to grow and trust to develop, it is not enough simply to know in advance how our partner will behave. A sense of predictability must be based on the knowledge that our partner will act in *positive* ways. As the relationship progresses, we begin to focus more on our partner's specific qualities, such as dependability and trustworthiness, and less in terms of predictable behavior. This leads to the second element of trust, dependability.

Dependability can be defined as the knowledge that our partner can be relied on when we need her or him. Both predictability and dependability are based on the assumption that people will behave in a fairly consistent manner (the same in the present as they did in the past). But because human behavior is changing, there is no guarantee that this will be so. Therefore, we often remain committed to a relationship based on sheer faith.

Faith allows people to go beyond previous observed behaviors to feel assured that the partner will continue to be loving and caring. Faith is rooted in predictability and dependability, but it goes beyond what has actually happened in the past.

Each of these components helps form the basis for a trusting relationship; none by itself is sufficient. Rather, the extent to which we trust our partner rests on the degree to which each component is interwoven with the others. Based on the findings of two studies using their trust scale, Rempel and Holmes developed a profile of the typical patterns a person follows, depending on how trusting she or he is. You can use the trust scale (see the box titled "Getting to Know My Own Level of Trust: A Self-assessment Scale") to measure your own level of trust and perhaps to share it with your partner so that you become familiar with her or his level of trust as well.

JEALOUSY AND ENVY

Although love can provide us with wonderful feelings and experiences, it often has a dark side as well: jealousy. Most of us have experienced jealousy at one time or another. Some of the most important relationships have been destroyed by it. So what is this powerful emotion, what causes it, who is most likely to exhibit it, and what consequences does it have for our relationships?

As is the case with love, there are perhaps as many definitions of jealousy as there are people who experience it. It has been defined somewhat tongue-in-cheek as "a cry of pain," "the fear of annihilation," and "the shadow of love" (Adams, 1982:39). On a more serious side, however, most researchers on the subject define **jealousy** as the thoughts and feelings that emerge when an actual or desired relationship is believed to be threatened. It is the fear of losing someone whom you love or who is very important to you. To precipitate feelings of jealousy, the perceived threat

PERSONAL REFLECTION

Trust Scale

Read each of the following statements, and decide whether it is true of your relationship with your partner. Indicate how strongly you agree or disagree by choosing the appropriate number from the scale below and placing it in the space provided in the left-hand margin.

1 = **strongly disagree**
2 = **moderately disagree**
3 = **mildly disagree**
4 = **neutral**
5 = **mildly agree**
6 = **moderately agree**
7 = **strongly agree**

Initial Score   *Final Score*

———— **1.** I know how my partner is going ————
to act. My partner can always
be counted on to act as I
expect.

———— **2.** I have found that my partner is a ————
thoroughly dependable person,
especially when it comes to
things that are important.

———— **3.** My partner's behavior tends to be ————
quite variable. I can't always be sure
what my partner will surprise me
with next.

Initial Score   *Final Score*

———— **4.** Though times may change and the ————
future is uncertain, I have faith that
my partner will always be ready and
willing to offer me strength, come
what may.

———— **5.** Based on past experience, I cannot, ————
with complete confidence, rely on my
partner to keep promises made to me.

———— **6.** It is sometimes difficult for me to ————
be absolutely certain that my partner
will always continue to care for me;
the future holds too many uncertain-
ties and too many things can change
in our relationship as time goes on.

———— **7.** My partner is a very honest person ————
and, even if my partner were to make
unbelievable statements, people
should feel confident that what they
are hearing is the truth.

———— **8.** My partner is not very predictable. ————
People can't always be certain how my
partner is going to act from one day
to another.

———— **9.** My partner has proven to be a ————
faithful person. No matter
who my partner was married to,
she or he would never be unfaithful,
even if there was absolutely no chance of
being caught.

of loss does not have to be real; instead, it can be potential or even completely imaginary. The key is that we believe the relationship is threatened. Researchers have also found that jealousy involves not one but a number of interrelated emotions including anger, anxiety, uncertainty, fear of loss, vulnerability, hatred, shame, sorrow, humiliation, abandonment, betrayal, loneliness, hopelessness, suspicion, and pain.

Jealousy is sometimes confused with or considered the same as envy. The two are, however, different emotions. **Envy** refers to unhappiness or discontent with ourselves that arises from the belief that some-

thing personal about ourselves (our personality, achievements, possessions) does not measure up to someone else's level. Envy involves feelings of inferiority, coveting what someone else has, rather than the fear of losing someone (Parrot and Smith, 1987).

A great deal of the research on the topic of jealousy has been conducted by psychologists and social psychologists and thus reflects their concern with the effects of interpersonal attributes on attitudes and behavior. In contrast, a sociological analysis of jealousy would focus far more on love in terms of the social-structural properties, such as norms or collective agree-

—— **10.** I am never concerned that —— unpredictable conflicts and serious tensions may damage our relationship because I know we can weather any storm.

—— **11.** I am very familiar with the —— patterns of behavior my partner has established, and he or she will behave in certain ways.

—— **12.** If I have never faced a particular issue with my partner before, I occasionally worry that he or she won't take my feelings into account.

—— **13.** Even in familiar circumstances, I —— am not totally certain my partner will act in the same way twice.

—— **14.** I feel completely secure in facing —— unknown new situations because I know my partner will never let me down.

—— **15.** My partner is not necessarily some- —— one others always consider reliable. I can think of some times when my partner could not be counted on.

—— **16.** I occasionally find myself feeling —— uncomfortable with the emotional investment I have made in our relationship because I find it hard to completely set aside my doubts about what lies ahead.

—— **17.** My partner has not always proven —— to be trustworthy in the past, and there are times when I am hesitant to let my partner engage in activities that make me feel vulnerable.

—— **18.** My partner behaves in a consistent —— manner.

Scoring

This is how to score yourself: For questions 3, 5, 6, 8, 12, 13, 15, 16, and 17, reverse numbers. That is, if you put down a 1, change it to a 7, and write this in the space provided in the right-hand margin. In the same way, if you scored a 2 change it to a 6, 3 to a 5, 5 to a 3, 6 to a 2, and 7 to a 1. A neutral score of 4 remains unchanged.

When you have reversed the scoring for the items listed above, take the scores for the remaining items and write them in the right-hand margin just as they are. Add all the scores in the right-hand margin to obtain your final trust score.

If you are interested, you can add up the scores for the following questions to arrive at a score for each subscale of trust: Predictability, add 1, 3, 8, 11, 13, and 18. Dependability, add 2, 5, 7, 9, 15, and 17. Faith, add 4, 6, 10, 12, 14, and 16.

Source: John Rempel and John Holmes, 1986, "How Do I Trust Thee?" *Psychology Today* (February): 30–31. Reprinted with permission from *Psychology Today* Magazine. Copyright © 1986 (Sussex Publishers, Inc.).

ments that govern whom and how we should love and under what circumstances we feel jealous, of a particular society or of particular groups within the society.

THE NATURE AND PATTERN OF JEALOUSY
The causes of jealousy vary from externally to internally induced factors. External factors include behaviors such as flirting or spending excessive amounts of time with someone other than the partner. Studies such as those by social psychologists Ayala Pines and Elliot Aronson (1983) report that most episodes of jealousy arise from external factors. Some cases, however, stem from inter-

nal factors that reside in the individual personality and can include feelings of insecurity and distrust learned from previous experiences. Some studies have found, for example, that jealousy is closely associated with low self-esteem and a high level of dependence on one's partner. One study, for example, found that among married couples the individuals who tended most often to be jealous were those who felt insecure about themselves and believed that they would not be successful in getting someone else if their partner left them (Hansen, 1985).

The experience of jealousy varies greatly from relationship to relationship and from individual to indi-

GLOBAL PERSPECTIVES

HIGH- AND LOW-JEALOUSY CULTURES

Jealousy is not found in all societies. Some social scientists have suggested that sexual jealousy is essentially a cultural phenomenon, occurring only in societies that place emphasis on sexual exclusiveness in intimate relationships (Brehm, 1992). Social psychologist Ralph Hupka's (1981) cross-cultural study goes a long way toward providing support for this premise. According to Hupka, societies with little or no *stratification*—the ranking of whole categories of people according to their access to scarce resources—exhibit a low level of jealousy. In contrast, highly stratified societies such as the United States exhibit a high level of jealousy. *Low-jealousy cul-*

tures discourage individual property rights, and sexual gratification and companionship are easily accessible to all people. Such cultures place little value on descent or the need to identify children as one's own progeny. For example, among the Todas of Southern India, jealousy is rare because there is little to be jealous of. This culture takes a sharing attitude toward people and things; neither are defined as personal property. In addition, the Todas place few restrictions on sexual pleasure, and neither marriage nor heirs are prerequisites for social honor and prestige.

A Native-American group, the Apaches of North America, repre-

sent an example of a *high-jealousy culture*. Among the Apaches, great emphasis is placed on female virginity and on male sexual gratification. Male sexual pleasure must be earned after a prolonged period of deprivation, and it must be judiciously protected from all intruders. Apache wives and children are so important to the status of Apache men that when the men are away from their families they engage close relatives to watch their wives secretly and report their wive's behavior to them when they return home.

Hupka concluded that jealousy is a learned emotion: We learn what our particular culture defines as valuable and in need of protection.

Source: Adapted from Ralph Hupka, 1981, "Cultural Determinants of Jealousy," *Alternative Lifestyles* 4:310–356.

vidual. Researchers have found, however, that those who are most likely to be jealous are women, people in open or multiple relationships, people who are unhappy with their lives overall or with their love relationship, less educated people, younger people, and people who are unfaithful themselves (Pines and Aronson, 1983; Salovey and Rodin, 1989).

Jealousy also varies from one historical period to another and from culture to culture. Examining research studies and records spanning the past 200 years, social psychologist Ralph Hupka (1981, 1985) found consistent differences across cultures in both the degree to which jealousy is present in a society and the ways in which it is expressed. This finding led him to classify societies as either high-jealousy or low-jealousy cultures. The Global Perspectives box provides a brief discussion of each type of culture.

Hupka's findings support the notion that jealousy is a social emotion learned through the socialization

process. The existence and expression of jealousy depend very much on how love and love relationships are defined; which people, things, and relationships are valued in a particular society. In other words, jealousy is rooted in the social structure of a society insofar as cultural norms provide the cues that will or will not trigger it. For example, sociologist Kingsley Davis (1977) argued that jealousy is the product of the practice of monogamy. If you are socialized in a society that practices monogamy, cultural norms require you to think of your partner in exclusive terms. Thus, adultery or nonexclusivity is resented and causes jealousy.

GENDER DIFFERENCES IN JEALOUSY The literature on jealousy indicates that women and men may experience this emotion differently. Some of the more prevalent findings concerning the differences between U.S. women and men in terms of the ways in which they feel and act when they are jealous are

There are probably as many definitions of jealousy as there are people who experience this emotion. As with love, women and men differ in terms of how they view and experience jealousy.

Source: Reprinted with special permission of King Features Syndicate.

- Women experience or feel jealousy more intensely than men.
- Jealousy causes women greater suffering and distress than it does men.
- Men are less likely than women to stay in a relationship that makes them jealous (Pines and Aronson, 1983).
- Women are more likely than men to fight to win back a lost lover rather than give up the relationship (Reik, 1946). When men feel jealous they try to repair their self-esteem, whereas women try to repair the relationship (make themselves and the relationship better so that he won't desire another partner) (Shettel-Neuber, Bryson, and Young, 1978).
- Women's feelings of personal inadequacy lead to jealousy, whereas men feel jealousy first, which then leads to feelings of inadequacy, that something is wrong with them.
- Men are more likely than women to express their jealousy in the form of violence. They are also more likely to shift the blame for both their jealousy and their violent response from themselves to a third party (Hoff, 1990).
- Women, more often than men, consciously attempt to make their partner jealous as a way of testing the relationship (see if he still cares), of increasing rewards (get their partner to give them more attention or spend more time with them), of bolstering their self-esteem, of getting revenge, or of punishing their partner for some perceived transgression (White, 1980).

DESTRUCTIVE JEALOUSY Although in the past jealousy was considered to be an indication of love, today it is increasingly seen as destructive and as a sign of some deficiency in the individual or the relationship. Jealousy can be destructive in terms of the toll it takes on the individual psyche, in the form of deep depression, fear, anxiety, self-doubt, and low self-esteem. It can also be physically damaging and life-threatening when it is expressed in terms of anger, violence, and the desire for revenge.

Some researchers (Smith and Clanton, 1977) have found that jealousy has some legitimate functions, such as to alert us to threats to our personal security and to our important relationships. Just as physical pain alerts us to threats to our physical well-being, the psychological pain of jealousy alerts us to threats to the security of our love relationships. Jealousy can also be a way of releasing pent-up anxieties and emotions, that otherwise could lead to violence. More often than not, however, jealousy is destructive to our relationships.

MANAGING DESTRUCTIVE JEALOUSY If jealousy is such a damaging emotion, what can we do either to prevent it or to deal with it in a constructive manner? Social researchers Lynn Smith and Gordon Clanton (1977) suggest four options for dealing with jealousy: (1) Get out of the relationship, (2) ignore or tolerate those behaviors that make you jealous, (3) attempt to change your partner's behavior, and (4) work on your own jealousy. The ways in which we manage jealousy depend on the type of jealousy we feel and how committed we are to the relationship. If we are interested in maintaining and enhancing our relationship, we must bring jealousy out in the open and not try to repress it. This process involves self-examination: How does jealousy make me feel? How would I prefer to feel? Which actions cause me to feel jealous? Which behaviors or thoughts can I modify to reduce or eliminate my feelings of jealousy?

As we try to answer these questions, we must look beyond the specific incidents that disturb us to the underlying causes of our jealousy. For example, is my jealousy caused by my partner's behavior, or is it really rooted in my own feelings of inadequacy and low self-esteem? If the latter, perhaps you should begin with discovering ways to bolster your self-concept and develop self-confidence.

We must also evaluate our situation realistically. For example, is this situation the best for me? Does my partner return my love? Is the relationship worth saving? If we decide the relationship is worth maintaining, perhaps we could move beyond our self-analysis of jealousy and share our feelings with our partner. We can share our expectations and goals for our relationship and reiterate or redefine what we expect from each other—the kinds of behaviors that are and are not acceptable. In this way we can begin to work together to change some of the factors (behaviors, attitudes) that spark jealous episodes. If these actions fail, you might consider counseling or therapy. Whatever course you follow, it should be a collaborative effort. Both parties must agree about how they see the relationship and what they want for the future.

ROMANTIC LOVE IN THE 1990s

Heterosexual love and romance in the 1990s reflect the changes that have been evident in the roles of women and men since the emergence of the contemporary women's movement. In the past, female and male roles in love and romance were clearly, if not rigidly, defined, usually as a power relationship characterized by male dominance and female submission. Today, however, dramatic changes have taken place in the relationships between heterosexual lovers, especially among the middle classes. At the same time, however, many traditional aspects of dating, intimacy, and mate selection remain firmly entrenched in U.S. society. The result is a great deal of anxiety and uncertainty as couples try to balance traditional norms with current developments in the absence of clear-cut rules and guidelines.

The contemporary women's movement and the subsequent rise in the level of education and employment opportunities for women, in combination with the sexual revolution, have affected the ways in which women and men relate to one another in their intimate relationships. Women have become more independent and more vocal about their desire to control their own destinies. Unlike their foremothers, many women today no longer define themselves in terms of a man or the lack of one.

The changing nature of female and male roles in intimate relationships has left some couples confused about how to relate to each other and has presented a number of problems that hamper the development or maintenance of love relationships. For other lovers or potential lovers, the challenge to traditional male-dominated intimate relations has set the stage for the development of a new, more equitable type of relationship. Many women and men are confronting the conflicts generated by changing gender roles by changing themselves. In general, women and men in the 1990s have accelerated the trend identified by social researchers in the 1980s, dealing with each other in a new way, "not as one-dimensional entities who fit into narrow and rigid roles but as whole and complete human beings" (Simmons, 1988:139).

SUMMARY

Love is a central feature of life in Western societies. References to love can be found throughout the popular culture. Because each of us expresses and experiences love differently, there are a variety of definitions of love and many different kinds of love. However, romantic love can be distinguished from other kinds by its erotic component. It can be defined as the intense feelings, emotions, and thoughts coupled with sexual passion and erotic expression that one person directs toward another, as well as the ideology that upholds it.

Researchers have found that love is extremely important to our physical and emotional health and well-being. Studies of children and adults who have suffered extended isolation from other humans indicate the learned nature of love and our dependence on other people to provide us with the experiences of love. There is great diversity in the ways in which people express romantic love. Some researchers have attempted to define love by isolating various components of love, whereas others have defined love in terms of several styles of loving. Still other researchers have distinguished love from friendship, infatuation, and liking.

Ira Reiss uses a wheel analogy to explain love as a developmental process. Love can also be considered in terms of limerence, characterized by extreme attraction, complete absorption or obsessive preoccupation of one person with another. Researchers have noted a variety of ways in which women and men differ in terms of how they feel and express love. For example, men fall in love more quickly than women and remain in love longer.

Love is experienced by lesbian and gay couples as well as by heterosexuals. For gays, on average, a sexual relationship precedes a love relationship, whereas lesbians tend to settle into stable, long-term relationships characterized by strong commitment and intense feelings of love. Regarding race, it seems that African-American women and men are facing a relationship crisis that is rooted in the historical fact of slavery and the continuing racism and discrimination they face.

A number of social and political obstacles hamper the development or maintenance of a loving relationship. These include traditional gender-role socialization, patriarchy, the lack of trust, and jealousy. Jealousy is the dark side of love and can be detrimental to the development or maintenance of a long-term love relationship. As with love, there are gender differences in the expression of jealousy. We can manage or eliminate jealousy by looking inward and working out the problems that make us susceptible to jealousy, or we can talk to our partner. We can also share with her or him our feelings and expectations for the future of the relationship while coming to an agreement about what behaviors are and are not acceptable within the relationship.

Heterosexual romance in the 1990s reflects the changes that have been evident in the roles of women and men since the contemporary women's movement. In general, women and men in the 1990s have accelerated the trend from the 1980s toward dealing with each other on a more equitable basis.

KEY TERMS

romantic love	wheel theory of love
ideology	limerence
capitalism	androgynous
Protestant work ethic	trust
infatuation	jealousy
liking	envy

QUESTIONS FOR STUDY AND REFLECTION

1. What is love? What does being in love mean to you? Have you ever been in love with someone who did not share your feelings? How important is reciprocity in a love relationship?

2. Using Ira Reiss's wheel theory of love, consider your own love relationships. How do they fit into this model of love as a developing process? Does your love relationship deviate from the Reiss model? How would you explain this? Are all of his stages healthy for a love relationship?

3. Is there a fundamental difference between liking, loving, and infatuation? Have you ever loved someone without liking her or him? Is it important that you like the person you love? To be her or his friend? Why or why not? Can a love relationship last if a couple neither like each other nor are friends?

4. Virtually everyone has experienced some degree of jealousy and envy. Differentiate between the two concepts. Are you jealous concerning your partner? What are some of the factors or contexts that make you jealous? Is your jealousy destructive to the relationship? What steps have you taken to change the situation?

FURTHER READING

CANCIAN, FRANCESCA M. 1987. *Love in America: Gender and Self-development.* New York: Cambridge University Press. An examination of the history of love and the emergence of androgynous love in the twentieth century. Androgynous love combines both love and self-development and gives both partners responsibility for the relationship.

FRANKS, DAVID D., AND E. DOYLE MCCARTHY (eds.). 1989. *The Sociology of Emotions: Original Essays and Research Papers.* Greenwich, CT: JAI Press. An interesting collection of articles dealing with a range of topics including liking, love, sexuality, eroticism, and jealousy.

FROMM, ERICH. 1956. *The Art of Loving.* New York: Harper & Row. This book is a classic on the subject of love. Fromm presents an insightful discussion of love as an active choice to care for another person.

HENDRICK, SUSAN, AND CLYDE HENDRICK. 1992. *Liking, Loving, and Relating.* Belmont, CA: Wadsworth. An up-to-date and comprehensive overview of personal relationships including discussions on attraction, love, and sexuality. It includes recent research, data, and case studies.

Chapter 5

DATING, COUPLING, AND MATE SELECTION

When she was 3 years old, Nyceema came to the United States from India with her family. She grew up in an upper-middle-class suburban community, attended high school and college, but she did not date. She is currently finishing law school at a prestigious university in the United States. Three years ago, her family decided it was time she married, so they placed an ad in an Indian newspaper in this country. The paper carries over 350 matrimonial ads each week. Their ad read: "Well-established parents seek a matrimonial match for their attractive daughter, who is a citizen of the United States. She is also a vegetarian, 22 years of age, 5'2", a law student at a good university, and comes from a respectable family." Nyceema's parents also checked the mammoth matrimonial directory at their temple in search of a suitable mate for their daughter. In addition, they contacted a family in India with whom they were friendly and who had a 25-year-old son who was completing his studies for a law degree.

After reviewing the matrimonial directory and sorting through the responses to their ad, Nyceema's parents decided that their friend's son was the best match for their daughter. His parents agreed that the two young people were suitable marriage partners because they were of the same nationality, social class, religion, and age, and both would soon be practicing lawyers. Therefore, a few months later, Nyceema and her family flew to India to meet for the first time her husband-to-be. One week after she met Kamau, they were married.

Nyceema describes her marriage as a logical step that she took with her eyes open. She says that she is very happy and has no regrets. She says that she and her husband become fonder of each other as the months go by. When her American friends asked her why she allowed her parents to arrange her marriage, she replied that she had seen the pressures on Americans to find the right person and she didn't want to go through that process. It not only horrified her, but she found it humiliating as well—the competition for male attention, the pressure to create the right impression, and so on.

How does the pattern of mate selection portrayed in this scenario fit with the American belief in romantic love as the justification for marriage? Do you think romantic love is the best basis for marriage? Do you think Nyceema's marriage will last? How do you feel about her views on mate selection in the United States? Would you let your parents select your marriage partner? Do you think your chances for dating and marital success are greater than Nyceema's? Why or why not?

"Dating, coupling, and mating": When these concepts are used together, they call up a variety of images. Close your eyes. What images come to mind when you think about dating in U.S. society today? Do you think of youth, "swinging," sex, "singles," fun, marriage, or love? These are some of the most familiar images associated with dating and mate selection, images that are relentlessly transmitted through the media. Do these images match the realities of the lives of most unmarried people? Do they match realities of mate selection for your parents? Your grandparents?

As this mental exercise might have illustrated, for many people the idea of dating and mate selection brings to mind love and marriage. Traditionally we have assumed that attraction leads to dating, dating to love, and love to marriage. Indeed, we have assumed that the major function of dating is to teach people to form intimate heterosexual relationships and to prepare people for marriage. Although this might have been true in the past, today it is frequent-

ly not the case. For one thing, an increasing number of people are either delaying marriage or not marrying at all. Others are pursuing alternatives to marriage (see Chapter 7). In addition, not all dating is heterosexual. Moreover, many dating relationships are based solely on material or sexual interests and not on notions of romantic love.

So what does this mean for current relationships among both heterosexual and homosexual couples? Is today's pattern of mate selection a continuation of trends of the past? Are dating relationships and mate selection different today than they were 50 years ago? One hundred years ago? Are they the same around the world?

Specific courtship procedures, like mate selection generally, have varied considerably from one culture to another and from one historical period to another. In the next section we explore some of the historical and cross-cultural trends in courtship, dating, and mate selection.

MATE SELECTION IN HISTORICAL AND CROSS-CULTURAL PERSPECTIVE

Did you know that dating is not a common practice in most countries? In general, when we speak of **dating** we are referring to a process of pairing off that involves the open choice of mates and engagement in activities that allow people to get to know each other and progress toward mate selection. In places such as China, India, South America, and most countries in Africa dating is very rare. In addition, it is forbidden in most Muslim countries including Iraq, Egypt, Iran, and Saudi Arabia. Only in Western societies such as the United States, Great Britain, Australia and Canada is dating a common form of mate selection. In these countries, dating is perhaps the single most important method by which people get acquainted with each other, learn to interact heterosexually, and select a mate.

Sociologists use the term **mate selection** to refer loosely to the wide range of behaviors and social relationships individuals engage in prior to marriage and that lead to long- or short-term pairing or coupling. An essential element in mate selection is **courtship**, a process of selecting a mate and developing an intimate relationship. Dating is simply one stage in the courtship process, a process that involves an increasing level of commitment that might culminate with the ultimate commitment, marriage. Whatever its end, mate selection is an institutionalized feature of social life. According to family sociologist Ira Reiss (1980), all societies ever discovered have exhibited some form of courtship, marriage, and family that ensures the production and nurturing of young people. The process of mate selection has ranged from agreements and arrangements among religious or community leaders or the families of prospective partners to choices made by the partners themselves with only limited consultation with parents or other relatives.

Mate selection in the United States has been described by some social commentators (for example, Waller, 1937) as a "courtship game" that has its own set of rules, strategies, and goals. Over time the rules and expectations of mate selection have been adapted and modified and have culminated in the process we recognize today. Thus, contemporary patterns of mate selection are linked to our past.

EARLY U.S. COURTSHIP AND THE DEVELOPMENT OF DATING

In the early history of this country mate selection primarily involved couples keeping company under family supervision. Keeping company was a very formal and upright relationship that developed only after people had become attracted to or felt romantic about each other. Keeping company involved a variety of activities, and couples kept company in some unique and interesting ways.

For example, in colonial New England unmarried couples practiced bundling, in which they spent the night in bed together, wrapped in bundling blankets or separated only by a long wooden "bundling board" down the middle of the bed. Only the outer garments could be removed, and the woman sometimes was placed in a sack that was sealed at the neck. This arrangement evolved in response to harsh winters and the difficulty of traveling, both of which made it difficult for a young man to return home after an evening of courting. Although such a practice would seem to discourage sexual contact, it apparently did not. Researchers Daniel Smith and Michael Hindus (1975) have estimated that approximately one-third of all eighteenth-century brides were pregnant at the time of their wedding.

In colonial United States marriage was considered to be of utmost importance in bringing order and stability to daily family living. Thus, there was a stress on coupling and mate selection. During this period couples came together through a variety of means, including matrimonial advertisements and third-party go-betweens. Demographic considerations as well as very precise cultural norms often dictated the ways that couples came together (Ramu, 1989). For example, due to a severe shortage of women in the American colonies, different patterns of mate selection evolved: Some men cohabited with Native-American women, and others imported brides from across the Atlantic.

In the eighteenth century, very explicit rules continued to govern the courting process. Although parents could not legally choose a partner for their offspring, they did exercise considerable power over mate selection. Daughters, in particular, were strictly supervised. If a young man wanted to keep company with a young woman, he had to meet her family, get their permission to court her, and be formally introduced to her. Even after two people were formally introduced they were often chaperoned (especially upper-class women) at social events.

Significant for the evolving pattern of dating in the United States were industrialization; the rise of free, public, coeducational, and mandatory schooling; and the mass movement of women (predominantly working-class women) into the mills and factories, allowing them increased contact with men. These events helped loosen parents' hold on their children. The mass production of the automobile probably had the most profound impact on the course of mate selection in North America. The automobile increased the mobility of young people and made a number of activities and places accessible to them. It also gave young people a new and private place for *getting together*, a pattern of dating that involves women and men meeting in groups, playing similar roles in initiating dates, and sharing equally in the cost of activities. Courting thus moved from the parlor to the front seats and backseats of cars, resulting in the emergence and institutionalization of dating. Some social scientists have gone so far as to suggest that the automobile became, in some sense, a "bundling bed on wheels."

DATING IN THE UNITED STATES: THE 1920s THROUGH THE 1970s

Dating as part of the mate-selection process developed in the 1920s amid the increased affluence and leisure of the white middle classes. This affluence and leisure gave rise to a youth culture whose members were relatively free to pursue their personal interests and social life. The rigid Victorian sex ethic (see Chapter 6) of the past was replaced with a new sexual intimacy as part of the courtship process. Couples dated for fun, pleasure, relaxation, and recreation. This new method of mate selection moved from one controlled by parents to one based on open and mutual choice.

The term *dating* originally referred to a specific date, time, and place of meeting. Thus, to speak of dating simply meant that two people of the opposite sex met at a mutually agreed-upon place and time and engaged in conversation. Dating has not remained constant over the decades. A variety of

sociopolitical and historical factors such as the Great Depression of the 1930s, World War II, and the middle-class prosperity of the 1950s helped to shape dating as we know it today.

During the 1920s and 1930s dating was especially visible on college campuses. Although college students represented only a small and select portion of America's youth—primarily white and middle class—their activities and behavior became the model for other youth. In a pioneering study of college dating patterns sociologist Willard Waller (1937) described dating on college campuses in the 1920s and 1930s as a competitive system that involved rating prospective partners based on clear standards of popularity. Material signs included owning an automobile, possessing the right clothing, belonging to the right fraternity or sorority, and, of course, having money. With the stock market crash of the late 1920s, the prohibition of liquor, and the depression of the 1930s, the national mood changed dramatically. However, the changes that occurred in popular culture and their impact on mate selection and dating continued to be visible in later decades.

During the 1940s and 1950s, dating spread from college campuses to most cultural groups in the United States. During this period, dating became essentially a filtering process in the sense that a person dated many people before settling down with one person. Only then did serious dating or courtship begin, with the ultimate goal being marriage (Ramu, 1989). Acceptance of the idea that dating should culminate in marriage seems to be reflected in the fact that the 1950s had the highest percentage of married adults on record (Cherlin, 1981).

During the 1950s, a variant of the traditional dating pattern that developed and became popular among young people was **going steady**—an exclusive relationship with one person. One researcher, Ersel LeMasters (1957), described going steady as an important intermediary stage in the dating pattern of the 1940s and 1950s. According to LeMasters, dating involves six stages of progressively deeper commitment from the first date in the junior high school years to marriage in the late teens or early 20s. Going steady, the third stage, occurred somewhere in the late high school years and involved a transition from the first two stages, the noncommitment of casual dating in junior high school and the random dating in the early high school years. The fourth stage occurred in college,

Dating in the 1950s often involved a specific activity, such as going to a prom. Today, dating is far more spontaneous, relaxed, and casual.

when the couple entered into an informal agreement to date each other exclusively. The final two stages are engagement and marriage. This sequential model of dating tended to be more common among the middle classes than among other classes. Lower-income and working-class youth tended to speed up the process and generally married at an earlier age.

Like other cultural patterns, dating patterns incorporate many of the values of the larger society. Thus, dating in the 1940s and 1950s clearly revealed U.S. society's emphasis on traditional gender roles, marriage, and the sexual double standard, with the male being the aggressor and the female playing a submissive role. For example, it was up to the male to initiate the date, and the female, in a dependent mode, had to wait to be picked or asked out. The male then was expected to pick up the female at her home, take her to a place of his choosing, pay for all expenses, and return her to her home at a respectable hour. The sexual double standard was also evidenced in the desired outcomes of dating. For males, a primary expected outcome of dating was sex, whereas for females it was commitment and marriage.

During the 1960s and 1970s, changing sexual norms, the increasing availability of contraceptives, a decline in parental authority, and the increasing activism of young people helped reverse the conservative dating trends of the 1940s and 1950s. Dating was transformed into a casual and spontaneous form of courtship. Greatly influenced by the women's movement, women no longer waited to be asked out but instead began to initiate dates and intimate relationships. There was an increasing emphasis on "going Dutch," where each person paid her or his own way. Going Dutch was particularly common among middle-class youth, who were financially more independent than poor and working-class youths (Ramu, 1989). Paying one's own way was seen as a way of reducing the exploitation of young women by males who, in the past, expected sexual favors in return for the money spent on dating.

By the late 1960s people were delaying marriage to a later age. Sexual intimacy, which had traditionally been closely confined to marriage or the courtship period that led directly to marriage, became a common part of dating. The increasing separation of sex from marriage during the 1960s and 1970s was probably most evident in the rising number of couples living together outside the legal marriage contract. During the 1970s, *cohabitation*—living together without being legally married—became a common extension of the traditional dating continuum, especially on college campuses among urban middle-class whites, and served as either an alternative or adjunct to steady dating and engagement (Gwartney-Gibbs, 1986). Cohabitation is discussed in detail in Chapter 7.

CONTEMPORARY TRENDS IN DATING: THE 1980s AND BEYOND

There is some consensus among sociologists that although most Americans continue to find mates through dating of some sort, dating is no longer what it was prior to the mid 1960s (Murstein, 1980). Not only have the structure and content of dating changed, but so has the terminology. Although some people still date in the traditional pattern, where each person has specific roles to play, most people today prefer to say they are "going out" with someone. Even though the term *dating* is less commonly used, however, the practice nonetheless continues, albeit in different forms.

Dating today starts at an earlier age and lasts longer than it did in the past. Adolescents as young as 13 years of age participate in some form of dating and pairing off. This represents a decrease in age of 3 years since World War I (Hennessee, 1983). Furthermore, if we consider the fact that the average age at first marriage is somewhere around 25 years of age, then the average person in the United States dates and courts for over 10 years. As the age at first marriage continues to increase, more people are spending more time in a number of dating relationships with a variety of people before marrying, if they marry at all.

The longer period of dating for most people has changed the ways dating is structured and perceived. In the 1990s, dating is based far more on mutuality and sharing than on traditional gender roles. There is a greater emphasis today on dating as recreation and entertainment and an emphasis on sociability. This has caused a change in the pattern or progression of intimacy and commitment from initial meeting to marriage. Dating today includes considerably more casual sexual involvements and fewer committed relationships than in the past. Although some couples still follow a traditional pattern, for many couples dating, sexual intimacy, living together, becoming engaged, and sometimes having a child have become a common part of a heterosexual relationship that may or may not culminate in marriage.

Moreover, dating today involves not only the very young but also an increasing number of older people who either have never married or are divorced or widowed. Although dating among these older singles differs somewhat from dating among high school and college students, many similarities exist. This is especially the case in terms of dating as recreation and entertainment. Dating also has become very time-contained, sometimes existing only for the moment for sexual or recreational purposes with no pretense that it is a prelude to courtship or marriage (Staples, 1981a). Although much of the discussion of contemporary dating patterns is descriptive of the white middle class, with some limitations it can be generalized to other groups. Later in this chapter we pay particular attention to the intersection of race, class, gender, and sexual orientation in patterns of dating.

The cultural diversity of U.S. society has given rise to a number of dating and mate-selection patterns. For example, among some groups courting occurs only after the marriage vows. Naturalized U.S. citizens from a variety of foreign cultures have continued to practice arranged marriages in this country. As the chapter opening vignette shows, this is particularly true of immigrants from India, whose numbers in this country in the 1990s have reached nearly 1 million. Despite their Western citizenship and education, many young Indians who have grown up in this country are going through the traditional networks—parents and other matchmakers, newspapers, and acquaintances—and agreeing to marry individuals they barely know. For some of these young people, however, the rules of this form of mate selection are changing. Influenced to some degree by U.S. individualism, they are demanding greater input in their marriage plans. In many cases their parents are allowing them veto power. This freedom to refuse parents' choice seems to be an important part of the appeal of arranged marriage (Chandra, 1991).

FUNCTIONS OF DATING: PAST AND PRESENT

As we have seen, dating no longer implies that marriage is inevitable, or even desirable. Of all the stages in the mate-selection process, dating is the one that carries the least commitment to continuing the relationship. So why do people date? The reasons are many and varied; however, researchers have identified some specific functions dating fulfills for the individual. The meaning and functions of dating, of course, depend in large part on the person's age and sex and the particular stage in the dating process. One researcher, G. N. Ramu (1989), summarizes the functions of dating in terms of socialization, recreation, status grading and achievement, and mate selection leading to marriage. As you consider the following functions of dating, bear in mind that they have been formulated primarily with young heterosexual couples in mind.

SOCIALIZATION The socialization function usually occurs in the early stages of dating. Through dating, people learn the norms, roles, and values that govern heterosexual relationships. One impact of the women's movement has been to change the ways in which some women and men define their roles in intimate relationships. Thus, for example, if a man finds he cannot accept an aggressive, self-confident, and self-reliant partner, or a woman finds that she will not accept a passive role, dating helps them to discover this and to realize what kind of roles they are willing to play in an intimate relationship. Dating is a competitive situation in which an individual can test and refine a number of interactive skills with respect to the opposite sex. For young people, dating also provides an opportunity for sexual experimentation and growth. Obviously the socialization function of dating is not limited to heterosexual or young couples. Socialization does not end in our youth, and it therefore continues to be an important function of dating even as we grow older.

In addition, the socialization function of dating can serve to enhance the ego or sense of self. According to anthropologist Margaret Mead (1935), a major way that we develop a personality and gain a sense of self is through our relationships with other people. If a positive self-concept is attributable in part to successful experiences with others, then an important stage in an individual's personality development can occur during successful dating experiences.

RECREATION For most people, regardless of age, dating provides an opportunity to relax, have fun, and enjoy themselves in the company of someone they like. Ramu (1989) and other social scientists distinguish between adolescent and adult patterns when discussing the recreational function of dating. The assumption is that dating in adolescence serves a recreation function (the seeking of fun and thrills); it

Dating is no longer necessarily the means to the end of marriage. Getting together, hanging out, or generally sharing fun activities on a date is now an end in itself.

is often an end in itself. In contrast, in adulthood it involves courtship, often directed toward finding a marriage partner.

STATUS GRADING AND ACHIEVEMENT Most Americans view dating in positive terms. Thus, the more one dates, the more likely one's status and popularity will increase. Status grading and achievement in dating is a process whereby women and men are classified according to their desirability as dating partners. For example, on college campuses, people try to date those people who are rated as the most desirable on campus, for example, females seeking to date the most popular athletes on campus and males seeking to date the most attractive females, to boost their own status and prestige.

According to Ramu (1989), although this principle may have been operable in the 1930s, the changing values governing sex roles today and the importance attached to qualities other than beauty and athletic prowess have reduced the importance of status seeking among contemporary dating couples. Do you agree? Has status grading and achievement decreased in dating today? On college campuses in particular? Do college women still attempt to date the most popular athletes or other high-status men on campus? Do college men still try to date the most popular or most attractive women? Does status play a role in your dating behavior?

MATE SELECTION Although mate selection is no longer the primary objective of dating, dating continues to be the primary strategy for mate selection in the United States. The increasing divorce rates notwithstanding, Americans are still highly committed to marriage. Thus, although dating initially simply brings people together for recreational and romantic purposes, over time it can become a means of socialization for marriage. An accumulation of dating experiences helps those who want to marry in their efforts to find a marriage partner. Given the longer dating period today, dating continues to fulfill the function that researchers S. A. Lloyd and R. M. Cote (1984) described as **anticipatory socialization**—socialization that is directed toward learning future roles, in this case for marriage.

Not only does dating perform different functions, but these functions can vary according to an individual's reasons for dating. A person's primary reason for dating will influence that person's behavior in the dating relationship. The general change in the reasons that Americans date accounts for the significant changes we see in contemporary patterns of dating. One study, conducted by researchers James Skipper and Gilbert Nass (1966), suggested that a person's motivation for dating can be placed on a continuum ranging from completely expressive (dating as an end in itself) to completely instrumental (dating as a means to some larger goal). Skipper and Nass suggested further that a person's emotional involvement in the dating experience may also be placed on a continuum ranging from no emotional involvement to complete emotional involvement. A person's motive will determine her or his place on these two continuums.

For example, if the primary motive is mate selection, the person will probably have a strong instrumental orientation (dating should lead to marriage) and a strong emotional involvement. If, in contrast, the motivation is either recreation or status achievement, the individual is likely to have both low instrumental orientation and low emotional involvement. Skipper and Nass suggest that dating couples will seek to continue their relationship if either the emotional involvement or the instrumental orientation is high.

? *Think for a minute about your most recent dating relationship. Would you categorize your attitude as more expressive or instrumental? What about your degree of emotional commitment? How would you rate your partner on these criteria?*

THE INTERSECTION OF RACE, CLASS, GENDER, AND SEXUAL ORIENTATION

Dating, like all other social behaviors, is rooted in social as well as historical conditions of life. People's experiences (including their dating experiences) emerge from the social, political, and economic structure of a society. As we discussed in Chapter 1, race, class, gender, and sexual orientation are basic and central categories of experiences that set particular limits on behavior and engender specific kinds of experiences. If we are to move away from an analysis that stems only from the experience of the white middle and upper classes, we must consider how race, class, gender, and sexual orientation influence dating and mate-selection patterns for different groups.

Although we cannot provide a comprehensive picture of dating and mate selection for all groups, we can provide some insight into these processes. Unfortunately, the literature in this area is highly limited. The most extensive literature deals with African Americans. Little work has been done on courtship among Native Americans, Asian Americans, and Latinos. For example, although we know that family networks continue to make up the fabric of contemporary Native-American social organization and are central to the day-to-day functioning of Native Americans, we do not know how these families are formed vis-à-vis courtship and mate selection. We do not know, for example, whether Native Americans have been affected by the larger cultural patterns of dating and courtship. Moreover, despite the existence of a growing body of data on lesbian and gay relationships, most studies focus specifically on sexual behavior rather than more generally on mate selection.

DATING PATTERNS AMONG AFRICAN AMERICANS

The practice of dating among African Americans varies by region, historical period, social class, and age. According to Robert Staples (1991), a sociologist who has written widely on African-American singles and mate selection, in the past, when African Americans lived in small, cohesive communities in the rural and urban South, what might be called dating behavior centered on the neighborhood, church, and school. Generally, dating was a casual process in which women and men met, formed emotional bonds, and eventually married. Individuals generally were encouraged to date people whose reputation was generally known to members of the community. As African Americans began to move to urban areas outside the South, however, the greater anonymity associated with urban life modified dating patterns. The school and house party became major centers for heterosexual fraternizing, particularly among the lower class. Dating patterns among the middle class did not differ significantly from those of the larger society and included activities like movies, dances, and bowling.

According to most research, dating among blacks, as among whites and other groups, is still primarily a middle-class phenomenon. For the African-American middle class, dating is typically sequential, occurring over the course of several stages: getting together in the teen years; keeping company on the porch and, eventually, in the house, under family supervision; group dating; and, finally, individual one-on-one dating, engagement, and, most often, marriage (Scott, 1988). Moreover, since the 1970s, blacks, like whites and several other groups, have been delaying marriage until later ages, which means they are dating or getting together for longer periods of time than in the past.

A notable characteristic of contemporary African-American dating patterns is the significant increase in interracial dating, especially on college campuses. This pattern is attributed, in part, to the desegregation of many of the nation's public school systems, workplaces, and other social settings. It probably also is due to the liberation of many white youth from parental control and the rejection of racist values conveyed throughout society. In the case of African-American women, dating across race is also due, in some part, to the historically low **sex ratio**—the number of men to every 100 women. Rates of interracial marriage continue to be very low, however—less than 5 percent of all marriages—providing further evidence that dating does not necessarily lead to marriage.

THE IMPACT OF GENDER

Perhaps more than most relationships, dating is affected by gender roles and stereotypes. Society traditionally has conveyed certain messages concerning dating: We should mate with the opposite sex; women are supposed to want a masculine man; men are supposed to want a feminine woman; men should initiate the relationship and sexual behavior, although women may guide them through flirting; men should be dominant and women submissive; and sexuality is supposed to be more important to men, and love or commitment to women. As we shall see later in this chapter, although these messages are still widespread, they frequently do not reflect the realities of contemporary relationships.

Discussing gender differences in dating in the context of social-learning theory, social scientist Susan Basow (1992) contends that men's dating scripts focus on planning and paying for the date as well as initiating sexual behavior, whereas women's scripts focus on enhancing their appearance, making conversation, and controlling sexual behavior. Many of us apparently have learned these sexual scripts well. For example, researchers have documented that women and men have different orientations to romantic love and that this difference continues when they consider a prospective mate (Dion and Dion, 1973). Women and men have traditionally differed in terms of the characteristics they look for in a mate. Women, on the one hand, prefer men who are well educated and have financial stability (Melton and Lindsey, 1987). They place greater value on qualities of a prospective mate such as working, saving, and paying bills. Men, on the other hand, especially upwardly mobile men, emphasize physical and sexual attractiveness.

Americans aren't the only people who display these gender differences. According to a University of Michigan study, of 37 cultures in 33 countries regardless of the culture, most men want intellectually smart, good-looking, young wives. Women, too, want husbands who are intellectually smart, but they also want husbands who are a bit older, ambitious, and have bright financial prospects (United Press International, 1990). One implication of studies such as this is that the social construction of a dating reality, like other traditional realities, exaggerates differences between the sexes and constrains behaviors within the sexes.

DIFFERENCES IN DATING ACROSS CLASS

Although dating as a method of mate selection is a universal practice in the United States, there are significant differences among the various classes.

UPPER CLASS   Dating within the upper strata of U.S. society tends to be far more regulated than it is for other classes. Upper-class families still exert considerable influence over mate selection. Most of the activities of young people in this class are closely supervised by parents or other adults who chaperon young people's activities. Dates are sometimes arranged by parents, and dating partners are almost always selected from within their own ranks. Seldom do upper-class members date someone from the middle or lower classes, and dating a number of partners is the norm. Adults also exercise more control over the sexuality of young people than is true of other classes. When upper-class women reach 18, they are formally presented to society. After this "coming out" they engage in a number of activities, during which they encounter a number of eligible men. If the couple become engaged, the man presents the woman with an expensive ring, and the engagement is announced in the society pages of the print media. The wedding, which is generally a very formal affair attended by the rich and famous, is also announced in the newspapers.

MIDDLE CLASS   Dating behaviors among middle-class youths are also supervised by adults, although not to the same degree as are those of their wealthier counterparts. Dating activities among middle-class couples include going to sports events and engaging in sporting activities such as ice skating and tennis, going to the beach, going out to dinner, and entertaining at home. Going steady remains common among the middle classes and usually leads to an engagement. Engagements of middle-class couples, like those of wealthy couples, are usually announced in the print media. Weddings are fairly elaborate and expensive and are often performed in a church or synagogue.

LOWER CLASS   Most research on dating suggests that lower-class families tend to exercise the least control over mate selection. Dating among this group is very informal and often includes simply "hanging out"—getting out of often small and cramped living quarters in favor of such places as bowling alleys and local bars. Serious, unsupervised dating usually begins in the mid teens and is often exclusive or monogamous. Lower-class couples often skip the engagement phase and progress directly to marriage. When engagements occur, they are not usually announced in the press, and weddings are often small, inexpensive, and informal. Sometimes they are conducted in the home of one of the partners.

LESBIAN AND GAY DATING

We know very little about the dating and mating behavior of lesbians and gays because relatively little research in this area has been done. Moreover, the research that exists deals primarily with sexual behav-

As with many heterosexual couples, dating among gay and lesbian couples often leads to the development of strong and enduring love relationships.

ior and lifestyles. Because society continues to stigmatize homosexual behavior, much of the mate-selection behavior is carried on in the privacy of homes and recreational establishments frequented only by lesbians and gays. Like heterosexual couples, most lesbians and gays date for recreational and entertainment purposes, but the development of love relationships is also an important goal. In this regard, the function of dating for some lesbian and gay couples is to find a mate with whom they can share love, psychological and economic support, and perhaps children (Parrot and Ellis, 1985). Because lesbians and gays are legally prohibited from marrying, for some lesbians and gays the ultimate goal of mate selection is a type of symbolic marriage, such as a domestic partnership, in which cohabiting lesbians and gays officially register as a couple. (Chapter 7 contains more detailed discussions of these topics.)

As with heterosexuals, there appears to be some fundamental gender differences in the dating and mate-selection behaviors of lesbians and gays. Lesbians tend to meet their partners through lesbian friendship networks (Tanner, 1978), with the period of courtship lasting on average 2 to 3 years (Harry, 1983). Their partners tend to be women they have known for a while and with whom they have had no prior sexual relationship. Lesbians tend to practice a kind of serial monogamy in that they may have several partners over the course of their lifetime but are involved in only one intimate relationship at a time. In contrast, as we noted in Chapter 4, the courtship period for gays—as for heterosexual men—is often relatively short and is often preceded by sexual relations.

In general, dating and mating patterns among lesbians and gays do not appear to be significantly different from those found among heterosexual women and men. Thus, they seem much more reflective of female and male socialization patterns than of patterns specific to lesbians and gays (Harry, 1983).

AFRICAN-AMERICAN LESBIAN AND GAY DATING

Research pertaining to lesbian and gay mate selection across race is especially scarce. One study by Vickie Mays and Susan Cochran (1991) of 530 middle-class African-American lesbians provides some insights into mate selection among this group. The study does not convey a comprehensive picture of the dating process, but it does provide some important data. For example, although two-thirds of the subjects were in a serious relationship, only one-third lived with their partner. The average age at which the women reported first being attracted to a woman was about 16. Their first lesbian experience did not occur until approximately age 19, however. Prior to their current relationship, almost all the women had been involved in a sexual relationship with another African-American woman. In addition, two-thirds had at least one such relationship with an Anglo woman, and 39 percent reported a lesbian relationship with some other woman of color. The median number of sexual partners was nine, which is similar to that reported by research on white lesbians.

Regarding males, according to some research (for example, Cochran and Mays, 1991), dating and mate selection among African-American gays may be influenced by sociocultural factors such as the unavailability of same-race, same-sex partners; residential immobility; fewer social and financial resources; and a general lack of employment opportunities. Thus, African-American gays, like many African-American heterosexual women, often have difficulty finding a potential partner. The traditional networks where mate selection takes place in the white gay subculture such as gay bars, baths, and other public gathering places are not always accessible to black gays due to actual or perceived racism. Thus, courtship among African-American gays is more likely to center around home entertainment.

An interesting finding about African-American gay sexuality comes from a 1978 study comparing the sexual behavior of black and white gays. In this study, Alan Bell and Martin Weinberg reported that black gays tend to be more bisexual in their behaviors than white gays do. This finding implies that African-American gays may be dating both women and men either concurrently or alternately over some specified period of time. If such behavior occurs, it might be attributed to the intense homophobia alleged to exist within the African-American community.

Other comparisons generated by the Bell and Weinberg study of black and white gays include the following: Black and white gays reported equivalent numbers of sexual partners, both lifetime and over a 12-month period; black gays were significantly less likely than white gays to engage in brief relationships with anonymous partners; over two-thirds of the blacks reported that more than half of their partners were white men. This last finding is in stark contrast to white gays in the same study, none of whom reported that more than half of their partners were black. Thus, it seems that as in heterosexual dating and mate selection, a shortage of eligible potential mates may encourage coupling with people of other races and ethnicities.

THEORIES OF MATE SELECTION

Thus far we have discussed mate selection historically, cross-culturally, and within the context of U.S. society. We have also paid particular attention to issues of race, class, gender, and sexual orientation in dating behavior. A complete understanding of mate selection in these contexts requires a theoretical framework that shows how these and other social, economic, and political factors are variously related and influence mate selection. Obviously no one theory can accomplish this. In the next section, we present some of the most frequently used theoretical explanations of mate selection: exchange theories—including stimulus–value–role theory and equity theory—and filter theory.

EXCHANGE THEORIES

Exchange theory is perhaps the most often used explanation of interpersonal attraction and mate selection. Although it was not developed specifically to explain mate selection, it provides some interesting insights into this process. You might recall from Chapter 2 that exchange theory revolves around the notion that individuals attempt to maximize their rewards and minimize their costs to achieve the most favorable outcome possible. Applied specifically to mate selection, exchange theory holds that people looking for mates try to maximize their chances for a rewarding relationship. In other words, we enter into and remain in an intimate relationship as long as we perceive that the rewards outweigh the costs. If each person maximizes outcomes, then stable relationships will develop between people who have very similar levels of resources, because they will exchange comparable resources.

Social scientist John Edwards (1969) refers to this principle as the *exchange theory of homogamous mating*. According to Edwards, within any pool of eligibles, a person looking to get married will seek out a person who she or he thinks will maximize her or his rewards. We therefore enter or do not enter into a romantic relationship depending on whether the other person possesses both tangible resources, such as money, and intangible resources, such as physical appearance. People with equivalent resources are most likely to maximize each other's rewards. Because couples with equivalent resources are most likely to have homogamous characteristics, mate selection is homogamous with respect to a given set of characteristics. As the relationship progresses, a couple engages in many other exchanges, including those involving power. Seldom are both parties equally interested in continuing the relationship. Thus, the one who is least interested has an advantage and is in a position to dominate. Some researchers have described this as the *principle of least interest*, where, in essence, the person with the least interest trades her or his company for the other person's acquiescence to her or his wishes (Waller and Hill, 1951).

Under traditional mate selection, men maximized their rewards because they generally had a range of rewards to offer, such as social status, economic support, power, and protection. In contrast, women generally had a limited set of resources, which primarily involved their physical appearance and their ability to bear and care for children. Today, however, women have more rewards to offer and thus can be more selective in choosing a mate. Instead of the traditional male tradeoff of economic security, many women today are looking for men who are expressive, sensitive, and caring. Along the same lines, instead of the traditional female tradeoff of physical attractiveness and nurturance, many men today are looking for women who are assertive, creative and self-confident, and who can contribute to the economic support of a family.

STIMULUS–VALUE–ROLE THEORY A popular variation of the general exchange theory of mate selection is Bernard Murstein's (1980) *stimulus–value–role theory* of interpersonal attraction. According to Murstein, in a situation of relatively free choice, attraction and interaction depend on the exchange value of the assets and liabilities that each person brings to the situation. In the mate-selection process couples move through three stages: stimulus, value, and role. In the *stimulus stage*, two people are attracted to each other. If both partners feel the situation is equal concerning the exchange of resources, they will likely proceed to the *value stage*. In this stage, the compatibility of the couple is tested with regard to a variety of mutually held values, including religion, politics, and marital and family expectations. The more similar the two people's values, the stronger their attraction becomes. Couples with similar values may move on to the *role stage*. This stage provides each partner with the opportunity to see how the other acts out her or his roles in real-life situations. If mutual benefits at this stage are positive and fairly equal, the couple may choose to get married. The key here is that successful passage through all three stages may lead to a long-term relationship, culminating in marriage.

EQUITY THEORY Yet another variation of exchange theory that is used to explain mate selection is *equity theory*. When used in this sense, the term *equity* signifies fairness. Equity theory proposes that a person is attracted to another by a fair deal rather than by a profitable exchange (Walster, Walster, and Traupman, 1978). It argues that most people believe that they should benefit from a relationship in proportion to what they give to the relationship. People are attracted to those from whom they get as much as they give. Two people do not usually seek the exact same things in a relationship. However, they are attracted by a deal that is fair to them. Values involved in judging equity range from physical attractiveness to family background to anything that a given person might value.

FILTER THEORY

As our discussion thus far indicates, mate selection involves a complex process of making choices within the context of a range of factors that can restrict or enhance our ability to choose. David Klimek (1979) describes this process in terms of a series of filterings. As Figure 5.1 suggests, individuals use a series of filters to sort through a large number of potential mates to arrive at the final choice. Each filter, in descending order, reduces the pool of eligible mates until relatively few eligibles are left. We then choose a mate from among this group. *Filter theories* or *process theories* as they are sometimes called, suggest that many factors are involved in the marital choice. In the next section we discuss some of the most prevalent of these factors, including marriage squeeze and gradient, propinquity, race, sex, class, age, religion, and family and peer pressure. After reading this section you should be more conscious of the fact that even Americans do not have complete freedom of choice in mate selection.

MATE SELECTION: FINDING AND MEETING PARTNERS

"There's supposed to be more women than men, so where are they?" "I know there are a lot of good men out there—you just have to know where to find

them." Do these comments sound familiar to you? Increasingly over the last decade single women and men looking for "Ms. Right" or "Mr. Right" have lamented the mounting problem of finding or meeting someone to date or marry. And, once they meet, how does each one know that the other is the right person? What attracts them to each other? How people meet and where, how or why they are attracted to each other and not someone else are some of the most basic questions surrounding mate selection. As you will see in the following discussion, finding a mate has become almost a national pastime in the United States. Some people go to great lengths to meet a potential mate, as revealed later in the chapter in the discussion of the new dating technology.

? *Do you know how your parents met? Was it love at first sight? How alike are they? What about you? Are you looking for a mate or partner? What characteristics do you look for in a mate? Character? Social conscience? A strong religious conviction? Money? Is it difficult to find someone who meets your standards? Think about your own dating and mate selection experiences and priorities as you continue reading this chapter. At the end of this chapter you may find that your thinking has shifted, or perhaps you have become aware of priorities and feelings that you never realized you had.*

FIGURE 5.1   The Filter Theory of Mate Selection.

Source: Adapted from David Klimek, *Beneath Mate Selection and Marriage: The Unconscious Motives in Human Pairing,* 1979 (New York: Van Nostrand Reinhold), p. 13.

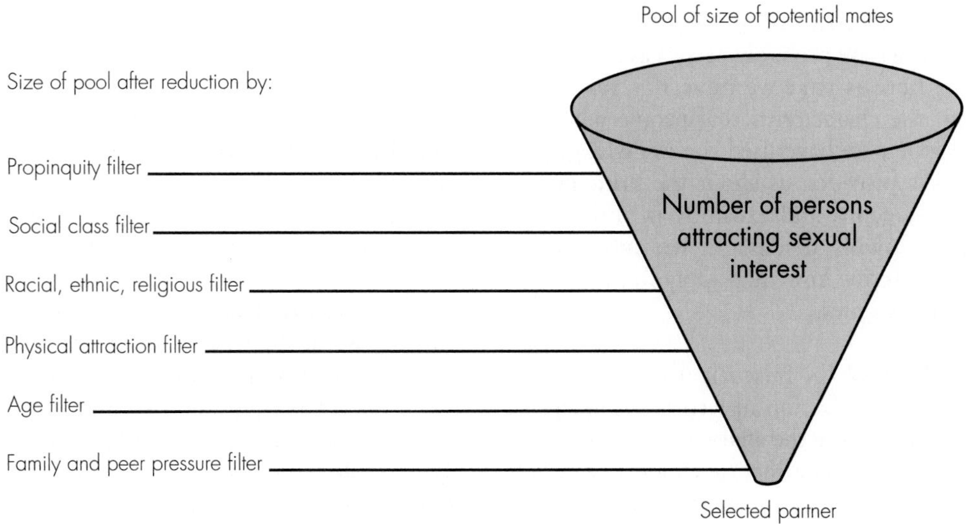

Pool of size of potential mates

Size of pool after reduction by:

Propinquity filter _____

Social class filter _____

Racial, ethnic, religious filter _____

Physical attraction filter _____

Age filter _____

Family and peer pressure filter _____

Number of persons attracting sexual interest

Selected partner

THE MARRIAGE MARKET AND THE POOL OF ELIGIBLES

Throughout our history various romantic theories of love and mate selection have suggested that when the time is right we will meet "Prince Charming" or a "fair maiden" without much effort on our part. Most such notions imply that mate selection is a rather unsystematic and random event determined by the "luck of the draw" or by a power higher than ourselves.

In reality, meeting prospective mates, choosing partners, developing a dating relationship, and falling in love are not random activities but are all predictable and are structured by a number of social and demographic factors. For example, if you are a female college student in a dating relationship, without meeting you or your partner we could predict fairly accurately many things about your partner. For example, he is probably a college student like you (or he has already completed college or attended college at some prior time), he is probably of the same racial or ethnic background and social class as you, he is probably a little taller than you, a few years older, and as religious or spiritual as you are. We might even predict that he is similarly attractive as you. (And if he isn't you probably will not have a lasting relationship; research shows that we are attracted to and tend to marry people who have a similar level of physical attractiveness.) Most likely the two of you are similarly intelligent.

Likewise, if you are a male student in a dating relationship the same predictions apply, with a few differences: Your partner is probably your age or 1 to 5 years younger, and she is probably your height or shorter. Although we may not be 100 percent correct, for many of you we are probably very close.

The point here is that we have not randomly guessed about the characteristics of people who date and marry. Rather, we have used the knowledge that sociologists have provided us about the principles of homogamy, endogamy, and exogamy in mate selection. In the following discussion we define these principles and describe how they apply to mate selection in the United States.

MARRIAGE MARKET Historically, sociologists have described mate selection in terms of a **marriage market**. That is, they use the analogy of the commercial marketplace to explain how we choose the people we date, mate, live with, and marry. The marriage market concept implies that we enter the mate-selec-

tion process with certain resources and we trade these resources for the best offer we can get. In this sense, the marriage market is not a real place but a process.

Regardless of how we choose mates, as exchange theory suggests, some sort of bargaining and exchange probably takes place. For example, in societies and subcultural groups where marriages are arranged by someone other than the couple, the parent or matchmaker carefully tries to strike the best possible bargain. Large **dowries**—sums of money or property brought to the marriage by a female—are often exchanged for valued characteristics in a male, such as high status. Indeed, valued resources like dowries can also act to make up for a person's supposed deficiencies. Thus, if a woman is considered unattractive but has a large dowry, she might be able to exchange the dowry for a highly prized mate. Although the idea of swapping or exchanging resources in mate selection may seem distant and applicable only in those cultures in which marriages are arranged, this process is very much a part of mate selection in the United States.

Although the nature of the marital exchange has changed, the market has not been eliminated. Despite some improvements in their bargaining position, women remain at a disadvantage vis-à-vis men in the mate-selection marketplace. Although women have entered the labor force in record numbers and become increasingly independent, their actual earnings are far below that of their male counterparts, as is their ability to earn. Furthermore, many of the traditional resources that women could offer, such as child care, housework, and sexuality, can be obtained by men outside marriage and thus have less value in the marriage market. Women are further disadvantaged by the sexual double standard attached to aging: As women age they are considered to be unattractive and undesirable by men.

Does this description of the marital marketplace sound cold, calculating, and unromantic? Even if we are uncomfortable with the idea, most of us engage in the exchange of various personality and social characteristics in our quest for a mate.

POOL OF ELIGIBLES Theoretically, every unmarried person in the United States is a potential eligible mate for every other unmarried person. Realistically, however, not every unmarried person is equally available or accessible to every other unmarried person. The people whom our society has defined as acceptable marriage partners for us form what sociologists call a **pool of eligibles**. For almost all of us, the pool of eligibles consists of people of the same race, class, and educational level as ourselves. With amazing consistency, we are very much like the people we meet, fall in love with, and marry—far more so than can be attributed simply to chance. Sociologists refer to this phenomenon as **homogamy**: the tendency to meet, date, and marry someone very similar to ourselves in terms of important or desirable characteristics.

Two of the most common sets of social rules governing mate selection and the pool of eligibles are exogamy and endogamy (see Figure 5.2). **Exogamy** refers to marriage outside particular groups. So, our

FIGURE 5.2 Exogamy and Endogamy in Mate Selection.

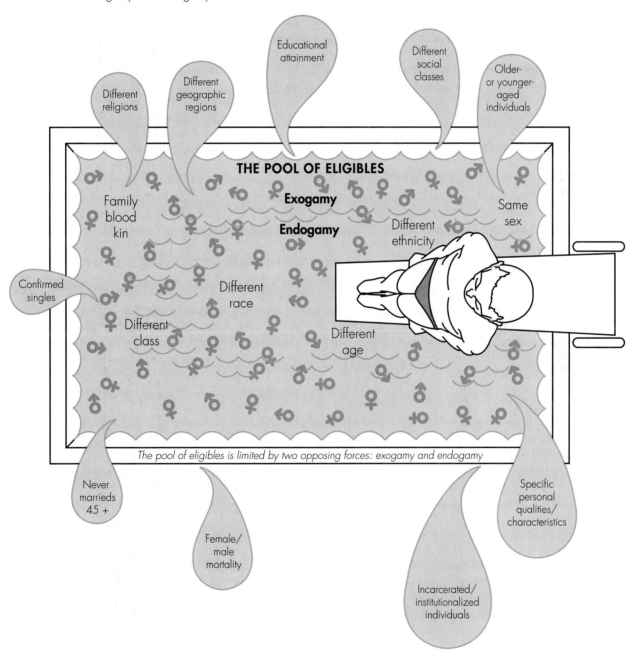

pool of eligibles is first narrowed by society's exogamous norms. The most common exogamous norms in the United States are those that prohibit us from dating or marrying someone who is a family member or who is of the same sex. As you know from Chapter 1, the incest taboo is a universal norm that narrows our pool of eligibles by eliminating close blood relatives. Regarding same-sex partners, people of the same sex are considered to be socially unacceptable mates and are also excluded, at least theoretically.

The opposite of exogamy is **endogamy**, marriage within a particular group. Endogamous norms can be formal, such as the laws in many U.S. states prior to 1967 that prohibited interracial marriage. Most, however, are informal. For example, social convention dictates that we marry someone near our own age.

FREEDOM VERSUS CONSTRAINT IN MATE SELECTION

Our freedom to choose a mate is restricted by cultural norms that sort people according to race, ethnicity, religion, social class, residence, and related factors. The romantic belief that mate selection is based on love and that we freely choose our mates notwithstanding, these factors best predict who meets, dates, falls in love with, and marries whom. Let's look at how our pools of eligibles are loosely or closely organized around these factors. Although all of these factors are interrelated, we will examine each one separately. Two of the most important factors are the marriage squeeze and the marriage gradient.

THE MARRIAGE SQUEEZE   Why do you think some people who want a mate and are actively looking cannot connect? Why do women complain more often than men about having difficulty finding a mate? Is there someone out there for all of us, no matter what resources we have to offer? Or will some of us not find a mate no matter how hard we look? In reality there is not someone out there for everyone. If those people being advised to "sit tight and wait" are women born after World War II, they may be waiting for a very long time. Demographic data reveal that at any given time in the United States since World War II, there has been a greater number of women than men who are eligible for marriage and looking for a partner. Sociologists have defined this imbalance in the ratio of marriage-aged men to marriage-aged women as a **marriage squeeze**, where one sex has a more limited pool of eligibles.

Although demographers predicted that the marriage squeeze would reverse itself by the mid 1980s, this did not happen. In the 1990s the marriage squeeze continues to limit the range of choices of mates for women, although its impact is experienced differently across race and age and even geographic location. African-American women, it seems, are particularly vulnerable to the marriage squeeze. In our earlier discussion of dating patterns among African Americans, we mentioned the historically low sex ratio in the African-American community. According to Staples (1991), this low sex ratio will continue to deny large numbers of African-American women a comparable mate. The lower life expectancy for black men (it is lower than for white males and all females), coupled with the increasing numbers of young black men who are victims of homicides and the disproportionate numbers who are incarcerated, has contributed to the current low sex ratio (Lindsey, 1990). By the time African-American women reach 18 years of age they begin to outnumber African-American males; the comparable age for white women is 32 (Spanier and Glick, 1980). The result of this is a seriously restricted field of eligibles for African-American women.

Not only is the marriage squeeze more evident for some racial and ethnic groups than for others, but it is also more evident in some geographic areas and for some age groups. For example, for every 100 unmarried 37-year-old women in Minneapolis, there are 46 eligible men; in St. Louis, the number is 45. In contrast, cities like Houston, San Diego, and San Francisco rank as some of the better marriage markets for women, with more than 70 eligible men for every 100 women (Westoff and Goldman, 1988:39–44). How are you affected by the marriage squeeze? Do you live in a city where there is an abundance of marriage-aged women and few eligible men? Take a look at Table 5.1. If you live in one of the 20 cities listed in the table you will find the ratio of men to women for your city and you may infer your chances for finding an eligible mate. Men who are seeking a mate can get a fair picture of their chances for realizing this goal by reversing the ratios in the table.

An even more notable feature of the marriage squeeze is the age factor. In most U.S. metropolitan

TABLE 5.1

"Where Are the Men?": Ratios of Eligible Men Available for Each 100 Women Aged 20–59, Living in 1 of the 20 Largest Metropolitan Areas in the United States

City	Ratio	City	Ratio
San Diego	75.1	Cincinnati	56.5
Houston	73.5	Minneapolis–St. Paul	56.5
San Francisco	73.2	Newark	55.6
New Orleans	70.2	Indianapolis	55.4
Los Angeles	69.9	San Antonio	54.5
San Jose	68.2	St. Louis	54.2
Fort Lauderdale	66.7	Buffalo	54.1
Washington, D.C.	66.5	Columbus	52.5
Denver	65.6	Pittsburgh	52.2
Seattle	64.7	Nassau–Suffolk Counties, N.Y.	49.2

Note: These figures are based on calculations of whites.

Source: Charles F. Westoff and Noreen Goldman, "Figuring the Odds in the Marriage Market." In J. Gipson Wells, *Current Issues in Marriage and the Family* (New York: Macmillan, 1988):40.

areas, at all ages over 25 the number of unmarried women significantly exceeds the supply of eligible men. As women get older, the shortage of men becomes more pronounced. For example, single women aged 25 to 29 face a shortage of eligible mates of almost 25 percent (77 eligible men for every 100 eligible women). For women aged 35 to 39 the sex ratio drops to 48 eligible men per 100 eligible women, and by the time women reach ages 45 to 49, the number is 38 (Westoff and Goldman, 1988). Thus, as women age they become more likely to feel the marriage squeeze.

THE MARRIAGE GRADIENT Another factor that affects the availability of eligible mates in the marriage market is the marriage gradient. In most cultures, including the United States, informal norms require women to marry men of equal or higher social status. Numerous studies of U.S. mate selection and marriage bear out this pattern. For example, only about 33 percent of women with 4 or more years of college marry men with less education, whereas 50 percent of men with 4 or more years of college marry less-educated women (Westoff and Goldman, 1988). The tendency to marry upward in

social status is referred to as **hypergamy**; marriage downward is known as **hypogamy**. Thus, in most cultures, women practice hypergamy, and men practice hypogamy.

As we have already indicated, hypergamy is much more descriptive of American mate selection than hypogamy. When men marry outside their social-class level, they more often marry downward than upward. Furthermore, the higher a man's occupational level, the more likely he will marry downward. Conversely, when women marry outside their social class, they most often marry upward. This pattern of marriage gives rise to a phenomenon we call the **marriage gradient**. Because women marry upward and men marry downward, men at the top have a much larger field of eligibles than do men at the bottom. The reverse is true for women: Women at the top have a very small pool of eligibles, whereas women on the bottom have a much wider range of men to choose from. This pattern therefore works to keep some of the highest-status women and lowest-status men from marrying. Although the description here is of marital patterns, the same general trend has been found to operate prior to marriage as well. This tendency has been called by some a *dating* or *mating gradient*.

Although the marriage gradient traditionally provided most women with upward mobility, this is not necessarily the case today. The increasing economic independence of some women has made marriage less of a mobility mechanism. Because of the shortage of men (real or perceived), many women are dating and marrying downward instead of upward. For example, a woman with a college degree was heard to say: "If I could find a kind plumber with a sense of humor, I'd marry him."

As with the marriage squeeze, the marriage gradient is very prominent for African-American women. One study (Staples, 1981b) found that as income level rises, so does the number of men who are married and living with their wives. In contrast, African-American women who have a college degree are the least likely of all African Americans to have married by the age of 30. And the African-American men least likely to marry or remarry are those with less than a high school education. A fundamental problem for middle-class or high-status African-American women is that men who have a similar status are either already married or are seeking a younger mate. Thus, the largest number of African-American men in their pool of eli-

Think about the structure of mate selection in U.S. society generally and in the various social groups to which you belong. Write a short essay that includes an analysis of your mate selection in terms of the following questions. Ask your parents or others to whom you are close and whose opinions you value, whom among the following they would object to if you dated or married.

Race: African American, white American, Asian American, Native American, Puerto Rican, Mexican American, other Latino, other race.
Age: 15, 20, 25, 30, 35, 40, 45, 55, 65, 75, 76 or older.

Educational Level: Fifth grade or below, eighth grade only, some high school, high school graduate, some college, college graduate, graduate or professional school.
Religion: Catholic, Baptist, Methodist, Muslim, Buddhist, Mormon, Lutheran, Unification Church, Orthodox Jew, Jehovah's Witness, atheist, other.
Blood Relatives: First cousin, second cousin, third or more removed cousin.
Gender: Same sex.

Also think about the following questions, and incorporate your responses in the essay. How do you feel about interracial mar-

riages? Do you know anyone who is dating or married to a person of a different racial group? What problems have they encountered? Have you ever been involved in an interracial relationship? If not, would you consider such a relationship? What barriers do you think you would encounter if you were a partner in such a relationship? Are any members of your immediate family married interracially? If yes, how do you feel about these relationships? To what extent do parents, relatives, and friends' attitudes about interracial dating and marriage affect your dating and marital choices?

---

gibles are those with a lower status. Therefore, educated African-American women who are interested in a mate often must date or marry down.

Moreover, with the increasing number of marriages that are now ending in divorce and the high proportion of remarriages, the marriage gradient can be seen operating in second marriages as well. As in other examples, women tend to be most vulnerable to the marriage gradient. Researchers Jerry Jacobs and Frank Furstenberg (1986), for example, found that when women, particularly those with children, remarried, they tended to marry downward instead of upward.

RACE Some of the most important norms in mate selection in the United States revolve around race and ethnicity. Dating, mate selection, and marriage are probably most endogamous and homogamous in terms of race. We currently have little reliable data on the number of contemporary couples who date interracially. We do know that about 98 percent of marriages in this country occur within the same racial group (Bovee, 1993). Although marriage is not an exact barometer of who dates whom because all dat-

ing does not result in marriage, it can give us some indication of who chooses whom as a mate. We discuss interracial marriage in detail in Chapter 8.

Think about your own dating history and that of people you know such as family members. You can use the exercise in the box titled "Applying the Sociological Imagination" to analyze some of your attitudes and those of people you know concerning the issue of race and intimate relationships.

SOCIAL CLASS Sociologists typically measure class using a composite scale consisting of level of educational attainment, occupation, and level of income. As we have seen, much of our behavior is affected by our location in the status hierarchy. People who share a similar social-class background tend to share common interests, goals, lifestyles, and general behavior. These kinds of compatibility of interest and general homogamy are the bases of intimate relationships. As with race, Americans mate with people from their own socioeconomic class with far greater frequency than could be expected simply by chance. This is especially true among the upper classes of all races. It has often been observed that the upper classes expend more efforts to control the mate selection of their offspring than do other classes because they have much more to lose if their children marry outside their social class (Ramu, 1989). Even on those occasions when a person marries someone of a different race, ethnicity, religion, or age group, the couple will most likely be from the same social class.

Because social researchers do not agree on the nature and number of social classes in U.S. society, it is difficult to determine accurate statistics on class endogamy. We know, however, that courtships and marriages tend to be highly endogamous for such class-related factors as education and occupation. Educational homogamy is most observable for women with 4 or more years of college, who tend to marry men with comparable or higher levels of education, and for men who have never attended college (Rawlings, 1978).

AGE Are you involved in a relationship with a person who is much older or younger than you? Do you know others who are? What about your parents? Is your mother older or younger than your father? When you see a much younger woman with an older man do you think: "Gee, she must be looking for a father figure." or "My God. He's robbing the cradle"? Age norms represent yet another important constraint on our freedom to choose a mate. Although no laws require us to date, live with, or marry people within our age group, informal norms and pressures operate to keep mate selection fairly homogamous in terms of age. Most Americans mate with people from a closely related age group. For most of us this means that we date and marry people roughly within 2 to 5 years of our own age. Although the sanctions for dating or marrying someone very much older or younger (within the law) than oneself are mild, most people adhere to the age custom in selecting a mate. In later marriages or remarriages, age differences are likely to be a little wider, although they continue to follow the general pattern of age homogamy.

RELIGION How important is religion in your choice of a partner? Several studies conducted over the years have found that people tend to select partners who are religiously similar to themselves (see, for example, Kerckhoff, 1976; Glenn, 1982; Shehan, Bock, and Lee, 1990). As with race, many of these studies deal primarily with marriage; nonetheless, we can assume some degree of congruency between whom people date and whom they marry. Thus, religious homogamy is yet another factor that limits our pool of eligible mates.

SEX AND GENDER When discussing factors that limit our pool of eligible mates we cannot overlook sex. As we have indicated repeatedly, heterosexuality is the norm in mating, dating, and mate selection in the United States. Most Americans are so socialized into a heterosexual frame of reference that it is outside their scope of reality even to consider a same-sex relationship as an alternative. So important is the value of heterosexuality to many Americans that exogamous norms regulating this behavior have been encoded into law to ensure that people mate heterosexually. The stigma attached to same-sex relationships, legal constraints, and the physical abuse that such couples frequently experience ("gay bashing") can act as deterrents for some people who might otherwise choose a partner of the same sex.

OTHER FACTORS THAT AFFECT MATE SELECTION

As we have seen, mate selection in the United States is an individual decision, yet many social and structural barriers and limitations act to constrain our freedom to choose a partner. Besides race, class, age, religion, and sex, these barriers can also include propinquity and family and peer pressure. Let us take a brief look at these factors.

PROPINQUITY We have already touched on the subject of propinquity and its role in mate selection, particularly as we discussed racial and ethnic homogamy. **Propinquity** is a term used by sociologists to denote proximity or closeness in place and space. Traditionally, Americans met, were attracted to, and married people who lived in the same community. This factor of residential proximity in mate selection was first introduced in a pioneering study of mate selection conducted by James Bossard in 1932. In his study of who married whom in the city of Philadelphia, Bossard found that more than half the couples who applied for marriage licenses lived within 20 blocks of each other. One-sixth lived only a block apart, and one-third lived within 5 blocks of each other. Subsequent research has reported similar results. Although we are no longer tied to our local communities in the way we were before mass transportation and the mass production of the automobile, residential propinquity continues to contribute to homogamy in mate selection.

Residential propinquity is closely tied to many of the factors we have already discussed: social class, race, sexual orientation, and to a lesser degree religion. Historically, people of the same general social characteristics have tended to live close together. For example, most, if not all, U.S. cities are racially and ethnically segregated, and many are class-segregated as well. It is not unusual to go to a city and find very distinct racial or ethnic communities: the African-American community, Little Italy, Chinatown, Greektown. These residential patterns increase the likelihood that we will meet, date, and marry people of similar social backgrounds.

Obviously propinquity is not limited to place of residence. In a mobile society such as ours, propinquity operates as much, if not more, in schools, the workplace, places of entertainment, and other institutions as we increasingly move out of our communities for a good portion of each day. Nevertheless, the probability of meeting someone and establishing an intimate relationship still depends on the likelihood of interacting with that person.

FAMILY AND PEER PRESSURE   Consider the following scenario:

> "I am working on a doctorate; my boyfriend has never attended college. We love each other, but my family and friends insist that I should break off with him because he is not on my level. I think they might be right because sometimes even I am embarrassed by the way he speaks and carries himself. I feel so pressured by them. Can love overcome the prejudices of society?"

Stated another way, this woman's question could well be: Can love overcome the pressures of family, friends, or peers? Who is or is not acceptable to parents and other relatives is of importance to most Americans. Parents in particular exercise direct and indirect influence on whom we meet and develop relationships with. Parents influence our choice of mate from the moment we are born through their teaching, their example, where they choose to live,

which schools they send us to, and so forth. How, where, and when we are brought up has a profound impact on our views and decisions concerning marriage and family. Additionally, the closer we are to our parents and kin, the more likely we will consider their views.

Peers, too, can be powerful forces in both whom we meet and whom we decide to date or pair with. If our peer relationships are significant and close, we are far more likely to consider our friends' views and feelings about the people we date and marry. If you have completed the exercise presented in the "Applying the Sociological Imagination" box, you probably have a more heightened awareness of just how influential parents, other family members, and peers can be in our choice of a mate.

PERSONAL QUALITIES AND MATE SELECTION

As we saw in Figure 5.1, social factors such as those we have just discussed act as an initial screening. Once our pool of eligibles is determined, other factors come into play, such as the personal qualities or characteristics of the people we meet and consider as potential mates. The personal qualities we consider cover a wide range that includes physical appearance, lifestyles, ability to communicate, values and attitudes, personality, and family background, to name but a few. Probably the most important, at least initially, is physical appearance, because first impressions are often based on whether or not we find a person attractive. In addition, first impressions are often lasting impressions. In the discussion that follows we take a brief look at attractiveness and companionship as classic examples of personal qualities that critically affect mate selection.

ATTRACTION   What does "Ms. Right" or "Mr. Right" look like? All of us have some image, vague though it may be, of who our ideal mate will be. Usually this image includes both physical and personality features, and we consciously or unconsciously rate or compare potential mates in accordance with these images. These ideas and images do not develop in a vacuum; rather, they are shaped in large part by the society in which we live. For most Americans, physical appearance is one of the most important ingredients in mate selection. Whether we admit it or not, how someone looks has a considerable impact on whether we choose that person as a friend or lover.

Researchers have found a number of interesting points about physical attractiveness and its influence on mate selection. One key point is that we tend to think we are better looking than other people do. Furthermore, men are more likely than women to exaggerate their appearance, whereas less-attractive females are more accurate in their self-evaluations. This is true, no doubt, because women get far more feedback about their appearance than men do. In any event, once people meet and dating begins, personality characteristics become important considerations, although attractiveness does not decline in importance (Patzer, 1985).

Dating and marriage relationships tend to be endogamous for physical attractiveness. Various studies have documented our general tendency to look for and end up with partners whose attractiveness is roughly equivalent to our own (Stroebe, Insko, Thompson, and Layton, 1971). Some of the physical similarities between people who become couples are probably the products of race and class endogamy. Some, however, are also probably a function of our definitions of what is physically appealing, including our assessment of where we fit in society's general definition of physical attractiveness.

COMPANIONSHIP Despite the increasing divorce rate, some demographers are predicting that many people who have married in recent times will likely stay married to the same person for the next 50 years or more unless death or divorce intervenes (Ramu, 1989). If they are correct, then qualities such as compatibility and companionship are critically important in mate selection. It is essential to choose a mate with whom we can communicate; enjoy sexually and socially; and depend on for friendship, support, and understanding. The presence or absence of these attributes can have a tremendous impact on the quality and longevity of the relationship. Ramu (1989) identifies communication and sexual adjustment as the two most crucial personal attributes that contribute to companionship in an intimate relationship. These attributes are complex and depend on a number of factors: the partners' intellectual compatibility, their sensitivity and empathy toward each other, each partner's ideas about the other's sexual behavior, simi-

larity in social class and other important social characteristics, and the importance to both partners of sexual relations in marriage.

THE LIFE CYCLE AND MATE SELECTION

The desire to date or participate generally in the mate-selection process does not begin and end with youth. The fact that many people are delaying marriage until later ages, coupled with the large and increasing divorce rate, better health, and an extended life expectancy, mean that an increasing number of older adults will enter or reenter into dating relationships, and some of them will look for a permanent mate. In some ways these older adults resemble their younger counterparts. They seek partners for companionship, for long- and short-term commitments, and to share their life with. They feel a need for emotional care and the same type of mutual aid that many younger couples share. They frequently differ, however, in terms of the ultimate goal of mate selection. Although many older adults say that they would like to remarry, few of them actually do. Many of them are independent and self-sufficient, and they want to remain that way. (See Chapter 15 for a fuller discussion of this topic.)

MEETING PARTNERS: WHERE AND HOW

"Looking for Mr. Right." "Suffering from a Man Shortage? Try Honey Hunting in the Boondocks." "Bachelors for 1991: Single Men from Coast to Coast Seek Sensible, Sensitive, Athletic and Sophisticated Mates." "A Few Good Men: Where?" "Where Are the Men?" "Where Are the Men for the Women at the Top?" "How to Meet Someone on the College Campus."

These quotes represent but a handful of the many titles that have appeared in recent popular and scientific literature. What do these titles suggest about mate selection in the 1990s? First, they suggest that single people in the dating market today face a great challenge, namely, finding a significant other. Moreover, they indicate that women more often than men express difficulty in finding a mate. Given what we already know about the marriage gradient and the sex ratios in many cities, this is not surprising.

Most of the literature on dating continues to focus on college students. In fact, studies of the college mixer as a typical place to meet or take a potential date are as outdated as the notion that dating is still primarily a white, middle-class, college-aged phenomenon. Today people who date come from all walks of life, represent a wide range of ages, and are increasing in number. This fact has not gone unnoticed by an increasingly competitive service industry that has recognized and capitalized on this phenomenon. Dating is now big business. One of the most significant additions to contemporary dating and mate selection is the highly developed dating technology that provides singles with increased opportunities to meet prospective partners by using a variety of new technologies. In this section we present a brief discussion of some of the ways that those who want to date look for a partner.

SCHOOL, CHURCH, AND WORK

The high school or college campus is a traditional place where pairing and dating takes place. Most high schools and colleges that used to be segregated by sex are now coeducational. Many campus dormitories are now desegregated, and even some fraternities have gone coed. These changes have increased the opportunities for heterosexual interaction and coupling. Students meet each other in the dormitories, in classes, or through friends. In addition, various groups sponsor activities such as dances and beach parties to bring people together.

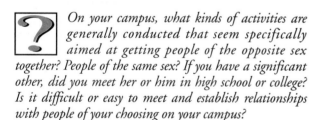 *On your campus, what kinds of activities are generally conducted that seem specifically aimed at getting people of the opposite sex together? People of the same sex? If you have a significant other, did you meet her or him in high school or college? Is it difficult or easy to meet and establish relationships with people of your choosing on your campus?*

Obviously, high school and college campuses are not sufficient places in and of themselves for meeting possible mates. Even on campuses we find those who want to date using a variety of other methods to meet people, such as being introduced by roommates, relatives, or

friends; advertising in the college or local newspaper; and using computerized dating services. In past times, the church or synagogue frequently brought people together. Today, however, as religion declines in importance in many people's lives, religious institutions and services less frequently serve this purpose.

Although the world of work at the turn of the century provided women with new and increased opportunities to meet and establish intimate relationships with the opposite sex in the sense that it got them out of the house and away from parents' supervision, it no longer provides the same level of opportunities for pairing. As in the past, the work women do is often sex-segregated or predominantly female, for example, elementary school teachers. Thus, it offers only limited contact with eligible males. In addition, the diversity of backgrounds that can sometimes be found in workplaces serves to limit the prospective pool of eligibles for women and men.

SINGLES' BARS AND GAY BARS

Singles' bars reached their peak in popularity during the 1970s and early 1980s. Once symbolic of the singles scene and a significant means of meeting potential mates, singles bars today are rejected by many people who see them as nothing but "meat (not meet) markets." In the past and to some degree today, singles' bars provided a space where people could feel comfortable and meet other single people. Studies of why people go to singles' bars indicate that the major reason is for companionship.

Gay bars are similarly rejected by some lesbians and gays as meat markets. The motivations for attending gay bars are not significantly different from those for attending heterosexual bars. Because of homophobia and discrimination against lesbians and gays and because many lesbians and gays do not feel free to express or be themselves in a predominantly heterosexual environment, gay bars continue to serve a significant mate-selection function.

SELF-ADVERTISING: PERSONAL ADS

Are you Italian? Petite, attrac. DIF 40+, degreed, seeking S/DIM 40+, must be finan/emot secure. No drugs/alcohol/smoking. Must like music, din out and travel.

One of the major problems for people who want to date is where and how to meet a prospective partner. Bars and dance halls that cater to singles are popular places for mate selection.

Attractive Aquarian. Gay, SWF, 33, tired of bar scenes. 5'5", 142 lbs., very romantic, honest, open-minded. Seeks honest open-minded gay SF, 30–40, non-drug user, for a long-lasting relat. Only serious need reply.

Sexy and Cute. SWF, 23, wants the best and won't settle for less! If you're attra., ambitious, prof. S/D white/Hispanic, fin secure please respond. Photo please.

SWM, 70, attrac., very active, outgoing & sincere, looking for a SWF who desires companionship & romance.

These fictitious ads are typical of those found in most local newspapers around the country. Such ads imply that any of us could find a potential mate through personally advertising for what we want. Resorting to such methods to find a mate is not a contemporary phenomenon. For example, in the 1800s settlers in the Northwest used a mail-order bride system, and several religious groups used matchmakers in the late nineteenth and early twentieth centuries (Steinfirst and Moran, 1989). The use of personal ads for dating and mating is not new, either. There is some evidence that personal ads appeared in newspapers during colonial times. Later, men moving across the frontier advertised in newspapers for brides (Carlier, 1972).

Not until the 1980s, however, did the use of personals became widespread and public. Since the 1980s, it seems that using personal ads has become not only acceptable but a fashionable way to meet people, especially among educated people (Steinfirst and Moran, 1989). Today, people who use the personals are no longer considered either perverted or desperate. In fact, some experts consider the use of personal ads to be a healthy and creative adaption to societal change (Bolig, Stein, and McHenry, 1984). In any case, with leisure time at a premium for many working people, with the dramatic increase in the numbers of singles, and with the difficulty of finding a partner through conventional means, an increasing number of people feel comfortable advertising themselves in the hopes of landing a mate.

A 1989 content analysis of personal ads by researchers Susan Steinfirst and Barbara Moran revealed some interesting gender differences in the way that women and men advertise for a mate. For example, women defined or offered themselves as attractive more often than men, and men sought attractive partners and requested photographs far more often than women. Men offered financial security much more than women, and women sought more permanent relationships than men.

A contemporary method of finding a partner is to participate in T.V. matchmaker programs such as "STUDS," a relationship show, where women and men are set up for multiple dates followed by an on-air discussion and selection of a partner.

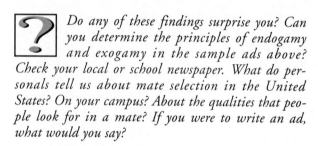 *Do any of these findings surprise you? Can you determine the principles of endogamy and exogamy in the sample ads above? Check your local or school newspaper. What do personals tell us about mate selection in the United States? On your campus? About the qualities that people look for in a mate? If you were to write an ad, what would you say?*

DATING CLUBS AND DATING SERVICES

Dating clubs and services advertise to and hope to attract those individuals who have difficulty meeting people through conventional routes or who are simply fed up with the commercialized nature of the singles' scene. A wide variety of dating clubs exist across the country that, for a fee, sort out compatible couples and bring them together. Rather than go the route of advertising in a newspaper or magazine, many people are joining or using the services of specialized dating clubs. A primary appeal of these clubs is that they provide immediate visual stimuli (which is important to those who are concerned with physical attributes and appearance). It also saves people from having to sort through pages of personals to find a person who fits what they are looking for in a mate and then, sometimes through trial and error, having to arrange to meet.

Many of these clubs are open to anyone interested in joining, but some are specialized and tailored to

the interests of a particular group. Specialized dating clubs can be especially appealing because they cater to a specific clientele. A number of such clubs around the country specialize in attracting members of a specific group, for example, professionals, vegetarians, bisexuals, Catholics, Jews, African Americans, single parents, lesbians, gays, and people who like to travel, to name but a few. There is even a dating club for the wealthy that charges its members a fee as high as $100,000 to match them with a marriage partner.

COMPUTER DATING

We should not be surprised that an increasing number of people now use computer technology in their search for a mate. Many unmarried people have joined computerized matching services that sell their members information on other members. Clients must complete a questionnaire covering a range of personal and demographic characteristics (sometimes as many as 200 traits) such as age, race, body build, religion, income, education, diet, tobacco use, political outlook, sense of humor, disposition, and sexual activity. This information is fed into a computer that matches it with other clients who have similar profiles. Members of computerized matching services pay a lifetime membership fee and then a separate fee for each computer match they receive.

Other people who want more control over the mate selection process use their personal computer to get in touch with prospective partners through dating networks called "dial-your-mate." People using these networks dial into a central computer and provide information similar to that contained in the questionnaires of the computerized matching services. "Dial-your-mate" services are geared toward heterosexual couples in that the information provided is compared with that of all opposite-sex participants and then ranked in terms of percentage of agreement. Subscribers can send information and messages back and forth on their computers, ignore the messages, exchange more information, or end the interaction at their discretion.

VIDEO DATING

Just as millions of Americans have turned to videocassettes as a basic source of entertainment, many singles now use videos to help in mate selection. Usually a company such as Amour or More Video Dating Service in Chicago prepares an audiotape or videotape of a client and put it on file. The company sends the client videotapes from its membership file as well as sending the client's videotape to other members. Video dating is generally fairly expensive, costing at least $600 per year. Despite the high cost, however, a growing number of people are using video dating technology.

THE FUTURE OF DATING

What is the future of dating? We cannot be sure. It is a safe bet, however, that dating will be around for some time to come, albeit in an increasingly modified form. Some "experts" project that dating in the twenty-first century will be so competitive as to resemble the classic Roller Derby. That is, it will be an intensive contest to determine who gets dumped first (Sunshine, 1990). Others are suggesting more creative ways of dating in the future. For example, David Coleman, director of student activities at a midwestern university, conducts "creative dating workshops" for college students who are tired of going to bars, movies, or dinner. According to Coleman, dating in the 1990s has become complicated by AIDS, drinking, and physical and sexual violence and abuse. Thus, he offers students approximately 300 ideas for innovative dates—most

of which do not involve alcohol. His master list of dating ranges from the "athletic" date to the "theme party" date and includes some offbeat ideas such as visit caves, take self-defense courses, and catch fireflies (Dodge, 1991). Whatever the future of dating, no doubt we as parents and grandparents some day will reminisce about the "good old days" when we were dating.

Although dating is often fun and can be a very positive experience in our lives, it can, and often does, involve negative experiences such as violence and abuse, and breaking up.

VIOLENCE IN DATING AND INTIMATE RELATIONSHIPS

Until the 1980s, the issues of date rape and violence received little public attention. Consequently, most people severely underestimated the extent of these problems. In recent years, however, due in part to the women's movement and a more open social attitude toward sexual issues in general, the media have begun to focus on all forms of intimate violence. As a result, our society finally is beginning to realize just how widespread are abuse and violence within dating relationships. Because of the seriousness and high incidence of violence, abuse, and rape in marriages and families, we devote a full chapter (Chapter 12) to its discussion. Here we are concerned specifically with dating violence and assault.

PHYSICAL ABUSE

Teenage dating violence is coming out of the closet today, and the numbers of teenagers involved in abusive relationships are staggering. One television special reported that 28 percent—or roughly one in four—high school students are involved in abusive or violent relationships. Most of the victims are females, most parents are unaware of the abuse, and most of the young women stay in the relationships. Hospitals report that these girls come in with facial injuries, such as a broken nose or black eyes, fractured wrists, and bruises on the neck and other parts of the body. Barrie Levy, a family therapist, reports that the pattern in these relationships is typically one where male

CRITICAL ISSUES

VIOLENCE AND ABUSE IN DATING RELATIONSHIPS

Family therapist Barrie Levy has spent a considerable number of years researching and lecturing to adolescents about violence, battering, and rape in dating relationships. Some of the most important violence-related facts that Levy has uncovered in her discussions with youth are that (1) many youth today consider sexual coercion or hitting justifiable under certain circumstances, including in dating relationships; (2) adolescent females are the primary victims of dating violence and abuse; and (3) adolescents as young as 12 years of age are sometimes involved in abusive or violent intimate relationships. Research estimates indicate that as many as one-third of high school- and college-aged youths

experience violence in an intimate relationship during their dating years (Levy, 1991:4). Fortunately, most of these young people survive the violence. But tragically some do not.

One teenager who did not survive the violence and abuse of her courtship was 15-year-old Jenny Compton. Her first boyfriend became her last. When Jenny tried to leave the relationship after a year of physical and emotional violence and abuse, including repeated death threats, her 18-year-old boyfriend killed her by stabbing her more than 60 times with a butcher knife. Like other females in abusive and violent relationships, Jenny was most vulnerable when she attempted to leave; she was at the greatest risk

at that time, and she paid dearly for it.

In your opinion, what factors of life in the United States might account for the high incidence of intimate violence in dating relationships? Why do you think that females are most often the victims of intimate violence? Are there battered males? What services on your college or university campus are available for victims of dating violence? In your community, city, and state? What legal remedies could be enacted to deal effectively with dating violence? If you were asked to testify before the United States Congress on the subject of intimate violence what would you say? How would you prepare for your testimony? What recommendations would you make?

jealousy escalates into controlling and restrictive behavior, accusations, and suspicions that ultimately escalate into violence (Levy, 1992).

Many victims, as well as their offenders, believe that the violence in their relationship is an indication of love and that it helps to improve the relationship. In one study of 15- to 19-year-olds, social scientists found that more than one-fourth of the victims and almost one-third of the offenders interpreted intimate violence in this way (Henton, Cate, Koval, Lloyd, and Christopher, 1983). Victims who hold this romantic view of violence frequently blame themselves for their mistreatment, rationalizing that because their partners love them, they must have done something to "deserve" the abuse (Gelles and Cornell, 1990).

An extension of this romantic illusion about abuse is seen in the fact that most girls and women who are battered during dating hold the unreal belief that the violence will stop after the wedding (Pagelow, 1984). Unfortunately, it does not. The available information

on violence among married and cohabiting couples suggests that if a woman continues in a relationship with a man who is violent before marriage or cohabitation, she can well expect that the violence will not disappear with the marriage vows or the moving in. Rather, the violence will likely be repeated and in some cases become more intensified. Most young women survive the violence they experience in their intimate relationships. But tragically some do not (see the Critical Issues box).

DATE AND ACQUAINTANCE RAPE

Just as our consciousness has been raised about intimate battering, we are also becoming increasingly aware of the widespread sexual violence suffered by females in relationships with males whom they know and, in some cases, trust enough to date. This problem received national attention in the early 1990s when

William Kennedy Smith, nephew of the late President John Kennedy, and Mike Tyson, former heavyweight boxing champion, were accused of sexual assault. In widely publicized trials, Smith was acquitted, and Tyson was convicted and sentenced to prison.

The public debate that surrounded these cases made many people aware that the majority of rapes are not committed by strangers. Rather, estimates are that more than 80 percent of all rapes in this country are committed by a man who is known to his victim (Bannister, 1992). Rape against a person who simply knows or is familiar with the rapist is called **acquaintance rape**. Rape against a victim who is actually "going out with" the rapist is known as **date rape**. These terms are so closely interrelated that they often are used interchangeably.

Although most rapes are date or acquaintance rapes, most *reported* rapes are stranger rapes. The reason for this is that most acquaintance rapes go unreported because many people still believe that a sexual encounter between two people who know each other cannot be rape.

The younger the woman, the more likely that she knows the rapist. In 63 percent of reported cases of rape in which the victim was between 12 and 18 years of age and 80 percent of the cases in which the victim was younger than 12, the victim knew her attacker (Renzetti and Curran, 1992). Date rape and acquaintance rape cut across race, social class, and sexual orientation and can be found in all geographic regions. They are probably most commonplace on college campuses, however. Although most such cases go unreported, it is estimated that between two and three out of ten college women are victims of courtship violence. Despite this fact, many educational institutions have been very slow to deal with this issue, if they deal with it at all.

A number of studies of date rape on college campuses have been conducted. One such study found that about one-third of the approximately 2000 men surveyed admitted having used some physical or emotional means to force a woman acquaintance to have sex with them even after she had indicated her unwillingness to do so. Most males and many females hold the attitude that the male use of force and aggression to have sexual intercourse is acceptable among acquaintances or dates (Koss, Leonard, Beezley, and Oros, 1985), at least under certain circumstances, such as if the female arouses the male (Giarrusso, Johnson, Goodchilds, and Zellman, 1979). One social researcher reportedly was told by a college male that he gets told "no" but that doesn't stop him; he keeps on going because "nobody complains afterward" (Barrett, 1982). Other research studies provide support for the finding that males who rape tend to consider sexual aggressiveness as acceptable and do not see themselves as having done anything wrong (Andersen, 1988).

BREAKING UP

As with marriage, one or both dating or cohabiting partners may feel the need to get out of the relationship. Breaking up can take many forms: The partners drift apart or stop calling or coming by, they have a fight over a minor incident or something said in anger; or in rare cases, both agree to terminate the relationship.

Some research indicates gender differences related to breakups before marriage. For example, in a study of relationships among a group of college-aged couples, Charles Hill and his colleagues (1976) reported that 51 percent of the breakups were initiated by women, 42 percent were initiated by men, and 7 percent occurred by mutual consent. The chances of the breakup being amiable were far greater if the man initiated the breakup.

How do we account for these findings? According to Hill, women depend far more on their husbands than husbands do on wives for income and status; therefore women are forced, more than men, to be practical when choosing a mate. Conversely, men can afford to be less practical and more romantic because they do not have as much at stake. Moreover, women are more concerned about the quality of a relationship than men are; consequently, women often expect more out of the relationship than men do. The practicalities that women exhibit in choosing a mate may function to help them better deal with breaking up than men can do.

Some social scientists claim that breaking up before marriage is less stressful than breaking up after marriage, when the couple have to deal with legally ending the relationship and possibly with custody issues as well. Even if this is true, breaking up is seldom easy, no matter what the relationship or who makes the break. When people who are emotionally involved break up, they frequently experience feelings of insecurity, anxiety, and guilt. "What's wrong with me?" "Will I find someone else?" "Will I be alone the rest of my life?" "What did I do to deserve this?" Unlike in marriage, there is no institutionalized means such as divorce to handle the breakup of a dating relationship, so there is little time to sort through and deal with the anger and hurt.

SUMMARY

Mate selection refers loosely to the wide range of behaviors and social relationships that individuals engage in prior to marriage that lead to short- or long-term pairing. It is an institutionalized feature of social life and can be found in some form in all human societies, although the exact processes that are followed vary widely from one society to another. In the United States, the mate-selection process, particularly for first marriages, is highly youth-centered and competitive. Dating, an American invention that first appeared in the 1920s, is the focus of our courtship system and incorporates a wide range of social relationships prior to marriage. The history of mate selection in this country has ranged from highly visible parental involvement during the colonial and preindustrial periods to the informal, indirect involvement of parents today. Dating became a widespread phenomenon in the 1920s and 1930s; in the 1940s and 1950s it filtered down to high school students, who started to "go steady"; in the 1960s and 1970s it became a more casual process; and during the 1980s and today dating has undergone many changes that reflect contemporary social and gender roles.

The functions of dating include socialization, self-image, recreation, and status grading and achievement. Like all other social behavior and organization, dating is deeply rooted in the social and historical conditions of life. Race, class, gender, and sexual orientation are basic and central categories in American life and thus must be considered in an analysis of mate selection.

A wide range of theories exists that attempt to explain who selects whom and under what circumstances. These theories include explanations in terms of social exchanges and rewards, role and value theories, and filtering theories. The process of mate selection can be viewed sociologically as a sequential or filtering process that stresses homogamy and endogamy. Mate selection in U.S. society is mediated by a range of structural and social factors: the nature of the marriage market, the marriage squeeze and marriage gradient, propinquity, race, class, sex, age, religion, education, family and peers, and cultural ideals about beauty and worth. Due to the impact of these factors we are very much like the people we meet, fall in love with, and marry—far more so than can simply be attributed to chance.

Not all intimate relationships lead to marriage or long-term commitment. Couples often break up under the pressure of a variety of sociopolitical factors. Moreover, a large number of dating couples are involved in physically or sexually abusive relationships. Battering and abuse among young couples as early as elementary and junior high school has reached epidemic proportions. The same can be said for date and acquaintance rape. In both cases, the victims are overwhelmingly female. Most intimate relationships, however, survive the problems of human frailty.

KEY TERMS

dating
mate selection
courtship
going steady
anticipatory socialization
sex ratio
marriage market

dowries
pool of eligibles
homogamy
exogamy
endogamy
marriage squeeze

hypergamy
hypogamy
marriage gradient
propinquity
acquaintance rape
date rape

1. "Cupid's arrow does not strike at random." Explain. Discuss the predictable factors that influence who meets, falls in love with, and marries whom.

2. Define the concepts of marriage squeeze and marriage gradient. How are the two related? How would the marriage squeeze and marriage gradient be significant in the lives of a 35-year-old female with a Ph.D. and a 35-year-old male who is a high school dropout? Why is the marriage squeeze so significant for African-American women?

3. Is breaking up before marriage any less painful or emotional than breaking up after marriage? Have you experienced either type of breakup? Do you know others who have? Ask a couple who broke up before marriage and a divorced couple about their emotional experience of breaking up, and compare their responses.

4. Explain the general exchange theory of mate selection. How does this theory help explain your involvement in your most recent intimate relationship? What specifically are or were the rewards and costs of that relationship?

FURTHER READING

BAILEY, BETH L. 1991. "The Economy of Dating." In Mark Hutter, ed., *The Family Experience*, pp. 288–94. New York: Macmillan. Bailey presents a social–historical analysis of the system of dating as it developed in this country in the 1920s. She pays particular attention to the economic underpinnings of the early dating system.

KAUFMAN, MICHAEL. 1992. "The Construction of Masculinity and the Triad of Men's Violence." In Michael Kimmel and Michael Messner, eds., *Men's Lives*, pp. 28–50. New York: Macmillan. Kaufman examines male violence in the social context of the construction of masculinity and the institutionalization of violence in the operation of most aspects of social, economic, and political life in the United States. He provides some interesting insights into male violence using the notion of a triad of male violence: violence by men against women, violence against other men, and violence against oneself.

LEVY, BARRIE, ed. 1991. *Dating Violence: Young Women in Danger*. Seattle, WA: Seal Press. This important book is divided into four parts that bring together professionals, activists, researchers, and young people in a manner that provides the reader with a comprehensive, cross-cultural view of dating violence. Both a call for action and a mechanism for change, this book presents the multifaceted issues of dating violence and offers clear models for intervention.

WESTOFF, CHARLES F., AND NOREEN GOLDMAN. 1988. "Figuring the Odds in the Marriage Market." In J. Gipson Wells, ed., *Current Issues in Marriage and the Family*, pp. 39–45. New York: Macmillan. This short but informative article provides an interesting view of the marriage market in the United States, one where the forces of supply and demand work in many of the same ways as they do in determining the prices of stocks or bonds.

Chapter 6

SEXUALITY AND INTIMATE RELATIONSHIPS

From all appearances it was not an unusual day. The alarm went off at the same time that it had gone off every morning for the last 6 years. Today, however, Sally was not going to work. Rather, she was scheduled to see a counselor about the results of her test for the HIV virus. When Sally was told by the counselor that she had tested positive for HIV (AIDS), she was too stunned to respond immediately. Her first impulse was to deny it. After all, she was not gay, she did not use drugs, nor had she ever had a blood transfusion. So how could she have AIDS? This could not be. There must be some mistake. She was a woman, and women generally do not contract AIDS. Or do they?

After the initial shock, Sally began to ask a number of questions: What does this mean? How could it have happened? Does my husband have it? If not, can I give it to him? Does this mean I can no longer have a sexually active life? Can I have children? If so, will it affect them in any way? Will they be born with AIDS? Am I going to die? Unfortunately, although the counselor was compassionate and caring, she could not answer most of Sally's questions. Instead, she handed Sally several booklets and pamphlets on AIDS and told her to read them and then contact her physician.

When Sally got home, she threw the information on the table and sat and stared into space for what seemed like hours. Finally, she arose from her chair and decided to confront the counselor's news by reading as much as she could about the AIDS disease, especially as it affected women. As she fingered through the reading material, she was shocked and then angered that every bit of the information was for men. Where was the information about AIDS in women? Were there no differences?

After some time and considerable effort Sally secured information that specifically addressed the impact of the virus for women. She is now taking life 1 day at a time as she and her husband and friends try to cope with the reality of this dreaded disease in their lives. She is happy that they have all chosen to stand by her. But she knows that unfortunately that is not the case for many women who have AIDS.

Do you know anyone with AIDS? Are they male or female? Are you aware of how many females contract AIDS? Are their symptoms different from those of men? Should both sexes receive the same medical treatment for the virus? Why do you think Sally had such difficulty finding gender-specific information on AIDS? Is this problem true in other areas of health care? What can women do to be better informed about AIDS? What would you do if you were Sally?

Probably no topic related to issues of marriage and family life is more shrouded with mystery and curiosity than is human sexuality. Human sexuality often is couched in terms of morality. The purpose of this chapter, however, is not to clarify or shape your morality but rather to increase your understanding of human sexuality, thereby enhancing your ability to make personal decisions concerning sexual behavior.

Because sexuality figures so prominently in marriage and family life as well as in other intimate relationships, this chapter, in conjunction with the supplementary materials presented in Appendix A, concentrates on sexual attitudes and behaviors before, during, and after marriage or a committed relationship as well as throughout the life cycle. We begin with a brief discussion of the historical roots of Western sexuality, from the Judeo–Christian tradition to U.S. sexual codes in the late twentieth century. We then consider the social basis of human sexuality by examining sexual

learning and how sexual scripts vary across gender, as well as trends in sexual attitudes and behavior, including sexual orientation. In addition, we discuss physiological aspects of sexuality such as human sexual response and expression. We also examine various codes of sexual conduct and patterns of sexual relationships across the life cycle. Finally, we examine human sexuality within the context of sexual responsibility and protecting yourself and your partners from AIDS and other sexually transmitted diseases.

Before we begin this discussion, take a minute to think about the topic of this chapter. How much do you know about human sexuality? If you're like most people you probably think you know almost all there is to know. Now is a good time to test yourself, before we get into a full discussion of sexuality. Take the quiz presented in the "Personal Reflections" box. Are you surprised at how much or how little you know about human sexuality?

PERSONAL REFLECTION

The following test consists of a series of statements, some of which are true and some of which are false. Take a sheet of paper and indicate whether you think each statement is true or false.

1. As a normal part of growing up, most people engage in some homosexual behavior.
2. Men are often capable of multiple orgasms, but women are not.
3. People who engage in premarital or extramarital sexual relations usually have a stronger-than-average sex drive.
4. For a certain period of time after an orgasm, neither women nor men are able to respond to further sexual stimulation.
5. The causes of impotence are almost always psychological.
6. The only normal method of sexual relations is when the penis is inserted into the vagina.
7. A woman's orgasm produced by vaginal penetration is more physically satisfying but requires more maturity than an orgasm resulting from direct stimulation of the clitoris does.
8. Oral–genital sex (mouth to sex organ) between a man and a woman often indicates homosexual tendencies.
9. Women who engage in sex before marriage are more likely than women who do not to have extramarital relations as well.
10. When women reach menopause, their sex drive may increase because the fear of pregnancy is removed.
11. Premature ejaculation (coming to climax too soon) is always the result of physical factors, such as an overly sensitive penis.
12. Women generally remain at the peak of their sex drive later in life than men do.
13. Alcohol is not a physical sexual stimulant.
14. The average teenaged female has a stronger sex drive than the average teenaged male.
15. A nymphomaniac is a woman who has a very strong sex drive, comes to a climax very easily, and is capable of multiple orgasms.
16. A woman's sex drive will not change even if she has her uterus removed.
17. Middle-aged and older women and men seldom masturbate.
18. If married persons masturbate, it is a sign of poor marital adjustment.
19. Although most males masturbate at one time or another during their lives, very few females do.
20. The size of her partner's penis is usually directly related to the sexual pleasure experienced by a woman during intercourse.
21. When a woman is sexually aroused, her clitoris becomes larger and firmer, just as a man's penis does.
22. There is little difference between homosexual and heterosexual sexual techniques and physiological responses.
23. People can be categorized as either exclusively heterosexual or exclusively homosexual.
24. Human sexuality is largely learned in the context of culture.

Answer Key: 1. T, 2. F, 3. F, 4. F, 5. T, 6. F, 7. F, 8. F, 9. T, 10. T, 11. F, 12. T, 13. T, 14. T, 15. F, 16. F, 17. F, 18. F, 19. F, 20. F, 21. T, 22. T, 23. F, 24. T

Source: Questions adapted from James L. McCary, 1978, *Human Sexuality: Instructor's Guide* (New York: Van Nostrand): 6–11.

HUMAN SEXUALITY: PAST AND PRESENT

Often people use the concepts *sex* and *sexuality* interchangeably. Thus, when someone talks about sexuality, we often assume that she or he is referring to sexual intercourse. On the other hand when we speak of sex it is not always immediately clear whether we are speaking of sexual activity such as intercourse or whether we mean a person's genetic sex (that is, biologically female or male). Although neither of these uses is incorrect, for purposes of clarification we use the term *sex* in this chapter to refer to genetic or biological sex only and *sexual activity* or *sexuality* to refer to a wide range of sexual behaviors, including intercourse.

Because human sexuality is so broad, no one all-encompassing definition is appropriate. In general terms, however, **human sexuality** refers to the feelings, thoughts, and behaviors of humans, who have learned a set of cues that evoke a sexual or an erotic response. It includes behaviors well known to us, such as sexual intercourse and masturbation, as well as behaviors we do not readily identify as sexual, such as breast feeding, giving birth, and talking affectionately with someone. In addition, human sexuality includes our feelings, thoughts, attitudes, and values (Albas and Albas, 1989b). Furthermore, human sexuality involves issues of power, authority, and emotional and physical vulnerability in relationships (Boston Women's Health Book Collective, 1992).

We are sexual beings, and a large proportion of our lives consists of sexual daydreaming, fantasy, and desire; sexual pleasure, activity, joy, and pain. Given the fact that sexuality is such an important dimension of human experience, all societies are involved, in some way, in controlling the sexual behavior of their members. Although the ways in which sexual behavior is controlled have varied over time and from culture to culture, all societies have a set of rules or codes that define appropriate sexual behavior. Throughout U.S. history, Americans have been subject to one set of sexual codes or another. The codes we adhere to today have their roots in sexual attitudes and practices that existed hundreds, if not thousands, of years ago.

Before we discuss the history of human sexuality in Western society, two points must be made:

1. Although the historical descriptions emphasize the sexual codes that were most prevalent during a given historical period, it is not our intention to imply that sexual ideas and behavior have progressed directly from very strict and repressive codes of sexual conduct to more liberal sexual norms. Rather, sexual ideas and behavior change according to cyclical patterns, with periods of extremely or moderately repressive norms followed by periods of more liberal norms. In addition, at any given time, many different sexual codes, ideas, and behaviors coexist.

2. Generalizations about human behavior are always risky. Human attitudes and behavior are so flexible that they are never the same for all people or all groups. Thus, there are many variations in sexual attitudes and behavior. The historical period in which people live; the political and economic climate; the social organization of race, class, and gender; and factors such as sexual orientation, age, and religion all affect human attitudes and behavior.

Consider, for example, the effects of gender on sexual behavior. Women historically have experienced sexuality in terms of: reproduction, oppression (powerlessness), and vulnerability (victims of sexual assault). In contrast, men have experienced sexuality primarily in terms of power and control, passion and emotions, and freedom in sexual choice and behavior. Furthermore, sex and sexuality traditionally have been defined in terms of heterosexuality and monogamy, with homosexuality labeled as a form of deviance. Thus, for lesbians and gays, the experience of sexuality has been far more repressive and has involved a high degree of public concern and social control by outside forces such as the state.

Similarly, the sexuality of various racial groups (African Americans, Latinos, Native Americans, and Asians) as well as poor people of all races has been defined primarily by outsiders. Thus, these groups have been defined in scientific research or the popular culture as sexually promiscuous and uncontrolled. These definitions of sexuality often have been used in conjunction with other ideologies of racial inferiority to rationalize oppression and unequal treatment. Therefore, as you read this chapter, keep in mind that human sexuality is not static but rather is a dynamic or changing process that is continually being shaped and reshaped through the social organization of many diverse factors at any given time.

JEWISH TRADITIONS AND HUMAN SEXUALITY

Ancient Jewish tradition placed great emphasis on marriage and reproduction. Women and men who did not marry and have children were considered sinful. Marriage was the only appropriate context for sexual intercourse, the sole purpose of which was reproduction. Although in principle the norm of premarital chastity applied to both sexes, it was more rigidly applied to women. A woman was supposed to be a virgin at the time of marriage. If she was not, she could be put to death. Moreover, women could not own property, nor could they obtain a divorce without their husband's consent. A further restriction placed on women's sexuality can be seen in the case of a menstruating woman. Because menstruation was considered to be unclean, menstruating women were isolated from their husbands and other family members and were forbidden to engage in sexual activities. Nakedness, masturbation, and homosexuality were strongly forbidden. Although homosexuality was not mentioned in earlier Hebrew codes, it was made punishable by death in later Hebrew documents. Some scholars claim that early Judaism represented a transition from a more positive view of sexual behavior, a view that was prominent in ancient times, to a more restrictive view characteristic of the early Christian period (Harmatz and Novak, 1983).

The two ancient Jewish notions about human sexuality—reproduction as a married couple's obligation and male dominance over women in sexual relations—became a part of Christian as well as non-Christian doctrine and, to some degree, can still be found in contemporary U.S. sexual codes.

CHRISTIAN TRADITIONS AND HUMAN SEXUALITY

Although in the Gospels Jesus refers to marriage as a sacred union, the values of women, marriage, and sexuality decreased as Christian ideas of chastity took hold. The early Christian sexual tradition seems to have been influenced most by St. Paul, who was strongly opposed to sex whether it occurred inside or outside marriage. Paul believed that celibacy was superior to marriage and that all humans should strive for a chaste life. A person who could not resist sexual temptations could engage in sexual intercourse, but only within marriage.

In the fifth century, the Christian scholar St. Augustine continued Paul's tradition of condemning sexuality, and his influence lasted throughout the Middle Ages. Church documents of the eighth century specified that only the male-superior, or "missionary," position was to be used, because any other position might cause some enjoyment. People who engaged in other than the male-superior position faced a range of penalties (Harmatz and Novak, 1983).

During the thirteenth century, the church, through the writings of St. Thomas Aquinas, renewed its position on sexuality. Sexual intercourse was seen as animalistic, an activity to be avoided. Celibacy and

virginity were the ideals (Strong, Wilson, Clarke, and Johns, 1978). In addition, nakedness, looking at parts of the body, dancing, singing, and touching other people were all considered sinful.

The Protestant Reformation of the sixteenth century ushered in a diversity of views and attitudes concerning human sexuality. Religious reformer Martin Luther, for example, renounced celibacy as an unnatural and unrealistic goal for human beings. Leaving the priesthood to marry, he considered sex to be a natural and appropriate act when carried out within the context of marriage. Likewise, other theologians, such as John Calvin, argued against celibacy, believing that sex was a holy act when it occurred within marriage.

Although Christianity exerted considerable influence over people, not everyone adhered to its teachings concerning human sexuality. For example, it has been noted that during most historical periods sexual behavior varies according to social class. Often the middle classes followed the prevailing sexual mores more closely than did the aristocrats (upper classes) or the peasants (lower classes).

SEXUALITY IN THE UNITED STATES: AN OVERVIEW

PURITAN SEXUALITY In the seventeenth century, Puritan immigrants from England brought their Calvinist sexual traditions to the United States. The Puritans defined marriage as a covenant of God and thus the only legitimate mechanism for sex and procreation. Inside marriage, sex was an act that brought a wife and husband together morally and physically. The Puritans also believed that a husband was obliged to satisfy his wife physically. Outside marriage, sex was a sin and a threat to the institutions of marriage and the family. Sanctions against premarital and extramarital sex thus were very rigidly enforced. As in prior historical periods, sexual codes of conduct were especially restrictive and rigid regarding female sexuality.

Some of the Puritan views on sexuality can still be found in U.S. sexual attitudes and behavior. Writing in 1983 about the historical development of human sexuality, social scientists Morton Harmatz and Melinda Novak claimed that many of the sex laws still on the books in various states in the country are a legacy of the Puritan forefathers. For example, in

The restricted sexual attitudes during the Victorian period were reflected in women's dress, which was specifically designed to hide the body.

some communities it is still illegal to kiss on Sundays (a law that is rarely enforced). In general, the Puritan codes of conduct continued to dominate U.S. sexual norms well into the nineteenth century, when the Victorians introduced a new and, according to some researchers, even more rigid set of sexual taboos.

VICTORIAN SEXUALITY The Victorian era was characterized by a number of sexual taboos. In general, sex, particularly premarital sex, continued to be thought of in negative terms. At the base of the Victorian view of sexuality was the notion that any kind of sexual stimulation, especially orgasm, sapped a person's "vital forces." Both women and men were fully clothed in several layers during sexual intercourse so that nudity and human flesh would not provide them with excessive stimulation (Harmatz and Novak, 1983).

According to the Victorian codes, sexuality was basically a male phenomenon. In contrast, women were idealized and considered to be morally superior

to men in matters of sexuality. The prevailing belief was that decent women did not experience sexual desire. In fact, sexual desire, passion, and enjoyment in women were considered to be sinful. A woman who dared to express sexual feeling or enjoy sexual intercourse was considered to have loose morals.

In contrast, males were considered sexual animals who were driven by their lust and desires whether inside or outside marriage. Because men were perceived this way, their sexuality, including premarital and extramarital affairs, was accepted (although not necessarily approved of), whereas similar behaviors by women were condemned. This differing set of norms based on gender is referred to as the **sexual double standard**.

Whereas single women were to refrain from sex altogether, married women were taught that sex with their husbands was their wifely duty; that they must tolerate and accommodate the animalistic nature of men. Given men's alleged greater sexual appetite and needs, wives were taught to look the other way when their husbands had extramarital affairs or engaged in sexual activities with prostitutes.

The degree to which people adhered to the Victorian sexual codes varied from one social group to another. As in earlier periods, the rich and ruling elites basically ignored the restrictions and enjoyed considerable freedom in sexual behavior. At the other end of the class structure, the poor were also exempted from the prevailing codes. Sexual purity was reserved for middle-class white women; working-class, immigrant and nonwhite women were viewed as strongly sexual. In fact, they were defined as depraved and loose. This stereotype functioned as a rationalization for the continued mistreatment of these groups, especially the repeated rapes of African-American women by white men (Basow, 1992).

SEXUALITY AND SLAVERY If Victorian norms regarding sexuality applied only to certain groups of whites, they did not apply at all to blacks. Whereas for middle-class whites sex was considered sacred and ideally was restricted to marriage, black female and male slaves legally were not allowed to marry (although as we saw in Chapter 1 there were some exceptions), and they were routinely forced to mate with each other to reproduce and increase the slave population. The control and manipulation of slave sexuality, although oppressive for both sexes, was experienced differently by slave women and men. For men it took the form of being used as studs or being castrated to render them even more powerless and helpless. For women it included the experiences of concubine, mistress, and rape victim as well as the bearer of new generations of slaves. Slave women were robbed of sexual choice and had no legal protection from the rape of any white male that so chose to exploit them.

SEXUAL ATTITUDES AND BEHAVIOR IN THE TWENTIETH CENTURY

In the twentieth century, sexual attitudes and behavior continued to change. Researcher Carol Darling and her associates (1989) have divided the century into three major eras in terms of sexual behavior. The first era lasted from 1900 to the early 1950s. Despite moral standards that defined sex as acceptable only in the context of marriage, this period witnessed an increase in the number of single women and men reporting sexual involvement prior to marriage. The sexual double standard, however, remained largely in force.

The second major era, from the 1950s to 1970, was characterized by greater sexual permissiveness. Darling refers to this period as an "era of permissiveness with affection," because sex outside marriage was acceptable as long as it occurred within a love relationship and the couple expected to marry each other. The prosperity of this era coupled with the groundbreaking work of sex researchers such as Alfred Kinsey, and William Masters and Virginia Johnson, sparked an exploration of alternative lifestyles and a new openness about sex, leading into the third and present era.

Since 1970, technological advances leading to greater travel and increased job opportunities for women and men have resulted in a decreasing emphasis on the nuclear family and an increasing view that sexuality can be recreational as well as an expression of love. Women as a group have become less sexually inhibited as they have become more independent in other areas of their lives. As in the previous era, many people view sexual intercourse as natural and expected for both women and men in love relationships. The difference now is that the couple do not have to plan to marry to justify their sexu-

al conduct. Sex before marriage is no longer defined as deviant; rather, it has become the norm.

These changes in attitudes and behavior did not happen by chance. Not only did the mass movement of women into the labor force influence sexual attitudes and standards, but other major changes during this century such as advances in birth control technology (especially the Pill), the contemporary women's movement, the 1973 Supreme Court decision (*Roe v. Wade*) legalizing abortion, innovative lifestyles on college campuses, the delay in marriage and childbirth, and the lesbian and gay liberation movements all helped move U.S. society toward less rigid sexual standards. These changes have exerted a tremendous impact on sexuality, the family, and heterosexual and homosexual relationships. For example, improved birth control technology enabled women to spend less time bearing and raising children. This had the effect of separating sexual intercourse from reproduction, which in turn contributed to a wider acceptance of sex outside marriage (Lieberman, 1985).

SEXUAL ATTITUDES AND BEHAVIORS IN THE 1990s The sexual liberalism that so many have written or spoken of in the past few decades may have peaked during the early 1980s, especially for people 18 to 29 years of age and for those who have completed some college (Basow, 1992). Specifically, people may be less likely to engage in casual sex. In general terms, however, the permissive pattern of the 1980s has continued into the 1990s. Females and males of all ages continue to be more sexually active than their counterparts of a few generations ago.

Given the more open sexual climate in which we live, people today receive a variety of messages about their sexuality and act on them in very different ways than in the past. The later age of marriage has increased the likelihood that women and men who marry will enter such a relationship sexually experienced. In addition, the high rate of divorce means that an increasing number of older adults are looking for new sexual partners. As previously indicated, a majority of people condone sex between unmarried people. However, many groups (such as some older adults and those who are religiously devout) continue to take a moral stance against what they perceive to be contemporary sexual permissiveness (D'Emilio and Freedman, 1988).

Sexual acts that were once considered deviant are widely accepted today. Although discrimination continues against lesbians and gays, Americans—particularly younger Americans—are more accepting of homosexuality. Despite these changes, however, some remnants of past traditions remain with us. For example, although the sexual double standard has diminished, males are still expected to take the initiative in heterosexual contact and in controlling sexual activities (Grauerholz and Serpe, 1985). Women, meanwhile, continue to face more restrictions on their sexuality than men. For example, they are required to be physically attractive, and their sense of self-worth is still often defined in terms of their sexual attractiveness. At the same time, however, they still must not be too sexually active or else they will be defined as "loose women."

THE MEDIA AND SEXUALITY During the 1970s and 1980s the mass media played a tremendous role in changing sexual attitudes and behavior by presenting and legitimizing a wide range of sexual role models and behaviors. Films, television programs, novels, and other media portrayed sexually active women and men, married and single, lesbian and gay, younger and older, engaging in a wide range of sexual behaviors. For females, major sex surveys conducted by popular women's magazines helped to popularize and validate a new sense of sexual freedom. Although most of these surveys were not highly scientific, they provided us with some interesting insights into female and male sexuality in the 1980s.

A SEXUAL REVOLUTION? Do these fundamental changes in sexuality represent a sexual revolution? Some people say yes, given the broad scope of the changes. Others contend that there has been no revolution, just the continued evolution of sexual norms. There is little doubt that attitudes and behavior have changed toward more liberal and permissive standards, but it is also a fact that many individuals and groups still hold securely to traditional sexual norms and values.

Some observers claim that the so-called sexual revolution of the last half of the twentieth century really amounts to a drastic change in female sexual behavior. Probably the most revolutionary shift in female sexuality reported by most researchers is the increase in and the convergence of the rates of sexual intercourse among unmarried females and males. Prior to 1970, the reported rate of sexual intercourse for single males was almost twice that for females. Since 1970, however, the reported rates for females and males are within 10 percentage points of each other (Darling, Kallen, and VanDusen, 1989), indicating that women have become more permissive in both sexual attitudes and behavior.

Researcher Morton Hunt (1974) has argued that a revolution has occurred only if institutional structures have changed such that traditional attitudes and behaviors have been replaced with a radically new set of attitudes and behaviors. In the case of sexuality, for example, a revolution would include the displacement of vaginal intercourse by other sex acts or an increase in sexual activities that would alter the relationship between marriage and sex, such as mate sharing or swapping and mutually agreed-upon extramarital sex. Until such institutional change occurs we cannot speak of a sexual revolution. Although Hunt's statement is over 20 years old, his linking of revolution to major institutional change is still relevant.

SEXUALITY AS SOCIAL LEARNING

Equally as important as the question of whether a sexual revolution has occurred are questions such as How do we become sexual beings? and What factors contribute to changes in our sexual attitudes and behaviors? Anthropologists have long shown that human sexuality is defined and learned within a particular cultural context. Thus, what constitutes sexuality will vary from one culture to another (Caulfield, 1985). In this section we consider sexual behavior as a learned social product.

Since the late nineteenth century, when Sigmund Freud first introduced his beliefs about the nature of human sexuality, the general public as well as professionals such as psychologists, social workers, and sex therapists have been influenced by his theories of human sexuality. According to Freud, the sex drive, which he viewed as a biologically determined force, is the motivator for all human behavior. In the twentieth century, Alfred Kinsey's extensive sex research reflected his agreement with Freud that human sexuality is biologically determined. Both men believed that humans have innate sexual desires that require gratification. Such desires cannot go unchecked in a society, however. Left unchecked, these desires would lead to uncontrolled sexual activity, which in turn would generate social chaos. Thus, through its sexual codes, society forces the individual to repress these desires or channel them into sexually appropriate behaviors.

Even if an innate sexual drive exists in human beings, it seems clear from a variety of research across academic disciplines that this drive is given shape and direction by culture. The sexual feelings and desires that we experience may seem innate, natural, and beyond our control, but we are not born knowing how to think, feel, or behave sexually. Cultural norms *prescribe* (tell us what we should do) and *proscribe* (tell us what we should not do) our sexual behavior. They determine what is or is not sexually attractive and stimulating, why we should or should not engage in sexual behavior, and how we should or should not feel sexually.

According to social scientists John Gagnon and William Simon (1973, 1984), sexual behavior is not very different from other behavior. It does not come naturally. Rather, it is socially constructed. Thus, from this point of view, what Freud commonly referred to as a *sex drive* is really something we have learned in a particular social environment. Like other behaviors, our sexual behavior is guided by cultural scripts that are similar to the scripts that guide the actions of actors. In learning our culture's sexual guidelines, we in effect create or invent our capacity for sexual behavior.

Sexual behavior is guided specifically by sexual scripts. **Sexual scripts** are simply our society's guidelines or blueprints for defining and engaging in sexual behaviors. We begin learning these scripts very early in life through the process of socialization.

SOURCES OF SEXUAL LEARNING

In earliest childhood, as we are learning other important norms of our culture we are also simultaneously learning about our sexuality, first from **significant others**, people such as parents, friends, relatives, and religious figures, who figure most importantly in our lives, and later from the point of view of **generalized others**, that is, the viewpoint of society at large. We also learn about our sexuality in school and from the

mass media. Some of the cultural information about our sexuality is consciously presented and learned; however, we learn much of it unconsciously.

LEARNING SEXUALITY IN THE FAMILY Many authorities on early childhood behavior believe that the family is the first and most significant agent of socialization. Where sexuality is concerned, however, the evidence suggests that children learn very little from their parents. For example, in a 1985 report of survey data on sexuality, almost one-half of those surveyed reported that their parents did not teach them anything about sexuality (Coles and Stokes, 1985). What little most children do learn about sexuality in the family is often in the form of prohibitions (for example, a negative response when a child touches her or his genitals).

Parents often go to great lengths to desexualize their children's lives. This often includes going out of their way to present themselves as asexual. They stop touching each other or showing any signs of intimacy when the children are around. They do not discuss sexuality around children except in hushed tones, and they often become embarrassed and speechless when their children ask them a frank question about some aspect of sexuality.

Although research (DeLamaster, 1987) indicates that sexual play during late infancy and early childhood is positive preparation for adult sexuality, many children are prohibited from engaging in such activities. This kind of reaction tends to define children's sexuality as something that is dirty, secretive, and distasteful. Another way in which parents give children a negative feeling about their sexuality is through their use of euphemisms for the sexual organs.

 What did you learn about sexuality from your parents? Did they discuss the issue with you in an open and honest manner? What information did they leave out? What happened when or if you explored your body? What euphemisms did they use for the genitals?

On an often hidden side of the family, thousands of children are sexually abused within their families every year. Although both sexes are victims of sexual abuse, females are far more likely to be abused than are males. (We examine child sexual abuse in more detail in Chapter 12.) Such abuse often has a negative affect on the adult sexuality of these victims in a number of ways. A growing body of evidence, for example, indicates that childhood sexual abuse may cause sexual problems in adult life, primarily by desensitizing the individual to her or his body. This might cause the person in adulthood to be either restricted or excessive in her or his sexual behaviors (Basow, 1992). New and interesting research has emerged that suggests a possible connection between female child sexual abuse and eating disorders in women (see, for example, Iazetto, 1989).

GENDER DIFFERENCES IN SEXUAL SCRIPTS

Parents also tend to communicate the content of sexual behavior to their children differently depending on the sex of the child. Despite changes in attitudes about gender-specific behavior, certain aspects of the double standard remain, and parents continue to pass these on to their children. For example, parents tend to be more open with daughters than with sons about reproduction and its relationship to sexual activities as well as the morality of sex. In fact, because females can become pregnant, the sexual scripts they learn tie sexual activity almost exclusively to reproduction and family life. Boys, on the other hand, learn that their sexuality is connected to society's notion of masculinity and their ability to achieve in different areas of life (O'Neil, 1981). Many parents also practice a sexual double standard whereby they place more restrictions on their daughters' sexuality than on that of their sons. Thus, female movements, social activities, and friendships are far more guarded and chaperoned than are male activities.

A number of researchers have identified several areas of gender difference in traditional sexual scripting:

- Interest in sex is part of the male sexual script but not part of the female sexual script.

- Males are expected to be the initiators and to take control of sexual activities; females are expected to be submissive and to conform.

- The sexual script for males emphasizes achievement and frequency of sexual activities; for females the emphasis is on monogamy and exclusiveness (for example, saving herself for the one right man in her life).

- Early or unmarried sexual activity carries little stigma for males. In fact, it sometimes elevates them in the eyes of their peers. Early or unmarried sexual activity for females carries a negative stigma and is subject to the criticism and moral judgment of others. Common epithets such as "whore" and "slut" are applied to their behavior.

- Exposure of the body is far more acceptable for males than females. Females are taught, early on, to keep their bodies covered by wearing restrictive clothing and sitting with their legs crossed.

Such sex-role socialization, it seems, produces some definite differences in the meanings that females and males attach to sex. In general, females connect sex with feelings of love, affection, and commitment, whereas males connect sex with achievement, control, and power, or purely in terms of sexual release. This is true for same-sex relationships as well as heterosexual relationships (Blumstein and Schwartz, 1983; Lawson, 1988). Moreover, women tend to have fewer sexual experiences overall than men, and their sexual experiences (especially their first) are usually with someone to whom they feel romantically attached. For women the major pleasures of sex are the feelings of love, attachment, and being needed; for men the physical aspect of sex generally is most pleasurable. Although these gender differences in the meaning of sex do exist, we should note that most men, like most women, prefer having love and sex together, and, like most women, most men rank love well ahead of sex in terms of overall importance for their life satisfaction (Basow, 1992).

Keep in mind that these are generalizations about sexual learning. Not all females and males learn traditional sexual scripts. The exact content of sexual scripts varies according to a number of factors including race and ethnicity, social class, and religious orientation. Thus, whatever sexual script we learn, our sexual behavior can change as circumstances change.

PEER INFLUENCE

By the time children reach adolescence, the influence of the family diminishes, and the influence of peers increases. Various studies have found that peer pressure is probably the single most important factor, next to physiological readiness, that determines when adolescents become sexually active (Smith, Udry, and Morris, 1985). Peer pressure to engage in sexual activity is especially strong among young males. Male peers tend to influence each other to explore their sexuality, while

Peer pressure to engage in sexual activity is especially strong among young males, whereas female peers encourage secrecy and abstinence.

Ads, such as this one, not only sell products, but they also shape and reinforce a cultural view of women as sex objects.

female peers encourage secrecy and abstinence ("How College Women and Men Feel," 1987). Peers also serve as an important source of information concerning sexuality. Unfortunately, much of what peers think they "know" is actually inaccurate. Thus, peers frequently mislead and misinform each other.

SEXUAL SCRIPTS AND THE MASS MEDIA   As previously discussed, sex has increasingly moved out of the privacy of the bedroom and into the public realm. One of the most visible manifestations of contemporary sexuality is the growth of a multibillion-dollar sex industry. Thousands of movie houses still feature X-rated movies, even though X-rated cable television stations have garnered a significant corner of the sex market. Sex magazines like *Oui*, *Playboy, Hustler*, and *Playgirl*, though diminishing somewhat in popularity, still enjoy a wide readership. Moreover, advertisers routinely use sexuality—particularly female sexuality—to sell a variety of products from heavy construction equipment to designer jeans to candy.

Similarly, television programming increasingly depicts sexual situations and behaviors. This trend is apparent in the content of daytime soap operas and talk shows, evening shows and movies, and perhaps most explicitly in cable channels devoted to sexual movies and shows. The personal ads, a feature of most major newspapers, also reflects the increasing openness of today's sexuality. In such columns, women and men publicly advertise for the type of sexual partner or experiences they want.

Celebrities have grown out of our new sexual openness. People like Dr. Ruth Westheimer have developed large followings by talking frankly and openly on radio and television talk shows about almost every conceivable aspect of human sexuality. Contemporary music, especially rock, rhythm and blues, and rap, often contains lyrics that are sexually explicit. Children as young as 3 or 4 years of age can be heard repeating lyrics such as "I want to sex you up," "Shake that bootie," and "Do it to me one more time." In addition, music videos are full of men grabbing or holding their crotch and gyrating women and men in sexually suggestive clothing, positions, and situations.

SEXUAL ORIENTATIONS

It is impossible to discuss human sexuality without discussing sexual orientation. Contrary to popular belief, sexual orientation, whether heterosexual or homosexual, is not synonymous with sexual behavior. **Sexual orientation** involves not only whom one chooses as a sexual partner, but, more fundamentally, the ways in which people understand and identify themselves.

Although Americans tend to think of sexual orientation in terms of clear-cut categories—for example, heterosexual versus homosexual—various sex researchers have concluded that fundamental categories of sexual desire do not exist for most of us. Rather, sexual desire is constructed in the context of social relationships and identities (Andersen, 1993). Cultural historian and sex researcher Shere Hite

As we have seen, the mass media are a major source of information concerning sexuality. Using a sociological perspective, conduct a content analysis of television programs from each decade starting with the 1950s, focusing on the sexuality and sexual activity portrayed or implied during each decade. Compare sexuality over time but also across race, class, gender, and sexual orientation. Wherever possible, include programs that have major nonwhite, lesbian, or gay characters and that represent different social classes. Develop a list of behaviors you want to observe and tally the number of times you find them in the programs you analyze. When you are finished, analyze your results, contrasting the portrayal of sexuality during different time periods and across different groups. In addition, compare the television portrayal of sexuality with research data of sexuality in the United States throughout each corresponding historical period.

(1976) believes that we are born with a natural desire to relate to people of the same as well as the other sex. Society, however, teaches us to inhibit all of our sexual desires except those for partners with whom we can procreate. Regardless of whether we accept Hite's hypothesis, it is clear that U.S. culture historically has espoused **heterosexism**, the belief that heterosexuality is the only right, natural, and acceptable sexual orientation and that any other orientation is pathological.

Heterosexism is so strong in U.S. society that most sex research is based on the assumption of heterosexuality. This assumption overlooks the fact that many people have a homosexual orientation and even more people have engaged in homosexual behavior at least once in their life. For example, by age 45, somewhere between one-fifth and one-third of all men and one-sixth of all women have experienced at least one homosexual encounter (Basow, 1992). Furthermore, research suggests that sexual orientation forms a continuum with at least four recognizable levels of orientation (see, for example, Maier, 1984). At the two extremes are exclusively heterosexual and exclusively homosexual orientations, with bisexuality and asexuality falling somewhere in the middle.

HETEROSEXUALITY

Heterosexuality refers to the preference for sexual activities with a person of the other sex. In a more sociological and political sense, heterosexuality also includes an individual's community, lifestyle, and core identity. Most research to date (for example, Maugh, 1990) indicates that more than 91 percent of Americans identify themselves as exclusively heterosexual. As the previous discussion indicates, however, some social scientists view sexual orientation, like other aspects of our identity, as an ongoing process that can vary considerably over the life course. For those who take this viewpoint, the degree to which we identify ourselves as heterosexual reflects in part the extent to which we have internalized society's messages and definitions of what is and is not acceptable. Given the stigma associated with sexual orientations other than heterosexuality, it is not surprising that most people claim (at least publicly) to be exclusively heterosexual.

Social scientists utilizing a feminist perspective maintain that in the United States, sexuality generally and sexual activities specifically that are associated with a heterosexual orientation are *phallocentric*, male-centered, and are defined almost exclusively in terms of genital intercourse and male orgasm. According to this point of view, the ideology of heterosexuality assumes that women exist for men, that their bodies and services are men's property. If a woman rejects this definition of normal sexuality she is stigmatized no matter who she chooses as a sexual partner (see Bunch, 1979). For men, the notion of heterosexual intercourse, with its assumptions of male power and control; male lust, passion, and aggression; and the male as the initiator of sexual activity, is the proving ground for acceptable male sexuality and identity in this society. It also provides the script that most men adopt, with some individual modification, as the foundation of both their masculinity and sexual activity.

Some feminist social scientists such as Adrienne Rich (1980) have argued that making heterosexuality compulsory stymies or restricts the sexuality of males as well as females. Rich suggests that both heterosexism and **homophobia**—an extreme and irrational fear or hatred of homosexuals—act to inhibit the possibility of some women and men finding emotional and sexual satisfaction with same-sex partners.

HOMOSEXUALITY

Like heterosexuality, **homosexuality** refers to both identity and behavior. It is part of a person's core identity and includes whom she or he defines as an acceptable sexual partner but does not consist solely of sexual preference. Thus, to label homosexuality entirely in terms of choice of sexual partner as is often done, distorts our perception of lesbians and gays. Certainly we do not define heterosexuals entirely or even primarily in terms of their choice of sexual partner. But, what if we did? Consider the questions in the "Heterosexual Questionnaire" presented in the FYI box. If you are heterosexual, do you find such questions offensive? Can you see and understand the indignity engendered when we routinely ask such questions of lesbians and gays?

Like heterosexuality, the exact determination of homosexuality is unknown. As we have seen, some scientists explain both homosexuality and heterosexuality in terms of social learning, social experiences, and role models. However, no specific social experience or type of social relationship has been found to be significant in the development of human sexual preference (Bell, Weinberg, and Hammersmith, 1981). At the same time, there is no conclusive evidence to support the argument that sexual orientation is determined entirely by biology. Nonetheless, the debate over the relative roles of social environment and biology in determining sexual orientation continues to spark controversy among a number of groups in society, including scientists, gay activists, and religious and political leaders.

Recently, those who take a biological stance in this debate have received a boost from research results that suggest that sexual orientation (at least in men) is determined in large part by genetic factors. If it turns out that sexual orientation is genetically determined, then can we continue to define either homosexuality or heterosexuality as sexual preference? In the next section we briefly examine some of the most recent research that suggests a biological basis of sexual orientation.

A BIOLOGICAL BASIS OF HOMOSEXUALITY   In a 1991 study, a psychologist at Northwestern University and a psychiatrist at the Boston University School of Medicine, interviewed a number of gay men

In contrast to popular images of the casual sexual behavior of gays, many gay couples share long-term monogamous relationships that often include adopted children.

1. When and how did you first realize that you were a heterosexual?

2. What do you think caused your heterosexuality?

3. Do your parents know? If so, how did they react when you told them?

4. Is it possible your heterosexuality is just a phase you may grow out of?

5. Is it possible your heterosexuality stems from a neurotic fear of others of the same sex?

6. If you have never slept with a person of the same sex, is it possible that all you need is a good gay lover?

7. If heterosexuality is normal, why are a disproportionate number of mental patients heterosexual?

8. If you choose to have children, would you want them to be heterosexual, knowing the problems they would face?

9. A disproportionate majority of child molesters are heterosexuals. Do you really consider it safe to expose your children to heterosexual teachers?

10. Why do you insist on making your heterosexuality public? Can't you just be what you are and keep it to yourself?

11. Why do heterosexuals place so much emphasis on sex?

12. Why are heterosexuals so promiscuous?

13. Why do you make a point of attributing heterosexuality to famous people? Is it to justify your own heterosexuality?

14. Why do heterosexuals feel compelled to seduce others into their lifestyle?

15. Just what do women and men do in bed together? How can they truly know how to please each other, being so anatomically different?

Source: Adapted from Martin Rochlin, 1982. "The Heterosexual Questionnaire." Reprinted from *Changing Men,* Madison, WI.

---

and their brothers. They discovered that in 52 percent of the cases in which a gay man had an identical twin, the twin was also gay. By contrast, such gay pairs were found in only 22 percent of the fraternal twins studied and 11 percent of adoptive (nongenetically related) brothers. Based on these results the researchers suggested a genetic contribution to sexual orientation, because brothers in the study who were most like each other genetically were most likely to be gay. Even so, however, sexual orientation is not completely a genetic trait. These researchers admit that environment is also important. It is not, however, just the social environment but also the biological environment, which includes diet, stress, and prenatal events, that might affect one twin and not the other (Griffin, 1991).

A few months before the findings from the twins study were made public, Simon LeVay, a neuroscientist at the Salk Institute, reported his research findings from an examination of autopsied brain tissue from 41 cadavers; 19 homosexual males, 16 heterosexual males, and 6 heterosexual women. LeVay found that a part of the brain believed to be responsible for the male sex drive was smaller in homosexual than in heterosexual men.

Both of these studies suggest that male sexual orientation is an innate condition that develops early and that is not socially influenced. Many people reject this conclusion and challenge the studies on which it is based. Some critics of the twins study say that instead of proving that genetics determines homosexuality, the study simply confirmed the obvious fact that twins are more likely to have the same sort of shaping influences. A more meaningful study, they contend, would examine twins raised apart. Critics of the LeVay study also claim that no single gene can account for a complex behavior like homosexuality. LeVay himself cautions that he found only a difference in the brain structure of gay and heterosexual men and not a conclusive answer to the question of sexual orientation ("Born or Bred?" 1992).

In both of these studies the subjects were predominantly male. Although no comparable research has been conducted on a significantly large sample of women, plans for such research are said to be underway in the United States. Because they have been left out of the research, many lesbians are wary of these findings, especially as applied to lesbians. For those lesbians who say that their choice of lesbianism is as much a feminist statement as a sexual one, the debate over the biological versus social environment determination of sexual orientation is of little interest.

In any event, a cautionary note is needed here. The research cited here is suggestive: It simply suggests that certain genes affect sexual orientation. Far from resolving the nature versus nurture debate, these studies have simply intensified it. For example, if sexual orientation is in the brain, when does it get there: before birth, during childhood, at puberty? Current research does not answer these questions (Griffin, 1991; "Born or Bred?" 1992). Further studies are needed to determine the roles of genetics and the environment in determining sexual orientation.

HOW WIDESPREAD IS HOMOSEXUALITY?

Because homosexuality is so stigmatized, it is difficult to determine with any precision how many women and men are homosexual. In the 1950s, Alfred Kinsey* and his associates (1953) reported that 28 percent of their sample of almost 8000 women had experienced a homosexual activity. Almost 25 years later, Hite (1976) reported that 8 percent of the women in her sample said that they actually preferred sex with another woman. A few years later, in her study of male sexuality, Hite (1981) found that 11 percent of the 7000 men in her sample preferred to have sex with a person of their same sex. Same-sex preference is clearly different from simply having a single homosexual encounter, as in the Kinsey study.

There is not total agreement about the extent or prevalence of homosexuality in today's society. A national study of male sexual behavior released in 1993,

for example, reported that only 2 percent of the men surveyed had engaged in homosexual sex and that only 1 percent considered themselves exclusively homosexual (Barringer, 1993). These findings challenge traditional estimates of male homosexuality, but they also raise questions regarding their own accuracy. Given the prevalence of AIDS and the stigma associated with this disease, are people telling the truth? In any event, a good estimate today is that somewhere between 3 and 10 percent of both women and men are primarily or exclusively homosexual, with more males than females reporting being homosexual (Basow, 1992).

This dichotomy of heterosexual versus homosexual, however, may be misleading. According to Kinsey (1948), few of us are completely and exclusively heterosexual or homosexual. Rather, there are some aspects of both orientations in all of us. Kinsey expressed this idea with a rating scale (0 to 6) of heterosexuality and homosexuality, in which each number on the scale represents the degree to which people have heterosexual or homosexual experiences (see Figure 6.1). Using this rating, Kinsey found that almost 80 percent of 25-year-old white male respondents in his study were exclusively heterosexual, and 3 percent were exclusively homosexual. The remaining respondents fell somewhere along the scale from 1 to 5.

Given Kinsey's earlier findings and the more contemporary work of sex researcher John Gagnon (1977), we cannot speak of homosexuality as if it were a monolithic behavioral and attitudinal pattern. Homosexuality varies in terms of importance, its

FIGURE 6.1 Heterosexual–Homosexual Rating Scale

Source: From Alfred Kinsey, W. B. Pomeroy, and C. E. Martin, 1948, *Sexual Behavior in the Human Male* (Philadelphia, PA: Saunders), p. 470. Reprinted by permission of The Kinsey Institute for Research in Sex, Gender, and Reproduction, Inc.

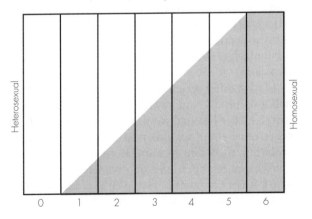

*Kinsey's trailblazing research on sexual behavior in the United States almost single-handedly touched off a sexual revolution of sorts. That is, Kinsey's goal was to tabulate human sexual behavior, and in so doing he brought sex out of the closet and into the minds of millions of people. Since his death in 1956 there has been very little follow-up research on Americas' sexual activities. Exceptions include the pioneering work of sex researchers William Masters and Virginia Johnson; Shere Hite's mail-in surveys on sexual behavior, including its methodological flaws; and a sprinkling of surveys using specialized groups such as college students as subjects or focusing on sexual attitudes as opposed to actual sexual behavior. As a consequence, over 45 years later, Kinsey's work (with its own serious flaws and outdated population sample) remains the definitive statement on sexual behavior in the United States, this in spite of the fact that his samples were not scientifically random and the subjects were almost all white, well educated, and young. Few, if any, were poverty-level people, and the sample was geographically skewed, centering primarily on the Midwest and the Northeast, with few subjects from the South or West (Lyon, 1992).

organization, and its actualization in people's lives. It is sufficient to say here that, except for the gender of one's partner, the sexual attitudes, behaviors, and relationships of lesbians and gays do not differ significantly from those of heterosexual couples. In Chapter 7 we provide a more in-depth discussion of lesbian and gay lifestyles.

BISEXUALITY

Bisexuality is difficult to define. On the one hand it refers to individuals who do not have an exclusive sexual preference for one sex over the other. Rather, a bisexual has partners of both sexes either simultaneously or at different times. On the other hand, as with other sexual orientations, bisexuality also represents an identity and a lifestyle. As we have already noted, an important aspect of sexual orientation is how one defines oneself. As with homosexuality, it is difficult to know exactly how many people are bisexual. One recent research report indicated that somewhere between 5 and 6 percent of Americans reported being bisexual since the onset of adulthood. In general, however, estimates are that from 10 to 25 percent of the adult population are bisexual (Maugh, 1990).

Like homosexuality, bisexuality is stigmatized in the larger society. In addition, bisexuals are often rejected by the homosexual community as well. Many people do not believe that people can really be bisexual; they have to be one thing (heterosexual) or another (homosexual) (Sapiro, 1990). This definitional problem, then, suggests that it is not possible to place people into neat categories of sexual preference or orientation. Therefore, Hite's (1981) suggestion that the terms *homosexual* and *heterosexual* be used not as nouns but as adjectives is noteworthy. Perhaps *bisexual* should also be used as an adjective to describe people's activities and not people themselves, particularly given that few people are completely bisexual.

As with other sexual orientations, the exact origins of bisexuality are unknown. Some evidence suggests, however, that bisexual women and men perceive and experience their sexuality somewhat differently. According to Phillip Blumstein and Pepper Schwartz (1977), for example, bisexual women feel that they have a variety of emotional as well as sexual needs, all

of which cannot be satisfied by either sex exclusively. In contrast, bisexual men place greater emphasis on a need for sexual variety.

The complex interaction of our biology and culture is evidenced in the fact that regardless of how we choose to express our sexuality, our bodies experience a physiological response pattern when we are sexually stimulated. Next we turn to a discussion of the human sexual-response cycle and some of the ways that we express our sexuality.

THE PHYSIOLOGY OF SEXUALITY

As noted earlier, until the mid 1960s, most of the available scientific information concerning our sexuality came from the studies of Alfred Kinsey (1948, 1953). Although Kinsey told us much about what people did, how they did it, and how often, his research told us little about what goes on in our bodies when we are sexually stimulated. For example, what, if anything, happens to our pulse? Our blood pressure? What about our genitals and other areas of our bodies? How do they respond to sexual stimulation? In the next section we address these and other questions concerning human sexual response. You can refer to Appendix A for an explanation and diagrams of anatomical references.

THE SEXUAL-RESPONSE CYCLE

Numerous studies of the sexuality of Americans have been conducted over the years. It was not until the pioneering work of sex researchers William Masters and Virginia Johnson (1966), however, that we began to understand, with more clarity, the physiological processes of sexual response in human beings. Based on over 10 years of systematic research on copulating couples (including the observation and manipulation of sex in a laboratory setting), Masters and Johnson recorded and described in some detail the physiological factors associated with sexuality and **erotic arousal**—the stimulation or awakening of sexual desires that we feel ourselves or that we invoke in others. According to Masters and Johnson, all people go through the same four phases of sexual response: excitement, plateau, orgasm, and resolution.

The sex research team of William Masters and Virginia Johnson destroyed many of the popular myths about human sexual behavior in their studies of how the body responds to erotic stimulation during masturbation and sexual intercourse.

EXCITEMENT PHASE The *excitement phase* begins the sexual response process and may last anywhere from a few minutes to several hours. In this phase the body responds to sexual stimulation. This stimulation can include any one or a variety of stimuli such as sights, images, sounds, touches, thoughts, and smells, and it varies from one individual to another. Most often this response is achieved through tactile stimulation of an **erogenous zone**—an area of the body that is particularly sensitive to sexual stimulation. The changes that occur in this phase include two important processes: *vasocongestion*, whereby body tissues became engorged or swollen with blood, and *myotonia*, whereby tension in the muscles increases as stimulation continues. The excitement phase is characterized by an increase in blood pressure and heart rate.

Females in this phase experience a secretion of body fluids that lubricate the vagina. If stimulation continues, the clitoris swells from engorgement. Internally, a *tenting* process occurs whereby the uterus expands (sometimes to twice its normal size) and elevates into the cavity of the body, pulling up the cervix and the upper end of the vagina. Other areas of the body may also exhibit change. For example, the breasts may enlarge, and the nipples may become hard and erect. (Nipple erection can occur in males as well.) For males, the penis becomes erect and moves away from the body as it fills with blood. The scrotum elevates, and the testes increase in size.

PLATEAU PHASE If sexual stimulation continues individuals move into the *plateau phase*, in which both heart rate and blood pressure intensify. In addition to the physiological characteristics of the excitement phase, the coronal ridge of the penile and labia minora glans enlarge further, and the color deepens from a pinkish to a bright red or deep wine coloring. This phase can last only a few minutes or for quite some time. For example, if a couple wish to prolong the plateau, they might decrease stimulation for a while and then begin it again.

For women in this phase, as the vagina responds to continued stimulation, the vaginal glands continue to secrete lubricating fluid, and the diameter of the vagina decreases by almost one-half, providing pleasurable friction for both partners during intercourse. In men, the head of the penis increases in size, and the abdomen and buttocks tighten. Almost involuntary pelvic movements begin, and if the male is within a couple of years of puberty, a few drops of a clear preejaculatory fluid may be secreted. Although the male has not ejaculated, the female can become pregnant because this preejaculatory fluid may contain some sperm cells.

ORGASMIC PHASE With continued stimulation both females and males enter into the *orgasmic phase*. In this phase, the sexual emotions and excitement built up in the previous phases reach a peak and are released in an **orgasm**, the involuntary release of pelvic congestion and accumulated muscular tension through rhythmic contractions in the genitals of both sexes and also through ejaculation in males. In this phase several physiological changes occur in the body: Heartbeat and blood pressure may double, the pattern of breathing may become deeper and faster, the facial muscles may contort the face, and brainwave patterns may change (Masters and Johnson, 1966). Orgasm is generally followed by a feeling of euphoria—a sense of contentment, well-being, and extreme relaxation.

According to Masters and Johnson's research, the clitoris, not the vagina, is the central organ of orgasmic response in women. This finding refutes the widely accepted Freudian notion that a vaginal orgasm is more sexually mature in women than a clitoral orgasm. For most men, orgasm usually includes **ejaculation**, the forceful release of semen through the meatus. Once ejaculation starts a man cannot voluntarily stop it.

Orgasm is not the same for all women and men, nor is it the same from one erotic experience to the next. For men, each subsequent ejaculation during a relatively short period of time will be less forceful and produce less semen. Orgasm can come as quickly as a few minutes after coitus for men, whereas women generally require between 10 and 15 minutes of foreplay and intercourse to achieve orgasm. Although women are capable of achieving multiple orgasms successively during a specific sexual activity, only 15 percent actually do, primarily because their partners stop sexual stimulation too soon (McCary, 1978). In contrast, few men can achieve successive orgasms during a given sexual activity. A few can achieve a second orgasm shortly after the first orgasm, but this ability decreases with age.

RESOLUTION PHASE   Finally, after orgasm and the cessation of stimulation, the body returns to its preexcitement physiological state. During this *resolution phase* physiological functions such as blood pressure, heart and pulse rates, breathing, and muscle tension return to their normal state. In females, the vagina decrease in size, and in males, the penis loses its erection. Masters and Johnson found that during this phase men experience a **refractory period**, a state of rest or relaxation that can last anywhere from a few minutes (in young males) to several hours (in older men). Men must remain in this period until it is completed. During this time they are physiologically incapable of rearousal (entering the excitement phase again) and generally lose all interest in sex.

For women the resolution period generally lasts only a few minutes, although this varies with age. Unlike men, women in this phase may continue to be sexually aroused and achieve subsequent orgasms. Figure 6.2 illustrates the sexual response patterns that were identified by Masters and Johnson for females and males. As the figures reveal, considerable variation exists between female and male responses. Although males generally exhibit the same pattern, females may experience any one of three patterns: (1) a response similar to the male response except with the possibility for multiple orgasms, (2) an attainment of the plateau phase and remaining without experiencing orgasm, and (3) rapid attainment of orgasm followed by a quick resolution.

Although the discussion of sexual response patterns refers to heterosexual sexuality, "neither male nor female sexuality is limited by genital geography" (Hite, 1976:389). From the point of view of physical pleasure we can relate erotically to either sex depending on our feelings (Hite, 1976). In the next section, we examine some of the social-psychological and emotional manifestations of human sexuality; some of the ways in which people express their sexual selves.

HUMAN SEXUAL EXPRESSION

Human sexual expression covers a wide variety of behaviors. Heterosexual intercourse is simply one of many ways to express human sexuality. Sexual expression ranges from activities involving only the self—**autoeroticism**—to activities involving one or more other individuals (such as "swapping" or group sex).

AUTOEROTICISM

Some of the most common and recognizable forms of autoeroticism are masturbation, sexual fantasy, and erotic dreams. Until recent times, U.S. society placed particularly heavy restrictions on autoeroticism. Today, however, a range of such behaviors is considered acceptable.

MASTURBATION   "Don't knock masturbation. It's having sex with someone I deeply love." This statement by film director Woody Allen reflects the attitudes of many people in this society for whom masturbation is a common form of sexual expression and enjoyment. **Masturbation** involves gaining sexual pleasure from the erotic stimulation of self through caressing or otherwise stimulating the genitals. Masturbatory behavior is said to begin in infancy when children accidentally discover the pleasure to be derived from rubbing, squeezing, caressing, or otherwise stimulating their genitals. For many people, this is the beginning of a lifelong way of expressing their sexuality.

Although masturbation is becoming more common among women, boys and adult men tend to masturbate more often than girls and women. In the 1950s, Kinsey and his colleagues found that 92 percent of males and 58 percent of females masturbated to achieve orgasm. A subsequent study found that about 67 percent of males and 20 percent of females reported having masturbated by the time they were 17 years of age (Wilson, 1975). As women and men age they masturbate less frequently, but they do not stop altogether. One study found that as many as 43 percent of men and 33 percent of women in their 70s masturbate (Brecher, 1984).

Not only are there gender differences in masturbation rates, but women and men also differ in terms of their attitudes toward masturbation. For example,

according to sex researcher Hans Hessellund (1976), masturbation functions more as a supplement to sexual life for men, whereas for women it functions more as a substitute for intercourse. Moreover, females tend to begin masturbation for orgasm at much later ages than males, sometimes for the first time in their 20s or 30s (Lindsey, 1990). Interestingly, Hite (1976) found that most women have more intense and quicker orgasms with masturbation than with intercourse.

Masturbation frequently continues after marriage. Husbands tend to masturbate more often than wives do. The majority of wives who masturbate rate their marriage as unsatisfactory (Petersen, Kretchner, Nellis, Leuer,

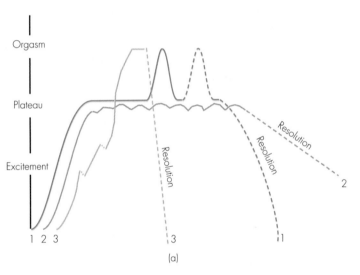

FIGURE 6.2 *Sexual-Response Cycles in Females and Males*

Source: William Masters, and Virginia Johnson, 1985, *Human Sexual Response* (Boston: Little, Brown).

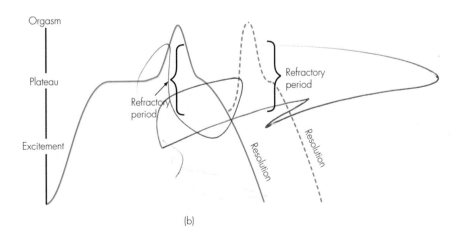

and Hertz, 1983). Many married and nonmarried couples participate in mutual masturbatory activities rather than have intercourse. Others find that manual stimulation of the genitals during intercourse heightens the likelihood that both partners will reach an orgasm.

It is interesting that so many people engage in a behavior that not long ago was thought to cause blindness, dementia (insanity), and a host of other mental and physical ills. So intense were past feelings about masturbation that children's hands and feet were often tied to bedposts to prevent them from masturbating during the night. Although many people still consider masturbation to be wrong, sex therapists have found that it serves some important positive functions such as providing a means for people (especially women) to explore and determine in private what is most sexually stimulating for them (Gagnon and Simon, 1973). Researchers June Husted and Allan Edwards (1976) found a positive correlation between depression and frequency of masturbation; that is, the more depressed people become, the more they masturbate. They concluded that masturbation reduces tension for depressed individuals. Despite the benefits of masturbation and the more liberal attitudes toward it today, many people find that their emotional needs are not met through self-stimulation.

SEXUAL FANTASY AND EROTIC DREAMS

Sexual fantasy and erotic dreams, like masturbation, are common methods of autoeroticism. People use these activities to supplement or enhance a reality that is less exciting than the images they can construct in their minds. Some researchers have suggested that sexual fantasies might help prepare women for experiences that are erotically satisfying (Shope, 1975). Whatever their particular function, fantasies help maintain emotional balance in the individual (Strong, Wilson, Clarke, and Johns, 1978). More males than females engage in sexual fantasy and erotic dreaming. Male fantasies appear to differ from female fantasies in that males tend to fantasize situations in which they are strong and aggressive and in which the sexual activity itself is basically impersonal. Women on the other hand tend to have more romantic fantasies (Shope, 1975). The most frequent fantasies for both women and men involve oral sex and sex with a famous person (Patterson and Kim, 1991).

Erotic dreams, often referred to as nocturnal dreams with sexual content, frequently lead to orgasm during sleep. This phenomenon is referred to as **nocturnal emissions** or **wet dreams**. Kinsey and his colleagues found that almost all men and the majority of women have nocturnal dreams with sexual content. Men tend to have more wet dreams than women: Four-fifths of all men, as opposed to one-third of all females, had nocturnal dreams that led to orgasm. Between 2 and 3 percent of a woman's orgasms may be achieved during nocturnal dreaming. In contrast, for men that number may be as high as 8 percent. The content of such dreams can cover a wide variety of erotic or sexual possibilities. The dream need not be overtly sexual, but it is usually accompanied by sexual sensations (Strong, Wilson, Clarke, and Johns, 1978).

INTERPERSONAL SEXUAL BEHAVIOR

In contrast to autoerotic behavior, which involves an individual acting alone, interpersonal sexual activity involves two or more people acting in concert for the purpose of giving each other pleasure.

PLEASURING   As far back as the mid nineteenth century, women were describing what to them was sexually pleasurable. Elizabeth Blackwell, the first woman to earn a medical degree in the United States, suggested that both women and men could experience sexual pleasure from each other without penile–vaginal intercourse. This idea of giving and receiving pleasure without intercourse was described over a century later by Masters and Johnson as **pleasuring**.

Pleasuring involves a couple exploring each other's bodies. It is erotic behavior that involves one person touching, exploring, and caressing nongenital areas of her or his partner's body for the purpose of giving erotic pleasure. After a while the partners exchange roles. This exchange can continue until orgasm, or it can function as foreplay followed by genital intercourse. However pleasuring is conducted, it seems that a large number of women find touching and caressing to be a natural eroticism and the most important part of sexual activity. Hite reported that one of the most basic changes that women wished for in their sexual relationships was touching and closeness for their own sake rather than only as a prelude to intercourse. One woman respondent, for example, said that "general body touching is more important to me than orgasms." Another said: "You can't love

Petting is an important form of sexual expression, and for many couples, it is a key part of the courtship experience.

sex without loving to touch and be touched. It is the very physical closeness of sex that is the main pleasure" (Hite, 1976:556).

PETTING AND ORAL SEX **Petting**, which involves a variety of types of physical contact for the purpose of sexual arousal, is a common activity among adolescent girls and boys. Petting includes kissing, oral contact with the body, finger insertions, and fondling. Kinsey once said that petting was one of the most significant factors in the sexual lives of high school and college females and males. If that was true in the past, it is even more true today. The great majority of young people today have experienced some type of petting behavior before they reach adulthood (Delora and Warren, 1977). Whereas in the past these behaviors were used most often as a substitute for copulation, for many couples today they are a prelude to copulation.

In many parts of society oral–genital sex is an unmentionable subject and taboo behavior. As late as the 1970s, social researcher Morton Hunt (1974) reported that oral–genital sex was still classified as a punishable crime against nature in the statutes of most states. By this time, however, **cunnilingus**, the oral stimulation of the female genitals, and **fellatio**, the oral stimulation of the male genitals, had become standard practices for a majority of white people of all social classes, single or married. Such behavior was evident to a far lesser degree among comparable samples of African Americans. For example, whereas 72 percent of single white males

and 63 percent of married white males reported active incidences of oral–genital activity, only 35 percent of single black males and 49 percent of married black males reported such activity. For white and black unmarried women, the rates were 67 and 48 percent, respectively, and for married women the rates were 60 and 50 percent, respectively. Although oral–genital sex has gained acceptance over the years, it may well be on the decline given the heightened sensitivity to various sexually transmitted diseases, especially herpes and AIDS.

COITUS **Coitus** refers only to penile–vaginal intercourse. Other forms of intercourse such as anal intercourse are not included in this term. Despite all the changes in sexual behavior that have occurred in the twentieth century, coitus remains the primary method through which heterosexuals seek erotic pleasure. Coitus can occur with the partners in any number of positions. The most common is the "missionary position," in which the female lies on her back and the male faces her, lying on top of her (D'Emilio and Freedman, 1988). Other positions include partners face to face with the woman on top, face to face with the couple lying on their sides, face to face with a pregnant woman sitting astride her partner, face to face standing, or rear entry where both parties are on their knees and the male enters the vagina from the woman's rear. Some couples also adopt a position popularly called "69," in which the couple lie down with their heads in opposite directions and simultaneously perform oral–genital sex on each other. These positions are not exhaustive or necessarily the "norm." Because sexual intercourse is personal and private, people usually create their own norm, whatever positions are mutually satisfying for them.

As we said earlier, the U.S. patriarchal structure of heterosexual relations assumes that coitus is the most satisfying sexual activity for women and men. Among heterosexuals, although most men find penile–vaginal coitus most satisfying, many women find clitoral stimulation, oral–genital sexual activity, and other methods of stimulation more satisfying than coitus (Hite, 1976). In general, women have more physiologically intense and quicker orgasms from manual clitoral stimulation, especially from their own stimulation, than from heterosexual intercourse (Basow, 1992).

SEXUAL EXPRESSION AMONG LESBIANS AND GAYS

As with other aspects of behavior, there is little difference in homosexual and heterosexual sexual expression and physiological response. Like heterosexuals, lesbians and gays engage in kissing, caressing, sexual arousal, and orgasm. Lesbians are more emotionally involved with their partners and are more likely to connect sex with love than gays are (Peplau, 1981). They express affection before actual sexual activity begins, and they often reach orgasm through mutual masturbation and cunnilingus. Contrary to popular belief, lesbians seldom use dildos or other objects in an attempt to simulate heterosexual intercourse. Such a belief is rooted in the heterosexist notion that heterosexual genital intercourse is the only normal way to express sexuality. Moreover, women tend to have a higher rate of orgasm in relations with other women than with men (Hite, 1976).

Gays often kiss, caress each other's penises, and reach orgasm through anal intercourse or through fellatio (Strong, Wilson, Clarke, and Johns, 1978). As indicated in Chapter 5, gays tend to have sex with more partners and in shorter-term relationships than do lesbians. Gays also tend to act on their sexuality earlier than lesbians, just as heterosexual males act earlier than heterosexual females. Some research indicates that these behaviors have changed in recent years due to the spread of AIDS.

SEXUALITY ACROSS THE LIFE CYCLE

As we have indicated repeatedly throughout this chapter, sexual behavior for most people begins earlier and lasts longer over the life cycle today than at any other period in U.S history. Adolescents at increasingly younger ages report being involved in some sort of sexual behavior. At the other end of the age spectrum, many people continue to enjoy sex into old age. The following discussion is a brief examination of sexuality in several key periods of the life cycle.

NONMARRIED SEXUALITY AND PREGNANCY

Although the terms *premarital sex* or *premarital intercourse* is commonly used in research studies of human sexuality, for two reasons it is outdated and inadequate

for discussing contemporary sexuality. First, it implies that marriage is the norm; that human life consists of two periods: before marriage and marriage. It also implies that sexual intercourse does not normally occur until after marriage. Neither of these assumptions is true any longer of the majority of the population. Thus, whenever possible we use the term *single* or *unmarried* whenever we refer to a nonmarried status.

The incidence of intercourse among singles has increased considerably over the last several decades. In addition, gender is no longer a distinguishing factor in unmarried sexual behavior. The behavior of white females dramatically illustrates both of these points. Over the last 3 decades the incidence of intercourse among single white females has increased significantly, narrowing considerably the gap in experience between them and their male peers. Among single African-American women a significant change has also occurred, although it has come primarily in terms of the earlier age at which coitus begins (D'Emilio and Freedman, 1988).

A review of recent research indicates not only an overall increase in sexual behavior among the single population but also a steady decline in the age of first intercourse: More adolescents are having intercourse at younger ages. For example, recent survey data on eighth graders (14-year-olds) from several rural counties in Maryland showed that 58 percent of the males and 47 percent of the females had experienced coitus. Even among those teens who are raised in conservative Christian families, the percentage who are sexually active is quite high (Rubin, 1990). Prior to the 1960s close to 10 percent of white females and 40 percent of black females had experienced coitus by the time they were 16 years of age (Gill, Glazer, and Thernstrom, 1992). By 1988, close to 33 percent of white and Latinas and almost 50 percent of black females had experienced coitus at least once by the age of 16. In addition, by age 16, about 50 percent white and Latino males and over 65 percent of black males had experienced sexual intercourse (Sonenstein, Pleck, and Ku, 1989).

How do social scientists account for this dramatic change in adolescent sexuality? Research on the subject reveals several key factors that contribute to the likelihood of a teenager becoming sexually active. Some of these factors include personal values and attitudes, dating experience, and family communication and structure. For example, adolescents who experience sexual intercourse at an early age generally place greater value on independence, are less religious, are less concerned with academic achievement, and are far more influenced by peers than by parents (Jessor et al., 1983). In addition, adolescents who begin dating early and develop steady relations early are more likely to be sexually experienced, to have had sexual relations with more partners, to have been more sexually active during the late teenage years, and to have more permissive sexual attitudes (Thornton, 1990).

Furthermore, some researchers have reported that parental sexual attitudes and family sexual communication are related to unmarried teenage sexual activity. For example, when parents are the main source of sex education, their adolescent children are less likely to engage in unmarried sexual activity (Fisher, 1986). Family structure is also a factor: Both teenaged boys and girls are more likely to engage in unmarried sex if they live in a home in which the father is not present (Newcomer and Udry, 1987).

The statistics on adolescent sexual behavior should not lead us to assume that nonmarried sexual activity is synonymous with casual sex. The majority of nonmarried intercourse among adolescents as well as among adults occurs within an affectionate, serious, and steady relationship (Thornton, 1990; Hendrick and Hendrick, 1992).

PREGNANCIES AMONG UNMARRIED WOMEN

A major problem associated with early coitus and declining and delayed marriage is an increase in childbirth among unmarried women. Today almost one-fourth of the births in this country involve single women. In the latter part of the 1950s, at the height of the baby boom, about 200,000 babies were born out of wedlock. Thirty years later, that number had risen to 930,000. This trend has affected almost every racial group. For example, in 1988, there were 177 births per 1000 births to single white women, an eightfold increase from 1957, when the figure was 21 per 1000. Among African-American women, the ratio of nonmarried births to total births had risen from 245 per 1000 at the end of the baby boom era in 1964 to 635 per 1000 in 1988 (Gill, Glazer, and Thernstrom, 1992). More educated women of all races and social status start their sexual activity at a slightly later age than less educated women and thus are less likely to have children outside of marriage.

TEENAGE PREGNANCY   According to one recent estimate, approximately 11 percent of unmarried teenaged females—over 1 million teenaged girls—become pregnant each year (Rubin, 1990). Although the overall number of births to teenaged women has declined since 1970, the rates of pregnancy and childbirth for single teenaged parents has increased dramatically. In 1970, over two-thirds of all babies born to teenagers were born to married couples. By 1988, however, this statistic had reversed: Two-thirds of babies born to teenagers were now born to single parents (National Center for Health Statistics, 1990). Slightly over one-half of all teenaged females between the ages of 15 and 19 are sexually active (Forrest and Singh, 1990), but less than half of them use contraception until they have been sexually active for at least 3 months (Zabin and Clark, 1981), and even then they do not use it on a consistent basis. There is some indication, however, that the increase in AIDS awareness has led to some increase in the use of contraceptives, especially among sexually active adolescent males (Sonenstein, Pleck, and Ku, 1989).

Insufficient knowledge and use of contraceptives help explain why the United States has a higher rate of teenage pregnancy and childbirth than any other industrialized country. It should be noted, however, that only 48 percent of teenage pregnancies actually result in live births. This is primarily due to the high number of stillbirths among pregnant teenagers and the high percentage of teenagers who utilize abortion services (Basow, 1992).

Teenage pregnancy and childbirth differ according to race. In 1987, 16.5 percent of Latina births, 22.6 percent of black births, and 10.4 percent of white births were to teenagers (Andersen, 1993). Among Native Americans, the full extent of nonmarried pregnancy is not known. The limited evidence however, suggests that it is relatively common, because no stigma is associated with having a child whether a woman is married or not. For example, in the mid 1980s, 47 percent of all births in the Native-American population in New Mexico and 62 percent of all births among the Native-American population of South Dakota were to unmarried women (John, 1988). Estimating teenage pregnancy for Native Americans is complicated by the fact that Native Americans are not a homogeneous people. Therefore, the rates may vary from group to group.

Teenage pregnancy is a particularly unsettling problem in this country, given that the majority of teen mothers live in or will live in poverty. Most teenaged parents, regardless of race, have low academic skills and high unemployment rates. They tend to come from poor families, most do not marry (at least not immediately), and they are likely to drop out of school, although black teenaged mothers are more likely than their white or Latina counterparts to continue attending school during and after pregnancy. According to sociologist Margaret Andersen (1993), regardless of their race and social-class status, teenaged mothers value marriage as an ideal, but they do not see it as a viable option given both expectant parents' general lack of economic resources.

MARITAL SEXUALITY: DOES GOOD SEX MAKE GOOD MARRIAGES?

The changes in sexuality we have discussed in this chapter have affected married as well as unmarried people. Most marriages today have moved toward greater variety in sexual behavior, more frequent intercourse, and higher levels of sexual satisfaction. For example, a comparison of married couples in the 1970s with those studied by Kinsey in the 1940s revealed that twice as many 1970s couples departed from the missionary position. Oral sex had been routinely incorporated into the sexual behaviors of married couples, except African Americans. Major surveys of women's sexuality during the 1970s and 1980s pointed out major shifts among heterosexual couples from penile–vaginal intercourse and simultaneous orgasm to a variety of sexual practices directed toward the needs and desires of women. These changes have weakened what some researchers have described as the male monopoly over the nature of sex (see, for example, Ehrenreich, Hess, and Jacobs, 1986).

Married couples are not only engaging in a variety of sexual behavior more frequently, they are also enjoying it more. This is not meant to imply that frequency of sexual intercourse leads to marital happiness. In fact, no such correlation has been found. Rather, the general quality of the marriage relationship has been found to be more important to a couple than is sex per se (Brehm, 1992). In general, however, when couples define their sexual activities as satisfying, they also define their overall relationship as satisfying (Blumstein and Schwartz, 1983).

EXTRAMARITAL SEXUALITY

Along with other changes in patterns of contemporary sexuality has come a change in the value attached to sexual exclusiveness in marriage. Research indicates that since the 1950s the incidence of extramarital relationships has increased substantially. Researchers estimate that by the 1980s as many as 65 to 70 percent of males and 45 to 65 percent of females had been involved in an extramarital relationship (Stayton, 1984). Obviously, even with the increasing tolerance of different lifestyles, an accurate assessment of the number of married people involved in extramarital relationships is difficult to determine because many of these relationships are conducted in secret. Thus, at any given time we can assume that the reported rates of extramarital relationships are significantly lower than the actual rate.

Why do people seek intimacy outside their marital relationship? There are probably as many reasons as there are individuals who engage in such relationships. Researcher Lynn Atwater (1982) noted some important attitudinal differences between husbands and wives who engage in extramarital relationships. Most wives indicated that they were dissatisfied with some aspect of their marriage, most often the expressive area. They also reported an improvement in their marital relationship, which they believed to be a direct result of their participation in an extramarital relationship. Husbands, on the other hand, more often participated in extramarital relationships because of the sexual excitement of such a liaison.

WHO ENGAGES IN EXTRAMARITAL RELATIONSHIPS? A number of demographic and social factors are associated with the likelihood that wives and husbands will remain sexually exclusive in marriage. Wives and husbands who are least likely to engage in an extramarital relationship are those who are conservative, religious, happily married, have children, have had limited sexual partners in their lifetime, reside in the same household with their spouse, feel a commitment to their marriage, and wish to please their spouse.

Discussions of extramarital relationships are complicated by the diverse number of relationships that are included in this category. Extramarital relationships can range from a one-night affair to a lifelong relationship. A husband can be involved with either a single or a married woman; likewise, a wife can be involved with either a single or a married man. A wife or husband can also have an extramarital affair with a person of the same sex. Thus, the frequency and nature of an extramarital relationship will vary not only with age, race, class, and other structural factors but also in terms of sexual orientation.

Overall, studies conducted throughout the 1970s and 1980s found that half of all wives and husbands aged 25 and younger were in extramarital relationships (Seagraves, 1989). As husbands get older they become less inclined than wives to enter into such a relationship. Whether a woman is in the labor force also seems to make a difference: Working wives are twice as likely as wives who do not work to be in extramarital relationships.

Finally, the frequency of extramarital relationships increases with length of time married. Thus, wives and husbands who have been married longer than 10 years are more likely to get involved in an extramarital relationship than newlyweds of 2 years of marriage or less. Contrary to the romantic myth that extramarital relationships involve good sex, research data indicate that extramarital relationships do not last very long, typically a year or less, and that the average frequency of sexual contact is less than five times over the course of the relationship (Harmatz and Novak, 1983).

What is perhaps ironic about the high percentage of married people who engage in extramarital relationships is that we as a society say that we find such behavior to be improper. In a 1989 nationwide poll, for example, over three-fourths of the respondents felt that extramarital relations were always wrong (cited in Smith, 1990).

Atwater (1982) has suggested that a primary reason for extramarital relationships is society's continued unrealistic views on love and the belief in the ability of one person to satisfy all the sexual needs of another person. How do you react to Atwater's hypothesis? Can one person totally satisfy another? Why do you think married people enter into extramarital relationships? Are such relationships ever justified? Why or why not?

POSTMARITAL SEXUALITY

As divorce and separation rates have increased and a growing number of widowed people—particularly women—are living into old age without a partner, a larger number of adults than in the past are confronted with the task of adjusting to a postmarital life. Popular cultural images have these individuals living either a life of great excitement, entertainment, and sexual activity, or, conversely, feeling depressed, devastated, and lonely, with no sexual life. As we shall see, neither of these images is accurate.

DIVORCED PEOPLE Most divorced people become sexually active within a year following their divorce, although older people are somewhat slower in this regard than people under the age of 40 (Masters and Johnson, 1985). Hunt (1974) found that among a sample of divorced women and men, 100 percent of the males and 90 percent of the females had been sexually active in the previous year. Divorced females reported having postmarital intercourse on average twice a week, the same rate reported by married women in the sample. Divorced men reported having postmarital intercourse more than twice a week, which was slightly higher than the married men in the sample.

In addition, divorced women and men are likely to have a number of different sexual partners until or unless they enter into an exclusive relationship. For example, the median number of partners in the past year for males was eight, compared with two for single males under the age of 25. The median number of partners in the past year for females was four, compared with two for single females under the age of 25 (Hunt, 1974).

Not only do divorced people appear to have sex as often as married or single people, but they commonly find postmarital sex more pleasurable and fulfilling than marital sex (Masters and Johnson, 1985). Such findings, however, should not cloud the fact that divorce often involves adjustments of many sorts, such as transition and recuperation, ending some relationships and developing new ones and adjusting to nonmarital sex. Some people find the world of postmarital sex to be anxiety-producing, particularly in terms of relearning the rules of dating and mate selection. Nonetheless, most divorced people manage to reintegrate their sexuality with their emotional needs. Many of them enter into intimate relationships that endure and deepen over time and very often lead to remarriage (Hunt, 1974).

WIDOWS AND WIDOWERS Widowed women and men sometimes choose to abstain from sex after their spouse's death, but almost one-half of widowers and widows engage in postmarital coitus (Masters and Johnson, 1985). Because there is little or no specific research on the sexuality of separated and widowed people, much of the information on them is speculative. The prevailing view at this time is that their sexual behavior does not differ much from that of the divorced population.

SEXUALITY AND AGING

The common stereotype of older women and men is that they are *asexual,* that is, they lose both interest in and the ability to engage in meaningful sexual activities. In addition, those elderly who remain sexually active are frequently dismissed as "dirty old women" or "dirty old men." When you think about older people, how do you perceive them sexually? Can you imagine your grandparents or great-grandparents engaging in coitus or oral–genital sexual behavior? In reality, researchers have consistently found that people who are healthy and happy with their lives can continue to be sexually active well into their advanced years.

It is true that as people become older they experience biological and psychological changes that can affect their sexual functioning. For example, some older adults take longer to become aroused, are less sensitive to stimulation, and experience less intense orgasms than younger people do. These exact experiences vary from one individual to another, however.

WOMEN, AGING, AND SEXUALITY   As women age, their reproductive ability declines gradually.* Somewhere around age 50, the menstrual cycle stops completely, marking the **menopause**. The onset of menopause and the symptoms that accompany it vary from woman to woman. Generally, however, the most common symptom in the menopausal process is the *hot flash,* a sudden feeling of warmth or heat over the top part of the body accompanied by sweating. Hot flashes affect about 80 percent of menopausal women. Hot flashes that occur during sleep are referred to as *night sweats.* Other symptoms of the menopausal process include thinning of the breasts and the vulva

---

*Unless otherwise indicated, the remainder of this section relies heavily on Masters, Johnson, and Kolodny (1992).

and *osteoporosis,* a loss of mineral content in the bones, resulting in a more brittle bone structure.

Although menopause does not automatically signal the end of sexual interest and desire, some menopausal women experience anxiety because they fear that they will no longer be able to enjoy sexual activity. This need not be the case, however. It is true that some specific physiological changes occur in the sexual-response cycle of postmenopausal women. For example, according to Masters and Johnson's research, there is little or no increase in breast size during sexual arousal, although the breasts continue to be sensitive to simulation. In addition, vaginal functioning changes in two important ways. First, the reduced elasticity in the walls of the vagina makes it less flexible during sexual activities. Second, the vagina produces less lubrication, making intercourse painful for some older women.

Experts disagree concerning the impact of menopause on female sexuality. Some studies suggest a decline in sexual interest and possibly the loss of female orgasmic response in the immediate postmenopausal years (Masters and Johnson, 1985). Other research (Masters and Johnson, 1966; Starr and Weiner, 1981), however, suggests that despite these physiological changes, menopausal women are still capable of experiencing orgasm, their sexual interest may increase, and for many of these women, the quality of their sexual experience seems to be higher than when they were younger.

MEN, AGING, AND SEXUALITY   Unlike women, men do not have a typical pattern of reproductive aging because there is no definite end to male fertility. Although the production of sperm abates after the age of 40, it continues into the 80s and 90s. Likewise, although the production of testosterone decreases after age 55, there is usually no major decrease in levels of sex hormones in men as there is in women. A very small percentage of men (approximately 5 percent) over the age of 60 experience what some sex researchers have labeled a *male climacteric,* which is similar to the female menopause in some ways. The male climacteric is generally characterized by some of the following: weakness, tiredness, decreased sexual desire, reduced or loss of potency, and irritability.

As men age, they experience a decline in sensitivity of the penis, and some experience an enlargement of the prostate gland. In older men, erections are also slower in developing, less precoital mucus is produced, the amount of semen is reduced, the intensity of the ejaculation is lessened and the refractory period becomes longer. On the other hand, as men age, they tend to experience an increased capacity to delay ejaculation, which some men (and women) find satisfying. In general, men tend to stay sexually active longer than women, although this may be explained in part by the fact that women outlive men and that the older a woman is the less access she has to a sexual partner.

Although older people generally can and do remain sexually active, the existing evidence suggests that most forms of sexual behavior decline significantly for women and men after age 75. In any event, a rising number of older adults are romantically and sexually involved in relationships, some of whom choose to carry out their relationships in cohabitation with their partner. (Issues related to the elderly are examined in more detail in Chapter 15.) These relationships reportedly are generally satisfying and rewarding and provide a positive example that sexuality can be pleasurable into old age.

SEXUAL DYSFUNCTIONS

Like other aspects of human experience, sex is not always smooth and problem-free. Most available research indicates that sexual discord or maladjustment of some sort is a widespread phenomenon in the United States. Masters and Johnson (1992) contend that some kind of sexual problem can be found in at least one-half of all marriages in this country. The fact is that almost everyone who is sexually active, even couples who are very satisfied with their relationship, experiences occasional sexual problems. These problems can range anywhere from lack of interest in sexual activities to an actual **sexual dysfunction**, the inability to engage in or enjoy sexual activities.

Although a few cases of sexual dysfunction can be traced to physical problems, the majority of cases are the result of social-psychological factors that interfere with or impair people's ability to respond as ordinarily expected to sexual stimuli. These factors range from anxiety about sexual performance to general life stresses. Sexual dysfunctions can be distinguished along gender lines. The most common sexual dys-

functions for women are related to penetration and orgasm: inhibited sexual desire, inhibited sexual excitement, inhibited female orgasm or anorgasmia, vaginismus, rapid orgasm, and dyspareunia. The most common sexual dysfunctions for men are related to erection and ejaculation: erectile dysfunction, premature ejaculation, inhibited male orgasm, priapism, dyspareunia, and inhibited sexual desire.

In our society a great deal of emphasis is placed on performance as a measure of people's personal worth. Sexual performance, like other performance, becomes a measure of our personal adequacy and value to others. Thus, when people do not perform sexually as expected, they often feel embarrassed, guilty, frustrated, confused, and depressed. This can often cause problems in personal relationships as well as in other aspects of people's lives. We will not go into detail here regarding the specifics of these sexual dysfunctions. Rather, they are presented in some detail in Appendix A. Suffice it to say here that whenever people recognize that they have a sexual dysfunction they should seek the help of a qualified physician, psychiatrist, or marriage or sex therapist, depending on the problem.

We end this chapter with a discussion of sexual responsibility and protecting oneself in the 1990s and into the twenty-first century, particularly as these issues relate to AIDS.

SEXUAL RESPONSIBILITY: PROTECTING YOURSELF FROM AIDS AND OTHER STDs

Sexually transmitted diseases (STDs), diseases acquired primarily through sexual contact, are fairly common in today's society. Such diseases can be caused by viruses (AIDS, herpes, hepatitis B, and genital warts), bacteria (syphilis, gonorrhea, and chlamydial infections), and tiny insects or parasites (pubic lice). Each year at least 12 million people acquire a STD. Because of the risks to physical and mental health, we must become more knowledgeable about STDs, and more responsible to ourselves and others in our sexual behaviors (Boston Women's Health Book Collective, 1992). With the exception of AIDS, which we discuss next, the STDs listed above are examined in Appendix B.

"How do I know you don't have herpes?"

Increasing public awareness and individual concern about sexually transmitted diseases have sparked a rise in humor about human sexuality. However, the contraction and transmission of STDs is a serious matter that should be discussed prior to having sexual relations.

Source: Reprinted with permission of V.G. Myers. © *Cosmopolitan*, 1982.

AIDS

According to a U.S. Public Health Service estimate, as of September, 1991 approximately 1.5 million people in the United States were infected with the **human immunodeficiency virus (HIV)**, which is believed to be the main cause of AIDS (Boston Women's Health Book Collective, 1992). Medical experts estimate that between 10 and 30 percent of people who possess HIV will actually develop AIDS. **Acquired immune deficiency syndrome (AIDS)** is a viral syndrome, or group of diseases, that destroys the body's immune system, thereby rendering the victim susceptible to all kinds of infections and diseases. Because the body is unable to fight off these infections and diseases, they eventually kill the victim. The most common diseases associated with AIDS deaths are *Pneumocystis* pneumonia, cytomegalovirus (CMV) infection, *Mycobacterium avium-intracellulare* (MAI), and Kaposi's sarcoma (KS), a form of cancer.

The AIDS memorial quilt is a means of expression for people who have lost a loved one to the disease. Since its first public showing in 1987, it has served to promote and encourage a better understanding of AIDS.

Currently, there is no cure for AIDS. People with the disease usually die within a few years after diagnosis. Of the more than 250,000 people in this country diagnosed with AIDS through December 1992, more than 170,000 had already died. Figure 6.3 illustrates the number of AIDS cases diagnosed and the number of AIDS deaths that occurred in each year through 1992.

THE TRANSMISSION OF AIDS AIDS is transmitted through blood and body fluids, such as semen, saliva, vaginal and cervical secretions, urine, tears, and breast milk. Although the AIDS virus can be transmitted through the use of an infected needle or syringe, the most common means of transmission is through sexual contact, as seen in Table 6.1. For children under 13 years of age the most common means of contracting the AIDS virus is from a mother either with or at risk for HIV infection (Centers for Disease Control, 1993).

According to the current evidence, HIV cannot be transmitted by casual contact. That is, AIDS cannot be transmitted through touching, coughing, sneezing, breathing, handshakes, or socializing, nor can it

FIGURE 6.3 AIDS Cases and Deaths in the United States Per Year, 1981 through December 1992

Source: Adapted from Centers for Disease Control and Prevention, 1993, *HIV/AIDS Surveillance Report* (February): 1–23, Table 12.

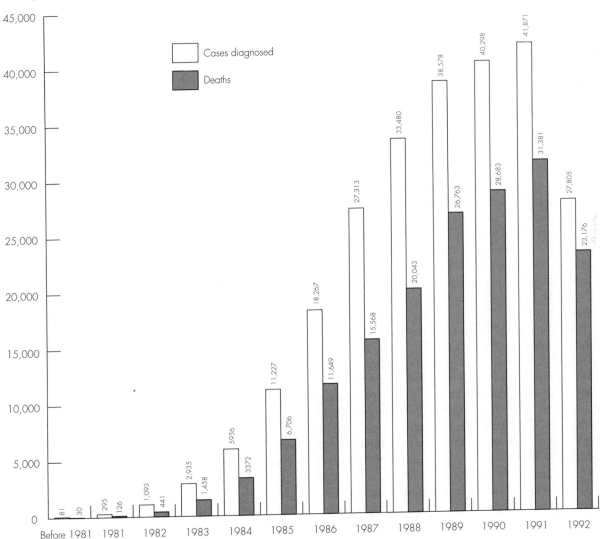

TABLE 6.1

Adult/Adolescent AIDS Cases by Exposure Category and Sex, Reported through December 1992.*

	Females (%)	Males (%)
Homosexual and Bisexual Men	——	64
Intravenous Drug Users	50	20
Homosexual Male Drug Users	——	7
Heterosexuals	36	3
Hemophiliacs and Recipients of Blood Transfusions	7	2
Other/Undetermined	7	4
Totals	100%	100%

*The Centers for Disease Control and Prevention tracks diagnosis of AIDS in terms of two basic age groups: adult/adolescents (13 years of age and older) and pediatric (children under 13).

Source: Adapted from Centers for Disease Control and Prevention, 1993, *HIV/AIDS Surveillance Report* (February): 1–23, Table 5.

be spread through toilet seats, food, eating utensils, drinking out of the same glass, water fountains, or insects. Right now, the most basic way to control the spread of the virus is believed to be through avoiding high-risk sex and through careful monitoring of transfusions of blood and other body fluids.

People may have the HIV virus without knowing it, given that the incubation period can be as long as 10 years. If a person has been exposed to the virus a blood test, the HIV antibody test, can be administered to test for AIDS virus antibodies in the blood. Although people commonly call this test "the AIDS test," it does not tell you if you have AIDS, rather, it indicates whether you carry the HIV. The majority of people who are infected with HIV develop antibodies within 6 months of exposure. A person who tests positive for HIV is regarded as infected and capable of transmitting the virus to others. In addition, other tests can be administered to determine conclusively if a person carries the infection. Some of the major symptoms of AIDS include persistent fever, diarrhea, a dry cough, night sweats, swollen glands, unex-

plained fatigue, dramatic weight loss, and bruises on the skin. Some of these are symptoms of other diseases as well.

AIDS TREATMENT As previously stated, no cure for AIDS presently exists. Certain treatments are available that relieve some of the symptoms of AIDS or prolong the lives of some AIDS victims, however. Among the most common AIDS treatments is CD4 cell (also known as T-cell) monitoring, which involves laboratory markers or tests that provide information on the progress of the disease. Antiviral medications such as azidothymidine (AZT) and dideooxyinosine (ddI) are also used. Some patients use a number of other treatments ranging from chiropractic treatment to Chinese herbs and acupuncture.

Access to medical treatment varies across race, class, and gender, although some physicians are unwilling to treat AIDS patients of all races and classes. The cost of treatment is often prohibitive, especially for poor and working-class people and those who do not have insurance coverage. Some sources claim that the cost of AZT treatment alone at the end of 1992 was somewhere between $16,000 and $18,000 dollars per year. Given that women and people of color are disproportionately found among those with limited resources, they often do not have access to the expensive AIDS treatments.

WHO GETS AIDS? As of December 1992, 89 percent of adult AIDS cases in the United States were men; 64 percent were gay men (Centers for Disease Control, 1993). All diagnosed cases among homosexuals are male (Kimmel and Levine, 1992). Although AIDS initially was identified with gays, the incidence of the disease is increasing among the sexually active heterosexual population. Although the actual percentage of heterosexuals infected with the AIDS virus is still relatively small, it has increased dramatically. In 1981, less than 1 percent of the reported cases of AIDS were caused by heterosexual transmission. By the end of 1992, this percentage had increased to 7 percent. The transmission of AIDS through physical contact can occur from male to female, female to male, and between people of the same sex. As of December 1992 the preponderance of AIDS victims were either males who had had intimate same-sex contacts or intravenous drug users who had shared a hypodermic needle (refer to Table 6.1).

Because the incidence of AIDS remains high among gays, there is still some feeling that the rest of the population is relatively safe from exposure to the virus. This could not be further from the truth. For example, estimates are that roughly one-fifth of gays marry heterosexually. Thus, heterosexual wives of gay men stand a high probability of being exposed to the virus. This does not include the possible exposure of women who are married to bisexual males.

In addition, some people's perception of the AIDS epidemic as a "gay disease" has contributed to open hostility toward and violence against gays. Many reporting agencies around the country report an increase in the 1990s of violent attacks against gays. At the same time, the AIDS epidemic has also generated among a number of people compassion, concern, and support for AIDS victims and their families and loved ones. It has also led many people to lobby for increased AIDS research and health care for AIDS victims.

AIDS AND WOMEN Although men are more likely than women to contract AIDS, women are increasingly at risk for AIDS. According to the Centers for Disease Control, AIDS is now among the top ten causes of death among women. Although women make up only 11 percent of adult AIDS victims, over half of all reported cases among females have been diagnosed since 1990. Although the reported cases of AIDS increased 5 percent between 1991 and 1992, the increase among women was 10 percent. The World Health Organization projects that by the year 2000 most new infections of AIDS will occur in women. Each passing year, the gap in transmission rates between women and men has narrowed in both developing and developed countries ("AIDS Growing Fastest," 1992).

Early symptoms of the HIV infection in women are similar to those found in men. In addition, women show special symptoms including recurring, hard-to-treat vaginal yeast infections and higher rates of abnormal Pap smears (Painter, 1992:6d). On average, women tend to die sooner after the diagnosis of AIDS than do men. This might reflect the fact that AIDS in women is generally diagnosed later than it is in men. One reason that women have not experienced early diagnosis and received specialized AIDS care is because most clinical research on AIDS has underrepresented women (Fowler, 1991). For years many symptoms specific to women were not included among the indicator diseases for AIDS. Consequently, women have typically been misdiagnosed or not diagnosed at all for AIDS. Those women who were diagnosed were often treated with methods tested on males. A recent American Hospital Association Health Report, however, indicated that accepted forms of treatment for men

The AIDS gap between the sexes is one gap that women are not fighting to close. Unfortunately, although almost one-half of newly infected adults have been women, some health specialists warn that AIDS prevention is still too focused on men.

Source: Reprinted by permission of William Costello for *USA Today.*

might cause potentially deadly side effects in women (Fowler, 1991).

Women's source of exposure to AIDS follows a somewhat different pattern than that of men. Whereas the majority of male victims contract the disease through same-sex contact, the most common mode of transmission for women is sharing drug needles, followed by sexual contact with infected men. Although we don't know how many women are actually infected with the AIDS virus, some studies indicate that the number of cases is rising rapidly in certain geographic areas. Moreover, race is a factor in female exposure to the AIDS virus. For example, through the end of 1992 53 percent of all women infected with the AIDS virus were African American. White women constituted 25 percent, Latinas 21 percent, and Asian-American and Native-American women only 1 percent (Centers for Disease Control, 1993).

AIDS AND CHILDREN Age also appears to be a factor in contracting AIDS. A disproportionately high number of adult AIDS victims are under age 30. In addition, the number of children under the age of 13 with AIDS is increasing.

In both 1991 and 1992 an almost equal number of females and males under age 13 were diagnosed with AIDS. At the end of 1992 there were 4249 pediatric cases of AIDS, 86 percent of whom contracted the disease from their mothers before, during, or after birth (for example, during breast feeding). The remainder of children with AIDS contracted the disease from blood transfusions. Today AIDS is a leading cause of death in children under the age of five. Although the number of children diagnosed with AIDS is projected to increase relatively slowly during the period 1993–1994, experts nonetheless estimate that 2300 new cases will emerge during this period. Four times as many black as white children have AIDS (Centers for Disease Control, 1992). The majority of these cases are found in poor, urban, inner-city neighborhoods. The mothers of these children often are intravenous drug users themselves or have partners who are. These women also have little or no access to drug treatment programs or health-care facilities.

Children with AIDS have not been exempt from the cruelty of those who do not understand the transmission of AIDS or are afraid of the AIDS virus. Many of these children have been cruelly taunted by neighbors and classmates and denied the right to a public education.

AIDS AS A NATIONAL AND INTERNATIONAL ISSUE In recent years AIDS has become a daily media topic. High-profile stars like Earvin "Magic" Johnson and the late Arthur Ashe who have contracted AIDS have heightened our sensitivities to the problem. City and state governments are attempting to promote safer and more responsible sexual behaviors. In Atlanta, for example, the city council passed an ordinance in 1992 that put condoms in all public washrooms. Controversies regarding federal dollars committed to AIDS research have arisen as AIDS activists push for more federal commitment to finding a cure.

The AIDS epidemic is not merely a U.S. problem. Rather, it exists in many other countries and is spreading rapidly. The World Health Organization estimates that as many as 13 million people are infected with the HIV virus in more than 74 countries around the world, the vast majority in Asia and Africa ("AIDS Growing Fastest," 1992). Whatever the actual figure, it appears that worldwide collaboration will be necessary to find a cure. Recognizing that our lack of knowledge about human sexual behavior limits our ability to intervene effectively and reverse the spread of AIDS, the World Health Organization is proposing a worldwide study of human sexuality.

AIDS PREVENTION AND SEXUAL RESPONSIBILITY Like most other human choices and behavior, our sexual choices and behaviors carry with them an expectation of responsibility. The romanticized notion of sex and sexuality has sometimes caused us in the past to ignore or avoid these responsibilities. However, the rising incidence of AIDS has focused the spotlight on sexuality and sexual responsibility and sparked a national campaign for **safe sex**. This campaign is geared toward informing people of how to protect themselves from AIDS and other sexually transmitted diseases through abstinence or by engaging in responsible sex. Thousands of taxpayer dollars are used to promote this campaign through mass-transit advertisements, billboards, brochures, and hotlines to explain the medical facts about AIDS (Kimmel and Levine, 1992). We are reminded repeatedly that we must take responsibility for our sexual behavior as well as for the consequences of that behavior.

Sparked by the AIDS crisis, posters and warning signs advising the use of a condom are now common features in public life.

nents. In addition, safe sex includes abstinence; communicating with your partner about her or his and your health, AIDS status, and sexual history; avoiding multiple partners and sex with high-risk individuals; and taking the appropriate occupational precautions if you are a health-care worker. Risk behaviors most often cautioned against are oral sex; penis–anus intercourse; finger play in the rectum or vagina; rimming (mouth–anus contact); and the use of sex toys, dildos, and vibrators. In addition, people should avoid the use of intravenous (IV) drugs. When drug use is necessary, people should use sterilized needles and should not share needles with other individuals (Boston Women's Health Book Collective, 1992).

Has all the recent publicity concerning the AIDS epidemic produced any positive results? Evidence suggests that some changes in sexual behavior have occurred since the rise of AIDS in the 1980s. There is some evidence that casual sex is on the decrease among both heterosexual and homosexual males. In addition, many sexually active people are practicing safe sex. For example, a 1988 survey of teenaged boys revealed that they were having sex less often and with fewer partners than were teenaged boys in the past. And when they were having sex, they were now using condoms (Sonenstein, Pleck, and Ku, 1989). Other studies (Gerrard, 1987) show that college students are also increasingly using protective practices in their sexual activities. In one study of college students (Carroll, 1988), over half of those who indicated that they were sexually active reported being more selective in terms of a partner and less sexually active than previous generations of college students. Roughly one-sixth of the respondents reported abstaining from sexual activity specifically because of their concern over AIDS.

Experts are uncertain whether sexual behavior is changing as a direct result of the increasing risks associated with AIDS. In any event, each of us has a responsibility to engage in sex in a manner that is protective of both our own and our partners' health and well-being.

The concept of safe sex involves four basic components:

1. Thinking and talking about HIV prevention before having sexual relations.

2. Being informed of what safe sex is and that it can be pleasurable.

3. Using barriers to protect yourself from potentially infected blood, semen, or vaginal fluids.

4. Avoiding drugs and alcohol that could impair your ability to comply with each of the first three compo-

SUMMARY

We are all sexual beings, and we spend a large amount of our time engaged in a variety of sexual behaviors. Although some people still believe the Freudian notion that our sexuality is biologically driven, sociol-

ogists stress the social basis of human sexuality. A sociological perspective of human sexuality focuses on the tremendous role that culture plays in creating and shaping the content of our sexuality. Like other behaviors, sexual behavior is guided by cultural scripts. In learning society's sexual guidelines, we in effect create or invent our capacity for sexual behavior.

As we learn other important norms of our culture, we also simultaneously learn about our sexuality from a variety of sources including the family, peers, and mass media. Parents generally try to protect their children's innocence and thus teach them very little about sex. In the peer group, children acquire ideas, knowledge, and much misinformation from people like themselves. Children also are exposed to society's ideas and definitions of sexuality through the mass media. Prime-time television programs, advertisements, films, and magazines continually bombard young people with sexual messages.

There is some debate over whether a sexual revolution has occurred. Whatever the verdict, it is clear that drastic changes have occurred in the approach to sexuality in the twentieth century United States. The most dramatic changes have occurred among women, across race, class, and age cohort. Women are dispelling traditional myths that defined them as less sexually responsive than men and capable of achieving orgasm only through penile–vaginal intercourse. More women today are sexually active and at younger ages. They are also engaging in a wider range of sexual activities, experiencing more frequent orgasms, and participating in more extramarital and postmarital relationships.

Although historically U.S. society has classified heterosexuality as the only acceptable form of human sexuality, humans actually express a range of sexual orientations or preferences. According to Alfred Kinsey these orientations fall along a continuum with heterosexuality and homosexuality at each extreme and bisexuality falling somewhere in the middle. Masters and Johnson found that a variety of physiological factors are associated with sexuality and erotic arousal, including changes in blood pressure, pulse, and breathing. According to Masters and Johnson, all people go through the same four phases of sexual response: excitement, plateau, orgasm, and resolution.

As with sexual orientation, sexual expression incorporates a wide variety of behaviors, ranging from activities involving only the self to those that involve two or more individuals. Masturbation and sexual fantasies and dreams are autoerotic activities in which the majority of people engage at some point in their lives. Petting and oral–genital sex are the most common interpersonal sexual behaviors in which humans engage.

There have been dramatic changes in human sexuality in every phase of the life cycle. Unmarried people are engaging in sexual activities with little expectation that such relationships will lead to marriage. Teenagers, in particular, are increasingly sexually active. One of the risks of early coitus is pregnancy, and the rate of pregnancy among teenagers has increased dramatically in recent years. Within marriages, wives and husbands are experiencing a wider range of sexuality and are more satisfied with their sexual relationships than in the past. In addition, a growing number of married people are engaging in extramarital relationships. And although physiological changes cause changes in the sexual response of older adults, most enjoy satisfying romantic and sexual relationships well into old age.

Although sexual attitudes in the United States have become increasingly open, liberal, and permissive, casual sexual behavior seems to have declined since the 1980s due to the growing incidence of AIDS. Other sexually transmitted diseases such as gonorrhea, syphilis, and herpes also have affected Americans' sexual behavior.

KEY TERMS

human sexuality	erotic arousal	petting
sexual double standard	erogenous zone	cunnilingus
sexual script	orgasm	fellatio
significant others	ejaculation	coitus
generalized others	refractory period	menopause
sexual orientation	autoeroticism	sexual dysfunction
heterosexism	masturbation	sexually transmitted diseases (STDs)
heterosexuality	nocturnal emissions	human immune deficiency virus (HIV)
homophobia	wet dreams	acquired immune deficiency syndrome (AIDS)
homosexuality	pleasuring	safe sex
bisexuality		

1. For the most part the media and mass advertising flaunt sexuality and define its content for all of us, including children. Consider how sexuality is presented in ads for popular products (cars, perfume, alcoholic beverages) as well as in rock videos. How have these images and definitions of sexuality affected your behavior? How close do they resemble your everyday life? What happens when the sexual messages of the media clash with your sexual upbringing? Do you think there is a relationship between media emphasis on sexuality and the high rate of unmarried pregnancies?

2. Do you know how AIDS is transmitted? What is the risk of contracting AIDS from living or working with a person infected with the virus? What kind of AIDS awareness, if any, takes place on your college campus? Has awareness of the disease affected sexual behavior on your campus? Do you think that people who have AIDS should be isolated from those who do not? What do you think about mandatory AIDS testing in schools and in the workplace?

3. How do your views differ from those of people you know in your own generation and those of your parents and your grandparents concerning sexual activity or pregnancy outside of legal marriage, oral–genital sexual activity, extramarital sexual behavior, homosexuality, bisexuality, and sexual behavior among older adults?

4. What were your feelings when reading this chapter? Did some subjects or topics make you feel uncomfortable? How comfortable are you discussing topics such as masturbation, wet dreams, and positions in sexual intercourse with a significant other? Parents? In a classroom? Your answers to these questions can be used as a way of getting in touch with your own orientation toward sexuality.

FURTHER READING

GEER, JAMES, AND WILLIAM O'DONOHUE, eds. 1987. *Theories of Human Sexuality.* New York: Plenum. The editors provide a wide variety of articles on human sexual behavior ranging in perspective from the theological to the feminist–political.

RICH, ADRIENNE. 1980. "Compulsory Heterosexuality and Lesbian Existence." *Signs* 5:631–60. A classic and influential work on the sociopolitical nature of female sexuality generally and lesbianism specifically.

GREENBERG, DAVID. 1988. *The Construction of Homo-sexuality.* Chicago: University of Chicago Press. An excellent and delightful book that presents homosexuality in sociohistorical context.

REINISCH, JUNE, AND RUTH BEASLEY. 1990. *The Kinsey Institute New Report on Sex: What You Must Know to Be Sexually Literate.* New York: St. Martin's Press. Over the years the Kinsey Institute has received hundreds of questions concerning human sexuality. This book attempts to address some of the most commonly asked questions surrounding topics such as AIDS, sexually transmitted diseases, and sexuality and aging.

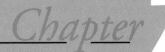

Chapter 7

NONMARITAL
LIFESTYLES

Betty finished talking to her mother on the telephone and returned to the living room, where her room-mate, Joan, was watching television. Betty's mother had called to ask Betty if she could come early on Thanksgiving to help get things ready for the family gathering. Her mother said that her younger brother and his new baby would be there along with an assortment of relatives, including several married cousins. She also told Betty that she had invited Bob, Betty's former boyfriend, now divorced. When Betty objected to Bob's inclusion, her mother said it was the neighborly thing to do because otherwise he would be alone on the holiday. Betty knew that her mother had always wanted her to marry Bob. Now that Betty was approaching 30, Betty's mother had intensified her efforts to introduce Betty to eligible men.

Betty, a successful real estate broker, had dated regularly during high school and college and continues to date now, but on an irregular basis. Last year she and Joan bought a townhouse together. Joan works for the airlines and is gone a great deal of the time. Both Betty and Joan like to travel and do so frequently. Both are happy with their current living arrangement, and neither wants to marry at this time. Betty told Joan that she is not enthusiastic about going home for Thanksgiving. She knows that with Bob being there and the new baby in the family, her single status will again be a topic of discussion. She knows her family finds it difficult to understand how she can be happy and satisfied without having a family of her own, and this makes her uncomfortable when she is around them.

How typical do you think Betty's situation is? Have you experienced any pressures similar to this in your life? Why do you think Betty's mother behaves this way? What if anything can Betty do about this situation?

Over the course of your lifetime you will be making a number of personal decisions, perhaps none more important than whether to marry. To make an intelligent decision, it is important to understand what the alternatives are and how they came to be. Although most Americans will marry at some point in their lives, increasing numbers of people are choosing to remain single into their 30s or even permanently. Others are forming relationships that differ in significant ways from traditional family structures. This chapter examines the lifestyles of people who, for one reason or another, do not marry, as well as the economic and social trends that help or hinder the development of nonmarital lifestyles. As is true of marriages and families today, nonmarital lifestyles represent a diverse range of social forms. Among the most common forms are singlehood, heterosexual cohabitation, lesbian and gay relationships, communal living, and group marriages. Each of these lifestyles is examined from both a historical and a contemporary perspective.

Before we examine what it was like to be single in America's early years, we must clarify exactly what we mean by *single*. The term is frequently used to describe anyone who is not currently married—the divorced, widowed, separated, and those who have never married. Including all of these diverse groups under one heading acknowledges that their members are similar in that they do not have legal spouses.

This practice, however, obscures the unique aspects of the lifestyles associated with each group. Thus, in this section of the text we apply the concept of "single" to never-married people only. Those who were formerly married—the divorced, separated, or widowed—are discussed in separate chapters.

HISTORICAL PERSPECTIVES

Most of the data available about singles in colonial America refer primarily to white settlers. The marital status and lifestyles of Native Americans and African Americans, both free and slave, went largely unrecorded during this time. Therefore, we do not know how many individuals in these groups remained unmarried or what such a lifestyle might have been like for them.

In addition, although there is a growing body of literature on single women in the eighteenth and nineteenth centuries, particularly middle- and upper-class women, scant information exists on the role of single men during this time. It is not that single men were nonexistent; in fact, quite the opposite was true: Single men made up a large proportion of immigrants to the United States at this time. But then as now, men's economic and political roles rather than their marital status were emphasized. Thus, the conclusions we can draw about the lifestyles of singles in

America's past are indeed limited and cannot be assumed to apply to all of the diverse groups living here at that time.

A survey of America's past reveals that for much of this country's history marriage was the cultural ideal and the norm. In fact, positive views concerning the permanently single were rarely articulated. Instead, a social climate evolved that tended to devalue singlehood and to discriminate against individuals who remained unmarried. Although the negative views of singles moderated over time, many stereotypes of the never married have persisted to the present day.

SINGLEHOOD IN EARLY AMERICA

Being single in early America was not easy; unmarried people often faced personal restrictions. For example, N. B. Shurtleff's (1853/1854) examination of public records of the Massachusetts Bay Company found that the authorities mandated "every town to

Throughout U.S. history never-married people have been victims of prejudice and discrimination. Even as notable a statesman as Benjamin Franklin (1745) compared the single man of his day to the "odd half of a pair of scissors."

dispose of all single persons and inmates within their town to service or otherwise" (quoted in Schwartz and Wolf, 1976:18). This "disposal" took the form of placing single people in the home of a responsible family, the belief being that all people needed to be associated with a family to ensure that they lived a proper life. The assumption that unmarried individuals could not be trusted to lead a proper life on their own gave rise to the view that the unmarried, regardless of age, were somehow not mature adults. This belief that the progression from engagement to marriage and then to parenthood represents normal growth and development still exists among some life-cycle theorists today (see Chapter 2).

STEREOTYPES OF SINGLES Unmarried women and men were commonly seen as defective or incomplete and were often the subject of ridicule. After studying this period, one investigator concluded that "bachelors were rare and were viewed with disapproval. They were in the class of suspected criminals" (Calhoun, 1917, I:67). Single women were not spared derogatory labels either. Those women not married by age 20 were referred to as "stale maids." Unmarried women 5 years older became known as "ancient maids." Even today, terms such as *old maid* and *spinster* convey negative connotations.

Why were single people treated this way? The devaluation of singlehood was in large measure a result of the high value attached to marriage, a value strongly associated with religious beliefs. The Bible stressed the importance of marriage and family life. For example, in the book of Genesis (2:24), men are enjoined "to leave father and mother and cleave to a wife." There were also practical considerations. The early settlers were concerned with economic and personal survival. Hence, there was an imperative to increase the population and to share the burdens of earning a livelihood in this new land. Writer Alice Earle (1893:36) took note of this in her reflection on New England customs: "What could he do, how could he live in that new land without a wife? There were no housekeepers—and he would scarcely have been allowed to have one if there were. What could a woman do in that new settlement among unbroken forests, uncultivated lands, without a husband?"

In sum, marriage was seen as a practical necessity, and singlehood was not considered an acceptable alternative because "the man without a family was evading a civic duty…and the husbandless woman had no purpose in life" (Spruill, 1938:137). Despite the negative ways in which single people were viewed and treated in colonial America, their numbers in the general population gradually increased as political, social, and economic changes combined to create new opportunities for them, especially for women.

SINGLEHOOD IN THE NINETEENTH AND EARLY TWENTIETH CENTURIES

The percentage of single women began to increase in the last decades of the eighteenth century and continued to do so into the nineteenth. At its height, the trend represented some 11 percent of American women, those born between 1865 and 1875 (cited in Chambers-Schiller, 1984:3). This historical increase is important to recognize, because we tend to think of developments in our own period as unique rather than as a continuation of long-term trends. Sociologist Edward Kain, in his book *The Myth of Family Decline* (1990), documents the fact that, contrary to popular belief, the increase in the numbers of never-married people since the 1970s is not a new phenomenon. Rather, it represents a return to historically higher levels of singlehood that began to decline markedly only after 1940. For example, in 1890, 15 percent of women and 27 percent of men aged 30 to 34 had never married. In 1940, the comparable figures for this age group were 15 and 21 percent, respectively; by 1970, they had dropped to 6 and 9 percent (Kain, 1990:75). By 1991, however, the rates had increased to 19 percent for women and 27 percent for men (Bureau of the Census, 1992a:15).

What accounted for the increase in the single population in the nation's early years? As we saw in Chapter 5, marriage rates are related to changing demographic, economic, political, and cultural factors. So, too, are changing rates of singlehood. In the early 1800s, industrialization created new jobs for both women and men, allowing them a measure of financial independence. Furthermore, some occupations were considered incompatible with marriage. For example, it was common for communities to have rules requiring teachers to resign when they got married (Punke, 1940). Thus, the choice to continue teaching was also a choice to remain single.

CHANGING ATTITUDES TOWARD SINGLEHOOD The Industrial Revolution was not the only event contributing to the growth of the single popula-

tion. Earlier, the American Revolution gave rise to a new cultural ethos that emphasized individualism, self-reliance, and freedom of choice in pursuing one's goals. According to historian Lee Chambers-Schiller (1984), in this climate, society's views of the unmarried woman moderated somewhat. Most Americans no longer thought of singlehood as a sin, even though to many it still seemed unnatural. An analysis of the professional and popular literature of the late nineteenth and early twentieth centuries reveals a changing attitude toward both singlehood and marriage (Freeman and Klaus, 1984). Particularly notable in this regard was the growing criticism of marriage and the perception that singlehood was preferable to a bad marriage.

The view that marriages should be happy rather than merely a duty evolved gradually during the early nineteenth century. The very title of Chambers-Schiller's (1984) study—*Liberty, a Better Husband*—provides insight into the decision to remain single. Marriage could now be viewed as an option, and more women chose not to marry; some even proclaimed their decision publicly. As one nineteenth-century woman explained: "I've chosen my life as deliberately as my sisters and brothers have chosen

Like many women in her day (1820 – 1906), Susan B. Anthony received several proposals of marriage. She refused them all, preferring her independence to being a wife and homemaker. She devoted her life to the pursuit of equal rights for women.

theirs.... I want to be a spinster, and I want to be a good one" (quoted in Freeman and Klaus, 1984:396). Other women saw their singlehood as a form of protest against the demands and restrictions of middle-class marriage and became advocates for women's rights. This criticism of marriage, the availability of employment, the opening of education to women, and the early women's movement all worked to the advantage of the unmarried, who were increasingly portrayed in a more positive light. Thus, there emerged a new ideology, called "the cult of single blessedness," which proved beneficial to families and the community at large. It became socially acceptable for unmarried women to care for aging parents, the orphaned, the sick, and the indigent members of the community. Over time such work came to be seen as appropriate vocations for women.

SINGLEHOOD TODAY: CURRENT DEMOGRAPHIC TRENDS

Although marriage remains the most common living arrangement for Americans today, significant numbers of people are choosing not to marry for all or for large portions of their lives. As of March 1991, 23 percent of all people 18 and over had never married (U.S. Bureau of the Census, 1992a:3). Most Americans who eventually marry do so by their mid-30s. Thus, as age increases, the proportion who have never married declines. This can readily be seen in Table 7.l, which compares the percentage of both sexes remaining single beyond the usual ages of marriage at two points in time.

The data in this table reveal several important patterns. Overall, the number of women and men who remain single into their late thirties has increased across all three racial and ethnic groups. Among both sexes, African Americans and Latinos have higher rates of singlehood than do their white counterparts. Some social scientists attribute these differences to the economic disadvantages experienced by these groups. Finally, in every age category the percentage of single men is higher than that of single women. This pattern holds true up until age 75, when the percentage of unmarried women surpasses that of unmarried men. This latter pattern is explained by two factors: Women have a longer life expectancy than men, and women tend to marry men older than themselves.

TABLE 7.1

The Never Married by Selected Ages, Race, Sex and Latino Origins, March 1971 and March 1991 (in percent)

	1971		1991	
	30–34	35–39	30–34	35–39
All Races				
Male	12.3	7.8	27.3	17.6
Female	6.9	5.6	18.7	11.7
White				
Male	11.9	6.9	25.0	15.6
Female	5.9	4.8	14.7	9.4
Black				
Male	16.4	12.8	43.7	31.0
Female	14.5	12.4	43.4	28.0
Latino Origin				
Male	———	———	26.5	19.3
Female	———	———	19.0	13.0

Source: Adapted from U.S. Bureau of the Census, 1971, *Current Population Reports*, Series P-20, No. 225, "Marital Status and Living Arrangements: March 1971" (Washington, DC: U.S. Government Printing Office): Table I, pp. 9–11; and U.S. Bureau of the Census, 1992a, *Current Population Reports*, Series P-20, No. 461, "Marital Status and Living Arrangements: March 1991" (Washington, DC: U.S. Government Printing Office): Table 1, pp. 15–17.

Comparable census data on the marital status of Asian Americans and Native Americans in these age categories are not yet available. There is evidence, however, that Asian Americans remain single longer than other groups. For example, in 1990, only 36 percent of Asian Americans aged 20 to 29 were married, compared with 42 percent of non-Latino whites (O'Hare and Felt, 1991:9).

Later in this chapter we examine the reasons people give for remaining single. Although we don't have this kind of information for all racial and ethnic groups, it is likely that part of the explanation for the different rates of singlehood is related to the availability of potential partners in their respective groups. As we saw in Chapter 5, in the United States people tend to select mates who have social characteristics much like their own.

DEMYSTIFYING SINGLEHOOD

In his analysis of the lifestyles of singles, sociologist Peter Stein (1976) observed that for many years most Americans, including social scientists, thought of single people as "those who fail to marry," not believing that anyone would want to remain single by choice. Stein's work has helped dispel this myth and show that the decision of whether to marry or stay single is conditioned by psychological, social, cultural, and economic factors. He characterizes these factors as a series of **pushes**, or negative factors in a current situation, and **pulls**, or attractions to a potential situation.

INDIVIDUAL DECISION MAKING

On the one hand, people are pushed toward marriage by pressures from parents, cultural expectations, loneliness, a fear of independence, and a feeling of guilt about staying single. On the other hand, parental approval, the marriages of friends, physical attraction and emotional attachment to another person, and a desire for security, social status, and children pull people toward marriage. In a similar vein, the perception of relationships as suffocating and as obstacles to self-development as well as an awareness of the high divorce rate may push people toward singlehood. Career opportunities, a sense of self-sufficiency, freedom, and the desire for psychological and social autonomy may pull people toward singlehood.

Although Stein's data represent common patterns of experiences, pressures, and desires, they are not necessarily experienced in the same way by everyone or even by the same person at different times in the life cycle. For example, some parents exert great pressure on their children to marry; others do not. Some people are self-sufficient in young adulthood but feel as they get older a greater need to be involved with someone else on a daily basis.

THE INFLUENCE OF SOCIAL AND ECONOMIC FORCES

The decision of whether or not to marry is influenced by many factors. Many Americans no longer view marriage as an economic or social necessity. The stigma attached to singlehood has lessened in recent years, and there has been a corresponding reduction in the perceived benefits associated with marriage. Furthermore, changes in gender roles (see Chapter 3) along with increased economic opportunities have provided increasing numbers of women

with the means to be financially independent outside of marriage. Research has shown that women in labor markets with favorable economic opportunities have lower rates of marriage than do other women (White, 1981). Researcher Judy Rollins (1986) found that most of her single respondents believe that being unmarried will help them establish their careers. Men may also delay marriage for the same reasons as women, choosing to devote their energy to finishing their education and establishing their careers. Declining economic fortunes, however, may contribute to an increase in the single population, especially for men. Women may perceive men who are unemployed or who earn low wages as less attractive candidates for marriage (Oppenheimer, 1988).

Other factors that affect the decision to remain single include the liberalization of sexual norms and the availability of contraceptive devices, both of which have freed women and men to pursue an active social and sexual life outside of marriage. Today, however, the fear of AIDS may constrain the expression of this freedom. Finally, the visibility of older unmarried people leading satisfying and meaningful lives has provided role models for younger adults to emulate. Nevertheless, not everyone who remains single does so by choice. As discussed in Chapter 5, some people find their desire for marriage frustrated by a marriage squeeze. This possible outcome can be seen more clearly by an examination of Stein's typology of singlehood.

TYPES OF SINGLES

Utilizing the reasons respondents gave for being single, Stein (1981) developed a typology of singlehood that places singles, including those who have never married and those who were formerly married, into four different categories based on the likelihood of their remaining unmarried:

- *Voluntary temporary singles* are currently unmarried and are not seeking mates. They remain open to the possibility of marrying someday, perhaps after completing their education or becoming established in a career.
- *Voluntary stable singles* choose to remain single and see themselves doing so on a permanent basis. Priests and nuns are included in this category.

- *Involuntary temporary singles* want to marry and are actively seeking mates.
- *Involuntary stable singles* desire marriage but have not yet found a mate. They tend to be older singles who have more or less accepted the probability of remaining single for life.

Sociologist Arthur Shostak (1987) also found four patterns corresponding to Stein's typology. However, he used more colorful terms to describe the same types of singles: *ambivalents, resolveds, wishfuls,* and *regretfuls.* Both typologies call attention to special characteristics of the single state: its heterogeneity and its fluidness. At any given time the population of singles is composed of individuals who either choose or hope to be single for only a limited period of time as well as those who plan to be or who will find themselves single for the rest of their lives. Research indicates that individuals who are voluntarily single tend to have a better sense of well-being than the involuntarily single (Shostak, 1987).

Regardless of which category of singlehood never-married people find themselves in, they enjoy certain advantages and cope with some disadvantages resulting from this lifestyle. Before reading the next section, reflect on your perceptions of a single lifestyle.

 What do you see as the advantages of being single? What do you see as its disadvantages? How do your perceptions compare with those identified by researchers?

ADVANTAGES AND DISADVANTAGES OF SINGLEHOOD

Studies have found a general agreement among single people regarding both the advantages and disadvantages of a single lifestyle. Among the most frequently cited advantages are personal freedom, financial independence, privacy, greater opportunities to pursue careers and other activities, and more time to develop a variety of friendships, including sexual relationships (Schwartz, 1975; McLeod, 1990; Ogintz, 1991). Consider what 34-year-old Vivian had to say about her life:

My life is my own. I can do housework in the middle of the night, be a total vegetable all weekend, eat at ridiculous hours, or not eat at all. No one messes up my place when it's clean; no one gripes when it's dirty.

I can keep fattening foods out of the house without depriving anyone. I can pig out without hiding. I see only the movies/shows/concerts I want to see. No one tells me how to spend my money. I may not be the best financial manager, but it's still my dough, and I'd rather spend it on clothes than stereo equipment." (Quoted in Lavin, 1991:3)

Given the negative view of singlehood in the past, it would be surprising if no disadvantages were associated with being single. Among the disadvantages singles report are loneliness and lack of companionship, being excluded from couple events or feeling uncomfortable in social settings involving mostly couples, not having children, and social disapproval of their lifestyle (Schwartz, 1975; Etaugh and Malstrom, 1981; Stein and Fingrutd, 1985). Jeffrey Ullman, president and founder of Great Expectations, a national video-dating service, summed up the view of many singles: "Nothing is wrong with being alone. However, it has a very ugly, nasty and debilitating side, and that is being lonely when you don't want to be alone" (quoted in Pauly, 1992:5).

These advantages and disadvantages are general categories and do not necessarily apply in every individual case or at all times in the life cycle. For example, not all singles are uncomfortable in social settings involving couples; some mix easily in such situations. Economic status also affects how singlehood is experienced, as singles with low incomes may not be able to implement the freedoms associated with being single. Changing family circumstances may alter a lifestyle in the direction of less freedom and more responsibility for others, as is often the case for single adult children who find themselves caring for sick or elderly relatives.

SINGLE LIFESTYLES

The major challenge facing single people through the ages has been building a satisfying life in a society highly geared toward marriage. Until recently, the general tendency in U.S. popular culture has been to portray singles as belonging in one of two stereotypical groups. On the one side is the "swinging single"—the party goer who is carefree, uncommitted, sexually adventuresome, and the subject of envy by married friends. Poles apart from this image is the "lonely loser"—the unhappy, frustrated, depressed single who lives alone and survives on TV dinners, a fate few people would envy. How accurate are these images? Research on the lives of single women and men contradicts these stereotypes and reveals a wide variety of patterns. For example, one in-depth study of 73 white, never-married, college-educated women and men over age 30 found significant variation in how these singles went about organizing their lives. Although there was some overlapping of activities, six different lifestyle patterns were observed, each having a central focus:

- *Supportive:* These singles spend much of their time in helping and supporting others and have careers in the teaching and nursing professions.
- *Passive:* These singles spend much of their time alone, have low levels of social participation and more negative outlooks on life, and show little initiative in shaping their lives.
- *Activists:* These singles center their lives around political or community involvement. They derive a great deal of satisfaction from working for social causes.
- *Individualistic:* These singles strive for autonomy and

self-growth. They see their independence, freedom, and privacy as an environment in which to grow and develop as a whole person. They enjoy reading, hobbies, and other solitary pursuits.
- *Social:* These singles have extensive personal relationships and spend little time alone. Friends and social activities have a high priority in their lives. They are deeply involved in hobbies, organizations, and family activities.
- *Professional:* These singles organize their lives around work and identify with their occupational roles. Most of their time and energy is spent on their careers. (Schwartz, 1976)

The single population, like their married peers, is not a homogeneous group. Singles differ not only in lifestyle orientation but also in the type of living arrangements they select. Figure 7.1 compares the living arrangements of never-married adults in three different age groups. "Of the 25.3 million persons aged 18 to 24 in 1990, 19.6 million (77 percent) had not yet married, 66 percent of them lived with their parents, 16 percent shared a home with nonrelatives, 12 percent shared a home with relatives other than their parents, and 6 percent lived alone" (U.S. Bureau of the Census, 1991a:11). This pattern

FIGURE 7.1 Living Arrangements of Never-Married Adults: 1990

Source: Adapted from U.S. Bureau of the Census. 1991a. Current Population Reports, Series P-20, No. 450, "Marital Status and Living Arrangements: March, 1990," Washington, DC: U.S. Government Printing Office, p. 11.

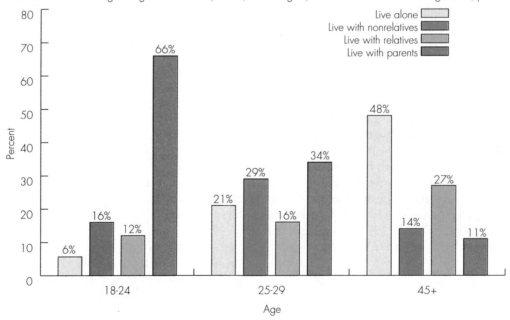

changes with increasing age. At each age group more singles leave their parental home to live alone or to share living arrangements with others. Among never-married people 45 years and older, 48 percent lived alone, 27 percent lived with other relatives, 14 percent lived with nonrelatives, and only 11 percent lived with parents.

A number of unmarried people live in specially designed singles areas—apartments or condominiums developed to meet the perceived needs of this population. These areas offer access to swimming pools, health facilities, restaurants, and singles bars. Although these complexes have attracted a number of singles, especially younger ones, the majority of the never married are dispersed throughout the general population. Some singles prefer the excitement of city living; others desire the less dense suburban areas or the openness of the countryside. With the changes in credit regulations beginning in the 1970s, more singles were able to get mortgages and become homeowners. The ability to buy a house, however, is dependent on income.

INCOME

Earlier we noted that one of the perceived advantages of being single is financial independence. How well off are single people? Are they better off economically than married people? These questions are difficult to answer because the needs of these populations may vary significantly. On the one hand, married people with children may need a larger living space than a single person does. On the other hand, singles may find that they spend more on food and traveling, as their married counterparts benefit from buying in quantity and sharing double-occupancy rates. We can, however, gain some insight into the relative status of single people by comparing their median income with that of their married peers. In 1990, female householders living alone had a median income of $12,548; the comparable figure for male householders living alone was $19,964. In contrast, married couples with both spouses present had a median income of $39,796 (U.S. Bureau of the Census, 1991a:13). What factors explain these differences?

One possible explanation is that singles, as a whole, are younger and less experienced than are

marrieds. This argument fails to hold up, however, when age differences are controlled. At the same age levels, singles still earn less than their married peers. Two factors are particularly significant in this regard. First, many married households have more than one wage earner, thus enhancing household earnings. Second, these earning differences may reflect a systematic bias against singles in the workplace. For example, certain data show that marital status affects men's wages. Blayne Cutler (1988:14) reports the biases single men experience in the workplace. Married white men who live with their wives earn about 12 percent more than never-married white men. The discrepancy in income is even more pronounced among black men, with married men earning about 20 percent more than never-married men. Overall, the wages of married men increase 1 to 2 percent more than those of single men, on the average. The probability of a promotion for married men is 11 percent higher than it is for single men.

What accounts for this wage difference? It may be a carryover from the past, when employers assumed that married men had greater financial needs than single men. Some employers still believe that married men are more stable, more dedicated to their careers, better able to get along with others, and less likely to cost the company money by changing jobs. Thus, they are more eager to hire married men and reward them more. Recent surveys of top executives found that although half of the top executive women were single, less than a tenth of the men were (Bradsher, 1989:3D). A 30-year-old graduate student told the authors about an experience he had looking for a job in public relations when he was 27: "When I was being interviewed, he [the personnel manager] kept referring to the social requirements of the job—entertaining, attending fund-raisers and such. I could tell by his attitude that he wanted someone who was married, so I said I was engaged. The funny thing was, I didn't get the job, but I did get married a year later."

There is evidence that these attitudes are changing, at least in some professions. Executives from job-search firms report that marketing and other jobs involving extensive travel now are likely to go to single men, even though administrative and supervisory positions, which often involve an after-hours social role, still go most frequently to married men (Bradsher, 1989:3D).

SUPPORT NETWORKS

As we saw in Chapter 4, everyone, regardless of marital status, has intimacy needs and must work at developing intimate and supportive relationships. Singles who live alone confront a greater challenge in meeting their need for intimacy. They respond to this challenge by establishing strong friendships. Schwartz (1975) and Simon (1987) report that singles, especially women, create their own "family," a support group of friends who function in much the same way as families do—exchanging services, traveling together, giving and receiving advice, celebrating birthdays and holidays, and creating shared rituals and meanings. Cockrum and White (1985) studied never-married women and men and found similar patterns. Both women and men valued friends, but in somewhat different ways. Women concentrated on establishing close, emotional bonds, whereas men focused on sharing their interests and their values with friends.

Another key intimacy need that is experienced by many people, regardless of marital status, is the bond that exists between parent and child. This need can present special problems for single people. Historically, great stigma has been attached to having children out of wedlock, and single women and men were denied the right to adopt children. However, changing attitudes as well as new reproductive technologies have made it possible for single people to bear and raise children. Consequently, more singles are doing so, a topic that will be discussed in Chapters 9 and 10.

LIFE SATISFACTION

No examination of the single lifestyle would be complete without a discussion of life satisfaction. How satisfied are never-married people with their lives? In the past, studies consistently found that married people reported higher levels of happiness and satisfaction (Cargan and Melko, 1982; Glenn and Weaver, 1988). However, these data must be interpreted with some caution. For a number of reasons, questions of happiness and life satisfaction are not always easy to answer. First, life satisfaction depends on a number of factors other than marital status: good health, satisfying work, personal growth, financial security, love, family, and friends (Simenauer and Carroll, 1982).

Second, every living arrangement contains advantages and disadvantages. Some people may experience more of the advantages, whereas others with different life circumstances may endure more disadvantages. Third, life satisfaction is not static; perceptions of satisfaction may vary over time depending on the changes occurring in an individual's life. Finally, the way society evaluates a lifestyle affects the perceived desirability of that status. Compared to the past, singlehood has become a more acceptable lifestyle in the United States. Hence, 10 years from now comparative lifestyle studies may reveal quite different patterns of happiness and life satisfaction. In a recent study, psychologist Janice Witzel found that this may be happening already, at least for the single women she studied. These women reported high levels of satisfaction and happiness (Ogintz, 1991).

A popular belief in the United States is that singlehood may be an exciting and satisfying lifestyle for young adults but that the opposite is true for older singles. How accurate is this belief? The next section focuses attention on a rarely studied population, the never-married elderly.

THE NEVER MARRIED IN LATER LIFE

Earlier in this chapter we discussed the fact that in the past marriage was perceived as the ticket to adult status. It was also assumed that marriage itself was a means of achieving security and well-being in old age. Conversely, it was popularly assumed that elderly singles must be lonely and isolated individuals. Do you know any older singles? Is this view simply another version of the stereotyped images of singles, or does it reflect the lifestyles of the never-married elderly? To answer that question, let us first find out who the elderly singles are. In 1991, approximately 1.4 million people 65 years of age and over had never married. Table 7.2 shows that the never married represent 4.8 percent of that age group. This percentage is fairly constant across all three racial and ethnic groups.

Our examination of the lifestyles of elderly singles is hampered by the fact that relatively little systematic research has been done on this population. Therefore, while instructive, the generalizations that we can make are limited and in need of further testing. Gerontologist Jaber Gubrium (1975, 1976)

TABLE 7.2

Never-Married People, 65 Years of Age and Over, by Age, Sex, Race, and Latino Origin, March 1991 (in Percent)

	Both Sexes	Male	Female
All Races	4.8	4.3	5.1
White	4.8	4.3	5.2
Black	5.2	5.2	5.1
Latino Origin	4.4	2.9	5.4

Source: Adapted from the U.S. Bureau of the Census, 1992a, *Current Population Reports,* Series P-20, No. 461, "Marital Status and Living Arrangements: March 1991" (Washington, DC: U.S. Government Printing Office): Table I, pp. 15–17.

reviewed what research had been done on elderly singles and concluded that (l) they tend to be lifelong isolates, (2) they are not particularly lonely, (3) they evaluate everyday life in much the same way that their married peers do (both groups are more positive than the widowed or divorced), and (4) due to their single status they avoid the desolation of bereavement that follows the death of a spouse.

THE "LIFELONG ISOLATE" RECONSIDERED
Later research has challenged some of these findings. For example, in his study of older men who live alone, Robert Rubinstein (1986) raises questions about the ambiguity of the meaning of "lifelong isolate." Rubinstein points out that the majority of the never-married men in his study spent many years living with other family members, particularly parents, and therefore could hardly be classified as isolates. These respondents did experience loneliness, but much less so than many of the widowers in his sample did. Although acknowledging that the married elderly may experience a unique form of desolation at the death of a spouse, Rubinstein argues that the death of a parent or sibling (and we would add friends) can be equally devastating to single people. We discuss how people cope with death and dying in Chapter 15.

Rubinstein's sample was small and exclusively male. Thus, we don't know if these patterns are typical of most older single men or to what extent these findings might apply to older women. Other research, however, indicates that there may be two distinct patterns among the older unmarried popula-

tion. Some elderly people do experience a degree of isolation. Pat Keith (1986:392), in his analysis of census data, reported that about 33 percent of the elderly never see neighbors, about 30 percent never see friends, and 21 percent of the men and 14 percent of the women never see relatives. These findings must be interpreted carefully, however. Factors other than marital status may be better predictors of isolation in old age. Older singles with health problems, lower levels of education, and low-status occupations tend to be the most isolated. A second pattern appears more frequently: Many elderly singles lead active social lives. For example, Keith found that more than 50 percent of all older singles interact with family, friends, and neighbors.

Katherine Allen's (1989) study of working-class women born in 1910, although a small sample, also shows the importance of family of origin in the lives of the elderly unmarried. Allen found that, like Rubinstein's respondents, the majority of the never-married women in her sample lived with one or both of their parents until their parents died. When this happened, however, they tended to replace the deceased parents with friends or other family members. Women appear to have an advantage over men in this regard due to early socialization experiences requiring them to concentrate more on developing interpersonal skills. Thus, single women often have a more extensive social support system than do single men. Allen also found that the majority of her respondents were pleased with their living arrangements, valued their independence, and had no regrets about not marrying.

Other researchers—for example, Kris Bulcroft and Margaret O'Conner-Roden (1986)—have examined heterosexual relationships and activities among older singles, including dating and sex. They discovered that in general, older singles, like their younger counterparts, enjoy movies, dances, travel, camping, plays, and romance. Further research is needed to see how race, class, and gender influence the pursuit of such activities.

IMPLICATIONS FOR SOCIAL POLICY
As we have seen, being single in later life presents some of the same challenges that it does in earlier years. Meeting the demands of daily living alone while building supportive networks gives the unmarried of any age a tremendous sense of accomplishment and

satisfaction. Nevertheless, changes in social customs and social policy could alleviate some of the problems encountered by the never married as they grow older. For example, we are all familiar with the rituals, showers, and gift giving that accompany the marriage ceremony. Yet rarely do we formally assist single people to establish their homes or symbolically, through a ritual celebration, recognize and give support to their lifestyle. Tax laws tend to favor homeowners (mostly marrieds), heads of households, and parents. Singles are often at a financial disadvantage, especially today as home ownership and material goods require more than one income. As single people age, they are likely to lose family and friends to death. If they are without children of their own, they may find themselves relatively isolated due to the age-graded character of our society. More opportunities for intergenerational contact and perhaps even intergenerational or some form of communal living arrangements could be investigated as a means of providing support for elderly singles.

HETEROSEXUAL COHABITATION

People who are not married choose a variety of living arrangements. One arrangement that has become increasingly popular among both the never married and the formerly married is **cohabitation**, popularly referred to as "living together."

HISTORICAL PERSPECTIVES

Historically, the number of cohabiting couples has been difficult to determine because such relationships were not publicly sanctioned; therefore, no systematic attempt was made to collect data on them. Nevertheless, such relationships did exist under a variety of forms. In our country's past, the people most likely to live together outside of a legal marriage were the poor or those individuals involved in unpopular relationships, for example, couples with mixed racial, religious, or ethnic backgrounds. Because of the prohibition against lesbian and gay marriages, homosexual couples have often lived together as well. As frequently occurs, however, when living together became widespread among the white middle class, researchers and other social commenta-

tors "discovered" it and gave it a new label, one not associated with poor, working-class, and nonwhite groups.

One form of living together that was visible in America's past is **common-law marriage,** "a cohabitive relationship that is based on the mutual consent of the persons involved, is not solemnized by a ceremony, and is recognized as valid by the state" (Stinnet and Birdsong, 1978:84). In sparsely populated areas of the country, clergy or judges often were not readily available to officiate at marriages. Thus, couples intending to wed went ahead and established a home together without any official ceremony. Later on, if the couple wanted legal recognition of their relationship, they had to prove to the state that they had lived as husband and wife for seven or more years and that they were legally eligible to be married. By the 1920s, most states had abandoned the concept of common-law marriage. Today only 13 of the 50 states (Alabama, Colorado, Georgia, Idaho, Iowa, Kansas, Montana, Ohio, Oklahoma, Pennsylvania, Rhode Island, South Carolina, and Texas) continue to recognize common-law marriages.

THE MEANING OF COHABITATION TODAY

The U.S. Census Bureau first began to collect data on unmarried-couple households, or what the Bureau calls *POSSLQS,* "persons of the opposite sex sharing living quarters," in 1960. Unmarried-couple households are defined as those households containing two unrelated heterosexual adults with or without children under 15 present. There are some problems with this definition—it may miss cohabiting couples in households with more than two adults, and it may include noncohabiting adults who may be boarders, roommates, or employees living in the household (U.S. Bureau of the Census, 1991a:14). Thus, although this definition is useful in measuring the number of nonrelated adults sharing living space, it does not convey the full meaning of the concept of cohabitation.

Cohabitation is similar to marriage in that couples create emotional and physical relationships with each other, and in some cases they also bear or rear children. It differs from marriage, however, in that it lacks formal legal, cultural, and religious support. And although attitudes are changing—over 50 percent of people in a national survey said they did not consider it morally wrong for unmarried couples to live together (Yankelovich, 1981)—it is likely that perceived parental or societal disapproval may still lead some couples to keep their relationship secret. Thus, our interpretation of past and current numbers of cohabiting couples must be somewhat tentative. In all probability the census data underestimate the total number of cases.

CURRENT DEMOGRAPHIC TRENDS Figure 7.2 traces the growth in numbers of unmarried-couple households since 1960, when they totaled only about 439,000. By 1990 this number had increased to almost 3 million.

Because census data capture living arrangements only at a given point in time, they do not reveal the full extent of the cohabitation experience in the United States. Three recent reports indicate that a fairly large number of Americans have cohabited. According to the Roper organization, one in ten people aged 18 to 29 years old is engaged in heterosexual cohabitation. Furthermore, about half of the population know a couple who is cohabiting (cited in Gonzales, 1988). University of Wisconsin researchers Larry Bumpass and James Sweet (1989) estimate that one-fourth of the U.S. adult population has cohabited at some point in their lives. For some people

today, especially among the younger population, cohabitation has become an extension of the courtship process. Young people are much more likely than their elders to have cohabited. Only 3 percent of females born in the beginning of the 1940s had cohabited before their 25th birthday, whereas 37 percent of females born in the beginning of the 1960s had done so (Bumpass and Sweet, 1989). During the 1960s, one in four remarriages was preceded by cohabitation; by the end of the 1980s seven out of ten were (Kierman, 1990). These data reveal the extent of cohabitation today but do not tell us who the cohabitants are. Do cohabitants differ in significant ways from the noncohabiting population?

CHARACTERISTICS OF COHABITANTS According to census data, in more than half of the unmarried-couple households both partners were in the same age group; in 55 percent of these households both partners were under 35 years of age. Of the 5.7 million people who were in unmarried-couple households, the largest proportion was 25 to 34 years of age (41 percent), followed by partners under 25 years (23 percent). Approximately 5 percent of adults in unmarried-couple households were 65 years of age and older. By marital status, never-married adults made up the largest share of the partners (56 percent), followed by divorced people (34 percent). Less

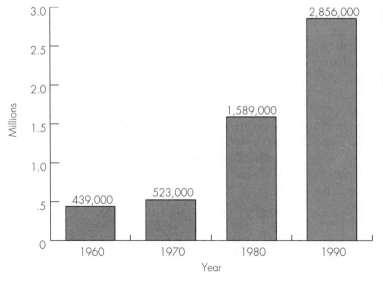

FIGURE 7.2 Unmarried-Couple Households, 1960–90

Source: Adapted from U.S. Bureau of the Census. 1991a. Current Population Reports, Series P-20, No. 450, "Marital Status and Living Arrangements: March 1990," Washington, DC: U.S. Government Printing Office, Table N, p. 14.

COHABITATION IN SWEDEN AND FRANCE

The United States is not the only country where cohabitation has become popular. Sweden and France have well-established patterns of cohabitation. However, their patterns differ from those in the United States in two important ways. First, living together has a longer history and is far more common in both countries. By 1980, cohabiting couples accounted for 15 percent of all Swedish households, compared with 2 percent in the United States. In 1982, 6 percent of France's households consisted of cohabiting couples.

Second, cohabitive relationships last longer in both Sweden and France than in the United States, where almost half of all cohabiting couples marry within 3 years of starting to live together. In Sweden the comparable rate is only 20 percent. By the end of the 1980s, approximately 50 percent of all births in Sweden were to cohabiting women. Cohabitation seems to be more of a substitute for marriage in Sweden than it is in the United States. In France, 30 percent of cohabitive relationships last at least 5 years, as compared to 10 percent in the United States. Because cohabitation is relatively new in the United States, whether it will follow either the Swedish or French model remains unclear at the present time.

Source: Andrew J. Cherlin, 1992, *Marriage, Divorce, Remarriage* (Cambridge, MA): 16–17.

than 4 percent of cohabitants were widowed. Approximately one-third of the unmarried-couple households contain children under 15 (U.S. Bureau of the Census, 1991a:14–15).

As noted earlier in this chapter, cohabitation initially was practiced by the poor. Then in the 1960s, middle-class college students experimented with it. Today, cohabitants are to be found among all classes, ages, and racial and ethnic groups. Nevertheless, cohabitation is not uniformly distributed throughout these groups. Comparisons of cohabitants and noncohabitants drawn from a 1983 national sample of never-married women, aged 20 to 29, revealed that cohabiting women tend to be older, less educated, less likely to identify with an organized religion, more likely to be unemployed, and live in large urban areas. Cohabiting women became sexually active at a younger age and have sex more frequently than their noncohabiting peers. White women are nearly one-and-one-half times more likely than black women to cohabit (Tanfer, 1987).

In an earlier study, however, Glick and Spanier (1981:199) found that while "the number of cohabiting couples is heavily concentrated among whites, the cohabitation rate among blacks is three times that of whites." The apparent discrepancy between the overall rates for whites and blacks and that for white and black women may reflect Glick and Spanier's finding that black male cohabitants were four to five times more likely than their married peers to live with a white female. Thus, black men and white women may have higher rates of cohabitation than black females do. Glick and Spanier speculate that the higher rate of interracial cohabitation is due to the social pressure against interracial marriages. Another probable explanation for the differences in black and white rates of cohabitation is the fact that a higher proportion of black than white adults have lower levels of education and are more likely to be poor.

Although we have comparative data on numbers and rates of cohabitation of these two racial groups, no systematic research on the cohabitive experiences of people of color has been done. Thus, we do not know if people of color attach the same meaning to this experience as do their white counterparts. Therefore, as we discuss in the next section the reasons for cohabitation, it is important to keep in mind that most of the data discussed here are based on white middle-class samples, frequently college students.

REASONS FOR COHABITATION

Perhaps some of you reading this book have had experience in a cohabitive relationship. Others of you may be contemplating such a relationship. Take a few minutes to reflect on why you (or others) might consider living together. In an earlier section of this chapter we discussed Stein's model of pushes and pulls to analyze the decision to marry or to remain single. These conceptual categories are also appropriate for understanding the reasons people give for cohabiting.

PUSH AND PULL FACTORS   Among the push factors cohabitants report are loneliness, high expenses of living alone, disenchantment with traditional dating and courtship, fear of marital commitment, awareness of the high divorce rate (and for the formerly married, fear of making another mistake), sexual frustration, and education or career demands that preclude early marriage. Among the pull factors are a strong physical attraction toward someone, being in a strong emotional relationship, desire for intimacy and sex on a regular basis, desire to experiment with a new living arrangement, desire for personal growth, example of peers, and desire to test compatibility for marriage (Macklin, 1972; Spanier, 1986).

Once again we can see the complexity of lifestyle choices. Cohabitation, like other options, is explained by a number of factors, both positive and negative. The meaning and experience of cohabitation varies considerably and reflects the different needs of individuals. For example, for some couples, living together is a new stage in a dating relationship, a "going steady" but with a live-in twist. A common pattern found among college students in the 1960s and 1970s was a gradual drifting into staying together, first spending the night, then the weekend, and then moving in (Macklin, 1972). For many of them, living together was a logical step in getting to know and share their lives with another person.

For other couples, cohabitation may represent a cheaper way to live. For example, sharing expenses might enable younger cohabitants to commit more time and energy to education or career development while at the same time providing them with companionship on a daily basis. For older divorced or widowed people with grown children, cohabitation is sometimes chosen over marriage to avoid possible complications with social security or inheritance issues. Because there are many different motivations for cohabitation, partners should never assume agreement about where a relationship is heading. Like people entering into any relationship, each partner needs to discuss and to understand the other's expectations.

For many people cohabitation has become a stage in the dating process. This couple enjoys sharing tasks together.

TYPES OF COHABITING COUPLES   Just as there are many reasons given for cohabitation, the relationships established by cohabiting couples vary in terms of individual needs and degree of commitment. In an early study of cohabiting couples, Carl Ridley and his colleagues (1978) identified four types of relationships:

- The *Linus blanket* type (named after the blanket-toting character in the "Peanuts" cartoon) has one partner who is highly insecure or dependent. These relationships generally do not last long because of the inequity of needs.

- In the *emancipation* type, at least one of the partners uses the cohabitation experience as a means of becoming independent from parental influence. Parents tend to be more relevant here than the partner, which often prevents the development of a truly intimate relationship.

- Relationships of *convenience* involve people who want financial benefits, sex, and a secure place to live but no legal ties. Gender is often a factor here. Men are less likely to desire marriage than women. If the relationship doesn't involve mutual convenience, it can easily become exploitive.
- A *testing* relationship is somewhat like a trial marriage. If cohabiting is satisfying, the couple may decide to marry.

In a later study, Macklin (1983) found types similar to the convenience and testing relationships. In addition, she identified three other types, each with varying degrees of commitment.

- In the affectionate *dating–going together* type of relationship, couples stay together because they enjoy being together and will continue to do so as long as it is a mutual preference.
- In the *temporary alternative to marriage*, couples are awaiting a more favorable time to marry.
- In the *permanent alternative to marriage*, couples have made long-term commitments similar to marriage but without legal and social sanctions.

Given these various reasons for and types of cohabitation, what then is gained or risked by living together?

ADVANTAGES AND DISADVANTAGES OF COHABITATION

Among the most common advantages of living together that cohabitants report are better understanding of self; greater knowledge of what is involved in living with another person; increased interpersonal skills, especially communication and problem-solving skills; growth in emotional maturity; better understanding of marital expectations; companionship; and the sharing of economic and domestic responsibilities. Cohabitation is not without its problems, however. Among the disadvantages cohabitants report are lack of social support for their relationship, which for some contributes to a sense of guilt about their lifestyle; conflict with partner over domestic tasks; potential instability of the relationship; loss or curtailment of other relationships; differing expectations with partner; legal ambiguity; and the emotional trauma of breaking up (Macklin, 1972; Olday, 1977; Stinnet and Birdsong, 1978; Newcomb, 1979).

Once again, we must not assume that each cohabiting individual experiences all of these advantages and disadvantages in the same way. The data on cohabitation, however, seem to suggest that regardless of the outcome, most individuals feel that they learned something from the experience. Furthermore, because cohabitation has become more widespread, it is likely that fewer individuals than in the past experience a sense of guilt about their living arrangement. For some couples, however, living together may go counter to their religious upbringing or to parental values; thus, their adoption of this lifestyle may trouble them. Such feelings may be intensified if a couple hides from family or friends the fact that they are living together.

COHABITATION AND THE DIVISION OF LABOR

How do cohabitants go about the daily tasks of living? Do they behave differently from their married peers? Research suggests the differences are relatively minor. Despite the fact that many couples may start out sharing household tasks, over time traditional gender roles emerge, with women assuming a larger share of the cooking and cleaning. Blumstein and Schwartz (1983) reported that even when women worked full-time and earned as much as their partners, they did more of the housework. This is not unlike patterns found among married couples. Sociologists Beth Shelton and John Daphne (1990) analyzed data from the national survey of families and households, comparing cohabiting and married couples, and found no difference between the amount of time married and cohabiting men devoted to housework or child care. This inequity in the household division of labor is often a source of conflict for cohabiting couples, just as it is for married couples, especially in situations where both partners are working (see Chapter 11).

COHABITATION AND MARITAL STABILITY As was discussed earlier in this chapter, one of the reasons cohabitants give for living together is to test their relationship for marital compatibility. Is cohabitation a good predictor of marital success? Several recent studies have examined the question of whether couples who cohabit before marriage have more sta-

Judy and Jim met at work. Judy, 23, worked in the personnel department, and Jim, 25, worked in the accounting office. They had many interests in common and soon started to date. After 6 months of dating, they fell in love. Neither felt ready for marriage, but they wanted to be together, so Judy moved in with Jim. At first, Judy's parents were upset by this arrangement and refused to go over to Judy and Jim's apartment when invited. However, after Judy told her parents that she and Jim planned to marry in the future, her parents had a change of heart, deciding that because Jim would be their son-in-law someday they should get to know him. Jim's parents divorced when he was 10. His mother is remarried and lives in another state. Jim rarely sees his father. From the start, Jim's mother approved of his living arrangement and told Jim that it was better to find out how well you get along with someone before risking marriage.

After living together successfully for 2 years, Judy and Jim decided to get married and start a family. After 3 years of marriage, however, they are experiencing problems. Judy complains that Jim has changed, that he hardly does anything around the house now. Judy feels that since they got married she is the one doing all the housework. Now she's taking care of a baby and working, too. Jim feels that all Judy does now is complain and that she's not the fun-loving girl that he married. Jim blames some of their problems on Judy's parents. Jim says that before he and Judy were married, they saw Judy's parents only occasionally. Now he claims they are over every week and that Judy's mother is always criticizing the way they take care of the baby. Judy and Jim have discussed a divorce, but because of the baby, they agreed to try counseling before making any final decision.

What do you think happened to Judy and Jim's relationship? Why were they able to have a successful cohabitive relationship and yet have a rocky marital relationship? What prediction would you make about their future? How typical do you think their problems are of couples who cohabit before marriage? What steps might they take to save their marriage?

ble and satisfying marriages than do couples who don't live together prior to getting married. The results of these studies are contradictory and ultimately inconclusive at this time. Some studies have indicated that cohabitants who married are more likely to remain together than are noncohabitants (White, 1987); others have suggested the opposite (Booth and Johnson, 1988; Bumpass and Sweet, 1989). Some researchers have taken a "neutral" position, concluding that cohabitation has no clear effect on marital success or satisfaction (Watson and De Meo, 1987; Teachman and Polonko, 1990). Obviously, more research needs to be done in this area.

It may well be that some cohabitants engage in behavior that in the long run is detrimental to marriage. In the cohabitive situation, they may put their best foot forward and share household responsibilities on an equitable basis. After exchanging marriage vows, however, one or both partners may, without consciously realizing it, change role expectations and fall back on traditional patterns in the division of household labor. There may be outside pressure as well. Parents and friends may be more tolerant of a "live-in lover" than of a spouse because they don't want to jeopardize the possibility of marriage. After marriage they may feel free to say or do things that could cause conflict between the now-married couple.

COHABITATION AND THE LAW

Cohabitation, like singlehood, can be temporary and fluid. Many cohabitants are together for only short periods of time. The average length of cohabitation is only 1.5 years (Bumpass, 1990). Cohabitants end their relationship for many reasons: growing apart, loss of interest, unequal commitment, value conflicts, outside pressures, or the need to relocate because of college graduation or a new job (Buunk and van Driel, 1989). Unlike the concept of a legal marriage, an assumption underlying cohabitation is that you are free to leave whenever the relationship becomes unsatisfactory. What happens, however, when cohabitants terminate a relationship? Who gets the apartment? The stereo? Can cohabitants expect compensation for their unpaid work or other contributions while living together? What are the legal aspects of cohabitation?

PALIMONY Even though you do not need a court decree to stop living together, there may be legal ramifications to ending a cohabitive relationship. Previous live-in partners may file suit for what has come to be called **palimony**, a payment similar to alimony and based on the existence of a contract (written or implied) between the partners regarding aspects of their relationship. For example, if there was a promise of future marriage, of an economic partnership, or of support for a child, courts may hold a partner responsible for legally fulfilling these obligations.

In 1976, widespread attention was focused on palimony when Michelle Triola Marvin sued Lee Marvin (she used his surname even though they were not legally married) after 7 years of living together. She claimed they had an agreement whereby he would support her and share his property with her in exchange for her domestic services, and that he had reneged on this promise. The court acknowledged that in the past such an arrangement would have been equated with prostitution and, therefore, have been unenforceable, but that times had changed and that such agreements now had to be honored. Subsequent legal action, however, set aside the court's award, and Triola received very little. Nevertheless, since that time, numerous suits have been brought against former live-in partners.

DOMESTIC PARTNERSHIPS So far we have been talking about what happens when cohabitants break up. However, a number of other areas to consider when living together could also have legal implications. For example, who is to be the beneficiary with regard to insurance and wills? Sometimes insurance companies require the beneficiary to have a conventional family tie. You cannot assume that because you live with someone you will be covered by her or his car or renter's insurance. Health benefits are problematic as well.

Some of this is changing as some communities and organizations make provisions for extending benefits generally reserved for married employees to other employees involved in what have come to be known as **domestic partnerships**. This term refers to unmarried couples who live together and share housing and financial responsibilities. About 25 localities in the United States now recognize some form of domestic partnership, although the rights and benefits involved in these arrangements vary from place to place. For example, a 1993 executive order allows lesbian and gay couples in New York City to register as domestic partners. The scope of this order is restricted to such areas as domestic leave for city workers, visitation rights in municipal hospitals and city prisons, and inheriting leases in apartment buildings owned or managed by the city. It does not address such issues as health insurance and tax status (Hicks, 1993). Madison, Wisconsin, allows lesbian, gay,

Cohabiting relationships are often of short duration. Like divorce, the break-up can involve conflicts over money and property. Lee Marvin's much-publicized break-up gave us the concept of "palimony."

and heterosexual couples to purchase a certificate of domestic partnership. The benefit is small—guaranteed family membership at the city's YMCA—but it does provide recognition of the relationship (Larson and Edmondson, 1991). Not-for-profit organizations like Columbia and Stanford Universities, American Friends Service Committee, the Museum of Modern Art, and the American Psychological Association also provide partnership benefits (Slavin, 1991).

Without such recognition cohabiting partners may have little to say in the medical treatment or other affairs of their partner. In case of death, who is to inherit property? Without a properly executed will, the state makes this determination, and the decision will likely favor family members over live-in partners. You can't automatically claim ownership to any property that does not bear your name even if you helped pay for it. The status of children can be ambiguous in cohabitive relationships as well. If the biological parent dies and there is no provision for naming the live-in partner the legal guardian, again the court may decide the matter. Often it does so contrary to the wishes of the cohabitants. These are just a few of the items that cohabitants need to consider as they establish their living arrangements. Unless they have made a binding agreement, cohabitants may have no legal rights in these matters.

LESBIAN AND GAY RELATIONSHIPS

Some of the legal issues we have just discussed concerning cohabitants apply to lesbian and gay relationships as well. As with our discussion of heterosexual cohabitants, our focus here is primarily on social relationships constructed by lesbian and gay couples.

Homosexual behavior has existed throughout history and in every known culture. Nevertheless, cultures have varied considerably in their attitudes toward this behavior. Certain peoples in Melanesia, Central Africa, and Egypt viewed sexual relationships between older and younger males as part of the normal socialization process. Similarly, records of classical Greece and Rome reveal acceptance of same-sex bonding for men. Historians know less about women's relationships during this period but have discovered some evidence that female same-sex bonding occurred then, too.

In U.S. society, homosexuality historically has been considered a form of deviant behavior. Medical research

into this "disorder" focused on its causes, with the emphasis on discovering a "cure." During the twentieth century, these negative attitudes began to change. Lesbians and gays began to organize to challenge laws and customs discriminating against them and condemning their behaviors. Although these groups initially were predominantly white, several African-American, Asian-American, and Latino organizations have emerged since the 1970s. In 1973, an important step in the redefinition of homosexual behavior occurred when the American Psychiatric Association removed homosexuality from its list of psychiatric disorders. The lesbian and gay struggle for acceptance and equal opportunity promises to be a major social movement.

METHODOLOGICAL ISSUES

Earlier in the chapter we noted the methodological problems surrounding the study of singlehood and heterosexual cohabitation. Similar problems of small, unrepresentative samples also limit the study of homosexual behavior. In addition, the long tradition of homophobia in the United States has kept many homosexual people from revealing their sexual orientation and from participating in research studies. Research studies with small samples of Asian Americans (Chan, 1989; Chun, 1990), Latinos (Espin, 1987; Carballo-Diequez, 1989), and African Americans (Loiacano, 1989; Peterson, 1992) suggest that people of color may be even more reluctant to identify themselves as lesbian or gay because of the intense cultural disapproval of homosexuality in their respective communities. Among many of these cultures homosexuality is widely viewed as a white, Western phenomenon. This view may be changing, however, as evidenced in a recent survey by state psychologists in Nanjing, China. This survey, the first by the state since the Communists took power in 1949, concluded that China has "a sizeable" lesbian and gay population and classified lesbians and gays as "normal" rather than mentally ill, as was believed to be true for years (Schmetzer, 1992).

There are many variations in lesbian and gay lifestyles. Some lesbians and gays live alone; others are cohabitants. Some have been involved in heterosexual marriages—one study puts the number at 33 percent for lesbians and 20 percent for gay men (Harry, 1988). Our focus here is on cohabiting same-sex couples; the Census Bureau counted 1.6 million of these couples in 1988 (Seligmann, 1990:38). Additionally, many lesbians and gays are parents and grandparents. Some had their children when they were part of a heterosexual union; others elected to have children outside of a biological relationship through artificial insemination (see Chapter 9). Lesbian and gay parenting is discussed in Chapter 10.

DEMYSTIFYING LESBIAN AND GAY RELATIONSHIPS

What images do you have of lesbian and gay cohabitants? No doubt you are aware of some of the many stereotypes about lesbians and gays. Among the most prevalent images are those depicting lesbians as masculine or "butch" and gay men as effeminate. The major stereotypes involving cohabiting same-sex couples assume that these couples imitate heterosexual patterns, with one partner acting as "wife" (submissive female) and the other partner playing the "husband" (dominant male). Current research, however, shows that these stereotypes apply to only a small minority of same-sex relationships, those in which partners tend to be older, male, and from lower socioeconomic and educational levels (Bell and Weinberg, 1978; Peplau and Gordon, 1983; Harry, 1984). In fact, most lesbians and gays feel negatively about such role playing (Jay and Young, 1977).

Richard Higginbotham (1991) argues that the problem with using the marriage model in studying lesbian and gay relationships is that it brings with it a set of expectations and norms that simply do not correlate with the realities of a same-sex relationship. Some researchers suggest that a friendship model, albeit with erotic and romantic elements, provides lesbians and gays with guidelines for their intimate relationships (Harry and DeVall, 1978). The difference between these two models is that the norms for friendship assume that partners will be relatively equal in status and power, as contrasted to traditional heterosexual marriage scripts, in which the husband is assumed to be the head of the family (Peplau and Gordon, 1983). What, then, are lesbian and gay relationships like? How do lesbians and gays handle the different dimensions of living together, for example, the division of household labor, finances, and decision making?

LIVING TOGETHER: DOMESTIC TASKS, FINANCES, AND DECISION MAKING

Because traditional gender distinctions are not relevant to same-sex relationships, lesbian and gay couples are in a unique position to create living arrangements tailored to their needs and interests. How, then, do same-sex couples resolve the day-to-day requirements of living? Research shows that there is considerable discussion and conscious joint decision making in these areas (Harry, 1984). One study found that over half of both lesbians and gays in the sample reported sharing housework equally (Bell and Weinberg, 1978). Sociologists Philip Blumstein and Pepper Schwartz (1983) found several factors that affect the division of household tasks. Among gay couples the number of hours spent at work determine the relative contribution of each partner—the one with the fewer outside hours does more of the household tasks. There were some constraints on this pattern, however. For example, these same authors found that "both heterosexual and homosexual men feel that a successful partner should not have to do housework" (1983:151). Among lesbians, preference and ability as well as the number of hours worked provide guidelines for the division of household labor. Lesbian couples work harder than either gay or heterosexual couples to create an equitable distribution of tasks.

Decision making, like housework, is often related to income; that is, the partner with the highest income tends to have the most power. In a comparative study of heterosexual and same-sex couples, Blumstein and Schwartz (1983) found this to be true for gay and heterosexual couples but not for lesbian couples. In this same study lesbian respondents reported less conflict over finances than did other couples. Among both heterosexual and gay couples, partners who feel they have equal control over how money is spent have a more tranquil relationship. Other researchers have reported equality in decision making for both lesbian and gay couples (Kurdek and Schmitt, 1986; Harry, 1982; and Peplau and Cochran, 1981).

THE SOCIAL AND LEGAL CONTEXT OF LESBIAN AND GAY RELATIONSHIPS

Lesbians and gays must deal with the same issues of living together that heterosexuals do: how to divide housework, decision making, and finances.

CRITICAL ISSUES

"COMING OUT"

The following conversation is based on an interview with a member of Parents and Friends of Lesbians and Gays. Think about how you might react if you were in Jane's situation.

Mary: When did you learn that your son is gay?

Jane: He told us his junior year in college. I'll never forget it. He was home for Thanksgiving, and we could tell something was bothering him but he couldn't bring himself to tell us until the night before he went back to school. I think he was afraid of how we would react.

Mary: How did you react?

Jane: Not too well, I'm afraid. My husband and I were shocked. We wanted to deny it. [Smiling] We tried to tell him it was just a phase he was going through and that he'd get over it. After all, he dated all through high school; he even talked about getting married. So how could he be gay? We stayed up all night talking, and he finally made us realize he is gay. He said he had known he was gay in high school but that he tried to deny it by doing all the macho things that men were supposed to do, but it did not work.

Mary: What happened after that?

Jane: We tried to be supportive when he left, but we were devastated. Ted [Jane's husband] cried. He couldn't accept it. We started to argue. We blamed ourselves and each other. We thought we must have done something wrong, that we failed our son somehow. Our hopes for grandchildren were gone. We felt embarrassed when friends asked us how Sam was doing. Sam didn't come home again for 6 months. I think he sensed our anguish. Things got so strained between my husband and me that we decided that if our marriage was to survive we had to get help. That was the turning point for us. We started reading books that the counselor had recommended, and we joined a support group. There we found we were not alone; other parents were going through the same kind of adjustments we were. We were relieved to learn that we had done nothing wrong, that being gay is not a disease that needs a cure.

Mary: How are things today?

Jane: We have a good relationship with Sam. We like his friends, especially Tom, whom he's lived with for over 3 years now. But there's still a part of me that wishes it were different. I worry about AIDS, and I'm afraid for him. Too many people don't understand.

Why do you think Sam's parents had such a hard time believing their son is gay? How do you think your family and friends would react if someone in your family "came out of the closet?" What can be done to help parents and children through this initial disclosure?

"Couplehood, either as a reality or as an aspiration is as strong among gay people as it is among heterosexuals" (quoted in Blumstein and Schwartz, 1983:45). Research comparing lesbians and gays with heterosexuals finds no significant differences regarding couple adjustment, feelings of attachment, caring, or intimacy (Cardell, Finn, and Marecek, 1981). As our discussion indicates, same-sex couples experience the same disadvantages and advantages of cohabitation as heterosexual couples. Additionally, however, they must deal with a society that remains largely intolerant of their lifestyle.

The 1980s and early 1990s have witnessed some improvement in the legal status of lesbians and gays.

According to the National Gay and Lesbian Task Force, an advocacy group based in Washington, D.C., 113 cities and towns in the United States have passed gay rights legislation, 55 of them in the last 3 years (Casuso, 1991). A New York court of appeals recognized the right of a gay man's surviving life partner to take over his interest in a rent-controlled apartment by holding that the surviving partner was part of the decedant's family. Several private companies, for example, Lotus Development Corporation and Ben and Jerry's ice cream firm, have granted their lesbian and gay employees the same spousal benefits as their married employees (Dorning, 1991).

However, lesbians and gays have also encountered a backlash among some voters. In 1992, Colorado passed an amendment to its constitution striking down laws banning discrimination in hiring and housing against lesbians and gays. Like heterosexual cohabitants, lesbians and gays in long-term relationships are generally denied legal and financial benefits such as community property rights, insurance coverage, tax breaks, leaves for the sickness or funeral of a partner, and inheritance protection.

DISCRIMINATION AGAINST LESBIANS AND GAYS

A major arena in which lesbians and gays experience discriminatory treatment is in the workplace, where sexual orientation is often used to screen out appli-cants. For example, the U.S. government still uses sexual orientation to deny security clearance to lesbians and gays. This restriction continues to exist despite the fact that a consistent body of research shows that lesbians and gays are no more likely than heterosexuals to suffer from personality disorders or stress, or to be psychologically unstable (Herek, 1990). Similarly, the U.S. military denies gays and lesbians the opportunity to serve their country and, consequently, to earn a living through this means. However, this policy is currently under review. In 1993 President Clinton announced he would work with Pentagon and congressional leaders to end discrimination against lesbians and gays in the military. The United States will not be the first country to do so. In October 1992, Canada's Department of National Defense ended that country's practice of barring gays and lesbians from the armed forces.

Every June in major cities throughout the country, lesbians and gays march to demonstrate their pride in who they are.

Lesbians and gays also confront other problems because of their sexual orientation: They are often the victims of name calling, ridicule, and even violence. The incidence of "gay bashing" has been increasing in our society over the last several years (Peters, 1991). In 1990, 1588 such incidents were reported, up 42 percent from the number reported in 1989 (Casuso, 1991). In such a climate, it is easy to understand why many lesbians and gays keep their sexual orientation hidden. Lesbians and gays who "come out of the closet" and acknowledge their homosexuality risk discrimination and the loss of family and friends.

Only limited research has been done on the process of "coming out" (Harry, 1988). The available data indicate that mothers are generally told first. Their reactions are mixed; mothers who consider themselves religious are more likely to disapprove of their child's life-style than are other mothers. Fathers often take a more extreme reaction, severing contact with their lesbian or gay child. Not all parents react negatively, however; many are very supportive. A number of supportive parents formed Parents and Friends of Lesbians and Gays (PFLAG), an international organization with about 250 chapters in eight countries.

LIFE SATISFACTION: ELDERLY LESBIANS AND GAYS

Given the difficulties homosexuals still face in the United States, we might expect lesbians and gays, especially those who are older, to be dissatisfied with their lives. Studies do not bear this out, however. Older gay men are generally well adjusted, experience high levels of life satisfaction, and are not isolated (Kelly, 1977). In fact, one investigator suggested that in some ways being homosexual may actually prepare men for old age (Berger, 1982). Because many gay men cannot look to a family of procreation for support, in contrast to heterosexual men they become more independent early on. Similarly, Monika Kehoe (1989) found that the majority of elderly lesbians in her study scored in the upper percentile on the Life Satisfaction Scale and felt positive about their lifestyle.

COMMUNAL LIVING AND GROUP MARRIAGE

Thus far, this chapter has focused primarily on single people who live alone or cohabit. Not everyone, however, is content to live alone or to cohabit with just one other person. Some people join a commune to satisfy their needs for intimacy and companionship.

A **commune** refers to a group of people (single or married, with or without children) who live together, sharing many aspects of their lives. Communes have existed from earliest times. In particular, they are likely to develop or expand in periods of political and social unrest (Mead, 1970). The communal movement in the United States originated around the end of the eighteenth century. Most of the early communes were religious in origin (see the box titled "Would You Like to Join the Shakers?"). The political instability in the years immediately preceding and following the Civil War produced about a hundred new communes. One of them, the Hutterites, a commune with a religious origin, still has members in the United States today. The economic turmoil of the 1930s and the political activism of the 1960s also led to new waves of communal development (Zablocki, 1980). It is estimated that there are over 1000 functioning communes worldwide (Springs, 1989). Among the more widely known communes in the United States today are Sandhill in Missouri, Twin Oaks in Virginia, and The Farm in Tennessee.

ADVANTAGES AND DISADVANTAGES OF THE COMMUNAL LIFESTYLE

Have you ever considered joining a commune or asked yourself what motivates someone to enter such a lifestyle? Studies of communes suggest that their members are motivated by a desire for egalitarian, personalized, cooperative, and satisfying intimate relationships—qualities they perceive are not readily available in the traditional nuclear family structure.

Among the advantages most frequently reported by members of communes are close intimate relationships with a variety of people; personal growth through group experiences; the sharing of economic resources, domestic tasks, and child care; companionship; social support; spiritual rebirth or strengthening; and a respect and reverence for nature. These

FOR YOUR INFORMATION

WOULD YOU LIKE TO JOIN THE SHAKERS?

The Shakers, a religious community named for the way they moved during prayer and song, came to the United States in 1774. Founded by Ann Lee, a working-class woman from Manchester, England, the Shakers believed that monogamous marriage and the nuclear family were detrimental to the spiritual health of the community. Therefore, any married couple who joined the group had to agree to live apart lest they be tempted to resume a sexual life. The Shakers practiced strict celibacy and advocated equality between women and men. To lessen temptation, the Shakers built their communal house with separate entrances for women and men. They ate their meals together, but the women sat at one table and the men at another. Because the Shakers did not reproduce, they depended on new converts for survival. They also took in orphans and reared them in the community. The Shakers regarded all commune members as family regardless of blood or marital ties. By 1830, the Shakers had about 6000 members living in communities from New England to as far west as Kentucky and Ohio.

Today only a few Shakers are left. The last Shaker community is located in Sabbathday Lake, Maine. It consists of 7 women and 2 men, ranging in age from 28 to 90. Visitors to the community will find these modern-day Shakers wearing jeans, watching television, driving cars, and engaging in much the same activities as other people. A typical day is spent in prayer and work. However, these Shakers also travel regularly throughout the country, visiting museums and art galleries to tell the Shaker story. They welcome inquiries from newcomers, but anyone wishing to become a Shaker must live with the community for a year or so before making a decision.

These two women remain members of the Shaker community founded in 1774 to promote equality between women and men through communal living.

Source: Barbara Brotman, 1992a, "Shaker Cares," *Chicago Tribune* (February 19): Sec. 5, pp. 1, 5. © 1992, Chicago Tribune Company. All rights reserved. Used with permission.

---

advantages also create some disadvantages, including limitations on privacy, restrictions on personal freedom, limitations on parental influence and control, lack of stability, legal ambiguity, financial problems, and the possibility of sexual jealousy (Stinnet and Birdsong, 1978; Zablocki, 1980; Cornfield, 1983).

Most communes last for only short periods of time. Many of the problems encountered in communes center on conflicts over power, authority, and ideology. Those communes that survive the longest share certain characteristics: religious orientation, strict admission requirements, strong member commitment, controls on sexuality, adequate financing, time and space for privacy, and clearly defined authority and distribution of tasks (Mowery, 1978; Zablocki, 1980; Cornfield, 1983).

COMMUNES AND THE FUTURE As with other lifestyles, communes are not for everyone, and we can only speculate on their future viability. Some writers believe that if the economy worsens or if new political turmoil develops, the number of communes will grow. Others predict that as the nation ages, some form of communal or group living will become a viable option for older Americans who otherwise might be forced to live alone (Dressel and Hess,

1983). If communes are to be a viable option, however, critical issues of social policy will have to be reexamined. For example, many zoning laws restrict residential occupancy to individuals who meet the traditional definition of the family. Such policies exclude the possibility of communes developing in many neighborhoods.

GROUP MARRIAGES

Group marriages represent a variation of communal living. Sociologists Larry and Joan Constantine (1973:29) define **group marriage** as "a marriage of at least four people, two female and two male, in which each partner is married to all partners of the opposite sex." The actual number of documented group marriages has been small. One of the best-known experiments with group marriage was the Oneida Community in New York, founded by the Protestant minister John Noyes. It lasted from 1849 to 1881 and had about 300 adult members.

Monogamous marriage and sexual exclusivity were not permitted. Children were reared in a communal nursery by specialized caretakers, and they were taught to consider all adults in the community as parents. Thus, the entire community was to be viewed as a single family. Hostile outside pressure contributed to the demise of this experiment in group marriage (Kephart, 1988).

No one knows for sure how many group marriages currently exist in the United States. Because group marriages are neither legal nor socially acceptable to most Americans, locating them is a difficult task. The Constantines studied group marriages in the 1970s and believed that there were less than 1000 marriages, perhaps even fewer than 100 (Constantine and Constantine, 1972). The most commonly reported reason respondents gave for their involvement with group marriages was their dissatisfaction with traditional monogamous marriage. However, the Constantines found a high rate of breakup among the group marriages they located; the ones they studied lasted on the average only 16 months.

SUMMARY

Over the last several decades the number of never-married people in the United States has grown. This increase is not a new phenomenon. Rather, it represents a return to historically higher levels of singlehood, which began to decline markedly only after 1940. In the past singlehood was a devalued status, and single people were often the objects of ridicule. Today there is greater acceptance of single people. Singlehood can be voluntary or involuntary, temporary or permanent. Singles engage in a variety of lifestyles. Some live alone, others live with relatives or friends, and some choose to cohabit.

In the past, cohabitation, or "living together," was more common among the poor. Today's cohabitants include people of all ages, races, and classes. Cohabitation, like living alone, can be temporary and fluid. For many, cohabitation has become an extension of the dating process. The number of unmarried-couple households has increased from 439,000 in 1960 to almost 3 million in 1990. Cohabitation is similar to marriage in that couples create emotional and physical relationships with each other, and in some cases they also bear or rear children. It differs from marriage, however, in that it lacks formal legal, cultural, and religious support. Some couples choose to cohabit prior to marriage. Studies of the impact of cohabitation on marital stability are inconclusive at this time.

Some communities now allow lesbian, gay, and heterosexual cohabitants to register as domestic partners and to receive some of the same benefits that married couples do. Lesbians and gays deal with the same issues of living together that heterosexuals do: household division of labor, decision making, and finances. Additionally, however, they confront discrimination and social disapproval of their lifestyle.

Some individuals, seeking an alternative to traditional marriage, join a commune or participate in a group marriage. These arrangements generally meet with disapproval from the larger community, and most are relatively short-lived.

KEY TERMS

push/pull factors   domestic partnership
common-law marriage   commune
cohabitation   group marriage
palimony

QUESTIONS FOR STUDY AND REFLECTION

1. Identify and discuss the structural changes that have led to the growth in nonmarital lifestyles. What are some of the problems that people face when they live a nontraditional lifestyle? What advice would you give to someone whose lifestyle meets with social disapproval?

2. Compare and contrast the legal status of married couples with that of cohabitants. What do you see as the advantages or disadvantages of the concept of domestic partnership? Do you favor or oppose granting domestic partnership status to cohabitants? Explain your position.

3. Compare and contrast the lifestyles of lesbian, gay, and heterosexual cohabitants. How would you react if your new neighbors were heterosexual cohabitants, lesbian cohabitants, or gay cohabitants? Explain your position.

4. Consider the dissatisfaction with traditional marriages that is reported by people who join communes and participate in group marriages. How valid are these complaints? Do you think that communes or group marriages can overcome these problems? Why or why not?

FURTHER READING

BERGER, RAYMOND. 1982. *Gay and Gray: The Older Homosexual Man.* Urbana and Chicago: University of Illinois Press. Based on in-depth interviews with ten older homosexual men, this book challenges the stereotypes of the lonely, unwanted, and isolated older gay man.

KEHOE, MONIKA. 1989. *Lesbians over 60 Speak for Themselves.* New York: Haworth Press. This book is the first attempt to research a nationwide representation of elderly lesbians. It provides rich data on their backgrounds and relationships with family and friends.

STAPLES, ROBERT. 1981. *The World of Black Singles: Changing Patterns of Male/Female Relationships.* Westport, CT: Greenwood Press. The number of black singles is increasing at a rapid pace. This work focuses on college-educated, urban singles between the ages of 25 and 45 and describes how they go about constructing their lives.

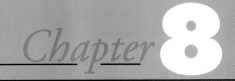

THE MARRIAGE EXPERIENCE

*M*arlene and Louis met in college, fell in love, and got married in a traditional church ceremony, on which Louis insisted. Both found jobs in their respective fields. Within the first year of the marriage Marlene discovered that she was pregnant. This unplanned pregnancy caused friction between the couple, with each blaming the other for being careless. Because Marlene was just establishing herself in her career, she planned to work during the pregnancy as long as her health would permit. She also planned to return to work as soon as possible after giving birth. Louis, however, did not agree with Marlene's plans. This resulted in many arguments throughout Marlene's pregnancy, with Louis insisting that Marlene quit work and stay home to be a full-time mother and homemaker. What Marlene once admired as Louis's masculinity and assertive personality now repelled her. She often told him he was not the man she married.

After the baby was born, Marlene reluctantly agreed to stay home. To compensate for the lost income, Louis decided to take on a second job. The couple continued to quarrel frequently, blaming each other for their problems and predicament. Marlene would accuse Louis of being insensitive, rigid, and unaffectionate, and would tell him he did not meet her needs. Louis would respond that he had unmet needs as well and that Marlene was unappreciative; she was lucky to have a man willing to let her stay home while he worked himself into poor health. The quarrels always ended with both partners feeling defeated and hopeless about the marriage.

Eventually Marlene began working part-time. For a while the couple rarely argued. Marlene, however, longed to resume her career on a full-time basis. As she became more vocal about this, the arguments resumed. At the same time, Louis lost his job and was forced to draw unemployment compensation. Creditors began pursuing the couple for unpaid bills. Under these circumstances the arguments became more intense and bitter. Sometimes the couple would go for weeks without even speaking to each other.

Suggestions by relatives and friends that perhaps it would be more healthful for everyone if the couple either sought professional counseling or separated were met with cold resistance. Marlene and Louis both claimed that in spite of their lifestyle and conflicts they loved each other and did not need a counselor, nor would they consider separating. They felt that they were a normal couple like thousands of others who simply disagreed from time to time.

What is happening in this marriage? Are Marlene and Louis a "typical" married couple? Are they really unconscious or unaware of the problems in their relationship? Who is at fault, if anyone? What are their fights really about? Do Marlene and Louis have compatible or conflicting marital expectations and goals? How and why do they believe that they are a well-adjusted couple with a few minor problems like all other couples? What, if anything, do you think needs to be done in this relationship?

Deciding whether to marry is one of the most important decisions we will make in our lifetime. This decision has implications for almost every aspect of an individual's life. Although U.S. society has experienced a significant rise in the divorce rate, in the number of couples who cohabit, and in the number of people who choose either to delay marriage or not to marry at all, most people in the United States marry at least once in their lifetime. Surveys continually reveal that Americans rank a good marriage at the top of their list of sources of satisfaction—above wealth, fame, good health, and a good job (Kidder, 1988). In addition, some researchers (for example, Kain, 1990) have predicted that the rates for both marriage and remarriage will continue to remain high into the twenty-first century. (See Chapter 14 for a full discussion of remarriage.)

These facts notwithstanding, as pointed out in Chapter 7, people in the United States today have more options concerning marital roles than they did in the past. The women's movement of the 1960s and 1970s has had a profound effect on social attitudes concerning the roles of women and men both inside and outside of marriages and families. Shifts in gender roles have altered not only how we view marriages and families but also how we experience them. In this chapter we examine the meaning of marriage in the United States in both traditional and contemporary terms. We pay particular attention to the legal aspects of marriage and their effect on marital relationships. In addition, we examine the nature of marriage relationships in the United States and the processes by which couples meet some of the many challenges of married life.

WHY DO PEOPLE MARRY?

Why is it that amid much discussion and speculation about the decline in marriage and family values, millions of Americans continue to marry each year? What is so attractive about marriage? What does it offer that other lifestyles do not? If you recall the discussion of love in Chapter 4, we indicated that most people in the United States believe that romantic love and marriage naturally go together; that marriage naturally follows falling in love. Given this notion about the interrelationship of love and marriage it should not be surprising that the single most important reason that people give for getting married is that they are in love. For many people marriage is a formal way for a couple to express their love, devotion, and commitment to each other and share their lives with the person of their choice. In this respect, marriage represents both a private and a public statement of commitment, trust, sharing, stability, intimacy, and the expectation of a permanent relationship.

In a discussion of couples who had been married for a long time and who described their relationships as happy, *Christian Science Monitor* staff writer Rushworth Kidder (1988) reported that when asked why they married or what they thought marriage offered, these couples most frequently focused on commitment and sharing. For example, Hattie Wilkerson, a retired cook married 48 years, responded, "To share with each other." Her husband, Melvin, responded in terms of the commitment needed to sustain a marriage (1988:54). According to Kidder, these two ideas in particular, sharing and commitment, are found throughout the responses of people who have strong marriages.

In addition to love and commitment, a number of social and economic reasons motivate people to marry. Some people marry purely for financial reasons, although this is less true now than in the past. This sometimes occurs among the upper classes, who build their lives around highly selective social encounters and relationships. It is also relatively common among many recently arrived ethnic groups whose subcultural norms may include arranged marriages, dowries, and bride prices.

Because social norms, values, and ideologies often equate adulthood with marriage, for some people achieving adulthood means getting married. People whose religious beliefs prohibit sexual intercourse and living together outside legal marriage marry to legitimize and sanctify their relationship. And some people marry because of peer or family pressure. Women in particular are often pressured to marry by well-meaning relatives and friends who do not want to see them end up "lonely old maids."

Another reason people marry is for companionship. Many people believe that being single inevitably leads to loneliness, even though there is no scientific evidence to support this view. Some evidence in fact suggests that people can be married and lonely; nonetheless, many people believe that marriage offers the best opportunity for steady companionship. Finally, some people marry to give legitimacy to a sexual relationship or to cohabitation, and others marry primarily for reproductive reasons—they want to have children or heirs who are recognized as legitimate by the state.

SOCIOLOGICAL PERSPECTIVES

On a theoretical level, there are several ways of explaining why people marry. A dominant point of view in the field of sociology has been a structural–functional analysis that ignores individual motivation, instead explaining why people marry in terms of society's need or demand for the legitimacy of children. The **principle of legitimacy**, the notion that all children ought to have a socially and legally recognized father, was first put forth by anthropologist Bronsilaw Malinowski (1929).

According to Malinowski, although many societies allow individuals the freedom to be sexually active whether or not they are married, only a very few societies allow their members the freedom to conceive children outside of marriage. Almost universally, marriage is based on the official control of childbearing. Because women give birth there is little doubt who is the mother of a child. There is, however, no visible means of identifying paternity. Thus, society must develop some means whereby men can be publicly (socially) and legally connected with their offspring. All societies, then, require that every child must have a man (a legitimately married father) who will assume the social role of father and protector and who will link the child to society.

In essence, such an explanation implies that people marry solely to have children. We know, however, that this is not the case for most people. The fact that a growing number of married couples do not have children gives us cause to question the viability of this principle to explain why people marry.

In contrast, a feminist perspective challenges theories such as the principle of legitimacy, maintaining that they place far more importance on the role of social father than mother in giving children social and legal status. Instead, a feminist perspective focuses on traditional gender-role socialization, in which girls are taught to consider love, marriage, and children the ultimate goals for women and the most fulfilling roles they can play in society (see Chapter 3). Thus, a woman's decision to marry can represent, in part, a response to social pressures and expectations.

Whatever reasons people have for marrying and whatever theories we use to explain why people marry, the fact remains that approximately 95 percent of us will marry at some time in our lives (*World Almanac*, 1990).

THE MEANING OF MARRIAGE

As we have seen, marriage means different things to different people. Virtually everyone, however, regards marriage as a relatively permanent and committed relationship. In addition, given the fact that most marriages take place within some religious context, we can surmise that most people also view marriage as a sacrament. How many of us, however, think of marriage in terms of a legal contract?

Marriage is not an isolated event. Rather, it joins together both the couple involved and their respective families. The relationships formed by marriage sometimes become complex and can require some regulation. For example, to prevent conflict the issue of inheritance and property rights requires a stable and consistent set of rules that prevails over time and applies fairly consistently across marriages and families. Thus, in the interest of order and stability, the state has set certain legal standards to which marriages and families must conform. These standards encompass such issues as whom we can marry, when we can marry them, who is a legitimate heir, and who has property and inheritance rights. Although the specific laws regulating marriages and families may vary from state to state, in all states marriage is a legal contract with specified rights and obligations.

In this section we take a brief look at marriage from three perspectives: as a commitment, as a sacrament, and as a legal contract.

MARRIAGE AS A COMMITMENT

Most researchers have found that commitment is a key factor in any intimate, emotionally satisfying, and meaningful relationship. When we pledge or commit ourselves to someone we generally assume (or certainly hope) the relationship will be long-term or permanent. According to some social scientists (Cherlin, 1981), human beings have a deep-seated need for secure, stable, and long-term relationships. Marriage is typically the type of relationship most people seek to fulfill this need.

In a survey of couples with long-term marriages, social researchers Jeanette and Robert Lauer (1985) found that a key factor contributing to the longevity of the relationship is the couple's belief in marriage as a long-term commitment and a sacred institution. Some of the couples viewed the marital commitment as analogous to a chain that binds the couple together whether or not they are happy. Others, however, viewed commitment as a vow to stay together and work through hard times. For example, one man in the study said: "Commitment means a willingness to be unhappy for a while…. You're not going to be happy with each other all the time. That's when commitment is really important" (1985:84).

Research (for example, Olson, 1986) has consistently indicated that strong families are those in which marital partners and family members are committed to each other; in which there is a high degree of togetherness and support. Commitment is not a single expectation or action. There are many aspects to commitment, some of which include the personal commitment between partners to each other, commitment to the relationship itself, commitment to the overall family unit, and long-term commitment. Commitment that includes these aspects tends to create individual as well as marital and family stability.

MARRIAGE AS A SACRAMENT

If you have not yet married but plan to in the future, what type of wedding will you have, and who will officiate at the ceremony? From a religious perspec-

Most first-time marriages in the United States are performed by some religious figure such as this rabbi.

tive marriage is regarded as a **sacrament**—a sacred union or rite. Did you know that the majority of people in this country who marry for the first time do so under the auspices of some religious figure such as a priest, rabbi, or minister? Although for economic and other considerations many people choose to bypass a religious ceremony, according to recent statistics at least three-fourths of first-time marriages and three-fifths of remarriages among divorced people take place within the context of some type of religious ceremony. Even widows and widowers frequently remarry within the context of a religious ceremony (U.S. National Center for Health Statistics, 1988). Is your choice of wedding ceremony consistent with these findings?

These statistics suggest that most people in this country regard marriage as a significant religious or holy institution based on a sacred commitment to each other and their God. In the Christian tradition, for example, the sacredness and joyfulness of marriage is often voiced in the story of Christ's first public miracle, which was said to have been the act of turning water into wine for a wedding celebration. In addition, marriage is considered to be a holy state ("holy matrimony") conducted under the direct authority of God ("What God has joined together let no man put asunder").

Marriage in the religious context is also considered to be a lifelong commitment. Recognizing that not all marriages will last a lifetime, however, some Protestant and Jewish denominations allow for the termination of marriage through divorce and sanctify remarriages based on the same principles of the sacrament. Some religions, however, most notably Catholicism, are quite literal in their interpretation of marriage as a holy union sanctioned by God. Thus, the Catholic church does not recognize divorce as a valid means of terminating a marriage. Under certain circumstances, however, the church may annul a marriage, declaring that the marriage never actually occurred.

MARRIAGE AS A LEGAL CONTRACT

Some marriage and family researchers have distinguished between what they call legal and social marriage. **Legal marriage** is a legally binding agreement or contractual relationship between two people that is defined and regulated by the state. In contrast, **social marriage** is a relationship between people who cohabit and engage in behavior that is essentially the same as that within a legal marriage, but the couple has not engaged in a marriage ceremony that is validated by the state. Thus, the relationship is not, under most circumstances, legally binding. Cohabitation and common-law marriage, both of which are discussed in Chapter 7, are examples of social marriage.

Marriage in the United States is a legal and financial contractual agreement that, like most other contractual agreements, is regulated by certain legal requirements. When two people marry, they agree to abide by the terms of the marriage contract. Although the marriage contract is very similar to an ordinary private contract, there are some very important differences. Unlike an ordinary private contract, the marriage contract is either unwritten or is not written in any one place. In addition, the terms and penalties of this contract are usually unspecified— that is, they are scattered throughout marriage and family laws and court decisions handed down over the years—or they are not very well known by the parties involved. In addition, the state, and not the married couple, specifies the conditions of the marriage contract. Therefore, unlike with a private contract, where the parties involved may break, modify, change, or restrict the contract by some mutual action, a married couple cannot on their own change or break the marriage contract.

Most contracts cannot be changed while they are in effect without the knowledge and consent of the parties involved. In contrast, the marriage contract, because its terms are defined by various policymakers such as judges and legislators, can be changed without the direct knowledge or consent of married couples. No other contract operates in this fashion. Because no one sends married couples a notification every time marriage laws change, most of us are unaware of these changes unless, of course, we keep abreast of them through media reports. Thus, for example, some states have proposed legislation that would require a wife to secure the consent of her husband before she could have an abortion. Even though the couple had little or no input into the proposed legislation, if it becomes law they are legally bound by it.

The most important marriage laws are state laws. The U.S. government has both created and defined marriage, giving the individual states the responsibility for ruling marriages. Each state defines the rights and obligations of married couples through a myriad of marriage and family laws, and only representatives of the state may marry people and terminate marriages. Even when people choose to be married by a member of the clergy, only those clergy that the state has granted the right to officiate at marriages may do so. In addition, state marriage laws cover only the residents of the particular state. Thus, if a couple marry in one state and later move to another state, their marriage is covered by the laws of the new state as soon as they become residents.

Most people probably do not think of marriage as a legally binding contract ruled by individual states. Most of us are not aware of marriage laws and the extent of the state's role in marriage until separation, divorce, or death occurs, or when inheritance or property rights are at issue.

SOME LEGAL ASPECTS OF THE MARRIAGE CONTRACT

Some of the more apparent legal aspects of the marriage contract specify who can marry whom and when. Every state in this country, for example, has laws that specify who can marry whom in terms of age and sex. In addition, until 1967 some states continued to specify who could marry whom in terms of race.

HETEROSEXUALITY In no state in this country can people of the same sex legally marry. This fact is not surprising given that most states define marriage

as a commitment by two people to carry on their lineage by conceiving and rearing children. Some people feel the legal prohibition of same-sex marriage prevents lesbian and gay couples from forming legal and public marital bonds that would secure their relationship rights and from publicly acknowledging their private commitments to each other (Bird and Sporakowski, 1992).

Marriage is a civil right that most heterosexuals take for granted. Although marriage has its drawbacks, some of its most striking benefits include the right of a surviving marital partner to inherit property, the right to file a joint income tax return (married couples filing jointly are taxed at a lower rate than single people and married couples who file separately), and the right to share in pension and health-care insurance benefits offered by many employers to their employees. In essence, then, the law sanctions heterosexual marriage and denies same-sex couples these legal benefits.

Same-sex marriage is not a new concept, nor is it an issue unique to the United States. In 1989, after a 40-year campaign by lesbian and gay rights activists, Denmark became the first country to legalize same-sex unions. Danish lesbians and gays can participate in a ceremony that legally joins a couple in a "registered partnership" that gives them most of the same rights as married heterosexuals (*Chicago Tribune*, 1989).

Believing that legal status should be given to committed relationships regardless of the sexual orientation of the couple, many gays and lesbians are participating in formal marriage ceremonies.

Although, as noted in Chapter 7, a few U.S. states recognize same-sex unions as domestic partnerships, this recognition does not include the same rights that married heterosexual couples enjoy. As an increasing number of lesbian and gay couples openly cohabit in more long-term relationships, they are placing greater pressure on business and government to extend to them the rights and privileges of married couples. As a result, we are witnessing a growing public debate between advocates and opponents of gay and lesbian marriage.

What do you think? Do laws prohibiting same-sex marriage violate the civil rights of gays and lesbians? The Critical Issues box titled "Should Lesbians and Gays Have the Right to Marry?" examines two different views on this controversial issue.

In addition to requiring heterosexuality in marital relationships, marriage law also requires monogamy. Under legal statutes people cannot have more than one spouse at a time. If an individual does, he or she can be prosecuted for **bigamy**—marrying one person while still being legally married to another. Although seldom enforced, many states have laws that prohibit **adultery**, extramarital sexual intercourse, and **fornication**, sexual intercourse outside legal marriage.

THE INCEST TABOO Not only does the marriage contract prohibit marriage between persons of the same sex, but it also prohibits marriage or sexual relations between a variety of relatives ranging from parents and siblings to non-blood-related in-laws. Although the specific set of blood relatives whom we cannot legally marry or have sex with differs from state to state, no state allows us to marry a parent, a sibling, an uncle or aunt, a niece or nephew, a grandparent, or a grandchild. The majority of states prohibit marriage between half siblings and first cousins. Some states also exclude second cousins and, in a few cases, third cousins. In addition, some states go so far as to prohibit marriage between **affinal relatives**, people related by marriage, such as a brother- or sister-in-law, even though they are not related by blood.

As we discussed in Chapter 1, although the range of relatives covered by the incest taboo has varied over human history, some theorists maintain that this taboo serves an important social and political function for families and society. By forcing families to mate and reproduce outside the immediate family network, marriage helps create political and economic relationships that are vital to society's structure and survival.

AGE RESTRICTIONS Marriage rules also define when we are considered mature enough to marry. In the past, the legal age at which people could marry was tied to puberty and the ages at which women and men could reproduce. If a person was old enough to reproduce, she or he was considered old enough to marry. Often the legal age for marriage was different for women and men.

Today, however, the concern is whether a person is mature enough to marry, regardless of the ability to reproduce. To ensure that a person is both old enough and mature enough, each state has set a legal age for marriage. That age varies, however, according to whether the couple have obtained their parents' consent. The marriageable age for women and men, with or without parental consent, is the same in most states. For example, in every state except one, the legal age at which marriage can be contracted without parental consent is 18 for both women and men. In Georgia, a female or male may contract a marriage without parental consent as early as 16 years of age. On the other hand, on the island of Puerto Rico individuals cannot contract a marriage on their own until age 21. (See Appendix F for a list of marriage requirements by state.)

With parental consent the picture changes. The typical age requirement for marriage with parental consent is 16. In as many as five states (Alabama, New Hampshire, New York, Texas, and Utah), however, females and males may marry as early as 14 years of age if their parents consent. Moreover, in a few states, parental consent is not required if a minor was previously married. And two states (California and Mississippi) have no age limits. In some states minors may obtain a marriage license if the female is pregnant, if a child has already been born to the couple, or under what some states define as "special circumstances." In other states a minor wishing to marry must not only have parental consent but must also get the permission of a judge.

BLOOD TESTS Regardless of age and whether parental consent is needed, when two people plan to marry they must file an application with the state and obtain a marriage license. In the majority of the states (approximately two-thirds), to obtain a marriage license a couple first must be tested to determine if they have a sexually transmitted disease. This procedure is commonly referred to as "getting a blood test."

SHOULD LESBIANS AND GAYS HAVE THE RIGHT TO MARRY?

Most people in the United States regard getting married and raising a family as a civil right that is so basic that they do not even question it. However, this civil right does not extend to lesbian and gay couples. Some lesbians and gays exchange vows and rings to symbolize their commitment to one another and to publicly challenge the heterosexual exclusivity of marriage. Others call for an outright ban on heterosexual marriage until same-sex marriage is recognized as a legal right. These actions and attitudes have contributed to a growing public debate on whether or not lesbians and gays should have the legal right to marry. Although people are generally divided on the issue of lesbian and gay marriage, the arguments supporting their viewpoint vary.

Supporters of lesbian and gay marriage believe that the right to marry is a civil right. They argue that lesbians and gays are human beings who, like heterosexuals, are citizens and taxpayers and thus should have the same basic human rights as other citizens.

Some supporters emphasize biology. They argue that the evidence is still mixed regarding the causes of homosexuality. Recent research, for example, indicates that there may be a biological link to homosexuality. If this is the case, they argue, then homosexuality is not simply a

matter of choice. Therefore, lesbians and gays should no more be penalized because of their orientation than heterosexuals.

Others argue that legalizing lesbian and gay marriage might eventually change people's attitudes toward homosexuality, ultimately leading to complete acceptance as people come to see lesbians and gays as family-oriented rather than as deviants.

Still others point to the heterosexual double standard: Although society encourages commitment and stability in intimate heterosexual relationships vis-à-vis marriage, these same characteristics are unacceptable when applied to lesbian and gay relationships.

Those against lesbian and gay marriage often use a biological or religious argument to support their position. For example, many detractors argue that homosexuality is unnatural in that two people of the same sex cannot reproduce—procreation being an activity they consider integral to marriage. In addition, some detractors argue that homosexuality not only contradicts natural biological laws but also the laws of God and Christianity. They quote the Bible chapter and verse to support their viewpoint that such behavior is sinful and should not be condoned through legal sanctioning of same-

sex marriages. Granting marital status to lesbian and gay relationships implies that the two are of equal social and spiritual value in society. This, they argue, would encourage more people to engage in what they believe to be a "deviant" lifestyle.

An interesting position taken by some detractors is that, although legal marriage secures social approval and provides economic benefits, the cost to lesbians and gays would outweigh these benefits. According to this position, legalized same-sex marriage would greatly constrain homosexual identities by mainstreaming lesbian and gay lifestyles. This would, in effect, create a climate where the uniqueness, distinctiveness, and diversity of lesbian and gay lifestyles would be ignored and heterosexuality would continue to be used as the standard by which to measure normalcy in all intimate relationships.

What do you think? Should lesbians and gays have the right to marry? Might legal homosexual marriage lead to societal acceptance of lesbians and gays? What do you think might be some of the consequences for society if lesbians and gays where allowed to legally marry? Would lesbian and gay marriage require a redefinition of marriage? If you know lesbian or gay couples personally, ask them their views on this subject.

Usually there is a brief waiting period between the time people are tested and the time they receive the marriage license. In several states individuals are tested for other diseases in addition to sexually transmitted diseases. For example, in eight states, people

(especially women) also must be tested for rubella (German measles) and their Rh blood type (see Chapter 10). In New York, certain applicants may be further required to take a test for sickle cell anemia, a condition that is far more prevalent among blacks than among whites, before a marriage license is issued. If the sickle cell condition is present, a couple can be denied a marriage license unless it is established that procreation is not possible (*World Almanac,* 1990).

Although most states require some type of medical test for sexually transmitted diseases, there is little routine testing for AIDS prior to marriage. For example, for a short period of time in the late 1980s, Illinois law required AIDS testing before a marriage license could be obtained. In 1989, however, the law was rescinded, due in part to the fact that many people, unhappy with the law, crossed state lines and married in surrounding states. In addition, the tests proved extremely expensive and uncovered only a small number of AIDS cases (Marriage License Bureau and Cook County Clerk's Office, 1993).

One last point is that some individuals do not do any of the things discussed in the previous paragraphs, yet their relationship is recognized by the state as a legal, or common-law, marriage. As discussed in Chapter 7, although common-law marriages were once widely recognized, today only about one-fourth of the states recognize them.

Thus, in answering the question, What is marriage? we have seen that marriage is a complex contractual agreement among not two but three parties: the couple and the state.

CHANGE AND CONTINUITY IN THE MEANING OF MARRIAGE

One of the most fundamental and significant premises on which U.S. marriage and family laws have been based is the historical notion that the family is the property of the husband, and therefore he is the head of the household. The other side of this argument is the belief that women are the weaker sex and need the care and protection of men. This belief reflects the common-law concept of **coverture**, the idea that a wife is under the protection and influence of her husband. From these assumptions flow many rights, obligations, and expectations about how a married couple should behave and relate to each other. Therefore, not surprisingly, we find that over the course of time many of the rules and laws surrounding marriage have treated women and men differently based solely on their biological sex.

Historically, marriage has extended the rights of men vis-à-vis women and children. Women, in contrast, have lost many legal rights when they married, because their marital obligations and rights have been defined primarily in terms of their service to husbands and children. Under this arrangement, for example, women have suffered a long history of violence at the hands of their husbands, who, until the late 1800s, could legally beat their wives. (Chapter 12 contains an in-depth discussion of this issue.)

PROVISIONS OF THE MODERN MARRIAGE CONTRACT

The provisions of the modern marriage contract are similar to those based on the old principle of coverture. Social scientist Lenore Weitzman (1977), for example, has identified four basic provisions of the traditional marriage contract that have been incorporated into marriage laws in this country: (1) The wife is responsible for caring for the home, (2) the wife is responsible for caring for any children, (3) the husband is head of the household, and (4) the husband is responsible for providing support for the family.

In the language of marital rights and obligations, these provisions assert that the wife owes her husband domestic and companionship services, and in return the husband owes his wife protection and economic support. Although marriage and family laws are becoming more equitable in the treatment of wives and husbands, the provisions listed above are not simply old-fashioned ideas that are no longer relevant. In many states women continue to lose legal rights when they marry, and they continue to be treated as the property of their husbands (Skolnick and Skolnick, 1987).

Although today the specific conditions of the marriage contract vary from one state to another, some common assumptions are evident. In the following discussion we examine some specific beliefs and practices from the past in terms of their impact on current marital patterns, noting both continuity and changes where they have occurred.

MARRIAGE AND RESIDENCE In the past, a woman was expected to take her husband's surname and move into his domicile (place of residence). Although a wife is no longer required to take her husband's name, a husband retains the

FOR YOUR INFORMATION

THE MARRIAGE CONTRACT: TRADITION AND RITUALS

As the previous discussion implies, in many ways the traditional marriage contract can be viewed as a transference of property among males: from a father to a husband. Indicative of the property status of women was the practice whereby a prospective husband had to receive the father's permission to marry his daughter. And at the time of the wedding the father gave his daughter to the groom. These are only two of many marriage traditions, almost all of which reflect in some way the unequal status of women and men.

Have you ever wondered about the origins and meaning of various rituals and traditions surrounding marriage in the United States? For example, why do you think that brides today need "something old, something new, something borrowed, and something blue"? This tradition apparently dates back to ancient Hebrew society, when brides wore blue ribbons on their wedding day to signify love, purity, and fidelity. In addition, the ancient Hebrews believed that if a bride wore an item borrowed from a married woman, the married woman's wedded happiness would transfer to the bride-to-be. How much do you know about other wedding rituals and traditions? See how many of the origins or stories behind the wedding traditions and rituals described below are already familiar to you.

The Bridal Shower
The first bridal shower is believed to have been held in Holland. This tradition supposedly began when a father denied his daughter permission to marry a poor man with whom she had fallen in love. When the man's friends heard this they gave the bride-to-be numerous gifts so that the couple could be married.

Bachelor Party
The ritual of the bachelor party dates back to ancient Greece. The night before the wedding a lavish dinner was held for the groom-to-be. It was not, at that time, referred to as a bachelor's party; rather, it was called the "men's mess."

The Honeymoon
Did you ever wonder why newlyweds keep their honeymoon a secret? In fact, sometimes the bride-to-be herself does not know where she is going for the honeymoon. It is probably not surprising that the honeymoon originated in France, a country that is synonymous with love and romance. Several hundred years ago, to escape relatives or others who opposed their marriage, the newlywed couple would seclude themselves in some secret place for a month until the opposition gave up and stopped looking for

legal right to decide where the couple will live, and marriage law imposes an obligation on the wife to live in her husband's choice of residence. Therefore, when a woman marries, if her place of residence is different from her husband's, his place of residence automatically supersedes hers. If a woman lives in a different state from her husband and she does not take her husband's place of residence as her own, the legal ramifications are many. For example, she must reregister to vote; she could lose the right to attend a university in her hometown as a resident student; and she could lose the privilege of running for public office in her home state (Renzetti and Curran, 1992).

Laws pertaining to the marital domicile reflect traditional gender inequalities in other ways. For example, if a husband gets a job in another city and his wife refuses to relocate with him, she is assumed by law to have abandoned him. If, on the other hand, a wife gets a job in another city and her husband refuses to relocate with her, she is still defined by law as having abandoned him.

In this sense, men are still assumed to be the head of the household and can therefore determine where the family will live (Sapiro, 1990). Over the years, however, some equalizing of marital roles and obligations has occurred. Thus, in many states today a woman can establish a separate household for a specific purpose. In addition, one state court recently ruled that a wife who is the primary breadwinner can decide where the couple will live (Renzetti and Curran, 1992).

216   *Chapter 8*

them. It is said that during this time of seclusion, the couple drank a special wine made with honey while watching the moon go through all of its phases. Thus, the term *honeymoon* literally means "moon of honey."

The Wedding Veil

The tradition of the wedding veil cannot be traced to one single country; rather, it has its origins in many cultures. In general, to protect the bride from the evil wishes of her rivals, her face was covered on her wedding day. In addition, the veil also represented the bride's purity at marriage. After the marital vows were exchanged, the veil was pulled back from the bride's face to symbolize her new status as wife. In ancient Rome and Greece, wedding veils were brightly colored, whereas the early Christian bride wore a white or purple veil to symbolize virginity.

Standing Arrangements at the Wedding Ceremony

It is said that the requirement that the bride stand to the left of the groom at the altar is a tradition dating back to a time when men carried swords to protect themselves and their loved ones. Tradition claims that the bride was required to stand to the left of the groom so that he could keep his right hand (his sword hand) free to protect and defend himself and his bride from his enemies or disgruntled in-laws.

Throwing the Bouquet

This ritual is said to have its basis in a bride's desire to save herself from an onslaught of wedding guests. In times past, it was the custom for guests to reach for the bride's garter. One bride, tiring of the practice, decided that throwing the bouquet would be safer. According to tradition, the unmarried woman who catches

Similar to the bridal tradition of tossing the bouquet, some contemporary grooms throw the bride's garter and, according to tradition, the single male who catches it will be the next one to marry.

the bouquet will be the next one to get married.

Source: Adapted from "Wedding Traditions Date Back for Centuries," 1988, *Chicago Sun-Times* (January 17): Special advertising sect., p. 2.

MARRIAGE AND PROPERTY RIGHTS In the past, a woman's property rights also came under the control and management of her husband once she married. Not only did a husband gain control of his wife's property on marriage, but he could also do with it as he pleased, with or without her knowledge or consent. Today, however, women have considerable property rights, although the specifics differ across states. In some states a wife and husband may own property individually, whereas in others their property may be considered community property.

Most U.S. states recognize the individual ownership of property. Whoever has proof of ownership of property owns it in the eyes of the law. If neither the wife nor husband has proof of ownership, however, most courts determine that the husband is the owner,

particularly if the wife has remained in the home as a homemaker during the marriage. The court's rationale is that because the wife had no income with which to acquire the assets, they belong to the husband, who has simply allowed her use of them over the years. Thus, for example, in some cases a joint bank account has been deemed by the court to belong to the husband if the wife did not earn an income.

As this discussion makes clear, common-law property states, as they are called, give quite an advantage to husbands. It is ironic that those women who conform most closely to the patriarchal norms that surround marital roles are the ones who are hurt most by marriage laws and regulations pertaining to property ownership. Women who have spent their lives in service to their husbands (and children) end up with few assets of their own. Moreover, because of their dependency on their husbands, they are the most vulnerable during and after marriage.

In the community property system, practiced in only a few states, wives and husbands own all assets jointly and equally whether or not the wife earns an income (Sapiro, 1990). This system does not penalize women for choosing to be full-time homemakers, although it does present other problems for wives which are discussed in more detail in Chapter 13.

As disadvantaged as married women were in the past and are today under the principle of coverture, men also were and still are restricted in several important ways. For example, it was argued that because marriage awarded a wife a right of inheritance, the husband's estate was reduced. In addition, marriage obligated a husband to support his wife and family, an obligation that poor and working-class men often found difficult to meet solely on their own. The continuation of this idea and the inequities it engenders for men are reflected in the fact that husbands today are still legally obliged to support their wives even if the wife works and earns a higher wage than the husband.

Given our discussion of marital rights and obligations thus far, are you wondering about the degree to which these principles are enforceable by law? We turn our attention next to an examination of this question.

MARRIAGE PRINCIPLES AND THE LAW

According to political scientist and women's studies professor Virginia Sapiro (1986), a husband's right to his wife's services is basically unenforceable by law in a direct sense. There are, however, some very important consequences of this provision of the marriage contract. As we discuss in more detail in Chapter 12, because of a husband's **conjugal rights**—rights pertaining to the marriage relationship—in about half of U.S. states a wife cannot charge her husband with rape. Furthermore, because the marriage contract obliges a wife to perform domestic labor for her husband, she cannot be directly compensated for her work, and until recent times her economic contribution to the marriage was not considered in the division of property at the

time of divorce. Interestingly, although the husband has no legal obligation to compensate his wife for domestic services, if a third party injures the wife, the husband can legally sue the party for the value of the domestic services that he lost.

Although a wife has a legal right to be supported by her husband, she has little control over the nature or amount of that support. Again, based on an accumulation of findings in various court cases, it seems that as long as a wife and husband live together the husband has a right to support his wife in whatever manner he chooses. If a wife feels she is not being adequately supported she has little legal recourse.

THE MARRIAGE CONTRACT TODAY

Since the 1970s, marriage and family law in the United States has changed substantially, although certain traditions and legal restrictions continue to leave women at a disadvantage. As pointed out, women no longer have to take their husband's surname. In many states, however, a wife who takes her husband's surname must seek his permission to return to using her maiden name. In the past the decision not to adopt the husband's surname often created legal problems and unnecessary difficulties for the couple. For example, employees in insurance companies, banks, and other bureaucracies often had difficulty dealing with married customers with different surnames. Thus, such customers were sometimes denied services meant for married couples, or they were seriously inconvenienced. Today, however, legal and business establishments have caught up with this practice, and a woman's decision to retain her family name does not appear to cause as many difficulties.

Rather than give up their family name upon marrying, a current practice for some women is to hyphenate their name after marriage (for example, Lillian Brown-Johnson). This practice, however, is not without problems. How will the couple name their children? Will their children carry the father's surname only? Will they carry the hyphenated name? If so, when the children become adults, can they hyphenate their already-hyphenated name?

Sometimes we get so caught up in our own traditions we think that they are the same for all people. However, different cultures define marriage differently and have rituals and traditions that are based on their unique sociocultural and political experiences. People studying different cultures have discovered interesting marriage practices that demonstrate the uniqueness of each culture.

China

The Chinese have a perfect solution for individuals who do not marry in their lifetime: a posthumous wedding. The "spirit wedding" is an ancient custom that is being revived in the Chinese countryside today. It is supposed to ensure that people who die unmarried will have a partner in the afterlife. In this custom an aging unmarried person buys a corpse in preparation for the "spirit wedding" when she or he dies. Upon death, the two will be "married" with a full ceremony and will be buried together. Under this practice, a 70-year-old man can marry a 7-month-old baby, or a young man can marry an old woman (*Chicago Tribune*, 1991).

Iraq

In the 1950s, Elizabeth and Robert Fernea lived in an Iraqi peasant village and studied the women's lives in detail. In this culture, parents arranged their children's marriages, and a couple could not meet before their wedding day without violating important cultural customs. For women, virginity was essential and had to be maintained at all costs until the wedding day. On the wedding day the couple consummated their marriage while their mothers, friends, and other relatives waited outside the couple's bedroom. When they finished, the mothers inspected the wedding sheets for blood from the young bride's broken hymen (a membranous fold of tissue partly closing the external opening of the vagina) and publicly announced the proof of the bride's virginity. If there was no blood, it was assumed that the bride was not a virgin, and her family suffered great humiliation. The bride herself was often put to death as a ruined woman (Fernea, 1965).

The Tiwi of Australia

Among the Tiwi, an Aboriginal people on the islands off the coast of Australia, there is no such thing as an unmarried female. Females are betrothed by their fathers before they are born into a system of reciprocity among males. Tiwi males gain prestige through the number of marriage contracts they make. Thus, marriage contracts are highly valued, even if some are with brides who are not yet born or who are not yet old enough to join the husband's household. In this system of polygyny for males and serial marriage for females, because the husband must be an adult before an infant female can be married to him, females are likely to outlive their husbands. Thus, when a husband dies, the wife's father or next male head of family has the right and responsibility to make a new marriage contract for her. She can never be unmarried. Given the prestige for males of having many marriage contracts, all Tiwi women, including the elderly, are valuable as wives (O'Kelly and Carney, 1986).

Other ways in which some people attack gender-stereotypic wedding rituals and traditions include brides having "best women" or best men, grooms having "men of honor" or females (rather than best men) stand up for them, both parents (as opposed to the father alone) giving away a daughter, one or both parents giving away the groom, or completely eliminating the ritual of someone giving the bride away.

MARRIAGE VOWS As more and more people change their views of marriage, they are also changing or at least modifying many of the rituals and traditions of weddings. For example, although some people continue to recite traditional wedding vows when they marry, others have modified or rewritten those vows to accommodate their preferences. The following sets of vows represent the traditional wedding vows and a set of vows written by a white middle-class couple (Mary and Richard) who married in the 1970s. How do they compare to the vows you recited or plan to recite?

Traditional Marriage Vows

I, _____, take thee, _____,
to be my lawful wedded wife (husband).
To have and to hold from this day forward
For better, for worse,
For richer, for poorer
In sickness and in health
To love (honor, and obey)* and to cherish
From this day forward
Till death do us part.

The Marriage Vows of Mary and Richard

Mary (Richard), to manifest my deep love for you,
I promise to cherish you, care for you,
and to share with you the difficulties, the
sorrows, and the hardships as well as the
joys, the beauty, and the happiness that
come our way.
I promise you a warm home and a dear and
understanding heart in it, so that we may
grow with and for each other.
I promise to work together with you to build
and to maintain this home and this love.**

Furthermore, many couples today are defining for themselves what their marriage will be; what their relationship with each other will be, including the economic and social obligations they will have to each other during their marriage. They are doing this by writing their own **personal marriage agreement**—a written agreement between a married couple in which issues of role responsibility, obligation, and sharing are addressed in a manner that is tailored to their own personal preferences, desires, and expectations.

PRENUPTIAL AGREEMENTS Today the marriage plans of many couples include the use of a personal marriage agreement in one of two ways. One is as a **prenuptial agreement** developed and worked out in

consultation with an attorney and filed as a legal document. The purpose of drawing up a prenuptial agreement in this manner is to negotiate ahead of time the settlement of property, alimony, or other financial matters in the event of death or divorce. The marriage agreement can also serve as a personal agreement between partners drafted primarily for the purpose of helping the couple clarify their expectations concerning their marriage.

Formal or legal marriage agreements such as prenuptial agreements are not new. Wealthy members of society have long used these agreements to protect family fortunes. It has been reported that prior to their marriage Jacqueline Kennedy and Aristotle Onassis drew up a 170-point prenuptial agreement (Totenberg, 1985).

Today, it is not just the rich and famous but an increasing number of middle-class couples, elderly couples, and divorced people who are ensuring before the wedding that in case the marriage ends their assets will go or remain where they want them. Because of the high rate of divorce, several divorce lawyers suggest that anyone (not just the rich) who is planning to marry should consider a premarital agreement. In addition, many attorneys suggest that cohabiting couples draw up a relationship contract even though some courts are still reluctant to enforce this type of agreement because they see it as potentially undermining the institution of marriage.

Although anyone can draw up a prenuptial agreement, for it to be upheld in court those involved must demonstrate that it is a fair agreement, signed voluntarily by both parties and entered into in good faith. To meet this criterion parties should secure the services of an attorney who is familiar with state laws governing marriage and community property. Even then there is no guarantee that courts will uphold all of the agreement's provisions. Although the specifications in the agreement may be morally binding, some, such as specifications concerning living arrangements, are not enforceable in court (Totenberg, 1985).

PERSONAL CONTRACTS The most popular version of the personal marriage agreement among couples today is the *personal contract*, created by the couple without advice or counsel from an attorney. Although these contracts serve primarily as guides to future behavior, they are sometimes filed as legal contracts. As

---

*Most couples, even if they recite the traditional vows, no longer vow to obey their partner.

**In addition, Mary chose to maintain her birth name.

THE MARRIAGE OF LUCY STONE: UNDER PROTEST

As far back as 1855, suffragist and feminist Lucy Stone and her husband-to-be, Henry Blackwell, wrote their own personal contract in protest against the inequality of women in marriage. Lucy Stone, who worked all of her adult life for women's rights and liberation, reluctantly gave up her freedom to marry Henry Blackwell, a well-known abolitionist. The couple drafted the following personal contract, which they later had read and signed as part of their wedding ceremony. In addition, Lucy Stone refused to take her husband's surname, preferring to be known instead as "Mrs. Stone."

Lucy Stone and Henry Blackwell's Personal Marriage Contract

While acknowledging our mutual affection by publicly assuming the relationship of husband and wife, yet in justice to ourselves and a great principle, we deem it a duty to declare that this act on our part implies no sanction of, nor promise of voluntary obedience to, such of the present laws of marriage as refuse to recognize the wife as an independent, rational being, while they confer upon the husband an injurious and unnatural superiority, investing him with legal powers which no honorable man would exercise, and which no man should possess. We protest especially against the laws which give to the husband:

1. The custody of the wife's person.
2. The exclusive control and guardianship of their children.
3. The sole ownership of her personal, and use of her real, estate, unless previously settled upon her, or placed in the hands of trustees, as in the case of minors, lunatics, and idiots.
4. The absolute right to the product of her industry.
5. Also against laws which give to the widower so much larger and more permanent an interest in the property of his deceased wife, than they give to the widow in that of the deceased husband.
6. Finally, against the whole system by which "the legal existence of the wife is suspended during marriage," so that in most States, she neither has a legal part in the choice of her residence, nor can she make a will, nor sue or be sued in her own name, nor inherit property.

We believe that personal independence and equal human rights can never be forfeited, except for crime; that marriage should be an equal and permanent partnership, and so recognized by law; that until it is so recognized, married partners should provide against the radical injustice of present laws, by every means in their power. We believe that where domestic difficulties arise, no appeal should be made to legal tribunals under existing laws, but that all difficulties should be submitted to the equitable adjustment of arbitrators mutually chosen.

Thus, reverencing law, we enter our protest against rules and customs which are unworthy of the name, since they violate justice, the essence of law.

(Signed) Henry B. Blackwell,
Lucy Stone.

Source: Miriam Schneir, 1972, *Feminism: The Essential Historical Writings* (New York: Vintage Books/Random House), pp. 104–5.

with the more formal and legal prenuptial agreements, personal contracts are not new. At different times in history couples have used the personal contract to satisfy a range of personal needs, including as a protest against the gender inequalities inherent in the traditional marriage contract. For an example of a personal contract designed as a means of protest, see the FYI box titled "The Marriage of Lucy Stone: Under Protest."

Many people view personal marriage agreements as cold, unromantic, and businesslike, and an indication of mutual distrust on the part of the couple. Other people consider premarital agreements to have several important benefits, including forcing a couple to communicate with each other their marital expectations, desires, and goals. Personal agreements are not limited to couples planning to marry. Any couple who are committed to each other or who live together as well as couples who are legally prohibited from marrying can benefit from such agreements.

Prenuptial or personal marriage agreements can include anything a couple consider appropriate, such as the general expectations a couple have for each other, the division of roles and tasks in the marriage or living arrangement, and whether they will have children. In Chapter 16 we invite you to write your own personal marriage or relationship agreement. We present many topics for your consideration. Are other topics relevant to your relationship? Did the contract between Lucy Stone and Henry Blackwell give you any ideas?

A personal marriage agreement notwithstanding, what happens once a couple is married? What kinds of changes take place in their lives? Do women and men experience marriage in the same way? In the remaining sections of this chapter we discuss marriage as it is experienced by women and men. In this regard, we examine gender differences in the marital experience, factors related to transitions and adjustments to marriage, some common typologies of marital relationships, heterogamous marriages, and the benefits of positive and open communication in marriages and intimate relationships.

MARRIAGE AND GENDER

Marriage and family researchers across academic disciplines increasingly are acknowledging that marriage is not experienced in the same way by women and men; that every marriage actually contains two marriages: hers and his. In her now classic book *The Future of Marriage* (1972), sociologist Jessie Bernard detailed the different experiential realities of wives and husbands. When asked identical questions about their marriage, husbands and wives answered so differently that Bernard called their marriages "her marriage" and "his marriage." Even when asked basic questions like how often they had sexual relations or who made decisions, wives' and husbands' responses were so different it was as though they were talking about two different marriages. Though largely hidden, the female–male differences in the experience of marriage have a tremendous effect on the mental and physical well-being of wives and husbands.

"HER" MARRIAGE

Does it surprise you that Bernard found that wives were much less happy in their marriages than their husbands? Some people believe that these are just a

few disgruntled wives; that couples who love each other live in a kind of identical harmony and peace. Several of Bernard's findings challenge this assumption. For example, although wives reported being happier with their lives than did single women, when compared with husbands they reported being less happy. In addition, married women reported much higher rates of anxiety, phobia, and depression than any other group in society except single men, and wives had a higher rate of suicide than husbands.

Research continues to uncover women's and men's different perceptions and experience of marriage. Reporting on a study of married couples between the ages of 17 and 69, for example, Daniel Goleman (1987) pointed out that husbands and wives differ dramatically in terms of how they evaluate their relationship. Men tend to rate almost everything as better than do their wives. They have a much more positive perception of marital sex, family finances, ties with parents, listening to each other, tolerance of flaws, and romance. Wives, on the other hand, tend to complain more about their marriage than husbands do.

Perhaps something about the nature or structure of marriage itself accounts for these gender differences. The structure of traditional marriage, particularly with regard to the housewife role, is revealing in this regard. For example, the division of labor in traditional marriages leads to fewer sources of gratification for housewives than for husbands. The imbalance of power in traditional marriages further alienates the housewife from her wifely role. According to Bernard, the housewife role has a "pathogenic" effect on wives. Often when women marry they lose their legal and personal identity and become totally dependent on their husbands. This dependency often leads to depression. Other researchers (for example, Gove, 1972) have concurred with this view, noting that the housewife role is so unstructured and devalued that wives often have low self-esteem, are highly self-critical, and are far more vulnerable to depression and unhappiness than their husbands are.

"HIS" MARRIAGE

Many of you have probably grown up on tales of men running from marriage, going to great lengths to avoid being "trapped." This folklore actually runs counter to the reality of women's and men's lives. In reality men seem to prefer marriage to being single. For example, when asked if they would marry the same person again, they respond in the affirmative twice as often as their wives do. In addition, most divorced and widowed men remarry, and at every age level the rate of marriage for these men is higher than the rate for single men. Furthermore, when compared with single men, married men live longer, have better mental and physical health, are less depressed, have a lower rate of suicide, are less likely to be incarcerated for a crime, earn higher incomes, and are more likely to define themselves as happy.

Although marriage is beneficial overall for men, it imposes certain costs. Bernard contends that a major cost of marriage for men is that they must give up their sexual freedom and take on the responsibility of supporting a wife and family. The provider role is costly in other respects, including the fact that it forces many men to work harder than they might otherwise. This cost, however, has been modified as women and men have become more sexually free both within and outside marriage and as more and more married women work outside the home and contribute to the family income. According to social scientist Marie Richmond-Abbott (1983), traditional marriage reinforces stereotypical masculine roles and may actually hurt men in such marriages.

TRANSITIONS AND ADJUSTMENTS TO MARRIAGES[*]

Getting married represents a significant change in the lives of a couple. The world of married couples is in many important ways different from the world of singles. As a married couple, two people must fit their lives together and meet and satisfy each other's needs. In simple terms **marital adjustment** is the degree to which a couple get along with each other or have a good working relationship and are able to satisfy each other's needs over the marital life course. One major adjustment that a married couple must make involves being identified with a partner and

[*]Although this discussion focuses specifically on marital adjustment, the information can apply as well to cohabitation or other relationships outside legal marriage.

Older married couples often must adjust to retirement and having more time to spend together as a couple.

thought of by the community as one unit, as opposed to the unique individual each person was before the marriage. Another set of marital adjustments regards seeing and relating to a partner on a daily basis and learning to live with that person and accommodate her or his wants, needs, expectations, and desires. Still other adjustments include sharing space, money, relatives, and friends with a partner, the division of tasks in the relationship, and adjustment to the partner's sexual attitudes and behaviors. Changing from a single to a married persona does not always run smoothly. Most couples, however, manage it with a minimum of problems.

Adjustment doesn't simply happen one day in a marriage; rather, it is an ongoing process. As pointed out in Chapter 2, some family sociologists hold that marriages and families move through a series of life events over the course of the marital life cycle. Research shows that couples must continuously make adjustments in marriage as they are confronted with new and different life-course events.

A TYPOLOGY OF MARITAL RELATIONSHIPS

What makes a happy, well-adjusted marriage? Most contemporary studies have concluded that there is no single model for a well-adjusted marriage. Helpfulness, love, mutual respect, and selflessness are but a few of the many characteristics associated with marital adjustment. Researchers John Cuber and Peggy Harroff (1966), in their study of 211 couples who had been married for 10 or more years and who expressed commitment to each other, concluded that satisfying, well-adjusted, enduring marital relationships can vary a great deal from each other and from societal ideals of a happy marriage. Although their work is more than 25 years old, it is still the most frequently cited research on adjustment and happiness in marriage. Cuber and Harroff identified five distinct types of marriages, representing a wide range of communication patterns and interaction styles: conflict-habituated, devitalized, passive-congenial, vital, and total.

THE CONFLICT-HABITUATED RELATIONSHIP

The first type, the *conflict-habituated relationship*, is characterized by extensive tension and conflict, although for the most part the tension and conflict are managed or controlled. The conflict-habituated couple engage in verbal arguments or fights about anything and everything: the past, children, politics. Sometimes the fights are private, but often they occur in front of the children, neighbors, friends, or relatives and come to be expected and tolerated. A high school son, for example, remarked somewhat nonchalantly: "Oh, they're at it again—but they always are" (1966:44). Such couples acknowledge that conflict and tension are pervasive in their relationship, but each knows how to keep the tension under control. Channeling conflict and hostility is so important to these couples it becomes a habitual part of their marriage. Some psychiatrists have suggested that the need to do psychological battle with each other is the factor that holds the marriage together.

THE DEVITALIZED RELATIONSHIP

The *devitalized marriage* involves little conflict but also little passion and attention to each other. In this type of marriage the couple were once deeply in love but have since lost their sense of excitement and passion. Most of the time spent together is now out of a sense of "duty." These couples console themselves by believing that their marriage is the way most marriages are. Although the relationship lacks visible vitality, these couples say that there is still something there. There are occasional periods of sharing, even if they are only memories of what the relationship was like in the past.

THE PASSIVE-CONGENIAL RELATIONSHIP

The *passive-congenial* mode of interaction is similar to the devitalized mode; the primary difference is that the passivity that characterizes this marriage was always there, whereas in the devitalized mode the couple has some exciting memories to draw on. In the passive-congenial marriage there is little conflict, but there is little excitement as well. For example, the wife of a prominent attorney, who had lived in the passive-congenial mode for 30 years, remarked:

> I expected to perform sex in marriage, but both before and since, I'm willing to admit that it's a much overrated activity. Now and then, perhaps it's better. I am fortunate, I guess, because my husband has never been demanding about it, before marriage or since. It's just not that important to either of us. (1966:52).

Couples in this mode share many common interests, but they are as involved outside the marriage as inside. They are simply not willing to invest total emotional involvement in the marriage. In fact, the passive-congenial couple feel that this type of relationship facilitates independence and security and allows them the time and freedom to pursue individual goals.

THE VITAL RELATIONSHIP

The *vital relationship* is in extreme contrast to the three relationships already discussed. Vital couples are highly involved with each other in important matters and events. The sharing and togetherness characterized by this mode of interaction provide the life force of the relationship. People in a vital relationship do not, however, lose their sense of identity or monopolize each other's time; rather, vital couples simply enjoy each other when they are together and make spending time together the focal point of their lives. In addition, unlike the conflict-habituated couple, the vital couple try to avoid conflict, and when conflict occurs it results, not from trivial matters, but from important ones. Furthermore, the vital couple try to settle disagreements as quickly as possible rather than let them drag on, as do the conflict-habituated couple.

THE TOTAL RELATIONSHIP

Whereas in the vital relationships the couples value their time together but maintain their individual lives as well, the *total relationship* is characterized by constant togetherness, and most if not all important life events are shared. Cuber and Harroff cite an internationally known scientist who after 30 years still considers his wife to be his friend, mistress, and partner. He still goes home as often as possible, sometimes at considerable inconvenience, to have lunch with his wife and spend vital time with her. There are few tensions and conflicts in this type of relationship primarily because tensions that do arise are dealt with as they occur. The main-spring of the total relationship is that when faced with tension, conflict, or differences the couple deal with the issues without losing the feeling of unity and vitality that is paramount to their relationship.

Total relationships are rare, and the total couple are often aware of their exceptionality. Such relationships do exist, however. In fact, Cuber and Harroff report that they occasionally found relationships so total that every aspect of the relationship was mutually and enthusiastically shared. In a sense, it was as if these couples did not have an individual existence.

? *Where do you fit in terms of these types of marriages or intimate relationships? Do you know couples who can be described in terms of one or more of these relationship types? What about your parents? Where do they fit?*

It is clear that the meaning of marriage as well as what represents marital happiness and adjustment differ among human beings. Cuber and Harroff stress the point that each of these relationship types simply represents a particular type of interaction in and adjustment to the marital relationship. Thus, people living in any one of the relationships described by Cuber and Harroff may or may not be satisfied. In addition, the categories are not mutually exclusive. Rather, some couples are on the border, and others may move from one mode of interaction to another over the course of their relationship. We should also keep in mind that the Cuber/Harroff typology represents relationships and not personality types. It is quite possible, for example, that a vital person could be living in a devitalized relationship, expressing her or his vitality through some other part of her or his life.

HETEROGAMOUS MARRIAGES

In addition to types of relationships, social scientists often classify marriages in terms of social characteristics such as race, ethnicity, and religion. Although people tend to select partners with whom they share these characteristics, some couples do come from different backgrounds or traditions. Marriages between people who vary in certain social and demographic characteristics are referred to as **heterogamous marriages**. Such marriages have become more common in recent years. The following section focuses on two major types of heterogamous marriage: interracial marriages and interfaith marriages.

INTERRACIAL MARRIAGES

Although many people interpret interracial marriage as referring to black–white couples, interracial marriages actually involve a wide range of combinations, including not only whites and blacks but also Native Americans, Asian Americans, and Latinos. Although the last legal constraints on interracial marriages were removed with a 1967 Supreme Court decision (see the FYI box titled "Antimiscegenation Laws"), the informal restrictions—sociocultural norms—concerning these marriages remain the most inflexible of all mate selection boundaries. Even though the number of interracial couples has almost doubled since the early 1980s—1 in every 50 marriages representing an interracial marriage (Bovee, 1993)—racial endogamy in marriage is still strong, particularly for certain groups. Thus, we cannot underestimate the power of informal social norms that operate in mate selection. For a better understanding of this, let us turn our attention to interracial marriages among various racial and ethnic groups in the United States.

AFRICAN AMERICANS Among various groups of color in the United States, African Americans have the highest rate of endogamous marriages and the lowest rate of exogamous marriages. Of the 53.5 million married couples in the United States in 1992, only 246,000 (0.5 percent) were black–white couples (Bovee, 1993). Approximately 93 percent of all African Americans who are married are married to another African American. As Figure 8.1(*c*) shows, however, when African-American women and men do marry interracially, most often their mate is white.

African-American men are twice as likely as African-American women to have a white mate. This fact notwithstanding, government statistics indicate that the number of black women marrying white men is growing. For example, the number of black women married to white men increased from 56,000 in 1987 to 83,000 in 1992, a 33 percent increase. In

FOR YOUR INFORMATION

ANTIMISCEGENATION LAWS: THE BAN ON INTERRACIAL MARRIAGES IN THE UNITED STATES

Although interracial marriages are legal in all states today, the legal right to marry outside one's race was gained only in 1967 with a Supreme Court decision (*Loving v. Virginia*) that declared state laws prohibiting interracial marriages to be unconstitutional. At the time of the Court's decision, 16 states still carried and enforced antimiscegenation statutes with penalties of up to $10,000 (Ramu, 1989). The case involved two native-born Virginians: Richard Loving, a white male, and his wife, Mildred, who was half African American and half Native American. The couple were married in 1958 in Washington, D.C. When they returned to Virginia they were arrested and charged with violating the state's 1924 law that prohibited interracial marriages. The couple were convicted and sentenced to 1 year in jail. The trial judge suspended the sentence on the condition that the Lovings leave the state and not return together for 25 years. After the conviction, the Lovings moved to Washington, D.C.

Five years later the couple returned to Virginia to visit Mildred Loving's mother, who was ill. They were arrested again, and this time they appealed their case to the U.S. Supreme Court. The Court ruled, in effect, that antimiscegenation laws violated the Fourteenth Amendment of the Constitution, which prohibits the states from depriving citizens of their basic rights, and thus were unconstitutional.

most cases, at least one partner in black–white marriages has been married previously. In addition, black men who marry white women are typically well educated, have a high income, and are usually older than their mate (Schoen and Wooldridge, 1989).

Although attitudes and behavior regarding racial intermarriages have changed somewhat, interracial couples, especially black–white couples, are still frequently subjected to a range of societal reactions from stares to cross burnings to physical attacks. These reactions reflect the importance Americans attach to the preservation of racial segregation and the role of informal norms in shaping our behavior.

NATIVE AMERICANS If African Americans represent the most racially endogamous end of the marital continuum among people of color, Native Americans are at the other end. Of six races studied by social scientist Richard Clayton in 1978, Native Americans were the least likely to exhibit racial endogamy in marriage patterns. In fact, Native Americans were involved in over 27 percent of all interracial marriages. The most prevalent interracial marriage included a white mate, and the least prevalent was with a black mate. This trend has continued into the 1990s. By 1991, only 47 percent of Native Americans were married to other Native Americans.

A number of explanations for this marital pattern have been proposed. The most common is the size of the Native-American population. Areas with small Native-American populations have significantly higher rates of interracial marriage than do those with large populations (Snipp, 1991). Likewise, interracial marriage is much higher for Native Americans living in urban areas than for those living on reservations (John, 1988).

ASIAN AMERICANS Historically, social scientists have used the rates of interracial marriage with whites as an indicator of the acculturation or assimilation of various groups of color into the American mainstream. If that is the case, then Asian-American families are becoming increasingly acculturated. Approximately 33 percent of Asian Americans are married exogamously, primarily with whites. Rates of interracial marriage vary from group to group. Groups with high rates include Japanese Americans and Chinese Americans. For example, 34 percent of Japanese Americans are married to non-Japanese. Interracial marriage is particularly prevalent among the younger generation (the Sansei or third generation), of whom almost 60 percent are married interracially. This younger generation of Japanese Americans exhibits considerable differences in marital

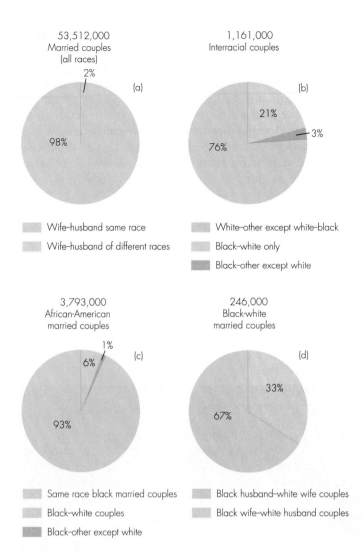

53,512,000
Married couples
(all races)

2%

(a)

98%

■ Wife–husband same race
■ Wife–husband of different races

1,161,000
Interracial couples

(b)

21%

3%

76%

■ White–other except white–black
■ Black–white only
■ Black–other except white

3,793,000
African-American
married couples

1%

6%

(c)

93%

■ Same race black married couples
■ Black–white couples
■ Black–other except white

246,000
Black-white
married couples

(d)

33%

67%

■ Black husband–white wife couples
■ Black wife–white husband couples

FIGURE 8.1 Interracial Marriages in the United States, 1992

Sources: Tim Bovee, 1993, "Interracial Marriages Now 1 in 50," *Times-Picayune*, February 12, pp. A1, A8; and U.S. Bureau of the Census, 1992a, "Marital Status and Living Arrangements" (Washington, DC: U.S. Government Printing Office): 7.

behavior from earlier generations. Whereas earlier generations were greatly constrained in marital choice by socialization and the power of the family, contemporary generations believe that parents should not interfere in the choice of marital partner. As this belief has become more widespread, the incidence of marriage between whites and Japanese Americans has increased considerably (Kitano, 1988).

In contrast, Korean Americans have relatively low rates of interracial marriage. In a comparison of three Asian-American groups in Los Angeles, sociologist Harry Kitano and his associates (1984) found Korean Americans to have the lowest rate of interracial marriage, 19 percent. Pyong Gap Min (1988) attributes

this low rate to the relatively greater number of Korean immigrants in that area. Of those Korean immigrants who marry interracially, the majority marry whites.

INTERETHNIC MARRIAGES

LATINOS As we have already seen, Latinos represent a diverse group. Although the rates of interracial marriage vary from one Latino group to another, overall the rates have increased in recent decades. Prior to the 1940s, never did more than 20 percent of Latino marriages involve a white partner (Moore and Pachon, 1985). In the 1980s, Mexican intermarriage with whites varied according to geographic location and ranged from 9 to 27 percent in Texas, 27 to 39 percent in New Mexico, and 51 to 55 percent in California (Becerra, 1988). By 1992, the U.S. Census Bureau reported 3.3 million married couples of Latino origin, of which 1.2 million were marriages between a Latino and non-Latino partner (U.S. Bureau of the Census, 1992a).

WHITES Interethnic marriage among non-Latino whites is now so commonplace that most people don't pay much attention to it. Estimates are that three-fourths of U.S.-born whites are married interethnically. As with other groups, ethnic intermarriage among whites varies with age and region of residence (Alba, 1985).

Although the data indicate that the rate of interracial marriage has been increasing and seems dramatic for some groups, we must be careful in drawing conclusions from them. Keep in mind that many of these statistics represent geographic or age-specific groups and should not be generalized to a total population. We should not lose sight of the fact that overall, interracial marriages are still an extremely low percentage of the total marriages in this country. In addition, we should remember that race is not experienced in a vacuum. As we learned in Chapter 5, race is interrelated with many other social factors that combine to have a significant effect on if and whom we marry.

INTERFAITH MARRIAGES

People today are probably more willing to cross religious than racial boundaries in selecting a spouse. Summaries of studies on interfaith marriages (for example, Eckland, 1968; Kerckhoff, 1976) have consistently

In the past, Jews have married within their own faith more often than has any other group. Today, however, a growing number of Jews are members of interfaith couples.

found Americans to be much like their partners in terms of religion. Most studies of interfaith marriages simply divide religion into three categories: Protestant, Catholic, and Jewish. A problem with this classification scheme is that it overlooks the diversity within various religious categories. For example, Baptists, Presbyterians, and Methodists are all Protestant denominations. If people from these different denominations intermarry, are their marriages endogamous or exogamous? Other problems arise in trying to define an interreligious couple. For example, if a Jew marries a Protestant who then converts to Judaism, is that an intermarriage, or do we consider it religiously homogamous? Or, what if one partner is of a religious denomination and the other is an atheist or agnostic?

With these limitations in mind, the statistics indicate the following: 93 percent of Protestants are married to Protestants; 88 percent of Jews are married to Jews; and 82 percent of Catholics are married to Catholics. If we take an average of these three categories, about 90 percent of all Protestants, Catholics, and Jews are married to people of the same religion (Glenn, 1982).

In recent years religious intermarriage apparently has increased as religion generally has lost some of its power and control over people's lives (Glenn, 1982). Some researchers, however, have pointed out that religious intermarriage varies according to location and population. Pace (1986), for example, found that cities such as New York, whose population includes a large number of Catholics and Jews, have a higher-than-average incidence of cross-faith (Jewish–Catholic) marriages. Likewise, Catholics and Lutherans exhibit a higher-than-average rate of intermarriage in states such as Pennsylvania, Iowa, and Minnesota, where the population is almost evenly split between the two religious denominations.

Although interfaith couples are less often the victims of society's disapproval than interracial couples are, cross-faith marriages are not without difficulties. Deeply held religious beliefs are an important part of our core personality. If we believe very strongly in a particular religious ideology, to what extent will we compromise? Partners from different religions must confront a number of issues such as choosing a religion for their children and deciding which holidays are to be observed. These are not insurmountable barriers, of course, but they do require that a couple closely examine the ramifications of marrying across faith and find solutions that are mutually satisfying.

Some studies indicate that racially and religiously heterogamous marriages have somewhat higher divorce rates and slightly lower levels of satisfaction than do homogamous marriages (see, for example, Price-Bonham and Balswick, 1980; Glenn, 1982; Heaton and Pratt, 1990). As with homogamous marriages, many factors affect the success of heterogamous marriages. Lack of family, societal, and religious support; cultural hostility; and differences in background can often undermine the stability and success of these marriages. Two other critical factors in determining the success of all marriages, heterogamous and homogamous, are the ability to communicate openly and honestly and the ability to manage conflicts that arise within these relationships. The concluding section of this chapter focuses on the issues of communication and conflict resolution.

COMMUNICATION AND CONFLICT RESOLUTION

Communication is essential to the success of marriages and other intimate relationships. Two key components of communication are what is said and how it is said. You have probably heard the expression: "It's not *what* you say, it's *how* you say it." For example, it is possible to say "I'm very happy in this relationship" several different ways. An individual could say it lovingly, sincerely or sarcastically. In good communication what we say should be consistent with how we say it. Also, communication involves not just words but gestures, actions, intonations, and sounds. Sometimes the messages couples give to each other are misinterpreted, misread, or missed all together. Missed messages and misinterpretations can build on themselves and result in conflict and hostility in a relationship. Clinical psychologist Joel Block (1981) gives this example:

A couple have just taken a moonlight walk by the ocean. They sit down by the water's edge. The woman says, "Let's go inside, I'm sleepy." The man responds, "It's nice out here. Why don't we lie and rest here?" The woman, angry, storms into the house. The man, equally angry, gets dressed and drives off to a local bar.

What has happened here is miscommunication. When the woman suggested going inside because she was "sleepy" she was actually attempting to communicate to her partner that she wanted to make love in

Some conflict in intimate relationships is inevitable. How conflict is managed is a key to a successful relationship.

identify, accept responsibility for, and resolve problems, as well as a willingness to listen and negotiate.

Several key areas of marriage and family life generally contribute to conflict in marriages: money, sex, children, power, work, in-laws, friends, religion, and substance abuse. When conflict arises in a relationship, as it inevitably does, it does not have to be destructive. Researchers have found that some conflict can be constructive. Conflict management is the key. When conflict is managed or resolved through negotiation and compromise, it can strengthen the bonds of affection between partners. When it is dealt with ineffectively it can lower satisfaction and even contribute to the dissolution of the relationship. Social researchers Don Dinkmeyer and Jon Carlson (1984) suggest some of the following strategies to resolve marital conflict: clearly define the problem, demonstrate a mutual respect for each other, agree to cooperate with each other, and agree to make decisions together.

Some social scientists (Sprey, 1979) believe that couples in lasting marriages do not really resolve most conflicts in the sense that the conflict is settled forever with a clear winner and loser. Rather, they manage most conflicts through an ongoing process of negotiation. Couples in successful marriages find ways of managing conflict that allow each partner to maintain her or his differences while working collectively to find a negotiated solution that is satisfactory to both parties.

the house. Her partner, on the other hand, was attempting to communicate his wish to make love on the beach under the moonlight. According to Block, neither communicated her or his wishes directly; thus, the evening ended with both partners feeling rejected and angry. When this type of miscommunication becomes a pattern of interaction in a relationship, a couple could find themselves continuously upset and irritated with each other.

One of the ways that couples can learn to communicate directly with each other is by conducting what Block calls "marital checkups." This activity involves identifying and appraising the assets and liabilities of the relationship. If done responsibly, the marital checkup can help the couple learn more about each other's needs, desires, and expectations.

In general, successful communication includes a number of conditions and skills. Two basic conditions are a nonthreatening, noncoercive atmosphere and mutual commitment. In addition, a couple must be willing to change as the needs and demands of the relationship change. Some of the skills that are important for successful communication are the ability to

Consider the intimate relationships in which you are or have been involved. Can you distinguish particular patterns of communication in these relationships? What are or were the major barriers to communication? What strategies of conflict resolution have you and your partners employed in these relationships? Did you learn anything about conflict resolution from your parents' relationship? How can you improve communication and conflict resolution in your close relationships?

SUMMARY

Although we have witnessed some important changes in marriage and family patterns, most Americans will marry at least once in their lifetime. People marry for a number of reasons, including to have a committed relationship and to have someone to share life with.

Marriage means different things to different people. For some people the key to marriage is commitment. For others, marriage is a sacrament, a sacred union or holy state under the direct authority of their God. Most people do not think of marriage as a legal contract. When two people marry, however, they are agreeing to abide by the terms of a marriage contract that they had no part in drafting. Although each individual state defines the rights and obligations of the marriage contract, all states specify who can marry whom and at what age they may do so.

Historically, the marriage contract put women at a decided disadvantage. Although the process of marriage is different today, in many states women continue to lose legal rights when they marry. Marriage in the United States is imbued with rituals and traditions, many of which date back to ancient societies. Although many people continue to abide by tradition when they marry, an increasing number of people are modifying, changing, or creating their own personal marriage rituals.

Like other experiences, marriage is experienced differently depending on factors such as race, class, and gender. For example, researchers point out that women and men experience marriage differently. This has led several researchers to describe marriage as containing two marriages: hers and his. The female–male differences in the experience of marriage, though largely hidden, have a tremendous effect on the mental and physical health of wives and husbands.

Getting married represents a significant change in the lives of a couple. Marital adjustment is an important part of the marriage experience. Couples must continuously make adjustments over the life course of the marriage. The success of the relationship depends, in large part, on the degree to which both partners are able to adjust. Satisfying, well-adjusted marriages vary a great deal. A typology of marital relationships representing marital adjustment includes the conflict-habituated, the devitalized, the passive-congenial, the vital, and the total relationship.

Whenever two people live together over some period of time, some conflict is bound occur. Conflict does not have to be destructive, however. Couples in successful marriages find ways of managing or resolving conflict that are satisfactory to both parties. An essential element in managing or resolving conflict is open, honest, and direct communication. If couples are committed to the relationship, they will try to manage or resolve conflict in a constructive way.

KEY TERMS

principle of legitimacy	affinal relatives
sacrament	coverture
legal marriage	conjugal rights
social marriage	personal marriage agreement
bigamy	prenuptial agreement
adultery	marital adjustment
fornication	heterogamous marriage

QUESTIONS FOR STUDY AND REFLECTION

1. Why do people marry? If you are married why did you marry? If you are not married but plan to wed, why are you going to marry? Ask three different married couples—one in their 60s, one in their 40s, and one in their 20s—why they married and what their expectations of marriage were. Do the women and men differ in their appraisals of marriage? Did you find any generational differences across couples? If so, how do you explain these differences?

2. Thinking about yourself, your parents, or some couple you are close to, do you (they) have a successful marriage? How important is communication to the success of the marriage? What communication skills does each partner possess?

3. Using the Cuber and Harroff typology of marital relationships, describe your marriage or nonmarital intimate relationship, and explain which category it best corresponds to. Which of the five types of relationships do you think is best? Why? Do you think that the Cuber/Harroff typology is useful to analyze all marriages regardless of the race and social class of the couple?

4. Jessie Bernard's typology of marriages along gender lines is a classic in the field of sociology. Do you agree that marriages are experienced differently by women and men? Can you give evidence from your own experiences or the experiences of people you know to support or refute Bernard's argument?

FURTHER READING

BLUMSTEIN, PHILLIP, AND PEPPER SCHWARTZ. 1983. *American Couples*. New York: Pocket Books. An in-depth examination of several aspects of the intimate lives of a diverse group of couples in the United States: married, heterosexual, lesbian, gay, and cohabitors. An important source of information on couple relationships.

NICOLSON, NIGEL. 1974. *Portrait of a Marriage*. London: Futura. A personal account of the author's parents, each of whom had homosexual affairs and practiced "open marriage." Despite their marital lifestyle they stayed together and loved each other in what was apparently an adjusted and satisfying relationship.

SELIGSON, MARCIA. 1973. *The Eternal Bliss Machine: America's Way of Wedding*. New York: Morrow. An interesting and enlightening discussion of various wedding ceremonies.

WEITZMAN, LENORE. 1981. *The Marriage Contract: Spouses, Lovers, and the Law*. New York: Free Press. Weitzman presents a classic examination and discussion of the law and the marriage contract.

Chapter 9

REPRODUCTION AND THE PARENTING DECISION

*M*ary and John married soon after graduating from law school. Before they were married they talked about when and how many children they wanted. They decided that they both should be established in their careers before having children. They wanted two children, a boy and a girl.

Tom and Susie married 3 years after graduating from high school and planned to start a family right away. Both had two siblings, and they wanted three children themselves. Tom worked in construction and experienced seasonal layoffs. Susie worked as a checker at their neighborhood supermarket and hoped to quit when she became pregnant.

Five years later neither couple had children; both were infertile, and became distraught when they found out. As a result, they experienced bouts of depression, guilt, and anxiety. At times their marital relationships seemed especially strained. Both couples continued to want children.

Why did these two couples experience psychological difficulties after learning they were infertile? What does their reaction suggest about the value of children? About adult status? What options are available to infertile couples who want children?

Today Mary and John have two children, a 4-year-old boy conceived through in vitro fertilization and a 1-year-old Colombian girl whom they adopted.

Despite equally strong desires for children, Tom and Susie are still childless. They have gone to a public adoption agency, and they remain on the waiting list.

How do you account for these different outcomes? Why were Mary and John able to realize their desires, whereas Tom and Susie were not? How do you feel about these different outcomes?

Fertility—the actual number of live births in a population—is both a biological and a social phenomenon. In all societies the timing and number of births are shaped by numerous social forces: the value attached to children and parenthood, marriage patterns and gender roles, political and economic structures, and knowledge about human reproduction. Thus, fertility patterns vary greatly across cultures. In some cultures children are highly valued as economic assets, and women are expected to begin childbearing at an early age and to have many children. Other societies view children in terms of their emotional value. These societies promote small families and encourage women to delay childbearing until their middle or late 20s. In some societies the birth of a first child precedes marriage; in others a birth outside of marriage is strongly condemned. Even within a given society fertility patterns may vary considerably across racial, ethnic, and class lines.

This chapter begins with a brief historical review of changing fertility patterns in the United States and then proceeds to look at the many factors that influence the decision whether to parent. The remaining sections examine the means for controlling fertility as well as the reproductive technologies that have been developed to help couples overcome problems of infertility. The chapter concludes with a discussion of reproductive choice and its social-policy implications.

HISTORICAL OVERVIEW: FERTILITY TRENDS IN THE UNITED STATES

Demographers use the term **fertility rate** to refer to the number of births per 1000 women in their childbearing years (ages 15 to 44). Evidence suggests that the fertility rate in early America was quite high. For example, the **total fertility rate**—the average number of children each woman has—in 1790, when the first census was taken, is estimated to have been 7.7 (Gill et al., 1992:41), in contrast to approximately 2.0 today.

NINETEENTH-CENTURY AMERICA

Figure 9.1 shows that by 1900 the total fertility rate had declined to half that of a century earlier. What happened to produce such a dramatic change in a relatively short period of time? Historians offer a number of explanations (Carlson, 1990). One focuses on the transformation of the United States from a rural-agricultural society to an urban-industrial society. In 1800, approximately 90 percent of the population lived in rural areas, with 80 percent involved in agricultural work. Children are an economic asset in an agricultural society, where many hands are needed to

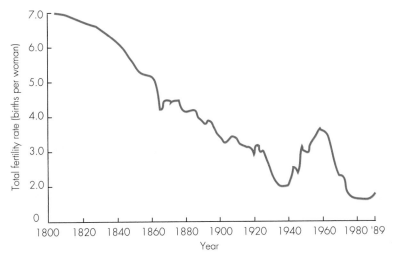

FIGURE 9.1 Total fertility rates in the United States, 1800 – 1989. Note the general decline in the average number of children, with the exception of the "baby boom" in the years following World War II.

Source: Adapted from Richard T. Gill, Nathan Glazer, and Stephan A. Thernstrom, 1992, *Our Changing Population* (Englewood Cliffs, NJ: Prentice Hall), p. 41. Reprinted by permission of Prentice Hall, Englewood Cliffs, NJ.

cultivate the land. In contrast, by 1900, only 39 percent of the labor force was engaged in agriculture (Gill et al., 1992:44). With the decline in the need for farmhands, the economic value of children also declined.

In a similar vein, Robert Wells (1978) suggested that the rapid advances in science and technology that accompanied the move to an urban-industrial society led to changes in people's views of the world. Wells believed that the adoption of "modern values" that focus on planning and the future led couples to conclude that controlling family size would have economic benefits. In addition, the changing technology of an urban-industrial society required a more educated labor force. Thus, not only did the economic value of children decline, but it also became more costly to raise and educate them.

A third perspective is offered by Carl Degler (1980), who examined the changing role of women in the nineteenth century. After analyzing their diaries and letters, Degler concluded that nineteenth-century women understood the benefits of limiting the number of children they had. In 1883, feminist Elizabeth Cady Stanton described in her diary a meeting in which she talked to working-class mothers about health, air, diet, and babies. "I also spoke to them of overpopulation. I think I made them clearly understand that so long as they filled their homes with infants their own conditions grew worse and worse with every generation" (quoted in Parker, 1972:268). Fertility control became an important part of the early struggle for women's equality.

TWENTIETH-CENTURY AMERICA

In the first decades of the twentieth century, the fertility rate continued to decline, particularly during the years of the Great Depression, when couples limited family size because of economic hardship. Demographers had predicted that the number of births would increase after World War II as couples put the depression and the war behind them. No one, however, anticipated the dramatic rise in the total fertility rate, which increased from about 2.5 in 1945 to a high of 3.8 in 1957. Between 1946 and 1965, a period called the "baby boom," 74 million babies were born in the United States. Although demographers do not agree completely on the causes of the baby boom, two factors seem to have played a key role. First, the expanding postwar economy enabled unprecedented numbers of people to marry and have children at an early age. Second, a number of government policies were aimed at helping young families get started. The GI Bill helped veterans get an education and, hence, better-paying jobs. Federal housing loans and income tax deductions for children and interest on home mortgages encouraged people to buy houses and start families.

The baby boom was not to last, however. In 1957, the total fertility rate again began to decline, falling by more than 50 percent in less than 20 years to a low of 1.7 in 1976. This rate had increased only slightly by the beginning of the 1990s. This drastic decline, called the "baby bust," was not anticipated either. Among the factors thought to be responsible for this change are a slowing of the economy, the introduction in the early 1960s of the birth control pill, the legalization of abortion, the continued increase in women's labor-force participation, and increases in both age at marriage and the divorce rate. The most likely explanation, however, is that the baby boom was simply a short-term deviation from the long-term decline that began in the nineteenth century. Whatever the reasons for the decline, another baby boom does not seem likely in the foreseeable future.

CURRENT FERTILITY PATTERNS

The fertility rate for the 12 months ending June 1990 was an estimated 67.0 births per 1000 women 15 to 44 years old (U.S. Bureau of the Census, 1991c:3). As Table 9.1 shows, fertility patterns are not uniform across all groups; rather, they vary according to income, race, ethnicity, and age. Before discussing these variations more closely, however, a point must be made. Even though fertility rates vary from one group to the next, all groups are affected by the same social forces. Thus, as the United States moved from an agricultural to an industrial society, fertility rates declined among all groups.

CLASS In general, the higher the income, the lower the fertility rate. Women with incomes of under $10,000 had a fertility rate of 87.5, compared to a rate of 55.9 among women with incomes of over $50,000. At first glance this pattern may seem illogical. After all, shouldn't we expect wealthier people to have more children because they can more easily afford them? University of Chicago economist and Nobel Prize winner Gary Becker (1981) explains the "demand" for children in economic terms. According to his argument, children are costly in a number of ways: medical costs of delivery; expenditures for food, clothing, shelter, and education; and cost of time spent in childbearing and child rearing—time that must be diverted from other activities such as careers. Although these costs are experienced by all parents, they are generally perceived as more costly by wealthier and more educated parents. These individuals often

TABLE 9.1

Births Per 1000 Women by Selected Characteristics, Year Ending June 1990

Characteristics	Total, 15 to 44	15 to 29	30 to 44
Total, all women	67.0	90.8	44.7
Race			
White	65.2	87.8	44.6
Black	78.4	107.2	46.3
Asian or Pacific Is.	58.1	79.0	40.4
Latina Origin			
Latina*	93.2	120.8	60.5
Non-Latina	64.4	87.4	42.2
Family Income			
Under $10,000	87.5	124.0	39.7
10,000–14,999	76.1	106.6	35.3
15,000–19,999	75.9	114.7	32.1
20,000–29,999	64.2	88.2	40.7
30,000–34,999	64.6	80.6	51.2
35,000–49,999	61.9	85.9	43.0
50,000 and over	55.9	54.3	57.0

*Latinas may be of any race.

Source: Adapted from U.S. Bureau of the Census, 1991c, *Current Population Reports*, Series P-20, No. 454, "Fertility of American Women: June 1990" (Washington, DC: U.S. Government Printing Office): Table A, p. 2.

delay marriage and childbearing so they can complete their own education. They also expect to send their children to college, which is a major expense. Moreover, they want to be engaged in time-demanding careers and other activities. Lower-income parents generally consider larger families more beneficial than costly. These parents are less likely to go to college, more likely to marry early, and more likely to see children as a means of providing adult status and identity.

ETHNICITY AND RACE Latinas have significantly higher fertility rates (93.2) than other women (64.4). Many Latinas have migrated from countries where large families are the cultural and religious norm. There is, however, considerable variation among Latino groups, with Cubans and Puerto Ricans having relatively lower rates, and Mexican Americans having the highest rates (Ventura, 1988). Regarding race, although the overall fertility rate for black women (78.4) was higher than that reported by white women (65.2), it varied by age. Black women aged 15 to 29 had higher fertility rates than white women in the same age category, but there were no significant fertility differences between the two races among women over 30 years of age. Fertility rates among Native-American women are 34 percent higher than those of white women (Weeks, 1989), and high fertility rates are more prevalent among those who live on reservations than those who do not. The most frequently used explanations for the different fertility rates across race and class are socioeconomic factors and perceived opportunity structures. Hence, women of color are believed to have more children because they are disproportionately represented in the lower classes and consequently have less opportunity to pursue alternatives to childbearing such as going to college and having a high-paying occupation (Hogan and Kitagawa, 1985).

In comparison to other racial groups, Asian Americans have the lowest fertility rates (Kitano and Daniels, 1988:163). Several factors contribute to this lower rate. Asian Americans tend to marry later than members of other groups, and Asian-American women are more likely than other groups to delay childbearing until their late 20s and early 30s (O'Hare and Felt, 1991).

In sum, the U.S. birthrate has been declining over the last 2 centuries. Much of this decline has been attributed to the changing economic value of children, older ages at marriage, and the decision of women to delay childbearing until their 30s. Although most people continue to want children, they want smaller families than in the past. According to the U.S. Census Bureau (1991c), nearly 61 percent of women aged 18 to 34 expect to have only one or two children. Of course, expectations are not always realized. In the next section we explore the many factors that affect the decision to have children.

TO PARENT OR NOT?

 Do you want to be a parent? For what reasons? If you are already a parent, was this a conscious and planned choice? Are you satisfied with the timing and number of children that you have? Is child rearing what you expected it to be?

All too often our exposure to child rearing is of its romantic side. Advertisers surround us with images of gurgling, laughing, adorable infants and toddlers who say and do the most clever things. What we don't often see are the temper tantrums and the rebellious "no's." Relatives and friends conspire in this romanticization of children, though probably unwittingly, by inviting us to christenings, birthday parties, graduations, and weddings, all of which reflect in their own way parental pride in their offspring. Rarely are we in on the parent–teacher conference about school problems or the police admonishment to control a wayward youngster. This dash of realism is not meant to negate the romantic side of parenthood but to suggest that parenthood, like any other activity, involves both costs and benefits that vary over the family life cycle and that people should consider before becoming parents. Even though people do sometimes change their mind after marriage, it is important to discuss the desire for children before marriage. Husbands and wives who disagree on whether to have children are likely to experience considerable marital conflict (Marciano, 1979). If the issue cannot be satisfactorily resolved, the marriage may dissolve.

THE COSTS OF PARENTHOOD

In contrast to previous eras, when children worked at various jobs, particularly on farms and later in factories, children today are primarily consumers.

Even when parents agree on having children, they may have quite different expectations of how a baby will affect their lives.

Source: FOR BETTER OR WORSE copyright 1990 Lynn Johnston Prod., Inc. Reprinted with permission of Universal Press Syndicate. All rights reserved.

Demographers estimate the cost of raising one child to the age of 18 in the United States to be $133,000, including college expenses (Crispell, 1989).

TIME, ENERGY, AND EMOTIONAL COSTS

Raising children involves more than financial outlays; it also requires a great investment of parental time and energy. Infants and toddlers are dependent on parents for all their physical and psychological needs. As children enter school, parents are likely to find themselves enmeshed in rounds of school activities, organized sports, religious events, scouting, music and dance lessons, family outings, and numerous other activities that compete for their time and attention. Raising children in today's environment also carries a high emotional cost in terms of parental worries over the easy accessibility of drugs, the lure of gangs, and random violence, all of which have taken a heavy toll on young people across all groups, but especially on the poor and children of color. An African-American mother of two sons observed: "I love my sons dearly, but if I had it all to do over again, I don't know if I would have children, especially boys. Every time my sons go out, my heart stops until they come home. Every day you read about some young African-American male being shot or beaten up for being in the wrong place."

LIFESTYLE DISRUPTIONS

The birth of a child can disrupt previously satisfying lifestyles. Not only do infants interrupt sleep and lovemaking and change household routines, they can alter a couple's social life and recreational pursuits. Babysitters are not always readily available, nor are babies easily compatible with work, hobbies, and leisure activities. Many parents find themselves in the position of having to forgo favorite pastimes at least until their children are much older. Although some parents find this a fairly easy exchange to make, others are unprepared for the degree of change in their lives. Some parents become resentful, and as a result, both the marital relationship and the parent–child relationship may be negatively affected.

Given these costs you may be tempted to agree with the authors of *Parents in Contemporary America*, who observed, "Rearing children is probably the hardest and most thankless job in the world" (LeMasters and DeFrain, 1989:21). Why, then, does anyone voluntarily become a parent? The answer to this question is twofold: Parenthood offers significant benefits to individuals, and in our society there are enormous social pressures for procreating.

THE BENEFITS OF PARENTHOOD

Although all parents experience to some degree the costs of having children, most parents believe the benefits of parenthood outweigh the costs.

EMOTIONAL BONDS Children are not only consumers and takers; they also give love and affection to parents. Furthermore, for many married couples their children are a tangible symbol of the love they share and the means for establishing "a real family life" (Neal et al., 1989). Couples who recall happy childhoods and positive family life experiences are especially likely to want to reproduce those feelings through having children of their own. Children also enlarge the social interaction network of parents by providing connecting links to other family members (grandparents, aunts, uncles, cousins) and to the larger community via schools, churches, neighbors, and places of recreation.

ADULT STATUS Many people see children as a means of achieving adult status, recognition, and personal fulfillment. From early on, girls are given dolls to play with to prepare them for the day they will become mothers themselves and affirm their womanhood to the larger community. Men, too, are socialized to affirm their manhood through procreation and financial support of their families. Beyond that, however, rearing children provides parents with a sense of purpose and gives their lives meaning. By transmitting societal values to a new generation, parents feel they are making a contribution and leaving their imprint on society. Watching their children grow and knowing they had a role in their children's development give parents a sense of pride and a feeling of immortality—that after their own deaths, part of them will live on through their children and grandchildren.

FUN AND ENJOYMENT Sometimes in the serious discussions of parenting another important benefit of having children is overlooked. Having children can be enormous fun. Through children adults can reex-

Traditionally, many fathers wanted sons who would someday join the family business. Today, it is not so unusual to include daughters in family enterprises.

perience some of the delights of their own childhood. They can recall their own sense of wonder of the world as they observe their children's new discoveries. The presence of children legitimizes many adult desires; for example, many parents delight in buying trains and other toys for their children so that they, too, can enjoy them. What adult has not at times looked wistfully on as children around them swing, swim, run, jump, and play Nintendo? Parents have the advantage of being able to do all these things with their children without needing to apologize or explain.

THE SOCIAL PRESSURES TO PROCREATE

Although many adults acknowledge the benefits of parenthood, in isolation, these benefits are probably not sufficient to produce a steady fertility rate. Obviously, reproduction is necessary for the continuation of a society. Without a fertility rate approaching the replacement level, and in the absence of immigration, a society would, over time, become extinct. Thus, it is in society's interest to promote a **pronatalist attitude**, one that encourages childbearing. Societies vary in their strategies for accomplishing this goal. In the United States we celebrate parenthood by having special days to honor mothers and fathers. Federal and state government bodies show their support for childbearing by a tax structure that rewards earners with children through a system of tax deductions. Family members and friends often participate in encouraging childbearing by constantly dropping hints: "When are we going to be grandparents?" "Hurry up, our Jimmy wants a playmate (cousin)." Some religious organizations, for example, the Catholic Church, promote reproduction by teaching that the purpose of sex is procreation and that artificial means of birth control, which we discuss later in this chapter, are contrary to that purpose.

DELAYED PARENTHOOD AND THE CHILD-FREE OPTION

Throughout most of U.S. history, having children was assumed to be the normal course of development for married couples. Until recently, a conscious rejection of parenthood was considered an unnatural and selfish act. About the only socially acceptable reason for not having children was biological incapacity, and those who were unable to have children were objects of sympathy and pity. Writing in the late nineteenth and early twentieth centuries, psychoanalyst Sigmund Freud argued that "anatomy is destiny." With that statement Freud asserted that the "natural" role of women was motherhood. He believed that women who rejected motherhood were also rejecting their feminine role. Freud did not make similar assertions for men. However, if it is unnatural for women to reject motherhood, is it not also unnatural for men to reject fatherhood?

Some contemporary psychoanalysts, like Erik Erikson, hold views similar to Freud's. Erikson believed that when couples decide not to parent, they are rejecting a major part of adult development that they may regret in later life. However, studies such as Marian Faux's *Childless by Choice: Choosing Childlessness in the 80s* (1984) challenge this perspective. More couples question whether to have children; approximately 5 percent of all married couples consciously choose to be child-free. The rate is almost three times higher among college graduates, however, and there are indications that the overall rate may be increasing. Charles Westoff, director of Princeton University's Office of Population Research, estimates that as many as 25 percent of women now in their 20s will remain child-free by choice (cited in Iaconetti, 1988:143).

DELAYED PARENTHOOD

The decision not to have children may be permanent or temporary. Some couples decide to delay having children until they have achieved other goals such as finishing college, establishing careers, traveling, strengthening the marital relationship, and buying a house. Figure 9.2 shows that since 1976 the number of births to women over age 30 has increased significantly compared to that for women in the traditional childbearing years of 25 to 29.

In earlier eras being pregnant at ages 35 and 40 carried substantial risks to maternal and fetal health. Today these risks have lessened, due in part to the fact that today's older first-time mothers generally are well educated, take good care of themselves, and have high

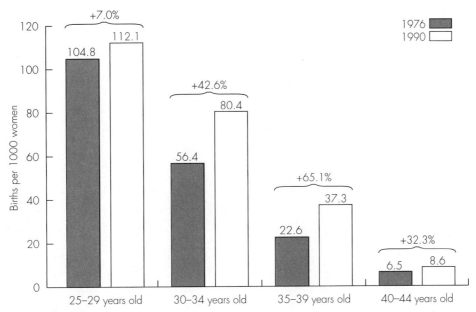

FIGURE 9.2 Births per 1000 women aged 25–44, 1976 and 1990. These data indicate a clear trend toward delayed parenting.

Source: Adapted from U.S. Bureau of the Census, 1991c, *Current Population Reports*, Series P-20, No. 454, "Fertility of American Women: June 1990" (Washington, DC: U.S. Government Printing Office): Table I, p. 13.

incomes. Additionally, the medical profession has developed improved techniques for dealing with pregnancies in later life. According to Dr. Samir Beydoun of the University of Miami, who conducted a study of mothers over age 40, the older mother has about the same chance of having a healthy baby as a younger mother (Shrieves, 1990:8). Nevertheless, the miscarriage rate is higher for these mothers, and they run a higher risk of having a baby with Down syndrome.

Sometimes, however, this initial decision to postpone childbearing evolves into acceptance of permanent childlessness (Veevers, 1980). Take, for example, the story of Bob and Betty, a child-free couple in their 50s. "We started out our marriage with the goal of establishing our careers and seeing the world. We thought when we reached our 30s we would have done everything we wanted, and we would be ready to settle down to raise a family. But we kept doing other things. When Bob turned 40, we decided that we were getting too old to start a family. We're happy and have no regrets, although it would be nice to have adult children at this time in our lives." (from author's files)

REASONS FOR REMAINING CHILD-FREE

Just as there are numerous reasons for having children, there are many reasons for not doing so. Among them are career and marital considerations, the desire for personal fulfillment, uncertainty about parenting skills, and the influence of **antinatalist forces**, policies or practices that discourage people from having children.

CAREER AND MARITAL CONSIDERATIONS
Couples vary in their choice of priorities in their lives. Some prefer not to have children, desiring instead to focus their energies on constructing satisfying careers and wanting to avoid the work and family conflicts typical of dual-career couples with children, a topic we discuss in Chapter 11. Other couples wish to concentrate their energies on the marital relationship itself, believing that children diminish the freedom and romance the couple value in the marriage. Children make great demands on parents, and as a result, parents often find themselves spending less time maintaining their relationship with each other.

APPLYING THE SOCIOLOGICAL IMAGINATION

PARENTING IN LATER LIFE

With today's reproductive technology it is possible for older women who have gone through menopause to become pregnant using donated eggs and carry their babies to term. In 1987, a 55-year-old grandmother delivered a healthy boy, becoming the oldest woman to give birth in Britain. The father was 65. In 1992, a 53-year-old grandmother in the United States gave birth to twins, the result of donated eggs fertilized by her 32-year-old husband's sperm. However, most cases of delayed parenting involve couples in their 30s and 40s.

To get a better sense of what delayed parenting is like for both parents and children, read Monica Morris, 1988, *Last-Chance Children: Growing Up With Older Parents* (New York: Columbia University Press). If you know someone who has experienced delayed parenting, either as a parent or a child, interview that person. Ask such questions as How do the ages of parents affect the

It is becoming more common for parents to delay childbearing until their 30s or 40s. As this couple is discovering, parenting at a later stage in the life cycle has its advantages and disadvantages.

parent–child relationship? What are the advantages and disadvantages for both parents and children when parenting is delayed? Should there be any age limits to delayed parenting?

PERSONAL FULFILLMENT Some couples prefer to invest the majority of their time and energy in hobbies, adult relationships, or in a variety of other activities they find personally fulfilling and satisfying. They contribute to society through working, performing volunteer activities, or interacting with and helping support other people's children, for example, students, friends, and relatives.

QUALIFICATIONS FOR PARENTHOOD In our country's past, the heavy cultural emphasis on having children rarely took into account the fact that most people can become biological parents but not all peo-

ple have good parenting skills. The high incidence of child neglect and abuse, which we discuss in Chapter 12, clearly indicates that not all people are equipped to do a satisfactory job of child rearing. Some couples, remembering their own unhappiness as a child, do not want to repeat the kind of parenting they received. Others question whether they have the knowledge, patience, aptitude, stamina, or communication or role-model skills to be a good parent.

ANTINATALIST FORCES Just as a society employs its institutions to encourage childbearing, it can also use them to discourage it. An example is China's one-child policy. As a means of fostering greater economic development, the Chinese government has expended much time and energy and many resources in attempting to limit its population. Some sociologists, like Joan Huber (1980) and Janet and Larry Hunt (1986), believe that antinatalist forces are at work in the United States today. They argue that current government and corporate policies are creating inequalities between parenting couples and child-free couples, and as a result are influencing couples who would otherwise have children not to do so.

One example of an antinatalist tendency is the long-term opposition to a national family-leave bill that requires employers to provide unpaid leave for new parents. This bill was opposed by many business organizations and vetoed twice by President Bush, before finally being signed into law by President Clinton in February 1993. Without even this limited kind of support after the birth of a child, some parents, mostly women, are forced to give up their jobs or reduce their hours if they can't find alternative child care. Consequently, their standard of living is lower than that of couples without children. When both parents work, they confront many problems as they struggle to integrate work and family roles. If social policy holds no ways for resolving these conflicts, more dual-earner couples may decide that the costs of having children are too high.

CONTROLLING FERTILITY

The decision whether or not to have children is one of the most important decisions people can make, for it affects not only their own lives but the society in which they live. Throughout history many groups and societies have attempted to control the timing and number of births to ensure an adequate supply of food and other resources for the entire community. Early efforts to control fertility took many forms. Some groups tried creating contraceptive barriers made out of animal intestines and various roots and grasses, and others ingested prepared herbs and potions that were thought to have preventive power. Over time other techniques were also employed: celibacy, late marriages, abstinence from intercourse for prolonged periods of time, prolonged breast feeding, physical actions such as jumping to dislodge the semen, and abortion. Because the process of human

reproduction was not completely understood until around the 1940s, many of these trial-and-error methods were unsuccessful. Thus, societies often resorted to other means of controlling their population; the most common of which was infanticide.

In contrast to these early methods, today efficient and safe methods of **contraception**—mechanisms for preventing pregnancy—are readily available. Most of us take the availability of contraceptives for granted. However, the distribution and use of contraceptives in the United States was outlawed in the latter half of the nineteenth century and remained illegal in some states until 1965. The battle to make contraception legal was ignited by Margaret Sanger, a public-health nurse who worked in the tenements of New York City in the early 1900s. Sanger was alarmed at the high maternal and infant mortality rates associated with the large families of the working poor she attended. Many of the mothers she nursed begged her for information about ways to prevent having more children. Sanger coined the term *birth control* as a positive description of family limitation and opened a birth control clinic in Brooklyn (McLaren, 1990:216). Although she was arrested and jailed, her efforts led to a successful social movement for planned parenthood.

In 1931, Margaret Sanger, a public health nurse, was chairperson of the National Committee on Federal Legislation for Birth Control and testified at a special Senate committee hearing on the issue.

Sexually active couples in the United States have fewer birth control options than their European counterparts. The federal government has yet to approve some of the new reproductive technologies available elsewhere. A case in point is RU-486, the French drug described as a "morning-after pill" and dubbed the "abortion pill" by its critics. This controversial drug is a steroid that counteracts the hormone progesterone and then provokes a miscarriage. The drug is used only in the first 7 weeks of pregnancy. Two days after taking RU-486 a woman takes prostaglandin, a drug that stimulates uterine contractions. The combination of the two drugs induces bleeding and a return to a normal menstrual cycle. Research has shown the drug to be 96 percent effective.

On the one side of the controversy are abortion foes who have brought enormous political pressure to keep the French drug out of the United States. They have threatened boycotts and other actions against drug companies involved in abortion research. Opponents of RU-486 argue that such a drug makes abortion too easy. On the other side, proponents of allowing the drug in the United States point to its promising applications in other areas. RU-486 can be taken once a month as a birth control pill. It acts to block key hormone systems involved in many disorders and thus has the potential for treating such diseases as cancer, osteoporosis, endometriosis, burns and other wounds, glaucoma, and a variety of immunological defects.

What is your opinion on RU-486? Should the United States permit researchers access to this drug? Should doctors be able to prescribe this pill to pregnant women? What does a controversy of this nature reveal about the political climate of the United States?

The struggle for contraceptive rights culminated in a series of Supreme Court rulings specifying that the decision to have a child is part of an individual's constitutionally protected right to privacy. In *Griswold v. Connecticut* (1965) the Court invalidated laws prohibiting the use of contraceptives by married couples. Seven years later, in *Eisenstadt v. Baird,* the Court extended this principle to unmarried adults. Then in 1977, in *Carey v. Population Services International,* the Court extended the same constitutional right to privacy to minors, stating that the state cannot deny them access to contraceptives.

Couples today can choose from a number of birth control methods (see Appendix E). Each method carries with it advantages and disadvantages. Some have health risks but are extremely convenient; others are safer but less convenient. Some have only a temporary effect; others are permanent. Some are costly; others are relatively inexpensive. Which method you choose should reflect your and your partner's values, needs, medical history, and desires. Decisions concerning contraception should be the responsibility of both parties and should not be left, as is frequently the case, to women simply because they are the ones who must worry about getting pregnant. Additionally, although a particular birth control device may prevent pregnancy, it does not necessarily provide protection against AIDS and other sexually transmitted diseases. Thus, more than one form of contraception may be advisable at any given time.

PATTERNS OF CONTRACEPTIVE USE

Not all contraceptives are equally available or popular. Table 9.2 gives the percentage distribution of all female contraceptive users aged 15 to 44. Gender plays an important role in the type of contraceptive used. Among all users, the female forms of contraception are the most likely choices: the Pill (31 percent), followed closely by female sterilization (28 percent). Male contraceptive methods are less likely to be chosen; the most popular are the condom (15 percent) and male sterilization (12 percent). Among married women, female sterilization is the most popular of all forms of contraceptive use (31 percent), followed by

TABLE 9.2

Characteristics of Female Contraceptive Users Aged 15–44, and Type of Method Relied On, 1988

Characteristic	Sterilization		Pill	IUD	Diaphragm	Condom
	Female	Male				
Total	28%	12%	31%	2%	6%	15%
Age						
15–19	2	0	59	0	1	33
20–24	5	2	68	0	4	15
25–29	17	6	45	1	6	16
30–34	33	14	22	3	9	12
35–39	45	20	5	3	8	12
40–44	51	22	3	4	4	11
Marital Status						
Never Married	6	2	59	1	5	20
Currently Married	31	17	21	2	6	14
Formerly Married	51	4	25	4	5	6
Education (20–44 only)						
0–11 years	52	7	23	4	1	6
12 years	34	15	29	2	3	11
13 or more years	21	13	29	2	10	16
Income (% of poverty level)						
0–149	37	4	36	3	2	13
150–299	32	12	29	2	5	14
over 300	22	14	30	2	8	16
Fertility Intentions						
More children	0	0	59	1	8	22
No more children	46	19	13	3	4	10
Race/Ethnicity						
Latina	32	4	33	5	2	14
Non-Latina white	26	14	30	2	7	15
Non-Latina black	38	1	38	3	2	10

Source: Adapted with permission of The Alan Guttmacher Institute from William D. Mosher, "Contraceptive Practice in the United States, 1982–1988," *Family Planning Perspectives, Vol.22*, No. 5, September/October 1990: Table 4, p. 201.

the Pill (21 percent), male sterilization (17 percent), and the condom (14 percent). The greater use of sterilization among married and formerly married women is most likely a result of their having reached the number of children desired.

Choice of contraceptives also varies markedly by life-cycle and socioeconomic characteristics. Female sterilization is most commonly used by older women, by formerly married women, by the least-educated and lowest-income women, and by African-American

women and Latinas. The Pill is more commonly used by women under 25, by never-married women, and by those who intend to have more children. Similarly, the condom is most popular among teenagers, never-married women, and women who intend to have children in the future. In 1988, about 60 percent of the 58 million U.S. women between 15 and 44 years of age were currently practicing contraception, up from 56 percent in 1982. This reflects in part a significant increase in contraceptive use among

Although we are treating sterilization as a contraceptive choice, we need to recognize that there have been (and may still be) major abuses regarding sterilization practices in the United States, primarily along class and race lines. Prior to 1979, when the federal government issued regulations to prevent involuntary sterilization, poor women, especially those of color, "were sterilized without consent, or consent was obtained on the basis of false or misleading information.... Information was given in a language women did not understand; women were threatened with loss of welfare or medical benefits if they did not consent; consent was solicited during labor; and abortion was conditional upon consent to sterilization" (Committee for Abortion Rights and Against Sterilization Abuse, 1988:27–28). A 1981 study reported that in the year 1972 alone, between 100,000 and 200,000 sterilizations took place under the sponsorship of federal programs (Davis, 1981).

Current government policies may still have a coercive effect on poor women. For example, the federal government and many state governments refuse to fund abortions but will cover, under Medicaid, the cost of sterilization. As recently as 1985, the Alan Guttmacher Institute, which specializes in studies of reproductive behavior, reported that the number of sterilizations of women of color still exceeded those of white women.

---

teenagers, from 24 percent in 1982 to 32 percent in 1988 (Mosher, 1990:199).

Approximately 6 million women become pregnant each year. More than half (3.4 million) of these pregnancies are accidents, the result of misusing contraceptives, using unreliable contraceptives, or using no contraceptives at all (Elmer-Dewitt, 1991). Given that there is a 2 to 4 percent chance of becoming pregnant after unprotected sex (which increases to 30 to 50 percent during ovulation), why do so many people risk the possibility of pregnancy by not using contraceptives?

REASONS FOR NOT USING CONTRACEPTIVES

As surprising as it might seem in this day and age, some young people believe they can't get pregnant the first time they have intercourse. If they were lucky and pregnancy did not occur the first time, they are likely to be tempted to have unprotected sex again, a pattern that researchers Jerry Burger and Linda Burns (1988) call the "illusion of unique invulnerability." There are a number of additional reasons why people do not use contraceptives, several of which are discussed below.

SYMBOLISM OF SEXUAL ACTIVITY For the young, especially for young women, being prepared with a contraceptive is a visible symbol of sexual activity. Their sexual awakenings may be in conflict with what they learned from parents, teachers, and religious leaders, who warned them against early sexual involvement. Thus, they may have feelings of guilt, fear, anxiety, or shame, all of which may prohibit them from taking proper precautions even though they are sexually active. Additionally, buying contraceptives in a public place like a drugstore carries with it the danger of being observed and, hence, identified as being sexually active.

ROLE OF PEERS AND PARENTS As with many other activities, peers play an important role in influencing contraceptive behavior. Friends share information and tend to behave in similar fashion. Thus, those whose friends aren't knowledgeable about or don't use contraceptives are also likely not to do so. The reverse is also true: Contraceptive users are likely to have friends who are users. Parents, too, may influence the contraceptive behavior of their children, explicitly and also subtly. Parents who have difficulty discussing sex with their children are more likely to have children who, if they become sexually active, will not use contraceptives. Again, the reverse is true. Children who can talk over sexual matters with their parents are more likely to use contraceptives.

CONTRACEPTION IS NOT ROMANTIC Some people complain that planning for and using contraceptives takes the spontaneity and romance out of a relationship. They prefer "letting things happen." Ignored or forgotten, however, is the possibility of a baby happening who will need them for at least the next 18 years of their lives. Even when pregnancy is considered, many women and men think of its benefits and not its negative consequences. Initially, young people may be proud of the pregnancy, believing it establishes her womanhood and his virility. In some cases one or the other party might believe, often falsely, that a pregnancy would strengthen their love or commitment to each other.

THE NATURE OF THE RELATIONSHIP Paradoxically, people are more likely to use contraceptives in the context of an ongoing, steady relationship than when they begin a new relationship. It may be that they don't expect to have sex until the relationship is well established or they want to see how well they get along first. Yet, if in the context of a new relationship a couple have sex and pregnancy results, they are less likely to be in a position to be supportive of each other. They may not even see each other after a night of unprotected sex.

As indicated in this foregoing section, contraceptive devices are not always used and, when used, are not always successful. Thus, many women faced with an unwanted pregnancy seek an abortion.

ABORTION

Abortion refers to the termination of a pregnancy before the fetus can survive on its own. This can occur either spontaneously (a miscarriage) or be induced through a variety of external methods (see Appendix D). Approximately 1.6 million abortions occur each year (25 percent of all pregnancies). Induced abortion has been a method of birth con-

trol throughout human history and for a major part of U.S. history as well. Today, however, induced abortions are the subject of an emotionally charged and highly politicized debate involving conflicting values regarding women's rights and the meaning of life. To understand the current controversy, it is necessary to place abortion in a historical context.

HISTORICAL PERSPECTIVES

Until the nineteenth century, American laws concerning abortion generally reflected the tradition in English common law that abortion was permissible until "quickening," the time (generally between the fourth and sixth months) at which a pregnant woman could feel the fetus moving in her womb. Abortions were advertised in newspapers, and recipes for abortifacients (anything used to induce abortions) were provided in popular books of the day. Estimates are that by the middle of the nineteenth century there was one induced abortion for every four live births, a figure comparable to today's rate (cited in Tribe, 1990:28).

Connecticut was the first state to regulate abortion. It did so in 1821 not on any moral grounds but to protect women by prohibiting the inducement of abortion through the use of dangerous poisons. Over time other restrictive measures followed. The most vocal supporter of these restrictions was the emerging medical profession, which desired to secure a monopoly over the practice of medicine by driving out non-physician practitioners such as midwives and women healers, who provided abortion services. In 1859, the fledgling American Medical Association called for an end to abortion, focusing much of its campaign on health and safety issues for pregnant women and the respect for life.

A second but no less significant force was also influencing the abortion debate. Significant numbers of married, white, middle-class Protestant women were choosing abortions as a means of controlling family size. Without the burden of an unwanted pregnancy, these women were free to pursue other interests. Many writers of the day saw this as a threat to traditional family structures. Additionally, racist fears motivated some people to try to outlaw abortions. People believed that the high birth rates of immigrant groups would threaten the existing social order by shifting the population balance away from established groups and toward the newly arrived groups. Hence, they encouraged middle- and upper-class women to have children. These forces combined to create an antiabortion climate. By 1900, abortion was illegal in the United States except when a physician judged it necessary to save a woman's life.

Criminalizing abortion did not end abortions, however. Rather, it drove them underground. Abortions became expensive, difficult to get, and often dangerous. Poor women, who unlike their wealthier counterparts were unable to travel outside the country or have a physician diagnose the need for a therapeutic abortion, suffered the most. Over time stories about botched abortions resulting in permanent injury or death began to surface. Two events in the 1960s became a catalyst for a new debate on the abortion issue. The first involved Sherri Finkbine, a mother of four who had taken the tranquilizer thalidomide while pregnant. When she discovered that the drug was associated with major birth defects, she elected to have an abortion rather than give birth to a seriously deformed child. After unsuccessful attempts to get an abortion in the United States, she went to Sweden, where she aborted a deformed fetus. The second event was a major outbreak of rubella (German measles) during the years 1962 to 1965. Rubella contracted by the mother during pregnancy causes major birth defects. During this period, some 15,000 babies were born with such defects. The medical profession, increasingly conscious of these tragedies, changed its position and advocated easing abortion restrictions. In 1973, the Supreme Court, by a 7 to 2 vote in *Roe v. Wade*, struck down all antiabortion laws as violations of a woman's right to privacy. Women again had the right to choose an abortion. Since that time, however, there have been renewed efforts to restrict this right.

RACE, CLASS, AND AGE

Although still legal, abortion has become increasingly less accessible. This is especially the case for poor women, women of color, and young women. In 1976, Congress passed the Hyde Amendment, which prohibited using federal Medicaid funds for abortions except in cases where the pregnancy threatens a woman's life. Over time, a majority of states followed the federal government's lead and prohibited state funding for abortions. Today only a quarter of states continue to fund abortions. Thus, although middle- and upper-class women, mostly white, are still able to choose whether or not to have an abortion, the rhetoric of choice is empty for poor women, regardless of race.

In the late 1970s, the first laws were passed requiring that parents be notified or give parental consent when a minor seeks an abortion. Today well over half of the states have such laws. These laws often drive teenagers underground and can have tragic consequences, as evidenced by the Becky Bell case. To prevent her parents from knowing about her pregnancy, this Indiana teenager had an illegal abortion and died as a result. These restrictions may also result in forcing women to have a child they do not want. Following the passage of a parental consent law in Minneapolis, the birth rate for 15- to 17-year-olds increased by nearly 40 percent (Freiberg, 1991).

Other states also passed restrictive measures that were challenged by abortion rights groups all the way to the Supreme Court. In 1989, by a 5 to 4 vote the Supreme Court in *Webster v. Reproductive Health Services* upheld Missouri's right to bar medical personnel from performing abortions in public hospitals. In 1992, in *Planned Parenthood v. Casey*, the Court narrowly upheld the right to abortion but at the same time allowed states to restrict the procedure. Few people on either side of the issue were satisfied with the decision. Congressional supporters of abortion rights almost immediately introduced the Freedom of Choice Act, which would make abortion legal in every state. President Clinton is expected to sign this measure if it reaches his desk. Later in this chapter we examine the major arguments on both sides of the abortion question.

THE ABORTION DECISION

The decision to abort is not an easy one to make, particularly in today's emotional and political climate. Yet each year more than 1 million women in this country make this choice. Who are these women? Table 9.3 shows that since the late 1970s the

CIRCUMSTANCES UNDER WHICH ABORTION IS AVAILABLE IN MAJOR EUROPEAN NATIONS

Austria, Greece, Hungary, Italy, Netherlands, Norway, Romania: On demand in the first 12 weeks.

Belgium: If woman is deemed in a "state of distress."

Britain: If two doctors feel continuing the pregnancy would involve greater risk to the life of the woman; injury to her physical or mental health or that of her children; or if there is substantial risk the child will be born with physical or mental defects.

France: During first 8 weeks, or

10 weeks since end of last menstrual cycle.

Germany: In 1993, Germany's highest court ruled that the country's liberal abortion law was unconstitutional. However, the court also said that women who undergo abortions in the first trimester and their doctors should not be prosecuted (Kinzer, 1993).

Ireland: Illegal.

Poland: If mother's life is in danger or if pregnancy seriously threatens her health, if the pregnancy result-

ed from rape or incest, or if the fetus is irreparably damaged.

Portugal: If mother's life is in danger or if pregnancy resulted from rape.

Spain: If mother's life is in danger, if fetus is malformed, or if pregnancy resulted from rape or incest.

Sweden: On demand through 18 weeks.

Switzerland: Allowed by a physician only if there is no other means to avert danger to the mother's life or the threat of serious, lasting damage to her health.

Source: Adapted from Associated Press.

---

typical woman who has had an abortion has been white, young, unmarried, and had neither previous abortions nor live births. What factors are involved in their decision to abort? Joanne Badagliacco (1991), a sociologist at Pomona College, suggests that a wide range of factors affect this decision and that these factors are different for women who are already mothers compared to those who are not yet mothers.

NONMOTHERS Among women who are pregnant for the first time, being unmarried and white, having income above the poverty level, having a partner who does not want the pregnancy, having access to legal abortions, and attending school are strongly related to the decision to abort. Combining childbearing and child rearing with school or work is difficult in our society, especially for women who do not have a partner willing to assist with child care and support. Thus, many women want to delay childbearing until they are better situated to raise a child. The freedom to chose this alternative is not available to all women,

however. Without government assistance, insurance, or other discretionary income, many poor women may have no other option but to continue a pregnancy. This is especially the case if they live in small towns and rural areas, where there are few, if any, abortion services.

Nonmothers who chose not to abort are more likely to be African American or Latina, religious, and married. The reasons for the racial and ethnic differences between aborters and nonaborters are not yet fully understood, but Badagliacco proposes some explanations. First, Latina and black women may be more tolerant than white women of accepting pregnancy outside of formal marriage. In addition, the influence of cultural or religious norms against abortion may be stronger for these women.

Being married also exerts a strong negative influence on the decision to abort, most likely because of the normative cultural expectations that marriage is the context within which childbearing and child rearing should take place. When race and marital status

TABLE 9.3

Selected Characteristics of Aborters in the United States, 1978 and 1987

	1987*	1978**
Age		
Under 20 years	30.0%	26.1%
20–24 years	35.0	33.1
25 or older	35.0	40.8
Race		
White	67.0	65.2
Nonwhite	33.0	34.8
Marital Status		
Married	26.4	17.6
Unmarried	73.6	82.4
Number of Live Births		
None	56.6	52.6
One	19.2	23.1
Two or more	24.2	24.3
Previous Abortions		
None	70.0	57.8
One	22.1	26.7
Two or more	6.9	15.5

*Stanley K. Henshaw, Lisa M. Koonin, and Jack C. Smith, 1991, "Characteristics of U.S. Women Having Abortions, 1987," *Family Planning Perspectives* 23, 2: 75–81.

**Centers for Disease Control, 1980, *Abortion Surveillance.* Annual Summary, 1978. Atlanta: Centers for Disease Control.

Source: Adapted from Joanne M. Badagliacco, 1991, "Abortion Choice Among American Women: 1976 and 1988." Paper presented at the 86th Annual Meeting of the American Sociological Association, Cincinnati, OH, August 24, Table 2, p. 23.

are examined more closely, however, different patterns emerge. Among unmarried women, whites are more likely than blacks to abort. In contrast, the reverse is true among married women (Trent and Powell-Griner, 1991). A plausible explanation for this pattern involves differences in the opportunities and costs that childbearing presents to black versus white women. According to this line of reasoning, poor, unmarried black women have less to risk in childbearing than unmarried white women because the latter have more opportunities for future education and employment. On the other hand, childbearing may be riskier for married black women than for married white women because black women have had greater ties to the labor market and historically

have contributed a larger share of family income. Thus, in comparison to white women whose husbands earn higher wages, black women can least afford the work disruption that childbearing entails. Further research on how race interacts with marital status and other variables is needed to determine the accuracy of these speculations.

MOTHERS For women who already have a child, the major factors affecting the decision to abort are their feelings and their partner's feelings about whether they want another child. The stronger the feelings that another child is unwanted, the more likely a woman is to abort. Other variables, however, may act to constrain that choice. For example, mothers who take an active role in religious activities are less likely to have an abortion than their nonreligious counterparts. In addition, married mothers have fewer abortions than nonmarried mothers. Age is also a factor. The older a mother is at the time of the pregnancy in question, the more likely she is to terminate an unwanted pregnancy. Yet another factor is ethnicity. Badagliacco found that Latina mothers are more likely to abort than white mothers. She speculates that although these women are less likely to abort first pregnancies than white women are, they may desire to control their future childbearing through abortion because cultural or religious norms prevent them from using effective contraceptive methods. Again, further research is needed to determine the validity of this interpretation.

THE AFTERMATH OF ABORTION Overall, studies of legal abortions show that most women who freely make the decision feel relief after termination of an unwanted pregnancy and suffer little if any psychological trauma afterward (Landers, 1989). This is especially true for women who have close and supportive social networks. In contrast, women who are experiencing the dissolution of a relationship or who are uncertain about or feel pressured into having an abortion are more likely to experience feelings of guilt and regret. Male partners have largely been ignored in research on abortion. Yet given their potential fatherhood, it is likely that they are emotionally vested in the abortion decision, even if in practice they exert little control. One of the few surveys that included would-be fathers found that men expressed higher rates of guilt than women (66 to 56 percent) and more of the men than women felt regret about the abortion (33 to 26 percent) (Skelton, 1989).

More follow-up studies are needed to determine how permanent these feelings are and to compare the subsequent experiences of women who opt to give birth with those who choose abortions. Along this line some studies comparing teenaged women who had abortions with those who gave birth found that those who aborted did better economically and educationally. To minimize psychological discomfort about the decision, it is important that women and men receive adequate counseling. This will enable them not only to make a reasoned decision but also to be knowledgeable about some of the adjustment problems they are likely to encounter depending on their choice.

THE POLITICS OF ABORTION

Legal scholar Laurence Tribe (1990) describes abortion as "the clash of absolutes," of life against liberty. Opponents of abortion (variously labeled anti-abortionists, anti-choice, right-to-lifers, or pro-life) believe that life begins at conception and that from that time on the embryo or fetus has the same rights as other human beings. Thus, to abort an embryo or fetus deliberately is tantamount to murder. Many people who oppose abortion make exceptions if there is a serious defect in the embryo or fetus or if the pregnancy was the result of rape or incest. However, most leaders in the pro-life movement draw a narrower line and believe that abortion is justified only when the pregnancy threatens the mother's life. According to the pro-life view, the solution for women facing an unwanted pregnancy is adoption. The goal of the pro-life movement is to make abortion illegal. One of the more radical segments of the pro-life movement, Operation Rescue, pursues a strategy of blockading and disrupting abortion clinics with the goal of shutting them down.

Those who favor keeping abortion legal (labeled pro-abortionists, abortion rights, or pro-choice) do not accept the view that life begins at conception. They argue that there is no biological basis for treating the early fetus as an independent human being with constitutional rights, because the fetus is viable (can survive outside the womb) at only about 6

months. For them, outlawing abortion is tantamount to forced pregnancy. Pro-choice advocates believe that women's rights must take precedence over those of the fetus; women must have the right to choose whether and when to become mothers. They also believe that bearing an unwanted child has negative consequences for both the mother and the child, and they point to the fact that many abused and neglected children were unwanted. Many in the pro-choice movement do not personally favor abortions, but they do not believe that they or anyone else has the right to impose this value on others. They recognize that contraception is not 100 percent effective and believe that if abortion were to be made illegal, it would only be driven underground again, with the same dangers to women as those that existed earlier.

Given these two sets of arguments, can you see any common ground for agreement between these two groups? Which arguments make the most sense to you? What is your personal viewpoint on abortion?

VALUES IN CONFLICT   One reason the abortion issue is so difficult to resolve in the United States is that its opponents and proponents tend to represent distinctively different social categories and to adhere to markedly different values. Sociologist Kristin Luker examined the contrasting worldviews of pro-life and pro-choice activists in her 1984 book *Abortion and the Politics of Motherhood.*

Pro-life activists, by and large, organize their lives around traditional gender roles. They believe that women and men are inherently different and, therefore, have different roles. Woman's natural and central role is motherhood, whereas man's role is family breadwinner. Women in the pro-life movement tend to be full-time housewives. If employed, they frequently work part-time, mostly in low-income jobs. To them motherhood is the most fulfilling role a woman can have, and they believe paid employment should not be allowed to interfere with childbearing or child rearing. Considering sex to be a sacred activity whose primary purpose is reproduction, they tend to be opposed to artificial means of contraception, and they find premarital sex disturbing. Religion is important in their lives, and they have larger families than their pro-choice counterparts.

Ever since the *Roe v. Wade* decision of 1973 legalized abortion in the United States, pro-life activists have demonstrated in an effort to reverse that decision. Pro-choice activists have countered with their own demonstrations.

In contrast, pro-choice activists reject traditional gender roles, believing that women and men are substantially equal. Pro-choice women are more likely to have careers, and their levels of education and income are higher than those of pro-life women. They believe that involuntary motherhood is destructive and that women's control over reproduction is essential for true equality with men. Pro-choice activists believe that sex is for pleasure and enhancing intimacy, and they view contraception as a matter of common sense. They believe that couples should postpone childbearing until they are emotionally and financially ready for the responsibility parenting entails.

Activists on both sides of the abortion issue are overwhelmingly white. The reasons for the limited participation of people of color in the abortion debate have not been systematically investigated. No doubt, a combination of cultural, religious, and economic issues are involved. For example, people concerned with subsistence issues generally don't participate in demonstrations or rallies. Andy Smith, a member of a Native-American women's group said, "The issue of reproductive rights has really no relevance to most Indian women. Most Indian women lost the right to abortion with the Hyde Amendment" (quoted in Brotman, 1992b:Sec. 5, p. 1). Also, the abortion issue is only one of many health and social issues confronting women of color. Thus, women of color who are activists may choose to focus on other issues they see as more central to their welfare.

PUBLIC ATTITUDES TOWARD ABORTION

As is evident throughout the preceding discussion, attitudes toward abortion are not static; instead, they are influenced by many factors: new information (particularly new medical knowledge), economic and political developments, media campaigns, and people's personal experiences. Polls conducted by the National Opinion Research Center at the University of Chicago show that 60 percent of Americans think abortion should be legal in some cases, 30 percent think it should be legal under all circumstances, and 10 percent do not believe it should be legal at all (Griffin, 1992). People are more likely to support abortions for "hard reasons": danger to the mother's life, severe birth defects, and cases involving rape or incest. They are less likely to support abortions for reasons of economics or desired family size.

The abortion debate is not likely to end soon. Americans could benefit by examining the history of abortion in other developed countries that have lowered their abortion rates by providing effective family-planning services. Little of the debate on abortion in the United States focuses on strategies to prevent abortion. Until the two sides in the debate can come to some agreement about the need for action that reduces the need for abortion, it is likely that the United States will continue to have the highest percentage of unplanned pregnancies of any developed country in the West.

Thus far, we have treated the decision of whether to have children as one of personal choice and control. Personal choices are not always realized, however. Just as some couples experience unwanted pregnancies, others want children but find they cannot have their own.

INFERTILITY

The medical profession defines **infertility** as the inability to conceive after 12 months of unprotected intercourse or the inability to carry a pregnancy to live birth. At any given time approximately 15 to 20 percent of all married couples experience some form of infertility (Higgins, 1990). After age 30, one out of four couples has difficulty in conceiving. When we examine who the infertile are and who is likely to seek and receive treatment for this problem, we find that race and class are critical factors. Reproductive impairments are more common among blacks and couples with low incomes. Yet whites and those with higher incomes are more likely and able to seek treatment (Hirsch and Mosher, 1987). Infertility treatments are costly. One couple reportedly spent $133,000 over a 7-year period on infertility treatments (Kauffold, 1990). Most insurance companies do not offer coverage for treatment, thus further limiting access for many couples.

CAUSES OF INFERTILITY

Because women show the visible signs of fertility—being pregnant—infertility, like birth control, is often viewed as a woman's problem. This tendency is reinforced by a cultural tradition that has associated masculinity with fertility. For this reason, some men are unwilling to consider the idea that they could be infertile. Men, however, are as likely to experience infertility problems as are women. About 40 percent of fertility problems are traced to the male partner and an equal percentage to the female; the remaining 20 percent involve both partners. Thus, if a couple are unsuccessful in their efforts to have a child, both should be examined for any possible problems. The causes of infertility are many and varied, and some of the same factors can affect both women and men. For example, prolonged exposure to toxic chemicals can produce sterility in both women and men. So, too, can sexually transmitted diseases. Other factors are specific to each gender. Regardless of the cause, however, infertility in either sex does not impede sexual performance.

FEMALE INFERTILITY A large percentage of female reproductive problems are connected with ovulation problems, for example, infrequent or no menstruation, whereby the egg is not released properly. In some cases fertility drugs are used to stimulate ovulation. However, this drug-induced stimulation can result in multiple births. Other forms of infertility are caused by a blockage of the fallopian tubes, which prevents conception from taking place. This blockage may be due to an inflammation, scar tissue, or **endometriosis**, a disease in which the tissue lining the uterus also grows outside the uterus, often in the fallopian tubes or on the ovaries, thus preventing the sperm from meeting the egg. Another cause of infertility can be the chemistry of the woman's reproductive system itself, which sometimes creates a hostile environment for the sperm or prevents the implantation of the fertilized egg.

MALE INFERTILITY Male infertility also takes several forms. A male's sperm production may be too low, the spermatozoa may not be sufficiently active (or motile), or the man may suffer blocked passageways. Mumps and other infectious diseases can impede sperm production, as can some medications like Tagamet, which is used to treat ulcers. Smoking marijuana can decrease sperm motility, but this effect can be reversed when marijuana use stops. Some men experience infertility because their testes have not descended into the scrotum, thus affecting production of healthy sperm. A higher body temperature can temporarily reduce a man's sperm count. Couples wishing to conceive may do well to avoid using hot tubs during this time.

CONSEQUENCES OF INFERTILITY

During the process of growing up, children commonly imagine themselves as future parents. Few, however, ever question the possibility of not being able to have children. Thus, for couples wanting to have children, the knowledge that they can't comes as a shock. Many experience a "crisis of infertility," an emotional state characterized by a feeling of loss of control over their lives. As a result, they experience a wide range of emotions: depression, disbelief, denial, isolation, guilt, frustration, and grief (Cook, 1987). Reactions to infertility vary by gender. Wives experience a deep sense of personal failure and often become preoccupied with the task of solving their infertility problems. Husbands are more likely to view infertility as an unfortunate circumstance. Their main concern with fertility focuses on their wife's unhappiness. These differing reactions can cause considerable strain in a couple's relationship. Some couples report an increase in conflict and a decrease in the frequency and level of satisfaction of sexual relationships after learning of their infertility. However, some of these same couples also reported that the experience of confronting the crisis together improved the quality of their relationship (Greil, 1991). A 34-year-old husband described how he felt about his and his wife's infertility: "At first it came as a shock, but then I figured it was something I could live with. But my wife went all to pieces. She was making herself sick going to doctors, and I wanted her to stop. We fought about it a lot; we even talked about divorce. We went to counseling, and that seemed to straighten us out. We don't talk about children much anymore. We keep busy doing things we enjoy, and we are happy."

In coping with their infertility, couples must ask themselves how important becoming parents is for them as individuals and as a married couple and how much medical testing, effort, expense, and marital tension they are willing to accept in seeking to become parents. If they decide they want to rear children, they have two options: adoption and a variety of reproductive technologies.

ADOPTION AS A SOLUTION TO INFERTILITY

Historically, about the only available solution for infertile couples was adopting someone else's children. Although both fertile and infertile couples adopt children, adoption rates are higher for infertile couples. Prior to the twentieth century, life expectancy was considerably less, and birth control methods were neither well known nor effective. Having a child

out of wedlock was considered scandalous. Women had few employment opportunities that paid a wage sufficient to support themselves, much less a child. Consequently, most unwed mothers felt pressured to give up their infants. Thus, many orphans and unwanted children were available for adoption.

These conditions have changed dramatically, however. With the increase in life expectancy, few children are orphaned at an early age. Birth control is more effective and is available to both the married and the unmarried. Abortions are legal, and people today are more accepting of unwed mothers. Today only about 6 percent of unwed mothers (aged 15 to 44) place their babies up for adoption. White babies are about 12 times more likely to be placed for adoption than black babies (Bachrach, 1986), who tend to become part of an extended family through an informal adoption process whereby relatives and friends simply incorporate them into their own families. African Americans informally adopt more than 10 times the number of African-American children placed for adoption through formal channels (Hill, 1977). All of these changes have led to a scarcity of adoptable infants, especially white infants. It is estimated that 3 million couples are seeking to adopt healthy, white infants but only 50,000 white infants are available (cited in Renzetti and Curran, 1992). This scarcity has created what sociologist Barbara Katz Rothman (1989) calls a "competitive market situation."

CLASS ISSUES IN ADOPTION Research on who adopts and who is adopted raises some serious political and ethical issues. Couples who adopt are most commonly white and affluent, with at least some college education (Bachrach, 1986; Bachrach et al., 1990), whereas children to be adopted come primarily from economically disadvantaged backgrounds. Part of this redistribution of children is the result of the strict requirements of adoption agencies, for example, a requirement that the adoptive mother not work outside the home.

Due to the shortage of healthy infants, prospective parents using an adoption agency face a waiting period of 1 to 5 or more years. Thus, many couples (as well as some unmarried women and men) have sought privately arranged adoptions through an attorney or a physician rather than an agency. Lynne McTaggart exposed some of the more exploitive aspects of such arrangements in her book *The Baby Brokers* (1980). Among some of the excesses she reports are solicitations for white babies through want ads placed in economically depressed communities. She also exposes some questionable practices involving babies from economically poor countries, including coercive pressure to relinquish parental rights, baby selling, and even kidnapping.

How do these private adoptions work? They may be closed or open. In a **closed adoption**, the adoptive parents and the birth parents do not meet. In **open adoptions**, however, the two parties meet and together work out the process of adoption. The birth mother may even take an active role in selecting the adoptive parents. In some cases the adoptive parents will invite the birth mother to live with them during her pregnancy. Some open adoptions are characterized by ongoing contact with the birth mother, the extent of which may vary from periodic reports of the child's progress to the birth mother's integration into the family as a friend or **"fictive kin"** (attribution of kinship terms to nonrelatives). The costs of these adoptions can exceed $20,000. Thus, this alternative to agency adoption is limited to the wealthier classes.

TRANSRACIAL (INTERRACIAL) ADOPTIONS

Race is also a factor in the politics and policies of the adoption process. Of the children eligible for adoption, 40 percent are African American, but many of them will remain in foster care indefinitely because prospective African-American parents can't meet agency income and housing requirements and because of the curtailment of interracial adoptions (Beck, 1988).

The 1960s and early 1970s witnessed a rapid growth in transracial adoptions. Between 1969 and 1974, more than 80 percent of the Native-American children adopted were placed with white families.

More and more couples who want to adopt are seeking children in other countries. This family welcomes their new daughter, who was adopted from the Philippines.

During the same time many Native Americans were rejected as adoptive parents because they did not meet agency criteria. By 1972, approximately 10,000 African-American children had been adopted by white couples (cited in McRoy, 1989). Over the last 2 decades, however, people of color have become more critical of interracial adoptions, raising concerns about the possible adjustment problems these children might have. This concern has not materialized; research has shown that adopted children raised in interracial homes generally adjust well. These children do struggle with identity issues, however (McRoy, Grotevant, and Surcher, 1988).

Because of the controversy, many agencies have reverted to race matching in adoption placements. Today only about 8 percent of adoptions are interracial (Bachrach et al., 1990). Consequently, many couples have turned to intercountry adoptions, seeking children from Korea, Colombia, India, Mexico, Vietnam, El Salvador, the Philippines, Honduras, Sri Lanka, Guatemala, Peru, and Romania. The majority of intercountry adoptions involve infants of color from economically disadvantaged countries. Some of these countries, however, are becoming sensitive to the loss of large numbers of their children and are now imposing stricter restrictions on such adoptions.

Until more progress is made in race relations, transracial adoptions are likely to be controversial and one-sided. The idea of people of color adopting white children is still largely unthinkable. The authors could find no evidence of formal adoptions of white children by people of color, although black foster parents in California tried unsuccessfully to adopt the white child they had in their care (Bunin, 1984).

Although approximately 8 percent of women who are infertile adopt (Bachrach, 1986), many others who wish to have children utilize one or more reproductive techniques.

REPRODUCTION WITHOUT SEX: THE NEW TECHNOLOGIES

Historical records show that as early as the eighteenth century, women actively sought help from the developing medical profession in having a child. Outside of providing advice to relax or to adopt children, doctors had little knowledge to offer women who wanted to conceive. It was not until 1940 that researchers had developed a clear understanding of the relationship between ovulation and the menstrual cycle. This breakthrough was immediately applied to attempts to reduce unplanned pregnancies by regulating conception, pregnancy, and menopause. The result of these efforts was the mass production of an oral contraceptive.

As contraceptive technology improved, fewer unwanted children were available for the infertile to adopt. Thus, pressure grew to find ways to overcome infertility. However, some of the reproductive technologies have generated considerable controversy because they have altered the relationship between sex and reproduction. In the United States the biological, rather than the sociological, aspects of parenthood have dominated our thinking and our social policies. Thus, as we shall see in the following section, some of these reproductive technologies challenge traditional definitions of parenthood and family and raise numerous ethical and legal questions.

ARTIFICIAL INSEMINATION

The reproductive technique known as **artificial insemination (AI)** involves the injection of sperm into a woman's vagina during her fertile period. Artificial insemination is a solution for male infertility as well as an option for single heterosexual women and lesbians who want to be mothers but who do not necessarily want to be married. This process is one of the oldest and most successful of the reproductive technologies, having been developed in the animal husbandry field several centuries ago. In the 1890s, a U.S. doctor, Robert Dickenson, secretly utilized the technique with women whose husbands were unable to produce sperm (Rothman, 1991). Since that time AI has become a popular method of infertility treatment.

The pregnancy rate following AI ranges from 40 to 90 percent depending on a number of factors: the woman's fertility potential, whether the sperm is fresh or frozen, and the timing and frequency of the insemination (Moghissi, 1989). For conception to occur, AI must take place at the time of ovulation. Although conception can occur after one insemination, two to five are more common. Compared to other reproductive technologies, the cost of AI is rela-

Artificial insemination has become a popular treatment for infertility and a means for unmarried and lesbian women to become pregnant. It is not without problems. Dr. Cecil Jacobsen was convicted of using his own sperm to artificially inseminate his patients while claiming other donors were involved.

sperm count is low. To enhance the possibility of conception, sperm from several ejaculations are collected and inserted into the wife's vagina. This method has wide social acceptance because any resulting offspring is biologically related to both the husband and wife.

Controversy arises, however, over the appropriateness of AI in cases where the husband is sterile or his sperm count is too low even for AIH. In such cases AID is utilized. Donors are usually screened for genetic problems and paid a modest fee for each ejaculate. The use of donor sperm raises legal and psychological issues regarding the lack of biological ties to the father. To minimize these concerns, attempts are made to find a donor who matches the husband's physical characteristics. In addition, the husband's sperm are mixed with those of the donor, thereby creating the possibility that the husband's sperm fertilized the egg. When husbands agree to AID and willingly accept paternal responsibility for any resulting offspring, most state laws view these children as legitimate and recognize the father's obligations to support them. Legal problems arise, however, when the husband was unaware of his wife's insemination. In such cases, if the husband rejects a paternal role, the courts will likely support him. In addition, some state laws still treat AID as adultery and the resulting offspring as illegitimate.

The use of AID raises other legal issues. For example, the courts have held separated lesbian partners accountable for children conceived in this manner. Also, in cases where the donor knows the mother, he may later demand parental rights even when he had initially signed an agreement disavowing them. Legal quandaries may also arise following a divorce. Can a sterile husband avoid child support by claiming he is not the biological father? On that same ground, can he be denied visitation rights? The answers to these questions have not been adequately resolved, and they raise another critical dilemma. Such legal proceedings move AI outside the realm of secrecy and into public view. Thus, some children conceived through AI are likely to be made aware of the circumstances of their birth in unplanned and uncontrolled ways. This knowledge can come as a shock and cause them great anxiety. Guidelines are needed to assist parents in discussing these issues with their children.

tively modest, ranging from $100 to $150 per insemination. Although the true extent of AI is unknown, the Office of Technology Assessment (1988), estimates that AI is responsible for 65,000 births each year.

The legal, ethical, and family issues surrounding AI stem from the fact that different sources of sperm are utilized in the procedure: *artificial insemination homologous* (AIH), where the husband's sperm is used; *artificial insemination by a donor* (AID), often anonymous and obtained from 1 of nearly 100 sperm banks in the United States; or a combination of the two. The AIH method is used when the husband's

FROZEN EMBRYOS AND EMERGING SOCIAL POLICY

In December 1988, Junior and Mary Sue Davis utilized in vitro fertilization to create seven embryos, which were then frozen and stored in a Tennessee fertility clinic. In February 1989, Davis sued his wife for divorce. He asked the court to prohibit any use of the embryos without his consent, arguing that he should not be forced to become a parent against his wishes. In August 1989, a judge issued a "life begins at conception" ruling and awarded custody of the embryos (what the judge called "children in vitro") to the ex-wife, who testified that she wanted control of the embryos so that she could use them in an attempt to bear children. This ruling was overturned by the Tennessee Court of Appeals,

which granted joint custody of the frozen embryos to the divorced couple, avoiding questions of whether the embryos are alive and deserving of legal protection, treating them instead as property of the marriage to be equitably disposed of in the event of a divorce.

Then in 1992, the Tennessee Supreme Court, citing privacy rights, ruled that Junior Davis shouldn't be forced into fatherhood against his will. The Court used the term *preembryos* to describe the organisms, claiming they were neither persons nor property but an interim category that entitles them to special respect because of their potential for human life. The court also stated that Mary Sue Davis Stowe, who in the interim had remarried,

had other reproductive options, including adoption. Consequently, her desire for the embryos could not automatically outweigh the desire of her ex-husband to avoid parenthood now that the two were no longer married. The ruling made clear that the embryos could not be implanted in Mary Sue or anyone else. Neither side planned to appeal the ruling.

Which decision do you favor, the lower court's or the Tennessee Supreme Court's? Do you think the ruling deals adequately with the concerns surrounding frozen embryos? Why or why not? What effect do you think the higher court's decision will have on abortion? If men should not be forced into fatherhood, should women be forced into motherhood?

IN VITRO FERTILIZATION

In vitro fertilization (IVF) is a more recent and more complicated reproductive technique. It is sometimes called "test-tube fertilization" because it takes place outside the woman's body, usually in a laboratory. The process begins with the insertion of a *laparoscope* (a tubelike instrument) through a small incision so that the follicle inside the ovary and where the eggs are produced can be viewed. A hollow needle is then inserted through a second incision, and the eggs and surrounding fluid are removed. The eggs are then fertilized by sperm from the husband or a donor, after which the resulting embryo is implanted in the woman's uterus, to be carried to term. The insertion of multiple embryos increases the chances of pregnancies, but it also increases the likelihood of multiple births.

The first publicly acknowledged human success of IVF occurred in England in July 1978 with the birth of Louise Brown. Three years later, the first IVF baby was born in the United States. Since that time, more than 5000 IVF births have been recorded in the United States. The success rate is in the range of about 15 to 20 percent. About one-third of the pregnancies result in a miscarriage, however. The costs are high, ranging from $4000 to $10,000 per procedure, out of the range of many couples.

Several objections have been raised to IVF. Some people question the "morality" of fertilizing more than one egg, given the possibility that the other fertilized eggs may be destroyed, a situation that they see as analogous to abortion and, in their view, the destruction of human life. Sometimes the additional fertilized eggs are not destroyed but frozen, to be implanted at a future date. This latter procedure, known as *cryopreservation*, has led to some complicated legal questions. For example, if the couple dies, what happens to the embryos? Who "owns" them? Do they have the right to exist, perhaps even inherit property and possessions from their deceased "parents," or can someone (the doctor, a relative) decide to destroy them or implant them into an "adopting" party? If the couple divorces, who has custody of the embryos? Can an ex-wife go ahead with an embryo implant over her ex-husband's objections? Social policy is just beginning to develop in this area.

Finally, IVF presents the possibility of **genetic engineering**, the ability to manipulate human genes and, hence, control heredity. Although most people applaud the use of technology to identify and manipulate defective genes that carry inheritable diseases, some fear that these same procedures will be used to attempt to create the perfect child—the right IQ, color of eyes, height, abilities, and even the right sex. Fertility experts are already working on methods of sex selection. One report gives the odds of getting the desired sex through these techniques as 80 to 20 for a boy and 70 to 30 for a girl (Kotulak and Gorner, 1991:16). If these methods are successful and become widespread, it is possible that a society that values one sex over the other will create a society in which there is a major imbalance of women and men.

GAMETE INTRAFALLOPIAN TRANSFER AND ZYGOTE INTRAFALLOPIAN TRANSFER

Developed around 1985, **gamete intrafallopian transfer (GIFT)** and **zygote intrafallopian transfer (ZIFT)** are two of the newest techniques for helping infertile couples. The first procedure involves the insertion of gametes—sperm and eggs—into the fallopian tubes. Women first take hormones to stimulate the production of multiple eggs, which are then collected from the ovaries. Shortly thereafter the eggs are inserted into the fallopian tubes along with the sperm. When male infertility is involved, the ZIFT procedure is used. Here zygotes—fertilized eggs—instead of gametes are placed into the fallopian tubes. In this way physicians know in advance that fertilization has occurred. The success rate for GIFT is slightly higher than for IVF. According to Michael DiMattina, founder of the first successful GIFT program in the

Washington, D.C., area, the success rate for GIFT and ZIFT is about 32 to 33 percent per procedure. Because microscopic surgery is involved, even though on an outpatient basis, the costs are quite high.

OVUM OR EMBRYO TRANSPLANT

The procedure known as **ovum** or **embryo transplant (OT)** is used when a woman is unable to produce viable ova. Hence, an ovum donor is used. A variety of fertilization techniques may be used (AIH, AID, or IVF). After fertilization is ascertained, the embryo is inserted into the uterus of the infertile woman. The perceived advantage of this method is that the husband will be the biological father and his wife, although not the biological mother, will experience pregnancy and childbirth, and thus the likelihood of early bonding with the child. This procedure has been refined and is now available to postmenopausal women who want to become pregnant as well as to women who want to avoid passing on a known genetic defect to their children.

Criticisms of embryo transplants revolve around two central issues. One is the possible exploitation of women donors. Although a woman may donate ova out of a desire to assist an infertile couple, some women, especially poor women, may feel pressured to sell their ova to help support themselves or their families. The second issue raises questions of what constitutes biological motherhood—the contribution of genetic material (via the ovum) or pregnancy and childbirth. This question has become even more complicated with the development of surrogate motherhood.

SURROGATE MOTHERHOOD

The term **surrogate mother** refers to a woman who becomes pregnant and gives birth to a child for another woman who is infertile or incapable of carrying a child. This is perhaps the most controversial of all the reproductive techniques because, like AID, it involves a third party. Unlike AID, however, the donor is intimately involved in the reproductive process.

Surrogate motherhood may occur in either of two ways. In the first, a third party is artificially inseminated with the husband's sperm (or donor sperm if he

Reproductive technology raises many questions about the meaning of parenthood.

Source: Reprinted by permission: Tribune Media Services.

Arlette Schweitzer (center), her daughter, son-in-law, and twin grandchildren leave a press conference in which Mrs. Schweitzer explained why she served as a surrogate mother for her daughter.

is also infertile). Here the term *surrogate* is somewhat misleading because the woman who is inseminated is also the biological mother. In the second, the wife's uterus will not allow a fertilized egg to implant itself and develop. In such cases the couple uses in vitro fertilization, but the resulting embryo is then transplanted in a surrogate mother. In both cases, however, after giving birth, the surrogate mother is expected to relinquish all claims to the infant in favor of the couple, who may or may not have a biological relationship to the child.

The surrogate can be a relative or a stranger. In the latter case the woman and the couple generally sign a contract. Generally, the provisions of the contract include a fee payment ($10,000 to $20,000) to the surrogate and coverage of all her medical expenses. In fact, however, the costs are much higher after legal and other fees are included.

Questions about the motivations of the two parties in such an agreement inevitably arise. For the infertile couple there is a desire to have a child that is genetically related to at least one of them. Several motivational factors are probably involved in the decision to be a surrogate mother. Detroit psychiatrist Philip Parker conducted extensive psychological tests on over 500 surrogate applicants and found strong altruistic aspects in their willingness to be surrogate mothers. They want to give the gift of a child to those who otherwise would not experience child rearing (reported in Gladwell, 1988). However, class factors may be operative as well. Most infertile couples who seek a child in this way are financially well off, whereas most surrogate mothers are young, poor-

ly educated, and have only limited employment prospects. Thus, the opportunity to earn money may play a role in their decision.

Critics of surrogate motherhood, such as the feminist writer Andrea Dworkin (1987), see it as reproductive exploitation whereby poor women's reproductive capacity becomes a commodity they are forced to sell to survive. Considering that gestation takes 9 months of 24-hour days, the sum these women are paid is considerably less than the minimum wage. Others see a potential for misuse in that it is now possible for fertile women wishing to avoid the discomfort of pregnancy or the interruption of a career by childbirth to utilize a surrogate.

SURROGATE MOTHERHOOD AND THE COURTS The legal issues surrounding surrogate motherhood are many. What if the surrogate mother changes her mind and decides to keep the child? This has proven to be a rare occurrence—only 6 out of approximately 4000 surrogate mothers have not relinquished their babies; an additional 10 others have expressed regrets for doing so (Curry, 1992). When a surrogate mother changes her mind, however, the results can be traumatic for all parties. One well-publicized example was the celebrated case of Baby M, whose biological mother, Mary Beth Whitehead, changed her mind after giving birth and wanted to keep the child. After a lengthy trial, the court ruled that the contract was valid. The judge awarded custody of the child to the biological father and adoptive mother, William and Elizabeth Stern, based on the longstanding legal principle of "the best interests of the child." The Sterns were seen as more stable and capable of parenting than the biological mother. Later, the New Jersey Supreme Court reversed the first decision, declaring surrogacy contracts invalid. The court upheld the custody decision but awarded visitation rights to the biological mother.

A more recent custody case involving surrogacy questioned the definition of *mother*. The surrogate mother, Anna Johnson, had contracted with Mark and Crispina Calvert to have their embryo, which had been obtained through in vitro fertilization, implanted in her uterus. After the child was born, Johnson sought maternal rights, claiming that through pregnancy and giving birth she had bonded with the infant and was therefore the baby's mother. The judge disagreed and awarded custody to the Calverts, stating that genetics, not giving birth, constitutes parentage. The judge compared the role the surrogate provides to that of a foster parent who temporarily stands in for a parent who is unable to care for a child.

Other issues may also arise in surrogate cases. What happens if a child is born with a major physical problem? Can the contract then be rescinded? If so, does the responsibility for the child rest solely on the surrogate mother? What rights does each party have—the unborn child, the child's biological mother, the child's biological father, and the contractual parents? Do the contractual parents have a right to demand certain behaviors from the surrogate mother during her pregnancy, for example, maintaining a particular diet, refraining from drinking alcohol, or undergoing surgery to improve the life chances of the fetus? These questions have spurred considerable legislative activity in attempts to regulate surrogate parenting. At this time, however, there is no consistent legal view across the country. At least 17 states have banned or restricted commercial surrogate contracts (Curry, 1992). Other states, like California, permit it. Most, however, have not yet decided on what approach to take in this matter.

FUTURE REPRODUCTIVE STRATEGIES

The successes of IVF and OT are fueling the development of even more radical reproductive techniques such as ectogenesis and cloning. **Ectogenesis** involves the insemination of an ovum and the development of an embryo outside the uterus. Although no one has as yet created an artificial womb that would support a fetus in its early stages, the development of incubators for premature babies suggests that this is a distinct possibility. In **cloning**, the nucleus of a mature unfertilized egg is removed and replaced with the nucleus of a body cell from an adult organism. In essence, the donor body cell fertilizes the egg. The result is that the new organism is genetically identical with the donor. Thus far, cloning has not involved humans, but it has been used to reproduce fruit flies, salamanders, and frogs. Those who advocate cloning believe the process could produce biological materials that could then be used to fight diseases and overcome physical impairments. Those who object to cloning fear the outcome of successful cloning—an exact duplicate (or possibly multiple copies) of its "parent." Such a technique, if successfully developed, raises race, class, and gender issues. Would some groups be cloned at the expense of others? Who would have the power to control this technology?

Ectogenesis and cloning both involve asexual reproduction, that is, reproduction without sexual intercourse. How would the advent of ectogenesis and cloning affect the relationship between women and men, who now must cooperate in the reproduction of children? How would such techniques affect society's views of parenthood and families? These questions remain unanswered.

In sum, the new reproductive technology has helped many infertile couples and unmarried women realize their goal of having and rearing children. "Eight times a day, a child is born in the United States who was conceived outside the womb. By the year 2010, such children are expected to number a million or more" (Hotz, 1991:11). Although decisions to have children are private matters, the technology created to assist the infertile has serious public implications. For example, the separation of sexual intercourse from reproduction undermines one of the traditional functions of marriage. Will widespread use of these technologies make marriage obsolete? Will these technologies change the meaning of parenthood as it has been understood historically? Will these reproductive techniques necessitate a whole different legal and social view of the family? Will biological ties cease to have much meaning? In an article titled "Asexual Reproduction and the Family," sociologist John Edwards (1991:504) suggests this latter possibility when he writes, "It will be possible for each child in the 'family' to be conceived in a different way, making the parent (her, him, or them) a different type of parent to each child."

IMPLICATIONS FOR SOCIAL POLICY

Throughout this chapter we have discussed a number of difficult issues that surround reproduction and the struggles for **reproductive freedom**, the ability of women to decide whether, when, and with whom they will have children. Reproductive freedom, however, does not exist in a vacuum. The legal right to use contraceptives, to seek treatment for infertility, to adopt, or to decide whether to abort a pregnancy in and of itself may not mean much if you do not have the economic or social resources necessary to translate a desired choice into a reality. Thus, public policy debates on reproductive rights need to address the way class, race, gender, and age affect the reproductive experiences of women and men. Kathryn Kolbert (1990:300), an attorney with the Reproductive Freedom Project of the American Civil Liberties Union, makes this point when she says, "Issues surrounding economic justice are closely related to and cannot be separated from reproductive rights issues."

SUMMARY

At the beginning of the nineteenth century the U.S. fertility rate was quite high. Since that time it has steadily declined to its current low rate, with the notable exception of the "baby boom" of the late 1940s and 1950s. Fertility rates vary across race and class; people of color and low-income groups have the highest rates.

Deciding whether to parent involves an evaluation of both costs and benefits. Increasing numbers of people are deciding to be child-free or to delay parenting until into their 30s. During the mid nineteenth century the use of contraceptives and abortion became illegal. After a long struggle, the Supreme Court invalidated laws prohibiting contraceptives, and in 1973 in *Roe v. Wade* it recognized a woman's right to an abortion. Since that time many efforts have been made to restrict abortion, and abortion has become a major issue in state and national politics.

The decline in the fertility rate, the legalization of abortion, and the tendency for more unmarried mothers to keep their babies have led to a scarcity of infants available for adoption. Thus, considerable research has gone into developing new reproductive technologies to help infertile couples achieve their desire to have children. These new reproductive techniques present many legal, ethical, and social challenges and raise questions about the nature of parenthood and the meaning of families. Social policy is only slowly emerging to deal with these questions.

KEY TERMS

fertility	endometriosis	gamete intrafallopian transfer
fertility rate	closed adoption	zygote intrafallopian transfer
total fertility rate	open adoption	ovum or embryo transplant
pronatalist attitude	fictive kin	surrogate mother
antinatalist forces	artificial insemination	ectogenesis
contraception	in vitro fertilization	cloning
abortion	genetic engineering	reproductive freedom
infertility		

QUESTIONS FOR STUDY AND REFLECTION

1. Trace and explain the changing fertility rates in the United States over the last 3 centuries. Project the patterns of fertility that are most likely to develop among various age, marital-status, race, and class groupings in the first half of the twenty-first century. Explain the rationale for your projections.

2. Compare and contrast the different reasons people give for wanting to parent or to be child-free. Given the current economic and political climate in the United States, do you believe there will be an increase or a decrease in the number of people choosing to be child-free? Explain your position.

3. Compare and contrast the opposing views on abortion. How would you go about developing a social policy that would seem to make sense in light of the divergent viewpoints that now exist? Describe your policy and the rationale behind it.

4. What is meant by *reproductive freedom*? Do you agree with this concept? Explain. How do issues surrounding contraception, adoption, and reproductive technology affect the likelihood of reproductive freedom in our society?

FURTHER READING

COREA, GENA. 1985. *The Mother Machine: Reproductive Technologies from Artificial Insemination to Artificial Wombs.* New York: Harper & Row. This book provides a provocative look at the historical background and methods of each technology, the risks involved, the social effects, and how the researchers themselves envision the use of these revolutionary techniques.

HARTMAN, BETSY. 1987. *Reproductive Rights and Wrongs: The Global Politics of Population Control and Contraceptive Choice.* New York: Harper & Row. A controversial book that examines reproductive policies of national governments and international agencies. The author calls for the expansion, rather than the restriction, of individual reproductive choice.

MCLAREN, ANGUS. 1990. *A History of Contraception: From Antiquity to the Present Day.* Cambridge, MA: Basil Blackwell. This book presents a highly readable account of contraceptive practices from ancient Greece to the late twentieth century and reveals the complex ways in which reproductive decision making is interconnected with social, economic, political, and gender relationships.

CHILDBEARING AND PARENTING

Justin and Debra, a couple in their late 30s, are very much in love. Both have previously been married. Debra has a teenaged son and daughter from her marriage; Justin does not have any children. The couple plan to marry at some point in the near future, but for the time being they are content with the relationship as it is. Although marriage is not in their immediate plans they have periodically discussed marriage, pregnancy, childbirth, child care, and other related issues.

Debra does not want more children, fearing that at her age she is likely to have a deformed or retarded child. In fact, the very thought of all aspects of pregnancy such as nausea, labor, a hospital stay, and the possibility of a baby born with a birth defect terrifies her. Justin, however, wants at least two children and rejects Debra's fears as irrational.

What do you think? Does Debra have good reason to be concerned about getting pregnant at her age? What should she do? Should she consider having two children, or at least one child, with Justin? If she refuses, is she being selfish? If she decides to have another child, what kind of medical advice should she seek? What would you do if you were in Debra's situation?

"It's a girl." "It's a boy." Every year millions of parents hear these words as they strain to get that first glimpse of the miraculous new life to which they have contributed. Whatever their feelings concerning pregnancy and childbirth, a majority of Americans have at least one child in their lifetime. As we saw in Chapter 9, at the end of the 1980s the total fertility rate was 2.0. Fertility rates vary considerably among different groups, and individual cases vary greatly as well. The *Guinness Book of World Records* (1990), for example, relates that in 1981 a woman in Chile gave birth to her fifty-fifth child. However many children an individual or couple has, the process always begins with the fertilization of an egg by a sperm. Between that moment and the birth of a child are many months of development.

In the previous chapter we examined the issue of fertility and various factors that affect the decision to parent. Once this decision is made, individuals and couples must turn their attention to matters of conception, pregnancy, childbirth, and child rearing. All of these activities effect considerable changes in the lives of the people involved. In this chapter we examine a number of factors associated with childbearing, including conception, prenatal care and concerns, and methods of childbirth. In addition, we examine what happens after the baby arrives; the adjustments and adaptations that individuals and families make when a child becomes part of the group.

CONCEPTION

Pregnancy and eventual childbirth begin with **conception**, the process by which a male sperm cell penetrates the female ovum (egg), creating a fertilized egg, or **zygote**. Until recently penile–vaginal intercourse was necessary for conception to take place. We saw in Chapter 9, however, that today conception can take place not only inside a woman's uterus but also within a petri dish. The latter procedure is sometimes distinguished from conception and referred to as *fertilization* or *cloning*. For the purposes of this book, however, the term *conception* will encompass all forms of fertilization.

What makes conception possible is the process of **ovulation**, the release of a mature egg. Female eggs develop in the ovaries, and during the female's monthly menstrual cycle an egg is released from one of the two ovaries. The egg, containing 23 chromosomes in its nucleus, moves in a fluid through the fallopian tube on a 3-to 5-day journey to the uterus. If the egg is not fertilized within 18 to 24 hours after ovulation, it disintegrates. The bloody uterine wall drops off in about 2 weeks, leaving the body through a process called **menstruation**. Under most conditions, females cannot conceive before they have begun to menstruate and ovulate. The period of fertility in females normally begins with ovulation and lasts until after the menopause (which occurs somewhere between 45 and 50 years of age, on average). There are always exceptions, however. In the United States girls as young as 10 years of age have conceived. The youngest female to conceive a child is recorded as a 5 1/2-year-old girl living in Peru, and the oldest is a 59-year-old woman who gave birth to a healthy baby in 1891 (*Guinness Book of World Records*, 1990).

Males are capable of participating in conception when they begin to produce sperm. This occurs around puberty. According to some authorities, men can produce viable sperm for 80 or more years. (This, of course, varies from one individual to another.)

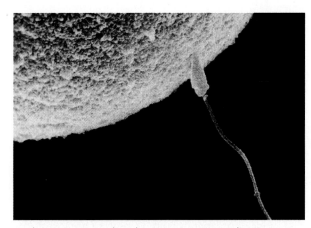

Fertilization occurs when the sperm penetrates the ovum.

Sperm cells develop in the testes. Each sperm has a nucleus or head that contains 23 chromosomes, a neck, a midsection, and a long, whiplike tail that gives it mobility to move toward the egg. The sperm travel to the penis and are released in semen during ejaculation. It is estimated that anywhere from 200 million to 400 million sperm are released with a single ejaculation. Sperm can survive for 48 hours after they are released. Most die in the vagina; only a few thousand reach the fallopian tube that contains the egg. These surviving sperm emit an enzyme that dissolves the outer layer of the egg until one sperm enters the egg and fertilizes it. Once the egg is fertilized it cannot be penetrated again by sperm. Therefore, after the egg has been fertilized, remaining sperm soon die. The egg is viable for approximately 24 hours. Thus, on the average, for conception to occur, a couple must have intercourse during or within 2 days prior to ovulation.

Within several hours after fertilization, the egg begins to divide. Division continues until the mass of divided cells, called a **blastocyst**, reaches the uterus anywhere from 5 to 14 days after conception. At that point implantation occurs; the blastocyst attaches to the uterine wall and begins to find nourishment from the lining of the uterus (see Figure 10.1). This first phase of prenatal development, from conception to implantation, is generally referred to as the *germinal period.* Following the germinal period is the *embryonic period,* which lasts from about 2 to 8 weeks after conception. During this phase the developing human organism is no longer referred to as a blastocyst but rather as an **embryo**. The third and final period of prenatal development is the *fetal period*—from 8 weeks through the end of pregnancy. From this point until birth we cease referring to the developing organism as an embryo and call it instead a **fetus**.

SEX DETERMINATION

At conception, the 23 chromosomes from the sperm join with the 23 chromosomes in the egg to produce 23 pairs of chromosomes. These paired chromosomes carry thousands of genes, which serve as a blueprint for the development of a unique human being. One chromosome from each parent is a sex chromosome. The sex chromosome in the ovum is always an X chromosome. In contrast, the sex chromosome in the

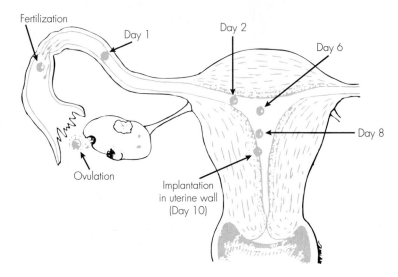

Fertilization

Day 1

Day 2

Day 6

Day 8

Ovulation

Implantation
in uterine wall
(Day 10)

FIGURE 10.1   Implantation in the Uterine Wall

Source: Copyright © 1971, 1973, 1976 by The Boston Women's Health Book Collective. Reprinted by permission of Simon & Schuster, Inc.

sperm may be either X (similar to the female X) or Y (uniquely male). Thus, when the male partner contributes an X, the baby will be a female (XX), and when he contributes a Y, the baby will be a male (XY). The environment (the acidic vagina) through which the sperm must travel to reach the egg is also considered by some to be a factor in sex determination. Genetic researchers, for example, have found that women who conceive when their vaginal environment is heavily acidic are more likely to produce a girl than when there is less acid in the vaginal area (Doyle and Paludi, 1991). Actually, all embryos will develop as females unless they are exposed to the Y chromosome and a sufficient amount of male hormones.

With increasing advances in reproductive technology a couple must no longer leave the determination of their unborn child's sex completely in the hands of nature. For example, the London Gender Clinic offers parents-to-be a chance to increase the odds of having a girl or a boy, whichever is their preference. Sex selection is a sensitive and controversial issue, however. Some experts in reproduction fear that the techniques used in sex selection might represent a health hazard to pregnant women. Some people are against the procedure on moral grounds and see it as interfering with the choice of God or nature.

Conception might seem like a simple process, but it is not. For a variety of reasons at least one in six couples cannot conceive. In about 16 percent of the cases in which human eggs are exposed to sperm, fertilization does not occur. The desire to have children among those who are infertile has led to a high demand for reproduction-aiding technologies (see Chapter 9). Moreover, for those who are not infertile, fertilization does not guarantee a successful birth. In fact, 18 percent of fertilized eggs are lost during the first week of pregnancy, and 32 percent are lost in the second week. Only around 37 percent of human zygotes survive to become live infants (Blank, 1988).

MULTIPLE CONCEPTION

Multiple conception, in which two or more children are conceived at one time, is relatively rare. The most common form of multiple conception is twins. Twins

Fraternal twins are often of a different sex and usually look no more alike than other siblings, whereas identical twins are always of the same sex and look very much like each other.

are born about once in every 90 births for whites and once in every 70 births for blacks. Asian Americans tend to conceive twins less often than any other racial group in the United States (Papalia and Olds, 1989). Triplets are fairly rare, occurring around once in every 9000 births. Even more rare are quadruplets, which occur once in every 620,000 births (Reeder and Martin, 1987). And rarer yet are quintuplets, which occur once in every 55 million births. Not surprisingly, the mortality rate for multiple births is higher than for single births. The greater the number of children born at one time, the greater the mortality rate.

There are two types of twins, fraternal and identical. Fraternal twins are the more common of the two. **Fraternal twins** develop when two separate eggs are fertilized by two different sperm. Because they are conceived from different sets of eggs and sperm, fraternal twins are no more alike genetically or physically (except, of course, in age) than are other full siblings. They do not necessarily resemble each other and may not even be of the same sex. In contrast, **identical twins** result when a single fertilized egg splits off into two parts. Because identical twins develop from the same fertilized egg, they are genetically the same. Consequently, they have the same physical characteristics, including sex, blood type, hair and eye color, and overall appearance. Identical twins represent only about one-third of all twins born.

PREGNANCY

Pregnancy officially begins when the blastocyst implants itself in the uterine wall. This process initiates many changes both physically and emotionally for the woman, her partner (if such a relationship exists) and the fetus. Major changes occur, for example, in the woman's hormone levels, body shape, and psychological state as the pregnancy develops. Pregnancy also brings about a variety of changes in the lives and relationship of the expectant parents. Their adjustment to the pregnancy is influenced to a large extent by whether the pregnancy was planned, their age at the time of pregnancy, their socioeconomic level, and their race and ethnicity.

The average length of a pregnancy from conception to birth is about 9 months (40 weeks or 280 days). This overall period of pregnancy is commonly referred to as the **gestation period**. The length of

gestation varies for different women. Thus, even under what are considered normal conditions, a pregnancy may last longer than 9 months or a few days or weeks less than 9 months.

Sometimes a woman suspects she is pregnant before she has a test to confirm her suspicions. Although conception itself does not produce recognizable symptoms, often a woman's suspicions are based on one or more typical signs of pregnancy that appear soon after conception. The most common of these signs is a missed menstrual period. Although a missed menstrual period is not always an indication of pregnancy, pregnancy is the most common reason why women between the ages of 17 and 39 miss a period. Some pregnant women, however, continue to have a period for the first 2 or 3 months of pregnancy. Sometimes at the onset of pregnancy a woman's breasts will swell and become tender, and they will become very dark in the **areola**, the circle around the nipple. As the milk glands begin to develop the breast might throb or tingle. In some cases the woman might begin to urinate more frequently than is normal for her. This frequent urination is generally caused by the pressure of the uterus expanding against the bladder.

One of the best known (and most uncomfortable) symptoms of pregnancy is nausea. This symptom is commonly referred to as "morning sickness," even though it can occur at any time of the day or night. Probably as many as one-half of all pregnant women experience some form of morning sickness. Other common symptoms of pregnancy include an overpowering sleepiness or constant fatigue (you've probably heard a pregnant woman complain of being tired or sleepy all the time); the retention of body fluids, resulting in the swelling of the feet, hands, or face; and an increase in the secretion of vaginal fluids, either clear and nonirritating, or white or yellow, foamy, and itchy.

Sometimes a woman claims to know intuitively that she is pregnant well before she has had a chance to experience (if she does at all) any of the above symptoms. As one woman observed:

> I realized I was pregnant the same night I became pregnant. I lay there all night. I'd had a very active sex life, and it was the first time I had ever felt this way. I wasn't expecting to get pregnant, but I felt different that night. (Boston Women's Health Book Collective, 1973:166)

In most cases, however, women want something more scientific or systematic than their intuition to confirm their suspicions of pregnancy. Thus, they generally consult a physician or use one of the many products on the market today that allow them to test themselves for pregnancy.

TESTING FOR PREGNANCY

THE "RABBIT TEST"   Most of you probably have heard of the so-called rabbit test. This term was once popularly used to cover a range of tests that involved administering a woman's urine to laboratory animals such as rabbits, mice, or frogs. The purpose of these tests—as of all chemical pregnancy tests—was to detect the presence of **human chorionic gonadotropin (HCG)**, a hormone found in the urine of pregnant women. In the case of the rabbit test, if HCG was in the urine administered to the laboratory animal, it would cause the animal to ovulate. The animal was then killed and its ovaries examined to determine the woman's pregnancy. If the ovaries were congested with blood, it was a positive sign of pregnancy. These tests were accurate for most women at about 27 days after conception, (at which point the menstrual period was about 13 days late (Boston Women's Health Collective, 1984). Such tests have become increasingly obsolete as technology in this area has advanced and the concern by animal rights groups over the routine killing of laboratory animals has increased.

THE PELVIC EXAM   The traditional pelvic exam is another way of detecting pregnancy. However, a considerable amount of time must have passed before pregnancy can be officially confirmed or negated. About 6 to 8 weeks after the last menstrual period a physician can detect pregnancy if (1) the tip of the cervix has become soft, (2) the cervix has changed colors from a pinkish to a bluish hue, (3) the uterus feels softer, and (4) the shape of the uterus exhibits a change, like a bulge where the embryo is attached to the uterine wall. These anatomical observations are sometimes referred to as *Hegar's sign.*

MODERN TESTS   Today much faster pregnancy tests are available that are easier to perform and give reliable results earlier in the pregnancy. These tests range from a relatively simple but expensive blood test to a urine test to home pregnancy tests that can be bought at the local drug store. The *beta subunit HCG radioimmunoassay test*, for example, can detect HCG in the blood as early as 8 days after conception. Although it is extremely reliable, it is also too expensive for most women, especially those who are poor and working class. The *agglutination test* involves putting a drop of the woman's urine in a test solution. If the solution coagulates, the woman is not pregnant. If she is pregnant, HCG in the urine will prevent coagulation.

EPTS   The *Early pregnancy tests (EPTs)*, commonly called home pregnancy tests, have become increasingly popular. They are relatively inexpensive, can be bought without a prescription, and can be conducted in the privacy of one's home. These tests claim to detect the presence of HCG as early as 9 days after a missed menstrual period. Although these tests are convenient, there are some problems with reliability. About 3 percent of the time these tests show a woman to be pregnant when she is not. Even worse, about 20 percent of the time these tests fail to detect a pregnancy. Thus, a woman who uses such tests should follow up with a test done by a doctor or a medical laboratory.

PRENATAL DEVELOPMENT AND CARE

The attitudes and behaviors of a mother during pregnancy greatly influence the health and well-being of the embryo/fetus and later of the human infant. In addition, race, class, age, and gender experiences significantly affect maternal attitudes and maternal behaviors during pregnancy (the prenatal period) and after (postnatal).

Almost all discussions of prenatal development and care divide pregnancy into three basic *trimesters*, periods of approximately 3 months. This division does not necessarily apply to all women, but it is a convenient way to discuss pregnancy. As we discuss each trimester we will also discuss various issues that might arise in each trimester. Keep in mind, however, that some of the issues discussed under a particular trimester may not be confined to one trimester but may occur throughout a pregnancy. We will note when such cases arise.

THE FIRST TRIMESTER

A woman's experience of pregnancy (both physical and emotional) changes as the pregnancy develops from one trimester to another. Early confirmation of pregnancy and prenatal care by a competent physician are critical both for the mother and the developing embryo/fetus.[*]

PHYSICAL CHANGES During the first 3 months of pregnancy a woman's body undergoes a series of changes that allow for the maintenance of pregnancy. One critical development is the formation of the **placenta**, a vascular membrane that holds the fetus in place inside the uterus and through which nourishment passes from the mother to the fetus. In addition, an *amniotic sac*, or *fetal sac*, of salty, watery fluid develops around the fetus to protect and cushion it throughout the pregnancy. Hormonal changes in the woman's body begin as soon as the egg is fertilized. Many other physical changes take place, such as those noted in our discussion of symptoms of pregnancy. Some women also experience moodiness or anxiety; for example, the fear of losing their individuality and becoming identified solely in terms of the pregnancy and the impending status of mother (Lubin, 1975). Fortunately most women soon get over these feelings.

By the end of the embryonic period, the developing embryo has grown to about 1 inch and developed rudimentary limbs. During the third month, the sex of the fetus can be detected, and the fetus increases in size to about 4 inches and weighs about six-tenths of an ounce.

EARLY CONFIRMATION A pregnant woman should begin prenatal care with a physician as soon as possible in the first trimester and should continue receiving this care on a regular basis throughout her pregnancy. Early confirmation and care enable a physician to gain an understanding of the woman and her pregnancy and to monitor her progress as well as to detect any problems early on. While early confir-

---

[*]We have already noted that the developing human organism is referred to as an embryo during the prenatal period of 2 to 8 weeks and thereafter referred to as a fetus. Although both terms apply in the first trimester of pregnancy, we use the term fetus in the remainder of this discussion. This decision was made purely for the sake of grammatical ease in referring to the human organism during this period.

mation and quality prenatal care are important, they are not evenly or equally available to all women or couples. Many women of color and poor women often avoid prenatal care because they do not have the resources or because of previous negative experiences involving the health-care system. Often these women deliver their babies in public hospitals and teaching institutions that can be insensitive to their needs.

PREGNANCY LOSS In addition to early confirmation and prenatal care, other important issues of concern include the possibility of a spontaneous abortion, tubal pregnancy, and Rh blood incompatibility. Although many of these factors are not confined to the first trimester, concern and attention to them begins here.

MISCARRIAGE *Spontaneous abortion*, more commonly referred to as a **miscarriage**, is the noninduced loss of an embryo or fetus. Although no one knows for sure how many pregnancies end in miscarriage, estimates are that between 10 and 15 percent of pregnancies result in a miscarriage before the fetus is mature enough to survive. About 75 percent of all miscarriages occur in the first trimester, and over 80 percent are due to genetic abnormalities of the fetus (Guttmacher, 1983). Although miscarriages generally do little or no physical damage to the mother, the psychological damage to both parents can be extensive. Some possible causes of miscarriages include structural problems of the uterus, weak cervical muscles, infection, environmental and industrial toxins, hormonal imbalances, and blood incompatibility between the mother and the fetus. Having a miscarriage does not mean that a woman is prone to miscarriages. There is a high probability that subsequent pregnancies will be successful.

ECTOPIC PREGNANCY The tubal or ectopic pregnancy is also a concern in the first weeks of pregnancy. **Ectopic pregnancies** occur when the fertilized egg implants itself in the fallopian tube, or more rarely, in the abdominal cavity, the ovary, or the cervix, instead of the uterine wall. Ectopic pregnancy can happen to any woman, although women who have had previous tubal surgery are at a higher risk. There has been a noticeable increase in ectopic pregnancies because of the increased use of intrauterine devices (IUDs), which can cause scar tissue to form on the tubes or can inflame the uterine lining, which then resists the implantation of the fertilized egg.

Ectopic pregnancy is difficult to diagnose early on because some of the early symptoms are the same as those for a normal pregnancy. When the condition is diagnosed, the fetus must be removed surgically. When the condition is not diagnosed, as the pregnancy progresses the fallopian tube stretches slightly, but it cannot expand indefinitely. Thus, somewhere between the eighth and twelfth week of pregnancy, the tube bursts. This can be extremely painful and dangerous and should be attended by a physician. Estimates of the frequency of ectopic pregnancies range from 1 in 100 to 1 in 300 pregnancies.

RH BLOOD INCOMPATIBILITY   The Rh factor refers to an antigen found in the blood. An *antigen* is a substance to which the body reacts as a hostile foreign substance. The Rh factor received its name from the fact that it was first discovered in rhesus monkeys. Most people have Rh antigens in their blood and are thus said to be *Rh-positive*. About 14 percent of the population, however, lack these antigens; they are classified as *RH-negative*. When someone with Rh-negative blood is transfused with Rh-positive blood, the Rh-negative blood will build up antibodies to protect the blood from what it interprets as the hostile Rh antigens. When it occurs during pregnancy, *Rh blood incompatibility* denotes a condition in which the mother and the fetus have different Rh blood factors: The mother is Rh-negative, and the fetus is Rh-positive, a condition inherited from the father.

During pregnancy, a small amount of blood naturally transfers between the mother and the fetus through the placenta. In the case of Rh incompatibility, exposure to the fetal blood causes the mother to produce anti-Rh antibodies. The mother's antibodies then pass back through the placenta to the fetus, where they destroy Rh-positive red blood cells. This can result in miscarriage or a stillbirth. Once an Rh-negative woman develops anti-Rh antibodies, the antibodies will attack the blood cells of each subsequent Rh-positive fetus. This produces a condition known as *hemolytic disease of the newborn*, in which the child is born with jaundice, anemia, and enlarged liver and spleen. Thus, the Rh factor should be checked early in the pregnancy. Couples for whom incompatibility is a potential problem are those in which the female is Rh-negative and the male is Rh-positive (Schiamberg, 1988).

What can be done when the Rh factor is a concern in pregnancy? Certain drugs and transfusion techniques enable most women with an incompatibility problem to give birth to a healthy infant. For example, the drug Rhogam, which prevents the body from producing antibodies, can be given to a woman within 36 to 72 hours after delivery, abortion, or miscarriage. In some areas of the country a woman can get a Rhogam shot free of charge. Also, certain techniques allow physicians to exchange invaded fetal blood for healthy blood while the fetus is still in the uterus or to exchange the baby's blood after the baby is born.

THE SECOND TRIMESTER

For many women, the onset of the second trimester signals the end of many of the first-trimester symptoms such as morning sickness and fatigue. By the fourth month of pregnancy, many of the major organs are present in the fetus, its heartbeat can be heard through a stethoscope, and it is large enough (about 6 inches) that the mother can feel its movements. Continued changes in the woman's body can bring on such conditions as edema and toxemia. These illnesses can be serious for both the mother and the fetus and should be attended by a physician.

PHYSICAL CHANGES   Although the fetus generally begins to make spontaneous movements around the fourteenth week of pregnancy, not until about the fourth or fifth month can the mother actually feel the movement of the fetus. (This occurs earlier in subsequent pregnancies.) Recall from Chapter 9 that these movements or flutters are referred to as *quickening*. As the pregnancy progresses these movements become more and more frequent and intense. For many women, the first experience of quickening is very emotional and moving. Some women have described it as the first realization that life is developing inside them.

During the second trimester, the fetus begins its bulkier growth. The woman's body shows corresponding changes: The waist gets thicker, and the womb swells below the waist. The greatest part of a woman's weight gain occurs before the twentieth week of pregnancy, when the uterus increases to perhaps 20 times its normal size. In addition, around the nineteenth week the woman's nipples may secrete a thin, yellowish substance called *colostrum*. This is not yet milk; however, the breasts, having been stimulated by hormones, are functionally complete for nursing if a couple chooses that route after the birth of the child.

EDEMA   During the second trimester a woman may experience **edema**—a swelling of the limbs, especially the lower legs and ankles, as a result of water retention. Hormones produced by the placenta cause the connective tissue throughout a woman's body to retain fluid. Some edema during pregnancy is considered normal, especially during the last half of pregnancy, and it is linked to healthy infants, higher birth weight, and lower infant mortality (Chesley, 1989). The proper amount of edema during pregnancy should be determined by the woman's physician.

TOXEMIA   **Toxemia** is a condition in which toxins produced by body cells at sites of infection enter into the bloodstream. *Toxins* are substances that have a protein structure and are capable of causing poisoning when introduced into the body. The earliest stage of toxemia—known as *preeclampsia*—is characterized by edema, high blood pressure, and protein in the urine. It usually occurs sometime after the twentieth to twenty-fourth week of pregnancy and can range from mild to severe. The second, or *eclamptic* stage is characterized by severe headaches or problems with vision. In the most severe cases a woman can experience convulsions and go into a coma. Toxemia can be fatal if untreated. A woman who develops toxemia but receives medical care will generally not proceed to the eclamptic stage.

Although there is some debate over the causes of toxemia, some doctors who work with poor women believe that toxemia of pregnancy is caused mainly by malnutrition. These doctors claim that when malnourished women are put on a balanced diet, the incidence of toxemia drops significantly. Very young women (under age 16), older women, and women with their first pregnancy are most susceptible to toxemia, as are women with diabetes, high blood pressure, and chronic kidney disease. Women who carry twins are also highly susceptible to toxemia.

Overall, by the end of the second trimester the fetus has all its essential structures. This fact notwith-

standing, the fetus is not ready for birth. In general, it would have a very slim chance for survival if it were born before or at the end of the second trimester.

THE THIRD TRIMESTER

As the uterus grows it becomes quite large and feels hard to the touch. Not only can fetal movements be felt, but by the third trimester they also can be seen as well from the outside of the body. Sometimes the shape of a protruding elbow, fist, or foot can be detected pushing against the abdomen. Sometimes it appears that the fetus is turning over, curling in a ball, or just flapping around. For the remainder of the pregnancy, development consists primarily of gains in weight and length and refinements in the developing fetus.

PHYSICAL CHANGES   The load on the mother's heart reaches its peak at some point during the third trimester and then decreases until the time of delivery. The uterus may exert pressure on the lungs, causing shortness of breath, or it may push up the stomach, causing indigestion. The diaphragm may move up as much as an inch. The body has gotten significantly heavier by this point, causing the mother to walk differently for balance. Anywhere from around 2 to 4 weeks before birth, and even as early as the seventh month, the head of the fetus settles into the woman's pelvis. This process is variously called *lightening, dropping*, or *engagement*. Somewhere around the third week prior to birth, painless uterine contractions may occur. However, they have no direct relationship to the onset of labor. Rather, they are thought to strengthen the uterine muscles in preparation for labor.

Some women view the profound changes within and outside their bodies at this time with mixed feelings. Some feel proud and beautiful, whereas others view their physical appearance with dismay, resentment, or a feeling of ugliness. Because of the inordinate stress placed on women's physical appearance as a measure of self-worth, many women are greatly concerned about their attractiveness during and immediately after pregnancy.

The most significant development for the fetus at this time is that it doubles in size. By the end of the eighth month the fetus weighs, on average, around 5 to 5½ pounds. Prior to the seventh month, the fetal lungs have not developed sufficiently for the fetus to live successfully outside the mother's body. During this last trimester, however, babies born before full term may survive. For a baby born at the end of 7 months there is a 50 percent chance of survival; for one born at the end of 8 months the chance of survival increases to 90 percent; and if born at the end of 9 months or term, a fetus has a 99 percent chance of survival. A fetus that is born in the seventh or eighth month and weighs less than 5½ pounds is considered *premature* and has a high risk of encountering problems during early childhood development (Harmantz and Novak, 1983).

As the end of the pregnancy period approaches many women feel an enormous sense of urgency for it to all be over with. And most often it ends with the birth of a healthy baby. Nine out of ten babies born in this country are healthy (Papalia and Olds, 1989). Although the chances of having a healthy baby are good, most parents want to do all they can to make this a reality.

PRENATAL PROBLEMS AND DEFECTS

Recent research findings are not entirely consistent concerning how many children in the United States are born with some sort of birth defect. Most estimates fall between 2 and 4 percent, but a few estimates are as high as 7 percent (see, for example, Papalia and Olds, 1989). Birth defects include any condition, such as abnormalities of body structure or function, that causes or leads to death or the lowering of the quality of life. Birth defects usually can be traced to one or more of the following factors: (1) the influence of the prenatal environment on the fetus, for example, exposure to toxic chemicals and the use of drugs, including alcohol and tobacco, by the mother; (2) heredity, that is, the parents' genes; and (3) injuries sustained at birth. Regardless of their causes, all defects present at birth are referred to as **congenital**. Parents who know or suspect that they might give birth to a child with a particular defect should seek some sort of counseling or professional advice.

Hundreds of birth defects are known to science. Among the most widely recognized are Down syndrome, spina bifida, Tay–Sachs disease, cystic fibrosis, sickle cell anemia, and hemophilia. *Down syndrome* is a nonhereditary disorder characterized by moderate to severe mental retardation; a short, flattened skull; and slanting eyes. About 1 in every 800 children is born with Down syndrome (Papalia and Olds, 1989). *Spina bifida* is a condition that results when the spinal covering fails to close. This condition usually causes severe mental retardation, physical disability, and sometimes death. *Tay–Sachs disease*, found most often among Jews of Polish and Russian descent, is a genetic disorder caused by an enzyme deficiency that prohibits the metabolism of fats in the nervous system. As a result, toxins accumulate in the brain and cause mental retardation, deafness, and certain death within a few months or years after birth. Millions of Americans carry the recessive gene responsible for *cystic fibrosis*, although they may not exhibit the disorder itself. This disease of the mucous glands causes pancreatic insufficiency and pulmonary disorders, including lung infections and digestive disorders.

Sickle cell anemia, a heredity condition, is most prevalent among African Americans and involves the presence of oxygen-deficient, abnormally crescent-shaped red blood cells. This condition causes episodic pain and leg ulcers. Approximately 1 in every 500 African Americans has sickle cell anemia (Cowley, 1990). *Hemophilia* is a hereditary blood disease characterized by excessive, sometimes spontaneous bleeding. It is transmitted by females, usually to their male offspring.

TESTING DURING PREGNANCY

Currently, about 4 percent of babies in the United States are born with a condition that requires some kind of medical or surgical intervention. Some women are against testing during pregnancy, and routine testing of all pregnant women is unnecessary. For most women, however, prenatal testing is a reasonable option if there is concern about the health or well-being of the fetus. Several prenatal tests can provide doctors with specific information about the condition of the fetus. The most commonly used are amniocentesis, chorionic villus sampling (CVS), ultrasound, and alpha-fetoprotein (AFP) screening.

AMNIOCENTESIS A physician who is concerned about a hereditary disease or the age or lifestyle of the pregnant mother, may suggest **amniocentesis**, a procedure in which a long needle is inserted through the abdomen into the uterus to collect cells cast off by the fetus. The genes within these cells are then examined for genetic disorders and biochemical abnormalities such as Down syndrome or any number of rare genetic diseases. Amniocentesis also provides information about the sex of the fetus. One of the major disadvantages of amniocentesis is that it cannot be performed until the second trimester. Given the risk involved in second-trimester abortions, a much earlier test for genetic disorders would alleviate some of the risk involved if a decision is made to abort. Amniocentesis can also increase the risks of fetal damage, premature birth, and spontaneous abortion. If performed properly, however, amniocentesis is generally a safe procedure. Several researchers have noted that the overwhelming majority of women who undergo amniocentesis eventually give birth.

CHORIONIC VILLUS SAMPLING (CVS) A newer diagnostic technique, **chorionic villus sampling (CVS)**, is now being used instead of amniocentesis by some physicians. During this procedure, an obstetrician guides a small tube through the cervix or abdominal wall into the uterus to extract cells from the *villi*, hairlike projections of the placenta, which are then examined for genetic abnormalities. A major advantage of CVS is that it is performed in the first trimester (ideally in the eleventh week of pregnancy), which allows for early diagnosis. On the other hand, critics of CVS cite several disadvantages of this procedure. Compared with amniocentesis, CVS presents a higher risk to the fetus and is less accurate in detecting abnormalities. Early research, for example, shows that women who use this technique experience higher rates of stillbirths, neonatal deaths (deaths after birth), limb deformities in born children, and miscarriages than do women who use amniocentesis. Also, CVS is quite costly, currently about twice the cost of amniocentesis (Rosenthal, 1991). Thus, this procedure might not be available to poor and working-class women.

ULTRASOUND Another prenatal test, **ultrasound** (sometimes referred to as *ultrasonic scanning*), allows a physician to observe the developing fetus directly by viewing electronically the echoes of sound waves pulsating through the pregnant woman's body. With ultrasound, a physician can predict within a couple of weeks when the child will be born and determine with 90 percent accuracy whether the mother is carrying twins and, in general, the size, position, and health of the fetus. Equally important, ultrasound can be used to detect various birth defects such as those that attack the skeleton of the fetus. Moreover, it can be performed early enough so that parents can safely choose an abortion if serious defects are detected. For many parents, one of the rewards of the ultrasound is the **sonogram**, which allows parents to see the fetus and any movements it makes.

AFP SCREENING **Alpha-fetoprotein (AFP) screening** is used to determine the level of AFP, a fetal blood protein, in the mother's blood. High levels of AFP can indicate certain neural defects in the fetus. This test is routinely administered as part of the preliminary tests for pregnant women. Like CVS, AFP screening can be performed early in a pregnancy, but it also presents some risks. A major shortcoming of AFP screening is that test results are not conclusive.

PROTECTING THE PRENATAL ENVIRONMENT

The majority of birth defects are caused not by heredity but rather by what happens in the prenatal and postnatal environment. Only about one-fifth of birth defects can be traced to heredity. Although we as individuals cannot control heredity we can, with the proper resources and support, control to some degree the prenatal environment.

Prenatal problems and defects are often linked to factors over which individuals have little or no control. Research has shown repeatedly that experiences such as those of age, race, and class have important effects on **morbidity** (illness) and **mortality** (death). For example, although more women 40 and older are having children today than in the past, it is believed that the optimum age for pregnancy is between 20 and 35 years of age. Thus, women younger than 20 and older than 35 are at greater risk of having a miscarriage, a *stillbirth* (the birth of a dead fetus), a premature birth, prolonged labor, or a child with a birth defect (Schiamberg, 1988). Although the overall risks to maternal and fetal health for pregnant women over 35 have lessened somewhat (see Chapter 9), in some areas of health and well-being these women are still more at risk than are younger women. Women over 40, for example, have the highest rates of babies born with Down syndrome. At the other end of the spectrum, the maternal death rate from pregnancy and its complications is 60 percent higher for adolescents than for mothers in their early 20s (Friede, Baldwin, Rhodes, Bueler, and Strauss, 1988).

Race and social class further affect a woman's chances of delivering a healthy baby. Although overall rates of infant and maternal mortality in the United States have declined significantly in recent years, their incidence varies among different racial and class groups. Black women, for example, are four times as likely as white women to die in childbirth (Gordon-Bradshaw, 1988). Blacks and Puerto Ricans are more likely than whites to have premature or low-birth-weight babies. This situation contributes to infant mortality and frequently has been associated with inadequate prenatal care and nutrition for the mother (Andersen, 1993). Essentially, the fewer resources women have such as adequate diet, financial resources and income, employment and housing facilities, and access to quality health care, the greater the likelihood of health problems or complications during pregnancy.

Moreover, the increasing cost of health care in this country prevents many pregnant women, particularly those with limited economic resources and inadequate (if any) health insurance, from receiving proper care during pregnancy. This problem is especially acute among Native Americans, Latinos, and African Americans. This situation points up the larger and continuing problem in this country of an inadequate health-care system of delivery for most individuals and families.

To protect the prenatal environment properly, a woman must take care of herself during pregnancy. Although it is desirable to see a physician on a regular basis, primary responsibility for protecting the fetus resides with the parents. A physician essentially monitors the care and protection parents give to the fetus.

PRENATAL CONCERNS

Contrary to popular myth, the majority of pregnant women are not in a delicate condition. They can for the most part carry on their lives as they did prior to pregnancy without fear of hurting the fetus. However, several areas of concern that sometimes accompany pregnancy can be detrimental to the fetus if unchecked or misunderstood.

NUTRITION What and how a woman eats is a major concern during pregnancy. The normal development of the fetus requires that a woman eat nutritionally balanced meals throughout the pregnancy. Because nutrients pass from mother to fetus through the placenta, the failure of the mother to eat properly can deprive the fetus of proper nutrition. This can result in any number of health problems for the fetus—including congenital defects and small stature—and it can cause a miscarriage or stillbirth. It can also increase the mother's susceptibility to disease, which can affect both the mother and the fetus. Maternal malnutrition is associated with diseases in the newborn such as rickets, cerebral palsy, and epilepsy. In fact, maternal malnutrition is one of the leading causes of fetal death. The probability of malnutrition during pregnancy is highest among teen mothers and poor and working-class women regardless of age (Schiamberg, 1988).

SMOKING Not only is smoking detrimental to the health of the smoker, it also has been shown to be detrimental to the health of the fetus. Cigarette smoke passes from the mother through the placenta to the fetus, lowering the amount of oxygen the fetus receives as well as impairing the circulation of the fetus's blood. Although the extent of damage caused by cigarette smoking during pregnancy is not fully known, the U.S. Surgeon General (1985) cautioned that smoking during pregnancy increases the risk of miscarriage, premature birth, low birth weight, and the probability of sickness, convulsions, or death in early infancy. A considerable amount of research on the subject indicates that nonsmoking mothers tend to have bigger babies (in terms of birth weight) than women who smoked during pregnancy.

Nonsmokers, pregnant or not, have been increasingly concerned about the indirect or secondary effects of smoking and the implications for their own health. In the case of pregnancy, there is reason to be concerned. Some evidence suggests that smoking by fathers may have an indirect and negative effect on the fetus in either of two ways: (1) Mothers can inhale the smoke secondarily, or (2) smoking can impair the male's sperm, thus producing an abnormal fetus ("Smoking and Sperm," 1981).

X-RAYS Current evidence indicates that X-rays can harm the embryo or fetus. A Johns Hopkins University study of older pregnant women found that the incidence of babies born with Down syndrome correlated highly with the number of X-rays a woman had undergone during her lifetime (Reeder, and Martin, 1987). Research indicates that some of the most common consequences for the fetus of direct exposure to X-rays are mental retardation—especially *microcephaly*, in which the child is born with a small, pointed head—deformity, stillbirth, and miscarriage. Most physicians claim that there is really no safe level of fetal exposure to radiation. Thus, they caution pregnant women to avoid X-rays.

ALCOHOL As with cigarette smoking, maternal alcohol consumption can have considerable negative effects both for the mother and the fetus. If a woman consumes alcohol and smokes, the effects on the fetus are highly intensified. Moreover, an alcoholic mother can give birth to a baby who is also dependent on alcohol. In the first few days of life these babies exhibit severe withdrawal symptoms. Alcohol consumption by itself or in conjunction with smoking can also lead to what researchers call **fetal alcohol syndrome**. This condition, which can sometimes affect the fetus as early as the first month of pregnancy (Sulik, Johnston, and Webb, 1981), is characterized by physical deformities such as facial abnormalities, an extremely small head, and heart defects; mental retardation; small birth size; and severe problems within the central nervous system. According to the U.S. Centers for Disease Control (1984), fetal alcohol syndrome is one of the foremost causes of birth defects in the United States.

Experts have yet to agree on a safe level of alcohol consumption by pregnant women. Although many people believe that an occasional glass of wine or beer is not harmful to the fetus, most physicians recommend that a pregnant woman refrain from all alcohol consumption. After the baby is born, if a woman plans to breast-feed, she probably should not consume alcohol because it can be transmitted to the nursing infant.

DRUGS AND OTHER SUBSTANCE ABUSE The majority of drugs, whether street drugs, common drugs like caffeine and aspirin, or prescription and over-the-counter medications contain chemicals that

have been found to have some effect on the fetus. Almost all drugs taken or ingested during pregnancy cross the placenta. The fetus is particularly vulnerable to drugs in the first trimester, when the vital organs are forming. Recall our discussion in Chapter 9 of thalidomide among pregnant women in the 1950s. The widespread deformity among infants of women who took this drug in the first trimester of pregnancy provides dramatic testimony to the devastating effects that certain drugs can have on the fetus.

The direct effects or extent of damage caused by drugs and various chemicals on pregnancy and the fetus fall into three general categories: (1) *teratogenic*, causing birth defects; (2) *toxic*, having a severe drug effect on the fetus; and (3) *addictive*, causing dependence (Boston Women's Health Book Collective, 1992:403). Drugs and chemicals that are dangerous or potentially dangerous to the fetus include insulin, cortisone, antithyroid drugs, antihistamines, tetracycline, quinine, various tranquilizers, and, of course, hard drugs like heroin and cocaine. In addition, inhaling cleaning products that contain chemicals like benzene can also be harmful. Thus, pregnant women should avoid these products. Fortunately, most cleaning products today do not contain these chemicals.

Every year a large number of babies are born to women who are addicted to or who heavily use hard drugs such as heroin, marijuana, cocaine, and phencyclidine (PCP). All such drugs can harm the fetus. For example, evidence indicates that heavy use of marijuana by the mother is linked to birth defects. Similarly, PCP seems to have long-term effects on children, who may as a result develop cerebral palsy and defective motor skills (Roark, 1985). Mothers who frequently use addictive drugs often give birth to babies who are also addicted to drugs. In 1990, about one in ten live births in the United States was a drug-addicted baby (Renzetti and Curran, 1992). These babies undergo withdrawal at birth and may vomit, tremble, perspire profusely, cry incessantly, and become hyperactive. The consequences of the mother's addiction to drugs can sometimes be fatal for the offspring (Papalia and Olds, 1989). Most often, however, these babies recover from withdrawal. But this does not mean that they are completely free of the effects of the mother's drug use. This is nowhere better seen than in the use of cocaine by pregnant women.

The late Mother Clara Hale devoted her life to caring for babies born addicted to drugs or alcohol or infected with AIDS. Here some of her "babies" help her celebrate her 83rd birthday.

The increasing use of cocaine and alkaloidal cocaine (crack) in the larger population is reflected in the rising incidence of cocaine use among pregnant women and the growing number of cocaine-addicted babies being born. In 1988, for example, 20 percent of the babies born at one hospital alone in Oakland, California, were addicted to cocaine. And in 1989, 25 percent of all babies born in inner-city hospitals were born addicted to cocaine (Brazelton, 1989). Like other drug-addicted babies, cocaine-addicted babies must endure the agony of withdrawal, which can sometimes last as long as 3 to 4 weeks after birth. In addition, many of these babies suffer long-term and often irreversible damage. The full consequences of cocaine-addicted babies for marriages, families, the school system, and society in general are not known at this time.

A growing number of people think that the fetus has a right to be born with the best possible chance for a healthy and long life. Some of these proponents of fetal rights believe that the answer to drug and alcohol abuse by pregnant mothers is legal prosecution of the mother. In the Critical Issues box titled "Protecting Fetal Rights: The Case of Cocaine Babies" we present this point of view for your reflection and discussion.

AIDS AND PREGNANCY Throughout this textbook we discuss the ramifications of AIDS for marriages and families. Here we limit our discussion specifically to the impact of AIDS on pregnant women and on the developing fetus.

Women who are HIV-positive face not only the probability that the infection will develop into full-blown AIDS but also face severe restrictions on their behavior, particularly their reproductive behavior. The results of studies of the effects of HIV on the health of pregnant women are inconsistent and inconclusive. In addition, we know very little about the rates, methods, and risks of transmitting HIV to the fetus. Nonetheless, many people, including health professionals, often encourage HIV-positive women either not to get pregnant or if they are pregnant, to terminate the pregnancy. Unfortunately, due to fear and a lack of information about AIDS, some physicians will not perform an abortion on an HIV-positive woman.

Current research indicates that pregnancy worsens AIDS in women who are in an advanced stage of the disease. In HIV-positive women who do not show any symptoms of AIDS, however, pregnancy does not intensify the disease or cause problems in the pregnancy. Pregnant women with AIDS frequently have miscarriages, however. Or if the fetus survives until birth, the newborn often dies early in infancy.

Medical evidence indicates that the HIV can be transmitted from a pregnant woman to the child during pregnancy or childbirth, although we don't know how this happens. Furthermore, there is a possibility that the virus can be transmitted to a child through breast-feeding. No one seems certain how many children born to HIV-positive women will develop the disease; estimates range from 30 to 40 percent. The more advanced the disease in the mother, the greater the probability that she will transmit it to the fetus. When HIV-infected babies are born they generally have prominent physical features that are linked directly to the HIV: small heads, slanted eyes that sit far apart from each other, a square forehead, a wide and flat nose, and loosely shaped lips. This physical appearance is referred to as **embryopathy** (Marion et al., 1986).

Because babies born to HIV-positive mothers have their mother's antibodies in their blood, they sometimes test positive for HIV even if they do not have the disease. Because such tests are inconclusive, these babies must be retested within a few months to determine if they are actually infected. Although there are not as yet any reliable tests that can detect the HIV

CRITICAL ISSUES

PROTECTING FETAL RIGHTS: THE CASE OF COCAINE BABIES

Women constitute a large and increasing number (about one third) of crack cocaine users. As the number of women using cocaine increases, the number of children affected by their mother's drug use will increase as well. Mothers who use cocaine during pregnancy have significantly higher rates of miscarriages, premature and low-birth-weight babies, and babies with small heads compared with those of nonusers (Chasnoff, Ellis, and Fainman, 1985; Cherukuri, Minkoff, Feldman, Parkeh, and Glass, 1988). They also have babies with a number of problems including strokes, seizures, brain damage, mental retardation, and congenital abnormalities. If this trend continues we will have an overwhelming number of severely drug damaged children that will stretch to their limits the capabilities of most major societal institutions to provide assistance. What must we do? What, if anything, is the responsibility of the parents? The state? The criminal justice system?

Increasingly women are being subjected to a sex-specific form of criminal prosecution for their drug abuse. By 1990, around 35 women in the United States who had used or abused drugs during pregnancy had faced criminal charges—which typically stated that these women had delivered drugs to a minor—for having abused drugs or alcohol while pregnant. Only one woman, however, had actually been convicted; she was sentenced to 15 years of probation. Prosecutors claim that criminal prosecution of drug-addicted mothers is the only way to force these women to get help for their problem while simultaneously protecting the unborn infant.

Without a doubt, this approach is very controversial. Apart from the constitutional issues it raises, it fails to recognize the need for drug treatment programs for women, especially pregnant women. Of the approximately 7000 drug treatment programs nationwide, only about 50 provide female patients

with obstetric and child care as well as special counseling. A 1990 survey of drug treatment programs in New York City found that 54 percent excluded all pregnant women, 67 percent excluded pregnant women on Medicaid, and 82 percent excluded crack-addicted pregnant women on Medicaid (Renzetti and Curran, 1992).

What do you think? Should a woman be prosecuted by a court of law for using drugs while she is pregnant? What is the responsibility of the court? Does it have the right to prosecute a woman or take custody of her child? What are the parents' rights? Should parents have complete and total freedom to do what they want during pregnancy? If not, who decides where to draw the line? Is drug abuse by a pregnant woman an instance of child abuse? Why or why not? Does a fetus have rights? If yes, what rights does it have? If no, why not? If the rights of the mother should conflict with those of the fetus, who determines which rights take precedence?

---

disease in the fetus, tests have been developed that can detect the virus in babies as young as 3 months old. Testing for the AIDS virus is still very controversial. Some policymakers have advocated the routine testing of all newborns for the HIV infection, but critics strongly oppose any testing that is performed without the informed consent of the mother.

Because of their limited access to drug treatment programs, medical information, and quality health care, poor communities and communities of color are especially at risk for HIV-positive babies. In fact, 91 percent of infants with AIDS are nonwhite. African-

American children constitute only 15 percent of this country's children, but they account for 53 percent of all childhood AIDS cases. Latino children, who represent about 10 percent of the nation's children, account for 23 percent of these cases (Renzetti and Curran, 1992). As many as 1 in 50 pregnant women in inner cities across this country may be infected with AIDS (Minkoff, 1987).

We discuss other sexually transmitted diseases such as syphilis and gonorrhea in Appendix B. These diseases can also affect a fetus and can also be contracted by the newborn. As with the AIDS virus, STDs in pregnant women can cause miscarriage, brain damage to the fetus (for example, from herpes), problems with eyesight (for example, from gonorrhea), and other medical problems.

SEXUALITY DURING PREGNANCY

What about sexual intercourse or other sexual activities during pregnancy? Can an active sex life be harmful to the developing fetus? Have you heard some of the tales that claim that penile–vaginal intercourse could lead to the puncturing of the amniotic sac and the harming of the fetus? Although most of us no longer operate under such myths, many people do not understand the relationship between pregnancy and sexuality.

Pregnancy can affect a couple's pattern of sexual relations. However, abstinence throughout pregnancy is not necessary to protect the fetus. Pregnancy may require a couple to change or adapt their sexual behavior so that it is compatible with changes in the woman's body and sexual desires, but there is no medical reason pregnant women cannot be sexually active as long as the pregnancy is normal (Hillard and Panter, 1985).

Until recent times, however, most physicians looked upon sexuality during pregnancy with a very restrictive eye. They commonly prescribed sexual abstinence during the last 2 months of pregnancy and the 6 weeks following delivery. Although this sexual prohibition was primarily against penile–vaginal intercourse, any activity leading to orgasm was considered to be dangerous. This point of view was based on several unproven notions: Sexual activities could rupture the membranes, leading to an infection in either the woman or the fetus; the pushing of the penis against the cervix could induce premature labor; uterine contractions of orgasm could induce labor. Also, many people apparently believed that sex during pregnancy was uncomfortable. In addition was the imputation of morality, that "good" or "nice" people abstained from sexual activity during the last months of this delicate condition and the early weeks after delivery.

Today, physicians are less restrictive about sexual activities during the last months of pregnancy as long as there are no problems such as bleeding, pain, or cramps, or risks such as miscarriage and disease.

Women who experience any of these problems should be cautious and consult with their physician. Furthermore, given the speed of recovery from childbirth today, sexuality does not have to be limited for a prolonged period after birth. Some women feel more sexual during pregnancy and immediately after than ever before, whereas others are ambivalent or cautious. Moods and desires may shift, but women and their partners can enjoy sexual activity as early or late in the pregnancy as individual bodies and preferences allow.

EXPECTANT FATHERS

Pregnant women are considered to be in a special condition, and we generally give them all of our attention and support. But what about the expectant father? Given that we expect men to play an increasingly active role in childbirth and child rearing, what do we know about their experiences through pregnancy and the birth of their children? Exactly what is the father's part in the process of pregnancy? Are men's experiences entirely social and psychological, or do men experience physiological symptoms as well?

Historically pregnancy has been viewed primarily as women's work. Expectant fathers were left in the background, unnoticed until the onset of labor. Few fathers participated in pregnancy and childbirth beyond offering general support to the mother. Today, however, a growing number of fathers are participating in the pregnancy and childbirth experience (recall the opening photo and vignette in Chapter 2). In response to this behavior a growing number of employers are granting men paternity leaves so that fathers may share the birthing experience and early weeks of life of the newborn with their mates.

THE CULTURAL DOUBLE BIND

In one of the few studies that examines the concerns and feelings of expectant fathers, psychologist Jerrold Lee Shapiro (1987) suggests that the pregnancy of a partner thrusts a man into an alien world. He is encouraged to be part of a process (pregnancy and childbirth) about which he knows little or nothing. He doesn't have role models because his father almost certainly didn't participate actively in his mother's pregnancy. These problems are not insurmountable, however, and can be overcome with care, preparation, and education.

A more important issue here is what Shapiro calls the "cultural double bind." On the one hand men are encouraged to participate in the pregnancy and birth of their children, but on the other hand they are treated as outsiders by everyone concerned. Although the expectant father's presence is desired, his feelings are not. At times, an expectant father might be as frightened, concerned, sad, and angry as his wife or partner. He needs to share these feelings and fears. But we allow only women to do this. The expectant father has neither the support systems nor the cultural sanctions for what he experiences. Some men unconsciously compensate for this by developing physiological aspects of pregnancy such as morning sickness, weight gain, or backache, but such symptoms are generally treated humorously by family and friends. When expectant fathers develop symptoms similar to those of the pregnant woman we sometimes refer to this as a sympathetic pregnancy or more formally as *couvade*. However humorous the pregnant-father syndrome may seem, many child psychologists believe that the more involved a man is with the pregnancy and birth of his child the more likely he is to be involved in child rearing.

Indifference to expectant fathers' feelings is reinforced through the media. Publishers produce a host of books and articles every year that although intended to aid new parents in the adjustment to their new roles are directed almost exclusively toward mothers and motherhood, with little or no information for and about expectant fathers. The continued invisibility today of men in the pregnancy process is ironic given our expectations for equality in parenting. The continued exclusion of fathers (and fathers to-be) in both the prenatal and postnatal processes reinforces the cultural notion that pregnancy, childbirth, and parenting are exclusively the domain of women. This perpetuation of sex-role stereotypes does not facilitate gender equality.

FEARS AND CONCERNS OF EXPECTANT FATHERS

Many expectant fathers experience fears and anxieties during their partner's pregnancy, but they often keep these feelings to themselves because they don't want to worry or burden their partner and because they don't want to be considered less than a macho male. Based on test results from his study of expectant and recent fathers 18 to 60 years of age and from all walks of life, Shapiro identified seven major fears and concerns expectant fathers typically experience:

- *Queasiness* The number-one fear among expectant fathers, including those who plan to be part of the event, is of the birth process itself. They are frightened that they will not be able to help their partner and make it through the delivery without getting sick or fainting. The fact that very few men actually have such trouble does not diminish this fear, which is often increased by the insensitivity of medical personnel.

- *Uncertain paternity* Many men acknowledge having some doubts that they are really the child's father. Their fears are based less on a feeling that their partner has been unfaithful and much more on a general insecurity brought on by being part of something as monumental as the creation of life or of being left out of the process.

- *Loss of spouse or child* Many men express a fear that neither their partner nor the child will survive the pregnancy. A related fear is that the child will be born brain-damaged or defective in some way.

- *Increased responsibility* Some men experience anxiety about the increased responsibility that comes with having a child. The birth of a child means financial as well as physical and emotional adjustments in the relationship, along with changes in role expectations and feelings of responsibility. Some men switch to more reliable jobs or work a second job to bring in more money.

- *Being replaced* Expectant fathers often fear they are going to be displaced by the fetus. They often begin to feel less vigorous in lovemaking, and when the woman is communicating with the fetus (for example, feeling its movements) the man feels left out.

- *Obstetrical–gynecological matters* Obstetrics and gynecological medicine is usually a mystery to most men, and medical personnel do not make matters any more comprehensible. Men report feeling out of place in the examining room and doctor's offices. Their questions concerning their partner's pregnancy are often silenced with looks that imply that they are stupid.

- *Life and death* Many expectant fathers start to think about human fragility and their own mortality. They start to take fewer risks (for example, they drive slower, avoid rougher areas of town, listening to a life insurance salesman) because there is now going to be someone who needs them. Many men report feeling closer to their own deaths after being so intimately involved with the beginnings of life.

In general, the number and severity of the fears expectant fathers experience increases under a number of conditions: if the man's partner is increasingly unavailable emotionally, physically, and sexually; if the man feels a need to reflect on changes in his life and does not have a close friend to confide in; if he believes that he should be strong enough to handle matters without help. The cultural double bind restricts intimacy between partners at a time when it is most needed by both partners. When men share their concerns with their partners, the relationship generally deepens, and closeness increases. Furthermore, when they participate in the pregnancy, including being in the delivery room, they tend to feel more comfortable with the father role and do a better job of parenting than fathers who do not participate.

CHILDBIRTH

Like pregnancy, childbirth has both physical and social-emotional aspects. The physical aspects involve the physiological changes that occur in a woman's body to enable the fetus to be expelled and enter the outside world. The social-emotional aspects relate to the feelings and attitudes of parents and other loved ones toward the impending birth. Included here are such questions as how and where the birth should take place, who should be present and what those present should do, and who will deliver the baby and under what conditions. In the next section we examine all these topics as we explore how a woman, her partner, and her family might prepare for the experiences of childbirth and becoming a parent.

CHOOSING A BIRTHPLACE

What kind of birth and postpartum experience will a woman have today? Increasingly, women can exercise choice in this matter. Women today generally have access to more information about birth practitioners and the settings within which birth can safely take place than did their mothers and grandmothers.

Women have not always delivered their children in hospitals, and male physicians have not always controlled the process. There was a time when healing, particularly in matters of birth and child rearing, was almost exclusively the domain of women. Until the

nineteenth century midwives and female family and friends presided over and assisted in most births. A **midwife** is a professional, most often a woman, who is trained either to deliver a baby or to assist in delivery.

Beginning in the nineteenth century, however, as the male-dominated medical profession became larger and more formalized, it increasingly took control of the birthing process. Today physicians routinely define pregnancy and childbirth in terms of a medical model in which they are more likely to prescribe drugs, to determine what constitutes a normal delivery, and to use some sort of medical intervention as an essential feature of the birthing process (for a history of this process, see Andersen, 1993).

Births in hospitals are typically cold, sterile, and impersonal. Today many hospitals offer birthing rooms for delivery. Sometimes referred to as alternative birthing centers (ABCs), these rooms are not without their problems. The general philosophy of birthing centers is nonintervention in a woman's delivery. However, hospital birthing centers typically intervene in delivery in such ways as speeding up or prolonging labor and giving the woman drugs or other medication for pain. In addition, they usually accommodate only one woman at a time; thus, if two women go into labor at the same time, the room may not be available for one of them. Furthermore, sometimes birthing-room regulations require women to qualify to be eligible to use the room (for example, a criterion might be a low-or no-risk pregnancy). Even when a woman qualifies, however, if her labor deviates from a predetermined notion of what is normal, she is likely to be moved to a more conventional labor room (Boston Women's Health Book Collective, 1984).

A small but growing number of women are avoiding hospital births altogether in favor of giving birth in *freestanding birth centers*. This term refers to places that are equipped to accommodate the birth of a child and that are separated from but near a hospital. Freestanding birth centers offer a homelike environment where women can deliver their babies with the help and support of family and friends. Women who use these centers claim that they offer the pregnant woman personal involvement and some control in the birthing process. In addition, these centers are economically accessible to a fairly large group of women.

The two major kinds of freestanding birthing centers around the country are nurse-midwife-directed centers and physician-directed centers. Some women feel that nurse-midwife-directed centers offer the best comprehensive care at the lowest rates. Skilled practitioners preside over the process. These centers use physicians as consultants and, like other centers, have a system whereby women can be transferred to a hospital if the need arises. In contrast, physician-directed centers are viewed by some women as minihospitals in that they tend to rely on nurses who may or may not be trained in midwifery skills.

In the United States today there are two main types of midwives: *certified nurse midwives (CNMs)* and *lay midwives*. Although their education and training differ, they generally share a similar philosophy of childbearing. This philosophy basically is centered on the notion that pregnancy and childbirth are healthy and normal conditions that are optimized by providing the best possible environment for the pregnant woman. For example, although CNMs independently manage the care of healthy pregnant women and their newborns, they are affiliated with a physician who is available for consultation and referral if necessary. Most CNMs deliver babies in hospitals or birthing centers, although they will deliver babies in the home if specific safety criteria are met (The American College of Nurse Midwives, 1991). Many countries such as England, Sweden, and the Netherlands routinely use midwives in home-birth deliveries. In contrast, in the United States midwives are involved in only a small percentage of births, although this percentage is increasing.

Some women prefer home births, believing that this experience offers the best opportunity for the woman and her family to participate in the delivery and greet the newborn, and for the woman to relax and set her own schedule. Although some people are still concerned over the safety of home births, the key to a healthy birth is not where it takes place but the care a woman gives herself during pregnancy as well as the training of the birth attendant. Not every woman is a candidate for home delivery. A woman with a high-risk pregnancy should plan to give birth in a place equipped to deal with any possible complications.

CONTEMPORARY CHILDBIRTH

No two childbirth experiences are exactly alike. Some women have long hours of labor; others have little or no labor before delivery. Some women are adminis-

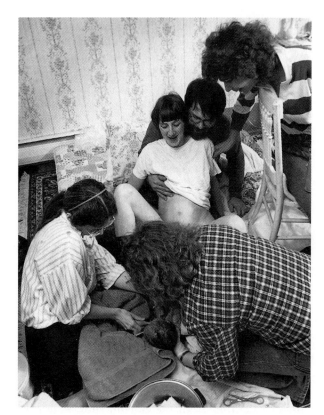

Deciding to deliver a child at home with a skilled midwife in attendance has many advantages, such as allowing friends and family to share in the birthing experience.

tered anesthesia during childbirth; others have *natural (undrugged) childbirth*. Some women have large babies; others have very small babies. Some fathers are in the birthing room with the mother; others are not. Some women experience *postpartum depression;* others feel euphoria after the delivery. However unique the birthing process for individual women and their partners, a general pattern can be discerned. Labor signals the end of a normal pregnancy and marks the beginning of the birth process. During labor, uterine muscles stretch the cervix for the baby to come out, and the muscles also push the baby down into the vaginal canal so it can be born.

FIRST STAGE OF LABOR Childbirth, like the development of pregnancy, can be divided into three stages. First-stage labor is characterized by three distinct phases: early, late, and transition. Early first-stage labor is generally characterized by mild contractions. Sometimes there will be some show of blood, and the amniotic sac may or may not break at this time (this is commonly called "breaking the water"). Late first-stage labor begins with contractions of the uterus, followed by dilation of the cervix from 5 to 8 centimeters to permit passage of the baby's head. After this, the transition phase of first-stage labor begins. This is the shortest and perhaps most painful part of labor. By the end of this stage contractions are very close together and very intense. These contractions indicate the beginning of the second stage of labor. Once the cervix has dilated to 10 centimeters, the second stage of labor begins.

SECOND STAGE OF LABOR   During the second stage of labor, the woman pushes the baby from the body. During this stage doctors often give the mother some type of anesthesia. When the baby's head appears—this is referred to as *crowning*—the physician may perform an **episiotomy**, a small incision to enlarge the vaginal opening and prevent tearing during delivery (see Figure 10.2). Although doctors have performed episiotomies routinely, it has been found that in most cases they are not necessary. With the proper attention from the doctor, most often the vaginal opening can stretch wide enough for delivery without tearing.

As the baby comes out the doctor usually drains mucus from its mouth and nose with a syringe. This allows the baby to gasp air into its lungs and to begin to breathe on its own. When the umbilical cord stops pulsating, the physician clamps it near the baby's abdomen and again about 4 inches away. The physician then cuts the cord between the 2 clamps. If the father has been participating in the delivery, he is permitted to cut the cord if he so desires. Immediately after birth, a baby's physical condition is evaluated in terms of the following vital signs: heart rate, muscle tone, respiratory effort, reflex response, and color.

THIRD STAGE OF LABOR   The third stage of labor is marked by the expulsion of the **afterbirth**, the placenta, amniotic sac, and remaining umbilical cord. Generally this happens somewhere between a few minutes and a half hour after delivery. The afterbirth is examined by the doctor to determine if it is intact and to check for signs of abnormality. If a piece of the placenta is left in the uterus, the mother may hemorrhage. After delivery, the uterus contracts and begins to return to its normal size. Once the afterbirth has been expelled the woman enters the *postpartum period*. Some people refer to this as a fourth stage in labor. During this period a woman is monitored very closely to ensure that her health is not in jeopardy.

FIGURE 10.2   An Epistiotomy

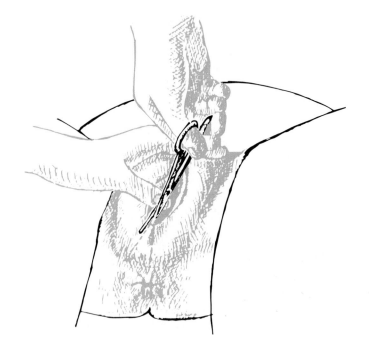

At the end of the birthing process parents embark on another set of experiences that often change their lives and their relationship with one another forever. In the last part of this chapter we present a brief and selective review of some of the experiences parents have after the birth of a child. In this regard, we examine the adjustment and adaptation to parenthood, the concepts of motherhood and fatherhood, and parenting strategies.

PARENTAL ADJUSTMENTS, ADAPTATIONS, AND PATTERNS OF CHILD REARING

Parenthood is one of the most demanding roles that individuals and couples face in their lifetime. Parents are often unprepared for the changes that this new family member will bring to their lives. Research has shown repeatedly that the addition of children to a relationship increases stress and lowers relationship satisfaction, particularly when children are still young and dependent (see, for example, Anderson, Russell, and Schumm, 1983; Field, 1988). Certainly, the addition of a new and dependent person requires that the couple make major lifestyle adjustments. Either one or both parents or someone acting on behalf of the parents must constantly be available and responsible for the care of the child.

What adaptations or adjustments do people make as parents? How does parenting change people's lives? Do women and men parent in different ways? In Chapter 3 we learned that gender expectations are rooted in cultural definitions of female and male roles. The ways in which people parent are significantly tied to how parenting roles and gender roles are culturally defined and the degree to which parents accept these definitions. Moreover, experiences such as age, race, class, gender, and sexual orientation interact to make the experience of parenthood different for different individuals and groups.

As we have indicated previously, having children can be a major event in people's lives. Parents must adapt to the birth experience biologically, (in the mother's case); psychologically; economically; and socially. For example, after the birth of a baby the mother's body must heal and return to a nonpregnant state. Parents must develop a mother or father identi-

ty. Also, particularly in the early months after the baby is brought home, parents have to adjust their sleeping habits to coincide with those of the newborn. Getting up in the middle of the night can be disruptive and exhausting and can affect the parents' job performance. Financial obligations also increase with the birth of a child, as do household and child-care responsibilities. All of these changes can increase stress within the family unit.

In addition to these adaptations, a couple often have to adjust their private and intimate time together to the schedule of a child. Sexual activity often loses out to the demands of child care. Work schedules, leisure time, and outside hobbies and interests all have to be adjusted or eliminated as a result of the addition of a child in the life of parents.

As we have already indicated, the sexual lifestyle of a couple may change drastically when a new child arrives. However, there is no set standard of sexual desire or behavior after childbirth. Thus, sexual activity varies greatly from couple to couple. Generally speaking, if the vaginal area is not painful or sore, if bleeding has stopped, and if the desire is there, there is no medical reason why a couple cannot engage in sexual behavior including sexual intercourse. Childbirth does not preclude the early resumption of sexual activities.

How does the presence of a newborn change the timing and performance of sexual activities? After childbirth, sexuality often loses its spontaneity as couples must now arrange sexual activities around working hours and at times when the newborn is asleep. Such adjustments can be long-term in that as children get older couples often continue to arrange sexual activities around times when children are at school or otherwise away from home.

PARENTAL ROLES

Traditionally, U.S. culture has made a clear distinction between motherhood and fatherhood. Both of these concepts reflect our ideas about gender-appropriate behavior and heterosexuality: Women are perceived as nurturant, caring, and supportive, and men as authoritative, strong, and protective. Researchers have found that for many people, the transition to parenthood means taking on more traditional sex roles. Why does this happen, and how does it make women's and men's experiences of parenting different? In this final section of the chapter we look at these issues. We begin with an examination of the concepts of motherhood and fatherhood in their social and cultural contexts. We then discuss gender differences in the experiences of parenting and styles of parenting within the context of gender, race, class, age, and sexual orientation.

MOTHERHOOD In Chapter 1 we discussed the general concept of the cult of true womanhood. That concept is important in our discussion here because traditional notions about motherhood are rooted in a *Eurocentric* (a worldview that places European culture at the center of analysis) middle-class ideology that emphasizes mothering as a woman's highest achievement and fulfillment in life. If we believe that motherhood is the only true and worthwhile role for women, then, by implication, those who consciously choose not to have children or who for various medical reasons cannot have children are less than complete women.

Some researchers (Hoffnung, 1984) have referred to such traditional ideas about motherhood as the **motherhood mystique**. The motherhood mystique also proposes that (1) the ultimate achievement and fulfillment of womanhood is through motherhood; (2) to be a good mother a woman has to enjoy being a mother and all the work that is defined as part of the mothering role; and (3) a woman's attitude about mothering will affect her children. The optimal situation for children is when women are devoted to mothering.

The motherhood mystique instills guilt in some women if they don't measure up to this ideal (Lindsey, 1990). For example, women who work outside the home are often made to feel guilty for not giving their children their undivided attention. Significantly, the same is not said of fathers who work. The myth that children need their mother's exclusive and continuous attention also serves to make women the scapegoat for whatever happens to children and also serves to support traditional gender roles that define women as subordinate to men. The motherhood mystique notwithstanding, the reality is that women can find satisfaction in a variety of roles. Not all women find motherhood fulfilling. In fact, not all women desire to mother. The best circumstance is one in which a woman freely chooses this option.

According to feminist sociologist Patricia Hill Collins (1991), the basic assumptions that underlie

Because an increasing number of women with children are working outside the home and because child care is still considered the primary responsibility of mothers, we are witnessing a growing number of latchkey children.

the traditional view of motherhood apply primarily to white middle-class families and most often do not reflect the realities of black families and other families of color. As an alternative to this view, Collins has proposed a model of African-American motherhood that consists of four basic themes:

- *Bloodmothers, othermothers, and women-centered networks.* Within African-American communities, the boundaries distinguishing biological mothers (bloodmothers) and other women (othermothers) are nebulous. In such communities a network of bloodmothers and othermothers (mothers, grandmothers, sisters, aunts, cousins, and friends) shares responsibilities for the others' children. This responsibility includes temporary and long-term child-care arrangements that, when necessary, can turn into informal adoption.

- *Providing as part of mothering.* African-American women make an essential economic contribution to the financial well-being of their families. They have long integrated economic activities into their mothering role, a combination that is looked on favorably in the African-American family.

- *Community othermothers and social activism.* African-American women's experiences as othermothers in their extended family networks are generalized to the larger community, where these women feel accountable for all of the community's children.

- *Motherhood as a symbol of power.* Because mothers not only raise their own children but also serve as community othermothers, motherhood is a symbol of power in the African-American community.

In recent decades the demographics of motherhood have changed considerably. Thus, contemporary women's views on motherhood can be seen as falling along a continuum identified by Collins. At one end of the continuum are traditionalists who want to retain the centrality of motherhood in women's lives; at the other end are those who want to eliminate what they perceive as a cultural mandate to mother. In the middle are large numbers of women who argue for an expanded but not essentially different role for women. In their view, women can be mothers as long as they are not just mothers. Many of these women are opting for both a career and motherhood. They continue to see motherhood as fulfilling but not as the only route to personal fulfillment.

FATHERHOOD   The traditional notion of fatherhood emphasizes an instrumental role of father as breadwinner and authority figure. Public policy, societal sentiment, state and federal legislation, and family law all echo this view. The traditional concept of fatherhood is as limiting as the traditional concept of motherhood. Attempting to adhere to this concept can deny a father an opportunity for meaningful relationships with his children.

Today four different views of fatherhood coexist, with some degree of overlap. First is the idea of the aloof and distant father. Second is father as breadwinner. Third is the notion of father as a gender-role model for the couple's children. Fourth is the idea of father as an active, nurturant parent. Although an increasing number of fathers are redefining their role in terms of this fourth category, the idea of father as breadwinner remains the dominant view (Basow,

Many fathers today are stepping outside conventional father roles and sharing the responsibility of taking care of their children.

1992). Even those fathers who actively participate in child care still see breadwinner as their primary role. They also see themselves as a helpmate assisting the main person, the mother (Astin, 1985). Research indicates that most fathers periodically "help" with child rearing, but they do not assume a long-term role of equal responsibility. In addition, mothers themselves are also likely to consider the father a helpmate (LaRossa and LaRossa, 1989).

Nonetheless, it would be erroneous to assume that fathers do not play a significant role in child rearing. As we saw in Chapter 3, more and more men are emphasizing their parental role and de-emphasizing their career role. According to some people, the increasing participation of fathers in parenting has been one of the biggest and most positive changes that has occurred in U.S. families in recent years. Some researchers (Risman, 1989) have found that when given the chance fathers are or can be just as nurturant as mothers.

Should Americans adopt the Japanese model of child rearing? The Japanese believe that society needs to pay better attention to how children are reared. In this regard, since the late 1970s a leading children's product exporter has conducted child-care seminars in Japan and is now conducting similar seminars in the United States for the purpose of sharing the Japanese child-rearing philosophy with Americans.

Japanese child-rearing methods are based on the belief that personal happiness is measured in large part by one's contribution to society. Thus, children are brought up to seek fulfillment with others rather than individually. The Japanese believe that such an approach to child rearing could contribute to worldwide peace and stability. At the heart of Japanese child rearing is a concept called *amae*, a sense of complete dependence based on a wish to be loved and cared for unconditionally. *Amae* is instilled in Japanese children through continuous love and attention from the mother. Japanese mothers typically spend every waking moment with their babies, bringing them into their beds at night and catering to their every whim. For example, if a child cries when the mother begins to leave a room, the child is rarely scolded. Rather, the mother will either stay in the room or take the child with her. In a typical Japanese household, the father works long hours and sees his children only on Sundays. Although the father bond is considered to be important, the father's primary role is to provide love and attention to his wife while she assumes

A traditional Japanese mother takes great pride in her children and typically spends every waking moment with them.

primary responsibility for raising the children.

GENDER DIFFERENCES IN THE EXPERIENCE OF PARENTHOOD

Is motherhood experienced the same way as fatherhood? As with much of the research on marriages and families, the majority of the information on gender differences in parenting focuses on white middle-class families. Thus, our ability to generalize to other groups is severely limited. Given that most people become parents, however, a brief overview of women's and men's experiences as parents is valuable.

Regardless of the division of labor before the birth of a child, after a child is born mothers are typically more involved in child-care activities than fathers are. New mothers find themselves with increased housework expectations and responsibilities. Mothers of babies and young children spend more hours on their family roles than do nonmothers or mothers with older children. This is true regardless of whether or not a woman works outside the home.

Men have generally claimed that the reason they do not participate more fully in child rearing is because of their job commitments and their general exhaustion at the end of a workday. In fact, however, women who are employed manage to do both. In less than 2 percent of married-couple families are fathers full-time homemakers, and in less than 15 percent do they equally share child-care and housework responsibilities. Although mothers spend more time taking care of children than fathers do, fathers spend more time than mothers in play behavior. The net result is that mothers' energies are more divided than fathers' energies, and their lives are more frantic (Sapiro, 1986).

In Japan, relationships and being part of the group are the most important elements in childhood socialization. Cooperation and teamwork are key to family and work life in Japan. Thus, *amae* is carried over into the schools, where children are taught to be cooperative with classmates and teachers. They are not encouraged to be assertive or competitive and in fact, are rewarded for cooperative behavior and punished for competitive behavior. They are taught that success is not an individual but rather a group achievement. It is widely believed that the Japanese drive and emphasis on cooperative effort is directly tied to the Japanese mother's coddling of her children.

The Japanese model contrasts with the typical child-rearing philosophy in the United States primarily because of the two countries' radically different histo-ries: Japan is a monoculture and historically has been isolated, whereas the United States is a culturally diverse society characterized by an emphasis on individualism. In addition, the two countries have different ideas about what constitutes a "good" person, which translates into different philosophies on how to raise children. For example, the Japanese hold loyalty, proper behavior, and attention to detail in the highest esteem. In the United States, the emphasis is on individualism, independence, and initiative, and we train children accordingly: Each stage of a child's development is meant to encourage self-reliance. Many U.S. parents would probably see the deferential treatment or doting of Japanese mothers as producing spoiled, self-centered, selfish individuals. The Japanese believe, however, that keeping children happy will motivate them to be cooperative. They also believe that U.S. child-rearing practices are too goal-oriented and produce individuals who are overly concerned with achieving personal success.

What do you think? Does the Japanese system sound appealing to you? What about the Japanese ideas of mother and baby having a socially approved period for bonding? Do we hold such values? Do you think that so much doting by the mother is really good for a child's development? Perhaps the fundamental issue that the Japanese model raises for U.S. parents is whether their children would benefit if cooperation, teamwork, and order were emphasized and autonomy and individuality de-emphasized. Is this what we want? How would adopting the Japanese model affect the sexual division of parenting in the family? If we reject the Japanese model, do we reject the whole model or just parts of it? Is there a middle ground? If so, what is it?

Source: Adapted from "Made-in-Japan Parenting," by Russell Shorto, *Health*, June 1991: 54–57.

Because of this greater responsibility for child care and housework, mothers tend to experience much greater stress than fathers do. Social scientist Robert Weiss (1979) has identified several sources of parental stress, which he labels responsibility overload, task overload, and emotional overload. Although all parents can experience these overload situations, they are more likely to affect mothers, particularly teenaged mothers.

Responsibility overload refers to a situation in which critical family decisions must be made by a sometimes less-than-mature person who has few if any resources to assist in decision making and follow-through. In **task overload**, the parent simply does not have enough time or skills and motivation to do all that is necessary in child rearing. Parents who experience increasing demands to be available in crisis situations

Because most teenaged mothers have low educational levels and few skills and receive little or no economic support from the father, their ability to support themselves and their children is severely limited.

both in the home and on the job often experience **emotional overload**. These overload situations can lead to a number of problems in terms of raising children.

Although many women experience stress and ambivalence about motherhood, they generally feel that the rewards of parenting outweigh the negatives. Some women, however, express a resentment at their partner's general lack of involvement in parenting. Thus, motherhood is at the same time both satisfying and dissatisfying for women, and most women express contradictory feelings about it (Basow, 1992).

When questioned about parenting responsibility, most Americans respond that from the outset both parents should take part in bringing up children. The notion that fathers should develop a special relationship with their children is not universally shared, however. The box titled "Made-in-Japan Parenting" contrasts child-rearing practices in Japan with those in the United States.

STYLES OF PARENTING

How parents rear their children and the effects of various child-rearing strategies are the subjects of a substantial literature. Professionals and the lay public alike dispense advice and analyses of what works and what doesn't. As a consequence, parents today are far better informed about child development and behavior than were parents at any other time in our history. Just as every pregnancy and child is different, so too are parenting styles. However, sociologists have identified some common patterns of parenting among families in the United States particularly within specified social classes.

Because one of the basic elements in sociological definitions of class is occupation, studies of parenting styles across class often examine the kinds of attitudes and values associated with different occupations and how these attitudes and values are related to child-rearing strategies. A classic statement using this approach is sociologist Melvin Kohn's (1977) discussion of parenting styles in terms of self-direction versus conformity parental-value orientations. According to Kohn, middle-class occupations require or allow workers much more self-direction in the ordering of activities and the selection of methods than do working-class jobs, which are more often routine and subject to strict supervision. In addition, middle-class occupations tend to call for individual action, whereas working-class occupations more often call for coordinated group or team action.

These occupational differences are reflected in general differences in values and parenting strategies among various social classes. According to Kohn, the *traditional* or *conformity* value orientation is more commonly found among working-class and lower-class parents, who emphasize order, authority, obedience, and respectability. In contrast, the *developmental* or *self-direction* orientation, most commonly found among middle-class parents, stresses the child's motives and the development of self-control. Emphasis is on internal qualities such as consideration, curiosity, and initiative rather than on external conformity.

Some social scientists have incorporated Kohn's findings into a model that divides parenting styles into three general categories: authoritarian, permissive, and authoritative. The *authoritarian* style, commonly associated with working-class parents, demands absolute obedience from children and often involves the use of physical punishment to control behavior. The *permissive* style of parenting, typical of middle-class parents, involves giving children autonomy and freedom to express themselves, and downplays conformity. Permissive parents most often use reason instead of physical punishment to modify their children's behavior. The *authoritative* style also encourages children to be autonomous and self-reliant. Authoritative parents generally rely on positive reinforcements while avoiding, as much as possible, punitive and repressive methods of discipline. These parents are in control of their children's behavior, while at the same time they allow the children much more freedom than do authoritarian parents. Although the first two parenting styles can be clearly found in families, some researchers dispute whether this third style actually exists in most families because no research evidence supports its existence.

In general, these parenting styles often overlap depending on a number of factors, such as the number of children, the unique personalities of the parents and child, parents' attitudes concerning child rearing, and the structure of the family. As we saw in Chapter 1, although some of the child-rearing functions of families have been taken over by other societal institutions, parents remain the major socializers of their children. Thus, their styles of parenting has important consequences for society.

RACE AND CLASS

AFRICAN AMERICANS Although these general parenting styles can be found among the total population there are some differences, modifications, and adaptations associated with race, age, and sexual orientation. Because most African Americans have encountered racism and discrimination in some form, African-American parenting styles and aspirations for their children tend to be similar across class boundaries. At the same time, however, they also exhibit class differences similar to those found among other groups in society.

For example, African-American middle-class families have a value orientation characterized by a high achievement motivation, social striving, and a high regard for property ownership. They also have high educational and occupational expectations for their offspring. Thus, they try to teach their children positive attitudes toward work and thrift. These families tend to be more egalitarian than patriarchal. Parents stress conformity, chastity, and fidelity and are more inclined to use persuasive approaches to elicit obedience and conformity than to use coercion and physical punishment. Yet they demand a high degree of respect for parental authority (Blackwell, 1985). In addition, African-American middle-class fathers are often integrally involved in parenting and are generally warm and loving and only moderately strict disciplinarians (McAdoo, 1986).

African-American working-class families hold similar attitudes concerning their basic goals, but their value orientation is much more affected by the constant struggle for survival, and they take great pride in the fact that they are self-supporting. The parenting style in working-class families includes an emphasis on respectability: Parents demand that their children behave well and not get into trouble with the police. Like their middle-class counterparts they stress conformity and obedience (Willie, 1981; Blackwell, 1985).

Perhaps the greatest class differences in parental attitudes and parenting styles are those between the African-American poor and middle class. Many poor African Americans are disenchanted, disillusioned, and alienated, and see little progress and even fewer possibilities for breaking out of their low economic status (Blackwell, 1985). As a consequence, according to sociologist Charles Willie (1981), many poor African-American parents are generally limited in their ability to guide their children and often have little control over their children's behavior. Often parental values and behaviors are those that are most expedient and offer hope of a livable or tolerable existence at the time. For example, parents are often grade school or high school dropouts, and to make their children obey and conform they sometimes hold themselves up to their children as negative images of what not to do.

NATIVE AMERICANS Other families of color, including Native Americans, Latinos, and Asian Americans, exhibit variations in parenting styles. Because Native Americans are a highly heterogeneous people, family behaviors vary considerably from group to group. Among the Navaho, for example, parents operate on the principle of the inviolability of the individual, which some researchers have translated as a principle of permissiveness. Navajo parents discipline their children through persuasion, ridicule, and shame rather than coercion and physical punishment. In addition, supernatural sanctions are used to control children's behavior.

The diversity of Native-American peoples notwithstanding, Native-American parents of all backgrounds tend to stress to their children a sense of family unity and tribal identity. They see their children as assets to both the family and the group. Some researchers have suggested that child rearing among Native Americans frequently is nonverbal: Parents communicate by giving stern looks or by ignoring inappropriate behavior. Furthermore, children are socialized by example and are expected to share with others, to be quiet and unassuming, to show deference to their elders, to control their emotions, to be self-reliant, and to make an economic contribution to the family from an early age (John, 1988).

LATINOS Certain Latino groups exhibit a similar emphasis on family interdependence and unity. Among Puerto Ricans, for example, females are charged with the responsibility of creating and maintaining these values in offspring. In general, the Puerto Rican parenting style can be characterized as authoritarian. Children are rarely consulted on matters that directly affect them. They are viewed as passive people whose attitudes and behavior must be completely shaped by the parents. Good behavior is taken for granted, and reasons for punishment are

Throughout this chapter and this textbook generally, we have emphasized the different effects of race, class, and gender on the experiences of people. In this chapter we paid particular attention to the intersection of these experiences in terms of prenatal and postnatal care and child rearing. Utilizing surveys or personal interviews conduct a small, qualitative analysis of the prenatal and postnatal care and child-rearing practices of pregnant women and new mothers. Try to include women of different races, classes, ages, and sexual orientations. Focus specifically on questions such as: What problems do they have? What commonalities exist? How do women in each of these categories differ from one another in terms of prenatal and postnatal care and child-rearing strategies?

---

seldom offered. Physical punishment is frequently used, especially by parents with the least social mobility and status. Parents born in Puerto Rico, more so than those born or raised in the United States, tend to perpetuate, although with some modifications, a double standard of conduct between the sexes. Females are trained to be modest, and overt expressions of affection are more common with girls than boys. Furthermore, mothers tend to be warmer and more playful with children than fathers are and interact more frequently with daughters than with sons.

ASIAN AMERICANS Parenting styles among Asian Americans vary according to the degree to which parents are acculturated into U.S. society. Newly immigrated or first-generation parents typically use traditional approaches based on authoritarian methods. Obedience and conformity are expected, and discipline is strict and involves physical punishment. In contrast, acculturated parents generally are more nurturing and verbal and give their children more autonomy (Young, 1972).

LESBIAN AND GAY PARENTS

An increasing number of lesbians and gays are choosing to have children through artificial insemination, heterosexual intercourse, or adoption and then sharing the prenatal and postnatal experiences with their partners. Although little is known about the parenting styles of lesbians and gays, the available research indicates that lesbians tend to form extended networks of support that operate like any other family except that they are not patriarchal. When lesbians and gays have children their children are generally accepting of their parents' lifestyle and they are not any less well adjusted than children who grow up in heterosexual households. Lesbian households also tend to be less structured around a gender-specific division of labor, and as mothers, lesbians tend to be more child-oriented than heterosexual mothers (Anderson 1993). In fact, some feminists have claimed that when lesbian mothers leave an unhappy heterosexual relationship where children are involved, the children may actually get more nurturing in a lesbian household where two or more women share the work of child care.

Unlike heterosexual parents, lesbian and gay parents spend a great amount of emotion and time protecting their custody rights to their children. This is probably due in part to the fact that they are often judged as parents not by their ability to rear and nurture their children but in terms of their sexual orientation and lifestyle. More lesbians have custody of their own or adoptive children than do gays. This partly reflects the fact that family law still more often gives women than men custody of children. Gays who raise children tend to be more nurturing and less rigid in terms of gender-role socialization and the gender division of household labor than heterosexual fathers. Gay fathers also tend to be more strict disciplinarians than are heterosexual fathers (Andersen, 1993).

In the final analysis, the question is not so much who mothers or who fathers as it is how much support we give to parents. Now that you have completed this chapter, you should exercise your sociological imagination. Complete the exercise described in the Applying the Sociological Imagination box, and ask yourself what kinds of resources parents need to raise their children successfully.

SUMMARY

Conception, pregnancy, and childbirth have a tremendous effect on the lives of individuals and couples. Conception begins with the fertilization of an egg by a sperm. From there the development of a child involves complex biological and physiological processes that culminate in birth. Once a woman or couple suspects pregnancy there are many ways of testing to confirm the pregnancy, including a number of home pregnancy tests.

Once pregnancy is confirmed, the woman should get immediate and continuous prenatal care. Research indicates that a number of factors, especially age, race, and class, affect the prenatal attitudes and behaviors of pregnant women. The pregnancy period is generally divided into three stages, or trimesters. Poor women and women of color are at a higher risk of receiving inadequate prenatal care due to a lack of economic resources. As a consequence babies born to these women are at greater risk of birth defects, diseases, and other physical or medical problems. Some of the most common risks to the prenatal environment are poor nutrition, X-rays, smoking, and drug and alcohol use. In addition, AIDS and other sexually transmitted diseases can harm the fetus.

In focusing on the pregnant woman, we often forget about the expectant father. Many expectant fathers now participate in their partner's pregnancy through a variety of actions ranging from donning empathy bellies to taking paternity leave for the birth of their child. Early on in a pregnancy an individual or a couple should decide where birthing will take place. Today, many women are opting to give birth in birthing centers or at home attended by a midwife instead of in hospitals attended by male physicians.

Becoming a parent is a major transition in a person's life. Not all people experience parenthood in the same way. Rather, parenthood varies for individuals and groups within as well as across a number of important areas of experience: race, class, gender, age, sexual orientation, and marital status. Within all groups, however, females and males seem to experience parenting differently. Although many individuals and groups no longer adhere as strongly to the traditional gender division of labor, women nonetheless tend to spend far more time in child-rearing and housework activities than men do. In the final analysis, no matter who does the parenting, more support is needed for parenting and those who parent.

KEY TERMS

conception	placenta	morbidity
zygote	amniotic sac	mortality
ovulation	miscarriage	fetal alcohol syndrome
menstruation	ectopic pregnancy	embryopathy
blastocyst	edema	midwife
embryo	toxemia	episiotomy
fetus	congenital	afterbirth
fraternal twins	amniocentesis	motherhood mystique
identical twins	chorionic villus sampling (CVS)	responsibility overload
gestation period	ultrasound	task overload
areola	sonogram	emotional overload
human chorionic gonadotropin (HCG)	alpha-fetoprotein (AFP) testing	

QUESTIONS FOR STUDY AND REFLECTION

1. Given the innovations in reproductive technology today, parents can now determine with some degree of accuracy the sex of their unborn child. What do you see as the pros and cons of predetermining the sex of offspring? How might widespread intervention into the determination of the sex of unborn fetuses affect U.S. society in the future?

2. Which aspects of the U.S. family system foster the gendered division of labor for mothers and fathers? What might be done to reduce or eliminate gender-based inequalities in parental responsibilities?

3. Why is the transition to parenthood stressful? Is it more stressful for mothers than for fathers? Why or why not? What can be done to make this transition less stressful?

4. What is your idea of a good mother? A good father? Based on these definitions, how do you rate yourself as a parent or prospective parent? What do you think are some of the important questions that people should ask themselves before they decide to become parents?

FURTHER READING

ARMS, SUZANNE. 1986. *Immaculate Deception: A New Look at Women and Childbirth in America*. New York: Bantam Books. One of the earliest exposés of the abuses of birth technology and medical intervention in normal childbirth and how women have lost their power over normal reproductive activities to male physicians. Although the tone is sometimes angry, the book provides a powerful and systematic discussion of an important topic.

ASHFORD, JANET ISAACS, ed. 1983. *The Whole Birth Catalog*. New York: Crossing Press. This is a delightful directory of groups, ideas, and products pertaining to pregnancy and childbirth, and it contains detailed descriptions of books on those subjects as well.

THE BOSTON WOMEN'S HEALTH BOOK COLLECTIVE. 1992. *The New Our Bodies, Ourselves*. New York: Simon and Schuster. This new version of the book that was first published during the 1970s contains an expanded and updated discussion of the leading women's health issues of the 1990s and beyond. It continues to break new ground and examine difficult and controversial topics. It is the most complete sourcebook on women's health-care issues to date.

JORDAN, BRIGITTE. 1980. *Birth in Four Cultures*. St. Albans, VT: Eden Press Women's Publications. An anthropological, cross-cultural comparison of birth rituals and customs in the United States with those in Holland, Sweden, and the Yucatán. Many of the birth practices that we think of as scientific are shown actually to be birth rituals.

EVOLVING
WORK
AND FAMILY
STRUCTURES

*B*oth Tim and Ellen Birch work. They are rarely able to spend time alone together. Ellen cares for their two children, ages 2 and 5, during the week, while Tim, who has his own printing business, works 50 to 60 hours a week. On the weekends Tim takes care of the children, while Ellen, a registered nurse, works 12-hour shifts at the local hospital. Neither Tim nor Ellen is happy with this arrangement. Although their work schedules have put a strain on their marriage, they say they can't make ends meet on Tim's salary alone. Ellen likes nursing but would prefer to work during the week so that the family could be together on the weekends. Affordable quality day care is not available locally, however, and they don't have any relatives in the area who could help them with child care.

How typical do you think Tim and Ellen's situation is? What kind of stress does such a work arrangement place on family members? What could be done to help couples like Tim and Ellen?

In our society we frequently think of work and family life as separate spheres. Research shows, however, that the worlds of work and family affect each other in significant ways. The quality and stability of family life are dependent to a large extent on the type of work available to family members. Work provides income, which determines a family's standard of living. As discussed in Chapter l, from about the 1830s until the 1970s, the typical U.S. family consisted of an employed husband and a wife who stayed home and took care of the children.

Because of changing economic and social conditions, however, a single income is no longer sufficient for most families. Many husbands remain major providers, but increasingly wives are sharing this role. As we will see throughout this chapter, reactions to these changes are mixed. Although many women want to work outside the home, some women feel that they carry a double burden—besides outside employment, they still do the majority of household and family work. Some men are relieved at not having to be the sole provider. Others, are dispirited, especially when their working spouses make demands on them to share household tasks and child care and to be more emotionally involved in family relationships. Additionally, growing numbers of families are headed by a single parent who must fulfill both the breadwinner and homemaker roles.

Work affects families in other ways as well. Work can have *spillover effects,* either positive or negative, on family life. An example of positive spillover is the carryover of satisfaction and stimulation at work to a sense of satisfaction at home. Negative spillover involves bringing home the problems and stresses experienced at work, making adequate participation

in family life difficult (Voydanoff, 1987). Similarly, family life can affect work in important ways. Family obligations can provide motivation for working hard, but problems at home, such as a child's illness, can hinder job performance as well.

This chapter focuses on the interconnections between the family and work, beginning with an examination of the changing composition of the labor force, notably the increasing participation of married women with small children, and the impact of this participation on marriage and family structures and functioning. We also examine the inequalities of wealth and resources as manifested in poverty, unemployment, and homelessness. The chapter concludes with an assessment of the kinds of changes that need to be made in the organization of work and in social policies to help individuals maintain a balance between the demands of work and family.

THE TRANSFORMATION OF WORK AND FAMILY ROLES

The idealized images of men as providers and women as homemakers continued into the second half of the twentieth century despite the fact that these roles were already being undermined. Figure 11.1 traces the changes in women's and men's labor-force participation rates from 1900 to 1990. The **labor-force participation rate** refers to the percentage of workers in a particular group who are employed or who are actively seeking employment. If people are not employed and are not actively seeking work, they are not counted in the labor force. As the twentieth century opened, only 20 percent of women aged 14 and

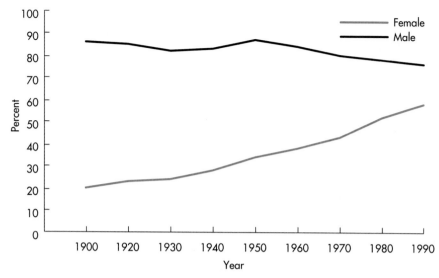

FIGURE 11.1 Civilian Labor-Force Participation Rates, by Sex

Sources: Adapted from U.S. Department of Commerce, Bureau of the Census, 1975, *Historical Statistics of the United States, Colonial Times to 1970.* Bicentennial edition, pt. I, (Washington, DC: U.S. Government Printing Office): pp. 131–32; U.S. Bureau of the Census, 1989a, *Statistical Abstract of the United States* (Washington, DC: U.S. Government Printing Office): p. 376; U.S. Bureau of Labor Statistics, 1991a, *Employment and Earnings* (Washington, DC: U.S. Government Printing Office): p. 208.

older were in the labor force, compared with approximately 86 percent of men in that age category. The comparable rates 90 years later were 58 percent for women and 76 percent for men 16 years of age and over. Thus, the labor-force participation rates for women and men are moving in opposite directions. The decline in the male participation rate is mostly due to older men retiring at earlier ages now than in the past and to the limited participation of African-American teenagers, for whom finding employment is increasingly difficult.

The narrowing gap between women's and men's participation rates reveals only part of the story, however. According to historian Alice Kessler-Harris (1982), a marked shift occurred in the participation patterns of women. Prior to World War II, the majority of women workers were young, single, poor, and women of color. As Figure 11. 2 shows, as late as 1970 just three out of ten married mothers with children under 6 years of age were in the labor force. Twenty years later, approximately six out of ten married mothers with children under 6 were in the labor force.

Historically, labor-force participation rates varied by race as well as by gender and marital status. In the past white women were less likely than women of color to be in the labor force. As white women began to delay marriage and to divorce in greater numbers, however, their rates have become similar to those of other groups of women. In 1990, black and white women had approximately equal rates of participation, 57.8 and 57.5 percent, respectively. Latinas had a slightly lower rate, 53.0 percent (U.S. Bureau of Labor Statistics, 1991a:208).

REASONS WOMEN WORK

Rarely do we ask men why they work; we assume they have no choice. They are expected to be family providers. But because the homemaker role was

FIGURE 11.2 Percentage of Married Working Mothers with Children under Age 6, 1970 – 91.

Source: Adapted from U.S. Bureau of the Census, 1992c, *Statistical Abstract of the United States* (Washington, DC: U.S. Government Printing Office): Table 620, p. 388.

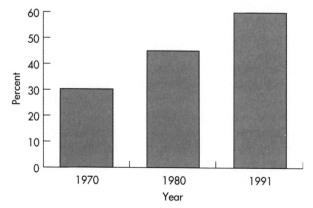

Historically, working mothers have always been confronted with child-care problems. During World War II, community nurseries like this one in Woodville, California, became common.

believed to be the traditional role for women, any departures from this role require explanation. A recent opinion poll found that the majority of women (55 percent) work for the same reasons men do—to support themselves or their family; an additional 32 percent work to bring in extra money (Roper Organization, 1990:62). Nevertheless, no single factor can explain these dramatic changes in women's labor-force participation rates. Rather, a complex interplay of demographic, economic, social, political, and personal factors have contributed to these changes. For example, in contrast to women in previous eras, women today are better educated, have fewer children, and live longer. Women who postpone marriage and childbearing to increase their level of education and to begin work are more likely to remain in the labor force after the birth of their children. Advanced education influences women in much the same way it influences men. Not only does education offer better job possibilities but it also raises awareness of personal options and creates a desire for self-expression and self-fulfillment. Women today also have more time in their total life span to pursue activities other than child rearing.

In recent decades both the U.S. and world economies have experienced major changes. In the United States many high-paying manufacturing jobs have disappeared: "Between 1981 and 1991, 1.8 million manufacturing jobs vanished in the United

States—a decline of 9 percent" (Barlett and Steele, 1992:xi). These jobs have been replaced by lower-paying service jobs. For example, when American Home Products closed its plant in Elkhart, Indiana, the average hourly pay of its workers was $13.40. One year later the average pay of the workers who found new jobs was $6.00 per hour (Barlett and Steele, 1992:97). During much of the 1970s and 1980s the real earnings of husbands remained stagnant or fell. At the same time, there was an increased demand for women workers to fill the expanding number of jobs in the service sector, for example, teaching, health care, social services, government, and real estate. The women's movement and affirmative action legislation also enhanced employment opportunities for women and people of color. Additionally, social attitudes have become more accepting of working women. These factors, combined with the desire for a higher standard of living, led many women into the workplace.

WORK AND FAMILY STRUCTURES

The rapid entrance of married women with children into the labor force has altered family life in many ways. A variety of work and family structures have emerged as a response to these economic and social transformations, creating both opportunities and problems for family members.

TRADITIONAL NUCLEAR FAMILIES

The highly idealized family structure consisting of a working husband, a wife who is a full-time homemaker, and dependent children living in a single-family house currently represents less than 11 percent of all households in the United States (cited in Renzetti and Curran, 1989:137). Within this family type, women and a small number of *househusbands*—men who stay home to care for home and family while their wives work—engage in activities that some authors are now calling *home production*: the nonmarket production of goods and services, usually for the family but occasionally on a volunteer basis for schools, churches, or other groups. What is traditionally known as "housework" is only one aspect of home production, which also includes household budgeting, grocery shopping, care of dependents, and other tasks that go beyond cleaning and laundry (Hodson and Sullivan, 1990:91). Randy Hodson and Teresa Sullivan point out the enormous value to families of these activities. If these nonpaid home production "workers" were compensated for their labor, their compensation would amount to billions of dollars per year.

Like all social roles, the role of home production worker (traditionally known as "housewife") has both costs and benefits (Oakley, 1974). On the positive side it provides the possibility of scheduling activities to suit one's own priorities and the opportunity to watch children grow and develop on a daily basis. Many parents, including some women and men currently in the labor force, would prefer staying at home at least while their children are young. Surveys conducted since 1970 showed a change in women's attitudes toward work. In 1991, for the first time since the survey began, the percentage of women who consider a career for working mothers an automatic right dropped below 50 percent. The number who favor part-time work for mothers increased noticeably (Balter, 1991). Caution is required in interpreting these changing attitudes, however. Although the attitudes of some women reflected a desire to be at home, the attitudes of other women reflected dissatisfaction with the quality of work available to them.

Among the disadvantages of the role are the repetitive and sometimes boring nature of activities such as cleaning and doing laundry and the overall social devaluation of housework, often reflected in the phrase, "I'm just a housewife." Important financial costs as well become major burdens for families with only a single source of income and become particularly significant when divorce or death disrupts the family. Homemakers are economically dependent on their partners. Unlike homemakers in several European countries, U.S. homemakers are not covered by pensions, insurance, or social security. Thus, when a marriage is dissolved in the United States the displaced homemaker frequently suffers downward social mobility (see Chapter 13).

THE TWO-PERSON CAREER

One variation of the traditional nuclear family/work relationship is what some writers have called the "two-person career" (Papanek, 1973; Mortimer and

Hillary Rodham Clinton had a law career of her own before becoming first lady. Since her husband's election, she has assumed the responsibilities of a supportive spouse in a two-person career.

London, 1984). This pattern, seen by Hanna Papanek as a "structural part of the middle-class wife's role" (1973:857), involves incorporating the wife into her spouse's job through the expectation that she will be available to entertain his business associates, engage in volunteer activities that will enhance his organization's image, attend company parties and other events, and socialize with her husband's coworkers off the job. Thus, men in these families symbolically bring two people to their jobs (Kanter, 1977). In contrast, when women hold similar positions, husbands are rarely expected to perform these duties.

Much of the research on the two-person career focuses on middle- and upper-class occupations. Many business, professional and political wives, for example, the first lady, are often viewed as typical of the two-person career. Such wives can be seen enacting stereotypical role behavior as they support and comfort their husbands and mother their children, all the while enhancing their husbands' images.

The two-person career marriage, like all others, has advantages and disadvantages. Employers benefit by having additional "workers" without having to pay for their efforts. Many husbands owe much of their career advancement to the social skills of their wives. In many cases the husband's work takes priority over family life. Thus, spouses often find they have little time to spend together. Because the husband is away from home much of the time, the wife becomes the exclusive home manager. Fulfilling this role gives wives status and a sense of accomplishment, leaving their husbands free to devote most of their energy to work. Among middle- and upper-class wives, the financial rewards for taking on this responsibility may be significant—a secure lifestyle, travel, and opportunities for cultural enrichment.

On the negative side many wives experience unhappiness in this role. Like other nonemployed homemakers, these wives perceive that their role is not appreciated or respected by the public. Furthermore, although much is demanded of them, they may not feel a part of their husband's work. Interviews with corporate wives reveal a frequent complaint that husbands don't have time or don't want to share their work with their wives (Reeve, 1991). Wives may feel enormously limited in their behavior, constrained in their choice of friends, and restricted in their own occupational goals because of the demands of their husbands' careers (Papanek, 1973; Kanter, 1977).

Economic shifts that require multiple family earners as well as the changing aspirations among women and men have led to a decline in the two-person career strategy. The traditional nuclear family of working husband, homemaker wife, and children is being replaced by dual-earner families, or, as some writers prefer, "two-paycheck couples."

DUAL-EARNER FAMILIES

Dual-earner families are not new. There have always been some families where both spouses were employed outside the home. These dual-earner families tended to be poor or nonwhite. In contrast, today's dual-earner couples constitute approximately 60 percent of all married couples and cut across all class and ethnic lines.

Nevertheless, dual-earner families do not all follow the same pattern. There is considerable variation in their commitment to work. At one end of the continuum are couples where one of the spouses, usually the wife, works part-time. At the other end is a small (approximately 7 percent) but growing number of couples in which both spouses are highly committed to work. These are what social scientists call *dual-career couples*. These households differ from other

dual-earner households in their approach to work. Rather than simply having a job, these couples invest in careers, which have several identifying characteristics. First, they require extensive training, usually a college or professional degree. Second, careers are more structured than jobs are, containing specific paths of upward mobility. Finally, careers involve commitment beyond a 9-to-5 workday. Sociologists Robert and Jeanette Lauer distinguish these families in the following way:

> The dual-earner family is one in which both spouses are involved in paid work, and one or both view the work only as a job. In other words, one of the spouses in the dual-earner family may be pursuing a career, while the other is merely holding down a job. In the dual-career family, on the other hand, both spouses are engaged in careers, which means that both are committed to employment that has a long-term pattern of mobility (1991:325–26).

Later in this chapter we will see that couples in dual-earner marriages experience satisfaction as well as stress and conflict as they struggle to solve important relationship problems such as the "problem over who will do the 'family work,' the housekeeping and child care that formerly was the work of the housewife" (Lauer and Lauer, 1991:326).

COMMUTER MARRIAGES

Some couples work in different geographic locations and because of distance must maintain two separate places of residence. Social scientists refer to these arrangements as **commuter marriages**. One form of commuter marriage has existed for a long time. Couples in which one spouse, most frequently the husband, is a politician, professional athlete, traveling salesperson, seasonal worker, prisoner, or serves in the military have had some experience with living apart while maintaining a marital relationship.

Today many commuter marriages develop because both spouses pursue careers but find that suitable jobs for each spouse are unavailable in the same location. Sometimes, too, the requirements of a job call for a transfer to a new area, and for whatever reason the other spouse can't or won't relocate. These arrangements are more stressful for younger couples, especially those with children and those who have been married for only a short time

Separations due to military service are common. The general pattern in the past, however, was for the husband to serve while the wife stayed home and cared for the children. Today it is not uncommon for both spouses to be in the military; in some cases the wife belongs to the military and the husband does not. With the creation of the all-volunteer army in 1973, a growing number of women, like their male counterparts, joined reserve and National Guard units to further their education and to develop skills for the civilian labor force. According to the Defense Department, about 140,000 people in various branches of the services are married to other military personnel, and there are about 67,000 single parents in uniform (*Chicago Tribune*, 1991a). Many military couples serve in the same or similar units.

During peacetime, separations for these couples and their families are often of short duration, usually for training purposes. During times of national emergency, like the Persian Gulf War of 1991 or the 1992–93 relief efforts in Somalia, however, a call-up of such units can trigger a period of separation, not only of spouses, but of parents from their children. Such separations are especially stressful for families because the duration of the separation is unpredictable and because one or both spouses (parents) may be injured or killed. There is the added burden that neither parent is able to remain behind with the children. During the Persian Gulf War, children from 17,500 families were affected by the loss of one or both parents (Priest, 1991). Finding alternative child care under these conditions can be especially difficult.

Race and class are important factors here as well. Because of limited opportunities in the civilian economy, the poor, the working class, and people of color disproportionately make up the volunteer army and reserve units and thus find themselves living in this type of commuter marriage. According to the Department of Defense, African Americans make up almost a quarter of the military, nearly double their percentage of the U.S. population, and accounted for nearly 30 percent of the front-line troops in the Persian Gulf War (Copeland, 1991:1).

Would you be comfortable as a partner in a commuter marriage? Consider some of the unique problems you would face in such a relationship. How would you handle social events? Would you attend events alone or in the company of a same-sex or an other-sex friend? How would you convey emotional support and intimacy from a distance?

(Gross, 1980). Couples in these relationships are pioneers. Few guidelines exist to help them, and they receive little social support, because living apart is contrary to the traditional American vision of married life.

In many ways being involved in a commuter marriage is like being single. On the one hand each spouse assumes all the responsibilities of maintaining a household, which can be burdensome. On the other hand, however, each spouse enjoys a considerable amount of freedom, especially in the use of time, much of which can be devoted to work and career advancement. Because of separate living arrangements, day-to-day conflict between work and family is not usually a problem.

Commuter couples, of necessity, have developed coping strategies for maintaining a sense of family. Many of these strategies require significant outlays of resources, particularly frequent telephone calls and travel to each other's place of residence. Interestingly, reports of women and men show that women feel more comfortable with commuter marriages than men do (Gross, 1980). This finding is consistent with other research that shows that men benefit more from marriage than women do. Living in a commuter marriage may liberate women from many domestic chores that they would otherwise have to undertake while forcing men to do for themselves what wives in the same location often do for them.

THE IMPACT OF WORK ON FAMILY RELATIONSHIPS

Much of the research conducted in the past on the impact of work on family life has been sex-segregated, that is, based on the assumption that work has a different meaning for women than for men. Although for women paid work was thought of as an option that had to be weighed against the disruption it would cause their families, for men it was considered a given. Men might have choices in the type of work they selected but not in whether they would work. Therefore, outside of their earning power, little attention was paid to how men's jobs affected their behavior in their families.

Studies of working women, in contrast, focused on different questions. Recall from Chapter 2 Talcott Parsons' functionalist view that a woman's role in the family is expressive and a man's is instrumental. According to Parsons, stepping outside these roles leads to family instability. Thus, prior to 1960 researchers assumed that the entry of mothers into the labor force would have negative consequences for the family, for example, children getting into trouble in school or with the law.

These traditional role definitions no longer adequately reflect the work and family experiences of women and men (if they ever did), especially those in dual-earner families. A new theoretical model is required that acknowledges the labor-force participation of both women and men. Thus, sociologist Joan Spade (1989) called for a sex-integrated model to understand the impact of work on the family. Such a model asks how the type of work women and men do shapes their orientations and behaviors in the home.

Given the increasing number of dual-earner families, this question takes on major significance. The attempts by dual-earner couples to integrate work and family experiences affect many aspects of family life: decision-making and power relationships, marital happiness, time together, and the household division of labor. In short, by examining dual-earner couples we can learn how gender roles in the family are changing in response to having both spouses in paid employment. (As you read the next section, keep in mind that some of the variations in behaviors and attitudes that can be observed among dual-earner families can be attributed to social class rather than to the presence of two wage earners.)

MARITAL POWER AND DECISION MAKING

One of the most consistent findings relating to the impact of work on family life revolves around the relationship between income and power in decision making. Money translates into power. When both spouses work, the traditional pattern of male dominance in the marital relationship shifts to one of greater equality in terms of more joint decision making (Godwin and Scanzoni, 1989). Spouses, most frequently wives, who do not contribute financially generally have little power in the relationship. The consequences of this may be severe. If the marriage is an unhappy one, the spouse without independent financial resources may feel compelled to stay in the relationship. On the other hand working may give an unhappy spouse the ability to leave the relationship. This relationship between independent resources and choice is illustrated by one of the respondents in a study of Chicana cannery workers. "It wasn't that my working hastened my divorce, in that it made my marriage worse, like Mario claims to this day. But rather it allowed me the freedom from a bad marriage" (Zavella, 1987:147).

This pattern of wives gaining more power as a result of their economic contribution holds true across most racial and ethnic groups. Researchers Jose Szapocznik and Roberto Hernandez (1988), for example, observed that Cuban women who migrated to the United States often found jobs sooner than their husbands did. Their economic contributions were then translated into gains in family decision making, thereby weakening the traditional Cuban patriarchal family structure. For the first generation of Cuban Americans these changes were often disruptive. Second-generation Cuban-American couples, who grew up in the United States, are less troubled by the greater equality in decision making and have tended to construct family relationships that are less male-dominated than those of their parental generation (Boswell and Curtis, 1983; Szapocznik and Hernandez, 1988). Similar patterns have been observed among Chinese- and Korean-American families as well (Min, 1988; Wong, 1988). Furthermore, given the consistently high level of labor-force participation of African-American women, it is not surprising to find that egalitarian decision making is common in African-American families as well (Gray-Little, 1982).

MARITAL HAPPINESS

Are couples with one earner happier than those with two? The results of research on this question are contradictory. Some studies have found homemakers to be happier than working wives (Stokes and Peyton, 1986; Saenz et al., 1989). However, these researchers found that much of the dissatisfaction of the working wives was attributable to the quality of the jobs they held—jobs with low pay, little status, and considerable stress.

Other studies, like the 1987 General Social Survey, found that working wives reported higher levels of happiness than did nonworking wives. Sixty-five percent of working wives reported their marriages to be "very happy," while only 1 percent reported that they were "not too happy." Nonemployed wives reported less happiness, with 55 percent identifying their marriages as "very happy" and 7 percent reporting their marriages as "not too happy." In contrast, men with working wives reported the same level of happiness as men with nonworking wives. In the same survey 69 percent of husbands both with and without a working wife reported their marriages to be "very happy" (Nock and Kingston, 1990:132–33).

What accounts for the differences in reported happiness between working and nonworking women? And what are we to make of the fact that married men report the same level of happiness whether or not their wives work? Perhaps the explanation for these patterns lies in the spillover effect discussed at the beginning of this chapter. Being happy at work may lead to happiness at home.

More important than work per se, however, are the couple's attitudes toward work. If the couple disagree about spousal employment or if the wife works only because of economic necessity, some tension and conflict are likely. On the one hand some husbands who adhere strongly to the good provider role might feel threatened or inadequate as a result of having a working wife. This is especially the case for some husbands whose wives earn more than they do. According to unpublished data from the 1991 Current Population Survey, more than one out of five wives earn more than their husbands. On the other hand, some women who desire only a domestic role may be embittered about their need to work. Thus, it seems that agreement on work and family roles is a key factor in marital happiness.

TIME TOGETHER The experience of marital happiness is related to another constraint confronting dual-earner families: finding time to be together, especially recreational time. "Couples with less time together express less satisfaction with their marriages" (Nock and Kingston, 1990:133).

Time is also related to two other important aspects of family living: household tasks and the care of children. Parsons' model of the family assumes that these are the wife's responsibilities and that they complement the husband's breadwinner role. Parsons didn't anticipate the contemporary widespread need for two incomes, however. What happens to housework and child care when wives share the breadwinner function? Do husbands reciprocate and share domestic responsibilities?

HUSBANDS AND THE DIVISION OF HOUSEHOLD LABOR

As more wives entered the labor force, social scientists began to investigate the degree to which husbands increased the amount of time they spent doing household work. Data collected from the 1960s to the mid 1970s showed that family work remained almost exclusively the province of women, whether or not they were employed. For example, a study of 1296 New York State families found that husbands spent about 1.6 hours per day in family work compared with 8.1 hours per day for housewives and 4.8 hours per day for working wives (Walker and Woods, 1976). It is not surprising then that compared to their spouses, wives experienced more **role overload**, a situation in which a person's various roles carry more responsibilities than that person can reasonably manage. As a result of role overload women have less free time for themselves and experience a diminished sense of well-being (Robinson, 1977).

Although there has been some change since the 1970s, husbands still do not make equal contributions to housework: "Husbands do less than one-quarter of the total work done by all household members" (Nock and Kingston, 1990:136). This observation has led some writers to describe women's dual role of worker and housewife as a "second shift" (Hochschild, 1989).

Inequity in family work has other consequences, too. Among wives there is a clear and positive connection between a fair division of family work and marital and personal well-being. Wives whose husbands do their share of family work are more satisfied with marriage than are other wives (Staines and Libby, 1986). Catherine Ross and her colleagues (1983) reported that wives whose husbands share housework are less depressed than other wives. According to a 1990 national opinion poll, next to money, "how much my mate helps around the house" is the single biggest cause of resentment among women who are married or living as if married, with 52 percent of the respondents reporting this as a problem. Women cite improvement in this area as one of the most important changes that would make their lives better (Townsend and O'Neil, 1990:28). In that same survey, 70 percent of the women respondents said that more help from men could help them balance the triple role of worker/mother/wife. In addition, 64 percent of the men agreed that by doing more at home, they could help balance work and family demands.

Thus, there seems to be some consensus among both women and men for the need to alter traditional gender roles. That some of this is occurring, albeit slowly, is indicated by Audrey Smith and William Reid (1986) in their study of role-sharing marriages and by Rosanna Hertz (1986) in her study of dual-career marriages. Hertz argues that dual-career couples generally do not start out with an ideology of equality in marital roles, but that it often emerges out of the opportunities and constraints they experience on a day-to-day basis.

Other researchers have found that men in dual-earner families who see themselves as co-providers with their wives do more domestic tasks than do men who still believe in the good provider role (Perry-Jenkins and Crouter, 1990). Some evidence suggests that this perception and behavior may vary by social class. For example, Jane Hood (1983) found that factory workers are more likely than professionals to see their working wives as co-providers, whereas upper-middle-class husbands had difficulty sharing the provider role with their wives (Fendrich, 1984). These different findings are related to the value a wife's earnings have to the welfare of the family. In working-class families the wife's contributions are more likely to be perceived as essential, whereas in middle-class families a husband with high earnings may view his wife's earnings as supplemental and not sufficient to compensate for the loss of a full-time homemaker.

CHILD CARE

Although some evidence suggests that fathers are taking a more active role in child care (see Chapter 10), the extent of their involvement has probably been exaggerated in the media. Both working and nonworking wives still do the majority of child care. This situation puts working women at a competitive disadvantage with male colleagues who are freed of this responsibility by their spouses. For women, having children constrains their labor-market activities. Women with small children have lower labor-force participation rates, and when they are employed, they are more likely to work

As more women enter the labor force, they become aware of the gender inequities in housework. Intellectually, many husbands also recognize the inequities, but most have not increased their share of housework to any marked degree.

Source: Reprinted with special permission of King Features Syndicate.

When both parents work, family roles often need to be renegotiated. Working women are asking for more equity in the division of household and child-care tasks. This father shares in the care of his young children.

part-time. For example, one study found that women responded to parenthood by reducing the number of hours they worked; men did not (Grant et al., 1990). This is especially true of poor women with limited education and skills. Finding a job that pays an income suf-ficient to cover child-care costs is unlikely for them. Compared to nonpoor families, who spend an average of 8 percent of their family income for child care, poor families spend 25 percent (Cattan, 1991).

SPLIT-SHIFT EMPLOYMENT AND PARENTING

When both parents work, child care becomes problem-atic. Some couples respond by split-shift employment and split-shift parenting, thereby enabling one parent to be home while the other is at work. By 1985 approx-imately 17 percent of all working mothers with chil-dren under 14 years of age had an evening or rotating shift job (McEnroe, 1991). This arrangement has costs as well as benefits. On the one hand parents rarely see each other, as was the case for Tim and Ellen, whom we met at the beginning of this chapter. This lack of time together can cause tensions that children also experi-ence. On the other hand children see their parents in equal roles, and they benefit from this dual parenting.

Couples who work the same shift face a different set of problems, the most serious of which is finding alternative child care. Table 11.1 shows the distribu-tion of primary-care arrangements for children in 1988. In 1977, 13 percent of employed women with

---

TABLE 11.1

Primary-Care Arrangements Used by Employed Mothers for Children Under 15 Years, Fall 1988

Type of Arrangement	Children Under 5	Children 5 to 14
Care in child's home	28.2	11.9
By father	15.1	7.1
By grandparent	5.7	1.1
By other relative	2.2	2.2
By nonrelative	5.3	1.5
Care in another home	36.8	4.0
By grandparent	8.2	1.4
By other relative	5.0	0.7
By nonrelative	23.6	1.9
Organized child-care facilities	25.8	2.5
Day/group-care center	16.6	1.7
Nursery/preschool	9.2	0.8
School-based activity	0.2	1.7
Kindergarten/grade school	1.3	75.5
Child cares for self	0.1	2.3
Mother cares for child at work	7.6	2.1

Source: Adapted from U.S. Bureau of the Census, 1992b, (August), *Current Population Reports*, Series P-70, No. 30, "Who's Minding the Kids?" (Washington, DC: U.S. Government Printing Office): Table D, p. 6.

a child under 5 years of age used organized day care. Eleven years later, 26 percent were using such facilities. Twenty-eight percent of the preschool children of working women were cared for at home, usually by the father or some other relative. Another 36 percent received care in someone else's home, primarily in the home of a nonrelative. Another 9 percent of children under age 14 were cared for by their mothers either at home or on the job. These mothers were frequently employed as private household workers or were themselves child-care workers who took in other children while caring for their own at home. The vast majority of children over 5 (76 percent) were already in school.

Regardless of the type of child-care arrangement in use, the majority of families who need child care confront two major problems: high cost and limited availability. Employers can help by subsidizing some of the costs of this care. About 2 percent of the nation's workplaces have opened child-care centers on the worksite, whose hours coincide with those of their parents (Kleiman, 1990). This arrangement allows parents to visit their children during work or lunch breaks, thus relieving parents of worry over how their children are managing without them. Yet affordable quality care is not readily accessible to all who need it, partly because many Americans still prefer mothers to be at home with their children. For years there has been a great debate about the impact of a mother's employment (but rarely a father's) on the well-being of children. The weight of the evidence today, however, suggests that children who receive *quality* child care suffer little, if any, negative consequences from maternal employment (Hamburg, 1992).

THE "MOMMY TRACK" The notion that child care is still primarily a woman's problem was highlighted when corporate consultant Felice Schwartz (1989) wrote an article for the *Harvard Business Review* outlining a controversial approach to the problem of child care and working women. She suggested that employers divide women into two groups based on whether they are career-primary or career-and-family women. Schwartz described the former group as women who are willing to put their careers ahead of family needs. She advised companies to identify these women early and put them on the same career track with talented men. The other women would make good workers, but to keep them Schwartz recommended that companies provide con-

siderations for their parental responsibilities, such as part-time employment, maternity leaves, and so on. The media labeled this position the "mommy track."

Criticism was swift to Schwartz's proposal. Some writers argued that such an approach would create a two-tiered system of women workers, with working mothers receiving fewer rewards for their work efforts. Ronnie Sandroff (1989) questioned why the adjustment for having children fell only on female workers. Rather than a "mommy track," there should be a "parent track." In fact, some fathers want to give more priority to their families. According to a 1991 article in the *Chicago Tribune*: "A recent survey showed that 75 percent of men would accept slower career advancement if they could have a job that let them arrange their work schedule so they could spend more time with their families" (1991d: Section 1A, p. 36).

The United States is about the only industrialized country that does not have a national child-care policy. This does not mean that the government does not support child-care programs. Rather, it means that the existing programs, such as Head Start, developed as isolated responses to specific problems rather than out of a consensus on the federal government's responsibility for assisting families at all economic levels.

INTEGRATING WORK AND FAMILY LIFE: RESOLVING ROLE CONFLICT

For the majority of people the transition to work, marriage, and parenthood requires taking on multiple roles. These roles frequently conflict with one another, placing a serious strain on families. **Role conflict** occurs when a person occupies two different roles that involve contradictory expectations of what should be done at a given time. Perhaps the most obvious and widespread example of role conflict in our society is the conflict between parent and worker. As more people (both married and single) find themselves occupying these roles, this form of role conflict will become even more common. Contributing to this problem are such elements as the absence of quality child care, troublesome work schedules, job-related travel, job transfers and relocations, and unanticipated emergencies.

The United States is not the only industrialized country with a rapid increase of working mothers in the labor force. Sweden and Canada have higher female labor-force participation rates than the United States; 63.9 percent and 58.4 percent, respectively (U.S. Bureau of Labor Statistics, 1991a:40). However, some of these industrialized countries invest considerably more public resources in child care than the United States does. For example, France and the Scandinavian countries have comprehensive child-care arrangements. In those countries widespread political support for child care has resulted in high-quality and widely used child-care facilities. The largest part of the cost is paid for out of tax dollars. Parents' fees cover only a minimal part of the cost. In Sweden, parents pay 10 percent of the cost of child care. Danish parents pay 23 percent. In France, child-care services are tax-financed, with parents paying 20 percent of the costs. France's system is a blend of child care, education, and health services based on free full-day preschool, subsidized day care, and licensed care in private homes. Approximately 90 percent of French children aged 3 to 5 attend preschools.

Why do you think the United States has been so slow in responding to the child-care needs of working parents? Should the United States implement tax-supported child care? What kind of child care do you or would you want for your child? How available is quality child care in the area where you live or work?

Source: David A. Hamburg, 1992, *Today's Children* (New York: Times Books), pp. 118–22.

STRATEGIES FOR CONFLICT RESOLUTION

Role conflict can be resolved in a variety of ways. Three common approaches are (1) establishing priorities within the home and workplace, (2) exiting one of the roles, and (3) making the role conflict public and demanding changes either within the family or within the larger society. There are benefits and costs to each of these solutions.

ESTABLISHING PRIORITIES   Establishing priorities requires making decisions about which activities are more important and will receive more energy and attention. This process is often complicated by gender, class, and the organization of work itself. For example, even though the gap in the labor-force participation rate of women and men is narrowing, society still assumes that men's first priority is work and that women's is the family. Hence, women who set work as their first priority and men who put their families first may confront considerable social pressure to change their priorities. Furthermore, many single-parent families as well as families requiring two earners may have limited options in selecting their priorities. Work may have to take precedence over family time. Finally, the way work is organized—starting times, days of the week, holidays and overtime requirements, and the need to bring work home—may present major obstacles to parents wishing to alter the balance of their work and family lives.

ROLE EXIT   A second method of resolving role conflicts involves exiting a role. This can occur in a variety of ways. A single parent or one of the spouses may leave the labor force or accept a less demanding job. This strategy may eliminate or minimize the immediate role conflict, but it can also be costly. Not only is family income reduced, but future employment opportunities for the affected worker may be diminished. Other people may choose to preserve the work role but to exit an unsatisfying marital role, either temporarily through a separation or permanently by divorce, a topic we discuss in Chapter 13.

PUBLIC AWARENESS   A third way to deal with role conflict is to make others aware of the problem. As more women enter the labor force, women

CRITICAL ISSUES

ROLE CONFLICT

Imagine yourself in each of these situations. What coping strategies could you use to resolve or minimize these conflicts?

Jim is a divorced father with custody of his two sons. He is also employed full-time as a systems analyst. Both of his sons are in school and in an after-school program, so Jim is able to manage the household without outside help. This morning his boss is expecting him to make a major presentation to a new client. His 6-year-old woke up with a temperature and a sore throat, which will force the child to stay home. Jim is in a quandary over how to handle this situation.

Marie is the mother of three children under 6 years of age. Her husband walked out on her a year ago, and she has been receiving welfare ever since. She wants to get a job, but she has only a high school education. The jobs she is

qualified for pay minimum wage. She has no one to help her care for her children, and were she to work and pay for child care, she would have less money than what she gets in public assistance. She enrolled in a community college to improve her skills, but she is having difficulty completing her courses because she is frequently absent due to child-care problems.

Barbara and Ted have been married for 35 years. Both are in their late 50s. Last year Barbara's widowed mother came to live with them after she was diagnosed as having Alzheimer's disease. Initially she was able to care for herself, but it is now clear that she can't be left alone. Barbara had promised her mother that she wouldn't put her in a nursing home. Barbara took a leave of absence from her job to care for her mother. Ted is increasingly

frustrated by the fact that Barbara is too tired to do anything with him in the evening and that they can no longer travel on weekends. He is insisting that Barbara make arrangements to institutionalize her mother.

After 10 years of marriage Sam and Betty have become a dual-career family. When their son Jason started school, Betty went back to work. Sam is heavily invested in his career as a stockbroker and rarely misses work or takes time off. When Betty was beginning her career, she would take time off to attend Jason's school plays and sporting events. She is now in a management track, however, and is afraid she will not be promoted if she devotes too much time to nonwork activities. Jason is complaining that they don't care enough about him to come to his activities.

and men frequently work side by side in offices and in factories. This arrangement has the potential for allowing women and men to see that gender inequality at work and at home adversely affects everyone's family well-being. Thus, greater numbers of working parents will demand that employers implement policies to assist them in meeting their dual obligations. Through negotiations, both collective and individual, employees are seeking changes in the organization of work (optional rather than required overtime, flextime, job sharing) and in benefits such as parental leave, child care, and equal pay for women. (These issues are discussed in more detail later in the chapter.) People are also pressuring the government to introduce or modify policies to help resolve conflicts between work and family responsibilities.

SPECIAL PROBLEMS OF WORKING WOMEN

Although the labor-force participation rates of women and men are converging, women still confront issues of inequity in the labor market that, in turn, can have a profound effect on their sense of worth and their family's economic well-being. Three issues are of special significance: occupational distribution, sexual harassment, and the gender gap in earnings.

OCCUPATIONAL DISTRIBUTION

Occupational distribution refers to the location of workers in different occupations. Although the media highlight stories of women and men who are in nontraditional occupations, for example, women construction workers and male nurses, most work is still thought of as either women's work or men's work. Table 11.2 shows the percentage of women and men in selected occupations. Women are more heavily concentrated in low-paying clerical or service jobs, whereas men are concentrated in higher-paying jobs of craftworkers and operators. Even though a slightly higher percentage of women than men are working in a professional specialty, women tend to be working in the lower-paid professions such as nursing or elementary school education, whereas men are more concentrated in the higher-paid professions of law, medicine, and engineering. As late as 1990, only 21 percent of lawyers and 19 percent of doctors were women (U.S. Bureau of Labor Statistics, 1991). Men have been even more reluctant to enter "women's" occupations in any significant numbers. Thus, job categories such as nursing and secretarial work remain over 95 percent female.

Race and ethnicity confound occupational distribution even further. Women of color are less likely than their white counterparts to be employed in managerial, professional, and sales jobs. Rather, they tend to be overrepresented in low-paying service and administrative-support jobs.

Occupational segregation restricts the options of both women and men. Additionally, however, evidence suggests that much of women's work is more stressful than most of men's work. According to a study conducted by the National Institute of Occupational Safety and Health, data-entry clerks (who are predominantly female) have the highest stress levels—higher than those of air traffic controllers. Secretaries have the second-highest incidence of stress-related diseases among workers (Reskin and Hartmann, 1986). These jobs share common characteristics. Tasks must be completed under pressure within limited periods of time, they offer little opportunity for creativity and autonomy, and they provide few rewards in terms of prestige or salary and benefits.

When women or men enter nontraditional occupations, they often encounter hostility from the other workers, adding to the level of stress. Often this takes the form of being excluded from the informal work groups that are so necessary to successful job performance and advancement.

SEXUAL HARASSMENT

Another problem workers—especially female workers—may experience is some form of **sexual harassment**—unwanted leers, comments, suggestions, or physical contact of a sexual nature, as well as unwelcome requests for sexual favors (Renzetti and Curran, 1992:95). Sexual harassment occurs in all types of work settings. Because of the sensitive nature of sexual harassment, accurate data on its extent are difficult to collect. Surveys of working women suggest, however, that 80 to 90 percent have been harassed at some point in their work life (Martin, 1989). Sexual harassment appears to be more prevalent in male-dominated occupations where some male workers seek to maintain control over women rather than recognize them as equals. For example, in a 1989 study of women lawyers, 60 percent reported they had been sexually harassed (Couric, 1989). One 29-year-old returning woman student provided a personal illustration of harassment at the job site: "I worked as a carpenter for 7 years. Many nights I came home and cried. I was the only woman on my first job. The men didn't want me there. They used to hide my tools and put obscene

TABLE 11.2

Selected Occupations by Percentage of Each Sex, 1990

Occupation	Women	Men
Executive, administrative, and managerial	40.0%	60.0%
Professional specialty	51.2	48.8
Technicians and related support	49.1	50.9
Sales occupations	49.2	50.8
Administrative support, including clerical	79.8	20.2
Service occupations	60.1	39.9
Precision, production, craft, and repair	8.5	91.5
Operators, fabricators, and laborers	25.5	74.5
Farming, forestry, and fishing	16.0	84.0

Source: Adapted from U.S. Bureau of Labor Statistics, 1991, (August), *Working Women: A Chartbook* (Washington, DC: U.S. Government Printing Office): Table A-1, p. 38.

notes in my lunch bucket. My next job was easier. There was another woman at the job site, and we ate lunch together. It helped to know I wasn't alone. After the men saw we could do the job, they left us alone; a few even became my friends after a while."

Although sexual harassment violates equal employment laws, enforcement is difficult. Many victims are afraid to report the harassment for fear of losing their jobs or being blamed for bringing it on themselves. These fears were crystallized for many women by the negative treatment University of Oklahoma law professor Anita Hill received when she testified before a 1991 Senate confirmation hearing that Supreme Court candidate Clarence Thomas sexually harassed her when she worked under his supervision at the Equal Employment Opportunity Commission. Workers who are sexually harassed report a number of problems both physical (chronic neck and back pain, gastrointestinal disorders, sleeplessness, and loss of appetite) and psychological (feelings of humiliation, helplessness, and fear). Harassment victims frequently bring these problems home with them, thereby adding tension to family relationships.

THE GENDER GAP IN EARNINGS

Regardless of how earnings are measured, women's wages are below those received by men regardless of race and ethnicity. Like occupational segregation, however, differences in earnings are exacerbated by race and ethnicity for both women and men. According to the U.S. Bureau of the Census (1991b), the median income for full time, year round workers in 1990 was:

White men	$30,186	Latinos	$19,134
Black men	$21,540	Black women	$18,518
White women	$20,840	Latinas	$16,186

For years researchers have struggled to explain why the wage gap persists even when workers are matched on the basis of years of experience, number of hours worked, education, occupation, and union membership. For example, one study found that educational attainment, work experience, and job tenure failed to explain the lower pay and status of female engineers compared to male engineers (Robinson and McIlwee, 1989). The general consensus of many of these studies is that discriminatory treatment is the major cause of the earnings gap. According to sociologist Beth Shelton, women's double workload holds down their earnings; the more time that is spent on housework, the less time one has for the job. In her research, Shelton found that "8.2 percent of the gender gap in earnings was due directly to women doing more housework then men" (cited in Kleiman, 1989:5).

Inequities in pay deprive families of greater purchasing power. One solution that has been proposed to narrow the gender gap in earnings is **comparable worth**, the principle of equal pay for different jobs of similar worth. To put this principle into practice requires evaluating jobs in terms of education, experience, and skill requirements, as well as the job's value to the community. To date only a few employers have put comparable worth into effect, mostly among state employees. Opponents argue that it is too expensive to do. Much work needs to be done in fostering more equitable pay for women and, hence, their families.

Some working parents have tried to resolve their work/family conflicts by working at home. What do you consider to be the advantages and disadvantages of this strategy? Would you like to work at home? Why or why not?

THE ECONOMIC WELL-BEING OF FAMILIES

All parents share a common desire to provide a decent standard of living for themselves and their families. Despite this goal, in 1990, 7.1 million families (11 percent) were poor, up from 5.3 million or 10 percent of all families in 1970 (Ahlburg and DeVita, 1992:36). Each year the federal government calculates the minimum level of income necessary to meet basic subsistence needs of families according to size and type. In 1991, the poverty level as determined by the federal government was $13,359 for a family of four and $6,652 for an individual.

POVERTY

Poverty rates are not randomly distributed across the population. They vary by family type, race, and ethnicity. Married-couple families have the lowest poverty rate (5.7 percent); followed by those with a male householder, no wife present (12.0 percent); and families with a female householder, no husband present (33.4 percent). Families headed by women accounted for the largest part of the increase in poor families since 1970. Children under 18 years of age account for 40 percent of the poor. As we will see in Chapter 13, over 60 percent of the children born since 1980 will spend some part of their life in a single-parent household. Thus, the proportion of children living in poverty is likely to increase (Kamerman and Kahn, 1988). This increase in the numbers of women and children who are poor is referred to as **the feminization of poverty**.

Although in absolute numbers most of the poor are white, white families had a lower poverty rate overall (8.1 percent) than black families (29.3 percent). Families of Latino origin had a poverty rate of 25 percent (U.S. Bureau of the Census, 1991d:7).

Many people believe that people are poor because they are lazy and don't want to work. Yet according to the Census Bureau, in 1990, in 59.6 percent of all poor families at least one person worked, and in 17.8 percent of all poor families two or more people worked. Being employed is not always sufficient to avoid poverty, however. Many jobs pay only the minimum wage and offer few, if any, benefits. Many are part-time or temporary jobs.

Women's wages play an important part in the economic well-being of families. In families where both husband and wife work full-time throughout the year, the wife's wages accounted for an average of 40 per-

cent of family earnings (U.S. Bureau of the Census, 1990d). Table 11.3 reveals the median weekly earnings of families in 1991. Half of all families have a weekly income above $669; half are below. This aggregate figure, however, conceals important differences by race and ethnicity and by type of family. White families, regardless of their structure, do better than families of color. However, family structure is an important factor in the economic well-being of families. The presence of two earners in the family increases the likelihood of achieving higher income levels. For every racial and ethnic group, dual-earner couples have the highest median weekly income, ranging from $940 for white couples to $757 for Latino couples. Not only do dual-earner couples have median weekly earnings nearly double those of single-earner families, but single-earner married couples earn considerably more than do families maintained exclusively by women. Moreover, single fathers earned considerably more than did single mothers. For example, families maintained by women had median weekly earnings of only $385, as compared with $514 for men. This discrepancy in women's and men's wages was true for white, black, and Latino families.

UNEMPLOYMENT AND UNDEREMPLOYMENT

To this point we have dealt with the complex connections between work and families. But what happens to families when this connection is broken? To date

TABLE 11.3

Median Weekly Earnings of Families by Type of Family, Race, and Latino Origin, 1991.

	All	White	Black	Latino
Total families with earners	669	695	484	495
Married-couple families	754	767	625	546
One earner	455	474	313	322
Husband	532	549	366	355
Wife	279	280	272	235
Two or more earners	911	922	776	732
Husband and wife only	929	940	796	757
Families maintained by women	385	399	339	343
Families maintained by men	514	529	401	462

Source: Adapted from Bureau of Labor Statistics, 1992, *Employment and Earnings* (Washington, DC: U.S. Government Printing Office): Table 52, p. 219.

the U.S. economy has not been able to provide jobs for everyone who wants to work. Moreover, the economy today is undergoing structural transformations that, in turn, affect the size and composition of the work force and, thus, family income. As a result of economic slowdowns, global competition, new technology, and plant closings, increasing numbers of people have been unemployed or underemployed for varying periods of time.

? *Have you ever been unemployed when you wanted to be working? Do you know anyone who is currently unemployed? How do the unemployed see themselves? How does society view them? How are family relationships changed when one or more members is unemployed?*

Unemployment affects individuals and families in many ways. Clearly, the immediate result of becoming jobless is the loss of or at least a lowering of income. This loss of income puts a severe strain on family budgets and in extreme cases can lead to homelessness. Unemployment can also have a negative impact on family and social life. For example, things often taken for granted—home entertaining, going out with friends for dinner or a movie, exchanging cards and presents—may no longer be possible. Children may feel isolated and rejected when they cannot participate in the activities of their friends.

Regardless of the causes, the impact of unemployment on family members can be enormous. To understand how devastating the experience of unemployment can be requires an appreciation of the role work plays in people's lives. Paid employment is a means for earning a living, for providing food, clothing, shelter, and other basic necessities for ourselves and for our families. Success or failure at this task is often the yardstick by which individual self-worth is measured. The unemployed repeatedly describe themselves as "being nothing," as "being looked down on," or as "having self-doubts." Being jobless can erode a person's self-esteem, which, in turn, can lead to other problems. As we shall see in the next chapter, a poor self-image may be a contributing factor to family violence. Besides giving us a sense of identity and worth, work also provides opportunities for social interactions and gives structure to our lives. Some people who lack this ordering in their lives frequently feel psychologically adrift and may seek to

escape these feelings through alcohol or other drugs. Other reactions to unemployment can be deadly. One researcher has statistically correlated the increase in the aggregate unemployment rate with increases in deaths, suicides, homicides, admissions to state mental hospitals, and sentences to state prisons (Bluestone, 1987).

UNEMPLOYMENT AND MARITAL FUNCTIONING
In addition to causing distress for individual family members, unemployment can affect the functioning of the family as a unit. Many researchers have found that unemployment is associated with lower levels of marital satisfaction, marital adjustment and communication, and harmony in family relations (Liem, 1985). Joblessness can also lead to a disruption in previously agreed-upon family roles, resulting in dissatisfaction for one or both partners. For example, Patrick Burman (1988) in his study of unemployment in Canada, found that when wives were unemployed, the egalitarian norms they had negotiated with their spouses disappeared. Consequently, the wives were forced back into the traditional role of housekeeper. As one of his respondents reported, "When I was working, it was more of a joint effort between my husband and I to get it done.... But when I was off then—I don't know if it was me or just the way things went—it became more my responsibility, which I really hated. There was no escape from...there would always be something to do.... I hate it" (quoted in Burman, 1988:171).

Burman also found that when husbands were unemployed, they tended to do more housework, but not all of it. Although there were only a small number of househusbands in his sample, he found that the men most likely to accept this role were middle class, had some familiarity with feminist ideology, and felt confident that they would find another job, at which time they could abandon the househusband role.

VARIATIONS IN FAMILY RESPONSES TO UNEMPLOYMENT
As in other areas of family life, families differ in their ability to respond to a member's unemployment. In some cases families can absorb the loss of income and provide emotional and physical support to their unemployed member until such time as new work is found. How family members react to unemployment depends a great deal on how the family functioned prior to the onset of unemployment as

well as on the reasons for the unemployment. Patricia Voydanoff (1983) uses family stress theory to explain the conditions under which unemployment contributes to family crisis or disrupts family functioning. The model she uses is Reuben Hill's (1958) formulation of the A, B, C, X model of family crisis. A is the event (unemployment) that interacts with B (the family's crisis-meeting resources) that interacts with C (the definition the family gives to the event). This produces X (the crisis—the degree to which family functioning is affected).

Unemployment (A) hits some families harder than others. Families who receive unemployment compensation or severance pay or who anticipate new employment might experience fewer financial and psychological hardships than families lacking these benefits. Among the unemployed, women are least likely to have these benefits. Families also differ in the number and effectiveness of the resources (B) they have for coping with stressful events. Family savings, homeownership, additional sources of income, good communication, and problem-solving skills can minimize the problems associated with unemployment. Additionally, how the family defines unemployment (C) is critical to the outcome. "If the family perceives the event as a crisis-producing situation, the likelihood of crisis is increased; if the family considers the event to be normal or manageable, family vulnerability to crisis is reduced" (Voydanoff, 1983:244).

Implicit in the family stress model are mechanisms for minimizing the negative consequences of unemployment. Leaving aside the need for more jobs, adequate financial assistance in the form of unemployment compensation and health insurance would help families get through a period of unemployment with fewer difficulties. Additionally, educational or counseling programs aimed at improving family functioning would help families cope with the stresses of unemployment. Finally, knowledge about the structural causes of unemployment would help families define unemployment in a realistic way and lessen the tendency to blame individual members for the problem.

AGE, RACE, ETHNICITY, AND UNEMPLOY-MENT Table 11.4 shows that like social rewards, unemployment is not evenly distributed throughout the population. In 1991, the unemployment rate for teenagers between the ages of 16 and 19 was 18.6 percent, compared with 6.7 percent for the popula-

TABLE 11.4

Unemployment Rates by Sex, Age, Race, and Latino Origin, 1991

Sex and age	Total	White	Black	Latino origin
Total				
16 and over	6.7%	6.0%	12.4%	9.9%
16 to 19	18.6	16.4	36.3	22.9
Women				
16 and over	6.3	5.5	11.9	9.5
16 to 19	17.4	15.2	36.1	21.9
Men				
16 and over	7.0	6.4	12.9	10.1
16 to 19	19.8	17.5	36.5	23.7

Source: Adapted from the Bureau of Labor Statistics, 1992, *Employment and Earnings* (Washington, DC: U.S. Government Printing Office): Table 44, p. 212.

tion 16 and over. The problem was even more severe for youth of color. The unemployment rate for black teenagers, nearly double that of white teenagers, was 36.3 percent. Teenage girls had slightly lower unemployment rates than their male counterparts.

Youth unemployment is troubling for a number of reasons. First, a family may depend on income contributions from teenage members for its economic well-being. Even when the teenagers' earnings go directly toward meeting personal needs—clothing, books, and entertainment—this contribution is likely to relieve some of the pressures on household budgets. Second, research indicates that adolescents who have a job are less likely than their unemployed counterparts to become involved in illegal activities such as drug dealing and theft. Finally, if this high unemployment rate continues, the likelihood that these teenagers will establish stable marriages and make long-term commitments to the labor force will diminish.

Similarly, in adulthood the burden of unemployment continues to fall more heavily on people of color despite the progress in civil rights and affirmative action of the last 3 decades. Among the hardest hit by unemployment are Native Americans. According to the Bureau of Indian Affairs (1985), 49 percent of the potential Native-American labor force or, alternatively, 39 percent of those who were actively seeking work were unemployed (cited in John, 1988:342–43).

Additionally, significant numbers of people experience what economists call **underemployment**. Underemployment takes several forms. Some of the underemployed are people who are employed part-time but who want to work full-time, a condition called *involuntary part-time employment*. In the second half of 1989 there were 5 million such workers (Foster, Siegel, and Von Brook, 1989:37). Other underemployed individuals work full-time but make very low wages. They are called the **working poor**, and their numbers are growing. The category of underemployed also includes workers with skills higher than those required by their current job. Like the unemployed, those who are underemployed worry about family finances and may also experience low levels of marital and family satisfaction as a result.

This discussion of unemployment and underemployment illustrates C. Wright Mills's distinction between personal troubles and social issues (see Chapter 1). Unemployment of this magnitude is not simply a personal trouble of affected families; it is also a social problem. Thus, solving the problem of unemployment requires action on the part of the larger society to create more jobs or to provide meaningful alternatives for those who cannot work. Two pieces of legislation—the Employment Act of 1946 and the Full Employment and Balanced Growth Act of 1978—recognize the federal government's obligation to use all practical means to secure the right to employment for all citizens. To date, however, neither the federal government nor the private sector has been able to reach this goal.

HOMELESSNESS

Unemployment can trigger many problems. One of them is homelessness. Although unemployment often leads to homelessness, employment does not always guarantee a place to live. In one study, 11 percent of all parents seeking help in finding shelter were homeless in spite of being employed (Maza and Hall, 1988). Other studies "have found that 5 to 10 percent of homeless adults are employed full time, and between 10 and 20 percent work half time or when they can find it" (Foster, Siegel, and Von Brook, 1989:5).

Homelessness is not a new phenomenon either in world history or U.S. history (Rossi, 1989). The minutes of seventeenth-century New England town meetings point to the existence of a transient homeless population that was composed mainly of single men and women but that also included a substantial number of two-parent families. The colonial authorities responded to the problem of homelessness by making social distinctions among the homeless population. Homeless members of the community would usually be provided for in some manner. Newcomers, however, especially those without visible means of support, did not fare well. Some were subjected to a process called "binding out," in which they were indentured to local families to work as servants or common laborers. Others experienced a "warning out" process whereby they were told to leave town. This latter process was given new meaning during the depression and in more recent years when local authorities removed the poor from their communities by providing them with bus tickets to other cities. This "Greyhound relief," as it was called, was aimed at curtailing the tax burdens of the towns by removing indigent people (Rossi, 1989; Wright, 1989).

THE HOMELESS TODAY The homeless population today is diverse and encompasses every age, race, religion, and marital status. The homeless inhabit every region of the country, from inner-city neighborhoods to the rural countryside. If you spend any time in parks or public facilities, be they bus or train stations, libraries or airports, you will encounter the homeless. What you will observe if you look closely is a population that includes the young and the old, the unmarried and family groups, veterans, the working poor, and people from all racial and ethnic groups.

How many Americans are currently homeless? No one can answer this question with certainty because there is no agreement on how to define homelessness. Sociologist Peter Rossi (1989) distinguishes two kinds of homelessness. The "literally homeless" are those who already live on the streets. The "precariously housed" are those who are in danger of losing their homes or who have lost their homes but have found temporary shelter with friends or relatives. Extended families often provide support by taking in homeless relatives, sometimes exhausting their own resources in the process. Therefore, if we use the first definition only, the number of homeless we count will be smaller than if we expand our definition to include those who are poorly or only temporarily

The American Dream of owning a home is beyond the reach of many families today. In fact, increasing numbers of families have slipped into homelessness. For this San Jose family, home is a car.

by the U.S. Department of Housing and Urban Development to a high of 1.3 to 2.0 million put forth by the National Alliance to End Homelessness (National Academy Press, 1988, cited in Foster et al., 1989:3). The U.S. Conference of Mayors (1988), in their survey of 25 cities, found that families with children make up 33 percent of the homeless population. Not only are children at risk of suffering physical and emotional problems because of their homelessness, but homelessness reduces their chances of staying in school or even remaining at their appropriate grade level. More significantly, homelessness may rob them of their parents. Twenty percent of the homeless families in one study had left minor children in someone else's care for extended periods of time (Maza and Hall, 1988).

CAUSES AND REMEDIES Although experts disagree on the exact numbers of the homeless population, researchers, social workers, public officials, and community activists are in general agreement that homelessness occurs as a result of a number of distinct but interrelated factors:

- A rapid decline in the supply of low-income housing
- An increase in the number of families living in poverty
- Mental illness, compounded by a shortage of adequate services and government policies of deinstitutionalization
- Family violence
- Adolescent runaways
- Unemployment and low earnings
- Substance abuse
- Budget cuts in public welfare programs
- Overall increases in the cost of living
- Racism and sexism

housed. Most studies of the homeless have used the first definition, thereby understating the extent of the problem.

The fact that homeless people tend to move in and out of shelters and public view on a regular basis also makes counting them difficult. For some people homelessness is short-term—the result of a fire, an eviction, family estrangement, or temporary financial difficulties—whereas for others it is permanent. Finally, we can count people only if we can locate them. Not all homeless people are in shelters. Many live in parks, cars, cardboard boxes, doorways, or other places not readily accessible to researchers. Thus, any published figures on homelessness must be interpreted with caution. Estimates range from a low of 192,000 to 586,000 in a controversial 1984 study

Because homelessness has many causes, no quick and easy solutions are likely. However, reducing poverty, adding to the supply of affordable housing, and expanding employment opportunities would ameliorate a good portion of the problem. The current visibility of the homeless and the discomfort they generate in the population may become a catalyst for political action. Congress took a tentative step in this direction in 1987 with the passage of the McKinney Homeless Assistance Act, which appropriated money for shelters, for medical care and services for the chronically mentally ill, and for a variety of

CRITICAL ISSUES

THE EXPERIENCE OF HOMELESSNESS

My name is Lisa McMullan. I am here with my husband, Guy, and my four children, Jamie, Ryan, Morgan, and Ryder. The story of my family's experience with homelessness began in Mile City, Montana, early in 1986. My husband and I owned a house there, but when my husband's job was phased out due to the farm crisis, we could no longer make the mortgage payments, so we gave the house back to the bank, sold everything, and came East in the spring.

We first stayed with my mother-in-law, but that didn't work out because there wasn't enough room for all of us. There were seven of us living in the basement. After a few months we moved to Baltimore, and my husband and I both held a number of jobs. In November or December 1986, we began to have problems paying the rent on our apartment. (Lack of construction work; day care too expensive.) After several eviction notices, we found ourselves without a place to live and with no place to go.

I called around, with the help of Social Services, to several shelters in Baltimore, but no one would take us as a whole family. Finally, the Salvation Army offered us a room to stay in. The room was very small with six people in it. The conditions at the shelter were very stressful for me and my family, and the children particularly became much more difficult to manage. The food was not that good, as you can probably imagine.

It was very crowded, and there's a weird feeling that goes along with being there. You feel like you're nothing because you suddenly don't have a home. You know you've done all you can do and it isn't your fault, but the whole situation makes you feel like you must have done something wrong.

What were the steps leading to the McMullan's homelessness? Could this happen in your family? How does the experience of homelessness affect people's sense of self-worth? What can be done to help families like the McMullans?

Source: James Wright, 1989, *Address Unknown: The Homeless in America* (New York: Aldine de Gruyter): 4, 5.

---

rehabilitation programs including vocational training. After years of neglect the public may now be willing to make homelessness a priority. In a 1987 survey conducted by the Roper Organization, 68 percent of the respondents favored spending more money on caring for the homeless (cited in Wright, 1989:34). Perhaps this will lead to the development of social policies aimed at providing a minimally decent standard of living for all.

RESTRUCTURING THE WORKPLACE

Throughout this chapter we have seen how the relationships between work and families have changed drastically. However, a gap exists between the current structures of families and the way other institutions continue to relate to them. For example, many businesses, medical facilities, and government offices are open from 9 to 5 when most people are at work. Such schedules may not present problems to traditional families with a single breadwinner and a full-time homemaker. Today, however, when the majority of families are composed of either dual-earner couples or single heads of households, such time conflicts have enormous consequences. This is true not only for parents with children but also for workers who are responsible for bringing an elderly parent or other relative to a doctor. A 1986 study by the Bureau of National Affairs found that such conflicts caused working parents to be absent from work about 8 days per year (cited in Zedeck and Mosier, 1990:244).

This situation is slowly changing. For example, some branch offices of the U.S. Post Office and some neighborhood medical clinics have extended or altered their traditional hours. Increasingly employers are aware they have to make concessions in this area. Given the low birthrates of the last 2 decades, employers will find themselves competing for workers. The majority of new entrants into the labor force by the year 2000 will be women and people of color. Those employers who institute organizational changes to help employees balance work and family demands will probably enjoy an advantage in attracting new workers.

WORKPLACE CHANGES

One of the major problems working parents face is getting children off to school in the morning and having a parent there to greet them when they come home. We are probably all familiar with stories of "latchkey children," children who return home after school to an empty house. According to the U.S. Department of Labor, 7 million children age 10 or under care for themselves after school (Robinson et al., 1986:4). Telephone companies report an increase in calls around 3 P.M. as parents and children check in with one another. Some school districts offer after-school programs to assist working parents, but most do not. Without outside support, families frequently find they must solve this problem by having one parent, usually the wife, work part-time rather than full-time. The economic consequences of this approach include low pay, few benefits, and little or no mobility for the affected worker.

One way companies could respond to this need is by providing permanent part-time employment with benefits for employees with young children. Another alternative is **job sharing**, in which two workers split a single full-time job. Each job sharer gets paid for half-time work, although most usually contribute more than a half-time performance. Thus, the existing evidence suggests that companies would benefit by getting more than half-time performances for half-time wages. Despite this, however, employers have been slow to experiment with this option. Such changes, however, would help only people in higher-income brackets who could afford to have reduced incomes. Other options are needed for workers in low-paying jobs.

A third approach to meeting family scheduling needs has met with slightly more success in the United States. **Flextime** arrangements that allow employees to choose when they arrive at and leave work—within specified time limits—can relieve some of this strain. Flextime is especially helpful when one parent can start work early and arrive home early, while the other works a later shift. To date only about 12 percent of U.S. workers have flextime, compared with more than 50 percent of the work force in Western European countries. Among U.S. employers with flextime programs are the federal government, IBM, Hewlett-Packard, Kimberly-Clark, and Washington National Insurance Company. Does allowing workers to select their hours hurt a company's chances of success? To date there is no evidence that flextime diminishes worker productivity; in fact, some evidence suggests the opposite. Hence, flextime can benefit both workers and employers.

FAMILY LEAVE

Much of the role conflict experienced by workers could be reduced by adequate family leave, which would include maternity and paternity leaves for the birth or adoption of a child as well as leaves to care for an elderly parent. Although more employers are attempting to meet the family needs of their workers, the majority have done little. Costs are often cited as the reason for not developing these types of programs. Some chief executives are now questioning this belief, however. In speeches to colleagues, the chairperson of the Evanston, Illinois–based Fel-Pro Company, which supplies parts to the auto industry and which provides extensive family benefits to employees, argues that most businesses are shortsighted. He argues that the typical cost–benefit analyses do not include the intangible gains of improved quality of life these programs can offer workers and their families, which, over the long run, can improve worker productivity. For example, 48 percent of female employees and 25 percent of male employees have spent unproductive time at work because of child-care issues (cited in Zedeck and Mosier, 1990:244). Work disruptions from failures in child-care arrangements affected 6 percent of the 1.5 million employed women with infants in 1988 alone (U.S. Bureau of the Census, 1992b:14).

Until as recently as 1993, the United States was one of the few industrialized countries that did not have a national family-leave policy. In 1990 and again in 1992, Congress passed the Family and Medical

Leave Act, which would have allowed either parent to take up to 3 months of unpaid leave for births, adoptions, and family emergencies. The bill excluded workers in companies with fewer than 50 employees. Because it provided only for unpaid leave, it would not help low-income workers. Despite its limited scope, the bill was opposed by many business interests and was twice vetoed by President Bush. Finally, in February 1993, Congress passed the bill for a third time, and President Clinton signed it into law.

Some business leaders oppose family-leave legislation, claiming that it is too expensive and that mandated benefits interfere with the free-enterprise system and should be determined by negotiations between employers and employees rather than by government policy. Proponents, on the other hand, argue that existing state laws mandating parental leave are neither costly nor difficult to implement. A recent study of parental-leave laws in Minnesota, Oregon, Rhode Island, and Wisconsin seems to support this argument. According to the Families and Work Institute, which conducted the study, "Only 9 percent of businesses polled said it was difficult to implement the laws; 71 percent had no increase in costs for training, and 55 percent said there were no administrative costs in implementing the policy" (Locin, 1991:3). The study also found that fathers took more leave after the laws went into effect, and, not surprisingly, women with higher household incomes took more weeks off than did women with lower household incomes.

Furthermore, unlike all other advanced industrialized countries, the United States has no statutory provision that guarantees a woman pregnancy leave, either paid or unpaid, or that guarantees that she can return to her job after childbirth. In the United States pregnancy leaves are covered by the Pregnancy Discrimination Act of 1978, which requires that pregnant employees be treated the same as employees with any temporary disability. One obvious limitation to this law is that employers who don't offer disability insurance to their other employees are not required to provide pregnancy leaves to their workers. Family sociologist Joseph Pleck (1988) points to an additional problem with using disability as the mechanism for dealing with childbirth: It excludes fathers from parental leave. Only a handful of U.S. businesses provide any paid parental leave, and relatively few men take advantage of it, most likely out of fear that to do so could hurt their careers. Researchers found that less than half of all women employees were covered by some form of disability or sickness benefits that provided income replacement for about 6 to 8 weeks of leave at the time of childbirth. They found no paid maternity leaves that extended beyond 12 weeks and no guarantee that women would get their jobs back if they took more than the standard disability time of 6 to 8 weeks. This is in marked contrast to Western Europe, where the minimum paid leave is 3 months (Kamerman et al., 1983). Sweden has one of the most generous parental-leave policies of any country. Either parent can take parental leave for 12 months, with the government providing 90 percent of the parent's income (Kamerman and Kahn, 1987).

Given the widespread movement of mothers into the labor force, the growing number of workers caring for elderly parents, the inability of many families to meet basic economic needs, and the lack of fit between workplace organization and other institutions, it is likely that pressure will build in the United States for a national family policy.

SUMMARY

Although we frequently think of work and family life as discrete activities, research shows that the worlds of work and family affect each other in significant ways. The quality and stability of family life depend to a large extent on the type of work available to family members. Work can have spillover effects, both positive and negative, on family life.

In 1900, only 20 percent of women aged 14 and older were in the labor force, compared with approximately 86 percent of men in that age category. Today, 58 percent of women and 76 percent of men 16 and older are in the labor force. Prior to World War II, the majority of women workers were young, single, poor, and women of color. As late as 1970, only 30 percent of married women with children were in the labor force. In 1990, the comparable figure was approximately 60 percent.

Women work for many of the same reasons men do, particularly to support themselves and their fami-

lies. The rapid entrance of married women with children into the labor force has altered family life in
many ways. The traditional nuclear family consisting
of a working husband and a full-time homemaker
with dependent children is in the minority today. The
typical family today is a dual-earner or "two-paycheck" family. The attempts by dual-earner couples to
integrate work and family experiences affect many
aspects of family life: decision-making and power relationships, marital happiness, time together, and the
household division of labor. Working couples often
experience role overload and role conflict as they
struggle to balance the demands of work and family.
Lack of affordable quality child care is particularly
stressful for working parents of preschool children.

Although the labor-force participation rates of
women and men are converging, women still confront issues of inequity in the labor market. Among
them are occupational distribution, sexual harassment, and a gender gap in earnings.

Unemployment and underemployment can have
severe negative impacts on marital functioning.
Unemployment is not evenly distributed throughout the population. It is particularly high among
teenagers and people of color. One of the problems
connected with unemployment is homelessness.
The homeless population today is diverse and
encompasses people of every age, race, religion, and
marital status.

Employers are becoming more sensitive to the
family needs of their employees. Some programs that
have been introduced to help workers are job sharing
and flextime. Given the widespread movement of
mothers into the labor force and the growing number
of workers caring for elderly parents, pressure will
likely build for a national family policy.

KEY TERMS

labor-force participation rate	comparable worth
commuter marriage	feminization of poverty
role overload	underemployment
role conflict	working poor
occupational distribution	job sharing
sexual harassment	flextime

QUESTIONS FOR STUDY AND REFLECTION

1. Describe the major changes in the characteristics
of the U.S. labor force that have occurred in the last
half of the twentieth century. How have these
changes affected the quality of family life in the
United States? Today approximately 60 percent of
families have two earners. For this reason many people argue that the United States needs a national
family policy. To what extent do you think the federal government and employers have a responsibility
for resolving some of the problems confronting
working parents? Would you be willing to see tax
dollars subsidize all or a portion of child care for all
working families? Explain.

2. How were household tasks divided in your family
of orientation? What was the basis for this division of
labor? Did family members perceive this division as

equitable? Do you plan to replicate this division of
labor in your family of procreation? Why or why
not? How is the division of household labor related
to marital functioning and satisfaction?

3. Imagine that you are part of a dual-career family
and that your spouse has been offered a promotion
that requires moving to a new community where you
don't know anyone. Such a move would mean that
you would have to resign your current position and
look for a new job. How would you make the decision? Would gender play a role in your decision?
What problems do families face when they have to
relocate? How can you minimize disruptions associated with job relocation?

4. Imagine that you (or your spouse or a parent)
suddenly lost your job. Using the Hill model of fami-

ly crisis, how well do you think you and your family would react to this event? What resources do you have to meet such a problem? What benefits would you be entitled to receive? If you suddenly lost your home, what would you do? Where would you go? How would you and your family manage in a homeless situation? Why do so many families have so much trouble dealing with unemployment?

FURTHER READING

BLEWETT, MARY H. 1990. *The Last Generation: Work and Life in the Textile Mills of Lowell, Massachusetts, 1910–1960.* Amherst: University of Massachusetts Press. The author uses oral histories to document the experiences of Irish, Jewish, Greek, and Polish millworkers during the first half of the twentieth century in a New England city in the throes of industrial decline.

KOZOL, JONATHAN. 1988. *Rachel and Her Children: Homeless Families in America.* New York: Crown. A journalist provides an intimate and sensitive look at life for America's homeless.

MILLER, ANGELA BROWNE. 1990. *The Day Care Dilemma: Critical Concerns for American Families.* New York: Plenum Press. The author focuses on the critical decisions parents make when they arrange child care for their children.

ROSEN, ELLEN ISRAEL. 1987. *Bitter Choices: Blue-Collar Women In and Out of Work.* Chicago: University of Chicago Press. This is an in-depth study of married blue-collar women, their work experiences in the electrical and apparel industries, and the consequences of employment and unemployment on workers and their families.

SCHWARTZ, JOHN E., AND THOMAS VOLGY. 1992. *The Forgotten Americans.* New York: Norton. The authors make visible the growing numbers of working poor and show how doing everything right—working full-time, year-round—no longer ensures a good life for families.

VANNOY-HILLER, DANA, AND WILLIAM W. PHILLIBER. 1989. *Equal Partners: Successful Women in Marriage.* Newbury Park, CA: Sage. Examines some of the changes in family structure brought about by the entrance of women into the labor force. Provides insight into what makes for successful marital relationships today.

Chapter 12

VIOLENCE
AND ABUSE

Joseph Bland expected his dinner to be ready and on the table when he arrived home from work. He had particularly strong feelings about how his wife, Bette, should cook his meat—medium rare. One day Joe became outraged when he found that his meat was too well done. He attacked Bette, first verbally and then physically. As had happened every time before, the neighbors closed their windows and doors and sighed, "There goes Joe again." In 15 years of battering, no one had ever tried to help Bette. When Joseph had tired himself out he stopped battering Bette and left to go to the local bar for a beer.

When Joe returned home late that night, Bette was asleep in bed. Still angry about the way his dinner meat had been cooked, he began battering Bette again and, in the process, kicked her out of the bed. When Bette hit the floor she broke her neck and spine, and died. After many delays and much red tape, Joe was prosecuted for Bette's murder and sentenced to 10 years in prison. A model prisoner, he was released for good behavior after 5 years.

Shortly after Joe got out of prison he remarried. His second wife, Joyce, was no better at cooking meat for Joe than Bette had been. No matter what type of meat she cooked, she never seemed to get it just right, and she suffered the same consequences as Bette had before her. One evening, a year and a half after the marriage and the battering began, Joe became so outraged when Joyce cooked his meat too rare that he picked up a carving knife and stabbed her to death. In Joe's second encounter with the criminal-justice system he encountered a sympathetic jury who saw the murder and battering as tragic but basically the result of a fit of passion. They therefore recommended that the judge grant Joe leniency. Based on the jury's recommendation, the judge sentenced Joe to 10 years. Joe can be free in another 5 years.

What does this scenario suggest about public attitudes toward woman battering and abuse? What does it suggest about the criminal-justice system's response to family violence, especially woman abuse? Why do you think these women stayed in the battering relationship with Joe? Is it fair to "blame" them for staying? Why do you think no one got involved? Are you in a battering relationship? Have you ever been? If yes, why did you remain for the time period that you did? What problems, if any, can you identify with the criminal-justice system and its handling of cases of violence against women? What can society do to reduce or eradicate family violence?

"Lizzie Borden took an ax and gave her father 40 whacks. When the job was neatly done she gave her mother 41." To many Americans, Lizzie Borden's behavior seems atrocious or inhuman. Surely if such violence occurs it is an unusual act of cruelty that only the most deranged person could commit. Families, after all, are "havens in a heartless world" (Lasch, 1977:8); they represent love and good feelings among members.

Unfortunately, this picture of families as havens of nonviolence is not accurate. Although most family members do not take an ax to each other, every year millions of Americans intentionally injure, abuse, assault, or murder members of their own families. Domestic or intrafamily violence is interwoven into the very fabric of U.S. society. It is believed to be the most common, yet least reported, crime in this country. In no other U.S. institution or group is violence and abuse more of an everyday occurrence than it is within the family.

THE ROOTS OF FAMILY VIOLENCE: A HISTORICAL CONTEXT

Many people think of family violence as a uniquely American phenomenon that has come into being only in recent years. Records, however, show that as early as the 1640s Americans recognized the existence and seriousness of family violence and abuse and attempted to prevent or punish such behavior (Pleck, 1989). The extent of family violence in America's past is difficult to ascertain, however, because official records were not always kept. Likewise, we know very little about the history of violence across cultures because most cultures around the world have not officially recorded such data. Nonetheless, based on his examination of cultures around the world, anthropologist David Levinson (1981) has concluded that family violence is not rare. Furthermore, wife beating is the most common form of family violence. Levinson's findings are consistent with those of most

SOME HISTORICAL FACTS ABOUT WOMEN AND VIOLENCE

- Under the Roman Empire, a husband could chastise, divorce, or kill his wife for adultery, public drunkenness, and other behaviors.
- In the Decretum (c. 1140), the first enduring systematization of Christian church law, women were described as "subjects to their men" and in need of punishment to correct them from their supposed inferiority and susceptibility to the influence of the devil.
- Well into the seventeenth century, in many European countries, including England, a man legally could kill his wife for certain behaviors.

- The eighteenth-century Napoleonic Civil Code, which influenced Swiss, Italian, French, and German law, gave men absolute family power, and violence was considered to be grounds for divorce only if the court believed that it constituted attempted murder. Thus, men could legally use violence against women up to the point of attempted murder.
- English common law held that men had a legal right to beat their wives so long as the stick they used was no thicker than the husband's thumb. (This law

is the basis of the contemporary saying "rule of thumb.")
- Sexual assault as well as physical beatings were an integral part of the female slave experience in the United States.
- In the 1800s in both Europe and the United States, men could use "reasonable" physical force against women, which included black eyes and broken noses.
- A nineteenth-century Mississippi court declared that husbands could use corporal punishment on their wives. Not until 1883 was wife beating banned in the United States.

---

social-science research into family violence in the United States, which finds that women are far more often the victims of violence and offenses against family members than are men. In fact, approximately 95 percent of the adult victims of domestic violence in the United States are women (National Woman Abuse Action Project, 1991).

VIOLENCE AGAINST WOMEN

The historical subordination of women and children is linked to their *experiences* of violence and assault in the family. Historical accounts by colonists and missionaries as well as anthropological studies inform us of the extent to which violence against women has been a part of the institutional structure of various societies throughout history. Consider for a moment the historical facts about women and violence presented in the FYI box.

The folkways and mores of various cultures show the universality of violence in women's lives.

According to feminist philosopher Mary Daly (1978), such practices as the binding of young women's feet in China, the Indian *suttee* (the burning of Indian women on the funeral fires of their husbands), European and American witch burnings, the mutilation of African women's genitals through female circumcision,[*] and past and some present gynecological practices in the United States, such as unnecessary surgery and forced sterilization, are all variations of the same thing: violence against women.

---

[*]Female circumcision takes several forms. The mildest form involves cutting the hood of the clitoris in a manner similar to the practice of male circumcision. The most severe form of female circumcision involves the removal of the clitoris, labia minora, and most of the labia majora, after which the vagina is stitched closed except for a very small opening to allow for the passage of urine and menstrual blood. Perhaps the most common form of female circumcision involves removing the clitoris and part of the labia minora. This latter type of circumcision is currently practiced in about 40 countries, primarily in East and West Africa, and it is not uncommon for as many as 90 to 98 percent of the female population to have undergone one or another form of circumcision without the aid of any anesthetics (Renzetti and Curran, 1992).

VIOLENCE AGAINST CHILDREN

Throughout history, children also have frequently been victims of violence and abuse, including sexual assault. Violence against children is linked to cultural values and attitudes that have defined children as the property of families. In many societies, families were ruled by fathers who virtually held their children's life in their hands. Historian Samuel Radbill (1980) reports that in ancient times a father had the power to withhold the right to life from his child by abandoning the child to die. Although there are no clear records of the actual number of children who died as a result of such practice, **infanticide**—the killing of infants and young children—appears to have been widely practiced throughout much of history. In some societies infants would be killed if they cried too much or if they were sick or deformed. Infanticide has been practiced by a wide range of groups, including some early Native-American cultures, where newborns were thrown into a pool of water and declared fit to live only if they rose to the surface and cried. Even adult children did not escape the power of fathers. In France, for example, fathers had the legal right to kill an adult son or daughter under certain conditions.

Historically, girls and children born to unmarried parents have been the primary victims of child violence, abuse, and murder. Like their adult counterparts, girls have been far more vulnerable to family violence and abuse than boys have. Female infanticide continues even today in some societies, such as in parts of China where boy babies are preferred.

In the past much of the violence against children was socially acceptable. Although such treatment is not generally acceptable today, some level of violence against children by parents continues to be condoned (or certainly tolerated) in the United States. Unlike Sweden, where a parent can be imprisoned for a month for striking a child, in the United States many parents believe in and use corporal punishment when disciplining their children.

VIOLENCE AGAINST THE ELDERLY

Another group frequently victimized by family violence is the elderly. Little is known about the historical incidence of elder abuse. We do have examples of societal violence directed against the elderly: Older women were the common targets of witchcraft trials, and older men were the most frequent murder victims. During the sixteenth, seventeenth, and eighteenth centuries, elders controlled the economic resources of the family, and independence for adult children came only with the parents' death. Elderly parents were thus frequently the targets of violence and abuse from adult children who sought to express their frustration or to take control of family resources. Following this period came the industrial era, during which adult children had opportunities to become independent of their parents. Parents often became financially dependent on their children rather than the other way around. This period seems to have witnessed relatively little reported elder abuse (Sigler, 1989).

VIOLENCE AGAINST SIBLINGS

Another kind of violence that historically has occurred within families is sibling abuse. To date, however, few systematic studies of nonfatal sibling violence in the United States have been conducted. One of the problems involved in documenting sibling violence and abuse is that historically parents have considered sibling conflict to be "normal" behavior and therefore have not generally reported it. Even today, there is little information on or public awareness of sibling violence.

Given the history of family violence around the world, why are Americans just discovering it as a serious problem? How much do you know about family violence? More likely than not, you probably know someone who is a victim of such behavior. Moreover, it is possible that you have been or will be a victim of family violence yourself. Why is violence of all types so common among members of the most intimate of all human groups—the family? In the following pages we explore this and other questions about family violence. In the next section we look at domestic violence and assault within the context of U.S. culture.

FAMILY VIOLENCE AND U.S. CULTURE

Crime statistics alone do not capture the full range of violent crime in this country. Nonetheless, in 1987 the Uniform Crime Reports indicated that an aggravated assault occurred every 38 seconds in this country; a forcible rape occurred every 6 minutes; and a murder occurred every 25 minutes. Despite our fears to the contrary, it is not a stranger but a so-called loved one or an acquaintance who is most likely to assault, rape, or murder us. In fact, Americans are more likely to be hit, beaten up, sexually assaulted, and killed in their own homes by other family members than anywhere else or by anyone else. Approximately one-third of all murders in U.S. society are perpetrated by one family member against another, and violent assaults within families have been estimated to account for nearly one-fourth of all serious assaults.

Violence, abuse, and assault are deeply rooted in U.S. history and culture, beginning with the founding of this country. The early European-American settlers subjected the native populations to widespread violence, abuse, and other atrocities, forcing them off their homelands and onto barren-land prisons called "reservations." Similarly, the American slave system was created and maintained through systematic violence and oppression.

Today, violence pervades U.S. popular culture. Among our most popular films, for example, are westerns, war movies, and crime dramas that contain (and sometimes romanticize) widespread death and destruction. The heroes of these films frequently are violent "macho" males portrayed by actors such as John Wayne, Clint Eastwood, and Sylvester Stallone. Many of the crime dramas in particular center around violence perpetrated by males against females. In these films, women are almost routinely terrorized, physically and sexually assaulted, and murdered. Television, like film, presents a constant stream of violent images. Prime-time television transmits 13 acts of violence per hour, with even higher rates of violence in cartoons that are watched primarily by children (Stephan and Stephan, 1990). By the time U.S. children reach the age of 15, they will have witnessed more than 13,000 television killings.

Similar trends appear in contemporary music, particularly rock videos. Violence is a recurrent theme, as are rape, mock rapes, the implication of rape, and the anticipation of rape and conquest by males. As sociologists Nijole Benokraitis and Joseph Feagin have concluded: "More than half of the music television videos (MTV) feature or suggest violence, present hostile sexual relations between men and women as com-

Films such as *Die Hard* glorify the macho, violent male.

monplace and acceptable, and show male heroes torturing and murdering women for fun" (1986:10). The audience for these videos includes many teenagers and young adults who are thus exposed to these attitudes and behaviors as they are growing up.

All the violations of women that we present in our popular culture contribute to what has been called a **rape syndrome** or *men's proclivity to rape*—the group of factors that collectively characterize men's likelihood to rape. For example, the unwanted, unsolicited pinch on a woman's behind, the wolf whistles and lewd remarks directed at women when they walk down the street, and the unwelcome compliments about a woman's anatomy are all acceptable behaviors among various groups of men. When we tolerate these so-called minor acts, other acts of aggression and violation seem more acceptable.

MYTHS ABOUT VIOLENCE AND ABUSE

A number of oversimplifications, myths, and distortions block our understanding of the nature and extent of marriage, family, and intimate violence. These myths involve issues of race, class, gender, and the mental state of the abuser. Although research has shown many of these beliefs to be overstated or blatantly false, many people continue to believe them. As a consequence, much family violence and abuse goes unrecognized and unreported.

In this section, as we discuss the various forms that family and intimate violence takes, we present and *debunk*—that is, expose the falseness of—several common myths associated with family violence. We begin by refuting three common myths: (1) Family violence is rare, (2) only mentally ill or "sick" people abuse family members, and (3) family violence is essentially a problem of the lower classes. We then turn our attention to the many victims, targets, and perpetrators of marriage, family, and intimate violence.

Myth 1: Family violence is rare.

Fact: Family violence is one of the most common of all crimes. Acts of family violence occur every 15 seconds in the United States (National Woman Abuse Action Project, 1991).

Until recent years, Americans considered family violence to be relatively rare. The fact that few reliable statistics on family violence were kept helped perpetuate this misconception. When researchers began to turn their attention to family violence, they discovered that it was far more common and severe than most of us thought.

Consider, for example, the following statistics. Approximately 11 percent of all reported criminal assaults are aggravated assaults between husbands and wives. In some states assaults between spouses constitute as many as one-half of all reported assaults (Gelles and Cornell, 1990). Violence will occur at least once in two-thirds of all marriages (Roy, 1982). Each year, an estimated 6 million American women are battered by their husbands or partners; 4000 of them are killed. One in four women who commit suicide was a victim of family violence at some point in her life (National Woman Abuse Action Project, 1991). The Federal Bureau of Investigation (1987) reported that 30 percent of female homicide victims are killed by their husbands or boyfriends, compared with 6 percent of male homicide victims who are killed by wives or girlfriends. About 2 million U.S. women have been victims of sexual abuse by a father or stepfather (Dunn, 1990). Every year, over 1 million children between the ages of 3 and 17 are abused (punched, kicked, beaten, or attacked with a knife or gun) by parents, stepparents, and guardians.

Because the majority of family life occurs in private, obtaining accurate statistics on the extent of family violence and abuse is difficult. The facts and figures presented above, however, go a long way in indicating the pervasiveness of family violence and shattering the myth that it is a rare occurrence.

Myth 2: Only mentally ill or "sick" people abuse family members.

Fact: Fewer than 10 percent of all cases of family violence and abuse are caused by mental illness or psychiatric disorders (Straus, Gelles, and Steinmetz, 1980).

When we consider some of the atrocities that family members have committed against each other, it is easy to understand why many people accept the myth that only the mentally ill could possibly be violent toward those they love. For example, a father has sexual intercourse with his 4-month-old daughter; a mother drowns her infant twin daughters; a mother and her common-law husband batter and scald their 2-year-old daughter in boiling hot water until she dies (Straus, Gelles, and Steinmetz, 1980). Shrugging off these events as atypical cases in which someone has simply "gone over the edge" misrepresents the realities of family violence and serves to maintain and perpetuate a psychopathology myth of family violence. In fact, the majority of abusive family members possess none of the symptoms or problems normally associated with people who are mentally ill or are suffering from personality disorders (Straus, Gelles, and Steinmetz, 1980). Whatever we think of their behaviors, these people are "normal" in the psychological sense of the word. In fact, we would probably have considerable difficulty identifying most perpetrators of violence and abuse as such if we met them at school, at work, or at a party.

It is probably less painful or easier emotionally for us to think that perpetrators of violence are "sick" or "deranged." This kind of thinking often allows us to separate ourselves from this behavior and view it as someone else's problem. The tendency to locate family violence within the personal characteristics of the abuser causes us to lose sight of or ignore completely the social and structural origins of family violence and abuse. As we will see later in this chapter, sociological explanations of family violence discount the idea that violence is located solely in the personality or temperament of the perpetrator and, instead, focus on interactions among family members and the interplay between families and their social environment.

Myth 3: Family violence is essentially a problem of the lower classes.

Fact: Family violence is not restricted to any one social class; it occurs throughout society.

A review of the research on family violence reveals that such violence occurs in every type of social, racial, economic, and age group. The 1987 death of 6-year-old Lisa Steinberg and the subsequent arrest of her parents—Joel Steinberg, a New York City attorney, and Hedda Nussbaum, a former editor of children's books at Random House—may have shocked many Americans, but they also made clear that family violence can be found throughout society at every social-class level.

In November 1987, New York City police, responding to a call for help, found Lisa Steinberg severely battered and abused and barely alive. Her 18-month-old brother was tied to his playpen and dressed in urine-soaked clothing. Lisa died shortly thereafter. During the trial for her murder (which ended with the conviction of her father, Joel), it was revealed that Hedda Nussbaum herself had been a constant victim of physical violence and abuse throughout her 17-year live-in relationship with her children's father. For almost 2 years this case received extensive media attention. Why do you think this particular case so captivated Americans? The answer probably is that the case did not fit the common stereotypes of family violence. Instead of being perpetrated in a run-down apartment in an inner-city neighborhood by lower-class, unemployed "minority-group" parents (as many Americans envision family violence), the abuse of Lisa, her brother, and her mother occurred within a white, middle-class, professional family environment.

The myth that family violence is confined to the lower classes is the second most pervasive myth about family violence behind the myth of mental illness (Gelles and Cornell, 1990). Perhaps like all myths, this one contains a grain of truth in that researchers have repeatedly found more reported family violence and abuse among the lower and working classes than among other classes.

These data do not mean, however, that lower-class families are more violent than other families. An

Society encourages men to express their hostility through physical aggression, whereas women are expected to suppress their anger. One result is that approximately 95 percent of adult victims of domestic violence are women.

important bias in these data is that they are confined to reported cases. Thus, they represent only those individuals or families who get caught in the act of family violence and abuse. Members of lower-class families run a far greater risk of being labeled "violent" or "abusers" than do college graduates or highly paid professionals (Newberger, Reed, Daniel, Hyde, and Kotelchuk, 1977). This is due, in part, to the fact that the lower classes have fewer resources and lack access to and power in institutions where such labeling takes place. Murray Straus and his colleagues, for example, report a case in which a physician declined to report a family for suspected child abuse because the suspected abuser was a fellow doctor (Straus, Gelles, and Steinmetz, 1980).

Overall, statistics reveal that one out of four middle-class women reports physical abuse (Steinmetz and Straus, 1974) and that educated, successful men such as lawyers, doctors, politicians, and business executives beat their wives as regularly and as brutally as do men in other classes (Saline, 1984). It is clear, then, that violence is not confined to lower-class families.

To understand the relationship between social class and family violence, we must first be aware of the factors that are most closely associated with woman battering. According to researchers, violence against women is most likely when the following circumstances are present: The husband is unemployed or employed only part-time, usually in manual labor; the wife is a full-time housewife; two or more children are present in the home, and disagreements over the children are common; family income is low; and both spouses are worried about economic security, or the wife is strongly dissatisfied with the family's standard of living. These factors tend to be more characteristic of lower-income families; therefore, rates of violence among such families may be slightly higher.

PHYSICAL ASSAULT: THE CASE OF BATTERED WOMEN

> A spaniel, a woman, and a walnut tree
> The more they're beaten the better they be.
>
> —Old English proverb

In this section we consider both the patterns of abuse and the strategies of resistance by victims of violence. Because 95 percent of all spousal assaults are committed by men, we pay most attention here to woman assault or battering. Woman assault has several dimensions. Those most commonly discussed in the literature are battering and sexual assault. Battering, in fact, is the single major cause of injury to women—more frequent than automobile accidents, muggings, and rapes combined (National Woman Abuse Action Project, 1991). Often the physical assault of women is accompanied by sexual assault, and it sometimes ends in the murder of the victim (Finkelhor and Yllo, 1985; Pagelow, 1988).

Most experts agree that woman battering is probably the most common and one of the most underreported crimes in this country. Approximately every 25 seconds a woman is battered. While you are reading this paragraph, four women will be severely beaten. The person who is responsible for raising our consciousness on this subject is Erin Pizzey, whose pioneering work titled *Scream Quietly or the Neighbors Will Hear* (1974) shocked many people. It also made public what had been hidden in the privacy of family life for decades, namely, that vast numbers of women were being physically and emotionally brutalized by their husbands or other men and these women basically had no place to go for assistance, support, or advice. Since Pizzey's book, woman battering, along with child abuse, has received a greater share of public, professional, and scientific attention than any other form of family violence.

Perhaps because the question of intimate violence was overlooked until recently, the research that has been conducted has certain limitations. One shortcoming is the tendency to group all battering against women as "wife battering." In fact, violent treatment is not restricted to married women. Rather, women in all marital categories are battered by men whom they date, are related to, cohabit with, or simply know.

Another limitation of the mainstream literature on woman battering is that it most often does not represent the experiences of women of color or lesbians. Like other experiences, the experience of intimate violence is not the same for all women. How exactly it differs, however, is not clear from most research. Although some of the research indicates that race, class, and to some degree sexual orientation are important factors in the incidence and nature of intimate violence, seldom do such discussions provide clear documentation. Most of this research adopts one of three approaches: It fails to mention the race of the women included, it acknowledges that only white women are included in the research, or it includes some women of other ethnic groups but not in proportions comparable to their numbers in the larger society (Asbury, 1987). Researchers have yet to investigate systematically, for example, whether there are any issues unique to women of color in violent relationships.

Much the same can be said about sexual orientation. Most of the research on intimate violence either fails to mention the sexual orientation of the people included in the sample or acknowledges that only heterosexuals were studied. The social pressures that contribute to family violence affect women and men of all sexual orientations and races. Due to continued prejudice against homosexuals, however, much of the violence that occurs in lesbian and gay relationships either goes unreported or is judged a "just reward" for people who pursue a "deviant" lifestyle. Moreover, many lesbians deny the very existence of lesbian battering. This denial no doubt is grounded in the desire to maintain an image of lesbian relationships as violence-free and egalitarian. Unfortunately, this approach has left many lesbians vulnerable, isolated, and at high risk (Levy, 1991).

WHAT IS WOMAN BATTERING?

In the family violence literature, the terms **woman battering** and *woman assault* are used interchangeably to refer to a range of behaviors that includes hitting, kicking, choking, and the use or threatened use of objects and weapons such as guns and knives. Because many battered women are also sexually abused, some discussions of woman battering include **sexual assault**—violence in the form of forced sexual acts that include vaginal, oral, and anal penetration; bondage; beating; torture; mutilation; bestiality; and group or gang rape. Still other discussions include emotional as well as physical assault.

In general, the pattern of the battering experienced by women is referred to as the **battered-woman syndrome** and is defined in terms of frequency, severity, intent to harm, and the ability to demonstrate injury. Following a classification scheme presented in 1979 by social scientist Murray Straus, most researchers today define and classify battering in terms of severity. Battering is said to be severe if it has a high likelihood of causing injury, it causes the victim to seek medical treatment, or it is considered grounds for arrest. Certain forms of battering like slapping, pushing, shoving, grabbing, and throwing objects at the victim do not fit this category.

Battering is generally cyclical in nature. Family violence researcher Lenore Walker (1984) has proposed a *cycle of violence theory* that includes three stages: (1) tension building, in which tension escalates gradually, making the woman increasingly uncomfortable in anticipation of the impending abuse; (2) acute battering, in which the woman is the victim of severe physical and verbal abuse; and (3) loving contrition, in which the man apologizes for his behavior, professes his love, and promises that he will never do it again.

Although defining woman battering so as to include every possible type of physical violence is difficult, the limitations of current definitions should not be overlooked. Limiting battering or assault to discrete physical actions excludes a wide range of violence that women experience. Battering is often accompanied by verbal abuse, psychological abuse, and threats or actual violence toward children and other loved ones. Moreover, ignoring "mild" or "less severe" violence overlooks the fact that any use of violence in a marriage or intimate relationship can have long-lasting detrimental effects on both the victim and the couple relationship (Frieze and Browne, 1989). Thus, a definition of battering that takes into account a fuller range of the violence and abuse is needed.

HOW PREVALENT IS WOMAN BATTERING? As of 1992 only three states had mandatory reporting laws for spousal violence. Consequently, researchers in this area must rely primarily on crime statistics, police reports, and scattered hospital records. The other major source of information on the incidence of woman battering is a body of research studies that rely primarily on the self-reports of women (for example, Walker, 1979, 1984; Straus, Gelles, and Steinmetz, 1980). Estimating the incidence of woman battering is difficult primarily because it typically occurs in private and more often than not goes unreported. Added to this is the fact that women who are battered or assaulted "only once" are rarely labeled as battered. For these reasons, some researchers estimate that the true incidence of woman battering may actually be double the rates reported in most studies.

The difficulties of self-reports of battering notwithstanding, a surprising number of women and men admit to committing or being the victim of a wide range of battering and violent acts within their intimate relationships. Some researchers estimate that as many as 25 to 33 percent of all U.S. women (around 12 to 13 million) are battered at least once in the course of their intimate relationships (Pagelow, 1984). Violence defined as less severe is even more common in intimate relationships (Edelson, Miller, Stone, and Chapman, 1985; Gelles and Straus, 1988).

Moreover, women who are physically violated by intimates face a much higher risk of being recurring victims of violence than do women who are victims of stranger violence. For example, a recent National Crime Survey revealed that one-third of the women who had been assaulted by an intimate were assaulted again within 6 months of the first reported assault, compared with approximately one-eighth of the victims in stranger assaults.

When woman battering is compared across marital status it has been found that women who cohabit are more likely to experience battering than are either single or married women. In fact, cohabiting women are four times more likely to suffer severe battering or violence than are married women (Yllo and Straus, 1981). How might we account for this? Possible explanations are that cohabiting women may simply report battering more often, that violence against cohabiting women is more likely to be labeled as battering than is violence directed against married women, and that cohabiting women may be less willing to accept a battering situation because they are less dependent economically and may not have children.

WHY DO WOMEN REMAIN IN ABUSIVE RELATIONSHIPS?

If the violence and abuse are so bad, why do women stay in these relationships? This question is often raised and is indicative of our lack of information concerning battered women. Probably one of the most pervasive gender myths pertaining to woman battering is that these women somehow enjoy being beaten. In addition, battered women bear the brunt of considerable **victim blaming**—essentially justifying the unequal treatment of an individual or group by finding defects in the victims rather than examining the social and economic factors that contribute to their condition. Many people maintain that female victims of domestic violence are somehow responsible for their mistreatment, which explains their unwillingness to leave the relationship. The fact is, however,

It is ironic that those people who claim to love or care about each other are the most likely to abuse each other.

that women do not enjoy, provoke, or deserve battering. For many women, however, leaving is not an option. Leaving a battering situation is not so simple as just packing up and leaving.

Research in this area indicates that women remain in battering relationships for a variety of reasons (see for example, National Woman Abuse Action Project, 1991; Dobash and Dobash, 1979; Hoff, 1990). One of the most common reasons is fear. A battered woman may be threatened or attacked if she tries to leave. She may also be concerned for the well-being of her children and may even fear that her abuser will kill himself if she leaves. In addition to fear, economic dependence and the lack of community support can keep a woman in an abusive relationship. Financial dependence on a man often means that a woman has no resources of her own with which to make changes. Moreover, the community may not have any programs or resources to help battered women or their children. Even if a woman is financially secure, she may not perceive herself as being able to deal with economic matters outside the relationship.

Sometimes women remain in battering relationships because of religious beliefs. Some women feel that their faith requires them to keep their marriage and family together at all costs and to honor and obey their husband, submitting to his will. Other times women remain in such relationships because they sincerely believe in the notion of the "cult of domesticity" and family harmony (Dobash and Dobash, 1979). Even though their situation does not fit this ideal, they continue to believe that the ideal is the way it should or can be. They often feel physically and emotionally trapped by society's expectation of them: Society labels them as stupid if they stay in the relationship and a failure if they leave.

Some women remain in battering relationships because they believe that children must be raised in a household with a father present. Thus, they endure physical and emotional abuse to keep the family together for the children's sake. Very often, it is when the violence is directed at her children that a woman will take the children and leave. More than half of the children whose mothers are battered also are victims of physical abuse.

In some cases the fear of being alone keeps women in an abusive relationship. Often women in battering situations have no meaningful relationships outside their marriage or intimate relationship. The husband or lover may have systematically cut off all her ties to family, friends, and other supportive people. Having nowhere to go and no one to turn to she remains with her abuser. Although some people might not understand this, some women in abusive relationships remain because of pity—they feel sorry for their abuser. They believe that he really loves them but he simply can't control himself. In pitying the abuser they often put his needs ahead of their own.

Finally, a common reason why women remain in violent relationships is love. Many women want the violence to end, but not the relationship. The relationship may have positive aspects that these women feel are worth saving. They love their partner and believe that he loves them as well. They may take many steps to try to stop the abuse; leaving the home may be their last resort.

Battered women actively seek help from a variety of sources in ending the cycle of violence. These sources include police, lawyers, health-care personnel, family members, and the clergy. Very often, however, the failure of these professionals and systems to provide adequate support keeps women in violent relationships. Some clinical psychological research suggests that women usually remain in violent relationships because they have been brutalized

into a state of submissiveness. Walker (1979) called this passive submission "learned helplessness," a situation in which battered women learn to anticipate violent attacks, but because they are unable to prevent the attack, they become passive and complacent and lose their initiative to leave the situation. Thus, to blame battered women for their situation of battering obscures the complex realities of the lives of these women.

In spite of all the reasons why some women remain in abusive relationships, most battered women do leave their abuser at some point, even if only temporarily (Dobash and Dobash, 1979). It is estimated that battered women who leave the battering situation do so, on average, seven times before they leave permanently (Bannister, 1992).

 Mentally put yourself in the shoes of a battered woman. Would you leave? Where would you go? How many services are available for women who are victims of courtship or marital violence at the college or university you are now attending? Are there offices you can go to? People who you can talk to? Do you know women who are in battering relationships? What reasons, if any, do they give for remaining in such relationships? Are they similar to or the same as some of those found above?

THE SEXUAL ASSAULT OF WOMEN

Battering is not the only form of abuse experienced by women in intimate relationships. Millions of women in the United States and around the world have suffered or will suffer some form of sexual assault. *Sexual assault* is a broad term that incorporates any behaviors, either physical or verbal, intended to coerce an individual into sexual activity against her or his will. Sexual assault is extremely widespread in U.S. society, with women and children representing the majority of the victims. In fact, the average woman is as likely to suffer a sexual attack as she is to be diagnosed as having cancer or to be divorced (Johnson, 1980).

Probably the most extreme form of sexual assault is rape. **Rape** is legally defined as sexual intercourse forced by a man upon a woman against her will. This definition overlooks the fact that men and boys sometimes are victims of rape as well. The overwhelming majority of rape victims, however, are female. Contrary to what some people believe, rape is not about sexual arousal. Rather, it is about the violent abuse of power. Most rapes are not committed by strangers but by people known to the victim. In fact, about 33 percent of all rapes in the United States take place in the victim's home, and 83 percent are perpetrated by husbands or acquaintances (Bannister, 1992).

Rape is the most frequently committed violent crime in the United States. It is also the least reported of all such crimes: Nine out of ten rapes go unreported (Bannister, 1992). The FBI (1987) estimates that 1 woman in every 12 will be a victim of rape or attempted rape during her lifetime. Estimates of rape would be even higher if they included assaults on young girls by their fathers, stepfathers, and other male relatives (usually categorized separately as incest) and cases of statutory rape. Statistics on rape provided by the FBI do not include these categories, nor do they include date and marital rape (Lott, 1987).

Females of all ages have been victims of rape. That no age is immune to rape is indicated in the findings from a study of a Washington, D.C., hospital in which those treated for rape ranged from a 15-month-old baby girl to an 82-year-old woman (Benokraitis and Feagin, 1986). Adolescent and young adult women are at the highest risk, however. Data concerning the likelihood of rape indicate a link between a woman's status, her race, and rape, with African-American, teenaged, and urban working-class girls running the greatest risk of being raped (Lott, 1987). Furthermore, divorced or separated women have been found to be more vulnerable to rape than have women who have never been married. Married women are much less likely to be raped than are divorced, separated, or never-married women. The likelihood of being raped is also higher for female heads of households and has a direct relationship to the amount of time a woman spends in public places (Andersen, 1988).

Men and boys are estimated to be victims in less than 10 percent of all rape cases (Renzetti and Curran, 1992). They are at greatest risk of being raped under conditions of incarceration. And they are even less likely than women to report that they have been raped. Gay men, like their heterosexual counterparts, seldom report this type of victimization.

RAPE MYTHS

An enormous amount of myth surrounds rape. Many people, male and female alike, hold erroneous notions about rape, rape victims, and rapists. You have probably heard most of these myths, and you might even believe some of them. Two of the most persistent rape myths are that: (1) male sexual violence is caused by the attitudes and behaviors of female victims, and (2) African-American males are the primary perpetrators of rape. In the following discussion we examine these two myths more closely.

RAPE AND RACE Many people mistakenly believe that the majority of rapists are African-American males who are usually strangers to their victims. In fact, as we have seen, in most cases the rapist knows his victim. Statistics reveal that most rapes, especially those of white and young female victims, occur within the same race. Therefore, the myth that African-American men commit the majority of rapes is just that—a myth.

Nevertheless, the myth of the black male rapist, especially of white women, persists. As some scholars have pointed out, such a myth is dangerous in that it diverts the attention of white women away from the most likely sources of sexual assault: white men. At the same time, it serves as a justification for negative attitudes toward and treatment of African-American males.

BLAMING THE VICTIM Another common myth surrounding rape is that most (if not all) women secretly desire to be raped. According to this belief, rape victims have generally acted in a manner that "invited" the rape; for example, they were a tease, had a sexy smile, were out too late, were too friendly, or were dressed seductively. The fact is that women actually fear rape; in fact, they fear it more than any other crime. Researcher Susan Griffin (1971), for example, expresses the view held by most women:

> I have never been free of the fear of rape. From a very early age I, like most women, have thought of rape as part of my natural environment...something to be feared...like fire or lightning. (Quoted in Lott, 1987:149)

Women must constantly act defensively; they must try not to be alone in public, especially at night. Such fear acts to pressure some women into accepting their oppression and subordination. Rape myths notwithstanding, no matter how a woman dresses, walks, or talks, when she says no she means no, not yes or maybe. A man who has forced sexual intercourse with a woman who says no is exercising his power and ability to dominate her, and he is committing the violent crime of rape.

MARITAL RAPE

The limited available information suggests that marital rape is widespread. As with other forms of intimate violence, the majority of victims are female. Victims of marital rape are often referred to as "hidden victims" because they seldom report their experiences.

The impacts of marital rape are no less serious and are sometimes more frightening than those of rape by strangers. Some researchers have found, for example, that the closer the association or prior association of the victim and the rapist, the more violent the rape tends to be (Russell, 1982). Consequently, wives who are raped suffer greater and longer trauma than other female rape victims do. They often feel betrayed because the person was someone they loved or cared for. As a consequence they stop trusting others. These feelings can lead to long-term anxiety and fear (Finkelhor, 1984a).

Researchers have identified several factors associated with marital rape. Among these factors, four have been most important: (1) the historical foundations of marriage in this country, (2) the establishment of marital exemption in rape laws, (3) the socially and economically disadvantaged position of women, and (4) the violent nature of U.S. society and its "rape culture" (Pagelow, 1988). The last two factors were discussed under family violence. Let us briefly examine the first two.

At the beginning of this chapter we pointed out the historical foundation of violence, which is firmly linked to the historical foundation of marriage. As you might recall from that discussion, husbands had absolute power over wives, including control over the wife's body. This idea, in conjunction with the British common-law notion that marriage represents a merger of husband and wife into a single identity—namely, that of the husband—provided the rationale for not legally recognizing the concept of marital rape. Thus, laws prohibiting rape contained spousal exemption clauses, which meant that a husband could not be prosecuted for sexually assaulting his wife.

Until the mid 1970s, marital rape was not a crime in this country. In 1977, Oregon became the first state to repeal the marital exemption clause to its rape statute. Since that time, similar clauses have been eliminated or modified by about half the states (Pagelow, 1988). In some states a husband may be prosecuted for rape only if the wife can show that the assault occurred after legal papers to end the marriage had been filed in court or that the couple were not living together at the time (Russell, 1990). At the same time, however, in 1980, 13 states broadened their marital rape exemptions to prevent the prosecution of a man who rapes the woman with whom he is living (Lott, 1987). This *cohabitor's rape exemption* or *voluntary social-companion rape exemption* further limits women's ability to pursue rape cases in the criminal-justice system.

THE CRIMINAL-JUSTICE RESPONSE TO WOMAN ASSAULT

Every part of the criminal-justice system—the police, prosecutors, judges, jurors—is critical to eliminating family violence generally and woman abuse specifically. Unfortunately, the system has refused to intervene on women's behalf, except when violence is extremely severe or death has occurred. It is often said that women are doubly victimized: first by their assailant and second by the criminal-justice system. A major reason for this is that the criminal-justice system, like society in general, historically has considered family violence to be a private matter, not a criminal issue. Consequently, offenders rarely have been arrested or punished, and victims have received little, if any, protection or support.

In this section we examine the criminal-justice response to woman assault in terms of the following two categories: (1) the attitudes and behaviors of people involved in the criminal-justice system, and (2) various court procedures and legal statutes that limit women's ability to receive redress.

ATTITUDES AND BEHAVIORS

The attitudes of police officers who respond to calls of family and intimate violence are critical in determining how these victims are treated. Although some progress has been made toward sensitizing police to the issues and concerns of battered and sexually assaulted women, many police still do not understand the battering cycle. These police often resent having to respond again and again to the same violent household. Most police calls for battering do not result in arrest. Based on cumulative studies of actions taken by police when answering family dispute calls, social psychologist Donald Dutton (1988) estimates that police arrested the alleged batterer in only 7 percent of the cases, even when women were injured. Moreover, when arrests are made, the offenders are generally released after a few hours. Very often they go home and continue their violent behavior.

Moreover, those involved throughout the criminal-justice system have not been immune to the racist, sexist, and homophobic ideas prevalent in U.S. society. Thus, women have often been faced with police who believe that women provoke men into violent acts and then stay with these men because they like to be beaten. African-American women have been further confronted with police and others who dismiss intimate violence as a natural part of African-American culture. The reactions of police to victims of lesbian and gay violence frequently have ranged from skepticism to outright hostility and violence.

If an arrest is made, the likelihood of the case going to court is very low. Prosecutors are often reluctant to prosecute men who batter or rape their wives. They rationalize their behavior by contending that the victim would probably not show up or prosecute her assailant if the case went to trial. It is true that some women do not pursue or follow up their complaints of physical and sexual assault. This is due, however, not to some hidden masochistic trait in these women but rather to the fact that the system with which they must deal is often indifferent and insensitive and officials often actively discourage them to pursue their complaints. As a result, they lack confidence that these people or the system generally will protect them and accord them proper redress.

If a woman's case gets to court, she often finds that she as much as her assailant is on trial. She is often questioned as if she did something wrong and "caused" the violence. Unfortunately many judges today are insensitive to or uninformed about the nature of domestic violence. This helps explain why male offenders usually are not convicted of a criminal offense. According to attorney and sociologist Shelly Bannister (1991), when males are convicted for their violence, judges tend to be lenient and seldom sentence the offenders to a prison term. Even men who kill their wives or partners and are convicted of homicide often do not get lengthy jail sentences. Moreover, men who kill their wives or partners are less severely punished than are women who kill their husbands or partners.

In highlighting the leniency of the court toward male batterers, Bannister cites actual cases in Denver, Colorado. During the 1980s the typical sentence for a batterer in Denver was a twenty-five-dollar fine even in cases where the victim suffered injuries such as brain damage. Bannister also examined the Hawaiian criminal-justice system, where state law mandates that a convicted batterer serve 48 hours in jail and receive counseling. Over a 5-month period in the late 1980s, however, only 1 in 111 convicted batterers in Honolulu was actually sent to jail, and only 8 of these men were ordered to receive counseling.

COURT PROCEDURES AND LEGAL STATUTES

In most states spouse abuse is considered simple assault, and police cannot make an arrest unless they witness the assault or the victim files a criminal complaint and a warrant is issued. In the past, in some jurisdictions, police used a *stitch rule* whereby they would arrest an abusing husband or intimate partner only if the victim had been injured badly enough to require a specific number of surgical sutures (Straus, Gelles, and Steinmetz, 1980). Currently, in some states, the police have the option of making an arrest if they believe there is "probable cause" (for example, visible weapons, injuries, witnesses). Only a few states have mandatory arrest laws where police are legally bound to arrest the abuser within a certain time period if there is evidence that he has committed an assault. These laws also call for evicting violent men from the home to ensure the safety of women and children. Evidence suggests that where such laws are enforced they help reduce repeated incidents of abuse. There is also evidence, however, that these laws frequently are not enforced (Renzetti and Curran, 1992).

Victims of battering and other violence can seek remedy in the criminal-justice system through an *order of protection,* a court order that prohibits a person from threatening, striking, or harassing a victim. Legally, if any part of the order is violated, the

CRITICAL ISSUES

THE RAPE OF MR. SMITH

The law discriminates against rape victims in a manner that would not be tolerated by victims of any other crime. In the following example, a holdup victim is asked questions similar in form to those usually asked a victim of rape. This brief scenario by an unknown author illustrates the injustices experienced by many rape victims. It also helps explain why the majority of victims choose not to report the rape.

"Mr. Smith, you were held up at gunpoint on the corner of 16th and Locust?"

"Yes."

"Did you struggle with the robber?"

"No."

"Why not?"

"He was armed."

"Then you made a conscious decision to comply with his demands rather than to resist?"

"Yes."

"Did you scream? Cry out?"

"No. I was afraid."

"I see. Have you ever been held up before?"

"No."

"Have you ever given money away?"

"Yes, of course…"

"And did you do so willingly?"

"What are you getting at?"

"Well, let's put it like this, Mr. Smith. You've given away money in the past—in fact, you have quite a reputation for philanthropy. How can we be sure that you weren't contriving to have your money taken from you by force?"

"Listen, if I wanted…"

"Never mind. What time did this holdup take place, Mr. Smith?"

"About 11 P.M."

"You were out on the streets at 11 P.M.? Doing what?"

"Just walking."

"Just walking? You know that it's dangerous being out on the street that late at night. Weren't you aware that you could have been held up?"

"I hadn't thought about it."

"What were you wearing at the time, Mr. Smith?"

"Let's see. A suit. Yes, a suit."

"An expensive suit?"

"Well…yes."

"In other words, Mr. Smith, you were walking around the streets late at night in a suit that practically advertised the fact that you might be a good target for some easy money, isn't that so? I mean, if we didn't know better, Mr. Smith, we might even think you were asking for this to happen, mightn't we?"

"Look, can't we talk about the past history of the guy who did this to me?"

"I'm afraid not, Mr. Smith. I don't think you would want to violate his rights, now, would you?"

How can we account for this discrepancy in the way victims of crimes are treated in the criminal-justice system? Do you think that if men were the primary victims of rape or other forms of intimate violence that these crimes would be taken more seriously? What can be done to help victims of violence receive better treatment in the criminal-justice system?

Source: Reprinted with permission from *Women Helping Women: Volunteer Resource Manual*, by Rape Crisis Services, Urbana, Illinois.

assaulter can be jailed, fined, or both. Unfortunately, these orders do not effectively protect most victims of violence. Many men, for example, routinely violate these orders and continue to batter and sometimes even kill their victim. Recently, some states have enacted *stalking laws*, which prohibit a spouse or intimate from following and harassing a partner or family member after the person has left the relationship.

The case of rape probably best illustrates women's continuing vulnerability in the criminal-justice system. The strict rules of evidence in rape cases basically put the burden of proof on the victim. For example, women who accuse men of rape must demonstrate that they are "real" victims; that they are not lying out of revenge or rejection. They must report the crime immediately, demonstrate emotional as well as physical trauma, and convince the police that they were not responsible for what happened to them. Furthermore, rape victims generally must have their testimony backed up by other witnesses and they must also establish that they tried sufficiently to resist their assailant. The box titled "The Rape of Mr. Smith" illustrates the irony of laws that require women who are raped to prove their innocence, in contrast to a victim of assault or robbery.

In recent years the treatment of rape and battered victims has improved somewhat. Since the 1970s many state legislatures have changed their laws so that women no longer have to prove that they "fought back" or to produce extensive evidence to corroborate their story. Also, several states have passed "shield laws" that prevent the victim's previous sexual experiences from being used as evidence in the trial. In addition, most police officers now receive special training to sensitize them to the trauma of victims, and an increasing number of victim-support and advocate services have appeared throughout the country.

On the national level, the country's first federal legislation dealing with domestic violence was introduced to Congress in 1991. Submitted by Senator Joseph Biden of Delaware, the Violence Against Women Act attempts to improve official responses to violence against women by imposing strict penalties on abusers, including federal penalties on those who cross state lines to track a fleeing partner. It also offers incentives to states that arrest spouse abusers and triples the amount of federal dollars available for battered-women's shelters.

FIGURE 12.1 Abuse can leave women with psychological and emotional scars. This drawing was done by a battered woman. What feelings and messages do you think she is trying to convey?

Source: Lee Ann Hoff, 1990, *Battered Women as Survivors* (New York: Routledge).

THE EFFECTS OF PHYSICAL AND SEXUAL ASSAULT ON WOMEN

There is a growing body of research that deals with the psychological effects of physical and sexual violence against women. There is also a growing recognition of battered women as "survivors." In this section we briefly explore some of the consequences of violence and abuse for the victim, then we examine some of the ways that assaulted women cope with and survive their experiences of violence.

The harm that men inflict on women takes many forms and has a wide range of effects. Research indicates that violent abuse exacts a tremendous toll on women: physically, psychologically, emotionally, and financially.

The physical effects are perhaps the most obvious and can range from bruises and temporary pain to scars, permanently broken bones, and disfigurement.

Less visible but perhaps more damaging are the psychological and emotional scars brought on by abuse (see Figure 12.1). Low self-esteem, self-hate, economic and emotional dependence on others (especially on those who perpetrate the violence), fear, self-destructive behavior such as alcohol and drug abuse, and suicide are not uncommon among abused women.

Research has found, for example, that during and after battering, women tend to think very poorly of themselves. Given their gender-role socialization, many abused women attribute the violence and abuse to something they did or did not do and therefore believe that they deserve to be treated violently

(Dutton, 1988). They frequently try to change themselves or the situations that they believe lead to the abuse (for example, not having dinner ready at a certain time or serving the coffee too hot or too cold). However, they usually come to realize that the abuse is unpredictable and could be triggered by almost anything they do. It is not surprising that women suffering under such conditions have a low sense of self-worth and a high sense of helplessness and hopelessness.

Women who have been victims of incestuous assault as children report feelings of severe depression throughout their lives, often to the point of suicide. Having been hurt by someone who was supposed to care for and protect them, they sometimes are unable to trust or participate in caring and intimate relationships. Along with the constant physical pain and bodily injury there is also the experience of fear, intimidation, humiliation, and degradation (Bannister, 1991). Probably the most extreme manifestation of battered-women's self-blame and recrimination is their tendency toward self-destructive behavior. Self-destructiveness can be considered both an effect and a coping strategy that abused women use to deal with their violent life experience and is discussed in more detail shortly.

COPING AND SURVIVAL STRATEGIES

Millions of victimized women develop coping strategies and learn survival tactics not only through their own personal efforts but also through close ties with others, especially other women. As with any stressful situation, coping with violence and abuse requires a variety of skills and resources. Research shows that battered women have developed a wide range of strategies, both constructive (seeking help, leaving the violent situation) and destructive (substance abuse, suicide, murder). Although the ways individual women cope vary from situation to situation, their coping and survival strategies can be classified in the following ways: psychological and emotional, self-destructive, and fighting back.

PSYCHOLOGICAL AND EMOTIONAL STRATEGIES One strategy employed by battered women is avoidance or prevention of violence. Victims of abuse sometimes develop plans to avoid future attacks. Sometimes they use sex (to the degree that they still

have some control over their sexuality) in an attempt to change the batterer or to avoid further beatings. Some battered women cope by trying to make the relationship work in spite of the obstacles, and others manage to cope and survive by insisting that the violence is not serious enough to end the relationship. Some women resort to dreams or fantasies that can range from being in a violence-free relationship to killing their mates. Still other women block out or repress their experiences of violence, though these experiences often resurface at some future time.

One strategy that is often discussed in the social-psychological literature is bonding. This concept is borrowed from research on people who have been held hostage. In the case of abuse, **bonding** refers to a situation in which the victim of violence grows attached to the abuser, often taking on his perspective. Several researchers have claimed that this response can be found among a variety of victims including battered women and children, and incest survivors. As a survival tactic, bonding with the abuser typically occurs when a woman perceives the violence and abuse to be a threat to her life, when she is isolated from others, or when she does not believe that she can escape the situation. In consequence, the victim turns to the abuser for nurturance and protection. Because her life may be at stake, she represses her anger against the violent side of her captor and bonds to his positive side in the hope that he will let her live.

SELF-DESTRUCTIVE STRATEGIES For many battered women self-destructive behavior is not only a consequence of battering and abuse; it is also a way of coping with the situation. Various addictions such as alcohol and drug abuse, overeating, and suicide are all forms of coping, although most people would consider them unhealthy, unwise, and ineffective.

Battering appears to be the single most important context for female suicide attempts. Battered women account for 42 percent of all attempted suicides. More than 25 percent of all female suicide attempts reported by hospitals are associated with battering. Of these women, 85 percent are seen in the hospital for at least one abusive injury prior to their first suicide attempt (Stark and Flitcraft, 1988). For African-American women, fully one-half of those who attempt suicide are abused. Indeed, the association among the experiences of violence, low self-esteem, and suicidal tendencies is quite strong among all female victims of violence (Counts, 1987).

Battering is also closely associated with female alcohol and drug abuse. Some researchers caution that it is unclear whether substance abuse is the context or the consequence of stress precipitated by violence (Allan and Cooke, 1985). That is, some researchers contend that alcohol abuse may contribute to a climate that makes abuse more likely. Other researchers respond that the rate of alcoholism among battered women is significantly greater than among nonbattered women. An examination of the recorded onset of alcoholism and of abusive injury among battered women reveals that three-fourths of the alcohol cases emerged only after the onset of abuse, suggesting that abuse leads to alcoholism among battered women, and not the reverse. Similarly, whereas drug abuse is no more common among battered women than nonbattered women prior to the onset of abuse, after abuse the risk of drug abuse is nine times greater than would normally be expected (Stark and Flitcraft, 1988).

Sometimes the self-destructive coping behavior of battered women is manifested in addictive behaviors such as overeating. Although a causal relationship between abuse and addiction to food has not been established, some battered women seem to use food as a way of coping with the violence in their lives (Dutton, 1988).

FIGHTING BACK Some women who cannot escape abusive relationships cope by fighting back. Most often their self-defense takes the form of hitting, pushing, or shoving the batterer. Only occasionally is women's self-defense more violent, such as pushing the batterer down a flight of stairs, biting him, kicking him in the groin, cutting him, or even shooting him. Some women now take self-defense classes to protect themselves against male attackers.

A small number of women who fight back eventually kill their abuser. Although a few of these women are acquitted by the courts on the grounds of self-defense, most are convicted and jailed. The majority of those convicted serve many years in prison despite their claims of self-defense and despite a large amount of evidence indicating that they had been severely abused by the men they killed. Some people consider women who respond to male violence by fighting back and who are then imprisoned to be

Probably one of the most widely publicized cases of violence against women was the 1977 case of Francine Hughes, an Iowa wife and mother who, after years of abuse and unsuccessful efforts to end her marriage, killed her sleeping husband by burning him to death. This case was immortalized in a book and later a movie, both titled *The Burning Bed*.

political prisoners (see, for example, Bannister, 1991). Whatever term we use to describe these women, the fact is that killing an abuser is more the exception than the rule. Only a small percentage of battered women use this strategy to end the abuse they suffer.

SHELTERS FOR BATTERED WOMEN

For many women, the first step in leaving a battering situation is escaping to a shelter. Prior to the establishment of battered-women's shelters during the 1970s, many battered women escaped to "informal safe homes and apartments" set up by other battered women (National Woman Abuse Action Project, 1991). In these safe places, as with shelters today, battered women and their children were free from intimidation by their abusers and safe from violence. Although shelters vary in philosophy and approach, all share the conviction that no one deserves to be beaten and that battered women need special resources and support to end the violence in their lives. The ultimate goal of these shelters is to give women the power to make their own choices.

Some people have gauged the success of this strategy by looking at the number of women who do not return to their abusers after staying in a shelter. Some researchers report that half of these women do not return to their abuser; other estimates go as high as between two-thirds to four-fifths. Even if these figures are somewhat inflated, shelters appear to be successful in helping women break the chain of violence and abuse. The longer a woman stays in a shelter, the less likely she is to return to her abuser, and the more likely she is to remain alive (National Woman Abuse Action Project, 1991). Even those women who return to abusive partners may progress toward a permanent solution to their situation as a result of their shelter experience (Sedlak, 1988). Some women may need to leave and return several times before they are ready to leave permanently (Walker, 1978).

Some people have argued that battered-women's shelters, although an important resource for women, are a "band-aid" solution to domestic violence. They question why women should have to leave their homes and sometimes their families, temporarily or permanently. Why shouldn't the abuser be made to leave? Proponents of shelters respond that shelters are not a band-aid solution but a life-saving response to a pervasive problem in the same way that ambulances and emergency rooms respond to medical crises.

 What do you think? Do you think the abuser should be made to leave the home? Do you think there should be laws to govern who should have to leave in these situations? If such laws existed, how could they be enforced?

A COMPARATIVE LOOK AT BATTERED MEN

A 30-year-old man moved out of an apartment it had taken him ages to find because of the couple who lived next door. What was it about the couple that made this young man give up his hard-found apartment? He said it was the fights: the shouting, the verbal abuse, and what sounded like physical abuse that

resounded from the apartment next door. What he found most disturbing was the fact that, in his view, the woman was the abusive and violent partner (Sims, 1989).

What evidence exists for female violence and male victimization? The suggestion that men are battered by women probably sounds implausible, if not silly, to some people. For others the image of a skinny little henpecked man chased by a large buxom wife with a rolling pin in her hand might immediately come to mind. In fact, some research during the 1970s and 1980s suggested that the phenomenon of battered husbands was as prevalent as that of battered wives. Suzanne Steinmetz (1977) was one of the first to call our attention to this issue by claiming that more women battered husbands than vice versa and that husband abuse was the most underreported of all forms of family violence. Studies based on national survey data in the 1980s found that in homes with couple violence, approximately one-fourth of the respondents indicated that men were victims and not perpetrators of violence; an additional one-fourth reported that women were victims and not offenders; and the remaining one-half reported that both wives and husbands were violent. More recently, around one out of eight wives reported having been violent toward their husbands at some point (Saunders, 1988).

Critics of the idea of widespread husband abuse caution that statistics such as Steinmetz's can be seriously misinterpreted. A major problem with claims that women use violence as often as men is that there is little or no clarification of how many of the women who use violence are actually acting in self-defense or retaliating against an abusive partner. Data from studies of violent relationships in which the police intervened (for example, Berk, Berk, Loeseke, and Rauma, 1983) clearly indicate that men are rarely the victims of battery. Research also clearly shows that men initiate violence in the majority of cases. Moreover, men who kill their partner do so in self-defense far less frequently than do women who kill their partner. In addition, rarely do battered women report initiating violence. The most frequent motive for violence in their self-reports is "fighting back" (Saunders, 1988), and the violent acts that they report tend, most often, to be protective or self-defense actions.

Given that women are, on average, smaller and physically weaker than men, they usually suffer much worse injuries than they inflict. Although some men are injured by a wife or lover, most women are unable to defend themselves effectively against male batterers. In fact, most battered women find it far safer to submit to the battering than to fight back and risk being seriously injured or even killed. In light of this fact it seems inappropriate to refer to women's behavior in this regard as "husband abuse" or "battering." This does not alter the fact, however, that domestic violence in all forms needs to be investigated and understood.

CHILD ASSAULT AND ABUSE

Although child abuse has existed throughout human history, in the United States it attracted public interest only in the early 1960s. At that time Dr. C. Henry Kempe and his associates (1962) published a national survey that described for the first time the series of behaviors known as the **battered-child syndrome**.

They defined this syndrome basically as "a clinical condition in children who have received severe physical abuse, primarily from a parent or foster parent" (Kempe, Silverman, Steele, Droegemueller, and Silver, 1962:17). Even then, however, child abuse was not widely acknowledged to be a major issue until the 1980s, when expanded media coverage brought the problem to the attention of millions of Americans. Public-opinion polls conducted in the 1970s revealed that only one in ten Americans considered child abuse to be a serious problem. By the 1980s that figure had increased to nine out of ten (Gelles and Strauss, 1987).

Trying to determine the overall incidence of child abuse is very difficult. Research data indicate that cases of child abuse reported to social-service agencies have risen at a rate of 10 percent each year since 1983. Higher reporting rates, however, do not necessarily mean that more children are being abused today than in the past. Because all states now have

Parental violence is among the five leading causes of death for children 1 to 18 years of age.

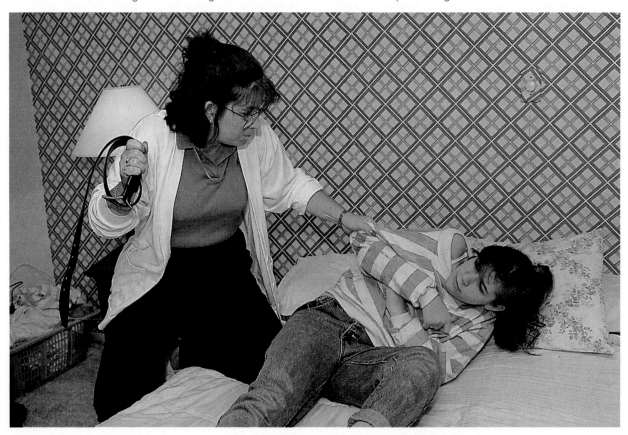

compulsory child-abuse reporting laws, people are more likely to report such abuse. Some researchers have suggested that the rate of child abuse has actually decreased since 1975 (Gelles and Cornell, 1990). Whatever the true incidence of child abuse, it is a significant social problem.

In some ways child abuse is even more difficult to deal with than is woman abuse. Children have few legal rights and are subject to the authority of their parents. Parents have a right and obligation to discipline their children, and few restrictions are placed on how they may do so. Perhaps more so even than woman abuse, parental violence against children historically has been considered a "family matter" with which the larger society should not interfere, except in extreme cases.

As with woman abuse, maltreatment of children takes many forms, including physical and sexual abuse. Children can also suffer *psychological abuse*, in which they are exposed to experiences that can cause emotional or mental distress, and *neglect*, the failure of parents and guardians to provide basic care such as food and shelter. Because of space limitations we will concentrate only on physical and sexual assault against children. This is not meant to diminish the seriousness or prevalence of other forms of child abuse, however.

THE PHYSICAL ASSAULT OF CHILDREN

Because adults have great latitude in terms of the methods they may use to discipline children, violence against children must be serious before it is labeled as abuse. (How many Americans recognize spanking as a form of violence?) Of all the types of child abuse, physical abuse is probably the most likely to lead to intervention by outside forces because it most often leaves visible evidence (such as bruises, lacerations, and broken bones) that can be introduced into a court of law as evidence of maltreatment (Sigler, 1989).

PHYSICAL ASSAULT: HOW PREVALENT? How prevalent is the physical assault of children? Because of a high rate of underreporting, the incidence of child assault is difficult to assess. This fact notwithstanding, the statistics we have on child assault and abuse are alarming. Survey data suggest that around 7 million U.S. children are abused each year by parents;

1.5 million of these children are seriously assaulted (Hotaling, Finklehor, Kirkpatrick, and Strauss, 1988). National surveys that ask Americans about violence in their homes have found considerable violence directed toward children. Most parents admitted using some kind of violence on their children during the preceding year. In one such survey, approximately 11 percent of parents admitted beating up a child at least once using severe forms of punishment, including threatening to use or actually using a gun or knife (Straus and Gelles, 1986). Parental violence is among the five leading causes of death for children between 1 and 18 years of age. Researchers estimate that every year about 2000 children are killed by their parents.

Child physical abuse cuts across all age groups. In some surveys 90 percent of parents who have 3-year-old children reported at least minor forms of physical punishment such as spanking or slapping, approximately two-thirds of parents with preteen and young teenagers said they "hit" their children, and one-third of parents of teenagers between 15 and 17 years of age admitted using such punishment (Gelles and Straus, 1987).

Although these figures are high, it is estimated that as many as one-third of all abuse and neglect cases go unreported or undetected, especially if they involve middle-class or wealthy families. We can safely assume that like most family violence, child abuse is often hidden in the privacy of the home, and most people do not admit to it. Furthermore, as with most statistics on violence, child assault statistics rely heavily on self-reports and on the reports of various professionals such as doctors, nurses, social workers, teachers, child-care workers, and police. Perhaps one primary reason that a significant amount of child assault goes unreported is because many of these professionals refuse to "get involved." Very often their biases concerning race and class affect their decision whether to report suspected cases of child assault. For example, doctors are twice as likely to label a black child a victim of abuse as a white child. Similarly, they are more likely to label a case as abuse if the child is from a janitor's family than if the child is from a lawyer's family (Besharov, 1987).

WHO ARE THE ABUSED? Child abuse victims are typically white. Over one-half (58 percent) of all white children are victims of major physical abuse, compared with 22 percent of black children and 11 percent of Latino children (American Humane Association, 1985). Current research seems to indicate that certain characteristics predispose a child to being abused. Children born to unmarried parents, premature infants, children who are congenitally malformed or mentally retarded, twins, and children born during a mother's depressive illness are most vulnerable to abuse. Usually only one child in a family is abused. That child most often is the youngest, followed, in terms of frequency, by the oldest. Prior to the age of 10 or 11, boys are more frequently abused than girls. At that point, the incidence of abuse of girls becomes greater.

Research also indicates that between 30 and 42 percent of abused children come from single-parent homes (Tower, 1989). In addition, they are more likely to have young parents and few siblings, to have been separated from their parents during the first year of life, and to have parents who were themselves abused as children (Smith and Adler, 1991). In addition, in 43 percent of the cases of child abuse examined in one study, at least one parent had a documented problem with alcohol or drugs (Murphy et al., 1991).

Until recently not much attention was paid to abused adolescents. Many people do not see adolescents as being particularly vulnerable because, unlike small children, they can run away, protect themselves, and get help. In fact, every year an unknown number of adolescents are abused. Many of them run away to someone or someplace, but most end up on the streets, unprotected and vulnerable to the abuse of a variety of unscrupulous people such as pimps, pornographers, and drug dealers. Sometimes when children reach adolescence they fight back. Some researchers estimate that almost 2.5 million teenagers commit acts of violence against their parents each year. Approximately 2000 parents die each year at the hands of a teenage son or daughter, often in self-defense or in retaliation against abuse (Gelles and Strauss, 1987). One common scenario involves a drunken, physically abusive father who is killed by a son who sees himself as the protector of the rest of the family (Pagelow, 1989). Overall, however, teenagers are more likely to employ violence against mothers than against fathers.

WHO ARE THE ABUSERS?   In 90 percent of child abuse cases, the abuser is a member of the immediate family. Although half of the reported cases of parental physical violence against children involve women and half involve men, most of the literature on child abuse claims that mothers are more likely than biological fathers to abuse their children, although the difference between the two is small. This finding should not be taken to mean that women are, by nature, more violent than men. Rather, women's general lack of power in the family, their isolation in the home, and the emotional tensions of mothering all lead to situations in which abuse is likely to occur. In fact, if we controlled for the amount of time spent in contact with children, rates of abuse would be higher for men.

Some researchers have found that women who are abused by their husbands or lovers are most likely to use severe violence against their children, although these women account for only a small overall percentage of such cases. Other researchers have found a relationship between work and child abuse, with women in the paid labor force (compared with all mothers) exhibiting the lowest rates of overall violence toward their children. Fathers whose wives work (compared with all fathers) also have the lowest rate of violence toward children (Gelles and Hargreaves, 1987). It seems too that a person's occupation is significantly related to the probability of abuse. People in working-class occupations are more likely to use physical punishment and abuse their children than are their counterparts in white-collar occupations. Moreover, children in homes where the father is either unemployed or working part-time are more likely to be abused than are children in homes where the father works full-time (Gelles and Cornell, 1990). Finally, young adults are more likely to abuse their children than are older parents, and stepfathers and boyfriends of single mothers are frequent abusers of children, especially sexual abusers (Renzetti and Curran, 1992).

Official reports of child abuse generally overrepresent poor people and people of color in comparison with their percentages in the larger population. In these reports, abusive parents are most likely to be poor and to exhibit cultural characteristics, such as early marriage and child rearing, attributed to the working class. Rates of reported physical abuse among lower-income families are two to three times those of upper-income families (Gelles and Cornell, 1990). Concerning race, although the rate of overall violence is the same for black and white families, the rate of reported abusive violence toward black children is about twice the rate of that toward white children.

THE SEXUAL ASSAULT OF CHILDREN

Child sexual abuse is a major problem today, and public concern about this issue has been heightened by numerous reports by adult survivors of its impact on their lives. The term *child sexual abuse* refers to the use of a child for the sexual gratification of an adult. Such abuse can be divided into two basic categories, depending on who the abuser is: familial abuse and extrafamilial abuse. Familial abuse is generally referred to as **incest**—the sexual abuse by a blood relative who is assumed to be a part of the child's family. Most definitions of incest include stepfathers and live-in boyfriends. Because most child sexual abuse is perpetrated by family members, our discussion focuses on familial rather than extrafamilial abuse.

Sexual abuse progresses over time, usually beginning with "trying out" behavior and progressing over time in intensity of abuse. It might begin with an adult undressing in front of the child and progress to the rubbing of the perpetrator's penis on the genital or rectal area of the child. Not every case of sexual abuse progresses in the same way. No matter what the cyclic order of child sexual abuse, however, it involves an adult using her or his power to force, coerce, or cajole compliance from a child who participates out of awe, fear, trust, respect, or love for the adult (Tower, 1989).

CHILD SEXUAL ABUSE: HOW PREVALENT?

How prevalent is child sexual abuse? Because of the extremely sensitive, embarrassing, and outrageous nature of incest, victims and perpetrators often keep it hidden. Family members and others outside the family cite personal reasons for not reporting known instances of child sexual abuse. The most common reason cited by adults is their reluctance to believe a child's claim of abuse and their hesitance to accuse an adult of such behavior. Thus, official reports of incest severely underestimate its actual occurrence. Taking into account the underreporting, a 1985 summary of all available national data estimated that incest occurs in 14 percent of U.S. families and can be found in all family types and social classes (*Developing a National Agenda*, 1985). Studies of adults who reported their past experiences with abuse have found that anywhere from 9 to 52 percent of the females and 3 to 9 percent of the males had some sexual exposure as children (Finkelhor, 1984b).

THE SEXUALITY ABUSED CHILD AND THE ABUSER

Can we make any generalizations concerning which children are sexually abused and who abuses them? According to the available research, the typical victim of abuse is female. Some researchers, however, claim that this conclusion is misleading because boys are less likely to report a sexual assault. Males who in early childhood are taught to be "strong" and "macho" may be unwilling or unable to admit that they have been victimized in this way. Recent research, in fact, suggests that boys are almost equally as vulnerable to incest as are girls (Tower, 1989). At the very least, these studies indicate that the incidence of abuse among male children is significantly higher than we imagine or is reported.

As with physical assault, white children are more likely than either black or Latino children to be sexually assaulted by a family member within the household rather than someone outside the household. Among victims of child sexual abuse, 75 percent of white children are assaulted by a member of the household, as opposed to 13 percent of black children and 9 percent of Latino children (American Humane Association, 1985). The average age of abuse victims is between 8 and 12. Some evidence suggests that boys are abused at an earlier age (8.5) than girls (12.4). In addition, the abuse of boys generally takes place for a shorter period of time. Furthermore, sexually abused boys are from poorer socioeconomic backgrounds than are abused girls.

A variety of factors have been identified that place some children at greater risk than others: children with various handicaps (physical or emotional), social isolation (unsupervised children), the mother absent from the home, a sexually punitive or religiously fanatic mother, a mother who did not finish high school or who kept herself isolated, and the presence of a stepfather in the home. The abuser can be anyone in the family circle, although in 95 to 98 percent of all reported cases the abuser is a male. In most cases the perpetrator was himself or herself sexually abused as a child (Smith and Adler, 1991).

THE EFFECTS OF CHILD ABUSE

Researchers have only recently begun to focus on the long-term consequences of child abuse. Among their findings are that a large percentage of sexually abused children become prostitutes or drug users and that sexually abused female runaways are more likely to be involved in deviant or criminal behavior than are nonabused females (Andersen, 1988). In addition, victims frequently suffer low self-esteem, severe depression, and alcoholism. Many attempt suicide. When they become adults, they often become abusers themselves or victims of spousal battering and abuse.

ELDER ABUSE IN THE UNITED STATES

As our earlier historical account of family violence illustrates, abuse of the elderly by their adult children (and sometimes grandchildren or other relatives) is not new, nor was it always viewed as a problem. Recently, however, elder abuse has gained widespread public attention and has been defined by some people as a major social problem. As we shall see in Chapter 15, a growing percentage of the U.S. population is over age 65. The greater longevity and visibility of older people have increased our awareness of and sensitivity to the many problems they experience, including violent treatment at the hands of family members. Like all other forms of family violence, elder abuse is greatly underreported. Older people in the United States are more likely to be abused by family members than by strangers. Currently, the abuse of parents by their children, popularly referred to as "granny bashing" in England, is estimated to range from 500,000 to 2.5 million cases per year for acts of physical violence alone; 1 million of these parents are seriously injured (Gelles and Cornell, 1990).

WHAT IS ELDER ABUSE?

The term **elder abuse** is a broad one that includes the physical, psychological, and material maltreatment and neglect of older people. Although many older Americans are independent and in good health, the chances of poor health and dependency increase with age, as does the potential for victimization in any one or more of the following forms: physical violence, psychological abuse (such as verbal abuse, threats, intimidation, isolation, and neglect), physical maltreatment (such as physical restraint, excessive medication, withholding medicine, food, or personal care), material abuse (such as theft or misuse of money or other personal property), and personal vio-

lation (such as physically removing them from their homes and placing them in other settings such as nursing homes against their will).

WHO ARE THE ABUSED AND THE ABUSERS?

As with women and children, some older adults run a greater risk of being abused than others: women, older people with physical or mental impairments, and those dependent on a caretaker to meet their basic needs. Current research suggests that women 75 years of age and older are the most likely victims of elder abuse. This probably reflects their lack of strength, their general lack of power, their devalued status, and the fact that they outnumber elderly men. Not everyone, however, agrees that elderly women run a greater risk of abuse than elderly men. One set of researchers, for example, found little difference in the victimization rates of older women and men, although women suffered more serious physical and psychological harm from the abuse (Pillemer and Finklehor, 1988).

Although the picture is still inconclusive, the abuser apparently is most often a male spouse who abuses his elderly partner (58 percent of the perpetrators), followed by children (28 percent), and then others (14 percent) (Pillemer and Finklehor, 1988). Violence perpetrated by an elderly male spouse is often a continuation of an earlier pattern of abuse. Elderly women who abuse their husbands may be enacting revenge for previous abuse by the husband (Renzetti and Curran, 1992).

Among children who abuse their parents, the most frequent offenders are adult daughters. This probably reflects the fact that because of gender-role socialization, daughters most often have the responsibility of caring for an aging parent or other relative. Often adult children who abuse their elderly parents were themselves abused and thus learned that violence toward intimates is acceptable behavior. In some cases, they may be acting in retaliation against an abusive parent (Kosberg, 1988). In other cases, the abuser is financially dependent on the older person, and the abuse stems from this dependency and lack of power in the relationship.

Although over two-thirds of U.S. states have enacted mandatory reporting laws to deal with elder abuse, some people question the effectiveness of these laws, given that they address the problem only after the fact. Critics have suggested that a more successful strategy might be to provide adult children with greater institutional assistance and support in caring for their elderly parents. (Chapter 15 contains a fuller discussion of the elderly.) Indeed, the abuse of the elderly is part of the larger problem of structured inequality. Like other low-status groups in U.S. society, older Americans are highly vulnerable to abuse.

SIBLING ABUSE

Who most commonly abuses children? Perhaps surprisingly, the answer is not mothers or fathers or other adults, but siblings. Although sibling violence is seldom discussed, according to some authorities on the subject, it is perhaps the most common form of family violence. In fact, siblings hit, slap, kick, and beat each other so frequently that few of us pay much attention to this behavior or consider it to be a form of family violence. Statistics on sibling violence suggest, however, that we reexamine our thinking about this behavior as "natural" and "inevitable."

A 1980 survey that included 733 families with two or more children found that 82 percent of the children between 3 and 17 years of age reported having used some type of violence against a sibling in the previous year (Straus, Gelles, and Steinmetz, 1980). Other studies estimate that upward of 29 million siblings physically abuse each other every year (Tiede, 1983). These acts are not minor acts of hitting. Rather, over half of them

could have resulted in legal prosecution had they been perpetrated by someone outside the family. Because of the historic acceptance of sibling violence we are unable to ascertain whether such behavior is becoming more or less common. Like the public, researchers have long ignored this pattern of violence. Even today, although recognition of sibling violence has increased somewhat, our knowledge as well as public awareness is still extremely low (Gelles and Cornell, 1990).

Who most often initiates sibling violence? Boys of all ages are more violent than girls, but the difference is relatively small. The highest rates of sibling violence tend to occur in families with only male children. Sibling violence is also higher among children in families in which child and spouse assault also occur. Sibling violence is more common during the youngest ages when siblings are home together and decreases as children get older and spend less time at home and with each other (Straus, Gelles, and Steinmetz, 1980). Some children both physically and sexually abuse their younger siblings.

Not much is known about the reasons for sibling violence. Some researchers have suggested that it is a learned response. Children raised in a violent environment learn that physical punishment is an appropriate way to deal with certain situations. In contrast, children raised in an environment free of violence learn other ways to resolve conflicts with siblings and later with other intimates (Gelles and Cornell, 1990).

SUMMARY

Family and intimate relationship violence is both deeply rooted in human history and widespread in contemporary society. The family is the major context within which most violence in this country occurs. A number of myths about family violence, ranging from the notion that it is a rare occurrence to the idea that women secretly desire to be raped, obscure our view of and knowledge about its pervasiveness.

Although any family member can be abused, women and children are the most common victims. Woman battering is perhaps the most common and one of the most underreported crimes in this country. It is cyclic in nature and has been described in terms of the battered-woman syndrome. Although we do not know a lot about battering across race and sexual orientation, we know that it can be found among all groups.

Family violence includes not only battering but also sexual assault. Here too, women and girls are the typical victims. Although information on the incidence and prevalence of marital rape is limited, there is a growing public awareness that husbands can and do rape their wives. This fact notwithstanding, the criminal justice system generally is unresponsive to battered and sexually assaulted women except in cases of severe violence or death. In fact, the attitudes of police officers, judges, prosecutors, and other personnel in the system as well as some laws and statutes often limit women's ability to receive relief from a violent life situation.

Some of the most visible effects of violence against women are low self-esteem, self-hate, economic and emotional dependence on others, fear, anxiety and self-destructive behavior. Victims also develop a number of survival strategies, some of which, such as overeating and substance abuse, are self-destructive. In addition, a growing number of women are dealing with their violent situation by fighting back. Women sometimes use violence against men, although they most often do so in self-defense against a threatened or actual physical attack.

Women are not the only victims of family violence: Around 7 million children are abused each year by parents or someone close to the family. We are only beginning to appreciate the extent of this problem today. Other, less visible victims of family violence include the elderly and siblings.

KEY TERMS

infanticide
rape syndrome
woman battering
sexual assault
battered-woman syndrome
victim blaming

rape
bonding
battered-child syndrome
incest
elder abuse

QUESTIONS FOR STUDY AND REFLECTION

1. Think about your own family or a romantic relationship you are involved in. What do you think is the likelihood that it will turn violent? What might you do to prevent this from occurring?

2. Which child-rearing philosophies and economic and social factors contribute to the prevalence of child abuse in the United States today? Should children be spanked? In your opinion, is there a difference between spanking and child abuse? Have you ever hit a child with something other than your hand? Do you think your behavior constituted battering? Why or why not?

3. In your opinion, is it possible for a man to rape his wife? A woman to rape her husband? Why or why not? To what degree would you be willing to remain in a marriage if your spouse raped you or you raped your spouse?

4. What factors might explain why some societies are more likely than others to abuse their elderly members? What possible reasons do you think a person could have for battering an elderly parent? Have you ever been physically or psychologically abusive to one or both of your parents? How might we deal with the problem of elder abuse?

FURTHER READING

GELLES, RICHARD J., AND CLAIRE PEDRICK CORNELL. 1990. *Intimate Violence in Families*. Newbury Park, CA: Sage. This is a handy little reader aimed at undergraduate students and designed to provide a basic overview of the subject of family violence. It examines violence against children, women, siblings, adolescents, parents, and the elderly.

KIMMEL, MICHAEL S., AND MICHAEL A. MESSNER. 1989. *Men's Lives*. New York: Macmillan. An excellent anthology focusing on the male experience. The book is organized around specific themes that define masculinity and the issues that men confront over their lifetime. Part 6 deals with men and women, including some poignant articles dealing with the American context of male violence and the rape of women.

LOBEL, KERRY, ed. 1986. *Naming the Violence: Speaking Out About Lesbian Battering*. (For the National Coalition Against Domestic Violence Lesbian Task Force.) Seattle, WA: Seal Press. A groundbreaking anthology on lesbian violence. It offers the reader personal stories of pain, empowerment, and healing. It includes articles and essays by lesbians active in the battered-women's movement and that examine the dynamics of abuse and various organizing strategies against lesbian violence around the country.

TOWER, CYNTHIA CROSSON. 1989. *Understanding Child Abuse and Neglect*. Boston: Allyn and Bacon. A comprehensive overview of all aspects of child abuse. The book begins with a historical analysis of child abuse. Subsequent chapters deal with topics ranging from the symptoms and effects of abuse to parental motivations, the social-service system, and the intervention process.

Chapter 13

THE PROCESS OF UNCOUPLING: DIVORCE IN THE UNITED STATES

riends and relatives regarded Bill and Terry as an ideal couple. The former high school sweethearts had been married for 14 years. Bill was the sales manager of a large car dealership. They had a home in the suburbs, took family vacations, and were active in the community. They seemed to have it all. Yet 2 months before their fifteenth wedding anniversary, Bill and Terry were divorced.

Neither Bill nor Terry is exactly sure what went wrong with their marriage. The first years were exciting. Both partners liked their work; they bought a house, and they maintained it together. They had two healthy children, and Terry stayed home and took care of them. She noticed that Bill stopped doing things around the house, but she didn't complain because he was earning the money. Terry enjoyed being home with the children, but once they started school, she became restless, especially when Bill's promotion required him to work longer hours. Over Bill's objections Terry returned to work. They seemed to have less and less to talk about, and Terry felt resentful when Bill refused to share the household chores, telling her she could always quit her job and stay home.

What do you think happened to Bill and Terry's relationship? Should they have seen early signs of trouble? Could they have done anything different to preserve their marriage?

The vast majority of people who promise to love, cherish, and comfort their spouse "until death do us part" really mean it. How, then, can we account for the fact that in 1990 approximately 1.2 million married couples in the United States divorced, up from about 600,000 in 1970 (U.S. Bureau of the Census, 1991e)?

The fact that divorce is so common today has led many to conclude that the family is a dying or at least a critically wounded institution. This thinking reflects the myths discussed in Chapter 1: In the past marriages were happier, families were more loving, and members treated each other with respect. People who feel this way tend to see divorce in a negative light, as a recent social problem that must be overcome. In contrast, some people see divorce as a solution to a problem of unhappy and sometimes abusive marriages. Both schools of thought find abundant evidence to support their positions.

As with so many social phenomena, however, the reality concerning divorce lies somewhere in between. Regardless of the quality of the marriage they left, few people undergo separation or divorce without experiencing some pain. In fact, some divorced people never get over the trauma they experience in the breakup of their marriage. This is especially true for the spouses who didn't want the divorce. Conversely, divorce allows people who were unhappy in their marriages to go on and build satisfying new relationships. To appreciate more fully these divergent outcomes of divorce, we need to see how the current institution of divorce came about. In this chapter we examine the historical controversies surrounding

divorce, with an eye to understanding current divorce laws and social policies. We also discuss who divorces and why as well as the consequences of divorce for family members.

HISTORICAL PERSPECTIVES

Contrary to popular belief, divorce is not a modern phenomenon. It has been a part of U.S. history since 1639, when a Puritan court in Massachusetts granted the first divorce decree in colonial America. This does not mean, however, that divorce was socially acceptable to all the early settlers. In fact, throughout U.S. history conflict has existed between those who favor divorce and those who oppose it.

DIVORCE IN EARLY AMERICA

Although early in their history the New England colonies permitted divorce, the grounds for divorce varied from one colony to another. Divorces were often adversarial in nature—one partner was required to prove that the other was at fault and had violated the marriage contract. Thus, friends, relatives, and neighbors were called as witnesses and, in effect, were forced to choose sides in what often became an acrimonious procedure. The finding of fault became the basis for harsh punishments for the "offending" party: fines, whippings, incarceration in the stocks, prohibition from remarrying, and even banishment from the colony. This fault-finding also became the basis for **alimony**, a concept originating in England in the 1650s whereby a husband deemed to be at fault for the dissolution of the marriage was required to provide his wife with a financial allowance. Conversely, if a wife was judged to be at fault, she lost any claim to financial support. Then as today, however, the law was one thing, and its implementation another. Because of incomplete or lost records we don't know how many divorces were actually granted in colonial America.

Although the population of the time included Native Americans and African Americans, their marriages were rarely recorded in the white courts. Thus, it is likely that few Native or African Americans sought an official divorce. However, one researcher did uncover the record of a divorce granted in 1745 on the grounds of his wife's adultery to a slave living in Massachusetts. The same researcher also found that in 1768, Lucy Purnan, a free black woman, received a divorce decree on the grounds of her husband's cruelty (cited in Riley, 1991:14). Additionally, Jesuit missionaries complained about frequent divorce among the Native Americans they came to convert (Amott and Matthaei, 1991:39).

Divorce was granted more infrequently in the middle section of the country than in the North. Most of the middle colonies did not enact explicit statutes regarding divorce, and records show that only a few divorces were granted in the colonies of New York, New Jersey, and Pennsylvania. For the most part the southern colonies did not enact divorce legislation until after independence was achieved. The reluctance of these colonies to legalize divorce should not be interpreted to mean that marriages were happier and more tranquil there than in the rest of the country. Formal and informal separations seem to have been widespread among the population, including Native Americans and African Americans both free and slave. Evidence of marital discord can be found in southern newspapers of this period, which carried stories and advertisements of runaway spouses, disclaimers of spousal debt, and other forms of marital strife.

Why did these early marriages dissolve? Historian Glenda Riley (1991) sees a variety of social and economic factors interacting to put strains on marriages and families. The growing mobility of the colonists, the movement west, and the emergence of a market economy along with new technology all combined to alter the role of the family as an economic unit and, thus, undercut to a degree a couple's sense of interdependency and common purpose. Additionally, the resistance to British rule and the ideology of the Enlightenment, with its emphasis on liberty, justice, and equality, caused people to examine their own level of personal well-being. On the individual level people sometimes made errors in their choice of spouse or married under duress of an unplanned pregnancy, only to regret their actions later on. Whatever the causes, on the eve of the American Revolution, divorce was fairly well established in the social fabric of the nation.

DIVORCE IN NINETEENTH-CENTURY AMERICA

The period following the American Revolution was a time of rapid social, political, and economic change. Each state assumed jurisdiction for divorce. Although there were individual differences among the various states, the general trend was to liberalize divorce laws and expand the grounds for divorce. Two major exceptions to this rule were New York, where adultery remained the sole ground for divorce, and South Carolina, where divorce was not permitted. These differing laws led to "migratory" divorce, whereby residents of one state traveled to another with more liberal laws. To discourage people from coming into their state solely to obtain a divorce, many of the more liberal states instituted minimum residency requirements.

Data on the number of divorces were not systematically collected until the end of the nineteenth century. Newspaper accounts and scattered divorce records, however, suggest that increasing numbers of people were utilizing the liberalized divorce laws. The apparent increase in the divorce rate sent shock waves across the United States. Passionate debates were carried on in newspapers and legislative chambers and from pulpits. Those opposing divorce, like newspaper editor Horace Greeley, saw it as immoral and responsible for most social ills of the day and argued that restricting divorce would deter hasty or ill-advised marriages.

On the other side, social critics of the day argued that marriage, not divorce, needed reform. Women's groups spoke out against wife abuse, which had gained public visibility by the 1850s. Female divorce petitioners frequently cited cruelty, including sexual abuse, as the reason for wanting to end their marriage. Proponents of divorce, like Indiana legislator Robert Owen, saw personal happiness and fulfillment as the primary purpose of marriage; they believed that marriage ought to end if these goals are frustrated.

In 1887, Congress responded to these public debates by authorizing Commissioner of Labor Carrol D. Wright to undertake a study of marriage and divorce in the United States. Wright found that 68,547 divorces were granted between 1872 and 1876, representing almost a 28 percent increase over the 53,574 divorces granted between 1867 and 1871 (cited in Riley, 1991:79). Wright found several interesting patterns in these data: Women obtained two-thirds of the divorces (a pattern still evident today); desertion was the most common ground for divorce; and western states granted the most divorces, and southern states the fewest. Although people in all classes and occupations sought divorces, more divorces occurred among the working class than among the middle and upper classes.

Although much of the public reaction to divorce focused on its frequency and availability, other problems connected with divorce were becoming evident. After divorce many women, especially those with custody of children, became impoverished. Although alimony was often granted by the courts, enforcement was difficult. Child custody was another problem area. The traditional view in colonial America was that children belong to the father, and therefore he should automatically get custody if a marriage was dissolved by either death or divorce. Thus, some women stayed in unhappy marriages rather than risk losing their children. With industrialization and the consequent notion of separate spheres for women and men, however, judges came to adopt the "tender years" principle that children under the age of 7 were better off with their mothers. This principle was based on the assumption that women are by nature more adept at nurturing than men are.

Men did not always agree with this interpretation. Sometimes heated custody battles ensued, especially if the mother was seen as the spouse at fault. Judges occasionally split siblings, giving girls or younger children over to the care of mothers and giving boys or older children to fathers. This decision, called **split custody**, is still made by some judges. As we shall see

later, the divorce reforms of the twentieth century have not been completely successful in resolving the debate over which parent should have custody of the children. In the reform efforts of the twentieth century the principle of tender years was modified, and child custody was, in principle at least, based on the best interests of the child.

Americans were also troubled by the destructive consequences that often accompanied divorce. Most of the criticism, however, focused on the divergent laws and procedures that existed in the various states. Many sought a solution to these problems by proposing a uniform divorce law that would encompass the entire country.

TWENTIETH-CENTURY AMERICA: EFFORTS AT REFORM

Generally, those favoring a more restrictive and uniform approach to divorce saw it as a moral evil to be stopped. This moral–legal view was challenged by a group of scholars in the newly developing social sciences. These analysts believed that divorce originates not in legislation but rather in the social and economic environment in which marriage is located. The changing patterns of divorce seemed to support this view. The divorce rate jumped considerably after World War I, when many marriages, some hastily conceived in the midst of war, floundered under the stress of economic and political uncertainty and the strains of separation and reunion. This war-related

When divorcing couples are unable to resolve their differences amicably, they often end up in costly legal proceedings.

Cultures vary significantly in their degree of acceptance of divorce and the rules governing who can initiate a divorce. In some cultures, like the Hopi Native Americans of the Southwest, both women and men could initiate divorce. Among the Yoruba of West Africa, however, only women could initiate divorce, and for centuries among many Asian cultures only men could ask for a divorce.

Researchers who studied the matrilineal Hopi 50 years ago found a high divorce rate: about one out of three marriages. The divorce process was easy. A wife could initiate divorce simply by placing her husband's belongings outside their dwelling. A divorcing husband simply moved back into his mother's house. If the couple had children, they stayed with the mother (Queen et al., 1985:49–50).

According to research conducted in the 1960s, the divorce rate among the Yoruba peoples was high. For the most part women were economically independent from their husbands. Divorce was not traumatic. Remarriages were frequent, and the concept of "divorcee" had little meaning (Lloyd, 1968).

According to sociologist Young I. Song (1991), women of Asia could not under any circumstance initiate divorce. A wife could be divorced unconditionally, however, if she broke any one of seven rules for marriage: "(1) If she does not serve her parents-in-law well; (2) if she cannot pro-

duce children, particularly male; (3) if she is lecherous; (4) if she is too jealous; (5) if she has an incurable disease; (6) if she talks too much; or (7) if she steals" (cited in Song, 1991:222). Men retained the property accumulated during the marriage and also received custody of the children. Although conditions are improving, Asian wives still have fewer rights and opportunities than their husbands do.

What is your reaction to these three different approaches to divorce? How do they compare with practices in the United States? Do you think there is any merit to making divorce as easy as it is for the Hopi and the Yoruba? Would similar models work in an urban, industrial society?

increase in divorce was not a new phenomenon but one that had been observed earlier in the United States in the period following the Civil War (and following all subsequent wars). Industrialization, the decline in economic functions of the family, employment and financial independence of women, weakening of religious beliefs, and the declining social stigma of divorce were also viewed as causes of divorce.

By the 1960s, the focus of the divorce debate began to shift once again. Although still concerned with the high rate of divorce, public attention increasingly turned to the effects of divorce on spouses and children. Numerous voices were raised against the adversarial nature of divorce, and various proposals for divorce by mutual consent were put forth, culminating in California's no-fault divorce bill signed into law by Governor Ronald Reagan (who was himself divorced) in 1969 (Jacob, 1988). Over the next 20 years state after state adopted its own version of **no-fault divorce**, believing that the most negative

consequences of divorce would be eliminated by this measure. Spouses no longer had to accuse each other of wrongdoing; instead, they could apply for a divorce on grounds of "irretrievable breakdown" or "irreconcilable differences." Indeed, no-fault divorce removed much of the acrimony of divorce while also lowering its economic cost. As we shall see later in this chapter, however, over 20 years' experience with no-fault divorce has shown that it was not the panacea its advocates anticipated. Issues of spousal support, division of marital property, and child custody remain problematic.

What lessons are to be learned from an examination of the history of divorce in the United States? Perhaps the most important is that neither marriage nor divorce can be understood apart from its social context. As Roderick Phillips (1988:640) observed: "It is entirely futile to expect marriage to remain constant or to have a consistent social meaning while social structures, economic relationships, demographic patterns, and cultural configurations have undergone the massive changes of past centuries." The historical record also makes it abundantly clear that efforts to eliminate divorce will in all likelihood fail. Therefore, it is probably more effective to focus social efforts on strengthening marriages and creating compassionate and fair systems of helping people whose marriages have failed.

CURRENT TRENDS

Calculating the actual extent of divorce today is not easy. Data concerning divorces are presented in a variety of ways, each having unique strengths and weaknesses for purposes of analysis. The five most commonly used measures are (1) the number of divorces per year, (2) the crude divorce rate, (3) the refined divorce rate, (4) the divorce-to-marriage ratio, and (5) the ratio of divorced to married people.

MEASURING THE INCIDENCE OF DIVORCE

NUMBER OF DIVORCES PER YEAR   The number of divorces granted in the United States in 1990 was 1,175,000 (National Center for Health Statistics,

1991:3). Does this number seem high or low to you? Without knowing the population total or the number of marriages, it is impossible to know if this number represents a high or a low divorce rate.

CRUDE DIVORCE RATE   A more meaningful measure is the **crude divorce rate** (CDR), the number of divorces per 1000 people in the population. The advantage of this measure is that it is easy to compute. However, changing characteristics of a population can affect the CDR. For example, in 1950 the rate was 2.5, whereas in 1980 it was 5.2. The higher rate in 1980 can be attributed in part to the increase in the number of marriages that took place in the 1970s as the large number of "baby boomers" took on adult roles. In brief, the marriage rate influences the crude divorce rate (Kain, 1990).

REFINED DIVORCE RATE   A third way of measuring divorce is the **refined divorce rate** (RDR). The RDR is more complicated but more accurate than the CDR. It represents the number of divorces per 1000 married women over age 15. In short, this statistic focuses on individuals who realistically are potential candidates for divorce. Figure 13.1 shows the differences between the crude and refined divorce rates. Both rates provide insight into how the frequency of divorce is affected by economic and political events. For exam-

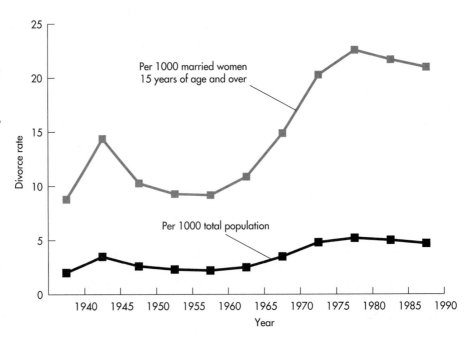

FIGURE 13.1 U. S. Divorce Rates, 1920–90

Source: National Center for Health Statistics, 1985, "Advance Report of Divorce Statistics, 1985," *Monthly Vital Statistics Reports*, 38, 8 (Hyattsville, MD: Public Health Service [Supplement, Dec. 7]): 2; "Population Update," 1991, *Population Today* 19 (July/August): 9.

ple, the divorce rate declined during the depression of the early 1930s, when couples simply could not afford to get divorced. It increased dramatically during and immediately after World War II, because of an improved economy and because previously separated couples had to readjust to living together. The RDR then remained relatively stable until 1965, when it began a sharp increase, peaking at 22.6 during the late 1970s and then leveling off somewhat in the recessionary period of the 1980s. Economic pressures led many wives to enter the labor force in the 1970s and 1980s, straining marital relationships.

DIVORCE-TO-MARRIAGE RATIO A fourth measure of divorce, the **divorce-to-marriage ratio**, compares the number of marriages with the number of divorces occurring in a given year. In 1990, the total number of marriages was 2,448,000, and the number of divorces was 1,175,000 (National Center for Health Statistics, 1991:3). Hence, we get a figure that makes headlines—approximately one out of every two marriages ends in divorce. This interpretation is misleading, however. The marriage statistic represents only couples married in a particular year, whereas the divorce statistic refers to all couples who divorce during that same year, regardless of when they married.

RATIO OF DIVORCED TO MARRIED PERSONS The fifth measure is the **ratio of divorced to married persons** (with spouse present). Although currently utilized by the U.S. Bureau of the Census, this method has one drawback. By failing to distinguish between people in first marriages and those in subsequent marriages, it excludes divorced people who have since remarried. Thus, it could be said to underestimate the extent of divorce. Based on this method, in 1990, there were 15,128,000 currently divorced people 15 years of age and over who had not remarried. These people represented 8 percent of the total adult population of the United States. Included in these figures were 12,643,000 whites, 2,146,000 blacks, and 952,000 Latinos (U.S. Bureau of the Census, 1991a:17).

RACE, ETHNICITY, AND DIVORCE

Table 13.1 uses the ratio of divorced to married persons to examine the divorce ratio since 1960. Several patterns are apparent in this table. First, the divorce

TABLE 13.1

Divorced Persons per 1000 Married Persons by Sex, Race, and Latino Origin, 1960–90

Year and Sex	Total	White	Black	Latino[*]
Both sexes				
1990	142	133	282	129
1980	100	92	203	98
1970	47	44	83	61
1960	35	33	62	NA
Male				
1990	118	112	208	103
1980	79	74	149	64
1970	35	32	62	40
1960	28	27	45	NA
Female				
1990	166	153	358	155
1980	120	110	258	132
1970	60	56	104	81
1960	42	38	78	NA

[*]Persons of Latino origin may be of any race. NA—not available.

Source: Adapted from U.S. Bureau of the Census, 1991a, *Current Population Reports*, Series P-20, No. 450, "Marital Status and Living Arrangements: March 1990" (Washington, DC: U.S. Government Printing Office): 3.

rate has increased for blacks, whites, and Latinos, with the highest increase occurring between 1970 and 1980. Second, women in all three groups had higher divorce ratios than men due to their lower incidence of remarriage. Finally, the ratios vary by race and ethnicity. In 1990, Latinos had a slightly lower rate than whites, and blacks had considerably higher rates than either of the other two groups.

DIVORCE AMONG AFRICAN AMERICANS How do we explain the different rates of divorce among racial and ethnic groups? In the past some analysts have viewed the higher rate of divorce among African Americans as the legacy of slavery (Frazier, 1939). Subsequent scholarship, however, has found that the increase in black marital instability is a more recent development, accelerating in particular since 1960 and corresponding to a decline in the economic situation of large numbers of African Americans (Gutman, 1976; Cherlin, 1981). Certain studies support the argument that higher divorce rates among African Americans reflect greater economic hardships. For example, one statistical analysis showed that a significant amount of black–white differences in marital stability can be explained by differences in levels of education and income among the two groups (Jaynes and Williams, 1989).

DIVORCE AMONG LATINOS Because Latinos also experience higher rates of poverty and unemployment as a result of discrimination, we might assume that the Latino divorce ratio would be closer to that of blacks than to that of whites. In fact, as Table 13.1 indicates, Latinos have the lowest overall divorce rate of the three groups in 1990. Two factors are often cited to explain the relatively high level of marital stability among Latinos: a cultural tradition that emphasizes the importance of the family unit, and a religion (Catholicism) that prohibits divorce.

Demographers Hugh Carter and Paul Glick (1976:246) raise another issue that may be relevant

Compared to black and white couples, Latino couples have lower rates of divorce. Nevertheless, a growing number of Latinas are single parents.

here. In their analysis of 1960 census data they found that the lowest ratios of divorced to married persons for a major group were among the foreign-born white population. They speculated that lack of familiarity with the U.S. legal system and a reluctance to become involved in court actions probably led many foreign-born couples to tolerate marital problems that might have resulted in divorce among native-born groups. These conclusions might apply to those Latinos who most recently have arrived in the United States.

Although all these factors may contribute to the lower divorce rates found among Latinos, the Latino ratio itself presents several problems. It does not distinguish among the diverse categories of Latinos whose economic status and rates of marital stability might vary. For example, according to the 1980 census, among Latino women aged 35 to 44, 28.5 percent of Puerto Ricans were divorced, compared with 14.2 percent of Chicanas and 13.4 percent of Cubans. In fact, the rate for Puerto Rican women approached that for black women (30.6 percent) and was over twice the rate of non-Latino white women (Sweet and Bumpass, 1987:224).

THE NEED FOR FURTHER RESEARCH It is apparent that more research is needed if we are to understand the interactive effects of economic status, race, and ethnicity on marital stability. In particular, more data are needed on groups such as Native Americans, who have high divorce rates, and on Asian Americans, who have low rates. In 1980, 48 percent of Native American women and 43 percent of men were no longer in intact first marriages (Sweet and Bumpass, 1987:188). These high rates are probably due largely to the high rates of unemployment and poverty among Native Americans.

Like Latinos and Native Americans, Asian Americans include a wide spectrum of groups with different cultural traditions. In 1980, for example, 15 percent of Chinese, 21 percent of Filipino, 22 percent of Korean, and 22 percent of Japanese women were no longer in intact first marriages. The corresponding figures for men were quite similar, except for a rate of 13 percent among Korean men (Sweet and Bumpass, 1987:188). Many Asian-American community leaders are concerned that as Asian Americans become more assimilated into mainstream U.S. culture, their traditional family patterns will change, and divorce rates will rise (O'Hare and Felt,

1991:10). Race and ethnicity are, of course, not the only factors affecting divorce rates. The next section examines a variety of social and demographic factors that affect the likelihood of divorce.

WHO GETS DIVORCED AND WHY?

If you are like most Americans, you are probably startled by the high rate of divorce. Perhaps the thought has occurred to you that you or people close to you are likely to end up divorced. Although no one can say with any degree of certainty which marriages will end in divorce, based on existing patterns, researchers can predict the statistical probabilities for different groups.

FACTORS AFFECTING MARITAL STABILITY

Divorce rates vary from group to group and are associated with a wide range of factors (Glenn and Supancic, 1984; White, 1990), including age at marriage, education, income, wife's employment, reli-

gion, parental divorce, and the presence of children. By understanding how these factors can influence a marital relationship, people contemplating marriage can better evaluate their chances of a successful marriage. For example, knowing that the age at marriage can increase or decrease the likelihood of divorce may lead people more realistically to evaluate their readiness for marriage.

AGE AT FIRST MARRIAGE Younger brides and grooms, especially those who are still in their teens when they marry, are more likely to divorce. "About half of both women and men who married under the age of 18 experienced marital disruption within 10 years of first marriage" (Sweet and Bumpass, 1987:184). Similarly, marrying at a late age (35 plus) can increase the probability of divorce during the first 15 years of marriage (Booth et al., 1986). In fact, Figure 13.2 shows that the risk of divorce for people who marry after age 35 approximates that for teenage marriages. The reasons for marital instability among the young come easily to mind: immaturity, lack of adequate financial resources,

Couples who marry in their teenage years run a high risk of being divorced.

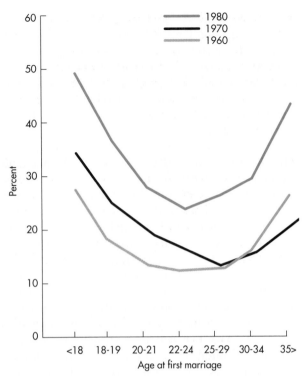

FIGURE 13.2 Percent of women married 10–14 years who are no longer in first marriages, by age at first marriage, 1960–80. Notice that the highest divorce rates occur among couples who marry in their teens and those who marry after age 35.

Source: Reprinted from *American Families and Households* by James A. Sweet and Larry L. Bumpass, ©1987 The Russell Sage Foundation. Used with permission.

different rates of personal growth, and often the pressures of early parenthood. By later ages, however, those problems should be resolved. Although fewer data on late marriages are available, some evidence suggests that late marriages tend to be more heterogamous and, thus, potentially more conflictual. Also, the pool of eligible marital partners becomes more restricted with increasing age. Thus, people wishing to marry may have to accept greater differences in values, ages, and educational and economic status in their partners than do younger people. It is also likely that late marriages involve a remarriage for one or both spouses; rates of divorce for remarriage are higher than those for first marriages. We examine the dynamics of remarriages in Chapter 14.

EDUCATION A complex relationship exists between divorce and levels of education for women. For example, women who drop out of high school experience the highest rates of marital disruption, whereas marriages of college graduates tend to be the most stable. This pattern reflects a number of different factors. High school dropouts are more likely to marry at an early age and to hold low-paying jobs. Thus, financial pressures on the marriage are likely to be substantial. Moreover, those who persist in school probably are better equipped to work out problems as they occur.

Interestingly, divorce rates are higher among women with 5 or more years of college education. This pattern, however, does not occur among comparably educated males (Glenn and Supancic, 1984). The reasons for these divergent patterns are not as yet well understood. Teresa Cooney and Peter Uhlenberg (1989) suggest that the higher level of divorce among professional women reflects the conflicts involved in balancing work and family responsibilities. In addition, professional women are less likely to be financially dependent on a spouse and thus can afford to leave an unsatisfactory relationship. This latter explanation is consistent with a pattern observed in earlier studies—women earning high incomes tend to have higher divorce rates than other women do (Glick and Norton, 1977; Houseknecht and Spanier, 1980).

INCOME The above finding is an exception to the general relationship that exists between income and marital stability. Overall, the lower the income, the more likely a couple is to divorce (South, 1985; Martin and Bumpass, 1989). Earlier we observed that low income and its accompanying stresses are a major factor in the higher divorce rate found among some groups. The significance of income is shown, for example, in its impact on early marriages. Young couples with sufficient financial resources had more stable marriages than similar couples with inadequate resources (Spanier and Glick, 1981).

WIFE'S EMPLOYMENT Numerous studies show that marital instability has increased along with women's labor-force participation (Moore and Sawhill, 1984; Cherlin and Furstenberg, 1988; Spitze, 1988). What is less clear, however, is why this relationship exists. One interpretation suggests that among marriages that are unsatisfactory for whatever reason, the costs of divorce are lowest for wives who are capable of self-support (Moore and Sawhill, 1984:157). Other explanations have been tied to changing gender roles. As discussed in Chapter 11, husbands may find it difficult to adjust to a co-provider role, and wives may feel overburdened by working outside the home while still being expected to do the bulk of the housework.

More recent research suggests that the relationship between the employment of women and divorce is not a simple cause-and-effect relationship. Other factors are at work here as well. For example, Theodore Greenstein (1990) found that the conditions under which wives work is the fundamental issue. He reported that divorce is less likely when the wife's earnings and her share of family income are higher. Having two wage earners may relieve financial tensions that often contribute to divorce; thus, a wife's employment may contribute to greater marital stability.

Under different circumstances, however, female employment can increase marital instability. As with men, for example, women in high-stress jobs frequently find that work-related pressures carry over into domestic situations and intensify marital difficulties. In addition, employment outside the home can provide women with greater opportunities for alternative relationships, which can weaken the marital bond. Clearly, then, we must avoid simple generalizations concerning the relationship between female employment and divorce.

RELIGION Historically, many religions have either prohibited or tried to discourage divorce among their members. On this basis we would predict that more religiously involved people would have lower rates of divorce, a view that is supported by a considerable body of research. Researchers Norval Glenn and Michael Supancic (1984) found that among white males, those who never attended religious services had a divorce rate over three times higher than those who attended on a weekly basis. Membership in a religious organization also promotes social cohesion (Durkheim, 1897, 1951) and provides a source of support in times of difficulty. This support helps couples work through problems that otherwise might lead to divorce.

Researchers also found differences among various religious groups. Protestant couples have the highest rates of divorce, Catholics are next, and Jewish cou-

ples have the lowest rates (Glenn and Supancic, 1984; Brodbar-Nemzer, 1986). Among the Protestant denominations there is also considerable variation, with Baptists and Pentecostals having higher divorce rates than Presbyterians and Episcopalians. Some caution is required in interpreting this last finding, however. The differences in rates may be the result of an interactive effect between religious membership and other factors such as education and income. Baptists and Pentecostals tend to have lower levels of education and income than do Presbyterians and Episcopalians.

PARENTAL DIVORCE Can the parents' divorce influence the outcome of their children's marriage? The answer apparently is yes. People whose parents divorced have higher divorce rates than do children who come from intact families (Keith and Finlay, 1988; McLanahan and Bumpass, 1988). Several factors may combine to produce this outcome. First, from their parents' example, children have learned that divorce can be a solution to marital difficulties. Thus, they may be more ready than their peers to seek a divorce when problems start. Second, as a result of a parental divorce, children may experience some long-lasting negative effects that they carry into their own relationships, causing them to be less committed. For example, women from disrupted families have more difficulty trusting and relying on men than do women from intact families (Southworth and Schwarz, 1987). A lack of trust can undermine a marital relationship.

PRESENCE OF CHILDREN A consistent research finding is that marital disruption is most likely when the marriage is childless (Wineberg, 1988) and least likely when there is a child younger than 3 (Heaton, 1990). This finding should not be construed to mean that marriages with children are happier than those without. In fact, couples with children still at home tend to be less happy than either childless couples or those whose children have left home (Spanier, Lewis, and Cole, 1975; Nock, 1979). Rather, parents who are having marital problems often delay divorce until all the children are in school.

Today, however, married couples are less likely to stay together because children are present in the home. The National Center for Health Statistics (1990e) reports that approximately half of all couples recently divorced now have children under 18. More than 1 million children have been involved in divorce annually since 1972. Overall, parents of sons are less likely to divorce than are parents of daughters (Morgan, Lye, and Condran, 1988). Researchers attribute this to a greater involvement of fathers with their sons. Graham Spanier and Paul Glick (1981), who reported the same pattern, suggest that it is related to a man's desire to have a son carry on his name, a desire especially strong among traditional fathers. Additionally, they speculate that mothers of sons might resist a separation in the belief that raising sons without a father would be more difficult than raising daughters alone. We examine the effects of divorce on children later in this chapter.

Thus far, we have examined a number of factors associated with divorce. Nevertheless, these factors do not tell us about the process of divorce or how or why individuals decide to divorce. Recall that we opened this chapter with a scenario of a formerly happy couple whose marriage failed. What, then, happens to marriages that look so promising when they begin? Although every marital disruption has its unique features, social scientists have identified several common stages through which most divorcing couples pass.

THE PROCESS OF DIVORCE

Divorce doesn't just happen. It is a complex social process in which a basic unit of social organization—marriage—breaks down over time, culminating in a legal termination of the relationship.

STAGES IN THE DIVORCE PROCESS

Divorce involves more than a legal decree officially symbolizing the end of a marriage. Some researchers, like Ahrons (1980) and Levinger (1979), identify three stages in the divorce process: (1) a period of marital conflict and unhappiness, (2) the actual marital dissolution itself, and (3) a postdivorce period. James Ponzetti and Rodney Cate (1986) see divorce as a four-step process: (1) recognition by one or both spouses of serious marital problems; (2) discussion of these problems with the spouse and possibly with

family, friends, or counselors; (3) initiation of legal action to dissolve the marriage; and (4) the postdissolution period, which involves adapting to a new status. Although both spouses go through the same stages, the timing may be different for each spouse, depending on who initiates the divorce.

Although these researchers propose different models, they all agree that the dissolution of a marriage occurs through a series of stages. The majority of separations and divorces follow a period of personal unhappiness, conflict, and deliberation, during which time individuals make decisions based upon three types of criteria: (1) an evaluation of the attractiveness of the relationship itself (the material, emotional, and symbolic rewards a spouse provides), (2) an evaluation of the costs and benefits of a divorce (monetary, social, and psychological), and (3) an evaluation of the attractiveness of possible alternatives, including new relationships (Levinger, 1965).

THE SIX STATIONS OF DIVORCE

Anthropologist Paul Bohannan (1970) has identified not one but six divorces that couples experience in dissolving their marital relationship. These he calls the **stations of divorce**: emotional, legal, economic, coparental, community, and psychic divorce.

The **emotional divorce** can be present in the marriage for a long time before any legal action is taken to end the relationship. Here one or both spouses question the viability or quality of the relationship and at some point share this view with the other. There is often a period during which one or both partners withdraw emotionally from the relationship. A loss of mutual respect, trust, and affection follows. During this period both spouses may hurt or frustrate the other deliberately. Yet despite the deterioration of the relationship and talk of separation, one or both spouses may not want a divorce for a variety of reasons: fear of living alone, concern about the children, desire to fulfill marriage vows, or the economic and social costs involved. Thus, some marriages may remain intact in form but not in substance for extended periods of time. Other spouses take action to move to the next stage. This may involve one spouse walking out or a mutual decision to begin a period of separation.

The **legal divorce** officially ends the marriage and gives spouses the right to remarry. Legal divorce generally follows a period of months or even years of deliberation. Sociologists Graham Spanier and Linda Thompson (1988:331) interviewed 50 separated and divorced people (22 women and 28 men) and found that the median length of deliberation between thinking that divorce is a possibility and the certainty of divorce was 12 months for the men and 22 months for the women. Women thought about divorce earlier than men. The divorce itself can be an adversarial process, especially when children and property are involved. In attempting to settle these issues the divorcing couple may lose control of the process itself to lawyers who advocate their client's interest generally without regard to the needs of the other party.

The **economic divorce** involves the settlement of property, a process that often involves considerable conflict. Most states now have laws specifying that both spouses are to receive an equitable share of the marital property. Equity is not always easy to determine, however. Tangible items like the house, the car, income, and bank accounts, whose values are easy to calculate, can be divided without great difficulty. But what about the current and future earning power of each individual? Should this be considered in a divorce settlement? For example, spouses with advanced degrees or special labor-market skills are at a real advantage after a divorce. Considerable controversy exists over the question of what constitutes a fair return on an investment in human capital. This question arises in cases where one spouse (most frequently the husband) earned a degree or learned a skill while the other spouse (most frequently the wife) played a major supportive role in making that possible, earning the money to pay for the spouse's education. Increasingly courts are wrestling with issues like this.

The economic station of divorce is less often applicable than some of the other stations. It assumes that all couples have tangible assets to divide. Although this is certainly true for middle- and upper-class couples, it is not generally true for the poor and even for many working-class couples, who live in rental units and depend on public transportation. According to Judith Seltzer and Irwin Garfinkel (1990), 40 percent or more of divorcing couples don't make any property settlement because they have nothing of value to divide.

The **coparental divorce** involves decisions concerning child custody, visitation rights, and the financial and legal responsibilities of each parent. This station can also be a source of conflict, particularly when parents are engaged in a custody battle. We'll return to the topic of child custody later in this chapter.

The **community divorce** involves changing social relationships. It can involve a loss of relatives and friends who were previously shared with the spouse. In one study of 60 divorced mothers, over three-quarters reported losing former friends, usually during or immediately after the divorce (Arendell (1986). The withdrawal of friendship may occur for several reasons. Those who were friendly with both spouses may not want to be drawn into taking sides. Others may see the divorce as a threat to their own relationships. For most of the women in the study the loss of friends was an unexpected occurrence that was painful and emotionally confusing. In this stage of divorce people may feel lonely and isolated.

The **psychic divorce** involves a redefinition of self away from the mutuality of couplehood and back to a sense of singularity. This process takes time and involves a distancing from and an acceptance of the breakup. Many people go through a mourning process similar to that experienced by people who lose a spouse to death (see Chapter 15). The time this

Maintaining a relationship with children is often difficult for the parent without custody. This divorced father reads to his children on one of their weekend visits.

takes and the degree of difficulty with which this station is passed through varies considerably from individual to individual.

We examine some of the dynamics of these stations of divorce in more detail when we discuss the consequences of divorce later in this chapter.

Although we now know how couples end their marriages, we still don't have an answer to the most frequently asked questions about divorce: Why? and What went wrong? What causes people to evaluate their relationships as problematic or unsatisfactory?

THE CAUSES OF DIVORCE

People who respond to a divorce by asking, What went wrong? frequently assume that some specific event or events disrupted the relationship. A key assumption here is that by eliminating the cause of the problem the marriage could have been saved. In fact, a growing body of research suggests that the search for causes of divorce may be futile.

FROM THE PERSPECTIVE OF DIVORCED PEOPLE

Paul Rasmussen and Kathleen Ferraro (1991) interviewed 32 divorced people, in most cases both husband and wife. Their findings raise questions about how we look at the causes of divorce. The behaviors most commonly cited as leading to divorce are extramarital sex, excessive drinking, and financial mismanagement.

Did these behaviors, however, actually "cause" the divorce? Many respondents considered these activities to be aftereffects of crises or problems that derived from other sources. Other respondents reported that these behaviors had occurred prior to dating, during dating, and during the marriage. Many of the spouses had remained committed to marriages in which such offending behaviors were present and openly acknowledged. Rasmussen and Ferraro concluded that these behaviors may exist for years without leading to divorce or even creating any serious problems. Conversely, they may be totally absent when divorce occurs.

According to Rasmussen and Ferraro (1991:387):

> Husbands and wives who share strong emotional ties require…[a] significant crisis to break the bond. While the typically listed causes of divorce played an important role in all the divorces studied, it was in their use as tools to facilitate the divorce rather than as direct causes. The "knife of crisis" used as a means of ending a marriage was often adultery, heavy drinking, or financial ineptitude. Spouses either indulged in or complained of problem behaviors in building a case for divorce.

Thus, it appears that divorced people cannot give a single reason for their divorce. Rather, a wide variety of "causes" are cited that pertain to a spouse's behavior, to perceived difficulties in the marital relationship, or to the impact of social and economic factors existing in the larger society. This doesn't mean, however, that researchers are unable to code their categories of complaints. For example, one sociologist was able to arrive at 13 "causes" reported by her respondents. "These ranged from clear-cut justifications, such as abandonment or 'becoming gay,' to rather fuzzy references to personality differences, poor communication, or simply the need to find a happier situation" (Johnson, 1988:69).

FROM THE PERSPECTIVE OF FAMILY THERAPISTS

One survey asked members of the American Association of Marriage and Family Therapists to rate the frequency, severity, and treatment difficulty of 29 problems frequently seen among couples experiencing marital difficulties (Geiss and O'Leary, 1981:516–17). The therapists were asked to rank the five areas they considered most damaging to couple relationships and the five most difficult to treat, giving their top choice a value of 5 and their fifth choice a value of 1. The ten areas rated as most damaging and their combined scores were

1. Communication (361)
2. Unrealistic expectations of marriage or spouse (197)
3. Power struggles (135)
4. Serious individual problems (126)
5. Role conflicts (95)
6. Lack of loving feelings (92)
7. Demonstration of affection (90)
8. Alcoholism (81)
9. Extramarital affairs (80)
10. Sex (79)

PERSONAL REFLECTION

This exercise is designed to help you assess some of the risk factors of divorce that may be present in your life. Circle yes if the question accurately describes you or those close to you.

1. Did you marry or do you plan to marry before your twentieth birthday?   Yes   No
2. Did you marry or do you plan to marry in your 30s or 40s?   Yes   No
3. Are your parents divorced?   Yes   No
4. Are any of your close friends divorced?   Yes   No
5. For females, do you plan to have a profession?   Yes   No
   For males, do you think your wife will have a profession?   Yes   No
6. Do you attend religious services only occasionally?   Yes   No
7. Will both you and your spouse work?   Yes   No
8. Do you prefer to avoid conflict rather than discuss problems?   Yes   No
9. Do you have difficulty managing your money?   Yes   No
10. Are you (or your spouse) reluctant to discuss problems and feelings with each other?   Yes   No

Scoring: Add up the number of times you circled yes. The higher the number of yes answers, the more risk factors you have for becoming divorced. However, this does not automatically mean you will be divorced at some point in your life. Rather, it indicates that you have some of the characteristics that researchers have found to be associated with a tendency to divorce and that you should be aware that these factors can present problems in a relationship.

The ten areas rated as most difficult to treat successfully and their combined scores were

1. Alcoholism (275)
2. Lack of loving feelings (178)
3. Serious individual problems (144)
4. Power struggles (129)
5. Addictive behavior other than alcoholism (104)
6. Value conflicts (92)
7. Physical abuse (90)
8. Unrealistic expectations of marriage or spouse (84)
9. Extramarital affairs (78)
10. Incest (62)

Now that you have reviewed the areas that are considered damaging to marital relationships, do you think restricting divorce through more stringent laws would be a wise public policy? Why or why not? Should couples who are experiencing marital difficulties be required to undergo counseling before being allowed to file for divorce? Should parents who are experiencing marital difficulties wait until the children are grown before divorcing? Why or why not?

IMPLICATIONS FOR STRENGTHENING MARRIAGE The second list implies that certain constructive measures can be taken to strengthen marriages. First, therapists can intervene in distressed relationships to help people improve their communication skills (see Chapter 8). Improved communication skills can help each partner understand the perspective of the other and perhaps avoid unnecessary conflict. Couples can also take certain steps to avoid entering marriage with unrealistic expectations of their relationship or each other. Discussion and negotiations (perhaps formulating a marital contract) prior to getting married as well as ongoing discussion and renegotiations are necessary if couples are to achieve satisfaction and agreement on their roles and responsibilities.

Finally, recognizing that some problems, like alcoholism, are difficult to treat effectively may encourage some people to take action sooner. For example, if a prospective spouse has a drinking problem or is abusive, perhaps marriage should be postponed until this problem has been addressed through counseling or some other means.

THE IMPACT OF DIVORCE ON SPOUSES

The consequences of divorce are many and varied. Although some of these are experienced by both spouses, a number of factors are gender-specific. We'll begin this section by looking at those issues that commonly affect both spouses, and then we'll isolate those features of divorce that affect women and men in distinctly different ways.

COMMON CONSEQUENCES OF DIVORCE

Charles Dickens could just as easily have been talking about divorce and its aftermath as about eighteenth-century London and Paris when he wrote, "It was the best of times; it was the worst of times." For most divorcing couples both statements are true. On the positive side divorce can free people from unhappy, conflict-ridden, or unsatisfactory relationships. On the negative side, however, divorce can produce considerable pain, guilt, and uncertainty. This duality is clearly visible in Cheryl Buehler and Mary Langenbrunner's (1987) research. They asked 80 divorced people (whose divorces had been finalized 6 to 12 months earlier) to identify which of 140 items they had experienced since they separated from their spouses. The results showed that divorced people are almost equally likely to report both positive and negative outcomes. The most frequently reported items appear in Table 13.2.

TABLE 13.2

Most Frequently Reported Experiences of Divorced Persons

I have felt worthwhile as a person	96%
I have experienced personal growth and maturity	94
I have felt relieved	92
I have felt closer to my children	89
I have felt competent	89
The cost of maintaining the household has been difficult	87
I have felt angry toward my former spouse	87
I have felt insecure	86
My leisure activities have increased	86
I have been depressed	86
Household routines and daily patterns have changed	85

Source: Cheryl Buehler and Mary Langenbrunner, 1987, "Divorce-Related Stressors: Occurrence, Disruptiveness, and Area of Life Change," *Journal of Divorce* 11:35.

Are you surprised to find that the most frequently occurring responses are positive? Many people are. However, this finding should not be interpreted to mean that the negative consequences of divorce are inconsequential. They are not. People in the process of divorce frequently encounter a number of problems. The most common problems experienced by both women and men are health problems (both physical and psychological), loneliness, the need for social and sexual readjustments, and financial changes in their lifestyles (Morgan, 1990). This latter problem is more common to women than to men, so we will consider it later under gender-specific problems.

HEALTH PROBLEMS Many people experience depression and sometimes despair in the wake of a divorce. The process of divorce involves a number of major lifestyle alterations: loss of a major source of intimacy, the end of a set of daily routines, and a changed social status—going from a socially approved category (married) to a still somewhat disapproved category (divorced). Based on her research with 104 separated and divorced respondents (52 women and 52 men), sociologist Naomi Gerstel (1990) found that the stigma of divorce has not completely disappeared. Gerstel argues that although divorce is now less deviant in a statistical sense than it was in the past and although the divorced are no longer categorized as sinful, criminal, or even wrong, the divorced still believe they are the targets of informal relational sanctions—they are excluded from social events, blamed for the marital breakup, and sometimes held in low regard. Hence, many divorced people respond to their new status with feelings of stress, guilt (especially for the initiator of divorce), and failure (especially for the partner who was asked for the divorce). Frank Trovato and Gloria Lauris (1989) report heightened levels of mortality and psychological and physical morbidity among divorced people in comparison to single, married, and widowed people.

LONELINESS Although people who live alone are not inherently more lonely than people who live together, a period of loneliness often accompanies the transition from being a part of a couple to being single again. This is especially true for childless couples and older couples whose children have already left home. However, divorce can involve more than the loss of a spouse. Relationships with former in-laws can be strained or broken off completely. Ann-Marie Ambert (1988) studied 49 separated and divorced spouses and found that only 11 percent of the respondents maintained positive relationships with their former in-laws after the separation. Conversely, blood relatives might choose to retain contact with the ex-spouse even against the wishes of their own kin. The latter pattern often creates social distance among family members.

SOCIAL AND SEXUAL READJUSTMENTS
Feelings of isolation and loneliness can lead to physical and psychological problems. Thus, divorced people are well advised to maintain old friends and companions or to seek new ones to offset the possible losses in their support network and to restore their self-esteem. In this regard, one of the major adjustments divorced people face is getting back into circulation. Dating is not easy at any age, but it is particularly problematic for older divorced people.

Newly dating divorced people must deal with two key issues: how to explain their unmarried status and whether to be sexually active. Divorce does not lessen social or sexual needs. Studies from Kinsey, Pomeroy, and Martin (1948) through today show that most divorced people have sex within 1 year of being separated from their partner. Besides filling a physical need, providing intimacy, and exploring a new-found freedom, sex is often used to validate a sense of self-worth that may have been seriously eroded during the divorce process. Both women and men need to know that others find them attractive and sexually desirable. Some need to test their sexual adequacy, especially if their performance was criticized by their previous spouse.

These needs are not always adequately met, however. Sexual encounters are not always satisfying. Women in particular often feel exploited by men who assume that because they are divorced, they will automatically welcome any casual sexual relationship. Although both divorced women and men are sexually active, overall men have more sexual partners than women do (Hunt, 1973).

GENDER DIFFERENCES IN DIVORCE

As discussed in Chapter 3, the U.S. sex–gender system structures women's and men's marital and family experiences in markedly different ways. In her study

titled *The Future of Marriage*, Jessie Bernard (1972) observed that every marital relationship contains two marriages that are often widely divergent. She called these "his" and "her" marriages. The same social structures and gender expectations that create differential marriage experiences for women and men also act to create differential divorces. These can be described as "her" divorce and "his" divorce.

"HER" DIVORCE   The most striking, even startling, difference, between women and men following a divorce is a monetary one. Media headlines about the divorce settlements of the rich and famous, like Johnny Carson and Donald Trump, suggest that women are the recipients of huge alimony payments. Volumes of research over the last 2 decades reveal a markedly different pattern, however. After divorce the standard of living of children and their custodial parents (predominantly women) drops sharply.

DOWNWARD SOCIAL MOBILITY   According to researchers Greg Duncan and Saul Hoffman (1985), women suffer about a 30 percent decline on average in their income in the year following a separation, whereas men experience a 15 percent increase. In a pioneering study of the economic impact of California's no-fault divorce law (discussed earlier in this chapter) on divorcing spouses, sociologist Lenore Weitzman found a larger discrepancy. Weitzman analyzed 2500 California court records covering a 10-year period, some before and some after the enactment of the law. She found that within a year of the final divorce the standard of living of women and their children declined by an average of 73 percent, whereas that of ex-husbands improved by an average of 42 percent (Weitzman, 1985:339). Duncan and Hoffman have come up with somewhat different numbers, but the general pattern they found is the same: downward social mobility for women and children, often to the point of impoverishment (McCarthy, 1985; Arendell, 1986). For example, close to 10 percent of white children and 14 percent of black children whose parents separated fell into poverty the following year (Duncan and Hoffman, 1985). A 1991 report of the U.S. Bureau of the Census found that 19 percent of children lived in poverty when their parents separated; 4 months later it was 36 percent. This same study found a 37 percent drop in family income available to children after their fathers moved out (*Chicago Tribune*, 1991b:6).

This downward mobility for women and children is explained by two key factors: the earnings gap between women and men (see Chapter 11) and the failure of courts to award, and ex-husbands to pay, alimony and child support.

THE LEGAL SYSTEM AND WOMEN'S FINANCIAL WELL-BEING According to sociologists Frank Furstenberg and Andrew Cherlin (1991:48–49), "When marriages dissolve, the shift in family responsibilities and family resources assumes a characteristic form. Women get the children and, accordingly, assume most of the economic responsibility for their support. Men become nonresidential parents and relinquish the principal responsibility for their support." These patterns are directly related to U.S. legal practices.

The courts routinely award alimony (also called "spousal support" or "spouse maintenance") in only 17 percent of all divorce cases. The rate is even lower for women of color—only 11 percent of divorcing African-American women and Latinas were awarded alimony (U.S. Bureau of the Census, 1992c:372). Furthermore, alimony is actually received in far fewer cases than the awards indicate. Terri Arendell interviewed 60 divorced middle-class women and found that "only 6 of the women—all of them divorced after marriages of 15 years or longer—received spousal support awards. One of them received an award for life or until she should remarry; the others were given awards of specific and short duration" (Arendell, 1986:33). A similar pattern has been found in child support awards, a topic examined in greater detail in the Critical Issues box later in this chapter).

CAUSES OF INEQUALITY BETWEEN DIVORCED WOMEN AND MEN What explains this economic discrepancy between divorced women and men? Weitzman (1985) attributes it to the provisions of the no-fault divorce laws, which require that husbands and wives be treated equally. In the abstract this sounds eminently fair. In reality, however, it overlooks the fact, discussed in Chapter 11, that women historically either were not in the labor force, or if they were, they received lower wages than men. For example, the 1991 study by the U.S. Bureau of the Census, discussed earlier, showed that after their husbands left, women who were working or who found a job

for the first time earned an average of $860 per month, only half of the $1720 per month their husbands averaged (*Chicago Tribune*, 1991b:6). Thus, simply dividing marital property equally without regard for the resources (professional degrees, skills) or the earning power of the respective spouses puts women at a real disadvantage vis-à-vis men. Women's advocates point out that by assuming responsibility for the majority of housework and child care, women sacrifice their own employment and earning power (see Chapter 11) and enhance that of their husband. Thus, these advocates argue that an equitable divorce settlement would take into account women's contributions to a husband's present and future earnings.

THE CONSEQUENCES OF DIVORCE FOR WOMEN What happens to women who experience this downward mobility? Many women, especially those in traditional marriages, suffer a loss of status, identity, and their domestic sphere—the home. Under the doctrine of equal division of property, homes are often sold so that both spouses can receive their share of the value of the house. According to Weitzman (1985) the number of cases in which there was an explicit court order to sell the home rose from one in ten in 1968 to one in three in 1977. The sale of the home often means moving out of a familiar and comfortable neighborhood into a smaller, less expensive place in a different neighborhood. Consequently, school, neighborhood, and friendship ties are often disrupted when they are most needed. Even when the house is not sold, financial strains may make maintenance and a comfortable style of living difficult.

Women with sole custody of children are often doubly burdened—they must be full-time parents as well as economic providers. In the process they must watch their children do without many things that were taken for granted in the past. As the sole parent, divorced women may find little time for themselves or for social activities with peers. All of this exacts a toll. The women Arendell (1986) interviewed spoke of recurring struggles with depression and despair. Many lost a sense of the future and felt trapped by their economic circumstances. Of the 60 women interviewed, 26 reported that they had contemplated suicide at some time after the divorce.

Although there is abundant evidence that women suffer more economic stress than men, there is also evidence to suggest that women fare better in terms of divorce adjustment than do men. According to Judith Wallerstein (1986), women improve the emotional and psychological quality of their lives more than men do. For example, women are more likely than men to experience a sense of growth in self-esteem after a divorce (Baruch et al., 1983). One explanation for women's and men's differing reactions may be that as women take on more instrumental roles, for example, becoming the sole provider and family head, they feel more confident about their abilities. Such changes were expressed by a female respondent: "I'm learning how to do things.... There's no mystery about it now, I can get out an electric drill.... I got satisfaction from putting a bookcase together" (quoted in Riessman, 1990:168). Men, on the other hand, lose some of those roles. The roles they add, such as housekeeper and cook, are not highly valued in this society, and hence, adoption of these roles doesn't generally increase self-esteem (Gecas and Schwalbe, 1983).

"HIS" DIVORCE It is clear from the analysis of "her" divorce that men are better off economically after a divorce than women are. This is a result of many factors. Traditionally society has placed greater value on male workers and therefore paid them higher wages. Even when men pay child support, these payments often represent only a relatively small amount of their take-home pay. A combination of anger, emotional pain, irresponsibility, other debts, a desire for revenge, and remarriage often leads to noncompliance with court-ordered child support. Legal efforts to enforce compliance are often plagued by heavy case loads, inadequate budgets, a shortage of personnel, and, until quite recently, a societal indifference to the plight of divorced women and children. Thus, a divorced husband typically has more discretionary income to support himself than his ex-wife has to support both herself and their children.

Although the number of single-parent fathers has increased slightly, divorced men typically do not get custody of their children. Therefore, whether men desire it or not, divorce frees them from child care. Because they have more discretionary money, they are freer than their ex-wives to pursue social and leisure activities. Men's opportunities for remarriage are also greater than women's. Unencumbered by children, they are freer to date and to begin new relationships.

As we will see in the next chapter, men remarry at higher rates and more quickly than do women.

As is the case for women, however, dating for divorced men is not problem-free. Divorced men may feel uncomfortable in this new role and may hold back because of a fear of rejection. They confront other problems, too. One man explains these problems this way. "The relationships are shallow, let's put it that way. They're not long-range. I don't know how to put it to you. If you just get into bed with someone (names women), I suppose it satisfies your basic needs, let's put it that way. But it's not meaningful. That's the best way to explain it. So, in a sense you have your freedom. You can play the field, you're on the circuit, on the tour, as we call it. But I find that they're basically shallow. So I guess your freedom is basically shallow, as far as that goes" (quoted in Riessman, 1990:193). Many divorced men, especially those from traditional marriages, have trouble establishing a satisfying home environment and maintaining a household routine on their own. Because this was considered a wife's domain, many ex-husbands feel overwhelmed by shopping, laundry, cleaning, and cooking.

Although loneliness can be a problem for both women and men, divorced fathers without custody may feel it more intensely. Even with visitation rights, they miss out on the day-to-day contact with their children and may miss the ritual of family celebrations of special events and holidays. Dennis Meredith (1985) reports that some noncustodial fathers exhibit a child-absence syndrome, feeling depressed, anxious, and cut off from their children's lives. For some divorced fathers this triggers negative reactions. Visits with their children become more sporadic or stop completely, or the fathers become psychologically distant from their children (Furstenberg, Morgan, and Allison, 1987; Wallerstein and Blakeslee, 1989). Some fathers engage in more extreme behavior and kidnap their children. According to government statistics, 25,000 child stealings occur each year; some private groups claim the number is closer to 100,000 (Boneparth and Stoper, 1988:210).

Divorce also has a negative effect on men's contact with their adult children and on their perceptions of their children as potential sources of support. For example, in one study, over 30 percent of middle-aged divorced fathers had lost contact with one or more of their adult children, a situation almost

In the fall of 1991, Gregory Morey, identified by the media as the nation's worst deadbeat dad, was sentenced to 1½ years in prison for failing to pay $108,000 in child support and interest to his former wife. He surrendered to authorities after his name appeared at the top of a national list of fathers who were delinquent on their child support payments. This list is assembled by the National Council of State Child Support Enforcement Administrators. Morey is not alone.

Among the 58 percent of divorced and separated women who were awarded child support in 1989, only 51 percent received the full payment. Of the remaining women, 24 percent received a partial amount, and 25 percent received no payment at all (U. S. Bureau of the Census, 1992c:372). The situation was even worse for divorced women of color. Although 67 percent of white women were awarded child support in 1989, only 34 percent of black women and 41 percent of Latino women were, a slight decline for all three groups from

1987 figures (U.S. Bureau of the Census, 1990).

Why don't fathers pay child support? Tom, a 35-year-old divorced father, offered this explanation: "I paid child support faithfully every month for 2 years after our divorce. During that time I didn't get one thank you. I was to have the kids one weekend a month. Half of the time when I went to pick them up, they weren't ready or my ex-wife said something came up and they couldn't come. I didn't like the way the kids were dressed or how they behaved. Instead of buying them nice clothes, she'd use the money for music lessons or some other thing. We'd argue. Eventually, it was easier just to let her do what she wanted. She's working and can support the kids. I hardly see the kids anymore. I've met someone else and we are getting married soon. I can't afford to pay any more child support."

Concern over the economic plight of divorced women and their children led Congress to pass federal child support legislation in an effort to give some relief to the

custodial parent. A 1984 law required each state to develop guidelines for establishing minimum child support awards. Four years later legislation required judges to follow their state guidelines in decisions pertaining to child support. Any deviation from these guidelines had to be justified in the court record. This 1988 law also allowed states to withhold child support payments from the noncustodial parental paycheck when children were receiving welfare. By 1994, all new court-ordered child support will be subject to automatic withholding, regardless of parental income or children's status (Furstenberg and Cherlin, 1991). By the end of the decade, we should be able to evaluate the effectiveness of these measures.

Do you think there is any validity to Tom's rationale for not paying child support? Do you think harsher enforcement is the way to deal with divorced fathers who don't pay child support? Are there any policies or programs that could deal effectively with Tom's complaints?

nonexistent for never-divorced men (Cooney and Uhlenberg, 1990). Ninety percent of the never-divorced older fathers had weekly contact with at least one of their adult children; this was true for only one-third of the divorced fathers. This study raises questions about the degree to which family ties exist for divorced men as they age.

In sum, although men appear to benefit more than women do from divorce, particularly economically,

they also experience dislocation from the breakup. Social policy must address men's concerns as well as those of divorced women.

RECOVERING FROM DIVORCE

Given that the majority of divorcing couples face serious economic, social, and psychological problems, you may well wonder whether people ever recover from the trauma of divorce. Most do, although the process usually takes several years. For example, a study conducted over a period of 10 years by Judy Wallerstein and Sandra Blakeslee (1989) of 60 families disrupted by divorce found that women take an average of 3 to 3.5 years and men 2 to 2.5 years to reestablish a sense of external order after the separation. Not everyone recovers at the same speed, however. Wallerstein and Blakeslee found that some of their respondents had not recovered 15 years after their divorce.

Why do some people adjust more quickly than others? Do certain characteristics enable some people to cope with divorce problems more effectively than other people? An emerging body of research has begun to identify certain factors that affect people's ability to adjust to divorce. Wallerstein and Blakeslee (1989), for example, found that younger people fared better. This was especially true for women. Women under 40 fared better in terms of making life changes than did men and older women. These changes tended to cluster around two major areas: increasing competence in the management of daily life and developing a fuller sense of identity. Robert and Jeanette Lauer (1988) found that those who successfully coped with their divorce were able to redefine the divorce as an opportunity for growth. Other research suggests that women and men who are nontraditional in their gender orientation adjust better and more quickly to a marital breakdown. The explanation for this is that androgynous women and men have better coping skills with which to handle the trauma of divorce than do women and men who behave according to traditional gender-role expectations (Chiriboga and Thurnher, 1980; Hansson et al., 1984). This latter point has major implications for how we socialize children to prepare them for adult roles.

THE IMPACT OF DIVORCE ON CHILDREN

With the increase in the divorce rate, more and more children have been drawn into the process. Sandra Hofferth (1985) estimated that nine out of ten black children and seven out of ten white children (and most likely growing numbers of Native-American and Asian-American children) will spend part of their childhood in a single-parent household, most resulting from marital dissolution. Numerous social theorists have argued that the intact, two-parent family is necessary for the normal development and well-being of children. Thus, divorce is assumed to be contradictory to these ends. This view is most evident in structural–functional, social-learning, developmental, and symbolic-interaction theories (see Chapter 2), all of which see the family as one of the primary agents of socialization and role modeling for children. However, these theoretical perspectives ignore the fact that the effects of disrupted families on children might be short-lived or that the role of an absent parent might be filled by significant others (Demo and Acock, 1988).

SHORT-TERM VERSUS LONG-TERM EFFECTS

There is an extensive body of literature on the effects of divorce on children. For the most part there is agreement about the short-term effects of divorce. Some of these effects resemble those experienced by divorcing parents: rejection, anger, denial, sadness, despair, and grief. Children frequently feel guilty, blaming themselves for the divorce, especially if their parents have quarreled over them. They often entertain fantasies about reuniting their parents (Wallerstein and Kelly, 1980).

Just as with adults these stresses can result in health problems, both psychological and physical. Research shows that the physical health ratings of children from divorced families are poorer than those of children from intact families (Guidubaldi and Cleminshaw, 1985). Teresa Mauldon (1990) studied the health histories of 6000 children and found that in families where a divorce occurs, children average 13 percent more illnesses a year after their parents' divorce than before. She attributes the increase in health problems to the stresses generated from the divorce, particularly the dramatic decline in their living standard. Children living with their mothers are more likely to lack health insurance, making timely and quality health care problematic. Children with divorced parents see themselves as less competent and exhibit more depression and withdrawal than children from intact families (Devall, Stoneman, and Brody, 1986; Peterson and Zill, 1986). The duration and intensity of these feelings depend in some measure on parental behavior. If parental conflict continues after the divorce, the adjustment process for children may be prolonged.

In contrast, many of the findings of long-term effects on children are not as consistent. On the one hand some researchers believe that children, by and large, regain psychological equilibrium 1 or 2 years after the divorce and then continue on a "normal" pattern of growth and development (Hetherington, Cox, and Cox, 1979). On the other hand others like Wallerstein and Blakeslee (1989) feel that the effects of divorce are long-lasting and interfere with normal social–emotional development for a significant number of children.

It may be that the age of children at the time of divorce has an impact on the degree to which they experience disruption in their lives. The lives of younger children may remain more stable than those of older children, who may be more aware of changes in their family's economic and social status. Accurate assessments of the long-term impact of divorce require more study and more precise control for the complex variables that promote or hinder growth in children's lives. Much of the research in the past has been cross-sectional and limited to comparisons of differences between children from disrupted homes and those in intact families, with no control for variables of changed economic status or quality of family relationships.

DOES DIVORCE AFFECT CHILDREN'S BEHAVIOR? Some researchers report that children of divorce are absent from school more, do poorer schoolwork, and misbehave more than children from intact families (Kinard and Reinherz 1986; Guidubaldi, Perry, and Nastasi, 1987). Again, however, these findings must be interpreted cautiously. Factors such as race and class are important here as well. Most studies of the behavioral effects of divorce involve samples of white children. The few studies of black children report mixed findings. Frank Sciara (1975) found that the absence of a father was more harmful to the academic achievement of black children than that of white children, but other researchers have found the academic achievement of black children to be unaffected by family structure (Hunt and Hunt, 1975; Shinn 1978). Furthermore, when social class is controlled, the observed differences in academic achievement between children from intact families and children from disrupted families disappear (Shinn, 1978). Thus, unequal economic resources rather than differences in family structure may account for the observed differences in school performance.

Much of the research on children of divorce focuses on antisocial behavior. A consistent finding is that both girls and boys from divorced families engage in more deviant behavior than do children in intact families (Dornbusch et al., 1985; Kalter et al., 1985). Within divorced families misbehavior is more common among boys than girls. It is commonly argued that boys have more difficulty adjusting to divorce than do girls (Lowery and Settle, 1985; Demo and Acock, 1988). Some researchers have attributed boys' problematic behavior to the lack of living with the same-sex parent (Wallerstein, 1987). However, problems may develop because of a decrease in adult supervision. Sanford Dornbusch and his colleagues (1985) found that the presence of an additional adult in the home lowered the rates of misbehavior. This finding has important implications as it suggests that other adults can effectively substitute for an absent parent.

Not all research on the effects of divorce have found negative effects. David Demo and Alan Acock (1988) reviewed a number of studies that revealed positive outcomes for children. In female-headed families both mothers and children develop more androgynous behavior as they reorganize the household after the father has left. Additionally, assuming more responsibilities leads children to greater maturity and feelings of competence. Finally, of course, children may feel relief to be out of a conflictual and possibly abusive family situation. Children living in a stable single-parent family are emotionally better off than if they remain in a conflict-ridden two-parent family (Peterson and Zill, 1986; Wallerstein and Blakeslee, 1989).

CHANGING PATTERNS IN CHILD CUSTODY

In any marital disruption involving children, a question that must be resolved is, Who gets the children? We examine this difficult question in the following section, focusing specifically on the issues of sole custody, joint custody, and visitation rights.

SOLE CUSTODY Throughout U.S. history, in divorce cases courts have almost always awarded **sole custody**, in which one parent is given legal responsibility for raising the child. Earlier we noted that in colonial America, fathers were far more likely to get custody of their children following a divorce. By the twentieth century, however, this pattern had so reversed itself that today approximately 90 percent of all divorced mothers have custody. The courts accepted the cultural bias that women are inherently better at nurturing than men are. Thus, they adopted the view that children, especially in their early years, need to be with their mothers. So entrenched did this view become by the mid-twentieth century that the only way a father could get custody was to prove his wife an unfit mother (Greif, 1985).

In the last 2 decades a small but noticeable shift has occurred in child custody cases. Although most fathers do not request custody, those who do so are often successful. It is estimated that in such cases, about one-half to two-thirds of the fathers are awarded custody (Greif, 1985; Hanson, 1988). Given the poor economic resources of some women and changing gender roles, some mothers agree that fathers should be the primary parent, and they do not contest custody. Given the traditional view of women as nurturers and homemakers, women who agree to give custody to the father frequently are portrayed as unloving, uncaring, selfish, and unwomanly. These negative images have little to do with the woman's actual reasons for not seeking custody: inadequate finances, child's preference for living with father, difficulty in controlling children, and physical or emotional problems experienced by the woman (Greif and Pabst, 1988).

Not all women who lose custody do so voluntarily. In one study of over 500 noncustodial mothers, almost 10 percent reported losing their children in a court battle or relinquishing custody to avoid conflict (Greif and Pabst, 1988:88). Women's groups have expressed concern that some of these decisions could set precedents that would weaken women's chances for gaining custody. They point to cases in which the judge's decision was based primarily on the father's better financial position (Max, 1985). Using financial means as a criterion for child custody puts women at a real disadvantage because in the vast majority of cases fathers are better off economically.

Money is not the only issue over which custody battles are fought or decided. The sexual orientation of a parent also has become an issue. Some states, like Massachusetts, Indiana, and Alaska, have rejected the notion that homosexuality can be used as a reason for denying custody. Other states, like Arkansas, Utah, Missouri, and Virginia, have ruled that it can be. A judge in Illinois, relying on allegations of lesbianism, denied the mother's request for custody and ordered that the mother not visit with her daughter in the presence of any woman with whom she may happen to be living. The case remains under appeal. It is estimated that there are 1.5 million lesbians with children in the United States today (Grady, 1991). Thus, the outcome of the Illinois case could have major implications in the future.

JOINT CUSTODY In recent years, courts have begun to award **joint custody**, in which both parents are involved in child rearing and decision making. However, full joint custody in this sense is rare. In practice, most joint custody involves shared legal custody, with physical custody remaining with one parent, usually the mother. In that sense joint custody varies little from sole custody except for the assumption that decisions about the children's welfare will be made by both parents (Glendon, 1987). The motives behind joint custody are to provide children with continuing contact with both parents and to relieve one parent of the total burden of child care. Initial studies indicate that some of these benefits are being realized. For example, one study found that fathers involved in joint-custody arrangements take a more active role in parenting than do noncustodial fathers (Bowman and Ahrons, 1985). They are also more likely to provide financial support for their children.

Joint custody is not for everyone, however. It works successfully only in cases where divorcing couples have a fairly amicable relationship and desire a pattern of shared parenting. In the absence of these two characteristics, joint custody may simply perpetuate the conflict that led to the divorce in the first place. Because joint custody is relatively new, an evaluation of its effectiveness in minimizing the adjustment problems of children is difficult.

VISITATION RIGHTS Regardless of the form custody takes, provisions for visitation of the other parent must be agreed upon. Noncustodial parents with visitation rights enter into a new set of interactions with their children. Often both the

FOR YOUR INFORMATION

CAN CHILDREN DIVORCE THEIR PARENTS?

On September 25, 1992, juvenile court judge Thomas Kirk granted 12-year-old Gregory Kingsley's request that the parental rights of his natural mother be terminated, thus allowing the boy's foster parents to adopt him. This ruling is believed to be the first time in which parental rights were ended based on a legal suit brought by a minor. Judge Kirk based his ruling on what he deemed the best interests of the child. Gregory's mother, an unemployed waitress, had given him up for foster care three times because of economic difficulties. Gregory testified that he had lived with his mother for only 7 months in the last 8 years and that for almost 2 years while he was in foster care his mother never visited, called, or wrote him. This case will likely set a precedent for giving children legal standing in their own right in cases where there is a clear pattern of abuse and neglect, rather than relying on adults to initiate cases for them.

---

parent and the child are uncertain how to behave in this situation; thus, visitation itself becomes a source of stress. Logistics are a problem, too: Where to go? What to do? Whom to include? Often the spontaneity of parent–child relationships is transferred into a recreational relationship with the time together being spent in a constant round of activities, for example, going to the movies or to the zoo.

Parents and children often perceive the visits in different ways. Parents may think that by taking the children places they are being loving, whereas children may feel rejected because the relationship seems artificial. Wallerstein and Blakeslee (1989) observed that what matters is not the frequency of visits but the degree to which the child feels valued in the relationship.

Thus, in the best of circumstances problems can occur in visitations. The visits can become a source of real stress, especially in the period immediately after a divorce if parents haven't worked through their own feelings. Visitation can then become a battleground through which ex-spouses carry on their conflict with each other. This takes many forms: The noncustodial parent often overindulges the children to look good in their eyes; both parents may grill the children about the other parent's new lifestyle or speak ill of the other parent; one or both parents may consistently violate the spirit of the visitation agreement by changing plans at the last minute, not having the children ready on time, or bringing them back late. Child experts agree that such behaviors have a negative impact on children.

Noncustodial parents are not the only ones concerned about visitation rights. Grandparents can play an important role in helping their grandchildren adjust to a divorce. Grandparents symbolize stability and continuity (Sanders and Trygstad, 1989). Because of the acrimony of some divorces or the geographical relocation of the custodial parent, however, grandparents may be unable to fulfill this role.

Studies have revealed certain trends in relationships between grandparents and grandchildren following divorce. In general the custodial grandparents (parents of the custodial parent) have an advantage in maintaining ties with their grandchildren. Andrew Cherlin and Frank Furstenberg (1986a) found that several years after the divorce 58 percent of noncustodial grandparents saw their grandchildren less frequently than before the divorce, compared with only 37 percent of custodial grandparents. Because women are more likely to receive custody, relationships between maternal grandparents and grandchildren tend to be maintained and even strengthened, whereas ties with paternal grandparents frequently are weakened. Increasingly grandparents have gone to court in efforts to ensure continuing contact with their grandchildren. In 1977, only 6 states had laws that enabled a grandparent to petition a court for visitation rights to a grandchild; today all 50 states have such laws. Not all grandparents, however, are aware of this possibility, nor do all grandparents have the economic resources to pursue this avenue.

REACHING ACCORD: DIVORCE COUNSELING AND MEDIATION

Thus far, we have seen that divorce can cause a variety of problems, not only for the divorcing couple but also for their children, their extended family, and their friends. Because of the emotional content, most divorces can easily become bitter and acrimonious affairs, leaving deep emotional and psychological wounds. Therefore, a growing number of marriage counselors and other professionals have shifted some of their practice into **divorce counseling**. Their efforts are aimed at helping people conclude the psychic divorce. Essentially, their goal is to replace the adversarial and often destructive aspects that can accompany the legal divorce with a more cooperative spirit. At the same time divorce counselors try to help people withdraw and distance themselves from the relationship so that acceptance of the loss and subsequent healing can take place. When these goals are accomplished, people are better able to begin new relationships. Divorcing couples or individuals may seek such counseling during the process of the divorce or at a much later stage in their life. Some states, however, require **conciliation counseling** before the courts will consider granting a divorce. The purpose behind this kind of counseling is to see whether the marital problems can be resolved and the couple reconciled.

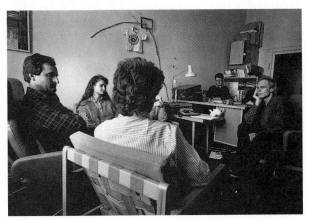

Children can sometimes be the source of conflict in a couple's marital relationship. In these situations marital counseling may lessen the likelihood of divorce.

Divorce mediation has a related but somewhat different emphasis. It is a procedure designed to help divorcing couples negotiate a fair and mutually agreed-upon resolution of such issues as marital property distribution, child custody, visitation rights, and financial support. Divorce mediators generally have backgrounds in law, social work, counseling, or psychology. In any given divorce one or more mediators may be involved. For example, divorce lawyers may work with counselors or therapists to help the couple reach accord. Some states actively encourage and even sponsor divorce mediation. Mediated settlements must be approved by the court to become legally binding on the parties involved.

Although divorce mediation is still relatively new, some evidence suggests that all parties benefit from the process. Couples can learn negotiating skills that will help them deal with each other in the future. Children do not see their parents embroiled in constant struggle over them. Because the spouses have helped to forge the agreement based on their own needs and those of their family, they are more likely to adhere to the terms of the agreement, thereby reducing the likelihood of future conflicts (Grebe, 1986).

OTHER FORMS OF MARITAL DISRUPTION

Thus far our discussion has focused on the legal concept of divorce. However, marriages can be disrupted in other ways as well, by separation, desertion, annulment, and death.

Separation refers to the termination of marital cohabitation and can take a variety of forms. Sometimes one of the partners simply moves out. This can be the result of an individual or a mutually arrived at decision. Its goal may be to give one or both partners some space and time to think about the relationship, or it may be the first step toward divorce. Because this is an informal arrangement, the courts are not involved, and the couple remains legally married.

In other cases, when the couple do not want to divorce or to continue living together, the courts order legal separation with specific regulations governing the couple's interactions, including custody, visitation rights, and economic support. Such separation orders may also provide for counseling or therapy and give a stipulated time frame for the duration of the separation. This can give the couple an opportunity to reassess and possibly learn to alter problem areas in their relationship. Couples may reconcile or divorce at the end of the legal separation. For some couples, however, a legal separation may become permanent. Some people reject divorce on religious grounds and therefore agree to live apart until the death of one spouse. Although either party may begin new relationships, neither is free to remarry.

Desertion refers to the abandonment of a spouse or family. The partner simply leaves, often without a word of warning. Desertion has sometimes been called the "poor people's divorce" because it frequently occurs when the family is experiencing economic hardship. However, desertion occurs among all classes, races, and ethnic groups. Although both women and men desert, men do so in greater numbers. This is perhaps the most difficult of all marital disruptions because the family is left without the financial and domestic support of the other spouse and the courts can't intervene unless the whereabouts of the deserting spouse are known. At the same time the deserted spouse is not legally free to remarry until a specified number of years have passed. Thus, the family's life is overshadowed by uncertainty and ambiguity.

An **annulment** has quite a different meaning from the other forms of disruption we have been discussing. In divorce, separation, and desertion there is agreement that a legal marriage had existed. In contrast, a civil annulment legally states that the marriage never existed and, thus, the parties are free to marry at will. Generally the basis for an annulment is that the couple did not meet the legal requirements for a marriage in the first place—they were underage, the degree of kinship is too close (first cousins, for example, are not legally permitted to marry in some states), the marriage was never consummated, or some form of fraud was involved. A civil annulment is distinct from the religious annulment granted by the Catholic Church. The church, after investigation, may decide that a religious marriage did not take place. In the eyes of the church the individuals are free to marry, but to do so legally they must obtain a civil annulment or a divorce.

Throughout much of U.S. history marital disruptions were generally caused by death, not divorce. This was due primarily to shorter life expectancies, harsher living conditions, and cultural patterns that discouraged divorce. Today widowhood most commonly occurs at later ages in the life cycle. We discuss the concept of widowhood as well as issues surrounding death and dying in Chapter 15.

SUMMARY

Calculating the actual extent of divorce today is not an easy matter. The most commonly used measures of divorce are the number of divorces per year, the crude divorce rate, the refined divorce rate, the divorce-to-marriage ratio, and the ratio of divorced to married persons. Each measure has its own strengths and limitations. Divorce rates vary from group to group and are associated with a wide range of factors. Among the most frequently cited factors are race and ethnicity, age at marriage, level of education and income, religion, parental divorce, and the presence of children.

Divorce doesn't just happen. It is a complex social process in which a basic unit of social organization—marriage—breaks down over time, culminating in a legal termination of the relationship. Researchers have identified several stages in this process: a period of marital conflict and unhappiness, the actual marital dissolution itself, and a period of adjustment following divorce. Both women and men in the process of divorce face some common problems: a decline in health, loneliness, and the need for social and sexual readjustments. However, there are also gender differences. Although women suffer more economic distress than men, they may fare better in terms of overall adjustment.

Increasing numbers of children are affected by divorce. Researchers generally agree that children experience some of the same short-term effects their divorcing parents do: rejection, anger, denial, sadness, despair, and grief. There is less agreement about the long-term effects of divorce on children. Some researchers believe that children gain equilibrium 1 or 2 years after the divorce; others feel that the effects are long-lasting and interfere with normal social–emotional development for a significant number of children.

Although the courts typically award one parent, generally the mother, sole custody of the children, more judges are awarding joint custody. It is still too early to assess the effectiveness of the latter approach for the welfare of children. Establishing fair and appropriate visitation rights for noncustodial parents (and increasingly for grandparents) is not an easy matter. Conflict over visitation rights can prolong the trauma of divorce. Divorce counseling, conciliation counseling, and divorce mediation increasingly are being utilized in an effort to reduce some of the conflicts in the divorce process.

KEY TERMS

alimony
split custody
no-fault divorce
crude divorce rate
refined divorce rate
divorce-to-marriage ratio
ratio of divorced to married persons
stations of divorce

emotional divorce
legal divorce
economic divorce
coparental divorce
community divorce
psychic divorce
sole custody

joint custody
divorce counseling
conciliation counseling
divorce mediation
separation
desertion
annulment

QUESTIONS FOR STUDY AND REFLECTION

1. Many cultures, including our own, believe that marriage should be a lifetime commitment. Numerous social changes may require a reevaluation of this goal, however. For example, in 1900, average life expectancy was 48.3 years for females and 46.3 years for males. Thus, when people married at age 22, they could expect to live together for about 25 years, most of which time would have been devoted to child rearing. Today, the life expectancy is 79 years for women and 72.1 years for men. Thus, even allowing for the later age at marriage today, couples can expect to live together anywhere from 40 to 50 years or more. Such a span of time can encompass significant individual physical and psychological changes as well as dramatic economic, social, and political changes, all of which can substantially alter the couple's original marriage bargain. Is the goal of lifetime marriage realistic in today's society? Considering the problems associated with divorce, might short-term or renewable marriage contracts be a better alternative? Explain your position.

2. Most marriages start out with many rituals. Among them are the engagement, the bridal shower, the bachelor party, the rehearsal dinner, and the wedding ceremony itself (often religious in nature).

Friends and relatives offer their support by cards, gifts, and attendance at these events. Divorce on the other hand is often a solitary experience. In fact, the partners are not even required to be physically present when the divorce decree is issued. Yet divorce, like marriage, marks a new beginning in a person's life. Do you think society should initiate divorce rituals aimed at helping people move on with their lives? If so, what would such rituals be like? In thinking about your response, consider the benefits rituals provide in many other aspects of our lives.

3. In U.S. society divorce is often viewed as a personal failure. Given what you have read about the "causes" of divorce and the factors frequently associated with divorce, how accurate is such an assessment? What advice would you give to people who want to know how to improve their chances for having a lifetime marriage?

4. As we have seen, children suffer many consequences in the aftermath of a divorce. What steps could be taken to lessen the trauma of divorce for children? How and what should children be told about their parents' divorce? Who should tell them? What reactions should parents expect from children during and after the process of divorce?

FURTHER READING

CHERLIN, ANDREW J. 1992. *Marriage, Divorce, Remarriage.* Cambridge, MA: Harvard University Press. The author examines trends in marriage, divorce, and remarriage. The consequences of and explanations for these trends are presented in a straightforward manner.

FURSTENBERG, FRANK F., JR., AND ANDREW CHERLIN. 1991. *Divided Families: What Happens to Children When Parents Part.* Cambridge, MA: Harvard University Press. In a lively manner, this book examines parental behavior and its impact on children. The authors question why so many fathers disappear from their children's lives after divorce and call for a radical change in the way all fathers—absent or present—relate to their children.

RIESSMAN, CATHERINE KOHLER. 1990. *Divorce Talk: Women and Men Make Sense of Personal Relationships.* New Brunswick, NJ: Rutgers University Press. The author provides a compassionate view of how women and men make sense of getting divorced. She found that when marriages end, women and men construct different lives, distinguished by gender-linked pressures and opportunities. Both women and men report that the divorce wasn't all negative. Rather, they claim it allowed them to discover new aspects of themselves.

VAUGHAN, DIANE. 1988. *Uncoupling: How Relationships Come Apart.* New York: Oxford University Press. This book presents a vivid look at the process of uncoupling, which everyone, married or unmarried, will experience at some time in their lives, whether it be falling out of love, separating, becoming divorced, or losing a loved one through death.

Chapter 14

REMARRIAGE AND REMARRIED FAMILIES

*S*ally and Tom met at a Parents Without Partners support-group meeting 7 months ago and began dating soon after that. Sally has been divorced for 3 years and with her ex-husband, Bill, shares joint custody for her two children. Although the children live with Sally, Bill sees them frequently, and he provides regular child support. Bill is also dating, but he has told the children he probably will not marry again. The children—Mike, who is 8 years old, and Sara, who is 10—are hopeful that their parents will get together again. Tom has been divorced for 2 years and wants to remarry. He also has two children—Sue, who is 12, and Ken, who is 14. The children live with his former spouse in another state but spend their summers and most of the holidays with him. Recently Tom told Sally he loves her, and he asked her to marry him. Sally is emotionally torn. She loves Tom but is uncertain about getting married again. Her children were upset when she started dating Tom on a steady basis. A close friend of hers remarried a man with children several years ago and is now in the process of a second divorce. This friend told Sally that if she had it to do over again, she would never have remarried someone with children. Sally's parents, however, like Tom and are encouraging her to marry him so she won't be alone.

Imagine that you are Sally. What fears would you have? What problems do you think you would face if you married Tom? Imagine you are Tom. How would you respond to Sally's concerns? What is the likelihood of a remarriage like this working out?

In the previous chapter, we discussed the high divorce rate in the United States. Some writers have erroneously interpreted this high rate of marital dissolution to mean that marriage is no longer popular among Americans. The remarriage statistics tell another story, however. The remarriage rate in the United States is the highest in the world. Over 50 percent of marriages in the late 1980s involved a second marriage for at least one of the partners, down slightly from the 60 percent rate of the mid 1980s (Bumpass, Sweet, and Castro-Martin, 1990).

The pattern of marriage, divorce, and remarriage has become well established in the United States today. According to the Census Bureau, 16 percent of all families with children at home are remarried families, an increase of 4 percent since 1980 (Margolis, 1992). Thus, statistically it is likely that you or several of your classmates have lived or will live part of your life in a remarried family. For purposes of our discussion in this chapter we use Esther Wald's (1981:2) definition of a **remarried family**: "A two-parent, two-generation unit that comes into being on the legal remarriage of a widowed or divorced person who has biological or adopted children from a prior union with whom he or she is regularly involved.... The children may or may not live with the remarried couple, but, in either case, they have ongoing and significant psychological, social, and legal ties with them."

Despite the large number of remarriages, social and legal changes have not kept pace with this new family form. According to sociologist Frank Furstenberg (1973), remarried people enter into a relationship where there are no rules or models to guide their behavior. The general societal approach to these relationships is to view them in much the same way as we do first marriages. Although all families share some of the same characteristics and face many of the same problems, families formed as a result of remarriage face additional problems that must be addressed if these relationships are to survive. William Beer (1989) identified ten fundamental ways in which the remarried family is different from the nuclear family.

1. Complexity: Remarried families take many forms: divorced individuals/single partners; divorced individuals/widowed partners; divorced individuals/divorced partners; widowed individuals/widowed partners. The presence of children increases their complexity.

2. A changing cast of characters: The membership of remarried families may shift. Some of the stepchildren may live together permanently; others may come and go depending on visitation arrangements; still others may appear rarely, if at all.

3. Unclear boundaries: Membership boundaries often are ambiguous in remarried families. For example, children may not include a noncustodial parent's new spouse in their definition of family. A stepparent's parents may not view themselves as stepgrandparents or be viewed that way by stepgrandchildren. The boundaries become further confused if there is a second divorce. Is the divorced stepparent then still a member of the family?

4. **Undefined rules:** Remarried couples often find agreeing on rules regarding discipline, money, and parenting responsibilities difficult.

5. **Unclear laws:** Although the biological parent–child relationship is well defined legally, considerable ambiguity remains regarding the legal rights and duties involved in stepparent–stepchild relationships.

6. **A lack of kinship terms:** American culture has relatively few kinship terms, and in remarried families the same word is used to denote very different relationships. For example, the word *stepparent* applies to a person who has married either a custodial parent or a noncustodial parent. It also refers to a new spouse of an elderly parent, for whom no parent–child relationship ever existed. The new spouses of both biological parents may see each other frequently and join in negotiations over stepchildren; yet there are no kinship terms for their relationship to each other.

7. **Instant families:** Nuclear families usually form gradually, over a period of years. In contrast, remarried families come ready-made, often without appropriate time for members to establish emotional bonds with each other.

8. **Guilt:** New spouses may have unresolved feelings about their previous marriage. Children may feel guilty for showing affection to the stepparent, believing this to be disloyal to the noncustodial biological parent.

9. **Grieving:** Remarried families have undergone a loss before their formation, and some members may not have completed the grieving process. Children may be particularly affected because they must now relinquish the dream of their parents reuniting.

10. **Myth of the recreated nuclear family:** Stepfamilies aren't like nuclear families. The more a remarried couple tries to make the stepfamily into a family like any other, the more likely they are to be disappointed.

These differences are only slowly being recognized. Thus, there are as yet few clearly defined role models for stepfamilies. Consequently, the participants generally lack preparation for the special complexities of remarried family life (Messinger, 1984). Members of stepfamilies often find themselves questioning their feelings and experiences, uncertain about how typical or "normal" their family situation is. In this chapter we explore the history and cultural meanings of remarried families, their special characteristics and problems, and strategies for strengthening these families. Before we do, however, a few words need to be said about the available research on this emergent family form.

METHODOLOGICAL ISSUES IN THE STUDY OF REMARRIED FAMILIES

Although remarriage has been part of the U.S. family system since the colonial period, with few exceptions, such as Jessie Bernard's pioneering 1956 publication titled *Remarriage*, social scientists did not begin to study this phenomenon until the 1970s, when both the divorce and remarriage rates began to accelerate. Since that time the amount of research on remarried families has increased substantially. Although such studies have provided us with significant insights into the process of remarriage and the overall functioning of remarried families, several major methodological problems hamper a complete understanding of this family form. Much of the information on remarried

Over half of all marriages today involve a second marriage for one or both partners.

Source: Reprinted by permission: Tribune Media Services.

families comes from small, nonrandom samples, thus making the generalization of findings to the larger population difficult. Here as in many other areas of family research, investigators have focused attention predominantly on small numbers of white, middle-class, remarried families. Although social scientists are now paying more attention to the structured relationships of race and class, there are still few empirical data on remarried families of color. Thus we do not know the degree to which the experience of remarriage is similar or different across all racial, ethnic, or class groupings. Several recent studies suggest that differences may exist across such groups.

In one study interviews with six African-American stepmothers suggested that the African-American community views stepfamilies as "natural" or "just another family" (Wade-Lewis, 1989). Sociologists Marilyn Coleman and Lawrence Ganong (1990) reported that African Americans exhibit less rigid family boundaries than do other groups. In fact, some scholars argue that the survival of the African-American family was due in large part to its ability to incorporate both relatives and nonrelatives into an integrated family unit (Staples, 1971). In a similar vein, Peter Uhlenberg and Kenneth Chew (1986) observed that African Americans depend less on formal definitions of marital status. They concluded that remarriage has less impact on family ties of African Americans than on those of other groups.

Further research is needed before any definitive conclusions in this regard can be drawn. In addition, research efforts must go beyond black and white comparisons. The information vacuum that exists regarding Latino, Asian-American, and Native-American families must be eliminated if we are to understand fully what is happening to U.S. families. Keeping these methodological limitations in mind, let's turn now to what we know about the pattern of remarriage in early America.

HISTORICAL PERSPECTIVE

In the previous chapter we saw that divorce has been a feature of U.S. family life since 1639. Remarriage has also been a part of family life from this country's beginnings. During the seventeenth and eighteenth centuries the proportion of remarriages among all marriages was approximately 20 to 30 percent

(Ihinger-Tallman and Pasley, 1987). The circumstances leading to remarriage were quite different in earlier times, however. Whereas in early America the overwhelming majority of remarriages followed the death of a spouse, today remarriages typically involve divorced individuals.

In the early colonies, the climate and harsh conditions as well as the lack of medical knowledge took a heavy toll on the inhabitants. For example, in Charles County, Maryland, marriages lasted an average of only 7 years and had only a 33 percent chance of lasting 10 years before one spouse died (Carr and Walsh, 1983). In seventeenth-century Virginia, 25 percent of children by the age of 5 had lost one or both parents; this figure rose to 70 percent by age 21 (Fox and Quitt, 1980). No group was immune to early death. For example, the fathers of Patrick Henry, Thomas Jefferson, George Washington, and James Madison all married widows (Calhoun, 1917).

Given the value attached to marriage in colonial America, remarriage following the death of a spouse was not only common but socially expected for both women and men, especially for those with young children. The time interval between the death of a spouse and remarriage varied from colony to colony. The Pilgrims of Plymouth Colony encouraged immediate remarriage to prevent the idolization of the dead spouse (Fox and Quitt, 1980). Such advice was often heeded: Most remarriages in Plymouth Colony occurred 6 months to 1 year after the death of a spouse. Other colonies instituted waiting periods, however. The colony of Pennsylvania, for example, passed a law in 1690 requiring widows to wait a year after a husband's death before remarrying.

After the American Revolution, the number of marriages ending in divorce increased, and the new states began to evolve social policies to deal with the affected parties. In general, most states permitted the remarriage of the "innocent party," but in some states the spouse found to be at "fault" for the marital breakup was denied this privilege. Although some religions continued to oppose remarriage for the divorced, civil law permitting even the "guilty" party to remarry gradually evolved throughout the entire country. Nevertheless, prior to the beginning of World War II, the most common participants in remarriages were still the widowed. According to demographer Paul Glick (1980), not until 1940 did the number of divorced men (aged 25 to 44) exceed

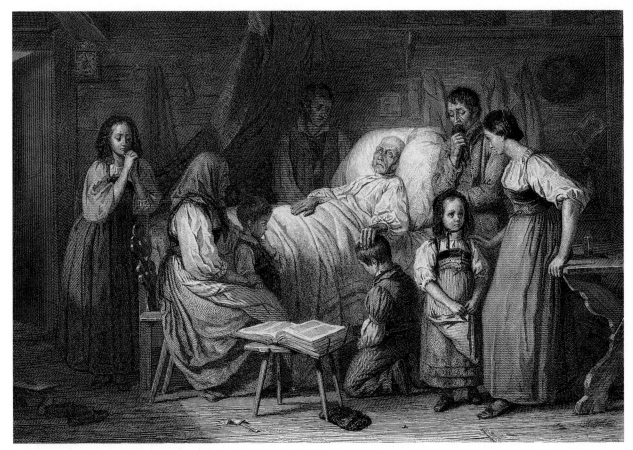

In the past, parents often died at an early age, leaving the surviving spouse with young children to raise. Remarriage following the death of a spouse was a common experience.

the number of widowers who remarried. The corresponding date for women in this age group was 1950. This pattern escalated to the point that by 1980, nine out of ten people entering a remarriage were divorced.

Little is known about the nature and quality of the early remarried families. They were considered to be the same as first families; no special records were kept on how well they fared. It is likely, however, that then, as now, remarriages faced some problems not encountered in first marriages.

What images come to your mind when you hear the term "stepfamily?" Are these images positive or negative? How did you learn about stepfamilies? As you read the remainder of this chapter, evaluate the accuracy of your views of stepfamilies.

CULTURAL IMAGES OF STEPFAMILIES

One basic problem stepfamilies throughout history have had to contend with is their cultural image. The original meaning of the term *step* in *stepfamily* comes from Old German and Old English terms associated with the experiences of bereavement and deprivation. The earliest designations of *step* referred to a child who was orphaned. Later on, the term was expanded to include the replacement parent, whether a stepmother or stepfather. Today, the use of the term *step* encompasses relationships established by the remarriage of a widowed or divorced parent to someone with whom the child of the prior marriage has no blood or legal ties and that may include stepsiblings. Hence, the term *stepfamily* refers to an entire family unit, not just designated individuals within it (Wald, 1981:46).

Throughout history many nursery rhymes and children's stories have depicted stepmothers as wicked and cruel.

The terms *stepchild, stepparent,* and especially *stepmother* have conveyed negative images from earliest times. Most of these images derive from folklore and fairy tales that through the medium of storytelling sought to provide guidelines for daily living. An analysis of children's fairy tales found that stepmothers, along with bears, wolves, giants, ogres, and witches, were the most frequent representations of evil (Sutton-Smith, 1971). Other analyses confirm the consistent image of the stepmother, but not the stepfather, as a cruel and evil person (Dainton, 1993). For centuries children have been entertained and frightened by "Hansel and Gretel," "Snow White" and "Cinderella," with their tales of maternal loss and cruel replacement.

Professionals and laypeople alike need to be aware of the fear and anxiety such images can create, especially for young children, who today increasingly live in stepfamilies. Such images also complicate the stepmother role, making it difficult and ambiguous. Negative images of stepmothers also imply that "step is less," as conveyed in the metaphor that anything of lesser value is "like a stepchild" (Wald, 1981). Again, such images can affect people's perceptions of stepfamilies. According to Coleman and Ganong (1987),

the stereotype of stepparents as being less loving and less kind than biological parents still exists even among some counselors and teachers, who may assume that a student's difficulties stem from living in a stepfamily. These researchers recommend, therefore, that those who deal with children and families receive professional training about both the strengths and problems associated with living in a stepfamily.

In an attempt to correct negative stereotypes, many stepparents, children's writers, and family professionals are publishing more accurate representations of today's stepfamilies. One result of this is an attempt to create more neutral terms to describe stepfamilies: *reconstituted, blended, merged, binuclear,* and *remarried families.* Some of these terms, however, create problems of their own. The notion of reconstituted, blended, or merged families implies that all members get along and fit comfortably into the new family structure. In fact, such a situation may never be achieved or at least may not be achieved for a number of years. The pressure to measure up to such standards may add further stress to a remarriage. Thus, we prefer the term *remarried families,* agreeing with Wald (1981:33) that the use of this term is "accurately descriptive, nontechnical, and value-free, and does not imply goals achieved." Throughout this chapter we use the term *remarried families* when referring to the family as a whole. Because there are as yet no agreed-upon terms for relationships within remarried families, however, we follow common practice and refer to these relationships as steprelationships.

THE PROCESS OF REMARRIAGE

Over time most divorced and widowed people are able to relinquish their strong emotional ties to the past. This, of course, does not imply that they do not have warm memories of the past or that they never think about their former partner. Rather, it means that they are able to focus on the present and plan for the future. When this happens, the widowed or divorced individual confronts the issues of whether to date and perhaps whether to remarry.

DATING AND COURTSHIP PATTERNS

Are dating and courtship different the second time around? Older adults report many of the same anxieties about dating that adolescents do: appropriate behavior for the first date, what to talk about, who pays, whether to be sexually involved, and how to end the relationship if it is going nowhere. Adults with children may find dating even more complicated. Children often have difficulty accepting a parent's decision to date. When the parental loss was due to death, children may interpret the surviving parent's dating as an act of disloyalty or betrayal toward the deceased parent. After divorce, children may fantasize about their parents getting back together again and thus react negatively to a parent's dating. Additionally, children may feel displaced by the dating partner so they may attempt to sabotage the relationship by behaving obnoxiously. Or they may pressure parents by promoting the relationship in hopes of finding a new parent.

Children are not the only ones to react to the resumption of dating. Relatives of a deceased spouse may feel hurt or betrayed if they believe the surviving spouse is dating too soon following the death of their loved one. Ex-spouses may also be hostile to their former spouse's dating. They may be jealous themselves or fear that someone else will replace them in their children's eyes. Thus, they may withdraw cooperation over visitation rights and delay or even end financial support.

We might assume that dealing with these complications would lengthen the courtship process. The opposite pattern seems to be the case, however. Divorced and widowed individuals tend to spend less time in dating and courtship than they did preceding their first marriage. Kathleen O'Flaherty and Laura Eells (1988) found that their respondents dated for

an average of 12 months, followed by a 5-month engagement, prior to their first marriage. In contrast, they dated for only 7 months, followed by a 2-month engagement, before their remarriage.

Other researchers suggest that more than time distinguishes dating and courtship before first and second marriages. For example, Frank Furstenberg and Graham Spanier (1987) found that dating among their divorced respondents was guided more by pragmatic than by romantic considerations. The style of dating among the divorced is more informal, and courtship often involves living together before marriage. Similarly, Ganong and Coleman (1989) found that the primary way that 59 percent of the 205 respondents in their study prepared for remarriage was through cohabitation. These individuals believed that in this way they would be less likely to have another unsuccessful marriage.

Beyond this cohabitation strategy, however, most people did little to prepare themselves for living in a remarried family. Only 38 percent of the women and 25 percent of the men in the Ganong and Coleman study sought professional counseling, although many more reported receiving advice from friends and self-help books. Furthermore, many couples did not use the dating or courtship period to discuss potential problems in a remarriage. For example, only 56 percent of the couples discussed the most serious problem observed by stepfamily experts: children from a previous marriage. Less than 25 percent discussed the second most serious problem: finances. A full 13 percent reported that they didn't discuss *any* issues very seriously. As a result of this lack of preparation, many people enter remarriage with nonverbalized expectations that, if not realized, become sources of conflict and disappointment.

Doni Whitsett and Helen Land (1992) examined the interrelationships among role strain, coping, and marital satisfaction of 73 stepparents. Many of their respondents reported that prior to their remarriage they had no clear idea of what is involved in being a stepparent or what their spouse expected of them. Although couples in first marriages may not be any more prepared than remarrying couples for entering a relationship, remarrying couples' lack of preparation may have more serious consequences for the stability of the marriage simply because the latter is more complex, especially when children are involved.

One of the decisions divorced people confront is whether to start dating again.

THE DECISION TO REMARRY

Given the pain and trauma surrounding many divorces, and given the complications of resumed dating, why do so many Americans choose to remarry? First and foremost, marriage remains an important cultural value, and it is still perceived as the normal way to form an intimate connection with another person. According to Ganong and Coleman (1989), many of the reasons women and men give for remarriage are similar to those given for first marriages: convenience, social pressure, love, and for a few, pregnancy. Other researchers found that remarried individuals, like first-time marrieds, are seeking companionship and support (Sager, 1983). Furthermore, given the persistent economic inequalities between women and men and the downward mobility experienced by many divorced and widowed women, remarriage for women may also be a rational economic decision that improves their standard of living (Riessman, 1990). Additionally, divorced and widowed custodial parents may be motivated to remarry to have help raising their children.

PATTERNS OF REMARRIAGE

As Figure 14.1 shows, remarriage rates generally fell in the 1970s and then stabilized in the 1980s. Between 1970 and 1984 the proportion of people who remarried within 5 years of their divorce dropped by 16 percent. This did not mean, however, that divorced people did not enter new relationships. During this same time the proportion who formed a union through cohabitation increased by 7 percent (Bumpass, Sweet, and Cherlin, 1991). Figure 14.1 also shows that divorced people remarry at much higher rates than do widowed people. In fact, the overwhelming proportion of remarriages (91 percent) involve people who were previously divorced; the remaining 9 percent were widowed (National Center for Health Statistics, 1990b).

Remarriage after widowhood is much less frequent than remarriage after divorce, for several reasons. First, unlike most divorced people, the widowed may continue an emotional attachment to the previous spouse. Thus, they may not be interested in establishing another relationship. Second, divorce usually occurs at younger ages than widowhood. In general, the

FIGURE 14.1 *Marriage Rates by Previous Marital Status, 1970–87*

Source: Adapted from National Center for Health Statistics, 1990b, "Advance Report of Final Marriage Statistics, 1987," *Monthly Vital Statistics Report* 38,12 (April 3): 3.

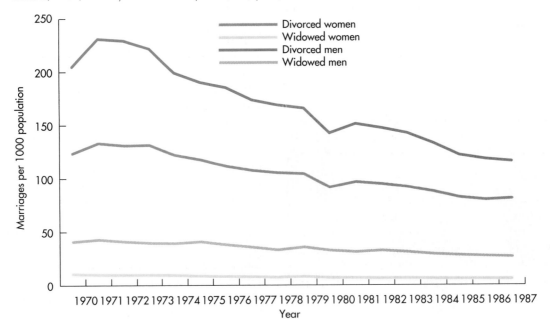

younger the age at divorce or widowhood, the greater the likelihood of remarriage. The relationship between age and rate of remarriage is especially true for women. Three of four women whose first marriage ends in divorce before they are age 30 remarry; for women aged 30 to 39 the comparable rate is three out of five. Women over 40 are less likely to remarry than are younger women or men of the same age. Only one of four women 40 years of age or older remarries (Levitan, Sar, and Gallo, 1988:33). There are several reasons for this. Some women choose to remain unmarried, preferring their newly found independence to a second marriage. Others desire to marry again but find themselves disadvantaged by cultural patterns that encourage men to marry younger women and disapprove of marriages between older women and younger men. Rates of remarriage also vary by social class, education, race, and the presence of children.

SOCIAL CLASS AND EDUCATION For both women and men, social class may be more important in the decision to remarry than age is. Men with higher incomes are more likely to remarry than are men with lower incomes (Glick, 1980). For men with low incomes the added burden of supporting two households may be prohibitive. Conversely, inadequate income may motivate some single mothers to remarry. As we saw in the last chapter, divorce adversely affects women's and children's economic well-being. By adding another (often higher) wage earner, remarriage reverses this process, especially for white women (Buehler et al., 1986).

A similar pattern emerges when we examine education. Women without college education tend to remarry quickly, whereas women with higher levels of education remarry later or not at all (Glick, 1984). Women college graduates are likely to be employed in relatively well paying jobs and thus may feel less pressure to marry for economic reasons than previously married women with low incomes.

SOCIAL CLASS, RACE, AND ETHNICITY Social class, however, does not operate the same way for all groups. Lower-income blacks are less likely to remarry than are their white counterparts. In fact, remarriage rates for black women across all socioeconomic levels are lower than those for their white counterparts (Staples, 1981b:71). For women whose marriages ended between 1965 and 1984, only 34 percent of black women had

remarried by 1988, compared with nearly 60 percent of white women and 45 percent of Latinas (cited in Ahlburg and DeVita, 1992:17). Sociologist Andrew Cherlin (1981) suggests that the overall disadvantaged economic position of blacks has led many of them to see the marital relationship as less effective than the larger kin network in providing support. Additionally, as we saw in Chapter 5, a sex-ratio imbalance places limits on the opportunities for remarriage among blacks.

The rates of remarriage for Latinas are between those of black and white women. As Table 14.1 shows, however, considerable variation exists among Latino groups. Puerto Rican women have the lowest rate of remarriage, and Cuban men have the highest. It is likely that a combination of factors is responsible for this variation among Latino groups: increased labor-force participation of Latinas, gender-role redefinitions, and the availability of alternatives to marriage, such as cohabitation. Variations in rates of remarriage are also found among Asian Americans, with Korean men and women having the highest rates and Vietnamese men the lowest. Native Americans have high rates of remarriage. Thus far, there is little research to help us understand the patterns among these populations.

TABLE 14.1

Percent of Divorced Individuals under Age 45 Who Are Married with Spouse Present, by Sex, 1980

	Men	Women
Non-Hispanic white	52.6	45.9
Black	31.2	17.7
Native American	47.4	39.6
Japanese	34.8	38.4
Chinese	36.0	35.2
Filipino	48.1	39.6
Korean	53.8	44.3
Asian Indian	45.8	40.0
Vietnamese	20.3	38.9
Hawaiian	44.5	37.2
Mexican	44.5	33.8
Puerto Rican	37.2	19.0
Cuban	51.3	34.0

Source: Adapted from James A. Sweet and Larry L. Bumpass, 1987, *American Families and Households* (New York: Russell Sage Foundation): 198.

THE PRESENCE OF CHILDREN   Finally, the presence of children affects the likelihood of remarriage for women and men in different ways. Divorced men with custody of children tend to remarry sooner than their female counterparts. Perhaps because they represent such a small minority and have not been socialized to be the primary caretaker, custodial fathers often more strongly feel the need for a partner to assist them with child care. Among women, those with young children and those with fewer children are more likely to remarry than are those with large families or older children (Glick and Lin, 1986). For all these people the decision to remarry begins a complicated series of adjustments that must be made if the new relationship is to survive.

THE STATIONS OF REMARRIAGE

In Chapter 13 we discussed the complex process of exiting from a marital relationship, utilizing Paul Bohannan's six stations of divorce: emotional, psychic, community, parental, economic, and legal. There is a similarity between the developmental tasks that must be mastered in the divorce process and the many personal changes and adjustments that accompany the process of remarriage. Clearly, remarriage involves more than the exchange of wedding vows. It requires individuals to adopt new roles, to unlearn old expectations from previous relationships, and to cope with an ambiguous legal status. Each stage of the remarriage process presents a challenge to the formation of a new couple and a new family identity (Goetting, 1982). Keep in mind that, as is the case for the stations of divorce, the six stations of remarriage do not affect all remarrying people with the same intensity, nor do they occur in exactly the same order for everyone. The presence of children, for example, can affect the intensity as well as the number of stages people experience in remarriage.

EMOTIONAL REMARRIAGE   The term **emotional remarriage** refers to the process of reestablishing a bond of attraction, love, commitment, and trust with another person. This can be a slow and difficult process for both the widowed and the divorced. The nature and quality of the previous marital experience affect the relationship with the new partner in different ways. On the one hand people who were happily married and then widowed may idealize the deceased spouse and thus see the new partner in a less favorable light. Such people can become overly critical of the new partner's behavior if it doesn't measure up to this ideal. On the other hand people who have been hurt and disappointed in previous relationships may be oversensitive to spousal criticism and may sense rejection by the new spouse when none is intended. For example, an intended compliment may be judged suspect because a former partner used similar comments as putdowns. Both the widowed and the divorced must be careful not to let the experiences of the first marriage unduly influence their new relationship.

PSYCHIC REMARRIAGE   The process known as **psychic remarriage** requires moving back from the recently acquired identity as a single person to a couple identity. This transition varies in intensity and perceived difficulty. For individuals who have accepted more traditional gender roles, regaining the status of husband or wife may be especially gratifying, and their adjustments to couple identity may be relatively minor. Other people, however, especially women who experienced a new sense of autonomy and personal independence after widowhood or divorce, may feel constrained after taking on a marital role.

COMMUNITY REMARRIAGE   **Community remarriage** involves changes in social relationships. Following the dissolution of a marriage, individuals often find that the nature and frequency of contact with relatives and friends is disrupted. As we have seen in Chapter 13, relationships with other married couples often suffer following a divorce. As a result, couple friends are often replaced with new unmarried friends. Often these friendships are deeper and more intimate because they are selected on the basis of one's personal interests and needs, and not those of a couple. Reentering the couple world may result in reverting back to less intimate and more couple-oriented relationships that can be shared more easily and "fit" more readily into a couple's lifestyle. Additionally, remarriage means that new in-laws must somehow be integrated into the family network. These changes, involving both gains and losses in the social network, carry with them both joy and sadness for all affected parties.

CRITICAL ISSUES

CHILDREN AND THE REMARRIAGE SERVICE

Planning for a remarriage ceremony at which children will be present can be a delicate matter. Sometimes children, especially young ones, want to take part. To meet this need, many religious bodies are modifying their wedding rituals to include children. When this happens, the children usually stand next to or behind the couple during the ceremony. Sometimes the marriage vows include a stepparent's promise to care for the spouse's children. In addition, as in the case of a Greendale, Wisconsin, congregation, the children occasionally are given medallions signifying their membership in the new family. Family therapists stress the symbolic importance of rituals in marking the new relationships and commitments remarriage brings. For children, participation in a formal ritual can make the new family seem more "real" (Visher and Visher, 1982).

Celebrating the wedding ritual together as a family serves another key function. A remarriage ceremony can be the first collective memory that the new family will share. For some children, however, the prospect of a parent's remarriage may be painful, and some older children may decline an invitation to participate in the ceremony or even to attend the wedding. Although couples may be hurt and disappointed by this reaction, it is generally best to let children decide this matter for themselves. Often when children know the decision is really theirs and that they will be welcome if they change their minds, they reverse their position and attend. Forcing children to attend against their wishes may set up a power struggle that will have a long-term negative impact on the quality of family life.

Remarriages can also affect adult children who are celebrating their first marriage. Deciding on whom to include in their own ceremony and wedding celebration can be difficult for these children. Have you attended any weddings where this was a problem? What problems can develop when adult children have both biological parents and stepparents? How can these problems be handled?

PARENTAL REMARRIAGE Remarriage in which one or both spouses have children from a previous relationship is known as **parental remarriage**. This stage of remarriage generally receives the most attention in social-science literature and in the media. An indication of how extensive this stage has become is the fact that "1300 stepfamilies are formed every day. One out of every five children has a stepparent" (Maglin and Schniedewind, 1989:13).

As staggering as these statistics may seem at first glance, they do not cover all individuals involved in steprelationships. Many of the statistics gathered on stepchildren include only minor children living with a remarried parent; they do not include those where custodial parents are cohabiting, whether with a same-sex or opposite-sex partner, nor do they include nonresidential steprelationships. Thus, in all likelihood the number of people living in a stepfamily environment at any given moment is considerably higher than these numbers suggest. There is every indication that this pattern will continue to increase into the next century due to the continuing high rate of divorce. Estimates are that over half of today's children will be stepchildren by the year 2000 (Glick, 1989).

Establishing good working relationships with stepchildren is perhaps the most challenging and emotionally trying aspect of remarriage. Both stepparents and stepchildren confront the emotional challenge of moving from the role of stranger to that of family member. This process takes time and is primarily one of trial and error. Such adjustments are often confounded by the presence of the nonresidential biological parent. The attitudes and behavior of the ex-spouse, if hostile, jealous, or uncooperative, may slow the integration of the stepparent into the family unit.

ECONOMIC REMARRIAGE **Economic remarriage** involves the establishment of a unit of economic productivity and consumption while at the same time working out mutually agreeable earning and spending habits. The presence of minor stepchildren can complicate the establishment of an economic plan for the new family unit in several ways. First, the remarried couple may be dependent to a degree on the economic behavior of people outside their immediate relationship. For example, when custodial parents remarry, they may be receiving alimony and child support from their ex-spouses. As we saw in the last chapter, child support might become sporadic or stop entirely after remarriage, adding a dimension of uncertainty to the family budgeting process. Second, new spouses may themselves be noncustodial divorced parents who are paying alimony and child support to their ex-spouses, thus diminishing the financial resources available to the new family unit. Friction may develop over resource distribution: Who should get how much of what is available?

Handling issues of financial equity, need, and flexibility may prove a daunting task. The nature of the financial arrangement may have an impact on the degree and speed of family integration. Some couples choose a "common-pot" approach, putting all wages and child support together and then allocating resources according to need rather than source of income. Others choose a "two-pot" arrangement, in which each spouse contributes a fixed amount to running the household but each biological parent is responsible for her or his children's expenses. Barbara Fishman (1983) found that the common-pot approach is more likely to unify the stepfamily, whereas the two-pot system tends to reinforce biological loyalties and individual autonomy. Which financial arrangement would you choose?

LEGAL REMARRIAGE **Legal remarriage** also requires people to make a number of adjustments. Taking on new responsibilities as a spouse does not absolve a person from responsibilities that accompanied the first marriage. Court-awarded payments of alimony and child support remain in effect. Other responsibilities to the first family are not as clear-cut, however. For example, do nonresident biological children or an ex-spouse have a right to any health or life insurance, retirement benefits, or inheritance from a noncustodial parent or former partner? Because these issues are not clearly dealt with in most states, increasing numbers of remarried couples sign a premarital agreement declaring which assets belong to the remarried family and which should be directed toward the ex-spouse or nonresidential children. These agreements notwithstanding, con-

flict may develop if circumstances change and one spouse feels that too many resources are being diverted to the other spouse's former family.

Additionally troubling is the legal ambiguity surrounding stepchild–stepparent relationships. Only five states have laws that obligate a stepparent to support a stepchild (Fine and Fine, 1992). This legal vacuum may create tension in several ways. On the one hand some stepparents may resent being asked to assume responsibility for someone else's children. On the other hand biological parents may feel guilty asking for help in supporting their children, or they may resent their new spouse's reluctance to help in this regard. A further complication for remarried families is the lack of legal rights on the part of stepparents where stepchildren are concerned. For example, in most states stepparents are not permitted to authorize medical treatment for stepchildren (Kargman, 1983).

Another area in which the legal system has failed to provide adequate support and guidelines for remarried families is in the area of sexual relations. Although all 50 states prohibit marriage and sexual relations between persons closely related by blood, few make similar provisions for family members in a remarriage—for example between a stepfather and stepdaughter or between stepsiblings. Although sexual relations between a minor stepchild and a stepparent are considered a criminal offense, and although sexual relations between stepsiblings are not socially condoned, neither behavior is defined as incest. This differential treatment of sexual relations in first marriages and remarriages can lead to tensions and even sexual exploitation in remarried families.

REMARRIED FAMILIES: ROLES, INTERACTIONS, AND REACTIONS

The dynamic interrelationships among these stations will become clearer as we examine the roles, interactions, and reactions of various members of remarried family households, beginning with stepchildren.

CHILDREN IN REMARRIED FAMILIES

Throughout this text we have emphasized that all families are influenced by people and events outside the immediate family unit. This is particularly true for stepfamilies formed after a divorce. Although members of nuclear families generally share one household, divorce creates two separate but **overlapping households**, with children having membership in both. This dual membership can have both positive and negative consequences for children. On the one hand if one or both biological parents remarry, children have more adults to guide, love, and nurture them. Interacting in two households, each with distinct members, expectations, activities, traditions, and family culture, can provide a richness of experience not found in any one household. On the other hand this dual membership can be a source of conflict and confusion for children. Each household has a set of rules that requires children to shift their behavior from one household to the next. For example, one of the author's young friends who is involved in overlapping households complained:

> When I'm at home I can go to bed anytime I want. Mom doesn't care as long as I get up right away when she calls me in the morning. When I'm at Dad's house, they make me go to bed when the other kids do, around 9 o'clock. I don't think that's fair. I'm older than they are.

Adults in both households need to understand that adjusting to two sets of rules is not easy for children; there must be time and space to allow for the transition from one set of rules to the other. Mixed emotions in these circumstances are not unique to children. Both parents and stepparents may feel insecure and jealous when children visit the other household and may communicate these feelings to children, who in turn may feel that to enjoy being in the other household is somehow disloyal to the other biological parent.

Whether overlapping households are beneficial to children depends in large measure on the attitude and behavior of the involved adults. If all parental adults cooperate in matters of visitation, refrain from criticizing each other in front of the children, and give the children permission to care about and enjoy their other family household, the positive benefits of dual household membership are likely to outweigh the negative consequences for both children and other family members. However, children, too, play a role in determining the nature and quality of overlapping households. They can cooperate or be a source of friction. A major factor in their behavior is the way in which they come to define family membership.

CHILDREN'S PERCEPTIONS OF FAMILY MEMBERSHIP Social scientists often report on the role of children in stepfamilies, but usually the source of this information is adults. Recently, however, Penny Gross (1987) studied 60 Canadian children, 30 females and 30 males between the ages of 16 and 18. Each had two living, divorced parents, at least one of whom had remarried. Utilizing a structured interview that focused on parent–child relationships, Gross asked the children who they considered family members. Four patterns emerged: retention, substitution, reduction, and augmentation.

RETENTION Twenty children (33 percent) defined the family as it was prior to the divorce, that is, with both biological parents but not the stepparent. Thus, some children lived with a stepparent but did not consider that person to be part of their family; and the nonresidential parent continued to play an important role in the lives of her or his children. Sons were more likely than daughters to include the nonresidential father as a family member.

SUBSTITUTION Eight children (13 percent) excluded one biological parent and included at least one stepparent in their definition of family. This was most common when children lived with the remarried parent. For these children, the household membership and the family were synonymous.

REDUCTION These families include fewer people than the original family. Fifteen children (25 percent) excluded their nonresidential biological parent as well as the stepparent, considering only the custodial parent as family. In most cases the custodial parent's remarriage had occurred recently, and the children still had negative feelings about this. These children were the most dissatisfied with their lives and revealed emotional stress during the interview.

AUGMENTATION Seventeen children (28 percent) added to their original family by including both biological parents and at least one stepparent as members. Most of these children lived with their biological fathers and their stepmothers but continued to have regular contact and a strong relationship with their biological mother. They felt free to move back and forth between the overlapping households without the fear of being disloyal to either biological parent.

A survey conducted in the United States also found variations in children's definitions of family membership. When asked, "When you think of your family, who specifically do you include?" 10 percent of the children did not list a biological parent, and 33 percent omitted a stepparent (Cherlin, 1991). Such research suggests that the realities for children involved in remarriages vary considerably. It also challenges definitions of the family that equate family membership with household membership. In the eyes of both children and parents, families may include more or fewer people than current household members. Further research is needed to examine the relationships among stepsiblings and half siblings and the degree to which children incorporate these relationships into their subjective views of family.

CONSEQUENCES OF PARENTAL REMARRIAGE FOR CHILDREN   How do children react to the remarriage of their parents? Do they experience more stress or behavioral problems than children in other family structures? To date, studies reveal no one answer to these questions. A review of an extensive number of studies found that the majority of children in stepfamilies did not have any more psychological or behavioral problems than did children from nuclear families (Ganong and Coleman, 1984:108). Marilyn Ihinger-Tallman and Kay Pasley (1987) also found that children in stepfamilies are similar to those in intact families in self-esteem, psychological functioning, and academic achievement. In the 1983 National Survey of Children, however, Frank Furstenberg and his colleagues reported that children living in stepfamilies are more likely to experience behavioral problems than children living in intact families. These problems may be more acute in remarried families where both parents bring children from previous families (Santrock and Sitterle, 1987). How are we to reconcile these divergent findings?

The first step is to recognize the timing and complexity of divorce and subsequent remarriage. As one research team observed: "Empirical findings suggest that the age of the child at the time of parental divorce and remarriage, sex of the child, and sex of the stepparent are important factors for understanding and predicting the influence of family change on children" (Ihinger-Tallman and Pasley, 1991:461). Let's examine these factors—age and sex—more closely.

AGE   Studies suggest that if parental remarriage occurs early in the child's life (before age 5), the child experiences few adverse effects. In contrast, school-aged children experience more stress after a residential parent remarries, and their schoolwork and social behavior are frequently adversely affected (Wallerstein and Kelly, 1980). In comparison with younger children, older children find adjusting to new people and new places more difficult, and they experience a complex set of emotions regarding both. As adolescents struggle to become more autonomous, the addition of another "parenting" adult to the household may be perceived as threatening to their desired independence. This may be especially true for the oldest child in a single-parent family. In that position the child may have had considerable authority over younger siblings and may have acted as confidant for the custodial parent. For some children relinquishing this responsibility may be a relief; others may resent the loss of power and status (Crosbie-Burnett, 1988).

SEX   When sex differences are taken into account, interesting patterns emerge. Research has consistently shown that boys have more problems adjusting to divorce than do girls. In contrast, boys experience fewer adjustment problems and express fewer negative behaviors in stepfamilies (Clingempeel and Segal, 1986; Peterson and Zill, 1986). For example, after a parental divorce there is an upswing in drug use among boys but not among girls. However, the pattern is reversed following a remarriage; drug use increases for girls but diminishes for boys (Needle, Su, and Doherty, 1990).

Observational studies have found that compared to stepsons, stepdaughters are more sullen and withdrawn and direct more negative behavior toward stepfathers (Hetherington, 1989). Other researchers report similar findings, particularly in mother-custody stepfamilies (Vuchinich et al., 1991). Joshua Fischman (1988) found that girls in stepfamilies showed more stress, exhibited more behavioral problems, and did more poorly on IQ tests than did girls from intact families.

Part of the explanation for this pattern lies in the nature of the relationships established after divorce. The most common structure in remarried families is a biological mother, her children, and a stepfather. Only 18 percent of all stepparents are stepmothers (Glick, 1989). This pattern reflects the fact that in the United

States divorced mothers overwhelmingly have custody of their biological children. Girls often become closer to their mother after a divorce and view the stepfather as an intruder or the stepmother as competition. In fact, closer mother–stepfather relationships are associated with more behavioral problems in girls. Additionally, the adolescent stepdaughter–stepfather relationship may be confusing for both parties. The emerging sexuality of adolescent girls may cause both individuals to be uncertain about the appropriate way to express affection for each other. Girls may feel uncomfortable with a nonbiologically related adult male in the household (Hetherington, 1989).

Boys, on the other hand, are initially angry that Dad was "sent away," but then they become comfortable with another male presence in the household. The presence of a stepfather often eases the mother–son problems that resulted from the divorce. Boys now find themselves with a source of support and companionship. E. Mavis Hetherington (1989) found that preadolescent boys who enjoy a close, supportive stepfather–stepson relationship display fewer behavioral problems and increased social competence. Although stepparent–stepchild relationships can be troublesome, most of these problems disappear by the third year into the remarriage. Perhaps the best advice for parents in such situations, therefore, is to be patient.

STEPSIBLING RELATIONSHIPS: RIVALRY OR SOLIDARITY?

Most of the research on remarried families has been conducted with adult respondents. As is the case with siblings in first marriages, stepsibling relationships have rarely been studied utilizing the perspective of children themselves. This is a critical omission, for, as we will see later in this chapter, children can affect the stability of the remarriage. For example, in one study over twice as many remarried individuals with stepchildren (15 percent) compared to those without children (6 percent) said if they could do it over again, they would not have remarried (White and Booth, 1985). As we have seen earlier, part of the difficulty lies in the relationship between stepparent and stepchild. However, a significant part of the tension in remarried families is centered on stepsibling relationships. Why is this the case? What is it like to be a stepsibling? How are stepsibling relationships different from sibling relationships in intact families?

Beer (1988) reviewed the literature on remarried families and found only indirect references to the subject of stepsiblings. When stepsiblings were discussed, it was generally in relation to one of four themes: (1) stepsibling rivalry, (2) changes in age-order, (3) stepsibling sexuality, and (4) the role of half siblings. The following discussion relies heavily on his work.

STEPSIBLING RIVALRY One of the main differences between siblings and stepsiblings is the origin of their relationships. In the idealized pattern children arrive after the marital relationship has been solidified. They share two biological parents and, hence, a sense of belonging to the same family unit. This does not mean, however, that their relationships are always harmonious. In fact, siblings sometimes experience intense rivalry for parental love.

Stepsiblings, however, start out in a different place than children in intact families. They were part of a family unit that was disrupted by death or divorce. Since that disruption they have formed close relationships with the custodial parent prior to a remarriage. Now they are asked to share this parent not only with another adult but with other children as well. In addition, they are asked to share living space, property, and other possessions that may be in short supply. Sharing space is less of a problem when the remarried family moves into new housing where no one has yet established territorial claims. This option, however, requires a degree of affluence that is not present for many remarried families. Thus, the more common pattern is for one part of the remarried family to move into the residence of the other. When this occurs, the former are likely to be seen as intruders and the latter are likely to regard them as unwelcome guests. As an 8-year-old stepdaughter reported: "We feel like guests in Jim's house. We are careful of what we do. It is like we are intruders. And I feel very bad that we took Tommy's room. They fixed up a room for him in the basement, with posters and all, but he's still mad at us for taking his room" (quoted in Fishman and Hamel, 1991:442). Consequently, neither party is really comfortable with this arrangement, at least in the beginning, and it may give rise to stepsibling rivalry.

Several other factors contribute to stepsibling rivalry. First, there is often a feeling of "them" and "us." Children feel their ties to their biological parent give them a greater claim in the competition for love and other resources: "She's my mom, not yours." Second, when the families were separate both units had their own rules. After remarriage stepparents may try to impose all the rules impartially on all stepchildren, both those who live in the same household and on those who only visit. This attempt at impartiality, however, may not be perceived as equitable by the stepchildren because the rules are often more familiar to one set of children than to the other. Third, differential treatment by others can lead to feelings of rejection, hostility, and envy. For example, grandparents may give generous gifts to their biological grandchildren and ignore their stepgrandchildren. Excluding some children in gift exchanges weakens the chances for establishing a sense of family integration, as it reflects the image that some are "outsiders." Finally, stepsibling rivalry can come about as a result of changes in the age-order of children in the remarried family.

When families are combined through a remarriage, sexual tension sometimes occurs between adolescents of similar ages.

CHANGES IN AGE-ORDER   In intact families the natural order of family births determines the age-order and age-interval of siblings, which, in turn, provide a relatively stable ranking system for children. Each position carries advantages and disadvantages for its occupant, and the children know where they fit in. When two sets of siblings are combined through remarriage, however, some siblings may find their age-order positions in the family altered. Some of these changes are easier to accept than others. For example, when an only child becomes the oldest child, a position of privilege is retained. To a degree benefits also accompany the transition from being an only child to becoming the youngest child. The most difficult change is losing the position of being the oldest to another child, especially of the same sex. Although these changes often cause tensions in the short run, over time children learn to adapt to the new sibling social structure. When the new sibling social structure includes adolescents of different sexes, however, drawing and maintaining sexual boundaries may become a critical task for remarried families.

STEPSIBLING SEXUALITY   Sexual tension is usually a greater problem in remarried families than in first marriages. Several factors interact to create this atmosphere. First, the parent–stepparent union is relatively new. As a couple, they are still likely to be in a honeymoon stage, showing affection for each other, which may be sexually stimulating for adolescents. In first marriages, parents have already worked out patterns for privacy over the years. By the time their children reach adolescence, most parents no longer display sexuality overtly (Visher and Visher, 1982). Second, when a teenaged girl and boy who have not grown up together come to live in the same residence, they may become sexually attracted to each other. Parents may unintentionally contribute to this process by encouraging mutual activities as a way of bringing the children together. Third, stepsibling relationships are not covered by the same incest prohibitions as the relationships between siblings are. This lack of clear rules may cause confusion and uncertainty in remarried families.

Given these conditions, it is not surprising that some sort of sexual activity sometimes occurs between stepsiblings. Nevertheless, at the present time no systematic attempt to measure the extent of such behavior has been made. What information we have on this behavior comes primarily from clinical reports of family therapists and social workers. However, not all sexual feelings between stepsiblings are acted out. A more likely pattern is for adolescents to convert this eroticism into expressions of hostility. Parents often report that stepsiblings seem to "hate each other." This anger can be temporary or long-term; if too severe it can threaten family stability. A more positive outcome results when children can convert their erotic feelings into warm, supportive relationships. Which outcome is more likely depends, to a large extent, on parental reaction. Open and honest discussions with the involved stepsiblings, reassuring them of the normality of such feelings and making clear that there is a difference between feelings and acting on those feelings, can reduce the possibility of a negative outcome.

As a result of such tensions, it is often difficult for remarried family members to feel like a "real" family. One way in which remarried parents try to overcome this perception and to create a cohesive family is by having a mutual child who will provide a blood tie among all members of the remarried family.

THE ROLE OF HALF SIBLINGS The decision to have a mutual child is quite common and occurs soon after remarriage. Over 54 percent of women are likely to have a child after remarrying, most within 24 months of the remarriage (Bumpass, 1984). This pattern holds true for both black and white remarried families (Wineberg, 1990). The rapidity with which this event takes place often causes confusion and adjustment problems for the other children. Although both adults may be biological parents in their own right, they are stepparents to each other's children, and they may or may not share responsibility for them. The birth of a mutual child adds a new role, a shared parental role. Although this new role may help solidify the couple relationship, it is not problem-free. A pattern may emerge whereby both parents exert authority over mutual children but only biological parents assert authority and take responsibility for their own children. This layering of authority and responsibility is a unique feature of remarried families and can produce problems, especially when disagree-

Remarried families are complex. The members of this family include a son from his first marriage, a daughter from her first marriage, and the child they had together.

ments over parenting styles arise (Giles-Sims, 1984). When this happens, there is often a tendency to form alliances—each parent siding with her or his biological offspring or each criticizing the other's children to produce what Emily and John Visher (1982) have called the "two-family-under-one-roof" syndrome.

Stepchildren may see the birth of a mutual child as adding yet another competitor for parental attention. Conversely, however, stepchildren may have positive feelings about the birth of a half sibling, believing that since they are now all related by a blood tie, they finally all belong to a "real" family. Some support for the beneficial role of having a mutual child comes from the pioneering research of Lucile Duberman (1973). Among her parent respondents who had a mutual child, 44 percent reported that relationships among the siblings were excellent, compared with 19 percent of those without mutual children.

In sum, we have seen that stepsibling and half-sibling relationships can be conflictual. That is only half the story, however. Living in a remarried family with stepsiblings or half siblings can also bring positive consequences. Stepsibling rivalry can help children distinguish themselves from others in the family, thereby giving them a strong sense of personal identity. For example, if an older stepsibling is active in sports, a younger stepsibling may turn to music to express her or his individuality. Competition among stepsiblings in some areas does not prevent them from cooperating in other areas. In fact, a sense of solidarity frequently emerges among stepsiblings.

STEPSIBLING RELATIONSHIPS OVER TIME
Sociologists Lynn White and Agnes Riedman (1992) undertook the first empirical research on adult step/half siblings, focusing on their relationships after growing up and leaving home. In general, they found evidence of continued contact and interaction. Although contact was more frequent among full siblings (one to three times a month) compared with the several times a year step/half siblings were seen, less than 1 percent of the respondents in that study were so estranged that they did not even know where their step/half sibling lived. Contact among step/half siblings was affected by three key factors: race, gender, and proximity. As was true among full siblings, African Americans, females, and those who lived near one another had the most frequent contact. To date we have relatively little information about the quality

of these relationships. However, Ihinger-Tallman (1987) hypothesizes that stepsibling bonding occurs most rapidly under conditions of similarity (age, sex, experience, shared values), interdependency, perceived mutual benefit of association, few perceived personal costs, and approximate equality in relinquishing aspects of a former lifestyle. Confirmation of this hypothesis awaits further research.

Children are not the only players in determining how well remarried families function. Stepparents also play key parts. Let's look first at stepmotherhood. The most typical form of stepmothering in the United States is part-time occasioned by the weekend and holiday visits of children to their remarried biological father.

STEPMOTHERS: A BAD RAP?

To what extent are the cultural images of the wicked stepmother valid? Although the empirical evidence does not substantiate the fairy-tale image of the "wicked" stepmother, it does suggest that stepmothering is more problematic than biological mothering. Deciding how to approach the new stepmother role is not easy. Margaret Draughon (1975) suggests three possibilities: (1) *other mother*, or second mother; (2) *primary mother*, who assumes major responsibility for day-to-day caregiving; and (3) *friend*, who is supportive and caring but does not try to be a substitute mother. According to Draughon, the choice of role should be based on the degree of emotional comfort the stepmother feels as well as on the child's emotional state at that time. Draughon believes that if the child is still mourning the loss of the biological mother, whether through death or divorce, the role of friend works best. If, however, mourning has ended, the primary mother role is probably more appropriate. This role, however, must be defined carefully. Generally speaking, defining it to mean primary caretaker instead of a replacement for the biological parent is likely to minimize stepparent–stepchild conflict. Draughon sees no particular advantage to the other-mother model.

STEPMOTHERS AND MOTHERING   How do stepmothers fare in the mothering role? Much of the research shows that stepmother–stepchild relationships are more tentative and difficult than are stepfather–stepchild relationships (Pasley and Ihinger-Tallman, 1987). This is due, in large part, to the greater expectations placed on women in families. Women are expected to take primary responsibility for the well-being of the family, especially in the area of child care, regardless of whose children they "mother." Such expectations can be more distressing for a woman who chooses a marital role but not necessarily a parenting role when she marries a noncustodial father. After remarriage she may find that his children visit more frequently than anticipated or that child custody has shifted unexpectedly to him. Furthermore, the nurturing expectations for women are so strong that stepmothers themselves often assume that "instant love" of stepchildren should be possible. For this reason, stepmothers frequently feel guilty when they don't as yet feel a strong attachment to their spouse's children.

A stepmother's attempt to create a close-knit family structure may be misinterpreted. The biological mother may accuse her of trying to take her place. The stepchildren may also perceive her behavior as a threat to their mother's position. On the other hand, if the stepmother chooses a less involved approach toward her stepchildren, she may be accused by them and her spouse of not caring enough or not being a good mother. A common reaction to these situations is stress: Stepmothers report significantly greater role strain than do stepfathers (Whittset and Land, 1992). Ann-Marie Ambert (1986) suggests this greater stress stems in part from women's traditional domestic role. She found that when stepchildren visit, the stepmothers, and not the fathers, usually acquire extra work, such as housecleaning and cooking.

We should remember, however, that not all stepparenting situations are alike. In a study of 109 stepparents, Ambert found that having live-in stepchildren is less divisive than are situations in which children live with the other parent and come for visits. The former situation allows the couple more control over their lives. Wives feel more "appreciated" by their spouses because of their child-rearing contributions, and they feel less threatened by the biological mother. Stepmothers develop a closer and deeper relationship with their live-in stepchildren than with stepchildren living elsewhere.

These findings offer an explanation for why stepfathers seem to experience fewer problems in their roles. Most stepfathers, in contrast to most stepmothers, have live-in stepchildren. What role, then, do stepfathers play in remarried families?

STEPFATHERS: POLITE STRANGERS?

Earlier in this chapter we discussed the cultural images of the "wicked stepmother." Although no comparable image or folktales exist for stepfathers, recently publicized cases of child abuse by stepfathers have focused renewed attention on this social category. Additionally, more is known about the role of stepfathers in remarried families than about stepmothers. This is due in large part to their greater numbers. Stepfather families are the most common remarried family structure and, as such, have been the focus of considerable social-science research.

A fairly consistent image of stepfathers has emerged from these investigations. Overall stepfathers tend to be more positive and responsive and less "bossy" toward children than are biological fathers. Samuel Vuchinich and his colleagues (1991) characterize such behaviors as the "sociable polite stranger" role. This pattern of stepparenting might explain the finding that stepfathers in stable stepfamilies generally enjoy better relations with their stepchildren than do stepmothers (Crosbie-Burnett, Skyles, Becker-Haven, 1988). However, this finding should not be interpreted to mean that stepfathers don't encounter problems in this role. They do. Elizabeth Einstein (1985) identified three areas of difficulty for stepfathers: sex, money, and discipline.

SEX   Stepfathers may feel uncomfortable in the presence of sexually developing adolescent stepdaughters. To prevent any misinterpretation by the stepdaughter or her mother, the stepfather often remains emotionally distant from his stepdaughter, with the result that the stepdaughter may perceive him as uncaring.

MONEY   Money may be a source of conflict for the stepfather in a number of ways. If he is a noncustodial biological parent, he may feel guilty for not playing a more active role in his own children's lives. Thus, he may give his children money or expensive gifts to compensate for his absence, thus creating envy among his stepchildren. This behavior may also cause

friction with both his current spouse, who feels the money is needed elsewhere, and with his ex-spouse, who fears he is buying his children's love by spoiling them. In other cases, the economic demands of a second family may be so severe that the stepfather stops supporting the children from his first family.

DISCIPLINE   Issues involving discipline revolve around two key questions: Who should discipline? and Under what conditions? The answers to these questions may be far from clear not only on the part of the stepfather but in the minds of other family members as well. The wife/mother in the remarried family may voice a desire to share authority with her new spouse, but when he takes her up on it, she may be emotionally unprepared to relinquish any of her authority over her children. Research shows that it takes approximately 18 to 24 months for stepparents to achieve an equal "co-management" role with the biological parent (Visher and Visher, 1982:64).

Stepchildren, too, may hold contradictory views regarding discipline by a stepfather. They may resent his efforts to make them behave. Yet if he doesn't try to discipline them, they may perceive him as indifferent and uncaring and respond angrily, "You don't care what I do; you don't love me." Researchers have found a correlation between stepchildren's perception of being loved by a stepparent and whether the stepparent makes them behave (Bohannan, 1985). The dilemma of discipline appears to be lessened in cases where a friendship has been established between the stepparent and the stepchild. When friendship exists, stepchildren are more likely to accept discipline from the stepparent (Wallerstein and Kelly, 1980).

EX-SPOUSES: DO THEY FADE AWAY?

Divorce ends a marriage, but it does not necessarily end the relationship between the former spouses. This is especially true for couples with children. How do couples come to view each other after divorce? One study of divorced fathers and their new wives found that most of these couples identified the children's mother as a major source of stress in their marriage. Both the ex-husbands and their wives described the ex-wife in negative terms (Guisinger et al., 1989). This finding seems to support the popular image of ex-spouses as warring factions.

In another study, however, researchers found that only half of the sample of divorced couples fit that description. Such couples were classified as either "angry associates," whose relationships are characterized by bitterness, resentment, and ongoing conflicts over visitation and support payments, or "fiery foes," whose relationships are extremely antagonistic. The lingering acrimony of their divorce made it impossible for them to cooperate with each other on any matter. In contrast, the other 50 percent of divorced couples in the sample maintained cordial relationships with each other, often as "cooperative colleagues," who are friendly and mutually concerned about their children's welfare. They managed to make decisions and celebrate their children's major life events together. A smaller number of ex-spouses remained "perfect pals." Their divorce was amiable;

they continued to like and trust each other, and they worked cooperatively to maintain a positive environment for their children (Ahrons and Wallisch, 1986).

Thus far, our discussion of remarried families has tended to focus on the numerous adjustment problems members face. This should in no way be interpreted to mean that there are few benefits to living in remarried families. Quite the opposite is true, as we will see in the next section.

THE STRENGTHS AND BENEFITS OF REMARRIED FAMILIES

The identification of strengths in remarried families is a relatively new phase in social-science research. Patricia Knaub and her colleagues (1984) were among

Integrating members of two different families can be difficult. Remarriage can also provide emotionally satisfying relationships for stepsiblings, however.

the first to undertake an empirical study of what makes remarried families strong. They asked 80 randomly selected remarried families to indicate what strengths were most important to their families. Their respondents listed love and intimacy (caring, affection, closeness, acceptance, understanding), family unity (working together; shared goals, values and activities), and positive patterns of communication (honesty, openness, receptiveness, and a sense of humor), characteristics that are important to all families. Further insight into the strengths of remarried families comes from a study of remarried couples in central Pennsylvania (Furstenberg and Spanier, 1984). These couples felt that their current marriage was stronger than their first marriage in three important ways. First, they had better communication skills. Second, they were more realistic about the existence of conflict in marriage, and perhaps as a result of having better communication skills, they reported having fewer conflicts in their second marriage. Third, the balance of power was more equal in the remarriage, and household tasks were more evenly distributed.

Remarriage offers a number of benefits to family members. A custodial parent gains a partner with whom to share family work as well as financial responsibility. In exchange the new stepparent shares in the joys of family life. For the new spouses, remarriage restores the continuity of a sexual relationship and provides companionship and a sense of partnership. Additionally, although it might be viewed as a mixed blessing, the ambiguity of roles in remarried families offers family members the opportunity to create new roles that may prove to be more satisfying in the long run. For example, stepparents don't have to try to replace parents; instead, they can be friends, counselors, teachers, or companions to stepchildren. Both stepparents and stepchildren can benefit by interactions that are less encumbered by unrealistic expectations of instant family love and unity. In a 1987 National Stepfamily Association newsletter, a stepchild described her stepmother in these words:

> Yet my own experience as a stepchild shows that it is possible to have a friendly relationship.... We established an amicable relationship...though I did not regard W——— as a mother, and I would have resented it if she had expected me to.... Our relationship isn't as close as that between natural parents and their children but there are certain benefits in this. Stepparents can be more detached, and there's no danger of them seeing the child as an extension of

themselves. Sometimes, because they're less involved, it is easier for them to see where the child's real interests lie. (Cited in Smith, 1990:44–45).

These are some of the tangible benefits of remarriages, but do they translate into emotional and psychological satisfaction? In short, are remarried couples happy and satisfied with their marital relationship?

THE QUALITY OF THE REMARITAL RELATIONSHIP

Despite all the problems we have just discussed, most remarried couples seem to find happiness in their new relationship. After comparing couples in first and second marriages, Elizabeth Benson-von der Ohe (1987:181) concluded, "In general, second marriages fared no better and no worse with regard to marital happiness, equality between husband and wife, incidence of crises of long-standing issues, or—measured near the outset of marriage—quantity and quality of communication and the number of 'touchy' topics." Similarly, other researchers who have examined the literature on remarriage concluded that the slightly higher level of satisfaction reported by people in first marriages compared with those in remarriages is not statistically significant (Coleman and Ganong, 1990).

When gender is examined, however, differences in levels of happiness and satisfaction emerge. Several studies found that remarried women reported lower levels of marital happiness and satisfaction when compared to remarried men (White, 1979; Glenn, 1981; Ishii-Kuntz, 1986). This finding is consistent with patterns observed in first marriages and supports the view that marriage tends to benefit men more than women. It may also be, as Norval Glenn suggests, that the remarriage market favors men. Consequently, women have a smaller pool of eligibles from which to select a partner. Hence, women may have more difficulty than men in finding an "ideal" mate, possessing all the qualities they desire.

Another factor that can affect a remarried couple's relationship is the form the stepfamily takes. For example, several researchers found that marital satisfaction was higher in mother–stepfather families where the stepfather had no children from a previous marriage than in stepfamilies where the stepfather coparented children from another marriage with an ex-spouse (Giles-Sims, 1984; Clingempeel and

Brand, 1985). These researchers explain this difference in terms of the nature of the coparenting relationship that exists with the ex-spouses. If the relationship is one of conflict over ongoing issues—for example, child support, discipline, visitation rights—the stress created is likely to have a negative impact on the remarried family. If the stepparent and ex-spouse have resolved their emotional problems and are able to relate to each other and to their children on a nonconflictual basis, however, then this situation should not exert stress on the remarriage.

As is true with first marriages, the presence of children in stepfamilies can affect the quality of family happiness. Studies of middle- and upper-middle-class families with adolescents reveal that the quality of the stepfather–stepchild relationship had a greater impact on family happiness than did the quality of the marital relationship (Crosbie-Burnett, 1984).

In sum, then, what can couples do to facilitate happiness in remarriage? Remarried couples who accept their children's loyalties to noncustodial parents, accept their spouse's ongoing coparenting relationship with an ex-spouse, and resolve the problems raised by their prior marriage are likely to have a happy remarriage. However, as we shall see in the next section, happiness in the remarried-couple relationship may not be sufficient to ensure the stability of the remarriage.

STABILITY IN REMARRIAGE

Songwriters Sammy Cahn and James Van Heusen popularized the notion that "Love is lovelier the second time around." Conventional wisdom would have us believe that second marriages should be more successful than first marriages. People often assume that divorced people possess characteristics that should enable them to build more effective relationships. On the average the divorced are older and seemingly more mature and experienced than those entering marriages for the first time. Thus, the argument goes, they should make more intelligent choices, have more realistic expectations, and have more negotiating skills with which to handle the stresses and strains that arise in married life.

As we have seen, the marital relationship in remarriages frequently is strong, and the level of marital happiness is similar in first and second marriages. In fact, however, statistics indicate that divorced people who remarry have a higher divorce rate than those in first marriages. Approximately 60 percent of all remarriages ultimately end in divorce, compared with approximately 50 percent of first marriages. Furthermore, remarriages dissolve more rapidly than first marriages. As Figure 14.2 shows, although the probability of divorce declines over the years, at each interval, it is greater than for first marriages.

FACTORS AFFECTING STABILITY Several factors combine to explain the higher divorce rate among remarried people. First, as we have already observed, remarriage is a complex process, requiring a number of adjustments that are outside the scope of first marriages and for which most remarried couples are not well prepared. To cite just one example, kinship terms and interactions may be a sticking point for all those affected by remarriage. If a biological father is called "Dad," what form of address should be used to refer to the stepfather? How do you integrate multiple sets of grandparents into holiday and family celebrations? What happens to previous family customs and traditions? Cherlin (1978) argued that "remarriage is an incomplete institution" that does not provide answers to these questions. Consequently, remarried families are left adrift to find their own

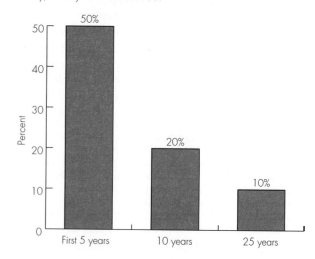

FIGURE 14.2 Greater Probability of Divorce in Remarriage Compared with First Marriages, Based on Number of Years Married

Source: Cited in Cynthia J. Pill, 1990, "Stepfamilies: Redefining the Family," *Family Relations* 39:186.

solutions to these problems. Without institutional-ized patterns of family behavior and support, family unity is likely to be precarious.

OUTSIDE SUPPORT AND PRESSURES   In addition, the attitudes of relatives, friends, and community members can affect the stability of remarriages. Positive and supportive reactions from friends and relatives contribute to successful remarriages. Conversely, disapproval of the remarriage by significant others can put added stress on the relationship. Sometimes the announcement of a remarriage may be greeted with little enthusiasm on the part of relatives. As one stepmother said in an interview:

> My mother was thrilled for me when I told her I was going to marry, but her manner changed completely when I told her he had a child. She was wary for me; she wanted me to think about it. It was not the dream she had for my marriage. (quoted in Smith, 1990:30)

ATTITUDES TOWARD DIVORCE   Moreover, the familiarity with the divorce process itself may remove some of the social barriers to a second divorce. Having survived a first divorce, some remarried people are less likely to stay in an unhappy or deteriorating relationship. Furthermore, because they have already dealt with the reactions of family and friends to their first divorce, they are likely to be less fearful of an adverse reaction to their course of action.

This seems to be especially true for some groups. For example, remarried white men are more likely to redivorce than are remarried white women (Glick, 1984). This seems strange given that women tend to report less happiness in second marriages than do men. Yet the reverse pattern is found among blacks: More black women than men divorce a second time. The most frequently cited explanation for these opposing patterns focuses exclusively on economic motivation. According to this argument, black women come closer to having economic equality with black men than white women do with white men. Consequently, remarriage may not represent the same level of financial security to black women as it does to white women. This interpretation clearly ignores many noneconomic factors. It may be that many black women, having been socialized to be assertive and self-sufficient (Hale-Benson, 1986) simply are less willing than other women to stay in an

unhappy relationship. It could also be that the black community does not view divorce with the same stigma that the white community does.

THE PRESENCE OF CHILDREN   Children may play a pivotal role in the parental decision to redivorce. Indeed, several studies have found that the divorce rate is higher in remarriages with stepchildren (Cherlin, 1978; White and Booth, 1985). Ihinger-Tallman and Pasley (1991) suggest three ways in which children can contribute to the dissolution of remarriages: personal adjustment, discipline problems, and disruptive behavior.

The presence of children makes adjustment harder for a remarried couple. Children limit a couple's privacy and the opportunity for intimacy. Couples may agree on aspects of their personal relationship but be at odds over what constitutes appropriate child behavior. This is especially likely considering the different parenting histories of each partner.

As we saw earlier, another source of conflict for remarried couples with children is discipline. Stepparents may feel that discipline was too lax in the "old" family and that new rules are in order. Stepchildren may resent such changes, and biological parents may feel caught in the middle. Consequently, all parties are likely to experience stress.

Finally, the actual behavior of children can be a powerful force in disrupting the marital relationship. Children can manipulate the biological parent into taking sides against the stepparent or stepsiblings. Also, by refusing to cooperate in matters of daily family living, children can create a tense and hostile environment.

Although at the present time remarriages are somewhat less stable than first marriages, this may change as remarriage becomes more common. Researchers can gain a better understanding of how stepfamilies fare over time by utilizing *longitudinal studies*, in which the same people are studied at different periods in time. Comparisons of stable remarried families with those that have dissolved should enable us to identify ways to help remarried families cope with the unique aspects of remarriage. For example, the experiences of therapists show that remarried families require a minimum of 2 to

FOR YOUR INFORMATION

STEPFAMILY ASSOCIATION OF AMERICA

Stepfamily Association of America (SAA) is a nonprofit organization created to provide support to stepfamilies. Its goals are far-reaching: to dispel the historical negative myths of stepfamilies, to educate society about stepfamily needs and concerns through greater media coverage and support of scientific research, and to provide needed information and support to remarried family units. SAA provides a wide range of services to its members. Educational and social programs are offered through local chapters. The association office serves as a clearinghouse for books and educational materials of special interest to stepfamilies. For information on the chapters in your area, write to SAA, 215 Centennial Mall South, Suite 212, Lincoln, NE 68508, or call 402–477–STEP.

---

5 years to begin to stabilize and develop their own customs, rituals, and history (Messinger, 1984). Knowing that this is a normal pattern for remarried families, some remarried couples who might otherwise contemplate divorce might stay together and wait for the "storms" to pass. Support groups for stepfamilies are increasing around the country, which should also help to stabilize this emerging family form.

In the meantime, however, existing research findings on stepfamilies suggest a number of ways in which social policy could be enlisted immediately to help support the growing number of stepfamilies in the United States.

RECOMMENDATIONS FOR SOCIAL POLICY

If any social policy is to be effective, it must first have a clear view of the targeted population it wishes to serve. As we have discussed throughout this text, most U.S. family policies are based on a traditional nuclear family model, yet only a small percentage of families fit this model. The processes of divorce and remarriage have created a wide variety of household forms. Thus, legal scholars and experts in family relations suggest that the conceptualization of the family change to include these households. Specifically with regard to remarried families their recommendations include clarification of legal norms, modification of the tax code, and development of educational materials about stepfamilies.

CLARIFICATION OF LEGAL NORMS

Researchers who have studied the problems of stepfamilies have identified three ways in which state laws affecting parent–child relationships could be modified to meet the needs of stepfamilies. First, they could include a form of legal guardianship that would allow stepparents to function more effectively in families. For example, stepparents should be allowed to sign school permission slips, view student records, sign emergency medical forms, and authorize driving permits. Second, lawmakers and judges need to be made aware of the probability of second or third divorces and take steps to ensure that the desires of stepparents and stepchildren regarding visitation rights be incorporated into divorce decrees. Although all 50 states now grant some third-party visitation, the laws tend to be directed more to the rights of grandparents than to those of stepparents (Fine and Fine, 1992). Third, to reduce ambiguities and sexual tensions that often exist in stepfamilies, incest laws could be broadened to include stepparents and their children and quite possibly stepsiblings as well (Crosbie-Burnett, Skyles, and Becker-Haven, 1988).

MODIFICATION OF THE TAX CODE

Throughout this chapter we have referred to the financial conflicts that often affect remarried families. Yet there is little acknowledgment of the financial contribution stepparents make to the parenting process. One recommendation to remedy this concerns the tax structure. Because many stepchildren are

APPLYING THE SOCIOLOGICAL IMAGINATION

WHAT'S IN A CARD?

The exchange of greeting cards on special occasions has become an accepted and expected pattern of behavior in the United States. However, the greeting card industry, like many other businesses, was slow to recognize the diversity of the U.S. population. In the past, outside of ethnic specialty shops it was difficult to find cards representing people of color. Today most stores stock these cards. Nevertheless, it is still difficult to find cards that represent other than traditional family forms. We searched a number of stores without success before finding this greeting card for stepparents.

Visit some of your neighborhood card shops. Can you find

I'm really glad now that we're part of the same family, but you probably know I wasn't so sure at first. I guess I was just afraid—afraid that there wasn't room for both of us in the same family, afraid I'd be forgotten or loved a little less than before you came along. But somehow we've managed to weather all that and to grow closer, too.

And now I realize how much you've brought to the family, how much you've added to my life— and I want to say thank you... for being such a patient, loving stepparent, such a very thoughtful, very special person.

Dorothy R. Colgan

cards for stepfamilies? What does the selection of cards in the section marked "For Relatives" reveal about our culture's attitude regarding stepfamilies? Do you think there should be greeting cards specifically for stepfamilies? For other groups? Why or why not? What purposes does the exchange of cards serve?

members of overlapping households, both households spend money on food, shelter, clothes, entertainment, travel, and many other items. Currently, however, dependent children can be claimed as a tax deduction for only one household. If the tax code were revised to allow stepparents to deduct their cost of shared child support, it would give these parents some financial assistance. Besides the monetary benefit, this change would symbolize society's recognition of the contribution stepparents make to the well-being of children and, hence, to the community at large.

EDUCATION

Schools at all levels are being encouraged to recognize the changing composition of families and to develop curricular materials that reflect the organization and functioning of various family structures. Proponents argue that this approach would serve several purposes. First, teachers and professional counselors would have the knowledge and

understanding to work with all kinds of families. This would enable them to change any existing policies and practices that devalue or ignore remar-

Relatively little public attention has been focused on stepfamilies. One notable exception to this was television's portrayal of "The Brady Bunch."

ried families. Two examples can illustrate this point: (1) Forms that students fill out can be changed to eliminate confusion about surnames by including all appropriate relationships, and (2) when students are asked to make cards or gifts for parents or grandparents, steprelationships could be included on a routine basis. Schools could also provide meeting space for support groups such as Stepfamilies of America (see the FYI box). Doing so would show stepchildren that some of their classmates experience similar problems of adjustment. This would lessen any stigma that they might feel about being different.

As information on the complexity of remarried families and successful coping mechanisms for dealing with this complexity become more available, and as the role expectations of family members become clarified, negative cultural images of remarried families are likely to be replaced with positive ones. As a result, participants in remarried families will no longer be made to feel that they are living in a "deviant" or "lesser" family structure, and they will feel more secure and accepted by the larger society. This, in turn, is likely to be reflected in the emergence of more stable remarried families.

SUMMARY

The pattern of marriage, divorce, and remarriage has become well established in the United States today. Most divorced people marry within 5 years of their divorce. Nine out of ten remarriages involve divorced individuals, in contrast to previous eras when most remarriages involved widowed people.

Despite the high rate of remarriage, relatively little is known about this family form, especially among different classes, races, and ethnic groups. Remarried families differ from nuclear families in fundamental ways: They are more complex; they have a changing cast of characters; their boundaries are unclear, and their rules are often undefined. Laws regarding remarried families are ambiguous, and there is a lack of kinship terms to cover all affected parties in a remarriage. Members of remarried families often feel guilty or are still grieving over previous relationships.

Divorced people who remarry tend to spend less time in dating and courtship than do people who marry for the first time, but like couples marrying for the first time, they spend little time discussing issues such as finances and children. The reasons for remarriage are similar to those for first marriage and include love, companionship, and social pressure. Men remarry more frequently and sooner than women do. Men with higher incomes are more likely to remarry than men with lower incomes.

College-educated women are less likely to remarry than other women. Whites have the highest rate of remarriage of any racial and ethnic group in the United States.

Children of remarried parents often find themselves living in overlapping households and having to adjust to two different sets of rules. Although stepchildren often have difficulties adjusting and may experience stepsibling rivalry, they also benefit from having new, extended families. A half sibling may be yet another source of competition for a parent's attention, but she or he may also help stepchildren to feel they are now part of a "real" family.

Both stepmothers and stepfathers face difficulties in establishing relationships with stepchildren, although stepmothers experience more stress than do stepfathers. Remarried couples report levels of marital happiness similar to those reported by couples in first marriages. Nevertheless, remarriages are more likely to end in divorce than first marriages are. The reasons for this discrepancy are related to the more complex characteristics of remarried families.

Legal scholars and family experts recommend that social policy be directed at disseminating knowledge about remarried families, clarifying the legal status of stepparents, and acknowledging the financial and other contributions of stepfamilies.

KEY TERMS

remarried family   parental remarriage
emotional remarriage   economic remarriage
psychic remarriage   legal remarriage
community remarriage   overlapping households

QUESTIONS FOR STUDY AND REFLECTION

1. Discuss the significance of viewing remarried families as distinct from nuclear families. In a similar vein, some sociologists have argued against referring to remarried families as reconstituted or blended families. How might these latter terms cause problems for individuals living in remarried families?

2. Imagine that you are getting remarried and that both you and your spouse are custodial parents with children of the opposite sex who are relatively similar in age. How would you arrange your home living space? What steps would you take to create a positive remarried family atmosphere?

3. Compare and contrast the roles of stepmother and stepfather in U.S. culture. Specifically, do you think that one role is more difficult than the other? Why or why not? What can society do to assist stepparents?

4. To what degree do you think remarried families are seen as a legitimate family form in the United States today? Be specific. Consider their relationships to other social institutions like the schools, laws, government, and the media. What changes, if any, would you make in these institutions regarding remarried families?

FURTHER READING

BEER, WILLIAM R. 1992. *American Stepfamilies.* New Brunswick, NJ: Transaction. The author utilizes a case study approach to examine the nature of stepfamily life. Anyone considering entering a stepfamily or who is currently in a stepfamily will find this volume a helpful resource.

MAGLIN, NAN BAUER, AND NANCY SCHNIEDEWIND, eds. 1989. *Women and Stepfamilies: Voices of Anger and Love.* Philadelphia, PA: Temple University Press. The varied experiences and perspectives of women in stepfamilies are revealed through poems, letters, essays, and journals. Women from different class, racial, and ethnic backgrounds share their stories.

PASLEY, KAY, AND MARILYN IHINGER-TALLMAN, eds. 1987. *Remarriage and Stepparenting: Current Research and Theory.* New York: Guilford Press. The collection of writings and studies in this volume deals with a wide range of historical, theoretical, and conceptual issues regarding the experiences of living in stepfamilies.

SOMERVILL, CHARLES. 1989. *Stepfathers: Struggles and Solutions.* Louisville, KY: Westminster/John Knox. The author uses a fictitious family to represent the problems and triumphs of stepparenting. Each chapter portrays a real life experience and provides a brief conclusion depicting ways for solving the problem.

Chapter 15

MARRIAGES AND FAMILIES IN LATER LIFE

Gus, age 78, and Millie, age 77, will celebrate their golden wedding anniversary next month. Their two children, Sara and Greg, who live out of state, have planned a small anniversary party for them. Sara and Greg also plan to use this occasion to have a family meeting to discuss Gus and Millie's living arrangements. They are concerned about their parents' ability to continue living in the two-story house Gus and Millie bought when the children were small. Gus had a stroke about a year ago, and Millie must help him with most of the activities that make up daily living. Although it is increasingly difficult for Millie to care for Gus, she promised she would never put him in a nursing home. He wants to stay in the house where things are familiar to him and where friends and neighbors still come to visit.

Sara and Greg fear that Millie will ruin her health if she continues to care for Gus. They want Gus and Millie to sell the house and move closer to one of them and they believe that the time is fast approaching when Gus will need to go to a nursing home. Sara has invited Millie to live with her in that event. Millie is uncertain about what to do. She likes her independence and doesn't want to be a burden. She loves her house and garden, but she knows that she can't continue to maintain them and also take care of Gus.

Imagine that this is your family. How would you approach this situation? Why would giving up the house be so difficult for Millie and Gus? Can you see any other alternative actions this family could take? Have you had any similar experiences in your family? As an adult child, would you want your elderly parents to live with you? Do you think they would want to live with you? Why or why not?

In the United States today, half of all people over age 65 with living children are members of four-generation families (Shanas, 1980). Four-generation and even five-generation families are far more common today than in the past because so many more people survive into later life. Thus, members of such families can be considered pioneers with relatively few role models to guide them. The result can be a great deal of confusion and uncertainty for all concerned. For the oldest relatives, the presence of great-grandchildren can be a source of pride and delight. It can also be a source of conflict and confusion, however, because different generations often adhere to different values and behaviors. The primary focus of this chapter is on what family expert Timothy Brubaker (1990) has called "later-life families"—families who are beyond the child-rearing years.

CHARACTERISTICS OF LATER-LIFE FAMILIES

Later-life families possess several characteristics that make them fascinating to study but that also have practical implications for developing meaningful social policies on aging. According to Brubaker, later-life families exhibit three characteristics: (1) they are multigenerational; (2) they have a lengthy family history; and (3) they experience a number of new life events for which they may have little preparation, for example, grandparenthood, retirement, and widowhood. As we will see

throughout this chapter, these characteristics greatly influence the nature and quality of family interactions.

In this chapter we look at some of the changes in family composition over time and at the new developmental tasks that accompany these changes. In this regard, our approach utilizes the theoretical model of the family life cycle introduced in Chapter 2. Evelyn Duvall's (1977) last two stages in the life cycle incorporate "later-life families." These stages encompass middle-aged parents who must deal with the "empty nest," the period after the last child leaves home, and the aging family, whose tasks include adjusting to retirement and the death of a spouse.

THE SANDWICH GENERATION

The middle-aged generation, sometimes called the **sandwich generation** because of the pressures its members experience from both ends of the age spectrum, finds itself playing many roles. Middle-aged parents must meet the challenges of their own lives—their own aging and approaching retirement from work and all the adjustments these entail. As their children reach adulthood, parents expect to be free from major family responsibilities and to have more time to spend on their own pursuits. For many parents, however, the economic realities of recent decades have put some of these expectations on hold. Many young adults find achieving financial independence difficult. Consequently, increasing numbers of adult children

Before we proceed to our discussion of the lifestyles of later-life families, take a few minutes to assess your degree of knowledge about the lifestyles of the elderly. Treat the following five statements as an ungraded quiz. Read each statement carefully, and indicate whether you believe it to be true or false.

_____ **1.** The majority of the elderly live in poverty.
_____ **2.** Most elderly people end up in nursing homes and other long-term care institutions.
_____ **3.** Most of the elderly are neglected by their children.

_____ **4.** The majority of the elderly are in poor health.
_____ **5.** Most elderly people are dissatisfied with their lives.

Scoring: If you answered false to all five statements, you already have considerable knowledge of the realities of later life. If you answered true to any of the statements, you, like many Americans, have some misconceptions about elderly people and the aging process. Throughout the remainder of this chapter we contrast these misconceptions with current realities.

Source: Adapted from Cary S. Kart, *The Realities of Aging: An Introduction to Gerontology*. Copyright © 1990 by Allyn & Bacon. Reprinted by permission of Allyn & Bacon.

---

remain at or return to the parental home: In 1991, 31 percent of unmarried adults aged 25 to 29 lived with their parents (U.S. Bureau of Census, 1992a:10). This living arrangement can be stressful. Conflicts of lifestyles and values are common. Both generations complain about a lack of privacy. Marital and parental satisfaction can decline under these circumstances.

Not only do middle-aged parents frequently have adult children living at home, but they often must care for elderly parents as well. Increasing life expectancy combined with lower birthrates, have brought about major shifts in the amount of time people spend in various roles. The middle generation, for example, will spend on average more years with parents over 65 than with children under 18 (Watkins, Menken, and Bongaarts, 1987). A new federal study of middle-aged Americans (ages 51 to 61) found that "30 to 40 percent of people in their 50s with children were helping them and a third were helping parents financially or in other ways" (Kolata, 1993:A16). Thus, the empty-nest stage is more a myth than a reality for increasing numbers of middle-aged parents.

DIVERSITY IN THE FAMILY LIFE CYCLE

As we saw in Chapter 2, the family life-cycle model has some inherent limitations that we will try to avoid. For example, our discussion of later-life families does not assume a nuclear-family model. Child-free couples, single-parent families, and families that have taken in other kin or friends—a pattern common among families of color—must also make changes and confront new tasks as their members grow older. Additionally, like families at other stages of development, later-life families take diverse forms. They include couples in a first marriage, mothers who have never married, widows and divorced people who have not remarried, and people who have remarried, some more than once. Diversity is further enhanced by the fact that these households cut across all social, economic, racial, and ethnic groups. Our discussion incorporates the diversity among and within later-life families to the extent that the existing data permit. Here again, however, much of the existing research involves white, middle-class families. Thus, our ideas concerning how the poor (and for that matter the rich) and people of color experience many of these later-life stages are largely undocumented.

For much of the twentieth century, the U.S. culture has emphasized youth. Consequently, many Americans have developed negative stereotypes of the elderly. Robert Butler, the former director of the National Institute of Aging and author of *Why Survive? Being Old in America* (1975), coined the term **ageism** to describe these stereotypes and the discriminatory treatment applied to the elderly. **Social**

Television's portrayal of the "Golden Girls" has challenged some of the stereotypes often associated with growing old.

gerontology, the study of the impact of sociocultural conditions on the process and consequences of aging, shows us that the impact of aging on marriages and families is multifaceted. Some older family members are frail and in need of care, whereas others are living independent, healthy, active lives. Some of America's elderly live in isolation in single-room occupancy hotels, but many others enjoy happy lives, interacting with family and friends and engaging in numerous new and exciting activities. Our goal throughout this chapter is to present these differing realities of America's elderly and their families. This approach requires that we balance the strengths and satisfactions of the elderly with the real problems many of the elderly confront on a daily basis.

CHANGING AGE NORMS

In general, life-course development tends to follow specific **age norms**, expectations of how one is to behave at any stage in life. These age norms currently show signs of being less restrictive than in the past. For example, today it is not unusual for people to marry for the first time in their 20s, 40s, or even 60s. Similarly, women are becoming mothers at both younger and older ages. Not only are teens giving birth but, due to new reproductive

technology, so too are menopausal women (Chapter 9). Divorced and remarried men in their 40s and 50s are starting new families. As late as the 1960s, students typically attended college for 4 years, starting at age 18 and finishing at age 22. Today your classmates may be 20, 30, 50, or even 70 years old, and they may take 4, 5, or even 8 years to complete their degrees. Although more people are opting for early retirement at age 55, others begin new careers at age 70. As these examples indicate, there has been an ongoing shift toward a loosening of age-appropriate standards of behavior (Neugarten and Neugarten, 1992).

As a result of falling mortality rates, most of us can expect to experience many of these later-life events—launching of children and the period of the empty nest, job changes, retirement, parental care, widowhood, and, particularly for females, an extended period of solitary living. By reflecting on the experiences of the generations ahead of us, we may better prepare ourselves to deal with these events. Such a reflection also allows us to confront some of the popular fears of aging that exist in our society.

THE DEMOGRAPHICS OF AGING: DEFINING "OLD"

Who are today's elderly? When does old age begin? One easy answer is at age 65, which was arbitrarily selected by government officials in 1935 as the age at which a worker could receive full social security retirement benefits. Defining old age is more complicated than this, however. Consider, for example, the active 78-year-old friend of ours who explained why she doesn't care to go to her local senior-citizen center: "The people there are all so old." By that she meant they are in their 80s and 90s and less active than herself. Her experiences confirm what many researchers have come to call *functional age*—an individual's physical, intellectual, and social capacities and accomplishments. People grow old at different rates. One person may be "old" at 60, whereas another is "young" at 75 (Shanas, 1980).

In 1900, only 3 million people in the United States were aged 65 or over, representing just 4 percent of the total population. By 1991, 31.7 million people were in this age group, constituting 12.6 percent of the population (U.S. Bureau of the Census, 1992a). By 2050 the number of elderly is expected to

APPLYING THE SOCIOLOGICAL IMAGINATION

IS AGEISM DEAD?

Imagine that when you woke up this morning you were suddenly 85 years old. How would people treat you? Would you experience ageism? Pat Moore, a 26-year-old industrial designer, decided to find out by taking on the appearance and demeanor of an 85-year-old woman. During the 3-year period of her research, she presented herself to people in two ways: as an old person and as herself. Her book *Disguised* (with C. P. Conn, 1985) provides a fascinating account of the ways in which the old Pat Moore was treated differently from the young Pat Moore. When disguised as the older woman, Moore frequently was treated with anger, disrespect, impatience, and even ridicule. For example, on two different occasions she shopped in the same store, behaved in the same way (uncertain about the product she wanted and slow to get her money out), wore the same dress, and was waited on by the same clerk. On her first visit to the store she disguised herself as the 85-year-old woman; the next day she appeared as herself. The clerk was impatient with and discourteous to the 85-year-old woman, whereas he treated the young woman with patience, respect, and good humor.

It is unlikely that you have time to replicate Moore's experiment. Nevertheless, you can imaginatively put yourself in the role of an elderly person. Write down your answers to the following questions.

What do you think you will look like at 85? How do you feel about the prospect of being that old? What factors are likely to affect the quality of your life at that age? Ask your family and friends to answer these questions as well. Compare your responses. What do these responses tell you about people's attitudes toward aging? The elderly?

---

climb to more than 68 million, or 23 percent of the population (U.S. Bureau of the Census, 1989b). Although the elderly share some common experiences, we will see in the following discussions how social characteristics such as age, gender, and marital status interact in ways that lead to different experiences for different groups of elderly.

AGE CATEGORIES OF THE ELDERLY

Including everyone over 65 in a single category called "the elderly" obscures significant differences in the social realities of older people. Recognizing the diversity among older people in terms of physical and social functioning, gerontologists now

To a degree, being old is a matter of self-definition. Some people may feel old at age 60; others may not feel old at age 80.

For Better or For Worse®   by Lynn Johnston

People over 85 constitute the fastest growing segment of the elderly population. By the year 2030, some 363,000 Americans are expected to be 100 years old or older.

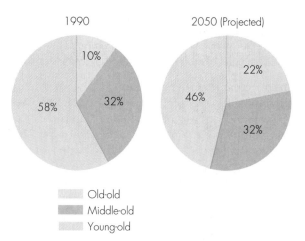

1990   2050 (Projected)

- Old-old
- Middle-old
- Young-old

FIGURE 15.1   Percentage of Older Americans by Age Group

Source: Adapted from Nancy R. Hooyman and H. Asuman Kiyak, *Social Gerontology: A Multidisciplinary Perspective*. Copyright © 1993 by Allyn and Bacon. Reprinted by permission of Allyn & Bacon.

GENDER AND MARITAL STATUS

Among the elderly population, especially those in the oldest category, women significantly outnumber men. Six out of every ten older Americans are female. This has led some researchers to characterize old age as primarily a female experience (Longino, 1988). This, however, is a relatively recent development. Only around 1930 did women's life expectancy begin to increase more rapidly than men's as female deaths connected with pregnancy, childbirth, and infectious diseases declined dramatically. Table 15.1 shows the change in the sex ratios in the different age groups of the elderly for 1960 and 1990. Women clearly have a longevity advantage over men. Why this should be the case is not fully understood. Science has not yet unraveled all of the reasons for the gender difference in mortality rates. Gerontologist Erdman Palmore (1980) attributes half of the difference to genetics and the other half to social roles and environmental factors.

Longevity for women, however, can be a mixed blessing. On the one hand it allows for a rich and meaningful life, and it provides an opportunity to share in the socialization of new generations. On the other hand it often means years alone as husbands and male relatives and friends die at earlier ages. For example, in 1991 there were almost five times as many wid-

speak of three distinct categories: the *young-old* (ages 65–74), the *middle-old* (ages 75–84), and the *old-old* (ages 85 and over). The older population itself is aging at a rapid rate. Figure 15.1 shows the changes expected in these ages categories by 2050. In 1990, only 10 percent of the elderly were 85 or older; in only 60 years 22 percent of the elderly will be that old. In fact, in 1989 an estimated 61,000 centenarians (people 100 years old or older) were living in the United States. By 2030 that number is expected to rise to 363,000 (Hooyman and Kiyak, 1993). These demographic changes present both opportunities and challenges. On the one hand families and the society at large have much to gain by utilizing the experience and wisdom of the older population. On the other hand families and social planners must also prepare to meet the anticipated health-care requirements and other service needs of an aging population.

TABLE 15.1

Changing Sex Ratios in the Older Population, 1960 and 1990 (number of males per 100 females)

| | Sex Ratio | |
Age Category	1960	1990
Young-old (65–74)	86	77
Middle-old (75–84)	76	59
Old-old (85+)	67	38

Source: Adapted from Robert C. Atchley, 1991, *Social Forces and Aging* (Belmont, CA: Wadsworth): 28.

ows (8.4 million) as widowers (1.8 million) in the United States. Figure 15.2 shows the marital status for all elderly people in 1991. Only 40 percent of all elderly women were married with spouse present; 58 percent were either widowed, divorced, or had never married. In contrast, 74 percent of elderly men were married with spouse present, and only 24 percent were either widowed, divorced, or had never married.

These differences in marital status also vary significantly by race and ethnicity. Among males 65 and older, blacks are the least likely to be married with spouse present (55 percent), compared with 76 percent of whites and 74 percent of Latinos. Similarly, among elderly women, 26 percent of blacks, 41 percent of whites, and 37 percent of Latinas are currently married with spouse present (U.S. Bureau of the Census, 1992a:15–17). These patterns are directly related to the different rates of marriage and remarriage among the different racial and ethnic groups that we discussed in Chapters 5 and 14.

Gender differences in survivorship rates are significant because older women across all racial and ethnic groups have fewer financial resources and are more likely to experience poverty in old age than elderly men are. In Chapter 11 we noted that historically women have been disadvantaged in the labor market. They earn less money, are segregated into less prestigious jobs, and are more likely to work part-time and to have their work life interrupted by child rearing than are men. Consequently, women have less access than men to pension plans and receive fewer benefits

FIGURE 15.2   Marital Status of Persons Aged 65 and Over, 1991

Source: Adapted from U.S. Bureau of the Census, 1992a, *Current Population Reports*, Series P-20, No. 461, "Marital Status and Living Arrangements: March 1991" (Washington, DC: U.S. Government Printing Office): 15.

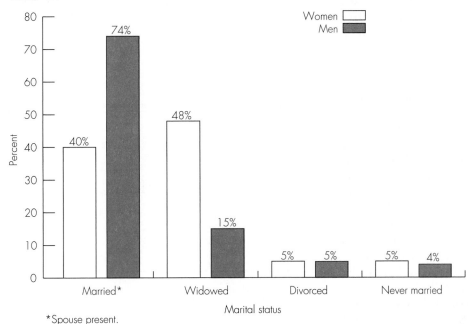

*Spouse present.

when they do have access. In 1989, the median income of widowed women was $8362, compared with $11,200 for widowed men (U.S. Senate Special Committee on Aging, 1992).

RACE, ETHNICITY, AND CLASS

In 1990, the overall racial composition of the population 65 and older in the United States was 89 percent white, 8 percent black, and 3 percent other races, which includes Native Americans, Eskimos, Aleuts, Asians, and Pacific Islanders. Latinos may be classified either as white or black; they constitute about 3.7 percent of the elderly population (U.S. Bureau of the Census, 1992a). Together, people of color make up 14 percent of the elderly population, and their numbers are increasing at a faster rate than those of the white elderly, due primarily to higher fertility and immigration rates. This trend is likely to continue well into the twenty-first century. Projections are that by 2050 people of color will constitute 32 percent of the population aged 65 or over in the United States (U.S. Senate Special Committee on Aging, 1991).

Although the gap in life expectancy rates for the white population and people of color is narrowing, these rates remain lower for people of color. For example, in 1990 life expectancy at birth was 78.6 for white females and 73 for white males. In contrast, it was only 75 for black females and 67.7 for black males (U.S. Bureau of the Census, 1992e). Native Americans and Latinos also have lower life expectancies than do whites.

What accounts for these differences? One major factor, of course, is social class. In general, families of color have fewer economic resources in old age than do their white counterparts. This is due primarily to the disadvantages they faced in the labor market in earlier years: low-paying jobs, longer and more frequent unemployment, and racial discrimination. Thus, they tend to have fewer health insurance or social security benefits than do the white elderly, and they are less likely to have supplementary retirement incomes from private pensions. For example, the 1990 median income for black families headed by people 65 and over was $16,585; for Latinos it was $17,966; and for whites it was $25,864 (U.S. Bureau of the Census, 1991f:52–55).

Although median income gives us a general picture of the economic situation of families headed by the elderly, it does not allow us to see the range of differences among elderly families. Not all elderly are poor, nor are all elderly of color poor. In 1987, for example, approximately 11 percent of households headed by an individual aged 65 or older had incomes of $50,000 or more. Nevertheless, the more typical pattern was one of low income; almost 32 percent of elderly families had incomes of less than $15,000 (Cockerham, 1991:23).

POVERTY AMONG THE ELDERLY Although a smaller proportion of elderly are poor today than in the past, poverty remains a problem for millions of elderly. Table 15.2 shows the changes in the poverty rate between 1959 and 1990. In 1959, 35 percent of the elderly over 65 were poor; by 1990 only 12 percent were so identified, although many others had incomes only slightly above the poverty line. The poverty rates for people of color are two to three times higher than those for whites. The initial decline in poverty rates was due to the nation's efforts to win the "war on poverty" in the 1960s. Many new social programs were instituted for poor people of all age groups, including the elderly.

Although many social-welfare programs were reduced or eliminated during the Reagan and Bush administrations, the programs that benefit the elderly remained largely in place. For example, social security benefits were improved by providing for increases in the cost of living. Many companies instituted pri-

TABLE 15.2

Poverty Status of the Elderly by Race and Latino Origin; 1959–1990

Years	All Races	White	Black	Latino
1959	35.2%	33.1%	62.5%	NA
1970	24.6	22.6	48.0	NA
1980	15.7	13.6	38.1	30.8
1990	12.2	10.1	33.8	22.5

Source: Adapted from the U.S. Bureau of the Census, 1991d, *Current Population Reports*, Series P-60, No. 175, "Poverty in the United States: 1990" (Washington, DC: U.S. Government Printing Office): Table 3, pp. 18–19.

vate pension plans for workers, which have provided workers with additional retirement income. Businesses instituted discount programs for senior citizens regardless of economic need. Attempts to reduce or eliminate these programs have been resisted by effective political lobbying by groups such as the American Association of Retired Persons (AARP), which has 32 million members. Today some public officials fear the possibility of a backlash among younger people who complain that such programs are costly and unfair to them.

LIVING ARRANGEMENTS

If you are like most Americans, you probably share the fear that when you get old you will be sent to a nursing home. Perhaps your parents, like Gus in our case study, have asked you to promise never to put them in a home. Disturbing stories of the plight of elderly in nursing homes frequently appear in the pages of newspapers. Perhaps this accounts for the widely believed myth that most aged persons end up

institutionalized. In fact, only a small proportion of older Americans live in an institutional setting. At any given time, only 5 percent of the elderly are in nursing homes, and they are primarily the infirm old-old (Cockerham, 1991:27). Because the old-old are the fastest growing part of the elderly population, however, we can predict an increased need for quality nursing-home care over the next several decades. Thus, many more families, perhaps yours included, will have to face the difficult decision of how to care for an elderly dependent relative.

As Figure 15.3 shows, the vast majority of older people live alone or in a household with their spouse. Living arrangements show a clear gender difference: Men are almost twice as likely as women to live with their spouse, whereas over three times as many women as men live alone. In 1991, although 74 percent of older men lived with their spouse, only 40 percent of older women did. In contrast, 42 percent of older women and 16 percent of older men lived alone. The remaining 2 percent of older women and men lived with nonrelatives in a variety of settings (U.S. Bureau of the Census, 1992a).

FIGURE 15.3 Living Arrangements of the Elderly by Sex, 1991

Source: Adapted from U.S. Bureau of the Census, 1992a, *Current Population Reports*, Series P-20, No. 461, "Marital Status and Living Arrangements: March 1991" (Washington, DC: U.S. Government Printing Office): Table J, p. 13.

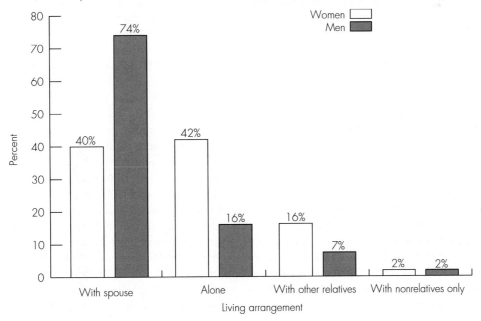

HOUSING PATTERNS

Of the elderly who live independently, 70 percent own their own homes; the remaining 30 percent are renters. Given these rates, at first glance we may be tempted to conclude that the elderly have few housing problems. A closer look reveals this is not the case, however. Much of the housing occupied by the elderly is of poor quality. Many of the houses are as old as or older than their owners and require constant maintenance that is often too costly for people on fixed incomes. An estimated 20 percent of the elderly live in dwellings that are substandard. Because of these housing problems the elderly are often exploited by unscrupulous individuals who promise to do home repairs but flee with the money without doing the work.

The situation for renters can be worse (Barrow, 1989:181). Renters typically live in apartments, including public housing of various quality. Some renters are boarders, and others live in residential hotels, including single-room occupancies (SROs). Increasingly SROs, especially those that cater to low-income elderly men, are demolished to make room for urban renewal projects. Not only does the destruction of SROs displace elderly residents, but, as we have seen in Chapter 11, it also contributes to homelessness.

Although younger Americans tend to be mobile, middle-aged and older people prefer staying in a familiar environment. Housing is more than a place to live. For many, it symbolizes continuity, independence, family history, and a sense of belonging. The majority of the elderly have lived in their current residence for 20 or more years.

As the family life cycle changes, however, so too do housing needs. Houses can become too big, too isolated, too expensive, or too difficult to maintain for a retired couple or the widowed after children have left home. In addition, housing that once was satisfactory may become inadequate as a result of the resident's illness or disability. The affected person may no longer be able to use stairs, reach cupboards or counters, get in or out of bathtubs alone, or maneuver a wheelchair through narrow halls or doorways. Sometimes remodeling or the intervention of outside help can take care of these problems. In other cases, relocation to more suitable housing is the only alternative. When a change is voluntary, the personal and psychological disruption it causes is likely to be relatively minor because the perceived benefits outweigh

Many senior citizen housing arrangements provide private rooms and apartments but also include common dining facilities.

the costs. When the elderly are forced to relocate, however, the result is often trauma, confusion, grief, and a sense of helplessness and isolation.

When asked by researchers which living arrangements they prefer, the elderly consistently say they want to be independent. An 80-year-old widow said:

> "My daughter feels I shouldn't be living alone. We are very close, but she and her husband have their own lives. They both work. They have a lovely home, but it is in a suburb with no sidewalks or public transportation. I'd be isolated and dependent on them for going anywhere. I like my independence. Here I can walk to the store and the bank, and I can see people every day. We keep in touch by phone, and I know they will come if I need them. That's all I want."

The elderly do not want to live with their children, and few do. Only 6 percent of older men and 11 percent of older women live with their children (Brotman, 1981). When parents live with children, the most common pattern is living with a daughter (Stone, Cafferata, and Sangl, 1987).

Race and ethnicity also affect housing decisions. In their analysis of 1980 census data, James Sweet and Larry Bumpass (1987) found that widowed Asian-American women and men were more likely than any other group to live with their adult children. Latinos were the second most likely group to do so. Among the old-old, black elderly are more likely to live with their children than are white elderly. Economic need and a cultural emphasis on the extended family are the most common explanations for these different patterns.

MARRIAGES IN LATER LIFE

Imagine being married to the same person for 50, 60, or even more years. Given current life expectancies, many married couples can expect to celebrate their golden wedding anniversary and beyond. What can we expect of a marital bond that endures this long? Does the quality of the relationship change over time? Is the poet Robert Browning correct in saying, "Grow old along with me / The best is yet to be"? We shall try to answer these questions by looking at two issues: marital satisfaction and adjustment to retirement.

MARITAL QUALITY AND SATISFACTION

Does marital quality improve with age? Linda Ade-Ridder and Timothy Brubaker (1983) reviewed more than 25 studies and found no consensus on this question. Some researchers found that marital relationships improved over time; others found just the opposite. Still other studies reported little or no change in marital quality in later life.

Studies showing improvement in marital quality report a pattern whereby couples start out with high levels of satisfaction, "the honeymoon phase." This period is followed by the childbearing and child-rearing years, during which stress and anxiety levels may be heightened, leading to a decline in marital satisfaction. Once the children are grown and leave home, couples can concentrate on each other again (Anderson et al., 1983). Spouses may rediscover or develop common interests and interdependence, resulting in increased feelings of affection and companionship (Dobson, 1983). Negotiating such role transition depends on a couple's prior adaptability and degree of marital satisfaction. Studies have found that couples celebrating golden wedding anniversaries (3 percent of all married couples) share similar values and belief systems and are good at negotiating with each other (Roberts, 1979–80; Parron, 1982).

Marriages in which couples share similar values and belief systems and are good at negotiating with each other are likely to endure for a lifetime. This couple is celebrating their fiftieth wedding anniversary with family and friends.

A second set of studies showed a gradual pattern of decline in marital love and companionship over the years (Blood and Wolfe, 1960). Finally, a third set of studies indicated little or no change in marital satisfaction. Couples who are happy in earlier years are likely to be happy in later years, and early unhappiness remains in later years (Clark and Wallin, 1965).

What are we to make of these different findings? Some of the differences may be related to the methodological techniques of the studies themselves. Much of this research involved studies of small samples of older couples taken at only one point in time. Comparisons of changes are difficult to make unless the same couples are retested at different times and unless a standardized measure of marital quality is used.

Throughout this text we have examined a number of factors that influence a couple's level of marital satisfaction. For example, in Chapter 6 we discussed sexuality among the elderly. A study by Ade-Ridder found that marital satisfaction is positively related to sexual behavior among older couples who are still sexually active. "Happier men and women report fewer changes in sexual activity and report them at a later age than do less happy people" (1990:63). This does not mean, however, that couples no longer participating in sexual intercourse had poor-quality marriages. Rather, Ade-Ridder concludes, "Sexual intercourse is not essential to a high-quality marriage in later life, but it has its rewards for those who still practice this form of intimate expression" (1990:64). Another important factor that affects later-life marriages is the way in which couples deal with retirement.

ADJUSTMENT TO RETIREMENT

Retirement, as a distinct phase in the family life cycle, is a modern phenomenon. Prior to the twentieth century, American workers typically worked until they died or were physically unable to continue working. When they stopped working, there was no pension or social security for their later years, and their welfare most frequently depended on other family members (Markides and Mindel, 1987). In the wake of the Great Depression, however, this situation changed. With the establishment of social security in 1935, the institution of retirement became part of the national culture.

Like so much of social life in the United States, the experience of retirement is affected by an individual's race, class, and gender. Years ago it was common to hear housewives say, "I married him for better or worse, but not for lunch." Such a line usually produced chuckles in the listeners because they could easily envision a newly retired man who suddenly has time on his hands wandering aimlessly around the house, interfering with his wife's daily routines. (Today it can as easily be a retired wife who is disrupting the household system.) Marital satisfaction is likely to decline under these conditions. However, this pattern was more applicable in the past, when more families had a traditional household structure in which the man was in the labor force and the wife kept house. Today, retirement increasingly means more time for couples to spend together in mutually enjoyable activities, thus increasing marital satisfaction (Zube, 1982).

TYPES OF RETIREMENT   To understand the impact of retirement today, we must ask "Whose retirement?" With over 58 percent of all women of working age in the labor force, couples must deal with more than one retirement. Given that men tend to be older than their wives, the timing of retirement, especially for employed wives, might be a source of friction. Brubaker (1985:31–32) has identified four patterns of retirement among older couples:

- *Single or traditional retirement*: Here one spouse, usually the husband, has been employed and thus only one spouse retires from paid employment.
- *Dissynchronized-husband initially*: In this situation the husband retires before his wife. She continues to work because she is usually younger or started her career after his.
- *Dissynchronized-wife initially*: This pattern, where the wife retires first, is rare. It may be that she has health problems or is needed to take care of an older relative.
- *Synchronized retirement*: In this situation both the husband and wife were employed, and they retire at the same time.

Most of the studies conducted on retirement have not taken into account these variations. It may well be that marital satisfaction is affected in different ways not by retirement itself but depending on the circumstances of retirement. For example, Gary Lee and Constance Shehan (1991) found that wives who continue to work after their husbands have retired have lower levels of marital satisfaction than wives in couples with any other employment status combination. This pattern may reflect in part the fact that retired husbands only marginally increase their domestic labor, and mainly in those activities traditionally associated with male gender roles, such as yard work and car maintenance. Perceived inequity in the division of household tasks is often a source of marital dissatisfaction (Brubaker and Henon, 1982). Researchers generally have found that retirement does not significantly alter the division of household tasks established in the earlier years of marriage (Keating and Cole, 1980). Given the consistent findings that early patterns are carried over into later years, people who desire a mutual sharing of tasks in later life are well advised to negotiate that status from the very beginning of their marriage.

Other factors also affect the quality of life after retirement. In 1986 Congress passed legislation ending mandatory retirement for most employees. Prior to that time most workers were forced to retire at 65 whether they wanted to or not. An extensive body of research revealed that involuntary retirement is likely to produce stress and depression. In contrast, when people want to retire and make plans to do so, retirement is more likely to be a positive experience. Finally, satisfaction during the retirement years also depends on the couple's financial status and health. If retirement income is sufficient to enable couples to pursue desired activities, retirement is likely to promote satisfaction. However, if couples have been unable to save much in the earlier years of married life or if their earnings have been so low that they receive only minimal social security benefits, they may experience considerable downward mobility with retirement.

Herbert Parnes and Lawrence Less (1983) report that after retirement a couple's income can decline by as much as 50 percent. Such drastic decreases can push some elderly into poverty. Although this is true to a degree for all groups, it is more likely to happen to white elderly. An analysis of data from two national longitudinal surveys showed that retirement led to a significant decline in income among white males but only a minor decline for black males (Fillenbaum et al., 1985). The reason for this is that the black workers had lower incomes than the white workers. The impact then is for blacks already in poverty to experience greater poverty and for whites, some of whom were middle class, to sink into poverty after retirement (Markides and Mindel, 1987:184).

When socioeconomic status is controlled, there appears to be little difference in the adjustment of blacks and whites to retirement (Jackson and Walls, 1978). Black workers, however, are less likely to experience voluntary retirement. Layoffs and poor health

often push African Americans out of the labor force. Kyriakos Markides (1978) found a similar pattern among Mexican Americans living in San Antonio, Texas. His research found that 55 percent of the Mexican-American respondents retired because of health problems, compared with 35 percent of the Anglo retirees. He also found that the Mexican Americans had more difficulty adjusting to the loss of the work role than did the more socioeconomically advantaged, older Anglos. Furthermore, the concept of retirement has little meaning for individuals whose jobs do not provide old-age benefits. They must keep working until they become physically incapacitated. This is particularly true for unskilled white workers and people of color, especially African-American women, who often work to an advanced age. Little systematic data exist on the retirement experiences of other people of color, especially Native Americans and Asian Americans.

INTERGENERATIONAL RELATIONSHIPS

The fact that the majority of elderly live alone or with their spouse gave rise to a belief that most old people are neglected by their children. On the contrary, studies have consistently found that approximately 50 percent of older people with children have at least one child within 10 minutes of their home; 80 percent live less than an hour away from at least one child; and 84 percent see or talk to an adult child at least once a week (Shanas, 1979, 1980). Similar patterns were found across different racial groups (Mitchell and Register, 1984; Chan, 1988). Substantial assistance in the form of financial aid, goods, and services flows in both directions (Peterson and Peterson, 1988). These patterns are particularly pronounced among African-American and Latino families (Tate, 1983). Additionally, a new study by the National Center for Health Statistics of 2,095 Americans over age 80 substantiates earlier findings of frequent contact between the elderly and their adult children. Among the oldest segment of the population, "as many as 85 percent of them saw or spoke to their children 2 to 7 times a week" (Kolata, 1993:A16).

Although there is considerable diversity in the way in which different generations relate to one another, family interactions are shaped to a large degree by the norm of reciprocity or complimentary exchanges. Contrary to popular belief older people are not primarily dependent recipients of aid; in many cases they are primarily donors (Bengtson et al., 1990). Older parents often remain a resource for their adult children, providing financial assistance, advice, and child-care services. This is especially the case when adult children have stressful problems, for example, getting divorced or becoming widowed. In exchange, both generations expect that adult children will assist their parents in times of need (Shanas, 1979; Finley, Roberts, and Banahan, 1988). Social class, however, may influence the direction of tangible aid. For example, wealthier older people are likely to continue giving financial assistance to middle-aged children, whereas working-class parents are more likely to be receiving assistance.

QUALITY OF RELATIONSHIPS

Although we know a great deal about the frequency of intergenerational contact, we know less about the qualitative aspects of these relationships. Frequency of contact in and of itself doesn't ensure a strong emotional bond. Nevertheless, researchers have found that most adult children and their elderly parents like one another and express satisfaction with their relationships (Bengston and Black, 1973). Gender seems to play an important role in this regard. For example, mother–daughter relationships tend to be particularly close and intimate during all phases of the life span (Troll, 1988). In contrast to sons, daughters are more likely to be chosen by the aging parent as a confidant and to stay in closer contact with parents (Aldous et al., 1985; Aldous, 1987). The maxim that "A son is a son until he takes a wife, but a daughter is a daughter all of her life" seems to have some empirical support.

PATTERNS OF SUPPORT

Do adult children really help their needy elderly parents, or do the government and taxpayers assume most of this responsibility? The weight of evidence in study after study indicates that families, not the formal system, provide the bulk of care for the elderly across all cultural groups. "Over 90 percent of the older disabled people who are not in institutions depend, in whole or in part, on family and friends for the care they receive: 70 percent rely exclusively on such helpers" (cited in Soldo and Agree, 1988:31). In addition to providing direct care, children often serve as mediators between institutional bureaucracies and elderly kin, providing older relatives with information on housing, pensions, insurance, and medical care (Sussman, 1985). Evidence also suggests that when people seek help outside the family, it is usually as a last resort. When we look more closely at the kind and degree of support the elderly receive and who is most likely to provide it, however, we find variations by gender, race, marital status, and presence of children.

RACIAL AND ETHNIC VARIATIONS Throughout this text we have presented data showing historically how race and ethnicity have functioned to provide some groups (mostly white) with access to societal resources and at the same time to restrict other groups (mostly people of color) from sharing in these resources on an equal basis. Partly as a response to the economic needs generated by this differential treatment, families of color have developed a wider range of informal support systems than have whites. For example, blacks have a higher incidence of extended family households than do whites (Stanford et al., 1988:232). One study comparing black and white family relations found that the black families were more involved in mutual exchanges of services across generations. When social class was held constant, the differences lessened, but helping patterns were still more evident among black families (Mutran, 1985).

Research on the functioning of informal support networks found that older blacks utilized a wider variety of resources than did whites. Although white elderly sought help from spouses and other specific family members when it was needed, black elderly relied on a more regular basis on family, friends, neighbors, and to a significant degree, fellow church members (Gibson, 1986; Taylor and Chatters, 1986). Latino elderly also tend to be involved in extended family networks that provide mutual aid and informal support (Mindel, 1983). Latino neighborhoods serve as important sources of help and opportunities for ongoing social interaction (Becerra and Shaw, 1984).

EVOLVING PATTERNS OF KINSHIP: GRANDPARENTHOOD

Changing mortality and fertility rates can have enormous consequences for the kin network. As recently as 1900, families with grandparents were rare. An analysis by Peter Uhlenberg (1980) showed that families in which three or more grandparents are alive when a child reaches age 15 have increased from 17 percent in 1900 to 55 percent in 1976. The social role of grandparent, let alone great-grandparent, is a fairly recent one and therefore is not well defined.

STYLES OF GRANDPARENTING

According to Nancy Hooyman and H. Asuman Kiyak (1993), 94 percent of older adults with children become grandparents. Nevertheless, there is great diversity in the timing of grandparenthood. Given the incidence of teenage pregnancies, some parents become grandparents as early as their 30s. Other parents who had children later in life may not become grandparents until into their 60s or 70s. This diversity in ages of grandparents contributes to the ambiguity surrounding this role. Although a great deal of folklore is connected with grandparenting, there is little agreement on how to fulfill this role. Thus, most of us will construct our grandparenting role out of our own childhood memories of our grandparents, our perceptions of the way our parents acted as grandparents, and the attitudes we pick up about grandparenting from the media and from those around us, especially our adult children.

Over the years researchers have investigated the role and meaning of grandparenthood and in the process have identified several styles of grandparenting. Bernice Neugarten and Karol Weinstein (1964:200–1) studied 70 middle-class grandparent couples and classified their interactions with their grandchildren into one of the following five categories:

- *Formal*: Grandparents follow what they see as a prescribed role for grandparents.
- *Fun seeker*: Grandparent–grandchild interaction is characterized by informality and playfulness.
- *Distant figure*: Interaction is limited to holidays and special occasions.
- *Surrogate parent*: Grandparents assume caretaking responsibilities for grandchild.
- *Reservoir of family wisdom*: Grandparents are the dispensers of special skills or resources.

Neugarten and Weinstein also found that age is a factor in the development of grandparenting styles.

Younger grandparents were more likely to be fun seekers, whereas older grandparents were more likely to adopt the formal approach.

This study and other early descriptions of grandparent roles have been criticized for their unidimensional approach (Roberto, 1990). In Neugarten and Weinstein's study each respondent was placed exclusively into one of the five categories. No provision was made for overlapping styles of grandparenting or changes in styles over time. Two decades after the Neugarten and Weinstein study was published, Andrew Cherlin and Frank Furstenberg (1986b:52–53) analyzed telephone interviews with 510 grandparents (and personal interviews with 36 of them) and found three styles of grandparenting:

- *Remote*: Grandparents interacted infrequently and maintained a ritualistic or purely symbolic relationship with their grandchildren.
- *Companionate*: Grandparents had an easygoing, friendly style of interaction with their grandchildren.
- *Involved*: Grandparents took an active role in rearing their grandchildren, exerted substantial authority, and imposed definite and sometimes demanding expectations.

These three styles correspond roughly to Neugarten and Weinstein's grandparenting styles of distant figure, fun seeker, and surrogate parent. However, Cherlin and Furstenberg's analysis takes into account the dynamic quality of such relationships. They found that grandparent–grandchild relationships can change over time. For example, grandparents may have a fun-seeking relationship with young grandchildren, but, when the children reach adolescence, the time spent together may decrease dramatically. Years later the relationship may change again with the arrival of great-grandchildren. Also, the same grandparent may exhibit different grandparenting styles with different grandchildren. For example, a grandparent may have a close companionate role with one grandchild and a remote relationship with another. Numerous factors influence the kind of relationship grandparents have with their grandchildren: age and employment status of grandparents, physical proximity, economic need, relationships between the grandparents and their adult children, number and ages of grandchildren, birth order, and gender and personality differences.

BENEFITS AND CONFLICTS

The grandparent role has the potential to benefit all three generations. One researcher, for example, discussed several contributions that the presence of grandchildren can make in a person's life. Grandchildren contribute to a sense of immortality, that something of the grandparent will continue after death. Playing the role of teacher, family historian, and resource person enhances the self-esteem of grandparents. Grandparents can take pride in the achievements of their grandchildren and boast about them to friends. Through social contact with grandchildren, grandparents can keep up to date on cultural and social changes. Finally, older grandchildren can provide assistance to grandparents—shopping, lawn care, running errands, and household chores (Barranti, 1985).

In exchange, grandparents can provide grandchildren with love and guidance minus the intensity, responsibility, and tension that frequently exist in parent–child relationships. Grandparents can give children a sense of continuity, identity, belonging, and values as they share with the children stories about the family's history. In so doing they often can help younger people understand their parents, and they frequently act as mediators between the two generations. Additionally, grandparents can be role models of successful aging for both their adult children and grandchildren. Finally, the parent generation can benefit by having someone they can trust assist them in their parenting role and if necessary act as surrogate parents in time of need. In this latter regard grandmothers have played a key role in the lives of adolescent mothers, especially in aiding them

Interaction between grandparents and grandchildren can be mutually beneficial to both generations. Through playing and sharing family history together, both generations can experience a sense of identity, continuity, and belonging.

in the care of their infants during the early months of the infant's life (Flaherty, Facteau, and Garver, 1991).

Such benefits, however, can also produce tension and conflict. Parents and grandparents may disagree about child-rearing strategies. Parents may resent what they perceive as grandparental interference or be jealous of the child's affection for the grandparent. Older grandchildren may become preoccupied with their own lives and forget to call or visit grandparents. As a result, grandparents often feel hurt and ignored. These problems notwithstanding, much of the research on grandparenthood shows that both grandparents and grandchildren tend to be satisfied with their relationships.

The research also indicates that there was more contact with maternal grandparents and that the maternal grandmother was consistently listed as the grandparent to whom grandchildren felt closest (Matthews and Sprey, 1985). Other studies show that grandmothers tend to be more satisfied with the grandparenting role than grandfathers are (Thomas, 1986).

In the past and to a great extent yet today, helping and caring for grandchildren are more traditionally associated with grandmothers. Sarah Cunningham-Burley (1987), however, found that some grandfathers attach great importance to the grandfather role, seeing it as an opportunity to experience the contact with babies and young children that they missed out on with their own children. Given that increasing numbers of today's fathers are more involved in child care than in the past, men might in the future become more involved in the grandparenting role.

Race and ethnicity also play a role in the degree of involvement in the grandparent role. Some research suggests that African Americans, Asian Americans, Italian Americans, and Latinos are more likely to be involved in the lives of their grandchildren than are other groups (Cavanaugh, 1993). The apparent greater involvement of ethnic grandparents may be a result of the greater extended kin network among these groups. For example, in a study of 48 black and 51 white grandfathers aged 65 and older, Vira Kivitt (1991) found that the grandfather role was more central in the lives of black men than it was for white men.

A high level of grandparent support has been found among Native Americans. One study found that 26 percent of Native-American elderly were caring for at least one grandchild and that about 67 percent of all older Native Americans live within 5 miles of their kin, with whom they engaged in various mutual support activities (National Indian Council on Aging, 1981).

Grandparents often ask their children to allow the grandchildren to live with them for a period of time so that the grandparents can teach the grandchildren about the Native-American way of life (Weibel-Orlando, 1990).

UNPLANNED PARENTING   Many grandparents routinely provide child-care services for their grandchildren, but in a growing number of cases, grandparents assume sole responsibility for their grandchildren. In 1991, over 3.3 million children under 18 years of age (5.1 percent) lived with their grandparents. In almost one-third of those cases, neither parent was present in the household (U.S. Bureau of the Census, 1992a). A decade earlier the comparable figures were 2.3 million children, representing almost 4 percent of children under 18. According to experts in the field, this increase did not result from an increase in the number of extended families. Rather, it is a direct result of the abuse and neglect of children due to current patterns of drug addiction among parents.

This type of unplanned parenthood brings with it many problems. Taking on this responsibility is emotionally and financially exhausting for many grandparents. In some cases the grandparents must abandon or fight their own children to allow the grandparents to provide their grandchildren with a healthy and stable environment. Keeping up with young grandchildren can be physically exhausting. Retired grandparents on a fixed income may find their household budget severely strained by the unexpected expense of children. In addition, the reality of unplanned parenting can be psychologically difficult to accept. The dreams these older couples have for spending time together, taking vacations, and pursuing other interests may be lost forever. Recently, support groups like Grandparents as Parents and Grandparents Raising Grandchildren have been formed to assist these families.

GREAT-GRANDPARENTHOOD

Now that four-generation families have become more common, a few researchers are beginning to examine the meaning of the great-grandparent role in later-life families. A study of 42 great-grandparents found that the majority expressed positive feelings about the experience (Doka and Mertz, 1988). They reported a renewed zeal for life and expressed satisfaction at the continuance of their families. Despite these positive reactions, most of the respondents reported having only a remote relationship with their great-grandchildren, interacting with them on a limited and mostly ritualistic basis.

The reasons for this kind of interaction pattern are not entirely clear. A partial explanation may be that because this is a new phenomenon, few cultural norms exist to guide individual behavior in these relationships. There is some indication, however, that at least among women of color, the great-grandparenting role is not significantly different from the grandparenting role; rather, it is a natural progression from that role (Scott, 1991). Further research is needed to study the costs and benefits of such relationships.

THE CHILD-FREE ELDERLY

Perhaps sometime in your life someone suggested to you that you should marry and have children so that you will have someone to take care of you when you get old. In fact the majority of today's elderly—approximately 80 percent—have surviving children (Brotman, 1981). But what about the other 20 percent, those who never had children or whose children have preceded them in death? They have no "natural" support system of adult children and grandchildren to rely on in old age. Are they then without potential caregivers, as folk wisdom would have us believe?

An examination of a national sample concluded that childlessness was a predictor of social isolation in later life. Compared with elderly parents, the child-free elderly had fewer social contacts. This was particularly true for those experiencing health problems (Bachrach, 1980). When marital status was controlled, however, an interesting pattern emerged. The unmarried child-free elderly interact more frequently with friends and neighbors than do the married child-free elderly. Some researchers believe this finding reflects the tendency of married couples to rely more on each other, thus limiting other social relationships (Johnson and Catalano, 1981).

In contrast, the unmarried elderly realize they may need help at some point in their lives and actively create a support network for themselves. For example, Robert Rubinstein and his colleagues (1991) interviewed 31 never-married child-free women 60 years of age and older and found that they consciously developed strategies to overcome the cultural emphasis on "blood ties." Not only did these women cultivate relationships with existing kin (nieces, nephews, and siblings) but they also constructed ties, often becoming fictive kin, interacting in ways traditionally associated with those who are related by birth. Many of our families include people we call "aunt" or "uncle" who are not formally related to us. These relationships are characterized by strong affective bonds and shared activities. Rubinstein's respondents described key friendships with other women as being "sisterlike." Although research on the role of friends in later life is just beginning, some preliminary findings show that these relationships serve as important sources of support (Chappell, 1991).

Despite the fact that unmarried elderly people are resourceful and have a fairly large social network, child-free elderly women have a greater chance of becoming institutionalized than do other categories of elderly (Cantor and Little, 1985). These women are often older and in poorer health than other elderly and thus require more care. Social programs need to take account of the fact that the child-free elderly are at greater risk of being without support than are the elderly with children. In the future, if fertility rates decline, the proportion of older people who need to rely on institutional programs is likely to increase.

SIBLING RELATIONSHIPS

The social relationships of the elderly are not restricted to the younger generations. Recent research on the elderly has pointed to the importance of siblings in later-life families. Sibling relationships are particularly valuable to the elderly for two reasons. First, elderly siblings share a similar family history. Second, the relationship is potentially the longest-lasting one an individual will ever have, covering as it does the entire life course. Thus, siblings can help each other fill important needs in later life. They can reminisce about the distant past, be social companions, and provide emotional support during times of stress. Additionally, because of their prior experiences, older siblings can serve as role models for resolving the developmental tasks of later life (Scott, 1990).

Upward of 70 to 80 percent of all elderly adults have at least one living sibling (Shanas, 1980; McGhee, 1985). Researchers have consistently found that contact with siblings in later life is strongly related to feelings of social and psychological well-being. This seems to be particularly true of siblings who were close during childhood. During young adulthood and middle age they may have had only limited contact because of the demands of their own families. As people age, however, they often renew or increase social contacts. Sister–sister relationships seem to be particularly important as support systems in later life (Scott, 1990). Even though much is made of sibling rivalry during childhood, research has found that few

respondents report poor sibling relationships in later life. The available evidence suggests that developing positive relationships with siblings in earlier years can be a good investment for the later years.

Siblings are likely to be a good source of support for some elderly well into the twenty-first century. This may not be the case for the elderly who follow them, however. Over the last several decades life expectancy has increased and birthrates have decreased. Thus, families are becoming verticalized in that they cut across more generational lines but have fewer siblings and other age peers within each generation (Hagestad, 1986; Bengston and Dannefer, 1987).

HEALTH AND ILLNESS

A common fear about growing old is the loss of health and independence. Although health problems increase with age, the health status of today's elderly is varied and is not as negative as is popularly portrayed. For example, a 1989 survey by the National Center for Health Statistics (1990a) found that 70 percent of the noninstitutionalized elderly described their health as good or excellent, whereas only 30 percent reported their health as fair or poor. Although self-ratings of health are subjective, they have been correlated with mortality. That is, older people who describe their health as poor are more likely to die within the next five years than are those who report their health as good (Kaplan et al., 1988). Thus, these self-ratings reflect with some accuracy an individual's overall health status.

A more common measure of health among the elderly is the activities of daily living (ADL), used by gerontologists to evaluate a person's performance of personal-care tasks such as getting in and out of bed, bathing, and dressing, as well as home management tasks such as managing finances, shopping, cooking, and light housework. The majority of the elderly manage these activities quite well. Only slightly more than 20 percent of the elderly are estimated to have an impairment that limits their ADL, and only approximately 4 percent are severely impaired (Hooyman and Kiyak, 1993:125). However, the extent of illness and the need for assistance in meeting the needs of daily living increase with age. Those aged 85 and older are four to six times more likely to be disabled and to require assistance than are those aged 65 to 74 (Manton and Liu, 1984).

Although at any time only a minority of elderly need assistance in their ADL, because the fastest-growing segment of our population is the old-old, increasing numbers of families will confront the need to provide elderly caregiving. Spouses are the first line of defense when illness strikes, followed by adult children. Compared with spouses, however, adult children provide care over a longer period of time (Chappel, 1991).

THE SPOUSE AS CAREGIVER

The longer a couple live together, the more likely that one of the spouses will become ill. When this happens, the healthier spouse generally assumes the caregiver role. Because men have higher rates of morbidity and mortality, wives make up the majority of spousal caregivers. The degree to which this arrangement represents a satisfactory response to a changed living condition depends on the severity of the illness or disability. In one study of working-class wives aged 59 to 81 with husbands with severe problems, researchers found that both spouses exhibited lower levels of morale than have been found in studies of nondisabled couples (Fengler and Goodrich, 1979). Frequently, wives are physically overwhelmed by the demands of caring for their spouse. If the husband needs to have someone in attendance at all times, wives may find that they have little free time for themselves, with the result that they become isolated from friends. Alfred Fengler and Nancy Goodrich refer to such wives as "hidden patients."

Sometimes these problems can be overcome by having outside help. Nurses, physical attendants, friends, and relatives may be able to relieve the primary caregiver on a regular basis. Some senior day-care programs have been created to enable the ill spouse to participate in social activities as well as to help the primary caregiver to keep going. Many elderly do not have a spouse to rely on for care, however, and they turn to their children for help.

ADULT CHILDREN AS CAREGIVERS

It is estimated that 5 million adult children are currently caring for parents. This does not include those who have previously cared for a parent or those who

Adult children, especially daughters, often assume the role of caregiver for elderly parents. This daughter feeds her father during a family picnic.

will do so in the future (Brody, 1988). Among the primary forms of assistance are emotional support, financial aid, help with instrumental activities (transportation, meal preparation, shopping, housework), personal care (bathing, feeding, dressing), and mediating with agencies to obtain services. All children are not equally likely to assume this role. The degree of filial responsibility is related to proximity (the child living closest to the parent frequently assumes this responsibility) and gender.

A wide range of studies has consistently shown that across all racial and ethnic groups the role of caretaker is most frequently filled by daughters (Stanford et al., 1990; Dwyer and Coward, 1991). Daughters, especially unmarried daughters or those past the childbearing stage, are more likely than sons to provide assistance with personal and home care. A son's contribution is more likely to be financial or in home repair and maintenance activities (Coward, 1987). The kind of help that caregivers provide is often mediated by social class. Middle-class adult children provide more emotional support and financial aid, often assuming a "care-manager" role whereby they identify needed services, help obtain them, and then supervise their delivery. Children from lower socioeconomic classes are more likely to provide the direct care themselves (Archbold, 1983; Rosenthal, 1986).

THE STRESSES OF CAREGIVING Although most children willingly help their parents when the need arises and express satisfaction in doing so, parental care can be stressful. Caring for an elderly relative can lead to financial hardship and can also jeopardize the caregiver's own health. The most severe consequences, however, tend to be the psychological and emotional stress that comes from seeing formerly strong and independent parents become dependent as well as from the restrictions on the caregiver's time and freedom. For example, one study found that daughters of elderly parents spend 30 hours per month helping their parents; sons spend 15 hours per month. Even more time is spent when adult children are unemployed or when the parent is disabled (Stoller, 1983).

The time demands of caring for an adult parent compete with other responsibilities and may result in conflict. Elaine Brody (1988) compared working and nonworking women who were caregivers for their widowed, elderly mothers and found that 28 percent of the nonworking respondents had quit their job because of their mother's needs for care. A similar number experienced conflict over this question and were considering giving up their job for the same reason. Leaving a job diminishes family income, in turn often producing additional strains. The direct caregiver is therefore not the only one affected by the pattern of caregiving. The family's lifestyle may be disrupted. Recreational activities and vacations may have to be postponed. If the elderly person is living with the caregiver's family, lack of privacy may become a problem. If spouses and other family members are supportive, however, the intensity of these strains is lessened.

If, however, the strains become too great, caretakers or their families may resort to extreme behavior, for example, elder abuse (see Chapter 12) or abandoning the elderly relative at hospital emergency rooms. Emergency room workers refer to this phenomenon as "granny dumping." An informal survey by the American College of Emergency Physicians drew 169 responses from emergency rooms across the country, reporting an average of eight abandonments a week. The problem has been observed most often in states with larger proportions of retired people—Florida, California, and Texas (*Chicago Tribune*, 1991e). Such behavior underscores the need for more outpatient and in-home services to help families cope with the demands of caring for an elderly relative. Certain situations arise, however, when regardless of the desires of the family, the ill spouse or parent can

no longer be cared for at home. Institutionalization may be necessary in these circumstances. If this is to be done with a minimum of dislocation, both socially and psychologically, family, friends, and professionals must play a supportive role in the process.

DYING AND DEATH

Someone once wrote that in all of life there are only two certainties: death and taxes. We have located the topic of death in the chapter on later-life families not because death is unique to the elderly, for it is not. Death can come at all ages, as evidenced by sudden infant death or fatal accidents. Most deaths, however, do occur among the elderly. As a result, death itself often seems to have little reality for the young.

Do you remember your first wake or funeral? How did you feel? Were you uncomfortable in that setting? Were you uncertain about the proper way to behave? If so, you are typical of many Americans today.

In the nineteenth century the overwhelming majority of Americans died at home, in the presence of family and friends. Information and skills on how to prepare the dead body were part of the common domestic knowledge of the day. The wake was held in the front parlor, and family and friends came there to pay their respects.

In contrast, by the twentieth century death had become culturally invisible (Aries, 1981). Physicians, hospitals, and nursing homes took control of the dying process. Today few people ever see an untreated dead body. Instead, professional funeral directors quickly remove the body and prepare it out of sight of family members in an effort to make it appear "natural" or "sleeplike." Rather than say that someone died, we use a variety of euphemisms like *passed away, departed*, and *left us* (DeSpelder and Strickland, 1988). In the process dying has become more depersonalized, and the rituals surrounding death have been shortened. One of the consequences of these changes is that survivors experience greater difficulties in receiving support throughout their period of bereavement and in expressing their grief openly. **Bereavement** refers to the state of being deprived of a loved one by death; **grief** is the emotional response to this loss.

Currently, however, another change in attitude is evolving. The AIDS epidemic as well as publicized discussions of **euthanasia** or elective death (see the Critical Issues box), have removed the invisibility of death. Increasingly, medical, religious, and legal personnel are advocating the concept of "death with dignity."

THE PROCESS OF DYING

Dying is a complex process. For our purposes we will utilize Robert Atchley's (1991) definition of a dying person, one identified as having a condition from which no recovery can be expected. Much has been written about how people react to the news that they are terminally ill. Psychiatrist Elizabeth Kübler-Ross (1969) invited dying patients to express their thoughts, fears, and anxieties about this last phase in their lives. On the basis of 200 interviews with dying patients of different ages, she identified five stages through which she believed the dying patient moves:

- *Denial*: "No, not me. It must be a mistake" is a common reaction.
- *Anger*: "Why me?" becomes the question.
- *Bargaining*: "Please let me live to see my daughter get married." "Please let me live to make amends for what I did." The appeal may be made to God or to one's doctors.
- *Depression*: This stage is characterized by generalized feelings of loss.
- *Acceptance*: The denial, anger, bargaining, and depression are replaced by contemplation of the approaching death with a quiet readiness.

In a later work Kübler-Ross (1974) pointed out that patients may skip a stage, experience overlapping stages, or move through the stages in any order. Kübler-Ross's stages of dying have not received any empirical support; nevertheless, many practitioners as well as family members continue to use them in an effort to understand and respond appropriately to the behaviors of dying people.

Critics of Kübler-Ross reject the notion of a progression through stages. They see the dying person as experiencing a variety of feelings and emotions and engaging in psychological defenses and maneuvers

People who know they are dying may choose to do so in a hospice setting where emphasis is on making the patient free of pain and providing companionship. Family members, like this son, are free to visit at any time.

CRITICAL ISSUES

THE RIGHT TO DIE

For centuries people have debated the ethical issues surrounding euthanasia, or as it is popularly called, "mercy killing." The term *euthanasia* derives from Greek words meaning "good death," or dying without pain or suffering. This debate has become more complicated because of medical advances that prolong the life of terminally ill patients but give no hope of improvement in the quality of life. Euthanasia can take two forms. In passive euthanasia, medical treatment is terminated, and nothing is done to prolong the patient's life artificially. Forty states and the District of Columbia have passed some form of natural-death legislation that allows patients or their families to refuse treatment in the final stages of terminal illness (Hooyman and Kiyak, 1993). This is usually done through what is called a *living will*, which stipulates a person's wishes in this regard.

A more controversial form of euthanasia is active euthanasia, which refers to actions deliberately taken to end a person's life. A Michigan doctor, Jack Kevorkian, who has assisted over a dozen people to die fueled the debate over active euthanasia, especially in the area of physician-assisted suicide.

Proponents of euthanasia believe it is cruel to prolong a terminally ill patient's suffering when she or he desires to die. They argue that people are capable of making rational decisions about the quality of life they want and therefore should have the right to die with dignity.

Opponents of euthanasia argue that euthanasia cheapens human life and puts society on a "slippery slope" that could lead to the killing of people who are considered a burden. They also argue that doctors are not always right and that "hopeless cases" have sometimes been reversed.

Public opinion appears to be moving toward acceptance of euthanasia. A 1990 Times Mirror Center survey found that 80 percent of the respondents agreed that there are circumstances when a person should be allowed to die (Cox, 1993). A 1991 national survey by KCR Communications Research found that 64 percent of the respondents favored physician-assisted suicide and euthanasia for terminally ill patients who request it (Hooyman and Kiyak, 1993).

Should euthanasia be allowed? Under what conditions? Do you support efforts to legalize physician-assisted suicide? How do you think you would react if you found out today that you had a terminal illness? How would you want those around you to react?

(Shneideman, 1980; Baugher et al., 1989–90). For example, Richard Kalish (1985) argues that what Kübler-Ross calls stages are simply common reactions to one's impending death. He believes that dying people also experience other reactions such as hope, relief, curiosity, and apathy. Despite such criticism, Kübler-Ross's work remains noteworthy for providing insights into the needs and tasks of the terminally ill and for initiating a much-needed discussion of these issues.

THE NEEDS AND TASKS OF THE DYING

One of the needs that most dying people have is to know that they are dying, yet access to this information is not always available. Although in recent years the tendency in the medical community has been to tell the patient, some doctors are still reluctant to do so. This need is strongly related to the tasks that the dying person must attend to—getting insurance and financial paperwork in order, making decisions about medical treatment, arranging for distribution of personal property, making a will, and letting people know her or his wishes regarding funeral arrangements. Too often these death preparations are not made until the last minute, if ever, thus leaving the grief-stricken spouse or family to cope with them during a period of enormous stress. No one likes to anticipate the loss of a loved one or to think of her or his own demise, yet doing so before the inevitable happens can make the necessary adjustments easier.

wife role and more interested in being accepted in their own right than as someone's wife. Some of these women find, however, that they must negotiate this new role with family and friends who still relate to them as "Mrs. John Smith" (Atchley, 1991).

Widows generally face a bleaker financial future than widowers do. Findings from a national sample of widows of all ages contradict the popular media portrayal of the "merry widow" grown prosperous as a result of a fat insurance policy. Instead, widowhood has a significant negative financial impact on women. The average living standard of widows dropped 18 percent following a husband's death. In addition, 10 percent of women whose income was above the poverty line prior to widowhood were pushed into poverty (Bound et al., 1991). Other researchers put the figure much higher. One study, for example, found that the average increase in poverty after widowhood was 30 percent, mostly attributable to a permanent decline in nonwage income, especially social security (cited in Logue, 1991:664). Although widowhood can cause financial distress for all women, women of color are particularly hard hit—36 percent of African-American widows and 25 percent of Latinas over 65 are poor, compared with 13 percent of white widows. (U.S. Bureau of the Census, 1987)

Inadequate income adversely affects the quality of life of the widowed. Widows with little money cannot afford to be active socially, which in turn increases their feelings of loneliness. Even widows with adequate income may experience problems related to finances. In many marriages husbands control the family finances, not wanting to bother their wives with these matters. Thus, some women have no knowledge of their family's financial status, nor do they acquire the necessary financial skills to cope with routine tasks of handling insurance premiums and claims, balancing a checkbook, paying bills, and making a budget. Having to learn to deal with these matters during their time of mourning may heighten their levels of anxiety and frustration and lower their self-esteem.

SPECIAL PROBLEMS OF WIDOWERS Widowers, too, face several problems related to traditional roles. Earlier studies like those conducted by Felix Berado (1968, 1970) concluded that many older widowers suffer because they are ill prepared to deal with day-

to-day domestic matters like cooking, cleaning, and laundry. As husbands come to share more of the household tasks with their wives, these problems are likely to be minimized.

In the social realm widowers often experience a double bind. Not only do they lose their major source of intimacy but they also find it more difficult than widows to move in with their children and to find a useful place there. Researchers have found that compared with widows, widowers have fewer contacts with their families and receive less social support from them following the death of their spouse (Longino and Lipman, 1981). This may be a continuation of a pattern begun years ago. In many marriages the wife is the primary initiator of family contacts; her death leaves a void in this area, lessening the interactions the widower is likely to have. Similarly, DiGiulio (1989) observed that women's support networks prior to and immediately following the death of their spouse were richer than men's.

Other research indicates that widowers experience higher rates of mental illness and depression than widows do (Gove, 1972). Widowers also have higher rates of death and suicide than widows during the first year following the death of their spouse (Walsh, 1980; Smith et al., 1988).

In sum, widowhood is a difficult stage for both women and men. There is increasing evidence, however, that a successful transition to widowhood depends on the variety of roles that make up a person's self-identity. People whose identities are multifaceted—who are involved in several activities and relationships—appear to cope better. They are less likely to become depressed or ill than are people with a more limited set of roles (DiGiulio, 1989).

BEYOND WIDOWHOOD

Thus far we have discussed the traumatic aspects of widowhood. However, in the wake of widowhood there can be positive role changes as well. After the period of mourning and grief subsides, those who cared for an ill spouse may feel a sense of relief and freedom. For many people, widowhood may provide an opportunity for a reunion with friends or for the making of new friends. During marriage, family responsibilities often prevent people from participating in other activities. Many widowed people use their new time to return to school, take up a hobby, do volunteer work, travel, and in some cases remarry. Phyllis Silverman (1988) compared widows and widowers and found that in this phase both make changes in their lives, albeit in different directions. Women's changes tend to be more internal. The experience of coping with widowhood leads them to be more self-confident, assertive, independent, and willing to satisfy their own needs. Men on the other hand focus more externally, becoming more aware and appreciative of friends and relationships. Nevertheless, both women and men are able to build satisfying lives after experiencing widowhood. For example, a recent study conducted by Ohio State University researchers found that women widowed an average of 12 years were as satisfied and optimistic about their lives as were married women in the same age group (*Modern Maturity*, 1992–93).

IMPLICATIONS FOR SOCIAL POLICY

Programs and policies that were successful in the past may not be adequate to meet the needs of the coming generations of elderly and their families. Many of today's elderly became poor after family illness, widowhood, or retirement. However, many of tomorrow's elderly, especially women and children and people of color, are already poor. Thus, unless we provide them with better education, job-training programs, and more extensive pension plans, the number of elderly poor will increase in the coming decades.

As the elderly population increases, greater pressure will be put on the health-care system. Yet according to the Health Insurance Association of America (1989), approximately one out of four Americans has no health insurance coverage. If unchanged, this trend will contribute to the creation of two very distinct groups of future elderly: those who are vital and healthy as a result of their access to high-quality health care, and those who are ill or disabled because of their history of inadequate care (Conner, 1992). Policy analysts argue that to keep health costs down, investments should be directed to preventing illness early on.

Finally, the kinship structure for many families now and in the foreseeable future will contain more elderly than younger members. Therefore, there will likely be a greater need for support models that combine both informal caregiving (family and friends) and formal caregiving (for example, adult day care, visiting nurses, housekeeping services). Social-support networks need not go in one direction only, however. The elderly represent a tremendous reservoir of skills and ability. Some public schools and universities have initiated intergenerational partners projects where the elderly serve as tutors and teachers' aides (Aday, 1991). Other elderly serve as "foster" grandparents and as business, craft, and hobby mentors. More elderly could be encouraged to use their talents for the social good either through paid employment or volunteer work.

SUMMARY

Throughout this chapter we have seen how family relationships have been altered by increased life expectancy and changing birthrates, resulting in highly verticalized kinship structures. Additionally, social and demographic changes are altering the composition of elderly cohorts. In comparison with older people today, the elderly of the twenty-first century will be more heterogeneous. Future cohorts of the elderly will include a higher proportion of people of color, and there will be greater numbers of single, divorced, widowed, remarried, and childless elderly, many of whom will be significantly older than current and past generations of old people.

Although most Americans fear ending their life in a nursing home, only about 5 percent of the elderly are in such institutions. The majority of older people live alone or in a household with their spouse. Elderly women are more likely to live alone, whereas elderly men are more likely to live with their spouse. Elderly of color are more likely to live with their adult children than are white elderly.

Studies of the level of marital satisfaction in later-life families have shown diverse patterns. Some older couples experience higher levels of satisfaction than in the earlier years of their marriage, some show less satisfaction, and still others show no change. Levels of marital satisfaction are related to patterns of retirement and family income. Poverty remains a serious problem for many elderly, especially widows and people of color. Later-life families are involved in reciprocal exchanges of services among the various generations. Spouses and adult children provide the vast majority of care for elderly family members who become ill.

Later-life couples must eventually deal with bereavement and grief. The experience of widowhood requires many adjustments for both women and men.

An understanding of the strengths and the needs of later-life families is critical to social planning for the future. The multigenerational structure of families and the resulting interdependence among generations can provide a model for intergenerational cooperation and interdependence at the societal level.

KEY TERMS

Sandwich generation
Ageism
Social gerontology
Age norms

Bereavement
Grief
Euthanasia

QUESTIONS FOR STUDY AND REFLECTION

1. Sharon Curtin wrote in her book *Nobody Ever Died of Old Age*, "There is nothing to prepare you for the experience of growing old." Based on your attitudes toward aging and your experiences to date, do you agree or disagree with Curtin? How do your own ethnic and cultural experiences affect your attitudes toward aging? How would you advise today's families to approach the aging of their members?

2. Reflect on the intergenerational relationships in your family. Do family members live in close proximity to one another? What kinds of services, if any, are exchanged by family members? In which generational direction do they flow? Are the patterns in your family typical of those for most later-life families?

3. Which style of grandparenting do you associate with your grandparents? If you become a grandparent, which style do you think you would adopt? What does this tell you about your view of grandparent-

hood? Should the role of grandparent be expanded? Why or why not? What kinds of problems do grandparents face when they assume the parenting role for their grandchildren? What kinds of resources and supports should society provide for such grandparents?

4. In Chapter 13, we asked whether the idea of a permanent marriage is a realistic option in today's society. In this chapter we noted that 3 percent of all married couples celebrated golden wedding anniversaries. Can you imagine yourself married for 50 or more years? What do you think it takes to stay married that long? The longer people stay married, the more likely they are to experience widowhood. Can or should married couples prepare for this eventuality? Would this make a difference in the way they experience widowhood? What advice would you give to a couple when one spouse is terminally ill? Explain your position.

FURTHER READING

BURY, MICHAEL, AND ANTHEA HOLME. 1991. *Life After Ninety*. London: Routledge. The authors interviewed almost 200 people aged 90 and older, living at home and in institutions. Their findings demonstrate that a good quality of life is often possible for the oldest-old and that life after 90 can be satisfying.

DAVIDSON, GLEN. 1984. *Understanding Mourning: A Guide for Those Who Grieve*. Minneapolis, MN: Augsburg. The author provides solid and practical guidelines for mourning and returning to a reorganized life.

KOCH, TOM. 1990. *Mirrored Lives: Aging Children and*

Elderly Parents. New York: Praeger. The author presents a case history of his father's illness and its effect on the entire family. His story raises an important question about the consequences of a cultural value that stresses independent living.

SCHREIBER, LE ANNE. 1990. *Midstream.* New York: Viking. The author provides a moving second hand account of her mother's death from cancer, revealing her own feelings and those of other family members.

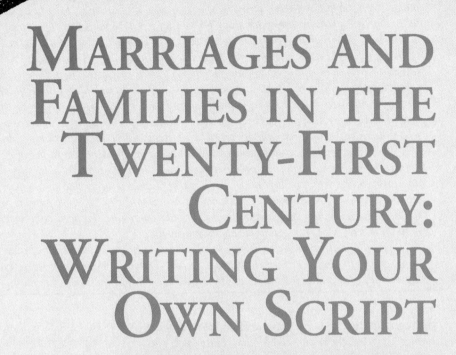

Chapter 16

Marriages and Families in the Twenty-First Century: Writing Your Own Script

Linda and Joe are both 22. They recently graduated from a midwestern college where they met 2 years ago when they were assigned a collaborative project in a marriage and family class. They enjoyed working on the project together and became friends. Both were dating other people at the time, but when those relationships ended, they wanted to date only each other.

Linda and Joe have discussed marriage, but they are aware that it may be risky for them at the present time. Although they love each other deeply and want to have a family together, they are hesitant about taking such a major step. Joe's parents were divorced when he was 15 years old. His dad was a steelworker who lost his job when the steel plants in the community where they lived closed down. After that, his father held a series of low-paying jobs. The marriage began to deteriorate, and eventually Joe's mother asked for a divorce. Joe believes that if his father could have been more successful economically, his parents would have stayed together. Joe is determined to be better equipped for the job market than his father was. Therefore, he wants to go to graduate school to get an MBA right away, even though it will mean increasing his debt load.

Linda majored in elementary education and was hired by the school district where she did her practice teaching. Because teaching salaries are low, Linda hopes to improve her economic prospects by returning to school during the summer months to get a master's degree in educational administration. Linda is an only child. Her mother had several miscarriages and had resigned herself to being childless. When she was 38 and her husband was 42, however, she discovered that she was pregnant. Although her mother still works, Linda's dad took early retirement because of poor health. Linda is very close to her parents and provides them with a great deal of emotional support. Linda expects her responsibility for her parents to increase as they get older, and she believes she should stay in the same city where they live. Joe feels that married couples need to be free to move to wherever the best economic opportunities are.

Given this brief description, what options do you think are available to Linda and Joe? Should they postpone marriage until they are financially more secure? Do their career goals seem compatible? How much weight should they place on their families of orientation in terms of their own life plans?

Throughout this book we have emphasized two key themes that have characterized U.S. marriages and families over the centuries: diversity and change. Although marriage and family were never static institutions, the pace of change appears to have accelerated in the last half of the twentieth century, causing many people to question how or if the family will survive in the future. We begin this chapter with a brief review of the major changes that have occurred in marriages and families since the 1950s, a time many people mistakenly think represents the historical norm of family life. We then consider the major trends that likely will carry us into the twenty-first century and highlight the major family-related problems that currently confront our nation. We close this chapter with a discussion of how social forces influence personal marriage and family scripts, providing you with some key questions to guide your own personal decision making.

Throughout this text we have discussed numerous changes that have occurred in marriage and family life since the 1950s. The most significant of these changes follow:

- The proportion of people living in family households, especially in traditional nuclear families, has declined (Chapters 1 and 11).

- The number of families with both parents working rose sharply after 1970. The dual-earner family currently represents the most common married family unit (Chapter 11).

- The average size of families has decreased. Many couples are choosing to have only one child, and an increasing number of women are choosing to remain child-free (Chapter 9).

- New reproductive technologies are enabling many infertile couples to have children (Chapter 9).

- People are marrying at later ages (Chapter 1).

- The percentage of people who have never married has increased, especially among people in their 20s and 30s (Chapter 7).

- The number of marriages ending in divorce has increased dramatically. Current estimates are that over one out of two new marriages will end in divorce (Chapter 13).

- The rate of remarriages climbed during the 1960s and 1970s and leveled off somewhat in the 1980s. Six out of ten remarriages end in divorce (Chapter 14).

- The number of single-person households has increased dramatically. With increases in life expectancy, more elderly and widowed people are living alone (Chapter 15).

- Single-parent households more than doubled between 1970 and 1990 (Chapter 10). Although the majority of these family units are created by divorce, a significant number of single-parent households are created by births to unmarried mothers.

- Both heterosexual and homosexual cohabitation has increased dramatically since 1960. A growing number of communities are granting limited rights to these couples through the institution of domestic partnerships (Chapter 7).

- Although growing in number, interracial marriages continue to represent only a small fraction of all marriages (Chapter 8).

MARRIAGES AND FAMILIES IN THE TWENTY-FIRST CENTURY

It is never easy to predict future trends. Given the scope and magnitude of the changes that have taken place over the last several decades, however, these trends will likely continue, albeit at a slower pace. For example, in recent years the rate of increase in the number of working mothers has slowed, and the divorce rate has declined slightly. According to a recent report by the National Center for Health Statistics, the divorce rate fell 11 percent from 1981 to 1991. Center spokesperson Sally Clarke noted that "people are still divorcing at a very high rate, but the change from 5.3 to 4.7 divorces per 1000 is statistically significant" (Peterson, 1992:4D).

It is too early to tell if the current decline in the divorce rate is a temporary pattern or if it is indicative of a long-term trend. There is a growing public awareness, however, that divorce often involves significant adverse consequences for the marriage partners and especially for their children. This awareness could lead to more widespread social attitudes that encourage couples to try harder to make their marriages work, thus slowing the rate of divorce.

RACE, CLASS, AND GENDER

Throughout this text we have pointed out how race, class, and gender affect the ways in which individuals experience family life. Over the last several decades some of these diverse experiences have converged, while others have diverged. Let's recall two brief examples we discussed in earlier chapters. On the one hand the difference in fertility rates between blacks and whites has narrowed considerably; on the other hand the gap between the marriage and remarriage rates of blacks and whites has widened.

Some of these patterns are also closely related to social class. For many low-income individuals regardless of race, the specter of long-term unemployment may preclude marriage or remarriage. Historically, people of color in the United States have suffered considerably higher rates of unemployment than have the white population. Until there is more equity in the marketplace, social class will continue to be a factor in marriage and family patterns. Gender, too, will continue to play a role in family composition in the future. Again, recalling one example from Chapter 15, life expectancy for women remains higher than that for men, which means that an increasing number of widows will live alone.

SATISFACTION WITH FAMILY LIFE

Despite many of the serious problems families face, there is considerable evidence that marriages and families will continue to play a central, if somewhat altered, role in people's lives. Throughout the 1980s, national survey data consistently showed that the vast majority of respondents reported a great deal of satisfaction with their family lives. Approximately 67 percent of married couples in those surveys rated their marriages as very happy (Cherlin and Furstenberg, 1983; Sabatelli, 1988). An even higher number, approximately 75 percent of adults surveyed, said they would choose the same spouse if they had it to do over again (Greeley, 1991). Children, too, tended to see their families in a positive light. In a national study 71 percent described their family life as "close and intimate" (Cherlin and Furstenberg, 1983:7).

Other data on family dissolution, however, indicate that families must enjoy a supportive environment to provide a sense of identity, emotional closeness, and security for their members. Families cannot fulfill these vital functions if they are preoccupied with obtaining the basic necessities of food, clothing, shelter, health care, and sustained employment. Therefore, as a society, the United States must find solutions to a number of family-related problems if the institutions of marriage and family are to remain strong and viable.

FAMILY-RELATED PROBLEMS

Among the family-related problems that are most significant as we move into the twenty-first century are the declining economic well-being of families, the declining welfare of growing numbers of children, and an increase in the number of frail elderly.

THE DECLINING ECONOMIC WELL-BEING OF FAMILIES All families share a common goal: to provide a decent standard of living for their members. For many families, however, this goal is becom-

The economic well-being of many families has deteriorated over the last decade. This couple moves their belongings after being evicted from their home.

ing more difficult to reach. According to the latest government statistics, 7.1 million families (11 percent of all families) were living in poverty in 1990, up from 5.3 million families (10 percent) in 1970 (Ahlburg and DeVita, 1992:36). Although overall income and wealth have increased in the United States over the last several decades, the pattern of distribution has been very uneven. Two Pulitzer Prize–winning investigative reporters from the *Philadelphia Inquirer*, Donald L. Barlett and James B. Steele (1992), have documented this inequality in a compelling book titled *America: What Went Wrong?* Their investigation points to a major transfer of wealth to the rich, resulting in a decline in the standard of living for the middle and working classes.

Consider these statistics. In 1959, the wealthiest 4 percent (2.1 million individuals and families) earned $31 billion in wages and salaries—the same amount as the bottom 35 percent (18.3 million individuals and families). In 1989, the wealthiest 4 percent (3.8 million individuals and families) earned $452 billion in wages and salaries—the same as the bottom 51 percent (49.2 million individuals and families) (p. ix). According to Barlett and Steele, "If the trend continues, sometime early in the next century the top 4 percent of individuals and families drawing paychecks will earn as much on the job as 60 percent of the rest of American workers" (p. xii). These figures, they remind us, deal only with wages and salaries and do not include interest and dividends or gains from the sale of stocks, bonds, and other capital assets—all of which flow overwhelmingly to the top 4 percent.

The nonpartisan Economic Policy Institute reports that even greater inequality occurred between 1983 and 1989. According to institute data, the richest one-half of 1 percent of U.S. families received 55 percent of the total increase in household wealth while the bottom 60 percent of families found their wealth either stagnating or falling during that same period. The author of that study, economist Edward Wolff of New York University, wrote that "U.S. wealth concentration in 1989 was more extreme than that of any time since 1929" (*Chicago Tribune*, 1992c:6).

Another point is worth noting. In the 1950s, the goods and services a family needed could be supplied in most cases by the efforts of one wage earner. As we have seen in Chapter 11, for a majority of families today, obtaining similar goods and services requires wages from both spouses. Families with children, families of color, families headed by women, and the unmarried elderly are especially vulnerable in this new economy. These economic shifts reflect certain structural changes in the U.S. economy: the loss of high-paying jobs; the stagnation of wages; the growth of part-time and temporary employment; increased individual, business, and national debt; and a changed tax structure that shifted some tax burdens from businesses to individuals and from the wealthy to the middle class. Thus, a reversal of these trends will also require structural changes.

THE DECLINING WELFARE OF CHILDREN

The economic shifts and changes in family life have had a negative impact on the lives of children in the United States. Although millions of children are flourishing and leading happy, healthy, and productive lives, increasing numbers of children are not. According to a 1990 National Commission on the Role of the School and the Community in Improving Adolescent Health: "Never before has one generation of American children been less healthy, less cared for, or less prepared for life than their parents were at the same age" (p. 3). Economist Sylvia Ann Hewlett, in her thought-provoking book *When the Bough Breaks: The Cost of Neglecting Our Children* (1991), cites a number of statistics that describe the plight of many children today.

- Twenty percent of all children are growing up in poverty, a 21 percent increase since 1970.
- Some 330,000 children are homeless.
- The rate of suicide among adolescents has tripled since 1960.
- Forty-two percent of fathers fail to see their children in the wake of divorce.
- Twenty-seven percent of teenagers drop out of high school.

According to Hewlett, the United States ranks second worldwide in per capita income but is not among the top ten in any significant indicator of child welfare. She points out that "compared with other rich countries, children in the United States are much more likely to die before their first birthday; to live in poverty; to be abandoned by their fathers; and to be killed before they reach the age of twenty-five" (p. 14). Hewlett argues that "over the past 25 years, slowly but relentlessly, American society has been tilt-

When both parents work, the amount of time parents spend with their children often declines. Some parents, like this father, try to avoid this by combining work at home with child care.

ing in an ominous new direction—toward the devaluation of children" (p. 17). As evidence she documents cuts in school budgets, construction of adults-only housing, and the increasing number of children who are growing up in poverty. Not only has U.S. society failed to spend sufficient resources on children's needs, but the amount of time parents spend with their children has declined sharply. This loss of time has resulted from the increasing labor-force participation of mothers, an increase in the average hours parents have to work, and the increasing divorce rate that removes one parent from the home on a daily basis.

One of the obstacles that we face in trying to improve the welfare of children is the deeply embedded notion that child rearing is a private endeavor that should result in a public benefit. Thus, parents are expected to enhance the well-being of the nation by raising a productive new generation. For many families today, however, that task is becoming more difficult, if not impossible, without outside support. Hewlett argues that child rearing must be seen as a collective responsibility and that public policies must be redrawn in the direction of supporting children through a variety of means:

- Free access to prenatal and maternity care and state-mandated parenting leave.
- Investment of a higher percentage of public money on child care and education, especially programs that have proven successful, like Head Start.

- Encouragement of employers to design family-friendly workplaces that offer working parents more time to spend with their children through flextime, compressed work weeks, and job sharing.
- Provision of substantial housing subsidies for families with children so that every child can grow up in a safe and stimulating environment.
- Enhancement and enforcement of child-support awards in the event of family dissolution.
- Encouragement of volunteer programs to support children and families.

Because many of these suggestions require government action and taxpayer dollars, they will generate considerable controversy. Nevertheless, if the debate over family values is to have any meaning, the United States must take seriously the future well-being of our families, especially our children, and develop an action plan that improves the quality of their lives and, hence, the health of the entire nation.

THE GROWING NUMBERS OF THE ELDERLY
Not only are children likely to need more support in the future but so too are people at the other end of the age spectrum. In Chapter 15 we examined the rapid growth of the elderly population, especially those over 75 years of age. More and more families, especially female family members, will find themselves facing the demands of caring for elderly relatives. As we move into the twenty-first century, however, the new generation of elderly will be at greater risk of being without needed support than is the current generation because there will be fewer children to care for them.

Furthermore, in the future more of the elderly will have experienced divorce and remarriage. This will add to the ambiguity of family roles and responsibility. Will children of divorced parents assume the care of an emotionally distant parent? Will stepchildren be as willing to care for a stepparent as biological children are for a natural parent? Even assuming that these family members are willing to provide care for an elderly relative, the economics of this care may prove to be too much for many families to bear alone. In less than 20 years the first of the baby-boom generation will turn 65. That gives us little time to plan for this surge in the elderly population. The decisions we make now about education, health care, pension and retirement programs, housing, and other social policies will determine the quality of life of the elderly as well as other family members.

These are complex problems, and solving them won't be easy. However, we should not be overwhelmed by them either. As indicated throughout this text, earlier generations confronted numerous family-related problems. Despite repeated fears that the family is a dying institution, it has survived by adapting to changing economic and political circumstances. Therefore, rather than worry about any specific changes in families or engage in nostalgia for a particular family form, social policies need to focus on the concrete realities within which families exist. Social policies that are truly "profamily" will recognize the diversity of U.S. families and the complexity of their needs. Having examined these general trends, you may be wondering how your marriage and family life will develop in the future. Let's turn to a consideration of your personal life choices.

PERSONAL LIFE CHOICES AND THE SOCIOLOGICAL IMAGINATION

A course on the sociology of marriages and families usually invokes concern and interest among students about how the general principles and descriptions in the textbook apply to their own lives. In this textbook we have stressed the application of the sociological imagination in everyday life. In this context, we have focused on social structure: how cultural values; historical context; economic and political changes; and various social-structural variables and social systems such as race, class, gender, sexual orientation, and age interact and affect the personal experiences of individuals and groups as they create, sustain, and change their marriages and families.

Although there are many benefits of applying a sociological perspective, four general ones stand out: (1) It allows us to take a new and critical look at what we have always taken for granted or assumed to be true; (2) it allows us to see the vast range of human diversity; (3) it allows us to understand the constraints and opportunities that affect our lives and those of other people; and (4) it enables us to participate more actively in society (Macionis, 1991). By utilizing the sociological imagination in making life choices you are apt to make more successful decisions, to be able to choose from a wider range of options, to choose more discriminatingly, and to exercise a greater degree of control over your life than you otherwise would.

Because our approach in this textbook has been interactive, encouraging you to become directly involved in learning by applying various concepts and information to real-life experiences (your own and those of others), it seems logical to conclude this textbook with a chapter that allows and encourages you to apply the sociological knowledge that you have gained from this textbook specifically to your own life.

Throughout our lives all of us are confronted with life events, living arrangements, and other activities about which we must make decisions. Some of the most important of these decisions are those concerning marriage and family living. Although we all exercise some degree of freedom in choosing among lifestyle alternatives, the choices we make are greatly shaped by the historical context within which we are located.

GAINING AWARENESS OF SOCIAL FORCES

Most people want to make the best possible decisions about their lives, but they often wonder how to go about doing that. We firmly believe that to choose wisely we need to be aware of the many options open to us, how those options are shaped by social and historical forces, and how societal norms and personal values affect the choices we make. In brief, to make "good" or "right" decisions for ourselves requires knowledge about the society in which we live, important social processes and pressures, and the major social-structural and political forces around us.

What does this mean in the context of a sociological perspective? It means that we must be able to see our personal lives as linked to society; we must understand and recognize the link between our personal experiences and larger social forces. Social-structural factors have an important effect on our personal choices in that they limit the options available to us. For example, as we discussed in Chapter 5, many highly educated African-American women who desire to marry will probably not do so because they outnumber eligible African-American men of comparable ages and educational achievement. Thus, the low sex ratio within this group constrains the marital choices of African-American women. Hence, an African-American woman may marry below her educational level, remain single, or wait and hope to marry someone of her same educational background. Her options are shaped to a large degree by the sex ratio, over which she has no control.

THE ROLE OF SOCIETAL NORMS

Another major factor influencing our choices is societal norms. Because we have internalized the norms of our culture and society, they are a part of our sense of self and are sometimes so ingrained that it is often difficult to go against them; it is often easier simply to follow society's rules. For example, in the past marriage and parenthood were so strongly sanctioned that many people married or had children whether they truly wanted to or not. Today, however, these norms are not nearly as rigid, and many people feel they can make these choices without fear of recrimination. In contrast, an area in which social norms continue to limit people's options is the situation of lesbian or gay couples who desire to marry but cannot do so legally. Thus, the choices they make—for example, to cohabit—are choices made within a range of options that excludes the possibility of legalized marriage.

KNOWLEDGE OF OPTIONS

Sometimes we make choices without full knowledge of the range of options available to us. For example, a couple may decide to pursue a mortgage at a 10 percent interest rate because they are unaware that other financial institutions are offering rates as low as 7 percent. In other cases people choose options that seem easier or less problematic than alternative courses of action. For example, some working women take on a "second shift" of housework and child care because they don't have the psychological energy to expend trying to get their partner to do a fair share of the family workload. They perceive the "easiest" course of action as simply doing the work themselves.

The sociological perspective then is especially well suited to help us make informed choices because it enables us to see and understand the power of social forces in our everyday lives. From a sociological perspective, the process of making life choices, which is at the core of our everyday lives, involves sociohistorical factors that shape the type and number of options available to us. Our knowledge of the range of options available to us; cultural and subcultural norms; family backgrounds; economic and political forces; our age, race, class, gender, and religion; and our personal values all affect the choices we make. We have tried to capture the essence of this process in Figure 16.1.

FIGURE 16.1 Factors that influence personal decision making.

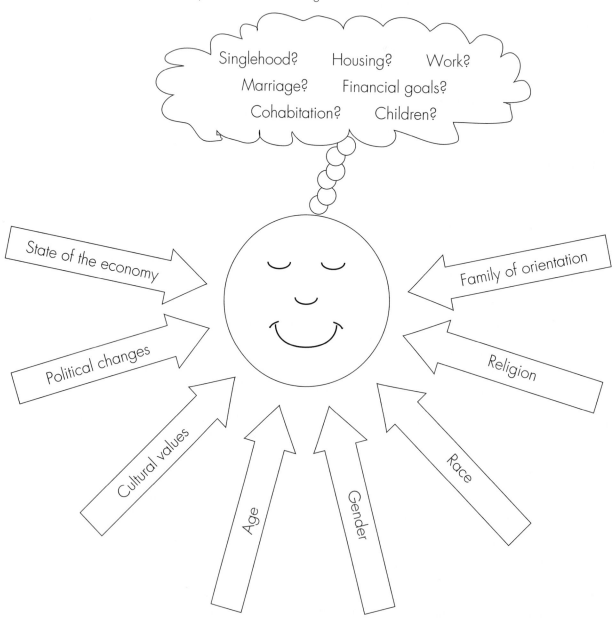

WRITING YOUR OWN SCRIPT

In the Preface, we suggested that you keep a personal journal of your thoughts and reactions to the material presented in the text. The remaining section of this chapter provides you with a more formalized process for reflecting on and planning your own life script. Now that you have read the entire text you are in a good position to evaluate your feelings and desires regarding the life choices you have made or will be making over the next few years. You can select only those areas of immediate concern to you, or you can work your way through all the life options presented here. The exercises correspond to key topics discussed in the textbook; you may want to refer back to those chapters as you think about your own life. The process of keeping a journal is meant to provide you with a means for engaging in *anticipatory socialization,* a process of preparing for and thinking about some of the expectations that accompany a potential future role. Even if you have already made some decisions, such as getting married and having children, this process can give you insight into how well your decision making worked and can perhaps suggest other areas where improvements can be made. You might also consider asking your partner to write down her or his feelings and desires regarding these life options. This method would provide you with a guide to consider whether the two of you have shared or conflicting expectations.

Rest assured what you do here now is not written in stone. The exercises contained in this chapter are simply a method that allows you to begin making informed choices by applying the sociological imagination. Some of these choices, like becoming parents, are permanent, whereas others, such as entering into or dissolving a relationship, can be altered. In addition, we should realize that the choices we make at various stages of our lives may affect later options. For example, a decision to delay marriage or childbearing into our 30s or 40s may result in fewer, if any, options to engage in these behaviors at a later date.

To think sociologically about your personal decision making, consider: (1) the factual information presented in this textbook, (2) the key life events and activities we will delineate shortly, (3) the options available to you in each area of decision making, (4) the larger social forces that may affect the range of options available to you, (5) the possible positive and negative consequences (advantages or disadvantages) of each option, and (6) how social forces and your own personal values may interact to influence your choices.

ROLE TRANSITIONS AND MARRIAGE AND FAMILY LIFE EVENTS

The following section presents a series of role transitions and major marriage and family life events. Some will apply to you at this point in your life, and others will not be relevant until later in your life course. Each life event or activity is introduced by a brief narrative description and is followed by a set of questions to help clarify the various options as well as personal preferences. In each case you should take the following steps:

- Consider the sociological knowledge you have concerning the event or activity.
- Consider the range of options available to you and from among which you will make choices.
- Consider the social forces and pressures that shape your options.
- Consider the possible positive and negative consequences or the advantages and disadvantages of each option.
- Consider the role of cultural norms and your own personal values and how each will affect your decisions.
- Make a choice.

GAINING SELF-AWARENESS   One of the most important factors in personal decision making is having a good sense of self; a sense of who we are. The person inside us is the person we need to consider most when making a decision. Thus, it is important to have a sense of who that person is. Therefore, in writing our life scripts, it seems most appropriate to begin by asking ourselves two questions: Who am I? and What kind of decisionmaker am I? To help answer these questions, complete the following exercises.*

*These exercises have been adapted from Alice G. Sargent, 1985, *Beyond Sex Roles* (New York: West).

Gaining knowledge about the society in which we live can help us make more informed lifestyle decisions.

1. In your journal write the words *Who am I?* at the top. Write at least 15 answers (more if you choose). After you have finished answering the question, rank your answers. Number one should be the quality or role without which you would not be yourself. In other words, it is the core of who you feel you are. After this, put a plus next to all of the most important descriptions of yourself and a minus next to those that you could give up.

2. *What is my sexual self?* Your exploration of self should include an understanding of your sexuality given that sexuality figures largely in many marriage and family life events or choices. A clear view of our sexuality is important because our degree of comfort with it or fear of it can affect our ability to establish close relationships with members of both the same sex and the other sex. Thus, after you have finished the "Who am I" exercise complete the following statements: "I am/am not heterosexual because…" "I am/am not homosexual because…" "I am/am not bisexual because…"

3. *What type of decisionmaker am I?* Now that you have reflected on who you are and on your sexual self, turn your attention to what kind of decisionmaker you are. To increase your awareness of the options available to you for making decisions, consider the following decision-making styles, that is, the decision-making strategies that are frequently employed in arriving at a course of action or, as the case may be, inaction.

- *Agonizing*: I get lost in all of the information I have concerning the issue or event. I become overwhelmed with deciding among alternatives. "I often don't know what to do."

- *Compliant*: I follow someone else's lead. I let others decide for me. "Anything you say is fine with me."

- *Delaying*: I procrastinate or postpone even thinking about the issue as well as making a decision. "I'll cross that bridge later."

- *Fatalistic*: I leave the decision up to fate; whatever happens is supposed to happen. "It's all in the cards."

- *Impulsive*: I give little thought to the issue or available options, or I take the first option or alternative that comes along. "I don't look before I leap."

- *Intuitive*: I make decisions based on some inner voice. "It feels right."

- *Paralyzed*: Although I want to accept responsibility for making a decision, I find that I am unable to do anything. "I can't face up to it."

- *Planning*: I try to see that my decision is a satisfying one. I try to use a rational approach to decision making by balancing cognitive and emotional aspects. "I weigh all the facts and then decide what's best for me."

 What did you learn about your style of decision making? How is it related to your overall sense of self? Are you satisfied with your decision-making style? Do you think it is effective? If not, which style would you prefer? Will you make a conscious effort to change your approach to decision making?

FORMING RELATIONSHIPS One of your first marriage and family life events or activities will involve the experience of having an intimate relationship. For some of you, evaluating whether to become involved in an intimate relationship may seem unromantic and even cold and calculating. Consider for a moment, though, the possible benefits of this process. What societal factors or pressures define intimacy? In the United States, we tend to think that such relationships just tend to happen; that people simply fall into them without much thought or preparation. In reality, however, we exercise a good deal of choice in whether to engage in such a relationship, as well as when, where, with whom, and how we will become involved.

QUESTIONS TO CONSIDER

1. What are my options? Do I want to become involved in an intimate relationship? If yes, what kind of relationship do I want (casual, serious, open, monogamous, platonic, sexual)? If I am currently involved in a relationship, how satisfied am I? Do I want to continue this relationship? If not, what steps do I need to take to end this relationship?

2. Deciding you would like to become involved in an intimate relationship involves other choices. Do I want to date? If so, what kind of person do I want to date? How should I go about meeting people to date? What are my goals in dating? If I decide not to date, is this a temporary or permanent decision? How may this decision affect my other life choices?

KNOWING YOUR PARTNER   Assuming you have decided to become involved in an intimate relationship now or in the future (or if you are already involved in such a relationship), what do you want or need to know about your partner? As we discussed in Chapter 5, research shows that on the average, the more a couple share such things as values, interests, religion, life aspirations, and lifestyles, the more likely the relationship will be successful. Conversely, the less similar the couple, the less likely the relationship will succeed.

In addition to knowing whether you and your partner are compatible in the areas we have cited, it is important to know about your partner's overall personality and behavior. With the high incidence of verbal, physical, and sexual abuse in intimate relationships it is also important to know as much as possible about our partners in terms of the likelihood that they could be abusive or violent. Although there is no specific profile of an abuser, the data presented in Chapter 12 suggest certain characteristics or factors that are prevalent among abusers, such as poor self-esteem, rigidity, and excessive dependency. The presence of these characteristics can alert us to the possibility that our partner can become abusive or violent.

QUESTIONS TO CONSIDER

1. What knowledge do I have about my partner? What else do I need to know? How do I find out what I want to know?

2. How similar are we? How significant are the differences between us? Do these differences cause problems or conflicts in our relationship? Can we resolve these differences?

3. Has my partner ever been abusive or violent toward me? Have I ever observed my partner being abusive or violent toward anyone else? Have I been abusive or violent toward my partner? What can we do if either of us becomes abusive or violent in our relationship? Will I be willing to seek counseling and encourage my partner to do the same? Will I be able to consider ending such a relationship even if I care for this person?

THE MARITAL DECISION   Do I want to marry? The answer to this question represents one of the most fundamental choices we will make in our lifetime. As we saw in Chapter 7, people are more likely today than in the past to consider alternatives to traditional marriage. Nevertheless, pressure to marry remains intense, especially for young adults. The popularity of marriage in the United States is still higher than in most other countries. Although increasing numbers of individuals are not marrying at all, delaying marriage to a later age, or divorcing at high rates, demographers predict that more than 90 percent of people born in the United States in recent years will marry at least once in their lifetime.

QUESTIONS TO CONSIDER

1. If I decide not to marry, is this a permanent decision or will I reevaluate this decision at some later time? What lifestyle will I choose? Will I cohabit with a partner or live alone? What are the advantages and disadvantages of a single or nonmarried lifestyle? If I choose not to marry will I be sexually active or remain celibate?

2. If I decide to marry, whom will I consider as a marriage partner? At what age do I want to marry? What do I need to consider before deciding to marry? How important is it for me to marry within my racial or ethnic background? How important are other factors such as age, economic background, and religion? How important is approval by family and friends of my choice of a marital partner? What expectations do I have for marriage?

3. If I choose marriage (or am already married), what do I need to know about building a successful marital relationship? If I am having marital problems, where can I get help? Will I be willing to seek counseling to solve these problems? What alternatives will I consider if my marriage is not going well? Will I consider separation or divorce if my partner and I cannot resolve our difficulties?

4. If I am widowed or divorced, will I consider remarriage? What are the advantages and disadvantages of remarriage? What do I need to know about building a successful remarriage?

WRITING YOUR RELATIONSHIP CONTRACT

The decision to marry or cohabit leads to a number of other related issues and areas of understanding that couples should consider, discuss, and resolve prior to establishing their living arrangement. Many couples have found it useful to write personal contracts that clarify their feelings and expectations for the marriage or cohabitative relationship. To be effective this exercise should be done with your partner. It may be easier, however, if you and your partner write separate contracts and then compare and discuss each other's contract before writing a final version that represents your collective view and consensus. Prenuptial and personal contracts include the expectations the couple bring to their relationship. In the exercise that follows we present the items commonly included in marriage and personal contracts. It is not necessary that you cover every item simply because it is here. Concern yourself only with those areas that are relevant to your particular situation. (*Note*: If you choose to remain single, either permanently or on a temporary basis, many of these items will apply to you as well. Although you don't need to consider a partner, reflecting on these items can help you to build a more satisfying lifestyle.)

RELEVANT HISTORY   Couples often assume they know all they need to know about each other without really discussing their past histories. However, a lack of knowledge can sometimes lead to problems later on.

QUESTIONS TO CONSIDER

Will we try to share all aspects of our history that might affect our intended relationship, for example, former marriages and our own and our families' health histories?

DIVISION OF LABOR AND RESPONSIBILITIES
A source of difficulty for many couples is the perception of inequity in the performance of household tasks. Often partners have different assumptions about who should do these tasks. Some people believe that household tasks should be allocated on the basis of gender even when both partners are employed full-time.

QUESTIONS TO CONSIDER

1. What rights do we each have as individuals, and what role expectations do we have for each other? How will we divide household responsibilities? Who will cook, clean, make the shopping lists, shop, do laundry, make house and car repairs, do yard work, wash windows, plan entertainment, take out the trash, care for children, take care of finances, pay bills, and perform all the other tasks of daily living?
2. How will decisions be made—individually or jointly? How will we resolve differences of opinion?

SEXUAL EXCLUSIVENESS   One of the reasons some people give for dissolving their relationships is a partner's extramarital affairs. Such behavior can lead to feelings of betrayal, jealousy, insecurity, and anger. Often couples don't discuss their views on sexual matters until after they are married or cohabiting, and sometimes they find that they have conflicting values in this area.

QUESTIONS TO CONSIDER

Will our relationship be sexually exclusive? What is our understanding about sexual access to each other? How will we communicate our personal desires? What are our feelings about outside relationships, both sexual and nonsexual? Would we feel threatened by outside relationships?

WORK: JOBS OR CAREERS? Work is an important activity in the United States. To a large extent our self-worth is tied to whether we work as well as the type of work we perform. Additionally, most families can no longer expect to survive with only the traditional male wage earner. There has also been a shift in people's attitudes toward work. Many women, for example, work not only out of necessity but also because of the intrinsic satisfaction that having a job or career affords. Some men today are redefining their work role, placing less importance on work as an indicator of their success and self-worth. For these men jobs or careers are taking second place to individual and family needs and desires. As we discussed in Chapter 11, the work status of individual family members profoundly affects the nature and quality of marriage and family life. There is still some ambivalence about working mothers. Thus, some women experience tremendous pressure to "stay home" or to work only part-time. Additionally, partners in a relationship have to make considerable personal adjustments if both are working, especially if they have children.

QUESTIONS TO CONSIDER

1. Do my partner and I want jobs or careers? Will one of our jobs or careers take priority over the other? How will we make employment decisions that involve the other partner? How will we deal with career moves, including geographical relocation, especially if one of us does not want to relocate? If we both work, how will that affect our division of household labor? How will it affect our decision if and when to have children?

2. If our family does not need two wage earners, will we both work anyway? Can either of us consider staying home to take care of the children? Why or why not? If we both need to or want to work, what options do we have for quality child care? What can we do to reduce the stress of work/family conflicts?

MANAGING FINANCES You have probably heard the saying "Money cannot buy happiness," and this may well be true. However, social researchers consistently have found that finances are a major source of tension and conflict within families. Being able to earn an adequate income and managing those earnings affects our lives in numerous ways—access to health care, education, food, clothing, shelter, transportation, entertainment, and other goods and services. Couples who develop skill, consistency, and agreement on financial management report higher relationship satisfaction than couples who have poor financial management skills. Conflict over financial matters is generally related to immature or poor attitudes toward spending and saving money.

Additionally, conflict over money may be a reflection of the couple's power relationship. For example, partners who earn the largest share of income may feel they have a greater claim to deciding how that money is spent. The partners who make less money or who don't work outside the home may resent this attitude. Family role expectations, if not shared, may also cause conflict. For example, men whose fathers controlled the family finances may expect to do the same in their relationships even though their partners are co-providers. Couples who strive for equity in economic decision making are more likely to be satisfied with their relationship.

Probably a minority of couples start out as good financial planners and money managers; most learn the hard way as they struggle to reduce tensions in their relationships. In today's uncertain economy, however, it is wise to begin planning early and to master money-management skills. Employees can no longer automatically assume that they will have long-term job security. Our current population of elderly have taught us that social security alone is not sufficient to maintain a comfortable retirement. Managing family resources is critical to a family's well-being. Qualified financial planners (always check their credentials and references) can provide guidance about family budgets, insurance, taxes, wills, investments, and savings tailored to individual family circumstances.

A critical task for any couple is preparing a family budget.

QUESTIONS TO CONSIDER

1. How will we handle the ownership, distribution, and management of property before and after marriage? How will we decide on the contribution of each person to the total family income and support? Will it matter if one of us earns more than the other?

2. As a couple, how compatible are our spending (including the use of credit cards) and savings patterns? Are we both comfortable with these patterns, or do we need to make any changes in them? What are our financial goals? What plans can we make to achieve these goals? Should we have joint or separate savings and checking accounts? What are the advantages and disadvantages of each arrangement?

3. Who will manage the family finances? How will we decide on a family budget? (See the FYI box titled "Establishing a Monthly Budget".) How will we decide how family money will be spent? Who will pay the bills and make the investments? How will we decide this? If one of us assumes this responsibility, how will that one keep the other informed about our financial matters? Will each of us be able to manage if something happens to the other?

CHILDREN Another major life choice many of us will make regardless of whether we choose to marry is whether we will parent. Choosing to parent will have significant consequences for us in terms of the time, energy, and resources required to perform this critical

FOR YOUR INFORMATION

CALCULATING A MONTHLY BUDGET

At some point we all must learn to manage a household budget. Take a few minutes to complete the following form, imagining that you are working and supporting a family. When you are finished, ask yourself whether this exercise has affected your feelings regarding family and parental responsibilities.

Income	Month _____		
Take-home pay	$_____		
Other	_____		
Total	$_____		
Fixed expenditures	projected	actual	(+) or (-)
Mortgage or rent	$_____	$_____	$_____
Property taxes	_____	_____	_____
Income and social security taxes not withheld by employer	_____	_____	_____
Alimony, child support	_____	_____	_____
Installment and credit card payments	_____	_____	_____
Insurance: auto	_____	_____	_____
homeowners	_____	_____	_____
life	_____	_____	_____
health and other	_____	_____	_____
Savings and investments: emergency fund	_____	_____	_____
investment fund	_____	_____	_____
vacation fund	_____	_____	_____
other	_____	_____	_____
Subtotal	$_____	$_____	$_____
Variable expenditures			
Food	$_____	$_____	$_____
Utilities: gas or oil	_____	_____	_____
electricity	_____	_____	_____
telephone	_____	_____	_____
water and sewer	_____	_____	_____
Home maintenance, furnishings, and improvement	_____	_____	_____
Automobile: gas and oil	_____	_____	_____
repairs	_____	_____	_____
Public transportation	_____	_____	_____
Day care	_____	_____	_____
Pocket money: hers	_____	_____	_____
his	_____	_____	_____
kids'	_____	_____	_____
Clothing (including dry cleaning): hers	_____	_____	_____
his	_____	_____	_____
kids'	_____	_____	_____
Personal care (haircuts, gym membership, etc.)	_____	_____	_____
Medical and dental bills not covered by insurance	_____	_____	_____
Educational expenses	_____	_____	_____
Entertainment, recreation, gifts	_____	_____	_____
Contributions	_____	_____	_____
Miscellaneous	_____	_____	_____
Subtotal, variable	$_____	$_____	$_____
Subtotal, fixed	$_____	$_____	$_____
Total	$_____	$_____	$_____

task. Our decision to have or not to have children affects not only our personal lives but also the life of our society. Fertility rates and the consequent size and composition of a nation's population have enormous social implications.

In the past, it was almost a foregone conclusion that a woman would reproduce. That was defined as her proper sphere in life, and she exercised relatively little choice or control in the matter. Deciding whether to parent is now much more a matter of choice than was true in the past.

QUESTIONS TO CONSIDER

1. Do we want children? What advantages and disadvantages are there to being child-free? What are our options if we have an unwanted pregnancy? Are there any conditions under which we would consider abortion? If we do not want children now or in the future, who is responsible for birth control? If we want children, how many do we want, and when do we want them? If one or both of us is infertile, will we consider other alternatives for having children? What are our attitudes toward reproductive technologies?

2. What are the advantages and disadvantages of parenting outside of legalized marriage?

FAMILY SURNAME   Names are important symbols of identity. In some cultures a newly married couple incorporate both family names into their surname. The cultural tradition in the United States is for a wife to take her husband's surname. Many couples, however, are questioning this practice.

QUESTIONS TO CONSIDER

Will we both carry the same surname? Will we hyphenate our name or use a new one? If we have children, what surname will they have?

SELECTING A PLACE TO LIVE   Where we live is an important decision that we make in adulthood. We spend a tremendous amount of time in the place we live. Thus, where and under what conditions we live is a major factor in how we perceive the quality of our lives. For example, overcrowding and lack of privacy can cause individual and family stress, whereas adequate space and privacy can improve family relations. For many people, the type and location of housing is a primary means of expressing their values about life. The more strongly people feel about values related to residence, the

Where we live is an important decision; it is a means of expressing our values about life.

more likely they are to make housing a priority in terms of life goals (Kennedy, 1986).

QUESTIONS TO CONSIDER

What type of housing do we want? How will we decide on our place of residence? How important are each of these factors in our decision: nearness to family, schools, work, convenience to community services and public transportation, the area's tax base, the overall safety and well-being of the neighborhood? What can we afford? Which is preferable for us, to buy or to rent?

RELIGION   Religion can be a source of comfort and support to couples, or it can be a source of conflict. If conflict occurs over religion, it may be because partners belong to different religions, have different values, or do not attach the same importance to religion.

QUESTIONS TO CONSIDER

What role will religion play in our relationship? Are we religiously compatible? Is this important to us? Will we attend services together? Separately? Will we raise our children in a specific religion?

RELATIONSHIPS WITH OTHERS   In many marriages today, couples often experience difficulty in trying to manage work, marriage, and other social responsibilities. Finding time to spend together may require making adjustments in the time devoted to other relationships.

How do we feel about each other's relatives and friends? How much interaction do we want to have with them? How will we decide where to spend our holidays and vacations? How will relationships with others be determined? How will we manage to keep time for ourselves?

CONFLICT RESOLUTION Every couple will experience conflict in their relationship at one time or another. The critical factor in the relationship is not the experience of conflict but rather how the conflict is handled.

QUESTIONS TO CONSIDER

What will we do when things don't seem to be working out right? What mechanisms can we create for resolving disagreements? Will we be willing to get counseling if we are having problems? Have our parents or any of our friends been divorced? What are our attitudes regarding divorce?

RENEWABILITY, CHANGE, AND TERMINATION OF CONTRACT People and conditions change over time. An effective contract allows for these possibilities. Couples are well advised to have periodic reviews of how the contract is working and what changes, if any, should be made.

QUESTIONS TO CONSIDER

How will we provide for a periodic reevaluation and change (if necessary) in this contract? Under what conditions will we terminate this contract?

These are only a few of the many issues and decisions we all face in the course of our lives. The decisions that are made will vary from one individual and family to the next. No single pattern can meet everyone's needs. Each individual and family must decide what arrangement is best for them. The most critical factor in all these areas is communication. All too frequently couples don't discuss these issues before becoming partners, with the result that they often begin a relationship with unrealistic expectations. Although communicating on these issues early in your relationship cannot by itself guarantee happiness or long-term stability, it can improve the probability of achieving these goals.

One final note: No marriage or family is ever completely free of problems or conflicts. Recognizing that fact and making yourself knowledgeable about the availability of outside resources and support can help reduce anxiety about the tensions and conflicts that may occur in your relationship from time to time. Realizing that other couples experience similar problems and that most of these problems can be overcome with effort and outside support increases the possibility of long-term stability in relationships.

SUMMARY

There is reason to assume that some of the marriage and family trends that we have observed since the 1950s will continue into the next century but at a slower pace. Families will continue to play a central, if somewhat altered, role in people's lives. Currently the vast majority of people report satisfaction with their family life, and there is every reason to believe that this trend will continue.

Nevertheless, families require a supportive social environment if they are to remain strong and vital. The United States faces several serious family-related problems that need attention: the declining economic welfare of families, the declining welfare of children, and the rapid growth in the numbers of the elderly. Most of the factors contributing to these problems are structural in nature and will require structural changes to solve them.

Applying a sociological perspective to our individual choices regarding marriage and family life can help us to make more effective decisions and to create an environment that may be more conducive to long-term stability in our relationships.

QUESTIONS FOR STUDY AND REFLECTION

1. Describe the marriage and family trends that you believe are most likely to continue into the twenty-first century. Which trends do you believe will change? What evidence is there for your position?

2. Describe what you consider to be the most serious problems confronting current and future families. What are the causes of these problems and what steps can couples and society take to minimize their impact?

3. How can the sociological perspective be applied to an individual's personal life? What are the advantages and disadvantages of doing so?

4. Given all that you have read throughout this text, how would you characterize the current status of marriages and families in the United States? What do you see as the main issues in the current debate over family values? How do you evaluate that debate?

FURTHER READING

BEAVERS, ROBERT W., AND ROBERT HAMPSON. 1992. *Successful Families*. New York: Norton. The authors develop a systems approach (see Chapter 2) to the process of building successful families.

HAMBURG, DAVID A. 1992. *Today's Children: Creating a Future for a Generation in Crisis*. New York: Times Books. A physician and nationally recognized authority on child development provides a comprehensive overview of the crisis today's children face and the decisions that society must make to protect them.

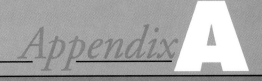

Appendix **A**

THE ANATOMY OF HUMAN SEXUALITY

In Chapter 6, we discussed the physiology of sexuality, what happens to our bodies when we are sexually aroused. We also discussed Masters and Johnson's typology of the stages of human sexual response. The following description of female and male sexual anatomy should help you understand the material presented in Chapter 6. We begin by describing the reproductive anatomy of the female body and male body. We then proceed to a brief overview of sexual dysfunctions.

FEMALE SEXUAL ANATOMY

Most of the female sexual organs are located inside the body. The external parts of the female genital organs are known collectively as the *vulva* (the Latin term for "covering"). As Figure A.1 shows, the female external genitalia extend from the mons pubis or mons veneris to the anal opening and include the clitoris, labia majora, labia minora, urethral and vaginal openings, hymen, and perineum.

The *mons veneris* ("mountain of Venus") is the fatty tissue over the pubic bone and is located approximately 6 inches below the navel. At puberty,

the mons develops a covering of hair that, in some cases, hides the vulva. The mons separates into two large, thick, and spongy folds of flesh called the *labia majora* (outer lips), which are dark colored and are covered with pubic hair. The labia majora extend from the mons to the hairless flat area of skin between the vaginal opening and the anus, called the *perineum*. Within the labia majora are the labia minora, clitoris, hymen, and the urethral and vaginal openings.

The labia majora act as protection or a cover for two inner folds of thin flesh called the *labia minora* (inner lips). The labia minora contain numerous nerve endings that are connected to pleasure centers in the brain. When stimulated, the labia minora become increasingly sensitive, an experience that many women find sexually enjoyable. In addition, the labia minora contain erectile tissues that, during sexual arousal, become engorged with blood, swell two to three times their unstimulated size, and protrude from the labia majora, clearing the way to the vaginal opening.

The *clitoris* lies at the base of the mons, just below the point where the labia join near the top of the vulva. When unstimulated, the clitoris is partial-

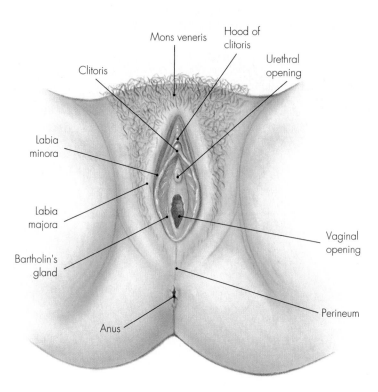

FIGURE A.1 Female Genitalia

ly covered by membranous flesh referred to as the *clitoral hood*. The clitoris has a *shaft* and a *glans*, or head. The clitoris is the center of sexual arousal for females. It contains an abundance of nerve endings and is extremely sensitive to touching and pressure, especially the glans. The overall length of the shaft and the glans clitoris combined is generally between $\frac{1}{4}$ inch and 1 inch. The clitoris is the primary source of sexual arousal and orgasm in females. In fact, Masters and Johnson's (1966) well-known work shows conclusively that all orgasms in women are caused by clitoral stimulation, whether direct or indirect. When the clitoris is erotically stimulated, the hollow areas of erectile tissue engorge with blood, the shaft becomes stiff and extends in length, and the glans becomes larger and harder. Immediately before and during orgasm, the clitoris withdraws beneath the clitoral hood and sometimes flattens and recedes to about one-half its unstimulated length.

Barely visible just below the clitoris is the very small *urethral opening*, through which urine is excreted. Some researchers have found that during sexual arousal, some women emit fluids from their urethra

(Strong and Reynolds, 1982). Below the urethral opening is the *vagina (vaginal opening)*, a muscular, elastic opening that is capable of expanding during sexual arousal to accommodate the penis and during childbirth to accommodate the passage of an infant (see Appendix C). The *Bartholin's glands*, two tiny, mucus-producing organs, lie on each side of the vaginal opening. These glands sometimes emit a small amount of fluid during sexual arousal, although the major amount of fluid that facilitates the insertion of the penis into the vagina is secreted through the vaginal walls.

Some researchers (for example, Whipple and Perry, 1981) claim that women have an erotically sensitive spot just inside the vaginal entrance. This spot, referred to as the *Grafenberg spot*, or *G-spot*, is simply a tiny bump on the anterior wall of the vagina. When stimulated, this bump doubles its usual size and causes sensations similar to those experienced during urination.

In some women, the vaginal opening may be partially closed by a thin membrane called the *hymen*, which is located just inside the entrance to the vagina. The hymen may be broken accidentally or intentionally before a woman's first copulation experience (for example, by athletic activities or inserting a tampon). If the hymen has not been ruptured prior to first intercourse it may tear at that time and cause bleeding, discomfort, or pain. The hymen has no role in sexual pleasure or reproduction but carries social significance in many societies, where chastity in women is highly valued and the unruptured hymen is considered to be an indication of virginity.

Finally, just below the perineum is the *anus*, the opening through which solid, or fecal, wastes leave the body. Although the anus is not part of the female sexual anatomy, it is surrounded by sensitive tissue and is sometimes stimulated as part of sexual activity (Donatelle, Davis, and Hoover, 1994).

MALE SEXUAL ANATOMY

The major male sex organs lie outside the body (Figure A.2). They are the *penis* and the *scrotum*. When a male is sexually unaroused his external sex organs hang loosely from his pubic area.

The penis is located at the base of the abdomen and consists of three distinct parts: the shaft and the glans, which are external or visible, and the root, which is internal. The *shaft* is the spongy part of the penis and is covered with thin, sensitive, loose skin. At the end or head of the penis is the *glans penis*, a smooth, cone-shaped tip. At birth, all males have a fold of skin, called *foreskin*, that folds over the glans. Most hospitals in the United States routinely remove this foreskin through a surgical procedure called *circumcision*. At the tip of the glans penis is the *urethral meatus*, a tiny opening through which urine and semen pass. The penis contains a high concentration of nerve endings, making it generally the most sexually sensitive part of the male body. Most of the penile touch-sensitive nerve endings are concentrated in the glans penis, particularly around the *coronal ridge*, the crown-shaped ridge at the rear of the glans.

The penis contains muscles, blood vessels, tissues, and nerves. Penile tissue consists of three parallel tubes of spongy erectile tissue: two large tubes, the *corpora cavenosa*, that lie above the third, the *corpus*

FIGURE A.2   Male Genitalia

Source: Adapted from Frederic Martini, *Fundamentals of Anatomy and Physiology*, 2d ed. Englewood Cliffs, NJ: Prentice Hall, 1992. Drawing by Craig Luce.

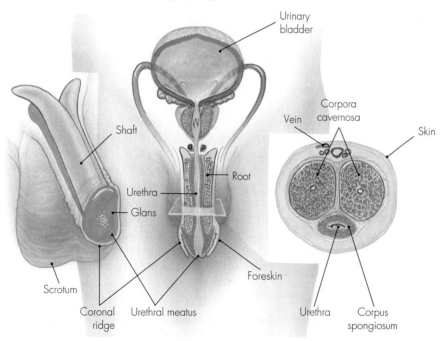

spongiosum. The flaccid (soft) penis lies on the scrotum and is generally 3 to 4 inches long. When the penis is stimulated, it becomes engorged with blood and thus becomes hard and erect, increasing in size to 5 to 10 inches.

Behind the shaft of the penis is a hanging sac or pouch of wrinkled, elastic skin called the *scrotum*. The scrotum holds two *testes* (or *testicles*), oval-shaped structures that produce sperm and the male hormone testosterone.

SEXUAL DYSFUNCTIONS*

Sexual dysfunction is a broad term that includes a number of specific problems. We describe the most common sexual dysfunctions found among women and men, distinguishing them as much as possible along gender lines.

SEXUAL DYSFUNCTIONS IN WOMEN

The most common sexual dysfunctions found among women are related to penetration and orgasm.

Inhibited sexual excitement refers to a lack of erotic response or feeling during sexual activity. A woman who experiences inhibited sexual excitement does not show any of the physiological manifestations of arousal such as expansion of the vagina, nipple erection, or vaginal lubrication. Consequently, sexual intercourse might be uncomfortable or even painful. In some cases a woman may never have experienced arousal (a *primary* dysfunction). In other cases a woman may have experienced arousal in the past but is not currently experiencing it (a *secondary* dysfunction).

Anorgasmia refers to the inability of a woman to reach orgasm. Prior to 1970, this dysfunction along with several others was lumped under the term *frigidity*. There are many forms of anorgasmia. In *primary anorgasmia*, no matter what type of stimulation has been tried, a woman has never experienced

orgasm. In *secondary anorgasmia*, a woman has been regularly orgasmic in the past but is not currently orgasmic. A third category, *situational anorgasmia*, describes a woman who experiences orgasm only under certain specific circumstances, such as in a hotel room but not in her own bedroom. Finally, *random anorgasmia* refers to a woman who has experienced orgasm in a variety of sexual activities but only on an infrequent basis.

The immediate cause of anorgasmia is an involuntary inhibition of the natural orgasmic reflex, but other factors can contribute to this condition, such as severe chronic illness, drug and alcohol abuse, hormonal deficiencies, diabetes, and various medications such as tranquilizers and blood pressure medications. In addition, social factors such as the double standard regarding the acceptability of sexual feelings in women and men can also contribute to anorgasmia. Some anorgasmic women find sexual activities pleasurable and satisfying even though they do not experience orgasm; others experience depression, a lack of self-esteem, or a sense of futility.

About 2 to 3 percent of adult women experience pain during penetration. *Vaginismus* is a condition in which the muscles around the outer part of the vagina contract involuntarily during penetration, closing the vagina almost totally. In most cases, vaginismus is specific to vaginal penetration and does not necessarily affect other aspects of a woman's sexual responsiveness. In some women, however, the same involuntary muscle spasms may occur in response to any attempt to enter the vagina. Therefore, foreplay, such as the insertion of a finger, or even gynecological exams will produce the involuntary spasms and vaginal closure.

Vaginismus may be caused by factors such as poor vaginal lubrication, the use of various drugs, some illnesses, vaginal infections, and pelvic disorders. Most often, however, it seems to be a result of psychological factors, for example, a strict religious upbringing, having been taught that sex is unpleasant and painful, fear of or hostility toward men, and psychological reactions to rape. Reactions by partners of a woman with vaginismus range from self-blame or passivity about sex to impatience, resentment, and open hostility. Sometimes vaginismus can be treated with simple relaxation exercises.

Another sexual dysfunction of women is *dyspareunia*, or painful intercourse, which can occur at any point during or immediately following intercourse.

---

*The discussion of sexual dysfunctions draws heavily on the following sources: William Masters and Virginia Johnson, 1985, *Human Sexual Response* (Boston: Little, Brown); and Morton G. Harmatz and Melinda A. Novak, 1983, *Human Sexuality* (New York: Harper and Row).

The pain of dyspareunia can range from burning sensations to sharp, searing pain or cramps and can occur in the vagina or in the pelvic region or abdomen. Although the exact incidence of dyspareunia is not known, it is estimated that approximately 15 percent of adult women experience painful intercourse a few times each year, and 1 to 2 percent experience it on a regular basis. The anxiety about the pain associated with intercourse can make a woman tense and decrease her sexual enjoyment or cause her to abstain altogether either from sexual intercourse or from all forms of sexual activity.

Finally, a very small number of women experience *rapid orgasm*, a condition in which a woman reaches orgasm too quickly. A minority of women who experience rapid orgasm lose interest in further sexual activity and may even find further activity to be physically uncomfortable. Most of these women, however, remain sexually aroused and interested, sometimes going on to have multiple orgasms. These women frequently view this condition as an asset rather than a liability. Sometimes the woman's partner will view this condition in personal terms, taking it to be symbolic of her or his unique lovemaking ability.

SEXUAL DYSFUNCTIONS IN MEN

The most common sexual dysfunctions among males are related to erection and ejaculation.

Erectile dysfunction refers to the condition in which a male cannot have or maintain an erection that is firm enough for coitus. Erectile dysfunction is sometimes referred to as *impotence* and can be classified as either *primary*, in which case a male has never experienced an erection that has been adequate enough to have sexual intercourse, or *secondary*, in which case a male has previously experienced one or more erections. Of the two, secondary erectile dysfunction is more common. Erectile dysfunction can occur at any age, and it takes many forms. In only a few cases is the man totally unable to have an erection. Usually the man has partial erections, but they are not firm enough for vaginal or anal insertion. In some cases, a man may be able to have an erection but only under certain conditions, such as during masturbation. Because losing or not having erections is so common among men, isolated incidents do *not* constitute a sexual dysfunction. Only when such incidents occur

in at least 25 percent of a man's sexual activities is the man said to be experiencing secondary impotence.

Although some physical conditions can cause primary erectile dysfunction, most cases are caused by psychological conditions such as a high level of anxiety or stress, a highly religious upbringing, early homosexual experiences that led to feelings of guilt and confusion, or a single traumatic sexual intercourse experience. Secondary erectile dysfunction is also caused by a number of factors. In most cases it is brought on by some precipitating event such as fatigue, work pressure, financial problems, drug or alcohol abuse, depression, or arguments. Men react to erectile dysfunction in a number of ways, the most common of which is a feeling of dismay. The partner of a male with erectile dysfunction may blame herself or himself, thinking that she or he is not skilled enough to arouse the man's passion.

Premature ejaculation, or *rapid ejaculation*, is a common dysfunction in which a male reaches orgasm too quickly. In most cases, the male ejaculates just before or immediately after entering his partner. Because ejaculation is so rapid, stimulation of his partner does not occur. As a result, both partners are often dissatisfied. Some men are not bothered by ejaculating quickly, whereas others become embarrassed or frustrated, develop low self-esteem, or question their masculinity.

Premature ejaculation is believed to be the most common male sexual dysfunction, affecting an estimated 15 to 20 percent of men on a regular basis. Less than 20 percent of these men consider this condition to be problematic enough to seek therapy. The primary causes of premature ejaculation are psychological factors such as anxiety or early experiences with rushing through intercourse or other sexual activity for fear of being caught (for example, having sex in the backseat of a car).

Another sexual dysfunction for men is *inhibited male orgasm*, sometimes referred to as *retarded ejaculation*, in which a man is unable to ejaculate during sexual intercourse despite a firm erection. Although the muscle contractions of orgasm do not occur, fluid containing sperm may leave the penis and enter the vagina; thus, pregnancy is possible. As with erectile dysfunction, inhibited orgasm can be *primary*, in which a man has never ejaculated during coitus, or *secondary*, in which a man who has experienced ejaculation and orgasm in the past suddenly develops a problem. In both instances, ejaculation is often possible by masturbation or some other noncoital stimulation. Drug and alcohol use accounts for about 10 percent of cases of inhibited male orgasm. Inhibited male orgasm should be distinguished from *retrograde ejaculation,* a condition in which the bladder neck does not close off properly during orgasm, causing the semen to spurt backward into the bladder.

Another male dysfunction, *priapism,* is a condition in which the penis remains erect for prolonged periods of time. Priapism results from damage to valves that are supposed to regulate penile blood flow. Under this condition, erection can last for days, but it is generally not accompanied by a desire for sex. Prolonged erection can be painful as well as embarrassing for most men.

Finally, men, like women, can suffer from *painful intercourse,* or *dyspareunia.* Typically, the pain is felt in the penis. Some men, however, experience the pain in the testes or even internally, where it might be related to a problem with the prostate or seminal vesicles. Both physical and psychological factors can contribute to dyspareunia. Physical factors include inflammation or infection of the penis, testes, urethra, foreskin, or prostate. A few men experience pain if the tip of the penis is irritated by vaginal contraceptive foams or creams.

Appendix B

SEXUALLY TRANSMITTED DISEASES

Sexually transmitted disease (STD) is a broad term used to describe a variety of bacterial, viral, yeast, and protozoan infections that are almost always transmitted by sexual contact and to refer to various other infections that are sometimes transmitted in nonsexual ways. In the past, many of these diseases were referred to as *venereal diseases*. Most STDs are transmitted through genital–genital, oral–genital, and anal–genital contact. Some STDs, such as AIDS and hepatitis B, however, can be transmitted through blood transfusions or the use of infected needles. In addition, as we pointed out in Chapter 10, some STDs can also be passed from the mother to the fetus through the placenta and from the mother to the newborn as it passes through the birth canal.

STDs vary greatly in terms of their symptoms, progressions, treatments, seriousness, and outcomes. Most STDs can be prevented with proper care and can be cured with drugs. Being cured does not mean that a person cannot contract the same STD again at a later time. In addition, it is possible for a person to contract more than one STD at a time. In this appendix we present some of the most common STDs: chlamydia, gonorrhea, syphilis, genital herpes, papilloma, hepatitis B, trichomoniasis, moniliasis,

lymphogranuloma venereum, and chancroid. A full discussion of AIDS appears in Chapter 6.

Chlamydia is probably the most common sexually transmitted disease in this country. It affects between 3 and 4 million people every year (McNair, 1988). Chlamydial infections are caused by a bacterium (*Chlamydia trachomatis*) that attacks the reproductive system. The majority of infected females and about one-third of infected males experience no symptoms. In the other two-thirds of males, symptoms include a whitish discharge from the penis. Sometimes infected females or males experience a mild irritation of the genitals and an itching or burning sensation during urination. Because chlamydia has symptoms similar to gonorrhea, it sometimes goes undetected. Untreated, it can result in sterility in both females and males, pelvic inflammatory disease (PID), infection of the uterus and tubes, infections in newborns, miscarriages, and stillbirths (Allgeier and Allgeier, 1988). Chlamydia can be cured with antibiotics such as tetracycline.

Gonorrhea is a highly infectious disease that can affect the genitourinary tract, tissues of the genitals, fallopian tubes, rectum, and cervix. It can also occur in other areas of the body such as the mouth, throat, and eyes. Gonorrhea is caused by the bacterium

Neisseria gonorrhoeae. It can be transmitted by any form of sexual contact ranging from sexual intercourse to fellatio, anal intercourse, and, in rare cases, cunnilingus and kissing. It is almost always transmitted through sexual intercourse, however, because the bacterium cannot live more than a few seconds outside the human body. It generally takes from 2 to 7 days after contact with an infected person for symptoms to appear. A woman who has intercourse once with an infected male runs a 50 percent risk of contracting gonorrhea, whereas a man who has intercourse once with an infected female runs only about a 20 to 25 percent risk of contracting the disease (Masters and Johnson, 1985).

Symptoms in women include a yellowish green vaginal discharge, pain in the abdominal area, burning during urination, fever, abnormal menstrual bleeding, and pain in the stomach. In males, symptoms include a thick yellowish green discharge from the penis, inflammation of the tip of the penis, burning during urination, and the appearance of pus or blood in the urine. As with chlamydia, many males and the majority of females show no symptoms during the early stages of the disease. When left untreated, gonorrhea can cause considerable damage to a person's reproductive capabilities, possibly causing sterility. It can also cause PID, heart disease, arthritis, and blindness. Gonorrhea can be cured with antibiotics, the most effective of which is penicillin G.

Syphilis is a chronic infectious disease caused by a type of bacterium known as a spirochete. Because the bacterium generally dies within seconds outside the body, it is usually transmitted through sexual intercourse, but it can also be contracted from a blood transfusion, or it can be transmitted from a mother to the fetus. Syphilis progresses through three stages of increasing severity: the primary, secondary, and tertiary stages. If allowed to run its full course, syphilis can cause paralysis, blindness, heart disease, nervous disorders, insanity, and even death. The incubation period for syphilis is 10 to 90 days.

Primary stage. Between 2 and 4 weeks after infection a hard, crusty, painless oval sore called a *chancre* appears on the vaginal wall, cervix, penis, scrotum, anus, tongue, lips, or throat. It begins as a dull red spot that develops first into a pimple and then into the chancre. If immediate attention is not given to these symptoms they may disappear, but this does not mean that the syphilis has cured itself. The

syphilis remains, and after several months the symptoms of the secondary stage appear.

Secondary stage. The secondary stage begins anywhere from 1 week to 6 months after the chancre heals if it has been untreated. In this phase, a person may experience reddish patches in the mouth and around the genitals that emit a clear liquid and are highly infectious. Other symptoms include a non-itching rash, sore throat, fever, headaches, and weight and hair loss. These symptoms can last from 3 to 6 months, but, as in the primary stage, they may disappear if they are not treated. For some people, these symptoms will appear and disappear many times if untreated. Between 50 and 70 percent of people with untreated syphilis remain in this stage for the rest of their lives. In the remaining cases, syphilis resurfaces after a latency period that can last for many years.

Tertiary stage. In this stage a number of more serious symptoms appear. Some people develop ulcers in the eyes, liver, lungs, or digestive tract. A few people suffer damage to the brain and spinal cord, which can result in paralysis, dementia, or fatal heart damage. Pregnant women with syphilis almost always pass it on to their offspring, who may be born blind, deaf, or deformed, or may die soon after birth.

Penicillin is the best treatment for syphilis and is effective at all stages of the disease. Although existing damage cannot be reversed, penicillin can prevent further damage.

The term *herpes* refers to any one of several viral diseases characterized by the eruption of blisters of the skin or mucous membrane. One type, *genital herpes,* received widespread attention in the 1980s as a result of its epidemic spread. Genital herpes is caused by the herpes simplex virus types 1 and 2. Genital herpes is usually transmitted by sexual contact but can also be transmitted by kissing or by touching your genitals after putting your fingers in your mouth. The incubation period for genital herpes is 2 to 6 days after being infected. Symptoms of the infection are similar for women and men. The first signs are itching, irritation, and a rash at the site of the infection. Other fairly common symptoms include pain or burning during urination, discharge from the urethra or vagina, soreness and swelling of lymph nodes in the groin, fever, weakness, and fatigue. Symptomatic blisters usually occur on the penis, scrotum, anus, vulva, clitoris, cervix, or mouth. These blisters are extremely painful and, over time, will rupture and eventually heal themselves even without treatment.

As with syphilis, the disappearance of the blisters does not mean that the virus is no longer in the body. Instead, the virus is still present, and blistering can recur at any time. Untreated, genital herpes can increase the risk of cervical cancer in women and can spread to women's and men's eyes from the hands. Women, more often than men, also develop aseptic meningitis, an inflammation of the covering of the brain. Pregnant women with herpes are likely to pass it on to their offspring, who might suffer blindness, brain damage, or even death. There is no cure for genital herpes, nor is there a single effective treatment. A drug called acyclovir is useful in lessening the severity of the symptoms. People with herpes should avoid having sexual contact during periods when the blisters are apparent.

Papilloma, or venereal warts, is one of the fastest-growing STDs. Venereal warts are dry, often painless, grayish white warts with a cauliflowerlike surface that grow on, inside, or near the genitals or anus. These warts are caused by a sexually transmitted virus and are not always visible. There may be one or a cluster of warts, and they may coexist with other STDs. Venereal warts may cause pain during sex and may multiply during pregnancy. If untreated, venereal warts increase the risk of cervical cancer in women and penile cancer in men. There is no known cure for venereal warts. They can, however, be treated with liquid nitrogen or podophyllin ointment, or they can be burned off surgically.

Hepatitis B is one of three main types of viral hepatitis (the other two are hepatitis A, and non-A, non-B hepatitis). It is a viral infection of the liver and varies in terms of seriousness from mild symptoms such as poor appetite or indigestion, to diarrhea, vomiting, fever, and fatigue; to more serious medical problems such as jaundiced skin and eyes. Although hepatitis B is generally transmitted through blood or blood products, many Americans contract the disease through sexual contact. Hepatitis B can also be spread by saliva, vaginal secretions, seminal fluid, and other body fluids. Many people with hepatitis B remain in a carrier state for years or even a lifetime. Hepatitis B increases the risk of liver cancer and other liver diseases.

Trichomoniasis is caused by a one-celled protozoan, *Trichomonas vaginalis*, that thrives and grows rapidly in moist, warm tissues such as the vagina and the urethra. The disease is most common among women. As many as 25 percent of women will probably contract trichomoniasis at some point. Trichomoniasis has probably received the least attention of all STDs. In fact, because it can be transmitted in many different ways besides sexual contact, some experts in the field do not consider it an STD.

Among women symptoms are generally a foul-smelling, foamy, yellowish green vaginal discharge accompanied by vaginal itching and irritation. In addition, sexual intercourse may be painful. Men experience itching, pain in the urethra, and a slight discharge similar to that caused by gonorrhea. Most infected people do not exhibit symptoms, however. Although lack of treatment does not carry any serious consequences, it does make control of the spread of trichomoniasis difficult. Trichomoniasis is commonly treated with the drug metronidazole, which is about 80 percent effective in both women and men.

Moniliasis, like trichomoniasis, is an infection that can be contracted through both sexual and nonsexual contact. Sometimes referred to as a *yeast infection*, moniliasis is caused by the fungus *Candida albicans*. Women and men seldom exhibit symptoms of this infection. When it invades the vaginal area of women, however, it sometimes produces a lumpy, white discharge that resembles cottage cheese. There is also itching and inflammation of the vaginal area, and intercourse becomes extremely painful. If untreated, moniliasis does not produce any serious complications, but it is extremely uncomfortable and severely limits sexual activity. It is generally treated with vaginal creams or suppositories that contain the drug nyastatin, but the infection can and does recur repeatedly with some women.

Lymphogranuloma venereum (LGV) is a bacterial infection caused by *Chlamydia trachomatis*, which invades the lymph system, a network of vessels in close contact with blood vessels. Of Asian origin, this disease was almost nonexistent in the United States before the Vietnam War. The first symptom of LGV is a small blister that usually appears on the external genitals between 5 and 21 days after contact. Sometimes, however, the blister appears inside the vagina or the urethra. The blister usually heals itself within a few days, but the disease moves on and settles in the lymph glands nearest the infected site. The glands swell and form a painful sausage-shaped mass that settles within the fold of the groin. Other symptoms are similar to those of the flu, including chills, fever, headache, pain in the joints, and upset stomach. If untreated, LGV can produce serious effects, including swelling of the inguinal (groin) lymph nodes, penis, labia or clitoris, and closure of the rectum. Although the disease is curable, treatment is often difficult because the infection responds very slowly to antibiotics. The most effective forms of treatment seem to be tetracycline and sulfa drugs.

Chancroid, like LGV, is a tropical bacterial infection that is usually transmitted by sexual intercourse, although it also can be contracted through less intimate contact. Chancroid is caused by the bacterium *Haemophilus ducreyi* and is particularly contagious if there are breaks or cuts in the skin. The primary symptom of chancroid is one or more ulcerated sores that appear on the genitals 3 to 7 days after exposure. In the beginning the sores appear as pimplelike bumps, that eventually burst into very painful and open sores that bleed easily. The lymph glands in the groin area may also become swollen, and in some cases the sores may spread over the entire genital area. If the disease is left untreated, chancroid gangrene can occur. Chancroid can be cured within a short period of time with tetracycline or sulfa drugs.

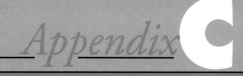

CONCEPTION, PREGNANCY, AND CHILDBIRTH

In Appendix A we discussed the sexual anatomy of women and men. Because our focus was on human sexual arousal, pleasure, and dysfunctions, we looked specifically at female and male external anatomy and physiology. Human sexual organs are used not only to achieve sexual gratification but also to conceive children. In this appendix our focus is on human reproduction; thus we describe the female and male organs that are critical to the reproductive process as well as to the female menstrual cycle. In addition, we present visual illustrations and a brief discussion of various aspects of conception, pregnancy, and childbirth to supplement the discussion of these topics in Chapter 10.

FEMALE INTERNAL ANATOMY AND PHYSIOLOGY

The parts of a woman's anatomy that are critical to reproduction are internal and include the vagina, ovaries, paired fallopian tubes, uterus, and cervix. Figure C.1 shows the female reproductive system and the major structures of the uterus.

Leading from the vaginal opening to inside the woman's body is the *vagina*, a thin-walled elastic structure 3 to 4 inches long. The vagina functions in a number of ways: It receives the penis during het-erosexual intercourse and serves as a depository for sperm during intercourse, as a passageway for menstrual flow, and as the birth canal.

The female body contains two *ovaries*, almond-shaped structures that lie on each side of the uterus. The ovaries produce ova (eggs) and the hormones estrogen and progesterone. Ova are embedded in folli-cles near the surfaces of ovaries; each follicle contains one ovum. A female is born with about 400,000 imma-ture eggs. Only about 400 of these eggs mature and are released over the course of a woman's fertile years, how-ever. More specifically, each month during a woman's reproductive years one or the other ovary releases one (or infrequently more than one) egg on a day approxi-mately midway between the menstrual periods into the abdominal cavity , a process known as *ovulation*.

Following ovulation the egg begins to migrate toward the *fallopian tubes*, small structures extending 4 inches laterally from each side of the uterus to the ovaries. Hairlike projections called *fimbria* at the end of the fallopian tubes create currents with lashing movements that draw eggs into and down through the tube. Fertilization generally occurs inside the fal-lopian tubes at the end closest to the ovaries.

Once fertilized, the egg continues its journey through the fallopian tube and into the *uterus* or *womb*. The uterus is a hollow, pear-shaped organ,

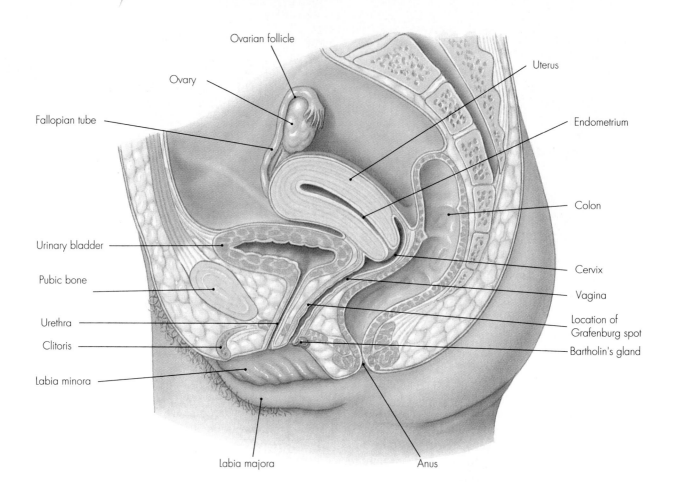

FIGURE C.1 Female Reproductive System (above), and Major Structures of the Uterus (right)

Source: Adapted from Frederic Martini, *Fundamentals of Anatomy and Physiology*, 2d ed. Englewood Cliffs, NJ: Prentice Hall, 1992. Drawings by William C. Ober, M.D., and Claire W. Garrison, R.N.

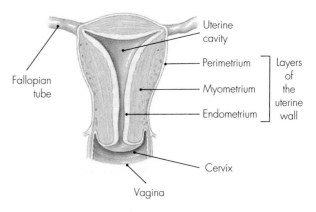

approximately 3 inches long and 3 inches wide, composed of three alternating layers of muscle: endometrium, myometrium, and perimetrium. The endometrium—the innermost layer—is rich in blood vessels after ovulation. If fertilization does not occur, the endometrium sloughs off and is discharged from the body during menstruation. If the egg is fertilized, it implants in the endometrium, where it develops, is nourished, and grows for approximately 9 months.

At the lower end of the uterus is the *cervix*, a narrow opening leading into the vagina. At birth, the baby forces itself through the cervix and the vagina to the outside world.

MALE INTERNAL ANATOMY AND PHYSIOLOGY

Male reproductive organs can be found both within and outside the body (see Figure C.2). The external organs (testes, scrotum, penis) are important in both sexual arousal and gratification as well as reproduction. The internal reproductive system includes the seminal vesicles, prostate gland, vas deferens, seminiferous tubules, Cowper's glands, urethra, epididymis, and interstitial cells.

The *testes* (*testicles*), the primary reproductive organs in males, produce both the spermatozoa necessary for reproduction and male hormones, primarily testosterone. Each testicle consists of three sets of tissue that come together to form a tube: seminiferous tubules, where sperm are produced; epididymis, where sperm are stored; and interstitial cells, where the male sex hormones are produced. From the testes the sperm travel through a duct system (epididymis, vas deferens, ejaculatory duct, and urethra) until they are expelled from the penis during ejaculation.

If ejaculation occurs, sperm leave the testes through the second part of the duct, two small tubes called the *vas deferens*, which lead from the testes to the prostate gland, where they form the urethra.

Contractions during ejaculation send the sperm into the two *ejaculatory ducts* that run through the prostate gland. After mixing with seminal fluid to form semen, sperm are propelled through the *urethra*, the tube through which males urinate and through which sperm leave the body.

Three male organs play key roles in helping the sperm move through the reproductive system to the penis and outside the body: the seminal vesicles, the prostate gland, and the Cowper's glands. The *seminal vesicles*, two small organs located behind the bladder, secrete fluids, many of which come from the prostate gland. These fluids add volume to the semen. The *prostate gland*, located under the bladder, where the vas deferens meet, adds an alkaline fluid to semen that protects the sperm. During orgasm it contracts, helping the semen to move out of the urethra. Located just below the prostate gland are two glands called *Cowper's glands*, or *bulbourethral glands*. These tiny glands produce an alkaline fluid that prolongs the life of sperm.

FIGURE C.2 Male Reproductive System and Structure of the Scrotum

Source: Adapted from Frederic Martini, *Fundamentals of Anatomy and Physiology*, 2d ed. Englewood Cliffs, NJ: Prentice Hall, 1992. Drawing by Craig Luce.

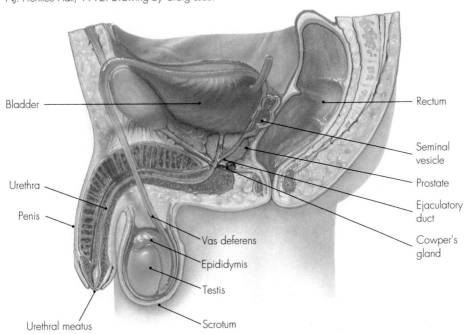

CONCEPTION, PREGNANCY, AND CHILDBIRTH

Conception, pregnancy, and childbirth are profound events. When female ovum and male sperm unite, conception occurs, marking the beginning of pregnancy. During the course of a pregnancy a woman's body experiences a number of internal and external changes as she carries a developing embryo and later fetus within her uterus. By the end of the fourth month of pregnancy, most women begin to "show" (their stomach swells as the fetus develops and grows) and can feel the fetus moving. Once the fetus is ready for birth it will turn its body so that its head is downward toward the cervix. Figure C.3 illustrates the various stages of labor and delivery. In most cases, the fetus is expelled from the uterus without complications.

FIGURE C.3 Labor and Delivery

Source: Adapted from Frederic Martini, *Fundamentals of Anatomy and Physiology,* 2d ed. Englewood Cliffs, NJ: Prentice Hall, 1992, p. 977, Figure 29–14.

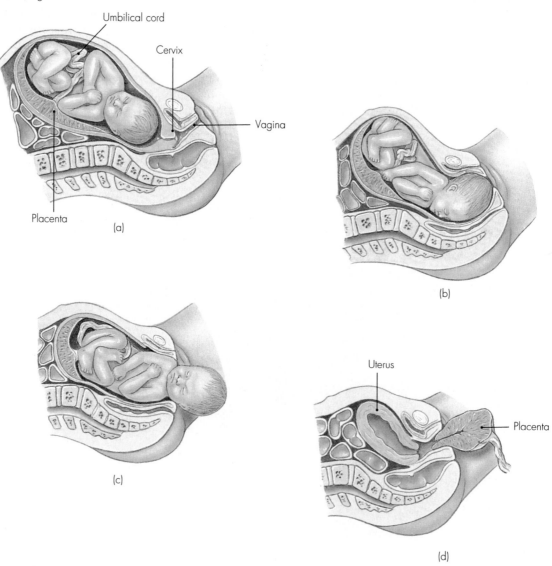

METHODS OF ABORTION

Approximately one-third of all reported abortions are spontaneous (miscarriages). In these cases the developing embryo or fetus is expelled from the uterus naturally. A number of factors can trigger a spontaneous abortion. Emotional shock, abnormal development of the embryo or fetus, wearing an IUD while pregnant, and any problems of the uterus that would prevent further development of the embryo or fetus are among the most common sources of miscarriages. Abortions can also be induced either medically or surgically.

MEDICALLY INDUCED ABORTIONS

Medically induced abortions are sometimes used during the second trimester. Abortifacients are either injected into the amniotic sac or are used as vaginal suppositories. Prostaglandins (a type of fatty acid), saline solutions, and other toxic solutions are among the most common abortifacients. These substances bring on uterine contractions that cause the cervix to open. As a result, the fetus and placenta are expelled, as in a normal delivery. The process takes anywhere from 12 to 36 hours. This procedure is riskier than surgical methods due to the possibility of complications such as infection, hemorrhaging, and embolism. Possible side effects include gastrointestinal cramping and fever.

More recently a substance called RU-486 (see Chapter 9), a synthetic prostaglandin that acts as an abortifacient if taken early in the pregnancy, was developed in France. Although RU-486 has been used in Europe for a number of years, protests against the drug by antiabortion groups delayed its testing in the United States until 1993, when a few research groups began clinical trials of the drug.

SURGICAL METHODS OF ABORTION

Abortion in the early stages of pregnancy is a relatively simple and safe procedure, although any surgical procedure runs some risk and can have varying degrees of discomfort. The most common surgical methods of abortion in the first trimester are dilation and curettage (D & C) and vacuum aspiration. Dilation and evacuation (D & E) and hysterotomy are the methods used in second-trimester abortions.

DILATION AND CURETTAGE (D & C) In this surgical procedure the cervix is dilated (made larger), after which a curette (a spoon-shaped surgical instrument) is used to scrape the uterine wall. This procedure is usually done in a hospital, with the woman under local or general anesthesia. Although some women experience pain and bleeding after this procedure, full recovery occurs within 10 to 14 days. After a D & C women are advised to abstain from sexual intercourse for several weeks.

VACUUM ASPIRATION   Most abortions today utilize the vacuum aspiration method (also called vacuum curettage) because it is quicker, involves less blood loss, and has a shorter recovery time than a D & C. The procedure is performed under local anesthesia and takes less than 10 minutes. It can be done in a doctor's office. The cervix is dilated by a speculum (an expanding instrument), after which a small tube attached to a vacuum is inserted into the uterus. The fetus, placenta, and endometrial tissue are gently suctioned out. Over the next few days the woman may experience some cramping and bleeding. She is advised not to use tampons or have sexual intercourse for a week or two after the procedure.

DILATION AND EVACUATION (D & E)   Dilation and evacuation is similar to a D & C but is performed later in the pregnancy, usually between the thirteenth and sixteenth weeks. Local or general anesthesia is used. Because the pregnancy is more advanced and the fetus is larger, the cervix requires more dilation, and the uterine contents are removed through a combination of suction equipment, special forceps, and scraping with a curette. Because this procedure is performed later in the pregnancy, it carries a higher risk. Women may experience cramping and blood loss after undergoing a D & E.

HYSTEROTOMY   Hysterotomy carries the most risk and therefore is rarely used. It is performed in the second trimester and involves removing the fetus through an incision made in the woman's abdomen. It is equivalent to a Cesarean section. Because it involves major surgery, hospitalization is required.

METHODS OF BIRTH CONTROL

Avoiding sexual intercourse is the surest, safest, and most cost-effective way to prevent pregnancy. Many sex education programs aimed at adolescents stress abstinence as a way to avoid both pregnancy and sexually transmitted diseases, including AIDS. However, abstinence is not a popular choice with people who desire a mutually satisfying sexual relationship but do not want children. The following section examines the birth control techniques that are legally available to couples living in the United States.

STERILIZATION

Surgical sterilization runs a close second to abstinence in both reliability and, if a long-term view is taken, cost-effectiveness. This is now the most popular form of birth control among married couples in the United States. In the past, female sterilization, called *tubal ligation*, involved a major operation done under general anesthesia, requiring a hospital stay of 3 or 4 days. In this procedure an incision is made in the abdominal cavity so that each of the fallopian tubes (the ducts between the ovaries and the uterus) can be cut and tied, thus preventing sperm and ova from reaching each other. As with any major surgery, there is some risk of infection (around 7 percent) and some amount of discomfort. In addition, the procedure is costly.

In recent years two new procedures have been introduced that reduce all three of these problems. The first of these procedures is *laparoscopy*. Here the surgeon inserts a laparoscope (a thin instrument with a viewing lens) into a small incision in the abdomen. The incision requires only a stitch or two to close; thus, the procedure has been dubbed the "band-aid" approach. Using this incision (or a tiny second one), the surgeon inserts another small instrument that cauterizes the interior of the fallopian tubes. This procedure leads to the formation of scar tissue, which seals the tubes.

The second method is *minilaparotomy*. As with laparoscopy, general anesthesia is used, and a small incision is made in the lower abdomen, bringing the fallopian tubes into view. The tubes are then tied off or sealed with clips, rings, or electric current. Compared with tubal ligation, these two procedures are less painful, quicker (about 15 minutes), less likely to cause infection (1 percent), require less recovery time, and, because hospitalization is generally not required, less expensive (several hundreds as compared with several thousands of dollars). Many insurance policies cover both female and male sterilization.

Male sterilization is called a *vasectomy*. It costs about $400, takes about 30 minutes, and is usually done on an out-patient basis. During the procedure small incisions are made on each side of the scrotum, and then the vasa deferentia (sperm-carrying ducts) are cut and tied. This procedure does not prevent sperm production. Rather, when sperm are produced, instead of being ejaculated they are absorbed in the man's body. Discomfort is minimal. Although men should refrain from lifting heavy objects for a few days after surgery, most miss little or no work after the procedure, and they can resume sex within a week of the surgery. However, live sperm remain in parts of the reproductive system for several weeks after the vasectomy, so to be safe a couple should use an additional form of contraception. This other form of contraception can be eliminated once the semen is examined and found to be sperm-free. Overall, vasectomies are successful. In only about 1 percent of cases has a severed vas deferens rejoined itself, allowing sperm to be ejaculated again (Masters, Johnson, and Kolodny, 1988). Periodic semen examinations can detect any possible changes.

Sterilization has several clear advantages. Once it is done, no further thought need be given to the task of prevention. It is 100 percent effective, except in rare instances when the procedures haven't been performed properly. Most women and men who have undergone sterilization report little or no decrease in sexual desire or sexual pleasure. Some even report more enjoyment after the fear of pregnancy is removed. Sterilization has the added advantage of not interfering with sexual spontaneity.

Sterilization has certain drawbacks, however. A small percentage of women and men experience some psychological problems after sterilization, equating their loss of fertility with diminished feelings of femininity and masculinity. The biggest drawback is that sterilization is permanent, so couples should use this method only if they are certain that they don't want any children. Problems arise when couples change their mind about wanting children or when they remarry and their new spouse wants children.

If a reversal is sought, women can undergo surgery or men can have a vasovasotomy (reconnecting the vas). Neither procedure is generally covered by insurance nor is guaranteed to be successful. Today affluent couples can now avoid concern over permanency by freezing and storing sperm and ova before sterilization (see Chapter 9).

HORMONAL METHODS: IMPLANTS

Among the newest contraceptives on the market, approved by the Food and Drug Administration (FDA) in late 1990, is a thin, matchstick-sized, soft capsule containing the hormone progestin. Doctors implant six silicone rubber capsules under the skin of a woman's upper arm; they are not visible but can be felt by touch. The procedure is simple, done in a doctor's office under local anesthesia. The capsules slowly release the hormone and are effective for up to 5 years. Although the implant method has not as yet been widely tested, preliminary studies show a failure rate of less than 1 percent. Another major advantage of implants is that they are easy to remove, and when removed their contraceptive effects are immediately reversed. There are some disadvantages. The initial cost is high. The implants called Norplant cost $200 to $300, not including the fee for the procedure. Thereafter, though, there is no expense until they are removed. Some women with implants experience menstrual irregularities, including prolonged periods and spotting between periods. At this time the FDA considers this method as safe and effective as any other contraceptive currently available.

DEPO-PROVERA INJECTIONS

Although Depo-Provera has been widely used as a contraceptive outside the United States, the FDA first approved its use for that purpose in 1992. Depo-Provera contains a synthetic progesterone that blocks ovulation. It is injected into the buttocks every 3 months, and effectiveness is 99 percent. Although some women experience irregular bleeding during the first year of use, most women stop menstruating entirely after a year. Depo-Provera has a number of beneficial effects: It relieves the breast tenderness, headaches, and cramping associated with premenstrual syndrome; it decreases the risk of inflammatory disease and yeast infections; and preliminary studies suggest that it may decrease the risk of ovarian cancer. On the negative side, women who use Depo-Provera may gain weight, experience mood swings or depression, and may be at greater risk for developing breast cancer.

ORAL CONTRACEPTIVES ("THE PILL")

The birth control pill, available since the early 1960s, contains synthetically produced hormones estrogen and progesterone, which would be present during pregnancy. The hormones work to prevent ovulation, and they thicken cervical mucus, which prevents the entry of sperm. In the event that fertilization occurs, these hormones inhibit implantation. Birth control pills are available only with a doctor's prescription. A woman's medical history may rule out use of the Pill. Women suffering from hypertension, poor blood circulation, and other risk factors should not take the Pill because of the danger of blood clots and high blood pressure.

Pills come in packages of 20, 21, or 28 and cost $15 to $20 per package. For the pills to be effective, a woman must take them according to a monthly cycle. The woman takes the first pill on the fifth day after the start of menstruation. Thereafter she takes one pill each day at about the same time for 20 or 21 consecutive days. Her next menstrual period follows 2 to 5 days later, and she repeats the pattern. Some women prefer taking the 28-day pills (7 of which contain no hormones) because they find it easier to remember to take a pill every day. If a woman misses one pill, she must take it as soon as she remembers, taking the next pill right on schedule. If she misses two pills, she can't rely on the method, and she must use an additional method of contraception to protect herself.

The advantages of the Pill are its convenience, its noninterference with spontaneity during intercourse, and its high rate of effectiveness, when used correctly about 95 to 98 percent. Use of the Pill may also reduce the risk of ovarian and endometrial cancers, although this is not certain. Additionally, many women report reduced premenstrual tension and cramps and lighter blood flows during menstruation. However, the Pill causes side effects in about 25 percent of users. Some of these side effects are slight and

The birth-control devices shown below include the vaginal sponge, the IUD, the male condom, oral contraceptives, and a diaphragm with foam and jelly.

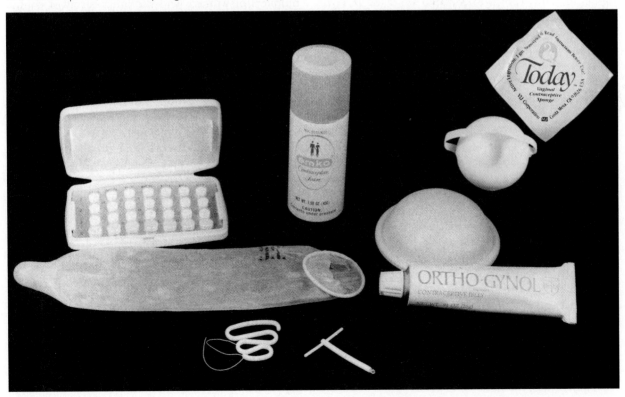

only temporary and can sometimes be eliminated by adjusting the dosage of hormones in the Pill. Others are so adverse as to warrant discontinuance of Pill usage. Among the more serious side effects are nausea, breast tenderness, weight gains due to water retention, migraine headaches, mood changes, and an increased tendency to develop yeast infections. More serious are visual disorders and the risk of cardio-vascular diseases. A yet unresolved controversy is a hypothesized link between long-term Pill use and cervical cancer. Women who have used the Pill for more than 5 years, who smoke, and who are over 35 are more prone to develop cardiovascular diseases.

INTRAUTERINE DEVICE (IUD)

The intrauterine device (IUD) is a small metal or plastic loop, ring, or spiral that is inserted into the uterus through the cervical opening. If not inserted properly, it can pierce the uterine wall and cause serious injury. For this reason an IUD should be inserted only by a medical practitioner. It can remain there for short or extended periods of time. Small strings are left in the vagina to allow women to check to see if the IUD is still in place. Spontaneous expulsions occur in about 10 percent of users, primarily during menstruation, so periodic checking is important. Expulsion is more common among younger women who have not yet given birth, so these women may be advised to use an alternative method. Although the IUD is quite effective (90 to 96 percent), requires little care, is reversible, is relatively inexpensive over the long term ($50 to $100 for insertion), and does not interfere with sexual spontaneity, it has been the subject of much controversy, resulting in decreased use in this country. Only a few types of IUDs remain on the market.

Part of the controversy stems from the fact that technically an IUD does not prevent conception; rather, it prevents the fertilized egg from implanting itself in the uterine wall. Some people equate this with abortion, which they find morally objectionable. However, the more publicized part of the controversy swirled around lawsuits brought in the 1970s against A. H. Robbins, the maker of the Dalkon Shield. This IUD was taken off the market after reports of high rates of uterine infections and an unusually high pregnancy rate among its users. Despite the problems with the Dalkon Shield, most users of other IUDs have few, if any, serious problems with these products. Nonetheless, some women experience cramping during and even after insertion, longer and heavier menstrual periods, and infections, in particular pelvic inflammatory disease.

MALE CONDOM

This contraceptive device has been around for a long time. In ancient Rome men used a condom made of animal intestine and bladder. A latex rubber condom became available in the United States in 1876. The condoms used today consist of a thin cover of rubber or processed sheep's intestine that is placed over the erect penis by either partner to prevent the sperm from entering the vagina. Condoms come in different sizes and colors. They are convenient (can be carried in a wallet or purse) and inexpensive (around 70 cents) and can be purchased over the counter in drugstores and supermarkets.

Condoms are about 90 percent effective. In addition, latex condoms protect against various sexually transmitted diseases, including AIDS. Increasing numbers of women who use other forms of contraception are buying condoms for the added protection they afford. The drawback to the condom is that it is put on after the man is aroused but before he enters his partner. Because sexual activity must be interrupted to do this, some couples neglect or forget to put it on. Some men complain that condoms interfere with sensation and spontaneity. Also, condoms can tear or slip off when in use and must be carefully removed after intercourse to avoid spilling the ejaculate.

FEMALE CONDOM

In 1992, a female condom became available in Switzerland and France and is now being tested in the United States. The female condom is a large, lubricated, thin polyurethane pouch with an inner and outer ring. The inner ring is inserted into the vagina and the outer ring is spread over the front of the vaginal area. The female condom has several advantages over the male condom. It tears less, and there is less chance of exposure to semen. Like the latex male condom, it can prevent the spread of sexually transmitted diseases, including AIDS. The female

The female condom.

condom is more expensive ($2.25) and more cumbersome than the male condom. Some couples find the pouch less spontaneous and somewhat comical.

DIAPHRAGM

The forerunners of the diaphragm, scooped-out halves of lemons and pomegranates, were used in Western Europe as early as 1600. The modern diaphragm is a flexible, dome-shaped rubber cup that is inserted into the vagina to cover the mouth of the cervix. It is used with contraceptive creams and jellies, and it functions as a barrier to sperm. A diaphragm is obtained by prescription after an internal pelvic examination. To be effective it must be properly fitted to conform to a woman's vaginal opening, and to ensure proper fit it should be checked every 2 years or after childbirth, an abortion, or significant weight changes. A woman (or her partner) inserts the diaphragm before having sex, and it must stay in place for 6 hours after intercourse so that the spermicide has sufficient time to kill all sperm. The diaphragm is about 85 to 90 percent effective. It can be inserted up to 2 hours before intercourse and left in place for up to 24 hours. Its main advantage is that it is reversible and does not interfere with a woman's hormonal system. Although there are few side effects, some women develop bladder infections or experience a mild allergic reaction to the rubber, cream, or jelly. Some

women see it as messy, and some feel that the preparation takes away from spontaneity. Initial cost is $50 to $75 for the fitting.

CERVICAL CAP

A cervical cap is a thimble-shaped device, similar to a diaphragm in appearance and function but considerably smaller. It is designed to fit snugly over the cervix and must be fitted by a trained practitioner. The cap is partially filled with spermicidal cream or jelly and placed inside the vagina. It must be left in place 6 hours after intercourse. The FDA approved the cervical cap in 1988; it is not yet widely used in the United States. Effectiveness ranges from 73 to 92 percent. Some women find the cervical cap more comfortable than the diaphragm. Like the diaphragm it does not interfere with body hormones, but it can become dislodged during intercourse.

CONTRACEPTIVE SPONGE

Approved for over-the-counter sales in 1983, the contraceptive sponge is a small polyurethane sponge containing spermicide. The sponge fits over the cervix, blocking and killing sperm. It can be inserted hours before intercourse and left in place for up to 24 hours. It is 75 to 90 percent effective, easily available, and convenient. However, there are as yet no long-term studies of its safety, and there have been some reports of users developing *toxic shock syndrome*, a systemic infection that can result in death, and *vaginitis*, an inflammation of the vagina.

CHEMICAL BARRIERS

A variety of chemical sperm-killing agents called *spermicides* (foams, creams, jellies, suppositories, tablets, and contraceptive film) can be purchased over the counter. They are more effective when used with a barrier method, but they can be used alone. They are inserted into the vagina and have a range of user effectiveness from 83 to 90 percent. A month's supply averages around $10, depending on frequency of intercourse. They are safe, simple to use, and reversible. However, some users complain of irritation and burning sensations. Some users find them messy, and because they must be used shortly before intercourse, couples sometimes feel they interrupt the sexual mood.

FERTILITY AWARENESS

Fertility awareness, also called natural family planning because it uses no mechanical or hormonal barriers to conception, makes use of the recurring pattern of fertile and infertile phases of a woman's body during the menstrual cycle. The goal of fertility awareness methods is to predict these phases so that couples can abstain from sexual activity during the fertile period. To determine the "safe" days, it is necessary to determine the time of ovulation. This can be done in several ways

1. The *rhythm method* uses a calendar calculation of unsafe days based on the length of a woman's menstrual cycle.

2. The *basal body temperature (BBT) method* calculates temperature change. A woman's temperature dips slightly just before ovulation and increases after ovulation.

3. The *cervical mucus method*, also called the *Billings* or *ovulation method*, examines the change in appearance and consistency of cervical mucus. The general pattern moves from no visible mucus for several days after menstruation to whitish, sticky mucus then to clear and slippery mucus during ovulation and then back to a cloudy discharge when ovulation ends.

4. The *sympto-thermal method* is a combination of BBT and mucus methods. This method is the most successful because it uses two indicators of fertility rather than one.

All of these methods are designed to help women check changing body signs so that they will know when ovulation occurs. Thus, the effectiveness of these methods depends on a woman's knowledge of her reproductive cycle as well as the couple's self-control (abstinence) during fertile periods. Although it is difficult to ascertain exactly when ovulation occurs, when these methods are used diligently they have a high effectiveness rate. However, risk taking during the fertile phase contributes to a fairly high failure rate. These methods are acceptable to most religious groups. They are also free, except for the purchase of a calendar, chart, and thermometer, and perhaps the expense of taking a class to learn to use the methods properly. There are no side effects. However, couples may experience frustration during periods of abstinence, which can last from 7 to 14 days.

WITHDRAWAL (COITUS INTERRUPTUS)

The withdrawal of the penis from the vagina prior to ejaculation can be an attractive form of contraception because it is simple, it doesn't require any devices, and it is free. Unfortunately, it also doesn't work very well. Withdrawal requires great control by the man, and it may limit sexual gratification for one or both partners. In addition, leakage of semen can occur prior to ejaculation.

DOUCHING

Douching, or washing out the vagina, is another old but unreliable method of birth control. Douching after intercourse may actually push some sperm toward the cervix. In addition, douching can lead to pelvic inflammatory disease.

FUTURE CONTRACEPTIVE STRATEGIES

Research to find safer, more effective, and less expensive methods of birth control is under way in many countries. For example, doctors in India are developing a birth-control vaccine for women. The vaccine would be effective for a year. Preliminary testing of the vaccine is encouraging, but the vaccine will not be available for several years. Most contraceptive research remains centered on the woman's reproductive system. However, some researchers are now investigating a male contraceptive pill that would inhibit sperm production. It is unlikely that such a pill will be available in the near future.

Appendix **F**

MARRIAGE LAWS AND DIVORCE LAWS

Wedding Laws in the 50 States and the District of Columbia

State	Age with parental consent		Age without consent		Physical exam and blood test for male and female			
	Male	Female	Male	Female	Maximum period between exam and license	Scope of medical exam	Waiting period	
							Before license	After license
Alabama*	14a	14a	18	18	—	b	—	s
Alaska	16z	16z	18	18	—	b	3 da., w	—
Arizona	16z	16z	18	18	—	—	—	—
Arkansas	17c	16c	18	18	—	—	v	—
California	aa	aa	18	18	30 da., w	zzz	—	h
Colorado*	16z	16z	18	18	—	bb	—	s
Connecticut	16z	16z	18	18	—	bb	4 da., w	ttt
Delaware	18c	16c	18	18	—	—	—	e, s
Florida	16a, c	16a, c	18	18	—	b	3 da.	s
Georgia*	aa	aa	16	16	—	b	3 da., g	s*
Hawaii	16d	16d	18	18	—	b	—	—
Idaho*	16z	16z	18	18	—	bb	—	—
Illinois	16	16	18	18	30 da.	b, n	—	ee
Indiana	17c	17c	18	18	—	bb	72 hrs.	t
Iowa*	18z	18z	18	18	—	—	3 da., v	tt

Wedding Laws in the 50 States and the District of Columbia (continued)

State	Age with parental consent		Age without consent		Physical exam and blood test for male and female			
	Male	Female	Male	Female	Maximum period between exam and license	Scope of medical exam	Waiting period	
							Before license	After license
Kansas*y	18z	18z	18	18	—	—	3 da., w	—
Kentucky	18c, z	18c, z	18	18	—	—	—	—
Louisiana	18z	18z	18	18	10 da.	b	72 hrs., w	—
Maine	16z	16z	18	18	—	—	3 da., v, w	h
Maryland	16c, f	16c, f	18	18	—	—	48 hrs., w	ff
Massachusetts	14j	12j	18	18	60 da.	bb	3 da., v	—
Michigan	16c, d	16c	18	18	30 da.	b	3 da., w	—
Minnesota	16z	16z	18	18	—	—	5 da., w	—
Mississippi	aa	aa	17gg	15gg	30 da.	b	3 da., w	—
Missouri	15d, 18z	15d, 18z	18	18	—	—	—	—
Montana*yy	16	16	18	18	—	b	—	ff
Nebraskayy	17	17	18	18	—	bb	—	—
Nevada	16z	16z	18	18	—	—	—	—
New Hampshire	14j	13j	18	18	—	l, zzz	3 da., v	h
New Jersey	16z, c	16z, c	18	18	30 da.	b	72 hrs., w	s
New Mexicoy	16d	16d	18	18	30 da.	b	—	—
New York	14j	14j	18	18	—	nn	—	24 hrs., w, t
North Carolina	16c, g	16c, g	18	18	—	m	—	—
North Dakota	16	16	18	18	—	—	—	t
Ohio*	18c, z	16c, z	18	18	30 da.	b	5 da., w	t
Oklahoma*	16c	16c	18	18	30 da., w	b	—	s
Oregon	17	17	18	18	—	—	3 da., w	—
Pennsylvania*	16d	16d	18	18	30 da.	b	3 da., w	t
Puerto Ricoy	18c, d, z	16c, d, z	21	21	—	b	—	—
Rhode Island*	18d	16d	18	18	—	bb	—	—
South Carolina*	16c	14c	18	18	—	—	1 da.	—
South Dakota	16c	16c	18	18	—	—	—	tt
Tennessee	16d	16d	18	18	—	—	3 da., cc	s
Texas*y	14j, k	14j, k	18	18	—	—	—	s
Utah*	14	14	18x	18x	30 da.	b	—	s
Vermont	16z	16z	18	18	30 da.	b	1 da., w	—
Virginia	16a, c	16a, c	18	18	—	b	—	t
Washington	17d	17d	18	18	—	bbb	3 da.	t
West Virginia	18c	18c	18	18	—	b	3 da., w	—
Wisconsin	16d	16d	18	18	—	b	5 da., w	s
Wyoming	16d	16d	18	18	—	bb	—	—
Dist. of Columbia*	16a	16a	18	18	30 da.	b	3 da., w	—

*Indicates 1987 common-law marriage recognized; in many states, such marriages are only recognized if entered into many years before. (a) Parental consent not required if minor was previously married. (aa) No age limits. (b) Venereal diseases. (bb) Venereal diseases and Rubella (for female). In Colorado and Wyoming, Rubella for female under 45 and Rh type. (bbb) No medical exam required; however, applicants must file affidavit showing non-affliction of contagious venereal disease. (c) Younger partners may obtain license in case of pregnancy or birth of child. (cc) Unless parties are over 18 years of age. (d) Younger parties may obtain license in special circumstances. (e) Residents before expiration of 24-hour waiting period; non-residents formerly residents, before expiration of 96-hour waiting period; others 96 hours. (ee) License effective 1 day after issuance, unless court orders otherwise, valid for 60 days only. (f) If parties are at least 16 years of age, proof of age and the consent of parents in person is required. If a parent is ill, an affidavit by the incapacitated parent and a physician's affidavit to that effect required. (ff) License valid for 180 days only. (g) Unless parties are 18 years of age or more, or female is pregnant, or applicants are the parents of a living child born out of wedlock. (gg) Notice to parents necessary if parties are under 21. (h) License valid for 90 days only. (j) Parental consent and/or permission of judge required. (k) Below age of consent parties need parental consent and permission of judge. (l) With each certificate issued to couples, a list of family planning agencies and services available to them is provided. (m) Mental incompetence, infectious tuberculosis, venereal diseases and Rubella (certain counties only). (n) Venereal diseases; test for sickle cell anemia given at request of examining physician. (nn) Tests for sickle cell anemia may be required for certain applicants. Marriage prohibited unless it is established that procreation is not possible. (p) If one or both parties are below the age for marriage without parental consent (3 day waiting period). (s) License valid for 30 days only. (t) License valid for 60 days only. (tt) License valid for 20 days only. (ttt) License valid for 65 days. (v) Parties must file notice of intention to marry with local clerk. (w) Waiting period may be avoided. (x) Authorizes counties to provide for premarital counseling as a requisite to issuance of license to persons under 19 and persons previously divorced. (y) Marriages by proxy are valid. (yy) Proxy marriages are valid under certain conditions. (z) Younger parties may marry with parental consent and/or permission of judge. In Connecticut, judicial approval. (zz) With consent of court. (zzz) Required offer of HIV test, and/or must be provided with information on AIDS.

Some Grounds for Divorce in the 50 States and the District of Columbia

Some grounds for absolute divorce

	Residence	Adultery	Cruelty	Desertion	Alcoholism	Impotency	Non-support	Insanity	Pregnancy at marriage	Bigamy	Separation	Felony conviction or imprisonment	Drug addiction	Fraud force, duress
Alabama	6 mos.*	Yes	Phys. only	1 yr.	Yes	Yes*	2 yrs.	5 yrs.	Yes	A	2 yrs.*	2 yrs.*	Yes	A
Alaska	*	Yes	Yes	1 yr.	1 yr.	Yes	No	18 mos.	No	A	No	Yes	Yes	A
Arizona	90 da.	No	No	No	No	No	No	No	No	No	No	No	No	No
Arkansas	60 da.	Yes	Yes	No	1 yr.	Yes	Yes	3 yrs.	No	No	18 mos.	Yes	No	A
California	6 mos.	No	No	No	No	A	No	Yes, A	No	A	No	No	No	A
Colorado	90 da.	No	No	No	No	No	No	No	No	A	No	No	No	A
Connecticut	1 yr.*	Yes	Yes	1 yr.	Yes	No	No	5 yrs.	No	A	18 mos.*	life*	No	Yes
Delaware	6 mos.	Yes	Yes	Yes	Yes	A	No	A	No	Yes	6 mos.	Yes	Yes	A
Florida	6 mos.	No	No	No	No	No	No	3 yrs.	No	No	No	No	No	No
Georgia	6 mos.	Yes	Yes	1 yr.	Yes	Yes	No	2 yrs.	Yes	A	No	Yes*	Yes	Yes
Hawaii	6 mos.*	No	No	No	No	No	No	A	No	A	2 yrs.*	No	No	A
Idaho	6 wks.	Yes	Yes	Yes	Yes	A	Yes	3 yrs.	Yes	A	5 yrs.	Yes	No	A
Illinois	90 da.	Yes	Yes	1 yr.	2 yrs.	Yes	No	No	No	Yes	2 yrs.*	Yes	2 yrs.	No
Indiana	6 mos.*	No	No	No	No	Yes	No	2 yrs.	No	A	No	Yes	No	A
Iowa	1 yr.*	No	No	No	No	A	No	A	No	A	No	No	No	No
Kansas	60 da.	No	No	No	No	No	Yes	2 yrs.	A	A	No	No	No	A
Kentucky	180 da.	No	No	No	No	A	No	No	No	No	No	No	No	A
Louisiana	1 yr.*	Yes	No	No	No	No	No	No	No	A	6 mos.	Yes*	No	A
Maine	6 mos.*	Yes	Yes	3 yrs.	Yes	Yes	Yes	A	No	A	No	No	Yes	No
Maryland	1 yr.*	Yes	No	1 yr.*	No	No	No	3 yrs.	No	A	1 yr.*	1 yr.*	No	No
Massachusetts	1 yr.*	Yes	Yes	1 yr.	Yes	Yes	Yes	No	No	A	No	5 yrs.	Yes	No
Michigan	180 da.	No	No	No	No	No	No	No	No	No	No	No	No	A
Minnesota	180 da.	No	No	No	No	No	No	No	No	No	No	No	No	A
Mississippi	6 mos.	Yes	Yes	1 yr.	Yes	Yes	No	3 yrs.	Yes	Yes	No	Yes*	Yes	A

Some grounds for absolute divorce

	Residence	Adultery	Cruelty	Desertion	Alcoholism	Impotency	Non-support	Insanity	Pregnancy at marriage	Bigamy	Separation	Felony conviction or imprisonment	Drug addiction	Fraud force, duress
Missouri	90 da.	No	No	No	No	No	No	No	No	No	No	No	No	A
Montana	90 da.	No	No	No	No	A	No	No	No	No	180 da.*	No	No	A
Nebraska	1 yr.*	No	No	No	No	A	No	No	No	A	No	No	No	A
Nevada	6 wks.	No	No	No	No	No	No	2 yrs.	No	A	1 yr.	No	No	A
New Hampshire	1 yr.*	Yes	Yes	2 yrs.	2 yrs.	Yes	2 yrs.	No	No	A	Yes	1 yr.*	No	No
New Jersey	1 yr.*	Yes	Yes	1 yr.	1 yr.	A	No	2 yrs.	No	A	18 mos.	18 mos.	1 yr.	A
New Mexico	6 mos.	Yes	Yes	Yes*	No	No	No	No	No	No	No	No	No	No
New York	1 yr.*	Yes	Yes	1 yr.	No	No	No	No	No	A	1 yr.	3 yrs.	No	A
North Carolina	6 mos.	No	No	No	No	A	No	3 yrs.	No	A	1 yr.	No	No	No
North Dakota	6 mos.	Yes	Yes	1 yr.	1 yr.	A	1 yr.	5 yrs.*	No	A	No	Yes	1 yr.	A
Ohio	6 mos.	Yes	Yes	1 yr.	Yes	Yes	Yes	No	No	Yes, A	1 yr.	Yes	No	Yes, A
Oklahoma	6 mos.	Yes	Yes	1 yr.	Yes	Yes	Yes	5 yrs.	Yes	Yes	No	Yes	No	Yes
Oregon	6 mos.*	No	No	No	No	No	No	No	No	No	No	No	No	A
Pennsylvania	6 mos.	Yes	Yes	1 yr.	No	No	No	18 mos.*	No	Yes	2 yrs.*	Yes	No	No
Puerto Rico	1 yr.	Yes	Yes	1 yr.	Yes	Yes	No	Yes	No	A	2 yrs.	Yes*	Yes	No
Rhode Island	1 yr.	Yes	Yes	5 yrs.*	Yes	Yes	1 yr.	No	No	Yes	3 yrs.	Yes	Yes	No
South Carolina	1 yr.*	Yes	Phys. only	1 yr.	Yes	No	No	No	No	No	1 yr.	No	Yes	No
South Dakota	none*	Yes	Yes	1 yr.	1 yr.	A	1 yr.	5 yrs.	No	A	No	Yes	No	A*
Tennessee	6 mos.*	Yes	Yes	1 yr.	Yes	Yes	Yes	No	Yes	Yes	2 yrs.	Yes	Yes	A
Texas	6 mos.*	Yes	Yes	1 yr.	*	A	No	3 yrs.	No	No	3 yrs.	1 yr.	No	No
Utah	3 mos.*	Yes	Yes	1 yr.	Yes	Yes	Yes	Yes	No	A	3 yrs.*	Yes	No	No
Vermont	6 mos.*	Yes	Yes	7 yrs.*	No	No	Yes	5 yrs.	No	A	6 mos.	3 yrs.	No	A
Virginia	6 mos.*	Yes	Yes*	1 yr.	No	A	No	No	A	A	1 yr.*	1 yr.*	No	A
Washington	bona fide res.	No	No	No	No	No	No	No	No	No	No	No	No	No
West Virginia	1 yr.*	Yes	Yes	6 mos.	Yes	A	No	3 yrs.	A	A	1 yr.	Yes	Yes	No
Wisconsin	6 mos.	No	No	No	No	A	No	No	No	A	1 yr.	No	No	A
Wyoming	60 da.*	No	No	No	No	No	No	2 yrs.	No	A	No	No	No	No
District of Columbia	6 mos.	No	No	No	No	A	No	A*	No	A	6 mos.–1 yr.	No	No	A

(*) indicates qualification—check local statutes; (A) indicates grounds for annulment.

Important: Almost all states also have other laws, as well as qualifications of the laws shown above and proposed divorce-reform laws pending. It would be wise to consult a lawyer in conjunction with the use of this chart.

GLOSSARY

abortion The premature termination of a pregnancy before the fetus can survive on its own. This either can occur spontaneously (miscarriage) or can be induced through a variety of external methods.

achieved status A position we hold in society by virtue of our own efforts, for example, becoming a teacher.

acquaintance rape Sexual assault by a person with whom the victim is familiar.

adultery Extramarital sexual intercourse.

affinal relatives People related by marriage and not by blood; for example, a brother- or sister-in-law.

afterbirth The placenta, amniotic sac, and remaining umbilical cord that are expelled following childbirth.

agape A selfless love; it is spontaneous and altruistic and requires nothing in return.

age norms The expectations of how one is to behave at specific ages in the life cycle.

ageism The application of negative stereotypes and discriminatory treatment to elderly people.

agents of socialization Individuals, groups, and organizations that help form an individual's attitudes, behaviors, and self-concepts.

AIDS (acquired immune deficiency syndrome) A viral syndrome that destroys the body's immune system.

alimony Court-ordered financial support paid to a former spouse following a divorce.

alpha-fetoprotein testing screening (AFP) A prenatal test used to determine the level of AFP, a fetal blood protein, in the mother's blood for the purpose of detecting neural defects in the fetus.

amniocentesis A prenatal test in which a needle is inserted into the mother's uterus to collect cells cast off by the fetus for the purpose of testing for genetic diseases or defects in the fetus.

androgynous Expressing a wide range of attitudes and behaviors with no gender-role differentiation. *Androgyny* is the combination of both culturally defined feminine and masculine traits in an individual.

annulment A legal declaration that a marriage never existed, leaving both parties free to marry.

anticipatory socialization Socialization directed toward learning future roles.

antinatalist forces Policies or practices that discourage people from having children.

areola The dark circle around the nipple of the breast.

artificial insemination The injection of sperm into a woman's vagina during her fertile period.

ascribed status A position we hold in society because we were born into it, for example, being female or male.

autoeroticism Sexual activities involving only the self, for example, masturbation, sexual fantasy, and erotic dreams.

battered child syndrome   A group of symptoms that collectively describe a clinical condition in children who have received severe physical abuse.

battered woman syndrome   A group of symptoms that collectively describe a general pattern of physical battering experienced by women. It is defined in terms of frequency, severity, deliberateness, and ability to demonstrate injury.

bereavement   The state of being deprived of a loved one by death.

bigamy   The act of marrying one person while still being legally married to another person.

bisexuality   Sexual attraction to members of both sexes.

blastocyst   A hollow mass of cells, formed around the fifth day after conception, that attaches to the uterine wall and develops into an embryo.

bonding   A situation in which the victim of violence grows attached to the abuser.

bundling   A courtship custom in colonial America that allowed couples to spend the night in bed together, wrapped in bundling blankets or separated by a wooden bundling board.

capitalism   An economic system based on the private ownership of the means of production.

caring cluster   A group of characteristics, typical of lovers, that includes giving the utmost and being a champion or advocate for another person.

case study   A research design that focuses on one example rather than a representative sample.

cenogamy (group marriage)   A situation in which the women and men in a group are simultaneously married to one another.

chorionic villus sampling (CVS)   A medical technique in which an obstetrician guides a small tube through the cervix or abdominal wall into the uterus to extract cells from the villi, which are then examined for genetic abnormalities.

cloning   The asexual production of a new organism identical to the donor from which the nucleus of a body cell is taken.

closed adoption   A form of adoption in which the adoptive parents and the birth parents do not meet.

cognitive-development theory   A theory that asserts that children take an active role in organizing their world, including learning gender identity.

coitus   Penile–vaginal intercourse.

common-law marriage   A cohabitive relationship that is based on the mutual consent of the persons involved, is not solemnized by a ceremony, and is recognized as valid by the state.

commune   A group of people (single or married, with or without children) who live together, sharing many aspects of their lives.

community divorce   This concept refers to the changing social relationships that often accompany a divorce—the loss of relatives and friends who were previously shared with a spouse and the replacement with new friends.

community remarriage   This concept refers to the changing social relationships that often accompany a remarriage—the integration of new in-laws and "couple-oriented" relationships and sometimes the loss of unmarried friends.

commuter marriage   A marriage in which each partner works in a different geographic location and therefore maintains a separate place of residence.

comparable worth   The principle of equal pay for different jobs of similar worth.

conception   The process by which a female ovum (egg) is penetrated by a male sperm cell, creating a fertilized egg.

conciliation counseling   Counseling intended to determine whether marital problems can be resolved and the couple reconciled. Some states require conciliation counseling before the courts will consider granting a divorce.

conflict theory   A theoretical perspective that focuses on conflicting interests among various groups and institutions in society.

congenital   Existing at birth but not hereditary.

conjugal rights   A set of rights pertaining to the marriage relationship.

content analysis   A research technique that is used to examine the actual content of books, documents, and programs.

contraception   Prevention of conception.

coparental divorce   The arrangements divorcing couples work out concerning child custody, visitation rights, and the financial and legal responsibilities of each parent.

courtship   The process of selecting a mate and developing an intimate relationship.

coverture   The traditional belief that a wife is under the protection and influence of her husband.

crude divorce rate (CDR)   The number of divorces per 1000 people in the population.

cunnilingus   Oral stimulation of the female genitals.

date rape   Sexual assault by a person with whom the victim "goes out."

dating   A process of pairing off that involves the open choice of mates and engagement in activities that allow people to get to know one another and progress toward mate selection.

debunk   To expose the falseness of a particular myth.

desertion   The abandonment of a spouse or family.

divorce counseling   Counseling intended to help couples replace the adversarial and often destructive aspects that frequently accompany divorce with a more cooperative spirit and to help them distance themselves from the relationship so that acceptance of the loss and subsequent healing can take place.

divorce mediation   A procedure in which trained professionals help divorcing couples negotiate a fair and mutually agreed upon resolution of such issues as marital property distribution, child custody, visitation rights, and financial support.

divorce-to-marriage ratio   A comparison of the number of marriages with the number of divorces occurring in a given year.

domestic partnerships   A category of relationships consisting of unmarried couples who live together and share housing and financial responsibilities. Some communities and businesses allow unmarried couples who register as domestic partners to receive certain legal rights similar to those of married couples.

dowry   A sum of money or property brought to a marriage by the female.

dysfunctional   Having a negative consequence or performing a negative service by hampering the achievement of group goals or disrupting the balance of the system.

economic divorce   The division of marital property and assets between the two partners.

economic remarriage   The establishment of a new unit of economic productivity and consumption.

ectogenesis   The insemination of an ovum and the development of the embryo outside the uterus.

ectopic pregnancy   A type of pregnancy in which the fertilized egg implants itself in the fallopian tube or, more rarely, in the abdominal cavity, the ovary, or the cervix instead of in the uterine wall.

edema   Swelling of the limbs, especially the lower legs and ankles, as a result of water retention.

ejaculation   Expulsion of semen from the penis.

elder abuse   Physical, psychological, and material maltreatment and neglect of older people.

embryo   The human organism at its earliest stage of development.

embryopathy   Prominent physical features in babies born with the HIV virus such as slanted eyes that sit far apart from each other, a small head, a flat forehead and nose, and loosely shaped lips.

emotional divorce   A period during which one or both partners withdraws emotionally from a marriage.

emotional overload   A situation of stress caused by increasing demands to be available in crisis situations both inside and outside the home. Although anyone can experience emotional overload, it most often affects young mothers, especially teenage mothers.

emotional remarriage   The process of reestablishing a bond of attraction, love, commitment, and trust with another person.

empirical evidence   Data or evidence that can be confirmed by the use of one or more of the human senses.

endogamy   The practice of requiring people to marry within a particular social group.

endometriosis   A disease in which the tissue that lines the uterus also grows outside the uterus, often in the fallopian tubes or on the ovaries, thus preventing sperm from meeting the egg.

envy   Unhappiness or discontent that arises from the belief that something personal about oneself does not measure up to the level of someone else.

episiotomy   A small incision to enlarge the vaginal opening and prevent tearing during delivery of the fetus.

erogenous zone   An area of the body that is particularly sensitive to sexual stimulation.

eros   Style of love that is selfish and sensuous, characterized by an intense emotional attachment and a strong emphasis on sexual pleasure.

erotic arousal   The stimulation or awakening of sexual feelings and desires in human beings.

ethnography (life history)   A research study of a particular culture, subculture, or group, most often through the use of participant observation or in-depth interviews.

exogamy   The practice of requiring people to marry outside particular groups.

experiment   A research method in which a researcher designs a series of steps that enable her or him to examine cause-and-effect relationships among differing phenomena under controlled conditions.

expressive traits   Personality traits that encourage nurturing, emotionality, sensitivity, and warmth.

extended family   A family consisting of one or both parents, siblings, if any, and other relatives, such as grandparents, aunts, uncles, or cousins.

family of orientation   The family into which a person is born and raised.

family of procreation   A family that is created when two people marry or enter into an intimate relationship and have or adopt children of their own.

family   Any relatively stable group of people who are related to one another through blood, marriage, or adoption or who simply live together, and who provide one another with economic and emotional support.

fellatio   Oral stimulation of the male genitals.

feminization of love   The idea that love is a central aspect of the female domain and experience and is defined purely in female terms.

feminization of poverty   The increase in the proportion of poor people who are women or children.

fertility   The actual number of live births in a population.

fertility rate   The number of births per 1000 women in their childbearing years (ages 15 to 44).

fetal alcohol syndrome   A condition characterized by physical deformities in the fetus caused by a mother's consumption of alcohol during pregnancy.

fetus   Name given to the embryo beginning 8 weeks after conception and until birth.

fictive kin   The attribution of kinship terms to nonrelatives.

flextime   An arrangement that allows employees to choose within specified time limits when they arrive at and leave work.

fornication   Sexual intercourse outside legal marriage.

fraternal twins   Type of twins that develop when two separate eggs are fertilized by two different sperm; they do not resemble each other.

fulfillment of personality needs   A concept used by sociologists to describe an interpersonal process of love in which each person in an intimate relationship is able to satisfy the needs of the other.

functional   Having a positive consequence or performing a positive service by promoting the achievement of group goals or helping maintain a system in a balanced state.

gender   The socially learned behaviors, attitudes, and expectations that are associated with being female or male; what we call femininity and masculinity.

gender identity   A person's awareness of being female or male.

gender-role socialization   The process whereby people learn and adopt the gender roles that their culture deems appropriate for them.

generalized others   The viewpoints of society at large—widespread cultural norms and values that are used as a reference in evaluating ourselves.

genetic engineering   The ability to manipulate genes to control heredity.

gestation period   The overall period of pregnancy.

getting together   A pattern of dating that involves women and men playing similar roles in initiating dates and sharing equally in the cost of activities.

going steady   An exclusive dating relationship with one partner.

grief   The emotional response to the loss of a loved one.

group marriage   A marriage of at least four people, two female and two male, in which each partner is married to all partners of the opposite sex.

Hawthorne effect   The distortion of research results that occurs when people modify their behaviors, either deliberately or subconsciously, because they are aware they are being studied.

hermaphroditism   A condition in which an infant's genitalia are ambiguous in appearance and the baby's sexual anatomy cannot clearly be differentiated.

heterogamous marriage   Marriage in which the partners are unlike each other in terms of various social and demographic characteristics such as race, age, religious background, social class, and education.

heterosexism   The notion that heterosexuality is the only right, natural, and acceptable sexual orientation.

heterosexuality   Preference for affectional and sexual activities with a person of the opposite sex—involves both personal identity (how a person sees herself or himself) and behavior (what a person does)..

homogamy   The attraction of people who are alike in terms of various social and demographic characteristics such as race, age, religious background, social class, and education.

homophobia   An extreme and irrational fear or hatred of homosexuals.

homosexuality   Preference for affectional and sexual activities with a person of the same sex—involves both personal identity (how a person sees herself or himself) and behavior (what a person does).

households   The persons who occupy a housing unit such as a house, apartment, single room, or other space intended to be living quarters.

human chorionic gonadotropin (HCG)   A hormone produced by the placenta which, if found in a woman's urine, indicates that she is pregnant.

human sexuality   The sexual character or potency of humans that includes feelings, thoughts, behaviors, and a learned set of cultural cues that evoke a sexual or an erotic response.

hypergamy   Marrying upward in social status.

hypogamy   Marrying downward in social status.

hypothesis   Statement of a relationship between two or more factors.

identical twins   Type of twins that develop when a single fertilized egg splits off into two parts.

ideology   A set of ideas and beliefs that support the interests of a group in society.

incest   Sexual abuse by a blood relative or someone who is thought of as a part of a person's family.

infanticide   Killing of infants and young children.

infatuation   A strong attraction to another person based on an idealized picture of that person.

infertility   The inability to conceive after 12 months of unprotected intercourse or the inability to carry a pregnancy to live birth.

institution   Patterns of ideas, beliefs, values, and behavior that are built around basic needs of individuals and society and that persist over time.

institutional racism   Systematic discrimination against a racial group by institutions of society.

instrumental traits   Personality traits that encourage self-confidence, rationality, competition, and coolness.

interview   A research method of collecting data in which a researcher asks subjects a series of questions and records the answers.

in vitro fertilization (IVF)   A reproductive technique that takes place outside the woman's body. Eggs are removed from a woman's ovaries and fertilized with sperm from the husband or donor, after which the resulting embryo is implanted in the woman's uterus.

jealousy   Thoughts and feelings of envy, resentment, and insecurity directed toward someone that a person is fearful of losing.

job sharing   An employment pattern in which two workers split a single full-time job.

joint custody   A situation in which both divorced parents are given legal responsibility for raising their children.

kinship   People who are related by blood, marriage, or adoption, or who consider one another family.

labor-force participation rate   The percentage of workers in a particular group who are employed or who are actively seeking employment.

latent functions   Unintended, unrecognized consequences or effects of any part of a social system or the system as a whole for the maintenance and stability of that system.

legal divorce   The official dissolution of a marriage by the state, leaving both former partners legally free to remarry.

legal marriage   A legally binding agreement or contractual relationship between two people that is defined and regulated by the state.

legal remarriage   The establishment of a new legally recognized relationship.

liking   A positive feeling toward someone that is less intense than love—a feeling typical of friendship in its most simple terms.

limerence   A style of love characterized by a complete absorption or obsessive preoccupation with and attachment to another person that is accompanied by extreme emotional highs when the love is reciprocated and lows when it is not.

ludus   Style of love that is perceived as a game or conquest; it is playful, nonpossessive, and challenging, without a deep commitment or lasting emotional involvement.

mania   A jealous love, characterized by strong sexual attraction and obsession, that demands constant displays of attention, caring, and affection from the partner.

manifest functions   Intended, overt consequences or effects of any part of a social system or the system as a whole for the maintenance and stability of that system.

marital adjustment   The process by which marital partners change, adapt, or modify their behavior, attitudes, and interactions to develop a good working relationship and to satisfy each other's needs over the marital life course.

marriage   A union between people that unites them sexually, socially, and economically; that is relatively consistent over time; and that accords each person certain agreed-upon rights.

marriage gradient   Phenomenon by which women marry upward in social status and men marry downward in social status. As a result, women at the top and men and the bottom of the social class ladder have a smaller pool of eligible mates to choose from than do members of the other classes.

marriage market   Analogy of the commercial marketplace to explain how individuals choose the people they date, mate, live with, and marry by "comparison shopping" and "bargaining for" the mate with the most desirable characteristics.

marriage squeeze   A condition in which one sex has a more limited pool of eligibles from which to choose. Sociologists use the concept to describe the phenomenon of an excess of baby boom women who had reached marriageable age during the 1960s compared to marriageable age men.

master (key) status   A position we hold that affects all aspects of our lives, for example, being female or male.

masturbation   Erotic stimulation of self through caressing or otherwise stimulating the genitals for the purpose of sexual pleasure.

mate selection   The wide range of behaviors and social relationships individuals engage in prior to marriage and that lead to long-term or short-term pairing or coupling.

matrilineal   The practice of tracing kinship or family lineage (descent) and inheritance only through the mother and her blood relatives.

menopause   A period in the female life cycle (typically between ages 45 and 50) characterized by the cessation of ovulation, the menstrual cycle, and fertility.

menstruation   A process occurring approximately every 28 days in women from puberty to middle age in which blood, unused tissue, and an unfertilized egg (ovum) are discharged from the uterus and discarded through the vaginal opening.

microstructuralism   A theoretical perspective that combines the interactionist theoretical focus on social behavior, statuses, and roles and the structural-functionalist focus on social structures to explain social behaviors such as gendered relationships.

midwife   Most often a woman who is trained either to deliver a baby or to assist a woman in childbirth. Most midwives today are professionals who practice in free-standing birth centers or who deliver babies at home.

miscarriage   Noninduced death and expulsion of an embryo or fetus.

modeling   A process of learning through imitation of others.

modified-extended family   Family in which a variety of relatives live, not necessarily in the same household, but in very close proximity to one another, interact on a frequent basis, and provide emotional and economic support to each other.

monogamy   Exclusivity in an intimate relationship. In marriage, it represents marriage to only one person at a time.

morbidity   The rate of occurrence of illness or disease in a population.

mortality   The rate of occurrence of death in a population.

motherhood mystique   The traditional belief that the ultimate achievement and fulfillment of womanhood is through motherhood.

mutual dependence   A concept used by sociologists to describe an interpersonal process of love in which partners rely upon each other for fulfillment; they come to need and rely on each other to share their lives, happiness, fears, hopes, dreams, and sexual intimacies.

myth   False, fictitious, imaginary, or exaggerated belief about someone or something.

nocturnal emissions (wet dreams)   Erotic dreams that lead to orgasm during sleep.

no-fault divorce   The dissolution of marriage on the basis of irreconcilable differences; neither party is judged at fault for the divorce.

norms   Cultural guidelines or rules of conduct that direct people to behave in particular ways.

nuclear family   A family consisting of a mother and father and their natural or adopted offspring.

occupational distribution   The location of workers in different occupations; for example, women are more heavily concentrated in lower-paying clerical or service jobs, whereas men are concentrated in higher-paying jobs of craft workers and operators.

open adoption   A form of adoption in which the adoptive parents and the birth parents meet and together work out the process of adoption.

orgasm   A climactic human sexual response at the height of sexual arousal characterized by the peaking and involuntary release of sexual tension through rhythmic contractions in the genitals of both sexes and accompanied by ejaculation in most males.

overlapping households The dual membership of children in the separate households of their divorced (and frequently remarried) parents.

ovulation A process that occurs approximately every 28 days in females whereby a mature ovum (egg) is released from a follicle in an ovary; part of the menstrual cycle.

ovum or **embryo transplant (OT)** A reproductive technique in which the ovum from a donor is fertilized and the resulting embryo is implanted in the uterus of an infertile woman.

palimony A payment similar to alimony made to a former unmarried live-in partner and based on the existence of a contract (written or implied) between the partners regarding aspects of their relationship.

parental remarriage A process that involves the establishment of relationships with the children of the new spouse.

passion cluster A group of characteristics, typical of lovers, that includes fascination or a preoccupation with each other and a desire to be together all of the time, exclusiveness, and sexual desire for each other.

patriarchal family A family organized around the principle of male dominance wherein the male (husband or father) is head of the family and exercises authority and decision-making power over other family members, especially his wife and children.

patrilineal The practice of tracing kinship or family lineage (descent) and inheritance only through the father and his blood relatives.

petting A variety of types of physical contact and activities for the purpose of sexual arousal and pleasure without engaging in penile-vaginal intercourse, common among adolescent girls and boys.

philos Style of love that is characterized by a deep and enduring feeling of friendship or brotherly love.

placenta Vascular membrane that holds the fetus in place inside the uterus and through which nourishment passes from the mother to the fetus.

pleasuring Engaging in activities during a sexual encounter that feel good; giving and receiving pleasurable feelings without the necessity of intercourse.

polyandry A form of marriage in which one female is married to two or more males.

polygamy A broad category applied to forms of marriage that involve multiple partners. In heterosexual marriage, polygamy involves a person of one sex being married to two or more people of the other sex (either *polyandry* or *polygyny*).

polygyny A form of marriage in which one male is married to two or more females.

pool of eligibles People who are potential mates by virtue of birth and societal definition as appropriate or acceptable partners.

pragma Style of love that is logical, sensible, rational, and based on practical considerations such as a potential partner's compatibility or the costs and benefits of a relationship. Combines the *ludus* and *storge* love styles.

principle of legitimacy The notion that all children ought to have a socially and legally recognized father.

pronatalist attitude A cultural attitude that encourages childbearing.

propinquity Proximity or closeness in time, place, and space; an important factor in mate selection.

Protestant work ethic An ideology or set of beliefs that emphasizes hard work and frugality.

psychic divorce A redefinition of self away from the mutuality of couplehood and back to a sense of singularity and autonomy.

psychic remarriage A process in which a remarried individual moves back from the recently acquired identity of a single person to a couple identity.

psychoanalytic/identification theory A theory developed by Sigmund Freud that asserts that children learn gender-appropriate behaviors by unconsciously identifying with their same-sex parent and that they pass through a series of stages in their psychosexual development.

push/pull factors Negative and positive factors in a current situation that influence our decision making.

qualitative research Research whose methods are designed to study conditions or processes that are difficult to measure numerically; based heavily on subjective interpretation.

quantitative research Research whose methods are designed to study variables or processes that can be measured numerically.

questionnaire A research method of collecting data in which research subjects read and respond to a set of printed questions.

rape Sexual intercourse forced by one person upon another against the person's will; usually perpetrated by a male against a female.

rapport A feeling of ease, comfort, or relaxation with another person. This concept is used by some sociologists to describe the first step in the interpersonal process of falling in love.

ratio of divorced to married persons A comparison of the number of currently divorced people 15 years of age and over who have not remarried with the number of people who are currently married.

refined divorce rate (RDR) The number of divorces per 1000 married women over age 15.

refractory period A stage in the sexual response cycle occurring after orgasm (in the resolution phase) in which a male experiences a state of rest or relaxation, during which he cannot become sexually aroused.

reliability The degree to which scientific research measures or instruments yield the same results when repeated by the same researcher or other researchers or when applied to the same individuals over time or different individuals at one time; consistency in measurement.

remarried family A two-parent, two-generation unit that comes into being on the legal remarriage of a widowed or divorced person who is regularly involved with biological or adopted children from a prior union. The children may or may not live with the remarried couple, but in either case, they have ongoing and significant psychological, social, and legal ties with them.

reproductive freedom The ability of women to decide whether, when, and with whom they will have children.

responsibility overload A situation of stress caused when a person must repeatedly make critical family decisions with few, if any, resources to assist in decision making and follow-through. Although anyone can experience this overload situation, it most often affects young mothers such as some teenage mothers.

role A set of socially prescribed behaviors associated with a particular status or position in society.

role conflict A situation in which a person occupies two different roles that involve contradictory expectations of what should be done at a given time.

role overload A situation in which a person's various roles carry more responsibilities than that person can reasonably manage.

romantic love A deeply tender or highly intense set of feelings, emotions, and thoughts coupled with sexual passion and erotic expression directed by one person toward another.

sacrament A sacred union or rite.

sandwich generation The middle-aged adults who find themselves pressured by responsibilities for both their children and their elderly parents.

scientific method A set of research procedures that includes gathering and analyzing information and then reporting the results.

scientific research Research that provides us with empirical evidence as a basis for knowledge or theories.

self-revelation A concept used by sociologists to describe an interpersonal process of love in which a couple feel enough at ease with each other to open up and disclose intimate and personal feelings.

separation The termination of marital cohabitation; the couple remains legally married, and neither party is free to remarry.

serial monogamy A system in which an individual marries several times but only after each prior marriage is ended by death or divorce.

sex The biological aspects of a person—the physiological characteristics that differentiate females from males. These include external genitalia (vulva and penis), gonads (ovaries and testes), sex chromosomes, and hormones.

sexism An ideology or set of beliefs about the inferiority of women and the superiority of men that is used to justify prejudice and discrimination against women.

sex ratio The number of men to every 100 women in a society or group.

sex typing The categorization of individuals according to personality traits thought to be characteristic of females or males.

sexual assault Violent behavior in the form of forced sexual acts that include vaginal, oral, or anal penetration; bondage; beating; mutilation; beastiality; and group or gang rape.

sexual double standard Differing sets of norms whereby certain behaviors are culturally accepted, when performed by men but are criticized or condemned when performed by women.

sexual dysfunction A psychological or physical condition in which a person is unable to engage in or enjoy sexual activities; impairment or malfunction of the human sexual response system.

sexual harassment Unwanted leers, comments, suggestions, or physical contact of a sexual nature, as well as unwelcome requests for sexual favors.

sexual orientation Affectional and sexual responsiveness to the same or different sex; the preference for an affectional and sexual partner as well as the way in which people understand and identify themselves sexually, for example, homosexual, heterosexual, or bisexual.

sexual script   Societal or cultural guidelines or blueprints for defining and engaging in sexual behaviors.

sexually transmitted diseases (STDs)   Contagious diseases transmitted or acquired primarily through sexual contact or which can be, but are not always, spread through sexual contact.

significant others   People who figure most importantly in a person's life such as parents, friends, relatives, and religious figures.

social construction of reality   The process in which individuals shape or determine reality as they interact with other human beings.

social exchange theory   A theoretical perspective that adopts an economic model of human behavior based on cost, benefit, and the expectation of reciprocity and that focuses on how people bargain and exchange one thing for another in social relationships.

social gerontology   The study of the impact of sociocultural conditions on the process and consequences of aging.

social-learning theory   A theory that asserts that gender roles and gender identity are learned directly through a system of positive reinforcement (rewards) and negative reinforcement (punishments).

social marriage   A relationship between people who cohabit and engage in behavior that is essentially the same as that within legal marriages except that the couple has not engaged in a marriage ceremony that is validated or defined as legally binding by the state.

social structure   Recurrent stable and patterned ways that people relate to one another in a society or group.

socialization   Lifelong process of social interaction through which people learn knowledge, skills, patterns of thinking and behaving, and other elements of a culture that are essential for effective participation in social life.

sole custody   A situation in which one divorced parent is given legal responsibility for raising children.

sonogram   A visual image of a fetus generated and printed out on a screen during ultrasound.

split custody   A court decision whereby siblings are split up between their two biological parents. When this occurs, a typical pattern is for mothers to have custody of daughters and fathers to have custody of sons.

stations of divorce   The multiple types of divorces that couples experience in dissolving their marital relationship: emotional, legal, economic, coparental, community, and psychic.

status   A social position that a person occupies within a group or society.

stereotypes   Qualities assigned to an individual solely on the basis of her or his social category. Stereotypes often are used to justify unequal treatment of members of a specific group.

storge   Style of love that is calm, affectionate, companionate, unexciting, and uneventful.

stratification   Hierarchical ranking of whole categories of people based on unequal access to scarce resources.

structural functionalism   A theoretical perspective that views society as an organized system, analogous to the human system, that is made up of a variety of interrelated parts or structures that work together to generate social stability and maintain society.

surrogate mother   The term used to refer to a woman who becomes pregnant and gives birth to a child for another woman who is infertile or incapable of carrying a child.

survey   A research method in which researchers collect data by asking people questions, for example, using questionnaires or face-to-face interviews.

symbolic interactionism   A theoretical perspective that defines society as a system of interacting individuals who communicate primarily through the use of shared symbols; a perspective that focuses on small-scale patterns of face-to-face interactions among people in specific settings such as in marriages and families.

symbols   Objects, words, sounds, or events that are given particular meaning and are recognized by members of a culture.

task overload   A situation of stress caused when a parent or guardian lacks adequate time, skills, or motivation to do all that is necessary in child rearing. Although anyone can experience this overload situation, it is most common among teenage mothers.

theory   A set of interrelated statements or propositions constructed to explain some phenomenon.

theory model   A set of interrelated statements or propositions that are intended to explain a limited set of facts, in contrast to broad theoretical perspectives such as structural functionalism.

total fertility rate   The average number of children women have.

toxemia   A condition that can develop during pregnancy in which the toxins produced by body cells at sites of infection enter into the mother's bloodstream and cause water retention, high blood pressure, and excessive weight gain. If left untreated it can cause convulsions, coma, and death.

trust Feelings of confidence and belief in another person; reliance upon another person to provide for or meet one's needs.

ultrasound A prenatal test that allows a physician to observe the developing fetus directly by viewing electronically the echoes of sound waves pulsating through the pregnant woman's body.

underemployment A concept that refers to several patterns of employment: part-time workers who want to work full-time, full-time workers who make very low wages, and workers with skills higher than those required by their current job.

validity The degree to which scientific research measures or instruments measure exactly what they are supposed to measure.

variable A factor or concept whose value changes from one case or observation to another.

victim blaming Justifying the unequal or negative treatment of individuals or groups by finding defects in the victims rather than examining the social and economic factors or conditions that create and contribute to their condition.

wheel theory of love A perspective of love developed by social scientist Ira Reiss in which love is viewed in terms of a four-stage, circular progression from rapport through self-revelation, mutual dependence, and personality need fulfillment as a couple interact with each other over time.

working poor Underemployed individuals who work full-time but make very low wages.

zygote A single-celled fertilized ovum (egg) that contains the complete genetic code for a human being.

REFERENCES

Adams, Virginia. 1982. "Getting at the Heart of Jealous Love." *Psychology Today* (May): 38–47.

Aday, Ronald H., Cyndee Rice, and Emilie Evans. 1991. "Intergenerational Partners Project: A Model Linking Elementary Students with Senior Center Volunteers." *Gerontologist* 31,2:263–66.

Ade-Ridder, Linda. 1990. "Sexuality and Marital Quality among Older Married Couples." In T. H. Brubaker, ed., *Family Relationships in Later Life*, 48–67. Newbury Park, CA: Sage.

———, and T. H. Brubaker. 1983. "The Quality of Long-Term Marriages." In T. H. Brubaker, ed., *Family Relationships in Later Life*, 19–30. Beverly Hills, CA: Sage.

Ahlburg, Dennis A., and Carol J. DeVita. 1992. "New Realities of the American Family." *Population Bulletin* 47,2 (August):1–44. Washington, DC.: Population Reference Bureau, Inc.

Ahrons, Constance. 1980. "Crises in Family Transitions." *Family Relations* 29:533–40.

———, and L. Wallish. 1986. "The Close Relationships between Former Spouses." In S. Duck and D. Perlman, eds., *Close Relationships: Development, Dynamics, and Deterioration*, 269–96. Beverly Hills, CA: Sage.

Alba, Richard D. 1985. "Marriage across Ethnic Lines." *Marriage and Divorce Today* 10:3.

Albas, Daniel, and Cheryl Mills Albas. 1989a. "Love and Marriage." In K. Ishwaran, ed., *Family and Marriage: Cross-Cultural Perspectives*, 125–42. Toronto, Canada: Wall and Thompson.

———. 1989b. "Sexuality and Marriage." In K. Ishwaran, ed., *Family and Marriage: Cross-Cultural Perspectives*, 145–62. Toronto, Canada: Wall and Thompson.

Aldous, Joan 1987. "New Views of the Family Life of the Elderly." *Journal of Marriage and the Family* 49:227–34.

———, Elizabeth Klaus, and David Klein. 1985. "The Understanding Heart: Aging Parents and Their Favorite Children." *Child Development* 56:303–16.

Allan, Carole A., and D. J. Cooke. 1985. "Stressful Life Events and Alcohol Misuse in Women: A Critical Review." *Journal of Studies on Alcohol* 46:147–52.

Allen, Katherine. 1989. *Single Women/Family Ties*. Newbury Park, CA: Sage.

Allgeier, Albert Richard, and Elizabeth R. Allgeier. 1988. *Sexual Interactions*. Lexington, MA: D. C. Heath.

Alpert-Gillis, L. J., and J. P. Connel. 1989. "Gender and Sex-Role Influences on Children's Self-Esteem." *Journal of Personality* 57:97–114.

Ambert, Anne-Marie. 1986. "Being a Stepparent: Live-in and Visiting Children." *Journal of Marriage and the Family* 48:795–804.

———. 1988. "Relationships with Former In-Laws after Divorce: A Research Note." *Journal of Marriage and the Family* 50:679–86.

American Association of University Women (AAUW). 1991.

Shortchanging Girls, Shortchanging America. Washington, DC: Greenberg-Lake Analysis Group.

American College of Nurse Midwives. 1991. "Today's Certified Nurse-Midwives." 1522 K Street NW, Washington, D.C., 20005.

American Humane Association. 1985. *National Analysis of Official Child Abuse and Neglect Reports.* Denver, CO: Author.

American Psychological Association. 1985. *Developing a National Agenda to Address Women's Mental Health Needs.* Washington, DC: Author.

Amott, Teresa L., and Julie A. Matthaei. 1991. *Race, Gender, and Work: A Multicultural History of Women in the United States.* Boston: South End Press.

Andersen, Margaret. 1988. *Thinking About Women: Sociological Perspectives on Sex and Gender,* 2d ed. New York: Macmillan.

———. 1993. *Thinking About Women: Sociological Perspectives on Sex and Gender,* 3d ed. New York: Macmillan.

———, and Patricia Hill Collins. 1992. *Race, Class, and Gender: An Anthology.* Belmont, CA: Wadsworth.

Anderson, S. A., C. S. Russell, and W. R. Schumm. 1983. "Perceived Marital Quality and Family Life-cycle Categories: A Further Analysis." *Journal of Marriage and the Family* 45:127–39.

Annadale, Ellen C. 1988. "How Midwives Accomplish Natural Birth: Managing Risk and Balancing Expectations." *Social Problems* 35:95–110.

Archbold, Patricia G. 1983. "The Impact of Parent-Caring on Women." *Family Relations* 32:39–45.

Arendell, Terry. 1986. *Mothers and Divorce: Legal, Economic, and Social Dilemmas.* Berkley, CA: University of California Press.

Aries, Philippe. 1981. *The Hour of Our Death.* New York: Knopf.

Asbury, Jo-Ellen. 1987. "African-American Women in Violent Relationships: An Exploration of Cultural Differences." In Robert L. Hampton, ed., *Violence in the Black Family,* 89–105. Lexington, MA: Heath.

Astin, A. W. 1984. "Freshman Characteristics and Attitudes." *Chronicle of Higher Education* 16 (January): 15–16.

Atchley, Robert 1991. *Social Forces and Aging,* 6th ed. Belmont, CA: Wadsworth.

Atwater, Lynn. 1982. *The Extramarital Connection: Sex, Intimacy, Identity.* New York: Irvington.

Bachrach, Christine A. 1980. "Childlessness and Social Isolation among the Elderly." *Journal of Marriage and the Family* 42:627–37.

———. 1986. "Adoption Plans, Adopted Children, and Adoptive Mothers." *Journal of Marriage and the Family* 48:243–53.

———, Patricia F. Adams, Soledad Sambrano, and Kathryn A. London. 1990. "Adoption in the 1980s." U.S. National Center for Health Statistics, Advance Data, No. 181, Jan. 5.

Badagliacco, Joanne M. 1991. "Abortion Choice among American Women: 1976 and 1988." Paper presented at the 86th annual meeting of the American Sociological Association. Cincinnati, OH.

Bailey, Ronald H. 1978. *The Home Front: U.S.A.* Alexandria, VA: Time-Life Books.

Balter, Joni. 1991. "Shifting Down: Yankelovich Survey Charts Big Change in Attitudes on Work vs. Family." *Chicago Tribune* (June 9): Sec. 6, p. 6.

Bannister, Shelly A. 1991. "The Criminalization of Women Fighting Back Against Male Abuse: Imprisoned Battered Women as Political Prisoners." *Humanity and Society* 15,4:400–416.

———. 1992. "Women and Violence." Lecture presented at North Park College, Chicago, IL.

Barcus, Earle F. 1983. *Images of Life on Children's Television: Sex Roles, Minorities and Families.* New York: Praeger.

Barlett, Donald L., and James B. Steele. 1992. *America: What Went Wrong?* Kansas City, MO: Andrews and McMeel.

Barnett, Alva P. 1991. "Sociocultural Influences on Adolescent Mothers." In Robert Staples, ed., *The Black Family: Essays and Studies,* 4th ed., 160–69. Belmont, CA: Wadsworth.

Barranti, C. R. 1985. "The Grandparent–Grandchild Relationship: Family Resources in an Era of Voluntary Bonds." *Family Relations* 34:343–52.

Barrett, Karen. 1982. "Date Rape: A Campus Epidemic?" *Ms.* (September): 48–51, 130.

Barringer, Felicity. 1993. "Sex Survey of American Men Find 1% Are Gay." *New York Times* (April 15): 1 Sec. A.

Barrow, Georgia M. 1989. *Aging, the Individual, and Society,* 4th ed. New York: West.

Baruch, G., R. Barnett, and C. Rivers. 1983. *Lifeprints: New Patterns of Love and Work for Today's Women.* New York: McGraw-Hill.

Basow, Susan. 1986. *Gender Stereotypes: Traditions and Alternatives.* Monterey, CA: Brooks/Cole.

———. 1992. *Gender: Stereotypes and Roles,* 3d ed. Belmont, CA: Brooks/Cole.

Baugher, R. J., C. Burger, R. Smith, and K. Wallstron. 1989–90. "A Comparison of Terminally Ill Persons at Various Time Periods to Death." *Omega* 20:103–15.

Bean, Frank, Russell Curtis, Jr., and John Marcum. 1977. "Familism and Marital Satisfaction among Mexican Americans: The Effects of Family Size, Wife's Labor Force Participation, and Conjugal Power." *Journal of Marriage and the Family* 39 (November): 759–67.

Becerra, Rosina M. 1988. "The Mexican American Family." In Charles H. Mindel, Robert W. Habenstein, and Roosevelt Wright Jr., eds., *Ethnic Families in America,* 141–159. New York: Elsevier.

———, and David Shaw. 1984. *The Hispanic Elderly*. Lanham, MD: University Press of America.

Beck, Melinda. 1988. "Willing Families, Waiting Kids." *Newsweek* (September 12): 64.

Becker, Gary A. 1981. *A Treatise on the Family*. Cambridge, MA: Harvard University Press.

Beer, William R. 1988. *Relative Strangers: Studies of Stepfamily Processes*. Totowa, NJ: Rowman and Littlefield.

———. 1989. *Strangers in the House: The World of Step-siblings and Half-siblings*. New Brunswick, NJ: Transaction.

Behrens, Leigh. 1990. "Study Shows Men's Capacity for Care." *Chicago Tribune* (October 28): Sec. 6, p. 2.

Bell, Alan P., and Martin Weinberg. 1978. *Homosexualities: A Study of Diversities among Men*. New York: Simon and Schuster.

———, and Sue Hammersmith. 1981. *Sexual Preference: Its Development in Men and Women*. Bloomington, IN: Indiana University Press.

Bell, Robert. 1971. *Marriage and Family Interaction*, 3d ed. Homewood, IL.: Dorsey.

Bem, Sandra L. 1983. "Gender Schema Theory and Its Implications for Child Development: Raising Gender-Schematic Children in a Gender-Schematic Society." *Signs* 8:598–616.

Bengtson, Vern, and Dean Black. 1973. "Intergenerational Relations and Continuities in Socialization." In P. B. Baltes and K. W. Schaie, eds., *Life-span Developmental Psychology: Personality and Socialization*, 208–34. New York: Academic Press.

Bengtson, Vern, and Dale Dannefer. 1987. "Families, Work and Aging: Implications of Disordered Cohort Flow for the 21st Century." In Russell Ward and Sheldon Tobin, eds., *Health in Aging: Sociological Issues and Policy Directions* 256–89. New York: Springer.

Bengtson, Vern, Carolyn Rosenthal, and Linda Burton. 1990. "Families and Aging: Diversity and Heterogeneity." In Robert H. Binstock and Linda K. George, eds., *Handbook of Aging and the Social Sciences*, 3d ed., 263–87. New York: Academic Press.

Benokraitis, Nijole V., and Joseph R. Feagin. 1986. *Modern Sexism*. Englewood Cliffs, NJ: Prentice Hall.

Benson-von der Ohe, Elizabeth. 1987. *First and Second Marriages*. New York: Praeger.

Berado, Felix M. 1968. "Widowhood Status in the U.S.: Perspectives on a Neglected Aspect of the Family Life Cycle." *Family Coordinator* 17:191–203.

———. 1970. "Survivorship and Social Isolation: The Case of the Aged Widower." *Family Coordinator* 19:11–15.

Berger, Raymond. 1982. *Gay and Gray: The Older Homosexual Man*. Chicago: University of Illinois Press.

Berk, Richard A., Sarah F. Berk, Donileen Loeseke, and David Rauma. 1983. "Mutual Combat and Other Family Violence Myths." In David Finkelhor, Richard J. Gelles, Gerald T. Hotaling, and Murray A. Straus, eds., *The Dark Side of Families: Current Family Violence Research*, 197–212. Beverly Hills, CA: Sage.

Berlin, Ira. 1974. *Slaves without Masters: The Free Negro in the Antebellum South*. New York: Pantheon Books.

Bernard, Jessie. 1956. *Remarriage: A Study of Marriage*. New York: Holt, Rinehart and Winston.

———. 1972. *The Future of Marriage*. New York: World.

———. 1982. *The Future of Marriage*. New Haven, CT: Yale University Press.

———. 1984. "The Good-Provider Role: Its Rise and Fall." In Patricia Voydanoff, ed., *Work and Family: Changing Roles of Men and Women*, 43–60. Palo Alto, Calif.: Mayfield.

Besharov, Douglas J. 1987. "Suffer the Little Children: How Child Abuse Programs Hurt Poor Families." *Policy Review* 39 (Winter): 52–55.

Bessell, Harold. 1984. *The Love Test*. New York: Warner Books.

Billingsley, Andrew. 1968. *Black Families in White America*. Englewood Cliffs, NJ: Prentice Hall.

Bird, Gloria, and Michael J. Sporakowski. 1992. *Taking Sides*. Sluice Dock, Guilford, CT: Dushkin.

Blackwell, James E. 1985. *The Black Community: Diversity and Unity*. New York: Harper and Row.

Blank, Robert. 1988. "Making Babies: The State of the Art." In J. Gipson Wells, ed., *Current Issues in Marriage and the Family*, 171–77. New York: Macmillan.

Blassingame, John. 1979. *The Slave Community*, 2d ed. New York: Oxford University Press.

Blau, Peter. 1964. *Exchange and Power in Social Life*. New York: Wiley.

Block, Joel. 1981. "Your Marriage Survival Kit." *Parents* (April).

Blood, Robert O., Jr., and Donald M. Wolfe. 1960. *Husbands and Wives*. New York: Macmillan.

Bluestone, Barry. 1987. "Deindustrialization and Unemployment in America." In Paul D. Staudohar and Holly E. Brown, eds., *Deindustrialization and Plant Closure*, 6–7. Lexington, MA: Heath.

Blumstein, Philip, and Pepper Schwartz. 1977. "Bisexuality: Some Social-Psychological Issues." *Journal of Social Issues* 33,2: 30–45.

———. 1983. *American Couples: Money, Work, Sex*. New York: Morrow.

Bohannan, Paul. 1970. *Divorce and after*. New York: Doubleday.

———. 1985. *All the Happy Families*. New York: McGraw-Hill.

Bolig, Rosemary, Peter J. Stein, and P. C. McHenry. 1984. "The Self-advertisement Approach to Dating: Male-Female Differences." *Family Relations* 33:587–92.

Boneparth, Ellen, and Emily Stoper. 1988. "Divorce and the Transition to the Single-Parent Family." In Ellen Boneparth and Emily Stoper, eds., *Women, Power, and Policy: Toward the Year 2000*, 206–18. New York: Pergamon Press.

Booth, Alan, and David Johnson. 1988. "Premarital Cohabitation and Marital Success." *Journal of Family Issues* 9:255–72.

———, Lynn K. White, and John N. Edwards. 1986. "Divorce and Marital Instability over the Life Course." *Journal of Family Issues* 7:421–42.

Borland, Delores M. 1975. "An Alternative Model of the Wheel Theory." *The Family Coordinator* 24 (July): 289–92.

"Born or Bred?" 1992. *Newsweek* (February 24): 46–53.

Bossard, James. 1932. "Residential Propinquity as a Factor in Mate Selection." *American Journal of Sociology* 38:219–24.

Boston Women's Health Book Collective. 1973. *Our Bodies, Ourselves*. New York: Simon and Schuster.

———. 1984. *The New Our Bodies, Ourselves*. New York: Simon and Schuster.

———. 1992. *The New Our Bodies, Ourselves*, (Revised). New York: Simon and Schuster.

Boswell, T. D., and J. R. Curtis. 1983. *The Cuban-American Experience: Culture, Images and Perspectives*. Totowa, NJ: Rowman and Allanheld.

Bound, John, Greg Duncan, Deborah Laren, and Lewis Oleinick. 1991. "Poverty Dynamics in Widowhood." *Journal of Gerontology* 46,3 (May): S115–24.

Bovee, Tim. 1993. "Interracial Marriages Now 1 in 50." *The Times-Picayune* (February 12): A1,A8.

Bowman, M. E., and C. R. Ahrons. 1985. "Impact of Legal Custody Status on Fathers' Parenting Post-divorce." *Journal of Marriage and the Family* 47:481–88.

Bradsher, Keith. 1989. "Employers Urge Men to Wed for Success." *News and Observer* (December 23): 3D.

Brazelton, T. B. 1989. Interview on Bill Moyer's "World of Ideas" (March 14).

Brecher, Edward. 1984. *Love, Sex, and Aging*. Boston: Little, Brown.

Brehm, Sharon S. 1992. *Intimate Relationships*. New York: McGraw-Hill.

Brod, Harry, ed. 1987. *The Making of Masculinities: The New Men's Studies*. Boston: Allen and Unwin.

Brodbar-Nemzer, Jay Y. 1986. "Divorce and Group Commitment: The Case of Jews." *Journal of Marriage and the Family* 48:329–40.

Brody, Elaine. 1988. "Parent Care as a Normative Family Stress." In Norval D. Glenn and Marion T. Coleman, eds., *Family Relations: A Reader*, 278–99. Belmont, CA: Wadsworth.

Bronstein, Phyllis. 1988. "Father–Child Interaction: Implications for Gender Role Socialization." In Phyllis Bronstein and Carolyn P. Cowan, eds., *Fatherhood Today:*

Men's Changing Role in the Family, 107–24. New York: Wiley.

Brotman, Barbara. 1992a. "Shaker Cares." *Chicago Tribune* (February 19): Sec. 5, pp. 1, 5.

———. 1992b. "A Silent Minority." *Chicago Tribune* (July 10): Sec. 5, p. 1.

Brotman, H. B. 1981. *Supplement to the Chartbook on Aging in America*. Washington, DC: White House Conference on Aging.

Broverman, Inge, Donald M. Broverman, F. E. Clarkson, P. S. Rosenkrantz, and S. R. Vogel. 1970. "Sex-Role Stereotypes and Clinical Judgments of Mental Health." *Journal of Consulting and Clinical Psychology* 34:1–7.

Brown, Bruce W., and Tony McCormick. 1988. "Family Coping Following Traumatic Head Injury: An Exploratory Analysis with Recommendations for Treatment." *Family Relations* 37:12–16.

Brubaker, Timothy H. 1985. *Later Life Families*. Beverly Hills, CA: Sage.

———. 1990. *Family Relationships in Later Life*, 2d ed. Newbury Park, CA: Sage.

———, and Charles B. Hennon. 1982. "Responsibility for Household Tasks: Comparing Dual-Earner and Dual-Retired Marriages." In Maximiliane Szinovacz, ed., *Women's Retirement*, 205–20. Beverly Hills, CA: Sage.

Buehler, Cheryl, and Mary Langenbrunner. 1987. "Divorce-Related Stressors: Occurrence, Disruptiveness, and Area of Life Change." *Journal of Divorce* 11:25–50.

Buehler, Cheryl, Janice Hogan, Beatrice Robinson, and Robert S. Levy. 1986. "Remarriage Following Divorce: Stressors and Well-being of Custodial and Non-custodial Parents." *Journal of Family Issues* 7:405–20.

Bulcroft, Kris, and Margaret O'Connor-Roden. 1986. "Never Too Late." *Psychology Today* (June): 66–69.

Bumpass, Larry. 1984. "Some Characteristics of Children's Second Families." *American Journal of Sociology* 90:608–23.

———. 1990. "What's Happening to the Family? Interaction between Demographic and Institutional Change." *Demography* 27 (November): 483–98.

———, and James A. Sweet. 1989. "National Estimates of Cohabitation." *Demography* 26,4 (November): 615–25.

———, and Andrew Cherlin. 1991. "The Role of Cohabitation in Declining Rates of Marriage." *Journal of Marriage and the Family* 53:913–27.

Bumpass, Larry, James A. Sweet, and Teresa Castro-Martin. 1990. "Changing Patterns of Remarriage." *Journal of Marriage and the Family* 52:747–56.

Bunch, Charlotte. 1979. "Learning from Lesbian Separatism." In Sheila Ruth, ed., *Issues in Feminism*, 551–56. Boston: Houghton Mifflin.

Bunin, Sherry. 1984. "Black, White, and Tan Family." *Parents* 59 (April): 88.

Burger, Jerry M., and Linda Burns. 1988. "The Illusion of

Unique Invulnerability and the Use of Effective Contraception." *Personality and Social Psychology Bulletin* 14:264–70.

Burgess, Ernest W. 1926. "The Family as a Unity of Interacting Personalities." *Family* 7:3–9.

Burman, Patrick. 1988. *Killing Time, Losing Ground: Experiences of Unemployment*. Toronto: Wall and Thompson.

Bussey, Kay, and Albert Bandura. 1984. "Influence of Gender Constancy and Social Power on Sex-Linked Modeling." *Journal of Personality and Social Psychology* 47:1292–1302.

Butler, Robert. 1975. *Why Survive? Being Old in America*. New York: Harper and Row.

Buunk, Bram B., and Barry van Driel. 1989. *Variant Lifestyles and Relationships*. Newbury Park, CA: Sage.

Calhoun, Arthur W. 1917. *A Social History of the American Family: From Colonial Times to the Present*, Vol. 1. Cleveland: Arthur H. Clark.

Campbell, Michael. 1992. "Eating Disorders Turn Up in Kids." *Chicago Tribune* (August 15): 1.

Cancian, Francesca M. 1989. "Gender Politics: Love and Power in the Private and Public Spheres." In Arlene S. Skolnick and Jerome H. Skolnick, eds., *Family in Transition*, 219–30. Glenview, IL: Scott, Foresman.

———. 1991. "The Feminization of Love." In Mark Hutter, ed., *The Family Experience*, 367–82. New York: Macmillan.

Cantor, M. H., and V. Little. 1985. "Aging and Social Care." In Robert H. Binstock and Ethel Shanas, eds., *Handbook of Aging*, 745–81. New York: Van Nostrand Reinhold.

Carballo-Diequez, Alex. 1989. "Gay Male Culture and Aids: Counseling Implications." *Journal of Counseling and Development* 68,1 (September/October): 26–30.

Cardell, Mona, Stephen Finn, and Jeanne Marecek. 1981. "Sex-Role Identity, Sex-Role Behavior, and Satisfaction in Heterosexual, Lesbian and Gay Male Couples." *Psychology of Women Quarterly* 5:488–94.

Cargan, Leonard, and Matthew Melko. 1982. *Singles: Myths and Realities*. Beverly Hills, CA: Sage.

Carlier, Auguste. 1972. *Marriage in the United States*. New York: Arno Press.

Carlson, Christopher. 1990. *Perspectives on the Family: History, Class, and Feminism*. Belmont, CA: Wadsworth.

Carr, Lois G., and Lorena S. Walsh. 1983. "The Planter's Wife: The Experience of White Women in 17th Century Maryland." In M. Gordon, ed., *The American Family in Social-Historical Perspective* 263–88. New York: St. Martin's Press.

Carrigan, T., Brian Connell, and Joseph Lee. 1987. "Toward a New Sociology of Masculinity." In Harry Brod, ed., *The Making of Masculinities*, 63–100. Boston: Allen and Unwin.

Carroll, Lee. 1988. "Concern with AIDS and the Sexual Behavior of College Students." *Journal of Marriage and the Family* 50:405–11.

Carter, Bill. 1991. "Children's TV, Where Boys Are King." *New York Times* (May 1): Secs. A1, C18.

Carter, Hugh, and Paul Glick. 1976. *Marriage and Divorce: A Social and Economic Study*, 2d ed. Cambridge, MA: Harvard University Press.

Casuso, Jorge. 1991. "Gays, Lesbians Shift Focus to Civil Rights and Win." *Chicago Tribune* (April 30): l, 6.

Catton, Peter. 1991. "Child-Care Problems: An Obstacle to Work." *Monthly Labor Review* 114 (October): 3–9.

Caulfield, M. D. 1985. "Sexuality in Human Evolution: What Is Natural in Sex?" *Feminist Studies* 11 (Summer): 343–64.

Cavanaugh, John. 1993. *Adult Development and Aging*, 2d ed. Pacific Grove, CA: Brooks/Cole.

Centers for Disease Control and Prevention. 1984. "Fetal Alcohol Syndrome." *Morbidity and Mortality Weekly Report (MMWR)*, 33,11.

———. 1992. "Projections of the Number of Persons Diagnosed with AIDS and the Number of Immunosuppressed HIV-Infected Persons, United States, 1992–1994." *Morbidity and Mortality Weekly Report (MMWR)*, no. RR-18.

———. 1993. *HIV/AIDS Surveillance Report* (February): 1–23.

Chafetz, Janet Saltzman. 1988. *Feminist Sociology: An Overview of Contemporary Theories*. Itasca, IL: Peacock.

Chambers-Schiller, Lee Virginia. 1984. *Liberty, a Better Husband: Single Women in America: The Generations of 1780–1840*. New Haven, CT: Yale University Press.

Chan, Connie S. 1989. "Issues of Identity Development among Asian-American Lesbians and Gay Men." *Journal of Counseling and Development* 68,1 (September/October): 16–20.

Chan, Florentius. 1988. "To Be Old and Asian: An Unsettling Life in America." *Aging* No. 358:14–15.

Chandra, Anupama. 1991. "Marriage Indian Style: The Arranged Marriage Is Alive and Well in the U.S." *Reader* 21,5 (November 1): 1–28.

Chappell, Neena. 1991. "Living Arrangements and Sources of Caring." *Journal of Gerontology* 46,1 (January): 51–58.

Chasnoff, Ira J., Jeffrey W. Ellis, and Zachary S. Fainman. 1985. "Cocaine Use in Pregnancy." *New England Journal of Medicine* (September 12): 666–69.

Cheal, David. 1989. "The Meanings of Family Life: Theoretical Approaches and Theory Models." In K. Ishwaran, ed. *Family and Marriage: Cross-Cultural Perspectives*, 33–42. Toronto, Canada: Wall and Thompson.

Cherlin, Andrew. 1978. "Remarriage as an Incomplete Institution." *American Journal of Sociology* 84,3:634–50.

———. 1981. *Marriage, Divorce, Remarriage*. Cambridge, MA: Harvard University Press.

———. 1992. *Marriage, Divorce, Remarriage*, rev. ed. Cambridge, MA: Harvard University Press.

———, and Frank F. Furstenberg, Jr. 1983. "The American Family in the Year 2000." *Futurist* (June): 7–14.

———. 1986a. "Styles and Strategies of Grandparenting." In Vern L. Bengston and Joan Robertson, eds., *Grandparenthood*, 97–116. Beverly Hills, CA: Sage.

———. 1986b. *The New American Grandparent: A Place in the Family, a Life Apart.* New York: Basic Books.

———. 1988. "The Changing European Family." *Journal of Family Issues* 9:291–97.

Cherukuri, R., H. Minkoff, J. Feldman, A. Parkeh, and L. Glass. 1988. "A Cohort Study of Alkaloidal Cocaine (Crack) in Pregnancy." *Obstetrics and Gynecology* 72:152–62.

Chesley, Leon. 1989. "Toxemia." In F. Gary Cunningham et al., *Williams Obstetrics*, 18th ed. Norwalk, CT: Appleton and Lange.

Chicago Sun-Times. 1980. "How to Decide Whether It's Love or Infatuation." Weekender Sec. p. 2.

———. 1988. "Wedding Traditions Date Back for Centuries." (January 17): Special advertising Sec. p. 2.

Chicago Tribune. 1989. "Danish Gay Couples Say 'I Do' Legally for 1st Time." (October 2): 1.

———. 1991a. "Pentagon Opposes Plan to Free Parents from Wartime Duty." (February 8): 18.

———. 1991b. "Study: Kids, Moms Poor after Divorce." (March 12): 6.

———. 1991c. "Chinese Find Perfect Solution for Those Who Put Off Marriage." (May 14): Sec. 1, p. 8.

———. 1991d. "Make Room for Daddy on the Job." (June 13): 1A, p. 36.

———. 1991e. "Elderly Abandoned at Hospitals: Granny Dumping Is a Variation of Baby-on-Doorstep." (November 29): Section 1,27.

———. 1992a. "Textbook Sexism." (July 12): Sec. 6, p. 1.

———. 1992b. "Aids Growing Fastest among Women." (July 21): 1,10.

———. 1992c. "Study: Rich Get Most of U.S. Wealth Increase." (October 30): Section 1,6.

Chiriboga, D. A., and M. Thurnher. 1980. "Marital Lifestyles and Adjustments to Separation." *Journal of Divorce* 3:379–90.

Chodorow, Nancy. 1978. *The Reproduction of Mothering: Psychoanalysis and the Sociology of Gender.* Berkeley, CA: University of California Press.

———. 1990. *Feminism and Psychoanalytic Theory.* New Haven, CT: Yale University Press.

Chun, Siong-Huat. 1990. "Asian Americans: Gay and Lesbian." In Wayne R. Dynes, ed., *Encyclopedia of Homosexuality*, 84–85. New York: Garland.

Clark, A. L., and P. Wallin. 1965. "Women's Sexual Responsiveness and the Duration and Quality of Their Marriage." *American Journal of Sociology* 71:187–96.

Clayton, Richard R. 1978. *The Family, Marriage, and Social Change.* Lexington, MA: Heath.

Cleary, Paul D. 1987. "Gender Differences in Stress-Related Disorders." In R. C. Barnett, L. Biener, and G. K. Baruch, eds., *Gender and Stress*, 39–72. New York: Free Press.

Clingempeel, W. Glenn, and Eulalee Brand. 1985. "Quasi-Kin Relationships, Structural Complexity, and Marital Quality in Stepfamilies: A Replication, Extension, and Clinical Implications." *Family Relations* 34:401–9.

Clingempeel, W. Glenn, and Sion Segal. 1986. "Stepparent–Stepchild Relationships and the Psychological Adjustment of Children in Stepmother and Stepfather Families." *Child Development* 57:474–84.

Coates, Jennifer. 1986. *Women, Men and Language.* New York: Longman.

Cochran, Susan D., and Vickie M. Mays. 1991. "Sociocultural Facets of the Black Gay Male Experience." In Robert Staples, ed., *The Black Family: Essays and Studies*, 4th ed., 289–96. Belmont, CA: Wadsworth.

Cockerham, William C. 1991. *This Aging Society.* Englewood Cliffs, NJ: Prentice Hall.

Cockrum, Janet, and Priscilla White. 1985. "Influences on the Life Satisfaction of Never-Married Men and Women." *Family Relations* 34:551–56.

Coker, Dana Rosenberg. 1984. "The Relationship among Concepts and Cognitive Maturity in Pre-School Children." *Sex Roles* 10:19–31.

Coleman, Marilyn, and Lawrence H. Ganong. 1987. "The Cultural Stereotyping of Stepfamilies." In Kay Pasley and Marilyn Ihinger-Tallman, eds., *Remarriage and Stepparenting: Current Research and Theory*, 19–41. New York: Guilford Press.

———. 1990. "Remarriage and Stepfamily Research in the 1980s: Increased Interest in an Old Family Form." *Journal of Marriage and the Family* 52:925–40.

Coles, Robert, and Geoffrey Stokes. 1985. *Sex and the American Teenager.* New York: Harper and Row, Colophon Books.

Collins, Patricia Hill. 1991. "The Meaning of Motherhood in Black Culture." In Robert Staples, ed., *The Black Family: Essays and Studies*, 4th ed., 169–78. Belmont, CA: Wadsworth.

Committee for Abortion Rights and Against Sterilization Abuse. 1988. *Women under Attack: Victories, Backlash, and the Fight for Reproductive Freedom.* Boston: South End Press.

Condry, John. 1989. *The Psychology of Television.* Hillsdale, NJ: Erlbaum.

Conner, Karen. 1992. *Aging America: Issues Facing an Aging Society.* Englewood Cliffs, NJ: Prentice Hall.

Constantine, Larry, and Joan Constantine. 1972. "The Group Marriage." In Milton Gordon, ed., *The Nuclear Family in Crisis: The Search for an Alternative*, 204–22. New York: Harper and Row.

———. 1973. *Group Marriage.* New York: Collier.

Cook, Ellen P. 1987. "Characteristics of the Biopsychosocial

Crisis of Infertility." *Journal of Counseling and Development* 65:465–70.

Cooney, Teresa, and Peter Uhlenberg. 1989. "Family-Building Patterns of Professional Women: A Comparison of Lawyers, Physicians, and Postsecondary Teachers." *Journal of Marriage and the Family* 51:749–58.

———. 1990. "The Role of Divorce in Men's Relations with Their Adult Children after Mid-life." *Journal of Marriage and the Family* 52:677–88.

Coontz, Stephanie. 1988. *The Social Origins of Private Life.* New York: Verso.

———. 1992. *The Way We Never Were: American Families and the Nostalgia Trap.* New York: Basic Books.

Copeland, Monica. 1991. "Black Women Push Alternatives to Army." *Chicago Tribune* (May 13): 1,10.

Cornfield, Noreen 1983. "The Success of Urban Communes." *Journal of Marriage and the Family* 45,1:115–26.

Counts, Dorothy Ayers. 1987. "Female Suicide and Wife Abuse: A Cross-Cultural Perspective." *Suicide and Life-Threatening Behavior* 17,3:194–204.

Couric, Emily. 1989. "An NLJ/West Survey, Women in the Law: Awaiting Their Turn." *National Law Journal* 11 (December): S1, S12.

Coward, Raymond T. 1987. "Factors Associated with the Configuration of the Helping Networks of Noninstitutionalized Elders." *Gerontological Social Work* 10:113–32.

Cowley, G. 1990. "Made-To-Order Babies." *Newsweek* special edition (Winter/Spring): 94–100.

Cox, Harold. 1993. *Later Life: The Realities of Aging*, 3d ed. Englewood Cliffs, NJ: Prentice Hall.

Crispell, Diane. 1989. "Three's a Crowd." *American Demographics* 11:34–38.

Crosbie-Burnett, Margaret. 1984. "The Centrality of the Step Relationship: A Challenge to Family Theory and Practice." *Family Relations* 33:459–64.

———, Ada Skyles, and June Becker-Haven. 1988. "Exploring Stepfamilies from a Feminist Perspective." In Sanford M. Dornbush and Myra H. Strober, eds., *Feminism, Children, and the New Families*, 297–326. New York: Guilford Press.

Cuber, John F., and Peggy B. Harroff. 1966. *The Significant Americans.* New York: Random House. (Published also as "Five Types of Marriage." In Arlene S. Skolnick and Jerome H. Skolnick, *Family in Transition*, 7th ed., 177–188, 1992. New York:HarperCollins).

Cunningham-Burley, Sarah. 1987. "The Experience of Grandfatherhood." In Charles Lewis and Margaret O'Brien, eds., *Reassessing Fatherhood: New Observations on Fathers and the Modern Family*, 91–105. Beverly Hills, CA: Sage.

Curry, George E. 1992. "New York State May Bar Mothers for Hire." *Chicago Tribune* (May 31): 17, 22.

Cutler, Blayne. 1988. "Band of Gold: The Earnings of Married versus Unmarried Males." *American Demographics* 10 (November): 14.

Dainton, Marianne. 1993. "The Myth and Misconceptions of the Stepmother Identity." *Family Relations* 42:93–98.

Daly, Mary. 1978. *Gyn/Ecology: The Metaethics of Radical Feminism.* Boston: Beacon Press.

Daniels, Roger. 1990. *Coming to America: A History of Immigration and Ethnicity in American Life.* New York: HarperCollins.

Darling, Carol, David J. Kallen, and Joyce E. VanDusen. 1989. "Sex in Transition: 1900–1980." In Arlene S. Skolnick and Jerome H. Skolnick, eds., *Family in Transition*, 6th ed., 236–78. New York: Scott, Foresman.

Darrett, B., and Anita H. Rutman. 1979. "Now Wives and Sons-in-Law: Parental Death in Seventeenth-Century Virginia Country." In Thad W. Tote and David L. Ammerman, eds., *The Chesapeake in the Seventeenth Century.* Chapel Hill, NC: University of North Carolina Press.

Davis, Angela. 1981. *Women, Race, and Class.* New York: Random House.

Davis, Keith. 1985. "Near and Dear: Friendship and Love Compared." *Psychology Today* (February 24): 22–28, 30.

———, and Michael Todd. 1985. "Assessing Friendship: Prototypes, Paradigm Cases and Relationship Description." In Steve Duck and Daniel Perlman, eds., *Understanding Personal Relationships: An Interdisciplinary Approach*, 17–38. London: Sage.

Davis, Kingsley. 1940. "Extreme Social Isolation of a Child." *American Journal of Sociology* 45,4 (January): 554–65.

———. 1947. "Final Note on a Case of Extreme Isolation." *American Journal of Sociology* 52,5 (March): 432–37.

DeBartolo, Anthony. 1991. "Men Still Unwelcome in Most Child-Care Jobs." *Chicago Tribune* (November 10): Sec. 2, p. 1.

Degler, Carl. 1980. *At Odds: Women and the Family in America from the Revolution to the Present.* New York: Oxford University Press.

Delamaster, John. 1987. "Gender Differences in Sexual Scenarios." In K. Kelly, ed., *Females, Males, and Sexuality*, 127–39. Albany, N.Y.: State University of New York Press.

Delora, JoAnn S., and Carol Warren. 1977. *Understanding Sexual Interaction.* Boston: Houghton Mifflin.

D'Emilio, John, and Estelle B. Freedman. 1988. *Intimate Matters: A History of Sexuality In America.* New York: Harper and Row.

Demo, David. H., and Alan C. Acock. 1988. "The Impact of Divorce on Children." *Journal of Marriage and the Family* 50:619–48.

Demos, John. 1970: *A Little Commonwealth: Family Life in Plymouth Colony.* New York: Oxford University Press.

———. 1974. "The American Family in Past Time." *American Scholar* 43:422–46.

Dermer, Marshall, and Thomas A. Pyszczynski. 1978. "Effects of Erotica upon Men's Loving and Liking Responses for Women They Love." *Journal of Personality and Social Psychology* 24:1–10.

DeStefano, Linda, and Diane Colosanto. 1990. "Unlike 1975, Most Americans Think Men Have It Better." *Gallup Poll Monthly* (February): 29.

De Spelder, Lynne A., and Albert L. Strickland. 1988. *The Last Dance.* Mountain View, CA: Mayfield Press.

Devall, Esther, Zolinda Stoneman, and Gene Brody. 1986. "The Impact of Divorce and Maternal Employment on Pre-adolescent Children." *Family Relations* 35:153–59.

DeVault, Marjorie L. 1990. "What Counts as Feminist Ethnography?" Paper presented at Exploring New Frontiers: Qualitative Research Conference, York University, Toronto.

Devor, Holly. 1989. *Gender Blending: Confronting the Limits of Duality.* Bloomington, IN: Indiana University Press.

DiGiulio, Robert C. 1989. *Beyond Widowhood: From Bereavement to Emergence and Hope.* New York: Free Press.

Dinkmeyer, Don, and Jon Carlson. 1984. *Time for a Better Marriage.* Circle Pines, MN: American Guidance Service.

Dion, K. L., and K. K. Dion. 1973. "Correlates of Romantic Love." *Journal of Consulting and Clinical Psychology* 41:41–56.

Dobash, R. Emerson, and Russell Dobash. 1979. *Violence Against Wives.* New York: Free Press.

Dobson, Cynthia. 1983. "Sex-Role and Marital-Role Expectations." In Timothy H. Brubaker, ed., *Family Relationships in Later Life*, 109–26. Beverly Hills, CA: Sage.

Dodge, Susan. 1991. "Creative Dating Offers Students Alternatives to Bars and Movies." *Chronicle of Higher Education* 37,27 (March 20): A37.

Doka, Kenneth, and Mary Ellen Mertz. 1988. "The Meaning and Significance of Great-grandparenthood." *Gerontologist* 28:192–97.

Donatelle, Rebecca J., Lorraine G. Davis, and Carolyn F. Hoover. 1994. *Access to Health*, 3d ed. Englewood Cliffs, NJ: Prentice Hall.

Dornbusch, Sanford M., J. Merrill Carlsmith, and Steven Bushwall. 1985. "Single Parents, Extended Households, and the Control of Adolescents." *Child Development* 56:326–41.

Dorning, Mike. 1991. "Software Giant Extends Benefits to Gay Couples." *Chicago Tribune* (September 7): Section l,14.

Downs, A. Chris. 1983. "Letters to Santa Claus: Elementary School-Age Children's Sex-Typed Toy Preferences in a Natural Setting." *Sex Roles* 9:159–63.

Doyle, James A., and Michelle A. Paludi. 1991. *Sex and Gender: The Human Experience.* Dubuque, IA: Brown.

Draughon, Margaret. 1975. "Stepmother's Model of Identification in Relation to Mourning in the Child." *Psychological Reports* 36:183–89.

Dressel, Paula L., and Beth B. Hess. 1983. "Alternatives for the Elderly." In Eleanor D. Macklin and Roger Rubin, eds., *Contemporary Families and Alternative Lifestyles: Handbook on Research and Theory.* Beverly Hills, CA: Sage.

Duberman, Lucile. 1973. "Stepkin Relationships." *Journal of Marriage and the Family* 35:283–92.

Duncan, Greg, and Saul Hoffman. 1985. "A Reconsideration of the Economic Consequences of Marital Dissolution." *Demography* 22:485–97.

Durkheim, Emile. 1951. *Suicide: A Study in Sociology.* J. A. Spaulding and G. Simpson, trans. New York: Free Press. (Originally published 1897)

Dutton, Donald G. 1988. *The Domestic Assault of Women.* Boston, MA: Allyn and Bacon.

Duvall, Evelyn M. 1977. *Marriage and Family Development,* 5th ed. Philadelphia, PA: Lippincott.

Dweck, Carol S., William Davidson, Sharon Nelson, and Bradley Enna. 1978. "Sex Differences in Learned Helplessness: II. The Contingencies of Evaluative Feedback in the Classroom. III. An Experimental Analysis." *Developmental Psychology* 14:268–76.

Dworkin, Andrea. 1987. *Intercourse.* New York: Free Press.

Dwyer, Jeffrey, and Raymond T. Coward. 1991. "A Multivariate Comparison of the Involvement of Adult Sons versus Daughters in the Care of Impaired Parents." *Journal of Gerontology* 46,5 (September): 5259–69.

Earle, Alice Morse. 1893. *Customs and Fashions in Old New England.* New York: Scribner.

Eckland, Bruce. 1968. "Theories of Mate Selection." *Eugenics Quarterly* 15:79.

Edelson, Jeffrey L., David M. Miller, Gene W. Stone, and Dennis G. Chapman. 1985. "Group Treatment for Men Who Batter." *Social Work Research and Abstracts* 2,3:18–21.

Edwards, John N. 1969. "Familial Behavior as Social Exchange." *Journal of Marriage and the Family* 31:518–26.

———. 1991. "Asexual Reproduction and the Family." In John Edwards and David Demo, eds., *Marriage and Family in Transition*, 497–505. Boston: Allyn and Bacon.

Ehrenreich, B., E. Hess, and G. Jacobs. 1986. *Re-Making Love: The Feminization of Sex.* Garden City, NY: Anchor Press.

Ehrhardt, Anke. 1985. "Psychobiology of Gender." In Alice Rossi, ed., *Gender and the Life Course*, 81–96. Hawthorne, NY: Aldine.

———, and Susan W. Baker. 1974. "Fetal Androgens, Human Central Nervous System Differentiation, and Behavior Sex Differences." In R. C. Friedman, R. M. Richard, and R. L. Vande Wiele, eds., *Sex Differences in Behavior*, 33–52. New York: Wiley.

Einstein, Elizabeth. 1985. *The Stepfamily: Living, Loving, and Learning.* Boston: Shambhala.

Elmer-Dewitt, Philip. 1991. "Why Isn't Our Birth Control Better?" *Time* (Aug. 12): 52–53.

Erikson, Erik. 1968. *Identity: Youth and Crisis*. New York: Norton.

Espin, O. M. 1987. "Issues of Identity in the Psychology of Latina Lesbians." In Boston Lesbian Psychologies Collective, eds., *Lesbian Psychologies*. Urbana and Chicago: University of Illinois Press.

Etaugh, Claire and Joan Malstrom. 1981. "The Effect of Marital Status on Person Perception." *Journal of Marriage and the Family* 43:801–5.

Ettelbrick, Paula. 1989. "Since When Is Marriage a Path to Liberation?" *Out/Look* (Fall).

Faderman, Lillian. 1989. "A History of Romantic Friendship and Lesbian Love." In Barbara Risman and Pepper Schwartz, eds., *Gender and Intimate Relationships*, 26–31. Belmont, CA: Wadsworth.

Fausto-Sterling, Anne. 1985. *Myths of Gender*. New York: Basic Books.

Faux, Marian. 1984. *Childless by Choice: Choosing Childlessness in the 80s*. Garden City, NY: Anchor Press/Doubleday.

Federal Bureau of Investigation. 1987. *Uniform Crime Reports*. Washington, DC: U.S. Government Printing Office.

Fendrich, Michael. 1984. "Wives' Employment and Husbands' Distress: A Meta-analysis and a Replication." *Journal of Marriage and the Family* 46:871–79.

Fengler, Alfred, and Nancy Goodrich. 1979. "Wives of Elderly Men: The Hidden Patients." *Gerontologist* 19 (April): 175–83.

Ferber, Marianne A. 1982. "Women and Work: A Review Essay." *Signs* 8 (Winter): 273–95.

Fernea, Elizabeth. 1965. *Guests of the Sheik*. Garden City, NY: Doubleday.

Ferrante, Joan. 1992. *Sociology: A Global Perspective*. Belmont, CA: Wadsworth.

Fillenbaum, Gerda G., Linda K. George, and Erdman B. Palmore. 1985. "Determinants and Consequences of Retirement among Men of Different Races and Economic Levels." *Journal of Gerontology* 40:85–94.

Fine, Mark, and David Fine. 1992. "Recent Changes in Laws Affecting Stepfamilies: Suggestions for Legal Reform." *Family Relations* 41:334–40.

Finkelhor, David. 1984a. "Marital Rape: The Misunderstood Crime." Address to the New York County Lawyer's Association.

———. 1984b. *Child Sexual Abuse: New Theory and Research*. New York: Free Press.

———, and Kersti Yllo. 1985. *License to Rape: Sexual Abuse of Wives*. New York: Holt, Rinehart and Winston.

Finkelman, Paul, ed. 1989. *Women and the Family in a Slave Society*. New York: Garland.

Finley, Nancy J., M. Diane Roberts, and Benjamin F. Banahan. 1988. "Motivators and Inhibitors of Attitudes of Filial Obligation toward Aging Parents." *Gerontologist* 28:73–78.

Fischman, Joshua. 1988. "Stepdaughter Wars." *Psychology Today* 22 (November): 38–45.

Fisher, Terri D. 1986. "Parent-child Communication About Sex and Young Adolescents' Sexual Knowledge and Attitudes." *Adolescence* 21,83 (Fall): 517–27.

Fishman, Barbara. 1983. "The Economic Behavior of Stepfamilies." *Family Relations* 32:359–66.

———, and Bernice Hamel. 1991. "From Nuclear to Stepfamily Ideology: A Stressful Change." In John N. Edwards and David H. Demo, eds., *Marriage and Families in Transition*, 436–52. Boston: Allyn and Bacon.

Flaherty, Sr. Mary Jean, Lorna Facteau, and Patricia Garver. 1991. "Grandmother Functions in Multi-generational Families: An Exploratory Study of Black Adolescent Mothers and Their Infants." In Robert Staples, ed., *The Black Family*, 192–200. Belmont, CA: Wadsworth.

Foreit, Karen G., Terna Agor, Johnny Byers, John LaRue, Helen Lokey, Michael Palazzini, Michele Patterson, and Lillian Smith. 1980. "Sex Bias in the Newspaper Treatment of Male-Centered and Female-Centered News Stories." *Sex Roles* 6:475–80.

Forrest, Jacqueline, and Susheela Singh. 1990. "The Sexual and Reproductive Behavior of American Women, 1982–1988." *Family Planning Perspectives* 22,5 (September/October): 206–14.

Foster, Carol D., Mark A. Siegel, and Patricia Von Brook, eds. 1989. *Homeless in America: How Could It Happen Here?* Wylie, TX: Information Plus.

Fowler, Susanne. 1991. "Women at Risk in Spread of AIDS, Study Warns." *Chicago Tribune* (6 October): Sec. 6, p. 1.

Fox, V. C., and M. H. Quitt. 1980. "Stage VI: Spouse Loss." In V. C. Fox and M. H. Quitt, eds., *Loving, Parenting and Dying: The Family Cycle in England and America, Past and Present* 49–61. New York: Psychohistory Press.

Franklin, Benjamin. 1745. "Advice to a Young Man in Choosing a Mistress." In L. Labare and W. Bell, Jr., eds., *The Papers of Benjamin Franklin*, vol. 3. New Haven, CT: Yale University Press (1961).

Franklin, Clyde W. 1988. *Men and Society*. Chicago, IL: Nelson-Hall.

Frazier, E. Franklin. 1939. *The Negro Family in the United States*. Chicago: University of Chicago Press.

Freedman, Estelle, and Barrie Thorne. 1984. "Introduction to the 'Feminist Sexuality' Debates." *Signs* 10 (Autumn): 102–05.

Freeman, Ruth, and Patricia Klaus. 1984. "Blessed or Not: The New Spinster in England and the United States in the Late Nineteenth and Early Twentieth Centuries." *Journal of Family History* 9:394–414.

Freiberg, P. 1991. "Parental-Notification Laws Termed Harmful." *APA Monitor* (March): 28.

Freud, Sigmund. 1974. "Some Psychical Consequences of the Anatomical Distinction between the Sexes." In J. Strachey, ed. and trans., *The Standard Edition of the Complete Psychological Works of Sigmund Freud*, vol. 19, 241–60. London: Hogarth Press. (Original work published 1925.)

Friede, A., W. Baldwin, P. H. Rhodes, J. Bueler, and M. Strauss. 1988. "Older Maternal Age and Infant Mortality in the United States." *Obstetrics and Gynecology* 72:152–62.

Frieze, Irene H., and Angela Browne. 1989. "Violence in Marriage." In Lloyd Ohlin and Michael Tonry, eds., *Family Violence*, 163–218. Chicago: University of Chicago Press.

Fromm, Erich. 1956. *The Art of Loving.* New York: Bantam Books.

———. 1970. *The Crisis of Psychoanalysis.* New York: Holt, Rinehart, and Winston.

Fuchs, Victor R. 1986. "Sex Differences in Economic Well-Being." *Science* 232 (April): 459–64.

Furstenberg, Frank, Jr. 1973. "Recycling the Family." In *Marriage and Family Review*, vol. 2. New York: Haworth Press.

———, and Graham B. Spanier. 1984. *Recycling the Family.* Beverly Hills, CA: Sage.

———. 1987. *Recycling the Family: Remarriage after Divorce.* Newbury Park, CA: Sage.

Furstenberg, Frank, Jr., and Andrew Cherlin. 1991. *Divided Families: What Happens to Children When Parents Part?* Cambridge, MA: Harvard University Press.

Furstenberg, Frank, Jr., S. Philip Morgan, and Paul D. Allison. 1987. "Parental Participation and Children's Well-Being after Marital Dissolution." *American Sociological Review* 52:695–701.

Furstenberg, Frank, Jr., C. W. Nord, J. L. Peterson, and N. Zill. 1983. "The Life Course of Children of Divorce: Marital Disruption and Parental Contact." *American Sociological Review* 48:656–68.

Gagnon, John H. 1977. *Human Sexualities.* Glenview, IL: Scott, Foresman.

———, and William Simon. 1973. *Sexual Conduct: The Social Sources of Human Sexuality.* Chicago: Aldine.

Ganong, Laurence H., and Marilyn Coleman. 1984. "The Effects of Remarriage on Children: A Review of the Empirical Literature." *Family Relations* 33:389–405.

———. 1987. "Sex, Sex Roles, and Familial Love." *Journal of Genetic Psychology* 148:45–52.

———. 1989. "Preparing for Remarriage: Anticipating the Issues, Seeking Solutions." *Family Relations* 38:28–33.

Gecas, Viktor, and Michael L. Schwalbe. 1983. "Beyond the Looking-Glass Self: Social Structure and Efficacy-Based Self-Esteem." *Social Psychology Quarterly* 46:77–88.

Geiss, S. K., and K. D. O'Leary. 1981. "Therapists' Ratings of Frequency and Severity of Marital Problems: Implications for Research." *Journal of Marital and Family Therapy* 7:515–20.

Gelfand, Donald E., and Charles M. Barresi, eds. 1987. *Ethnic Dimensions of Aging.* New York: Springer.

Gelles, Richard J., and Claire Pedrick Cornell. 1990. *Intimate Violence in Families.* Newbury Park, CA: Sage.

Gelles, Richard J., and Eileen F. Hargreaves. 1987. "Maternal Employment and Violence toward Children." In Richard J. Gelles, ed., *Family Violence*, 108–25. Newbury Park, CA: Sage.

Gelles, Richard J., and Murray Strauss. 1987. "Is Violence toward Children Increasing? A Comparison of 1975 and 1985 National Survey Rates." *Journal of Interpersonal Violence* 2:212–22.

———. 1988. *Intimate Violence: The Definitive Study of Cases and Consequences of Abuse in the American Family.* New York: Simon and Schuster.

Genovese, Eugene D. 1974. *Roll, Jordan, Roll.* New York: Pantheon.

Gerrard, Meg. 1987. "Sex, Sex Guilt, and Contraceptive Use Revisited: The 1980's." *Journal of Personality and Social Psychology* 52:975–80.

Gerstel, Naomi. 1990. "Divorce and Stigma." In Christopher Carlson, ed., *Perspectives on the Family: History, Class, and Feminism*, 460–78. Belmont, CA: Wadsworth.

Giarrusso, Roseann, Paula Johnson, Jacqueline Goodchilds, and Gail Zellman. 1979. "Adolescents' Cues and Signals: Sex and Assault." Paper presented at the annual meeting of the Western Psychological Association, April, San Diego, CA.

Gibson, Rose. 1986. "Blacks in an Aging Society." *Daedalus* 115:349–71.

Giles-Sims, Jean. 1984. "The Stepparent Role: Expectations, Behavior, and Sanctions." *Journal of Family Issues* 5,1:116–30.

Gill, Richard T., Nathan Glazer, and Stephan A. Thernstrom. 1992. *Our Changing Population.* Englewood Cliffs, NJ: Prentice Hall.

Gilligan, Carol. 1990. "Teaching Shakespeare's Sister: Notes from the Underground of Female Adolescence." In C. Gilligan, N. P. Lyons, and T. J. Hammer, eds., *Making Connections*, 6–29. Cambridge, MA: Harvard University Press.

Gladwell, Malcolm. 1988. "Surrogate Parenting: Legal Labor Pains." In J. Gipson Wells, ed., *Current Issues in Marriage and the Family*, 179–84. New York: Macmillan.

Glendon, Mary Ann. 1987. *Abortion and Divorce in Western Law.* Cambridge, MA: Harvard University Press.

Glenn, Evelyn Nakano. 1983. "Split Household, Small Producer and Dual Wage Earner: An Analysis of Chinese American Family Strategies." *Journal of Marriage and the Family* 45 (February): 35–46.

Glenn, Norval D. 1981. "The Well-being of Persons Remarried after Divorce." *Journal of Family Issues* 2:61–75.

———. 1982. "Interreligious Marriage in the United States: Patterns and Recent Trends" *Journal of Marriage and the Family* 44 (August):555–66.

———, and Charles N. Weaver. 1988. "The Changing Relationship of Marital Status to Reported Happiness." *Journal of Marriage and the Family* 50:317–24.

Glenn, Norval D., and Michael Supancic. 1984. "The Social and Demographic Correlates of Divorce and Separation in the United States: An Update and Reconsideration." *Journal of Marriage and the Family* 46:563–75.

Glick, Paul. 1980. "Remarriage: Some Recent Changes and Variations." *Journal of Family Issues* 1,4:455–78.

———. 1984. "Marriage, Divorce, and Living Arrangements: Prospective Changes." *Journal of Family Issues* 5:7–26.

———. 1989. "Remarried Families, Stepfamilies, and Stepchildren: A Brief Demographic Analysis." *Family Relations* 38:24–27.

———, and S. Lin. 1986. "Recent Changes in Divorce and Remarriage." *Journal of Marriage and the Family* 48:737–47.

Glick, Paul, and Arthur Norton. 1977. "Marrying, Divorcing, and Living Together in the U.S. Today." *Population Bulletin* 32:2–39.

Glick, Paul, and Graham B. Spanier. 1981. "Cohabitation in the United States." In Peter Stein, ed., *Single Life*, 194–209. New York: St. Martin's Press.

Glick, Paul, and Robert Parke. 1965. "New Approaches in Studying the Life Cycle of the Family." *Demography* 2: 187–202.

Godwin, D. D., and J. Scanzoni. 1989. "Couple Consensus during Marital Joint Decision-making: A Context, Process, Outcome Model." *Journal of Marriage and the Family* 51:943–56.

Goetting, Ann. 1982. "The Six Stations of Remarriage: Developmental Task of Remarriage after Divorce." *Family Relations* 31:213–22.

Goleman, Daniel. 1987. "Two Views of Marriage Explored: His and Hers." In Ollie Pocs, ed., *Marriage and Family 87/88: Annual Editions*, 58–59. Sluice Dock, Guilford, CT: Dushkin.

———. 1988. "Sex Roles Reign Powerful as Ever in the Emotions." *New York Times* (August 23): Sec. C1,C13.

Gonzales, Monica. 1988. "Do You Know One?: Unmarried Couples Who Live Together." *American Demographics* 10 (July): 21.

Goode, William. 1959. "The Theoretical Importance of Love." *American Sociological Review* 24,1 (February): 38–47.

Gordon-Bradshaw, Ruth. 1988. "A Social Essay on Special Issues Facing Poor Women of Color." *Women and Health* 12:243–59.

Gove, Walter. 1972. "The Relationship between Sex Roles, Marital Status, and Mental Illness." *Social Forces* 51:34–44.

Grady, William. 1991. "Child Custody Plea Raises Issue of Gay Rights." *Chicago Tribune.* (October 20): 1.

Grant, Linda, Layne Simpson, and Lan Rong Xue. 1990. "Gender, Parenthood, and Work Hours of Physicians." *Journal of Marriage and the Family* 52:39–49.

Grauerholz, Elizabeth, and Richard Serpe. 1985. "Initiation and Response: The Dynamics of Sexual Interaction." *Sex Roles* 12:1041–59.

Gray-Little, Bernadette. 1982. "Marital Quality and Power Processes among Black Couples." *Journal of Marriage and the Family* 44:633–46.

Grebe, Sarah C. 1986. "Mediation in Separation and Divorce." *Journal of Counseling and Development* 64:377–82.

Greeley, Andrew. 1991. *Faithful Attraction.* New York: Tom Doherty Associates.

Greenstein, Theodore N. 1990. "Marital Disruption and the Employment of Married Women." *Journal of Marriage and the Family* 52:657–76.

Greif, Geoffrey L. 1985. *Single Fathers.* Lexington, MA: Lexington Books.

———, and Mary S. Pabst. 1988. *Mothers without Custody.* Lexington, MA: Heath.

Greil, Arthur L. 1991. *Not Yet Pregnant: Infertile Couples in Contemporary America.* New Brunswick: Rutgers University Press.

Greven, Phillip. 1970. *Four Generations: Population, Land and Family in Colonial Andover, Mass.* Ithaca, NY: Cornell University Press.

Griffin, Jean Latz. 1991. "Study: Sex Preference Is Genetic." *Chicago Tribune* (December 16): Sec. 2, pp. 1–4.

———. 1992. "Most Take Middle Ground on Abortion." *Chicago Tribune* (July 2): 1.

Griffin, Susan. 1971. "Rape: The All-American Crime." *Ramparts* (September): 26–35.

Griswold del Castillo, Richard. 1984. *La Familia.* Notre Dame, IN: University of Notre Dame Press.

Gross, Harriet E. 1980. "Dual Career Couples Who Live Apart: Two Types." *Journal of Marriage and the Family* 42:567–76.

Gross, Penny. 1987. "Defining Post-divorce Remarriage Families: A Typology Based on the Subjective Perceptions of Children." *Journal of Divorce* 10,1/2:205–17.

Gubrium, Jaber F. 1975. "Being Single in Old Age." *Aging and Human Development* 6:29–41.

———. 1976. *Time, Roles, and Self in Old Age.* New York: Human Science Press.

Guidubaldi, John, and Helen Cleminshaw. 1985. "Divorce,

Family Health, and Child Adjustment." *Family Relations* 34:35–41.

Guidubaldi, John, Joseph D. Perry, and Bonnie K. Nastasi. 1987. "Growing Up in a Divorced Family: Initial and Long-Term Perspectives on Children's Adjustment." In Stuart Oskamp, ed., *Family Processes and Problems: Social Psychological Aspects.* Beverly Hills, CA: Sage.

Guinness Book of World Records. 1990. New York: Sterling.

Guisinger, Shan, Philip A. Cowan, and David Schuldberg. 1989. "Changing Parent and Spouse Relations in the First Years of Remarriage of Divorced Fathers." *Journal of Marriage and the Family* 51:445–56.

Gutman, Herbert G. 1976. *The Black Family in Slavery and Freedom: 1750–1925.* New York: Vintage Books.

Guttmacher, A. F. 1983. *Pregnancy, Birth, and Family Planning.* Revised and updated by I. H. Kaiser. New York: New American Library.

Gwartney-Gibbs, Patricia A. 1986. "The Institutionalization of Premarital Cohabitation: Estimates from Marriage License Applications, 1970 and 1980." *Journal of Marriage and the Family* 48:423–34.

Hagestad, Gunhild. 1986. "The Family: Women and Grandparents as Kinkeepers." In Alan Pifer and Lydia Bronte, eds., *Our Aging Society,* 141–60. New York: Norton.

Hale-Benson, Janice. 1986. *Black Children: Their Roots, Culture, and Learning Styles,* rev. ed. Provo, UT: Brigham Young University Press.

Hall, Roberta M., and Bernice R. Sandler. 1985. "A Chilly Climate in the Classroom." In Alice Sargent, ed., *Beyond Sex Roles,* 503–10. New York: West.

Hamburg, David A. 1992. *Today's Children: Creating a Future for a Generation in Crisis.* New York: Time Books.

Hansen, Gary L. 1985. "Perceived Threats and Marital Jealousy." *Social Psychology Quarterly* 48:262–68.

Hanson, S. M. 1988. "Divorced Fathers with Custody." In P. Bronstein and C. P. Cowan, eds., *Fatherhood Today: Men's Changing Role in the Family,* 166–94. New York: Wiley.

Hansson, Robert O., and Jacqueline H. Remondet. 1987. "Relationships and Aging Family: A Social Psychological Analysis." In Stuart Oskamp, ed., *Family Processes and Problems: Social Psychological Aspects.* Beverly Hills, CA: Sage.

Hansson, Robert O., Marieta F. Knopf, E. Anne Downs, Paula R. Monroe, Susan E. Stegman, and Donna S. Wadley. 1984. "Femininity, Masculinity, and Adjustment of Divorce among Women." *Psychology of Women Quarterly* 8,3:248–49.

Harmatz, Morton G., and Melinda A. Novak. 1983. *Human Sexuality.* New York: Harper and Row.

Harry, Joseph. 1982. "Decision Making and Age Differences among Gay Couples." *Journal of Homosexuality* 2:9–21.

———. 1983. "Gay Male and Lesbian Relationships." In E. D. Macklin, and R. H. Rubin, eds., *Contemporary Families*

and Alternative Lifestyles: Handbook on Research and Theory,* 216–54. Newbury Park, CA: Sage.

———. 1984. *Gay Couples.* New York: Praeger.

———. 1988. "Some Problems of Gay/Lesbian Families." In Catherine Chilman, Elam W. Nunally, and Fred M. Cox, eds., *Variant Family Forms,* 96–113. Newbury Park, CA: Sage.

———, and William DeVall. 1978. *The Social Organization of Gay Males.* New York: Praeger.

Hatfield, Elaine. 1983. "What Do Women and Men Want From Love and Sex?" In Elizabeth R. Allgeier and Naomi B. McCormick, eds., *Changing Boundaries: Gender Roles and Sexual Behavior,* 106–34. Mountain View, CA: Mayfield.

———, and G. William Walster. 1978. *A New Look at Love.* Reading, MA: Addison-Wesley.

Heaton, Thomas B., and Eugene L. Pratt. 1990. "The Effects of Religious Homogamy on Marital Satisfaction and Stability." *Journal of Family Issues* 11:191–207.

Heaton, Tim B. 1990. "Marital Stability throughout the Childrearing Years." *Demography* 27,1 (February): 55–63.

Hendrick, Susan, and Clyde Hendrick. 1992. *Liking, Loving, and Relating.* Pacific Grove, CA: Brooks/Cole.

———, and Nancy L. Adler. 1988. "Romantic Relationships: Love, Satisfaction, and Staying Together." *Journal of Personality and Social Psychology* 34,6:980–88.

Hennessee, J. A. 1983. "Monkey See, Monkey Do Dating." *Psychology Today* (May 17): 74.

Henton, J., R. Cate, J. Koval, S. Lloyd, and F. S. Christopher. 1983. "Romance and Violence in Dating Relationships." *Journal of Family Issues* 4:467–82.

Herek, Gregory, 1990. "Gay People in Government Security Clearances: A Social Science Perspective." *American Psychologist* 45,9:1035–40.

Hertz, Rosanna. 1986. *More Equal Than Others: Women and Men in Dual-Couples.* Berkeley: University of California Press.

Hessellund, Hans. 1976. "Masturbation and Sexual Fantasy in Married Couples." *Archives of Sexual Behavior* 5:133–47.

Hetherington, E. Mavis. 1989. "Coping with Family Transitions: Winners, Losers, and Survivors." *Child Development* 60:1–18.

———, Martha Cox, and Roger Cox. 1979. "Play and Social Interaction in Children Following Divorce." *Journal of Social Issues* 35:26–49.

Hewlett, Sylvia Ann. 1991. *When the Bough Breaks: The Cost of Neglecting Our Children.* New York: Harper Perennial.

Hicks, Jonathan P. 1993. "A Legal Threshold Is Crossed by Gay Couples in New York." *New York Times* (March 2): Secs. A1,B3.

Higginbotham, Richard. 1991. "Friendship as an Ethical Paradigm for Same-Sex Couples." Unpublished paper, Seabury-Western Theological Seminary, Evanston, IL.

Higgins, B. S. 1990. "Couple Infertility: From the Perspective of the Close-Relationship Model." *Family Relations* 39:81–86.

Hill, Charles, Zick Rubin, and Letitia Peplau. 1976. "Breakups before Marriage: The End of 103 Affairs." *Journal of Social Issues* 32,1 (Winter): 147–68.

Hill, Reuben. 1958. "Generic Features of Families under Stress." *Social Casework* 39 (February/March): 139–50.

Hill, Robert B. 1977. *Informal Adoption among Black Families*. Washington, DC: National Urban League Research Department.

Hillard, P. A., and G. G Panter. 1985. *Pregnancy and Childbirth*. New York: Ballantine.

Hirsch, Marilyn B., and William D. Mosher. 1987. "Characteristics of Infertile Women in the United States and Their Use of Fertility Services." *Fertility and Sterility* 47:618–25.

Hite, Shere. 1976. *The Hite Report: A Nationwide Study of Female Sexuality*. New York: Macmillan.

———. 1981. *The Hite Report on Male Sexuality*. New York: Knopf.

Hochschild, Arlie. 1989. *The Second Shift: Working Parents and the Revolution at Home*. New York: Viking.

Hodson, Randy, and Teresa Sullivan. 1990. *The Social Organization of Work*. Belmont, CA: Wadsworth.

Hoff, Lee Ann. 1990. *Battered Women as Survivors*. New York: Routledge.

Hofferth, Sandra L. 1985. "Updating Children's Life Course." *Journal of Marriage and the Family* 47:93–115.

Hoffnung, Michele. 1984. "Motherhood: Contemporary Conflict for Women." In Jo Freeman, ed., *Women: A Feminist Perspective*, 124–138. Palo Alto, CA: Mayfield.

Hogan, Dennis P., and Evelyn M. Kitagawa. 1985. "The Impact of Social Status, Family Structure, and Neighborhood on the Fertility of Black Adolescents." *American Journal of Sociology* 90:825–55.

Holmes, Thomas, and R. Rahe. 1967. "The Social Readjustment Rating Scale." *Journal of Psychosomatic Research* 11:213–18.

Homans, George. 1961. *Social Behavior in Elementary Forms*. New York: Harcourt, Brace and World.

Hood, Jane C. 1983. *Becoming a Two-Job Family*. New York: Praeger.

hooks, bell. 1984. *Feminist Theory: From Margin to Center*. Boston, MA: South End Press.

Hooyman, Nancy, and H. Asuman Kiyak. 1993. *Social Gerontology: A Multi-disciplinary Perspective*, 3d ed. Boston: Allyn and Bacon.

Horney, Karen. 1967. *Feminine Psychology*. New York: Norton.

Hotaling, Gerald, David Finkelhor, J. T. Kirkpatrick, and Murray Strauss, eds., 1988. *Family Abuse and Its Consequences: New Directions in Research*. Beverly Hills, CA: Sage.

Hotz, Robert L. 1991. "Ethics and the Fertility Business." *Chicago Tribune* (December 24): 11.

Houseknecht, Sharon K., and Graham B. Spanier. 1980. "Marital Disruption and Higher Education among Women in the United States." *Sociological Quarterly* 21:375–89.

Houseknecht, Sharon K., Suzanne Vaughn, and Anne S. Macke. 1984. "Marital Disruption among Professional Women: The Timing of Career and Family Events." *Social Problems* 31:273–84.

"How College Women and Men Feel Today about Sex, AIDS, Condoms, Marriage, Kids." 1987. *Glamour* (August): 261–63.

Huber, Joan. 1980. "Will U.S. Fertility Decline toward Zero?" *Sociological Quarterly* 21:481–92.

Hunt, Janet G., and Larry L. Hunt. 1986. "The Dualities of Careers and Families: New Integrations or New Polarizations?" In Arlene S. Skolnick and Jerome H. Skolnick, eds., *Family in Transition: Rethinking Marriage, Sexuality, Child Rearing and Family Organization*, 275–89. Boston: Little, Brown.

Hunt, Larry L., and Janet G. Hunt. 1975. "Race and the Father–Son Connection: The Conditional Relevance of Father Absence for the Orientations and Identities of Adolescent Boys." *Social Problems* 23:35–52.

Hunt, Morton. 1959. *The Natural History of Love*. New York: Knopf.

———. 1973. "Sexual Behavior in the 1970s." *Playboy* (October): 204.

———. 1974. *Sexual Behavior in the 1970s*. Chicago: Playboy Press.

Hupka, Ralph. 1981. "Cultural Determinants of Jealousy." *Alternative Lifestyles* 4:310–56.

Husted, June, and Allan Edwards. 1976. "Personality Correlates of Male Sexual Arousal and Behavior." *Archives of Sexual Behavior* (March).

Hyde, Janet S. 1984. "Children's Understanding of Sexist Language." *Developmental Psychology* 20,4: 697–706.

Iaconetti, Joan. 1988. "Coping with the Decision Not to Have Children." In J. Gipson Wells, ed., *Current Issues in Marriage and the Family*, 143–48. New York: Macmillan.

Iazetto, Demetria. 1989. "When The Body Is Not an Easy Place to Be." Ph.D. dis. the Union Institute, Cincinnati, OH.

Ihinger-Tallman, Marilyn. 1987. "Sibling and Stepfamily Bonding in Stepfamilies." In Kay Pasley and Marilyn Ihinger-Tallman, eds., *Remarriage and Stepparenting: Current Research and Theory*, 164–82. New York: Guilford Press.

———, and Kay Pasley. 1987. "Divorce and Remarriage in the American Family: A Historical Review." In Kay Pasley and Marilyn Ihinger-Tallman, eds., *Remarriage and Stepparenting: Current Research and Theory*, 3–18. New York: Guilford Press.

———. 1991. "Children in Stepfamilies." In John N. Edwards and David H. Demo, eds., *Marriage and Family in Transition*, 453–69. Boston: Allyn and Bacon.

Ishii-Kuntz, M. 1986. *Sex and Race Differences in Marital Happiness in First-Married and Remarried Persons: Update and Refinement*. Pullman, WA: Washington State University.

Jackson, J. J., and B. F. Walls. 1978. "Myths and Realities About Aged Blacks." In M. Brown, ed., *Readings in Gerontology*, 95–113. St. Louis, MO: C. V. Mosby.

Jacob, Herbert. 1988. *Silent Revolution: The Transformation of Divorce Law in the United States*. Chicago: University of Chicago Press.

Jacobs, Jerry, and Frank Furstenberg. 1986. "Changing Places: Conjugal Careers and Women's Marital Mobility." *Social Forces* 64:714–32.

Jay, Karla, and Allen Young. 1977. *The Gay Report*. New York: Summit.

Jaynes, Gerald D., and Robin M. Williams, Jr., eds. 1989. *A Common Destiny: Blacks and American Society*. Washington, DC: National Academy Press.

Jessor, Richard, Frances Costa, Lee Jessor, and John Donovan. 1983. "Time of First Intercourse: A Prospective Study." *Journal of Personality and Social Psychology* 44,3:608–26.

John, Robert. 1988. "The Native American Family." In Charles H. Mindel, Robert W. Habenstein, and Roosevelt Wright, Jr., eds., *Ethnic Families in America*, 3d ed., 325–63. New York: Elsevier.

Johnson, Allan G. 1980. "On the Prevalence of Rape in the United States." *Signs* 6:136–46.

Johnson, Colleen L. 1988. *Exfamilia*. New Brunswick, NJ: Rutgers University Press.

———, and Donald J. Catalono. 1981. "Childless Elderly and Their Family Supports." *Gerontologist* 21:610–18.

Kain, Edward. 1990. *The Myth of Family Decline: Understanding Families in a World of Rapid Social Change*. Lexington, MA: Heath.

Kalish, Richard A. 1985. *Death, Grief, and Caring Relationships*, 2d ed. Monterey, CA: Brooks/Cole.

Kalter, Neil, Barbara Riemer, Arthur Brickman, and Jade Woo Chen. 1985. "Implications of Parental Divorce for Female Development." *Journal of the American Academy of Child Psychiatry* 24:538–44.

Kamerman, Sheila B., and Alfred J. Kahn. 1987. *The Responsive Workplace: Employers and a Changing Labor Force*. New York: Columbia University Press.

———. 1988. *Mothers Alone: Strategies for a Time of Change*. Dover, MA: Auburn House.

———, and P. Kingston. 1983. *Maternity Policies and Working Women*. New York: Columbia University Press.

Kanin, Eugene J., Karen B. Davidson, and Sonia R. Scheck. 1970. "A Research Note on Male-Female Differentials in the Experience of Heterosexual Love." *Journal of Sex Research* 6,1 (February): 64–72.

Kanter, Rosabeth M. 1977. *Work and Family in the United States*. New York: Russell Sage Foundation.

Kaplan, Gloria, Vita Barell, and Avala Lusky. "Subjective State of Health and Survival among Elderly Adults." *Journal of Gerontology* 43:S114–20.

Karen, Robert. 1987. "Giving and Getting in Love and Marriage." *Cosmopolitan* (March): 228–31, 236–37, 293.

Kargman, M. W. 1983. "Stepchild Support Obligations of Stepparents." *Family Relations* 32:231–38.

Kart, Cary S. 1990. *The Realities of Aging: An Introduction to Gerontology*. Boston: Allyn and Bacon.

———, Eileen Metress, and Seamus Metress. 1988. *Aging, Health, and Society*. Boston: Jones and Bartlett.

Kauffold, Mary Peterson. 1990. "Seeds of Doubt: Bill Takes Aim at 'Test Tube' Baby Industry." *Chicago Tribune* (October 14): 4.

Keating, Norah C., and Priscilla Cole. 1980. "What Do I Do with Him 24 Hours a Day? Changes in the Housewife Role after Retirement." *Gerontologist* 20:84–89.

Kehoe, Monika. 1989. *Lesbians over 60 Speak for Themselves*. New York: Haworth Press.

Keith, Pat. 1986. "Isolation of the Unmarried in Later Life." *Family Relations* 35:389–96.

Keith, Verna M., and Barbara Finlay. 1988. "The Impact of Parental Divorce on Children's Educational Attainment, Marital Timing, and Likelihood of Divorce." *Journal of Marriage and the Family* 50:797–809.

Kelly, Jim. 1977. "The Aging Male Homosexual: Myth and Reality?" *Gerontologist* 17:328–32.

Kempe, C. Henry, F. N. Silverman, B. Steele, W. Droegemueller, and H. K. Silver. 1962. "The Battered Child Syndrome." *Journal of the American Medical Association* 181:17–24.

Kemper, Theodore, and Roslyn Wallach Bologh. 1981. "What Do You Get When You Fall in Love? Some Health Status Effects." *Sociology of Health and Illness* 3:72–88.

Kennedy, Robert, Jr. 1986. *Life Choices: Applying Sociology*. New York: Holt, Rinehart and Winston.

Kephart, William M. 1988. "The Oneida Community." In Norval D. Glenn and Marion Tolbert, eds., *Family Relations: A Reader*, 17–24. Belmont, CA: Wadsworth.

Kerckhoff, Alan C. 1976. "Patterns of Marriage and Family Formation and Dissolution." *Journal of Consumer Research* 2:262.

Kessler-Harris, Alice. 1981. *Women Have Always Worked: A Historical Overview*. New York: Feminist Press.

———. 1982. *Out to Work: A History of Wage-Earning Women in the United States*. New York: Oxford University Press.

Kidder, Rushworth M. 1988. "Marriage in America: Why Marry?" In Ollie Pocs, ed., *Marriage and Family 88/89:*

Annual Editions, 44–47, Sluice Dock, Guilford, CT: Dushkin.

Kiernan, Kathleen. 1990. "Ringing Changes." *New Statesman and Society* 3 (February 16): 25.

Kimbrell, Andrew. 1991. "A Time for Men to Pull Together." *One Reader* (May/June): 66–71.

Kimmel, Michael S., and Martin P. Levine. 1992. "Men and AIDS." In Michael S. Kimmel and Michael A. Messner, *Men's Lives*, 318–29. New York: Macmillan.

Kinard, E. Milling, and Helen Reinherz. 1986. "Effects of Marital Disruption on Children's School Aptitude and Achievement." *Journal of Marriage and the Family* 48:285–93.

Kinsey, Alfred, Wardell B. Pomeroy, and Clyde E. Martin. 1948. *Sexual Behavior in the Human Male*. Philadelphia, PA: Saunders.

———, and P. H. Gebhard. 1953. *Sexual Behavior in the Human Female*. Philadelphia, PA: Saunders.

Kinzer, Stephen. 1993. "Abortion Limited by German Court." *New York Times* (May 29): 1, 3.

Kitano, Harry H. L. 1988. "The Japanese American Family." In Charles H. Mindel, Robert W. Habenstein, and Roosevelt Wright, Jr., eds., *Ethnic Families in America: Patterns and Variations*, 258–275. New York: Elsevier.

———, and Roger Daniels. 1988. *Asian Americans: Emerging Minorities*. Englewood Cliffs, NJ: Prentice Hall.

———, Wai-tsang Yeung, Lynn Chai, and Herbert Hatanaka. 1984. "Asian American Interracial Marriage." *Journal of Marriage and the Family* 46 (February): 179–190.

Kivett, Vira R. 1991. "Centrality of the Grandfather Role among Older Rural Black and White Men." *Journal of Gerontology* 46,5 (September): 250–58.

Kleiman, Carol. 1989. "Men Clean Up in Wages as Women Keep House." *Chicago Tribune* (September 18): 4,5.

———. 1990. "Liability Is Still Standing in Way of Office Day Care." *Chicago Tribune* (March 12): Sec. 4, p. 6.

Klerman, Gerald L., and Myrna M. Weissman. 1980. "Depressions among Women: Their Nature and Causes." In Marcia Guttentak, Susan Salasin, and Deborah Belle, eds., *The Mental Health of Women*, 57–92. New York: Academic Press.

Klimek, David. 1979. *Beneath Mate Selection in Marriage: The Unconscious Motives in Human Pairing*. New York: Van Nostrand Reinhold.

Knaub, Patricia, Sharon L. Hanna, and Nick Stinnett. 1984. "Strengths of Remarried Families." *Journal of Divorce* 7,3:41–55.

Kohlberg, Lawrence. 1966. "A Cognitive-Developmental Analysis of Children's Sex-Role Concepts and Attitudes." In Eleanor Maccoby, ed., *The Development of Sex Differences*, 82–173. Stanford, CA: Stanford University Press.

Kohn, Melvin. 1977. *Class and Conformity*. Chicago: University of Chicago Press.

Kolbert, Kathryn. 1990. "Developing a Reproductive Rights Agenda for the 1990s." In Marlene Gerber Fried, ed., *From Abortion to Reproductive Freedom*, 297–306. Boston: South End Press.

Kosberg, Jordan I. 1988. "Preventing Elder Abuse: Identification of High-Risk Factors Prior to Placement Decisions." *Gerontologist* 28,1.

Koss, Mary P., Kenneth E. Leonard, Dana A. Beezley, and Cheryl J. Oros. 1985. "Non-stranger Sexual Aggression: A Discriminant Analysis of the Psychological Characteristics of Undetected Offenders." *Sex Roles* 12:981–92.

Kotulak, Ronald, and Peter Gorner. 1991. "Babies by Design." *Chicago Tribune Magazine* (March 3): 14–19.

Kübler-Ross, Elizabeth. 1969. *On Death and Dying*. New York: Macmillan.

———. 1974. *Questions and Answers on Death and Dying*. New York: Macmillan.

Kurdek, Lawrence A., and J. Patrick Schmitt. 1986. "Relationship Quality of Partners in Heterosexual Married, Heterosexual Cohabiting, and Gay and Lesbian Relationships." *Journal of Personality and Social Psychology* 51 (October): 711–20.

Lai, Tracy. 1992. "Asian American Women: Not for Sale." In Margaret Anderson and Patricia Hill Collins, eds., *Race, Class, and Gender*, 163–71. Belmont, CA: Wadsworth.

Lakoff, Robin. 1975. *Language and Woman's Place*. New York: Colophon.

Landers, S. 1989. "Severe Stress after Abortion Is Rare." *Monitor*: American Psychological Association (May): 32.

Landrine, Hope. 1985. "Race and Class Stereotypes of Women." *Sex Roles* 13:65–75.

Larche, Douglas. 1985. *Father Gander Nursery Rhymes: The Equal Rhymes Amendment*. Santa Barbara, CA: Advocacy Press.

LaRossa, Ralph, and Maureen Mulligan LaRossa. 1989. "Baby Care: Fathers vs. Mothers." In Barbara J. Risman and Pepper Schwartz, *Gender in Intimate Relationships*, 138–54. Belmont, CA: Wadsworth.

Larson, Jan, and Brad Edmondson. 1991. "Should Unmarried Partners Get Married Benefits?" *American Demographics* 13 (March): 47.

Lasch, Christopher. 1977. *Haven in a Heartless World: The Family Besieged*. New York: Basic Books.

———. 1978. *The Culture of Narcissism*. New York: Norton.

Laslett, Peter. 1971. *The World We Have Lost*, 2d ed. New York: Scribner.

Laswell, Marcia E., and Norman Lobenz. 1980. *Styles of Loving*. Garden City, NY: Doubleday.

Lauer, Jeanette, and Robert Lauer. 1985. "Marriages Made to Last." *Psychology Today* (June): 22–26.

Lauer, Robert, and Jeanette Lauer. 1988. *Watersheds: Mastering Life's Unpredictable Crises*. New York: Little, Brown.

———. 1991. *The Quest for Intimacy*. Dubuque, IA: Brown.

Lavin, Cheryl. 1991. "What's Best, and Worst, About Being Single." *Chicago Tribune* (July 21): Sec. 5, p. 3.

Lawson, A. 1988. *Adultery: An Analysis of Love and Betrayal*. New York: Basic Books.

Lee, Gary R., and Constance L. Shehan. 1991. "Retirement and Marital Satisfaction." *Journal of Gerontology* 44,6:226–30.

Lee, John Alan. 1974. "The Styles of Loving." *Psychology Today* 8,5 (October): 46–51.

LeMasters, Ersel. 1957. *Modern Courtship and Marriage*. New York: Macmillan.

———, and John DeFrain. 1989. *Parents in Contemporary America: A Sympathetic View*, 5th ed. Belmont, CA: Wadsworth.

Lengermann, Patricia Madoo, and Jill Niebrugge Brantley. 1988. "Feminist Theory." In George Ritzer, ed., *Sociological Theory*, 400–443. New York: Knopf.

Lever, Janet. 1978. "Sex Differences in the Complexity of Children's Play and Games." *American Sociological Review* 43:471–83.

Levinger, George. 1965. "Marital Cohesiveness and Dissolution: An Integrative Review." *Journal of Marriage and the Family* 27:19–28.

———. 1979. "A Social Psychological Perspective on Marital Dissolution." In George Levinger and Oliver Moles, eds., *Divorce and Separation*, 37–60. New York: Basic Books.

Levinson, David. 1981. "Physical Punishment of Children and Wife Beating in Cross-Cultural Perspective." *Child Abuse and Neglect* 5,4:193–96.

Levitan, Sar A., Richard S. Belous, and Frank Gallo. 1988. *What's Happening to the American Family? Tensions, Hopes, Realities*. Baltimore, MD: Johns Hopkins University Press.

Levy, Barrie, ed. 1991. *Dating Violence: Young Women in Danger*. Seattle, WA: Seal Press.

———. 1992. "A Closer Look." NBC television.

Lieberman, B. 1985. "Extra-premarital Intercourse." Unpublished manuscript, University of Pittsburgh, Department of Sociology, Pittsburgh, PA.

Liem, Ramsay. 1985. "Unemployment: A Family as Well as a Personal Crisis." In Jacques Boulet, Ann Marie Debritto, and Shirley Aisha Ray, eds. *Understanding the Economic Crisis*, 112–18. Ann Arbor: University of Michigan.

Light, Donald, Suzanne Keller, and Craig Calhoun. 1989. *Sociology*, 5th ed. New York: Knopf.

Lindsey, Linda. 1990. *Gender Roles: A Sociological Perspective*. Englewood Cliffs, NJ: Prentice Hall.

Lips, Hilary. 1993. *Sex and Gender: An Introduction*. Mountain View, CA: Mayfield.

Liss, Marsha B. 1992. "Home, School, and Playroom: Training Grounds for Adult Gender Roles." *Sex Roles* 26,3/4: 129–47.

Litwak, Eugene. 1960. "Geographical Mobility and Extended Family Cohesion." *American Sociological Review* 25:9–21.

Lloyd, Peter C. 1968. "Divorce among the Yoruba." *American Anthropologist* 70:67–81.

Lloyd, S. A., and R. M. Cote. 1984. "Predicting Premarital Relationship Stability: A Methodological Refinement." *Journal of Marriage and the Family* 46:71–76.

Locin, Mitchell. 1991. "Study: Parental-Leave Laws Work Well." *Chicago Tribune* (May 22): Sec. 1, p. 3.

Logue, Barbara J. 1991. "Women at Risk: Predictions of Financial Stress for Retired Women Workers." *Gerontologist* 31,5:657–65.

Loiacano, Darryl K. 1989. "Gay Identity Issues among Black Americans: Racism, Homophobia, and the Need for Validation." *Journal of Counseling and Development* 68,l:21–25.

Long, Bonita C. 1989. "Sex-Role Orientation, Coping Strategies, and Self-Efficacy of Women in Traditional and Nontraditional Occupations." *Psychology of Women Quarterly* 13:307–24.

Longino, Charles F., Jr., 1988. "A Population Profile of Very Old Men and Women in the United States." *Sociological Quarterly* 29:559–64.

———, and Aaron Lipman. 1981. "Married and Spouseless Men and Women in Planned Retirement Communities: Support Network Differentials." *Journal of Marriage and the Family* 43:169–77.

Lopata, Helen Z. 1973. *Widowhood in an American City*. Cambridge, MA: Schenkman.

Lott, Bernice. 1987. *Women's Lives*. Monterey, CA: Brooks/Cole.

Lowery, Carl R., and Shirley A. Settle. 1985. "Effects of Divorce on Children: Differential Impact of Custody and Visitation Patterns." *Family Relations* 34:455–63.

Lubin, B. 1975. "Mood and Somatic Symptoms during Pregnancy." *Psychosomatic Medicine* 37:136–46.

Luker, Kristin. 1984. *Abortion and the Politics of Motherhood*. Berkeley, CA: University of California Press.

Lynch, James J. 1977. *The Broken Heart: The Medical Consequences of Loneliness*. New York: Basic Books.

Lynn, David. 1966. "The Process of Learning Parental and Sex-Role Identification." *Journal of Marriage and the Family* 28:466–70.

Lyon, Jeff. 1992. "Keeping Score." *Chicago Tribune Magazine* (November 29): 14–16; 28–32; 34–35.

Maccoby, Eleanor, and Carol Jacklin. 1987. "Gender Segregation in Childhood." *Advances in Child Development and Behavior* 20:239–87.

MacDonald, Kevin, and Ross D. Parke. 1986. "Parent–Child Physical Play: The Effects of Sex and Age on Children and Parents." *Sex Roles* 15:367–78.

Macionis, John. 1991. *Sociology*. Englewood Cliffs, NJ: Prentice Hall.

Macklin, Eleanor D. 1972. "Heterosexual Cohabitation among Unmarried Students." *Family Coordinator* 21:463–72.

———. 1983. "Nonmarital Heterosexual Cohabitation: An Overview." In Eleanor Macklin and Roger Rubin, ed., *Contemporary Families and Alternative Lifestyles: Handbook on Research and Theory*, 49–73. Beverly Hills, CA: Sage.

Madsen, William. 1964. *The Mexican American of South Texas*. New York: Holt, Rinehart and Winston.

Maglin, Nan Bauer, and Nancy Schniedewind, eds. 1989. *Women and Stepfamilies: Voices of Anger and Love*. Philadelphia, PA: Temple University Press.

Maier, Richard. 1984. *Sexuality in Perspective*. Chicago: Nelson-Hall.

Malinowski, Bronislaw. 1929. *The Sexual Life of Savages in North Western Melanesia*. New York: Harcourt Brace.

Manton, Kenneth G., and Korbin Liu. 1984. *The Future Growth of the Long-Term Care Population: Projections Based on the 1977 National Nursing Home Survey and the 1982 Long-Term Care Survey*. Washington, DC: Health Care Financing Administration.

Marciano, Teresa D. 1979. "Male Influences in Fertility: Needs for Research." *Family Coordinator* 28:561–68.

Margolis, Jon. 1992. "Increase in Stepfamilies Introduces New Stresses." *Chicago Tribune* (November 27): 1, 12.

Marion, Robert, et al. 1986. "Human T-Cell Lymphotrophic Virus Type III (Htlv-III) Embryopathy." *American Journal of Diseases of Children* 140:638–40.

Markides, Kyriakos S. 1978. "Reasons for Retirement and Adaptation to Retirement by Elderly Mexican Americans." In E. P. Stanford, ed., *Retirement: Concepts and Realities of Minority Elders*, 83–90. San Diego, CA: San Diego State University.

———, and Charles H. Mindel. 1987. *Aging and Ethnicity*. Newbury Park, CA: Sage.

Marriage License Bureau and Cook County Clerk's Office. 1993. Telephone interview: "Marriage License Requirements for the State of Illinois." Chicago, IL.

Martin, Carol Lynn 1990. "Attitudes and Expectations About Children with Nontraditional and Traditional Gender Roles." *Sex Roles* 22:151–65.

Martin, Susan Ehrlich. 1989. "Sexual Harassment: The Link Joining Gender Stratification, Sexuality, and Women's Economic Status." In Jo Freeman, ed., *Woman: A Feminist Perspective*, 3d ed., 57–86. Palo Alto, CA: Mayfield.

Martin, Teresa Castro, and Larry L. Bumpass. 1989. "Recent Trends in Marital Disruption." *Demography* 26:37–52.

Martini, Frederic. 1992. *Fundamentals of Anatomy and Physiology*, 2d ed. Englewood Cliffs, NJ: Prentice Hall.

Masters, William, and Virginia Johnson. 1966. *Human Sexual Response*. Boston: Little, Brown.

———. 1985. *Human Sexual Response*. Boston: Little, Brown.

———. 1992. *Human Sexual Response*. Boston: Little, Brown.

Matthews, Sarah, and Jetse Sprey. 1985. "Adolescents' Relationships with Grandparents: An Empirical Contribution to Conceptual Clarification." *Journal of Gerontology* 40:621–26.

Maugh, Thomas H. H. 1990. "Sex American Style Trend to the Traditional." *Los Angles Times* (February 18): A1, A22.

Mauldin, Teresa A. 1990. "Women Who Remain above the Poverty Level in Divorce: Implications for Family Policy." *Family Relations* 39:141–46.

———, and Carol B. Meeks. 1990. "Sex Differences in Children's Time Use." *Sex Roles* 22,9/10:537–54.

Max, Ellen. 1985. "Custody Criteria, Visitation and Child Support." *Women's Advocate* (September): 1–4.

Mays, Vickie M., and Susan D. Cochran. 1991. "The Black Women's Relationships Project: A National Survey of Black Lesbians." In Robert Staples, ed., *The Black Family: Essays and Studies*, 4th ed., 92–100. Belmont, CA: Wadsworth.

Maza, Penelope, and Judy A. Hall. 1988. *Homeless Children and Their Families: A Preliminary Study*. Washington, DC: Child Welfare League of America.

McAdoo, J. L. 1986. "Black Fathers' Relationships With Their Preschool Children and the Children's Development of Ethnic Identity." In R. A. Lewis and R. E. Salt, eds. *Men in Families*, 159–68. Beverly Hills, CA: Sage.

McCarthy, L. 1985. *The Feminization of Poverty: Report of the Lieutenant Governor's Task Force on the Feminization of Poverty*. Sacramento, CA: State of California.

McCary, James L. 1978. *Human Sexuality: Instructor's Guide*. New York: Van Nostrand.

McEnroe, Jennifer. 1991. "Split-Shift Parenting." *American Demographics* 13,2 (February): 50–52.

McGhee, Jerrie L. 1985. "The Effects of Siblings on the Life Satisfaction of the Rural Elderly." *Journal of Marriage and the Family* 47:85–91.

McGrath, Ellen, Gwendolyn B. Keita, Bonnie R. Strickland, and Nancy F. Russo, eds. 1990. *Women and Depression: Risk Factors and Treatment Issues*. Hyattsville, MD: American Psychological Association.

McLanahan, Sara, and Larry Bumpass. 1988. "Intergenerational Consequences of Family Disruption." *American Journal of Sociology* 94:130–52.

McLaren, Angus. 1990. *A History of Contraception*. Oxford: Basil Blackwell.

McLeod, Beth. 1990. "Being Single and 30-Plus Is Not the End of the World." *Chicago Tribune* (October 14): Sec. 6, p. 5.

McNair, N. 1988. "Chalamydia is Not a Flower." *Health Call* 4, 2:3.

McRoy, Ruth G. 1989. "An Organizational Dilemma: The

Case of Transracial Adoptions." *Journal of Applied Behavioral Science* 25,2: 145–60.

———, Harold Grotevant, and Louis A. Zurcher, Jr. 1988. *Emotional Disturbances in Adopted Adolescents: Origins and Development*. New York: Praeger.

McTaggart, Lynne. 1980. *The Baby Makers: The Marketing of White Babies in America*. New York: Dial Press.

Mead, Margaret. 1935. *Sex and Temperament in Three Primitive Societies*. New York: Morrow.

———. 1970. "Communes: A Challenge to All of Us." *Redbook* 35 (August): 51–52.

Melton, Willie, and Linda Lindsey. 1987. "Instrumental and Expressive Values in Mate Selection among College Students Revisited: Feminism, Love and Economic Necessity." Paper presented at the annual meeting of the Midwest Sociological Society, Chicago, IL.

Meredith, Dennis. 1985. "Mom, Dad, and the Kids." *Psychology Today* (June): 62–67.

Messinger, Lillian. 1984. *Remarriage: A Family Affair*. New York: Plenum Press.

Middlebrook, Patricia Niles. 1974. *Social Psychology and Modern Life*. New York: Knopf.

Mills, C. Wright. 1959. *The Sociological Imagination*. New York: Oxford University Press.

Min, Pyong Gap. 1988. "The Korean American Family." In Charles H. Mindel, Robert W. Habenstein, and Roosevelt Wright, Jr., eds., *Ethnic Families in America*, 199–229. New York: Elsevier.

Mindel, Charles H. 1983. "The Elderly in Minority Families." In Timothy H. Brubaker, ed., *Family Relationships in Later Life*, 193–208. Beverly Hills, CA: Sage.

The Miniature Mother Goose. 1992. Philadelphia: Running Press.

Minkoff, Howard L. 1987. "Care of Pregnant Women Infected with Human Immunodeficiency Virus." *Journal of the American Medical Association* 258 (November 20): 2714–17.

Mintz, Steven, and Susan Kellog. 1988. *Domestic Revolution: A Social History of American Family Life*. New York: Free Press.

Mirande, Alfredo. 1985. *The Chicano Experience: An Alternative Perspective*. Notre Dame, IN: University of Notre Dame Press.

Mirchandi, V. K. 1973. "Attitudes toward Love among Blacks." Master's thesis, East Carolina University.

Mitchell, Jim, and Jasper C. Register. 1984. "An Exploration of Family Interaction with the Elderly by Race, Socioeconomic Status and Residence." *Gerontologist* 24:48–54.

Modern Maturity. 1992–1993. "Time Improves Lives of Older Widows." (December–January): 8.

Moghissi, Kamran S. 1989. "The Technology of Aid and Surrogacy." In Linda Whiteford and Marilyn Polan, eds.,

New Approaches to Human Reproduction. Boulder, CO: Westview Press.

Money, John, and Anke Ehrhardt. 1972. *Man and Woman, Boy and Girl*. Baltimore, MD: Johns Hopkins University Press.

Moore, Joan, and Harry Pachon. 1985. *Hispanics in the United States*. Englewood Cliffs, NJ: Prentice Hall.

Moore, Kristin A., and Isabel V. Sawhill. 1984. "Implication of Women's Employment for Home and Family Life." In Patricia Voydanoff, ed., *Work and Family: Changing Roles of Men and Women*, 153–71. Palo Alto, CA: Mayfield.

Moore, Pat, with C. P. Conn. 1985. *Disguised*. Waco, TX: Word Books.

Moore, Wilbert E. 1978. "Functionalism." In T. Bottommore and Robert Nisbet, eds., *A History of Sociological Analyses*, 321–61, New York: Basic Books.

Morgan, Leslie. 1990. "The Multiple Consequences of Divorce: A Decade Review." *Journal of Marriage and the Family* 52:913–24.

Morgan, S. Philip, Diane Lye, and Gretchen Condran. 1988. "Sons, Daughters, and the Risk of Marital Disruption." *American Journal of Sociology* 94:110–29.

Morris, Monica. 1988. *Last-Chance Children: Growing Up with Older Parents*. New York: Columbia University Press.

Mortimer, Jeylan T., and Jayne London. 1984. "The Varying Linkages of Work and Family." In Patricia Voydanoff, ed., *Work and Family: Changing Roles of Men and Women*, 20–35. Palo Alto, CA: Mayfield.

Mosher, William D. 1990. "Contraceptive Practice in the United States, 1982–1988." *Family Planning Perspectives* 22,5:198–205.

Mowery, J. 1978. "Systemic Requisites of Communal Groups." *Alternative Lifestyles* 2:235–61.

Moynihan, Daniel Patrick. 1965. *The Negro Family: The Case for National Action*. Office of Policy Planning and Research, U.S. Department of Labor. Washington, DC: U.S. Government Printing Office.

Murphy, Michael, et al. 1991. "Substance Abuse and Serious Child Mistreatment, Child Abuse and Neglect." *International Journal* 15,3:197–211.

Murstein, Bernard I. 1971. "A Theory of Marital Choice." In Bernard I. Murstein, ed., *Theories of Attraction and Love*, 100–151. New York: Springer.

———. 1974. *Love, Sex, and Marriage through the Ages*. New York: Springer.

———. 1980. "Mate Selection in the 1970's." *Journal of Marriage and the Family* 42:777–92.

———. 1986. *Paths to Marriage*. Beverly Hills, CA: Sage.

Mutran, Elizabeth. 1985. "Intergenerational Family Support among Blacks and Whites." *Journal of Gerontology* 40 (May): 382–89.

National Center for Health Statistics. 1985. "Advance Report of Divorce Statistics, 1985." *Monthly Vital Statistics*

Report, 38,8 (suppl.) (December 7). Hyattsville, MD: Public Health Service.

———. 1990a. "Current Estimates from the National Health Interview Survey: U.S. 1989." *Vital and Health Statistics*, Series 10, No. 176. Hyattsville, MD: Public Health Service.

———. 1990b. "Advance Report of Final Marriage Statistics, 1987." *Monthly Vital Statistics Report* 38,12 (suppl.) (April 3). Hyattsville, MD: Public Health Service.

———. 1990c. "Advance Report of Final Divorce Statistics, 1987." *Monthly Vital Statistics Report* 38,12 (suppl. 2) (May 15). Hyattsville, MD: Public Health Service.

———. 1990d. "Advanced Report of Final Natality Statistics, 1989." Monthly Vital Statistics Report 40,8 (suppl.). Hyattsville, MD: Public Health Service.

———. 1991. "Annual Summary of Births, Marriages, Divorces, and Deaths: United States, 1990." *Monthly Vital Statistics Report* 39,13 (August 28). Hyattsville, MD: Public Health Service.

National Commission on the Role of the School and the Community in Improving Adolescent Health. 1990. *Code Blue: Uniting for Healthier Youth.* Washington, DC: National Association of State Boards of Education and the American Medical Association.

National Indian Council on Aging. 1981. "1981 White House Conference on Aging: The Indian Issues." *National Indian Council on Aging Quarterly* 4:1.

National Woman Abuse Action Project. 1991. "Understanding Domestic Violence." Washington, DC: National Woman Abuse Action Project.

Neal, Arthur G., H. Theodore Groat, and Jerry W. Wicks. 1989. "Attitudes About Having Children: A Study of 600 Couples in the Early Years of Marriage." *Journal of Marriage and the Family* 59:313–28.

Needle, R. H., S. S. Su, and W. J. Doherty. 1990. "Divorce, Remarriage and Adolescent Substance Use." *Journal of Marriage and the Family* 52:157–70.

Neugarten, Bernice, and Dail Neugarten. 1992. "Age in the Aging Society." In Hugh Lena, William Helmreich, and William McCord, eds., *Contemporary Issues in Society*, 208–19. New York: McGraw-Hill.

Neugarten, Bernice, and Karol Weinstein. 1964. "The Changing American Grandparent." *Journal of Marriage and the Family* 26:199–204.

Newberger, E. H., R. B. Reed, J. H. Daniel, J. N. Hyde, and M. Kotelchuck. 1977. "Pediatric Social Illness: Toward an Etiologic Classification." *Pediatrics* 60:178–85.

Newcomb, Paul R. 1979. "Cohabitation in America: An Assessment of Consequences." *Journal of Marriage and the Family* 41:597–602.

Newcomer, Susan, and J. Richard Udry. 1985. "Oral Sex in an Adolescent Population." *Archives of Sexual Behavior* 14:41–46.

———. 1987. "Parental Marital Status Effects on Adolescent Sexual Behavior." *Journal of Marriage and the Family* 49:235–40.

Nezu, Arthur M., and Christine M. Nezu. 1987. "Psychological Distress, Problem-Solving, and Coping Reactions: Sex Role Differences." *Sex Roles* 16:205–14.

Niemi, Richard, John Mueller, and Tom W. Smith. 1989. *Trends in Public Opinion: A Compendium of Survey Data.* New York: Greenwood Press.

Nock, Steven L. 1979. "The Family Life Cycle." *Journal of Marriage and the Family* 41 (February): 15–26.

———, and Paul W. Kingston. 1990. *The Sociology of Public Issues.* Belmont, CA: Wadsworth.

Oakley, Ann. 1974. *The Sociology of Housework.* New York: Pantheon.

Office of Technology Assessment. 1988. *Infertility: Medical and Social Choices.* Washington, DC: U.S. Government Printing Office.

O'Flaherty, Kathleen M., and Laura Workman Eells. 1988. "Courtship Behavior of the Remarried." *Journal of Marriage and the Family* 50:499–506.

Ogintz, Eileen. 1991. "Goodbye to the Myth of Unmarried Women." *Chicago Tribune* (October 22): Sec. 5, pp. 1, 2.

Ogletree, Shirley, Sue Williams, Paul Raffeld, Bradley Mason, and Kris Fricke. 1990. "Female Attractiveness and Eating Disorders: Do Children's Television Commercials Play a Role?" *Sex Roles* 22,11/12: 791–97.

O'Hare, William P., and Judy C. Felt. 1991. *Asian Americans: America's Fasting Growing Minority Group.* Population Trends and Public Policy 19 (February). Washington, DC: Population Reference Bureau.

O'Kelly, Charlotte G., and Larry Carney. 1986. *Women and Men in Society: Cross-Cultural Perspectives on Gender Stratification.* Belmont, CA: Wadsworth.

Olson, Douglas H. 1986. "What Makes Families Work?" In S. VanZandt, et al., *Family Strengths 7: Vital Connections*, 1–12. Lincoln, NE: University of Nebraska Press.

O'Neil, James M. 1981. "Patterns of Gender-Role Conflict and Strain: The Fear of Femininity in Men's Lives." *Personnel and Guidance Journal* 60:203–10.

Oppenheimer, Valerie Kincade. 1988. "A Theory of Marriage Timing." *Journal of Marriage and the Family* 42: 777–92.

Pace, L. 1986. "Interfaith Marriage Barrier Proves Not Insurmountable." *Norwich Bulletin* (February 12).

Pagelow, Mildred D. 1984. *Family Violence.* New York: Praeger.

———. 1988. "Marital Rape." In Vincent B. Van Hasselt, Randall L Morrison, Alan S. Bellack, and Michel Hersen, eds., *Handbook of Family Violence*, 207–32. New York: Plenum.

———. 1989. "The Incidence and Prevalence of Criminal Abuse of Other Family Members." In Lloyd Ohlin and

Michael Tonry, eds., *Family Violence*, 263–313. Chicago: University of Chicago Press.

Painter, Kim. 1992. "Number of Female Cases Rising Rapidly." *USA Today* (July 23): 6D.

Palmore, Erdman. 1980. "The Facts on Aging Quiz: A Review of Findings." *Gerontologist* 20:669–72.

Papalia, Diane, and Sally Olds. 1989. *Human Development*. New York: McGraw-Hill.

Papanek, Hanna. 1973. "Men, Women, and Work: Reflections on the Two-Person Career." *American Journal of Sociology* 78,4 (January): 852–72.

Parker, Gail, ed. 1972. *The Oven Birds': American Women on Womanhood 1820–1920*. Garden City, NY: Anchor Books.

Parnes, Herbert, and Laurence Less. 1983. *From Work to Retirement: The Experiences of a National Sample of Men*. Columbus, OH: Ohio State University Center for Human Resource Research.

Parron, Eugenia M. 1982. "Golden Wedding Couples: Lessons in Marital Longevity." *Generations* 7,2:14–16.

Parrot, A., and M. J. Ellis. 1985. "Homosexuals Should Be Allowed to Marry and Adopt and Rear Children." In H. Feldman and M. Feldman, eds., *Current Controversies in Marriage and Family*. Beverly Hills, CA: Sage.

Parrot, W. G., and R. H. Smith. 1987. "Differentiating the Experiences of Envy and Jealousy." Paper presented at the annual meeting of the American Psychological Association, August, New York.

Parsons, Talcott. 1955. "The American Family." In Talcott Parsons and Robert Bales, eds., *Family, Socialization and Interaction Process*, 3–34. Glencoe, IL.: Free Press.

———. 1964. *The Social System*. New York: Free Press.

Pasley, Kay, and Marilyn Ihinger-Tallman. 1987. "The Evolution of a Field of Investigation: Issues and Concerns." In Kay Pasley and Marilyn Ihinger-Tallman, eds., *Remarriage and Stepparenting: Current Research and Theory*, 303–13. New York: Guilford Press.

Patterson, James, and Peter Kim. 1991. *The Day America Told the Truth: What People Really Believe About Everything That Really Matters*. Englewood Cliffs, NJ: Prentice Hall.

Patzer, Gordon L. 1985. *The Physical Attractiveness Phenomena*. New York: Plenum Press.

Pauly, Brett. 1992. "The Number of Happily Never-Marrieds Is on the Rise." *Chicago Tribune* (October 4): Sec. 6, p. 5.

Peplau, Letitia A. 1981. "What Do Homosexuals Want?" *Psychology Today* (March): 28–38.

———, and Sara L. Gordon. 1985. "Women and Men in Love: Gender Differences in Close Heterosexual Relationships." In Virginia E. O'Leary, Barbara Strudler Wallston, and Rhonda Kesler Unger, eds., *Women, Gender, and Social Psychology*. Hillsdale, NJ: Erlbaum.

Peplau, Letitia A., and Steven L. Gordon. 1983. "The Intimate Relationships of Lesbians and Gay Men." In Elizabeth R. Allgerier and Naomi McCormick, eds., *Changing Boundaries: Gender Roles and Sexual Behavior*, 1–14. Mountain View, CA: Mayfield.

Peplau, Letitia A., and Susan Cochran. 1981. "Value Orientations in the Intimate Relationships of Gay Men." *Journal of Homosexuality* 6:1–29.

Perry-Jenkins, Maureen, and Ann C. Crouter. 1990. "Men's Provider Role Attitudes: Implications for Household Work and Marital Satisfaction." *Journal of Family Issues* 11:136–56.

Peters, Jeff. 1991. "When Fear Turns to Hate and Hate to Violence." *Human Rights* 18,1 (Spring): 22–25, 30.

Petersen, James, A. Kretchner, B. Nellis, J. Lever, and R. Hertz. 1983. "The Playboy Reader's Sex Survey, Parts I and II." *Playboy* (February/March): 108, 241–50.

Peterson, Candida, and James Peterson. 1988. "Old Men's and Women's Relationships with Adult Kin: How Equitable Are They?" *International Journal of Aging and Human Development* 27,3:221–31.

Peterson, James L., and Nicholas Zill. 1986. "Marital Disruption, Parent–Child Relationships, and Behavior Problems in Children." *Journal of Marriage and the Family* 48:295–307.

Peterson, John L. 1992. "Black Men and Their Same-Sex Desires and Behaviors." In Gilbert Herdt, ed., *Gay Culture in America*, 147–64. Boston: Beacon Press.

Peterson, Karen. 1992. "More Couples Staying the Course of Marriage." *USA Today* (October 2): 4D.

Phillips, Roderick. 1988. *Putting Asunder: A History of Divorce in Western Society*. Cambridge, MA: Cambridge University Press.

Pill, Cynthia J. 1990. "Stepfamilies: Redefining the Family." *Family Relations* 39:186–93.

Pillemer, Karl A., and David Finkelhor. 1988. "The Prevalence of Elder Abuse: A Random-Sample Survey." *Gerontologist* 28,1: 51–57.

Pines, Ayala, and Elliot Aronson. 1983. "Antecedents, Correlates, Consequences of Secret Jealousy." *Journal of Personality* 51:108–09.

Pitcher, B. L., and D. C. Larson. 1989. "Early Widowhood." In S. J. Bahr and E. T. Peterson, eds., *Aging and the Family*, 59–81. Lexington, MA: Lexington Books.

Pizzey, Erin. 1974. *Scream Quietly or the Neighbors Will Hear*. Harmondsworth, England: Penguin.

Pleck, Elizabeth. 1989. "Criminal Approaches to Family Violence." In Lloyd Ohlin and Michael Tonry, eds., *Family Violence*, 19–58. Chicago: University of Chicago Press.

Pleck, Joseph H. 1988. "Fathers and Infant Care Leave." In E. F. Zigler and M. Franks, eds., *The Parental Leave Crisis* 177–94. New Haven, CT: Yale University Press.

Pomerlau, André, Daniel Bolduc, Gérard Makuit, and Louise Cossette. 1990. "Pink or Blue: Environmental Stereotypes in the First Two Years of Life." *Sex Roles* 22,5/6:359–67.

Ponzetti, James, Jr., and Rodney M. Cate. 1986. "The Development Course of Conflict in the Marital Dissolution Process." *Journal of Divorce* 10:1–15.

Powers, Edwin. 1966. *Crime and Punishment in Early Massachusetts 1620–1692: A Documentary History*. Boston: Beacon Press.

Price-Bonham, Sharon, and Jack O. Balswick. 1980. "The Noninstitutions: Divorce, Desertion, and Remarriage." *Journal of Marriage and the Family* 42,4:959–72.

Priest, Dana. 1991. "17,500 Families Divided: Data Given on Children Left without GI Parent." *Washington Post* (February 15): Sec. A1, A30.

Punke, Harold H. 1940. "Marriage Rate among Women Teachers." *American Sociological Review* 5,4:505–11.

Purcell, Piper, and Lara Stewart. 1990. "Dick and Jane in 1989." *Sex Roles* 22:177–85.

Queen, Stuart A., Robert W. Habenstein, and Jill S. Quadagno. 1985. *The Family in Various Cultures*. New York: HarperCollins.

Radbill, Samuel. 1980. "A History of Child Abuse and Infanticide." In C. Henry Kempe and Ray Helfer, eds., *The Battered Child*, 3–20. Chicago: University of Chicago Press.

Ramu, G. N. 1989. "Patterns of Mate Selection." In K. Ishwaran, ed., *Family and Marriage: Cross-Cultural Perspectives*, 165–78. Toronto, Canada: Wall and Thompson.

Rank, Mark R. 1989. "Fertility among Women on Welfare: Incidence and Determinants.," *American Sociological Review* 54:296–304.

Rasmussen, Paul K., and Kathleen J. Ferraro. 1991. "The Divorce Process." In John N. Edwards and David H. Demo, eds., *Marriage and Family in Transition*, 376–88. Boston: Allyn and Bacon.

Rawlings, S. 1978. "Perspectives on American Husbands and Wives." Current Population Reports, Series P-23, No 77. Washington, DC: U.S. Bureau of the Census.

Reeder, Sharon J., and Leonide L. Martin. 1987. *Maternity Nursing*, 16th ed. Philadelphia, PA: Lippincott.

Reeve, Catharine. 1991. "Corporate Wives." *Chicago Tribune* (March 17): Sec. 6, pp. 1, 7.

Reik, Theodore A. 1944. *A Psychologist Looks at Love*. New York: Lancer.

Reiss, Ira L. 1960. "Toward a Sociology of Heterosexual Love Relationship." *Marriage and Family Living* 22,2 (May): 139–45.

———. 1971. *The Family System in America*. New York: Holt, Rinehart, and Winston.

———. 1980. *Family Systems in America*, 3d ed. New York: Holt, Rinehart and Winston.

Rempel, John, and John Holmes. 1986. "How Do I Love Thee?" *Psychology Today* (February): 30–31.

Renzetti, Claire M., and Daniel J. Curran. 1989. *Women, Men, and Society: The Sociology of Gender*. Boston: Allyn and Bacon.

———. 1992. *Women, Men, and Society: The Sociology of Gender*. 2d ed. Boston: Allyn and Bacon.

Reskin, Barbara F., and Heidi I. Hartmann. 1986. *Women's Work, Men's Work: Sex Segregation on the Job*. Washington, DC: National Academy Press.

Rheingold, Harriet L., and Kaye V. Cook. 1975. "The Content of Boys' and Girls' Rooms as an Index of Parents' Behavior." *Child Development* 46:459–63.

Rich, Adrienne. 1980. "Compulsory Heterosexuality and Lesbian Existence." *Signs* 5:631–60.

Richmond-Abbott, Marie. 1983. *Masculine and Feminine*. New York: Random House.

Ridley, Carl, Dan J. Peterman, and Arthur W. Avery. 1978. "Cohabitation: Does It Make for a Better Marriage?" *Family Coordinator* 27:129–36.

Riessman, Catherine Kohler. 1990. *Divorce Talk: Women and Men Make Sense of Personal Relationships*. New Brunswick, NJ: Rutgers University Press.

Riley, Glenda. 1987. *Investing the American Woman: A Perspective on Women's History*. Arlington Heights, IL.: Harlan Davidson.

———. 1991. *Divorce: An American Tradition*. New York: Oxford University Press.

Risman, Barbara J. 1989. "Can Men Mother? Life as a Single Father." In Barbara J. Risman and Pepper Schwartz, eds., *Gender in Intimate Relationships: A Microstructural Approach*, 155–64. Belmont, CA: Wadsworth.

———, and Pepper Schwartz. 1989. *Gender in Intimate Relationships: A Microstructural Approach*. Belmont, CA: Wadsworth.

Roark, A. C. 1985. "Effects of PCP, Cocaine on Unborn: A Tragic Picture." *Los Angeles Times* (December 5): Sec. 2, pp. 1–3.

Roberto, Karen A. 1990. "Grandparent and Grandchild Relationships." In Timothy H. Brubaker, ed., *Family Relationships in Later Life*, 100–12. Newbury Park, CA: Sage.

Roberts, W. L. 1979–80. "Significant Elements in the Relationship of Long-Married Couples." *International Journal of Aging and Human Development* 10:265–72.

Robertson, John, and Louise F. Fitzgerald. 1990. "The (Mis)treatment of Men: Effects of Client Gender Role and Life-Style on Diagnosis and Attribution of Pathology." *Journal of Counseling Psychology* 37:3–9.

Robinson, Bryan, Bobbie Rowland, and Mick Coleman. 1986. *Latchkey Kids: Unlocking Doors for Children and Their Families*. Lexington, MA: Lexington Books, Heath.

Robinson, J. P. 1977. *How Americans Use Time*. New York: Praeger.

Robinson, J. Gregg, and Judith S. McIlwee. 1989. "Women in Engineering: A Promise Unfulfilled?" *Social Problems* 36:455–72.

Rochlin, Martin. 1982. "The Heterosexual Questionnaire." *Changing Men* (Spring).

———. 1992. "The Heterosexual Questionnaire." In Michael Kimmel and Michael A. Messner, *Men's Lives*, 482–83. New York: Macmillan.

Rollins, Judy. 1986. "Single Men and Women: Differences and Similarities." *Family Perspectives* 20:117–25.

Roper Organization. 1990. *The Virginia Slims Opinion Poll: A 20-Year Perspective of Women's Issues*. Storrs, CT: University of Connecticut.

Rosenthal, Carolyn J. 1986. "Family Supports in Later Life: Does Ethnicity Make a Difference?" *Gerontologist* 26:19–24.

Rosenthal, Elisabeth. 1991. "Technique for Early Prenatal Test Comes under Question in Studies." *New York Times* (July 10): C11.

Ross, Catherine E., John Mirowsky, and Joan Huber. 1983. "Dividing Work, Sharing Work and In-between: Marriage Patterns and Depression." *American Sociological Review* 48:809–23.

Rossi, Peter H. 1989. *Down and Out in America*. Chicago: University of Chicago Press.

Rothman, Barbara Katz. 1989. *Recreating Motherhood: Ideology and Technology in a Patriarchal Society*. New York: Norton.

———. 1991. *In Labor: Women and Power in the Birthplace*. New York: Norton.

Roy, Maria, ed. 1982. *The Abusive Partner: An Analysis of Domestic Battering*. New York: Van Nostrand Reinhold.

Rubin, Jeffrey Z., Frank J. Provenzano, and Zella Luria. 1974. "The Eye of the Beholder: Parents' Views on Sex of Newborns." *American Journal of Orthopsychiatry* 44:512–19.

Rubin, Lillian B. 1990. *Erotic Wars: What Happened to the Sexual Revolution?* New York: HarperCollins.

Rubin, Zick. 1973. *Liking and Loving: An Invitation to Social Psychology*. New York: Holt, Rinehart, and Winston.

———. 1974. "Lovers and Other Strangers: The Development of Intimacy in Encounters and Relationships." *American Scientist* 62:182–90.

Rubinstein, Robert L. 1986. *Singular Paths: Old Men Living Alone*. New York: Columbia University Press.

———, Baine B. Alexander, Marcene Goodman, and Mark Luborsky. 1991. "Key Relationships of Never Married Childless Older Women: A Cultural Analysis." *Journal of Gerontology* 46,5 (September): 270–77.

Russell, Diana. 1982. *Rape in Marriage*. New York: Macmillan.

———. 1990. *Rape in Marriage*, 2d ed. Bloomington: Indiana University Press.

Sabatelli, Ronald M. 1988. "Measurement Issues in Family Research: A Review and Critique of Contemporary Survey Instruments." *Journal of Marriage and the Family* 50:891–915.

Sadker, Myra, and David Sadker. 1985. "Sexism in the Schoolroom of the 80s." *Psychology Today* (March): 54, 56–57.

Saenz, Rogelio, Willis J. Goudy, and Lorenz Frederick. 1989. "The Effects of Employment and Marital Relations on Depression among Mexican American Women." *Journal of Marriage and the Family* 51:239–51.

Sager, Clifford J. 1983. *Treating the Remarried Family*. New York: Brunner/Mazel.

Saline, C. 1984. "Bleeding in the Suburbs." *Philadelphia Magazine* (August): 81–85, 144–51.

Salovey, P., and J. Rodin. 1989. "Envy and Jealousy in Close Relationships." In Clyde Hendrick ed., *Close Relationships*, 221–46, Newbury Park, CA: Sage.

Sanders, G. F., and D. W. Trygstad. 1989. "Stepgrandparents and Grandparents: The View from Young Adults." *Family Relations* 38:71–75.

Sandroff, Ronnie. 1989. "Why Pro-Family Policies Are Good for Business and America." *Working Women* (November): 126.

Santrock, John W., and Karen A. Sitterle. 1987. "Parent–Child Relationships in Stepmother Families." In Kay Pasley and Marilyn Ihinger-Tallman, eds., *Remarriage and Stepparenting: Current Research and Theory*, 273–99. New York: Guilford Press.

Sapiro, Virginia. 1986. *Women In American Society*. Mountain View, CA: Mayfield.

———. 1990. *Women in American Society*, 2d ed. Mountain View, CA: Mayfield.

Sargent, Alice G. 1985. *Beyond Sex Roles*. New York: West.

Saunders, Daniel G. 1988. "What Do you Know About Abuser Recidivism?: A Critique of Recidivism in Abuser Programs." *Victimology: An International Journal*.

Scanzoni, John. 1980. "Contemporary Marriage Types." *Journal of Family Issues* 1:125–40.

Schiamberg, L. B. 1988. *Child and Adolescent Development*. New York: Macmillan.

Schmetzer, Uli. 1992. "Puritan China Faces Gay Question." *Chicago Tribune* (September 27): Section 1,6.

Schneir, Miriam, ed. 1972. *Feminism: The Essential Historical Writings*. New York: Vintage Books/Random House.

Schoen, Robert, and John Wooldridge. 1989. "Marriage Choices in North Carolina and Virginia, 1969–71 and 1979–81." *Journal of Marriage and the Family* 51:465–81.

Schwartz, Felice N. 1989. "Management Women and the New Facts of Life." *Harvard Business Review* (January/February): 65–76.

Schwartz, Mary Ann. 1975. "Over Thirty and Never Married: An Analysis of Career Development." Unpublished Ph.D. diss. Northwestern University, Evanston, IL.

———. 1976. "Career Strategies of the Never-Married." Paper presented at the 71st annual meeting of the American Sociological Association, New York.

———, and Paula Wolf. 1976. "Singlehood and the American

Experience: Prospectives for a Changing Status." *Humboldt Journal of Social Relations* 4,1 (Fall/Winter): 17–24.

Sciara, Frank J. 1975. "Effects of Fathers' Absence on the Educational Achievement of Urban Black Children." *Child Study Journal* 5:45–55.

Scott, BarBara M. 1988. "The Making of a Middle-Class Black Woman: A Socialization for Success." Ph.D. dis. Northwestern University, Evanston, Illinois.

———. 1991. Unpublished interviews with African-American women.

Scott, Donald M., and Bernard Wishy, eds. 1982. *America's Families: A Documentary History.* New York: Harper and Row.

Scott, Jean Pearson. 1990. "Sibling Interaction in Later Life." In Timothy H. Brubaker, ed., *Family Relationships in Later Life*, 86–99. Newbury Park, CA: Sage.

Seagraves, Kathleen B. 1989. "Extramarital Affairs." *Medical Aspects of Human Sexuality* 23 (April): 99–105.

Sedlak, Andrea. 1988. "Prevention of Wife Abuse." In Vincent B. Van Hasselt, Randall L. Morrison, Alan S. Belack, and Michel Hersen, eds. *Handbook of Family Violence*, 319–58. New York: Plenum.

Seligmann, Jean. 1990. "Variations on a Theme." *Newsweek* (special ed.) (Winter/Spring): 38–46.

Seltzer, Judith, and Irwin Garfinkel. 1990. "Inequality in Divorce Settlements: An Investigation of Property Settlements and Child Support Awards." *Social Science Research* 19:82–111.

Shanas, Ethel. 1979. "The Family as a Social Support System in Old Age." *Gerontologist* 19:169–74.

———. 1980. "Older People and Their Families: The New Pioneers." *Journal of Marriage and the Family* 42,1:9–15.

Shapiro, Jerrold Lee. 1987. "The Expectant Father." *Psychology Today* (January): 36–9, 42.

Shehan, C. L., E. W. Bock, and G. R. Lee. 1990. "Religious Heterogamy, Religiosity, and Marital Happiness: The Case of Catholicism." *Journal of Marriage and the Family* 52:73–79.

Shelton, Beth A., and John Daphne. 1990. "The Division of Household Labor: A Comparison of Cohabiting and Married Couples." Paper presented at the 85th annual meeting of the American Sociological Association, Washington, D.C.

Shettel-Neuber, J., Jeff Bryson, and I. E. Young. 1978. "Physical Attractiveness of the 'Other' Person." *Personality and Social Psychology Bulletin* 4:612–15.

Shinn, Marybeth. 1978. "Father Absence and Children's Cognitive Development." *Psychological Bulletin* 85:295–324.

Shneidman, Edwin. 1980. *Voices of Death.* New York: Harper and Row.

Shope, D. F. 1975. *Interpersonal Sexuality.* Philadelphia, PA: Saunders.

Shorto, Russell. 1991. "Made-in-Japan Parenting." *Health* (June): 54–57.

Shostak, Arthur. 1987. "Singlehood." In Marvin Sussman and Suzanne Steinmetz, eds., *Handbook of Marriage and the Family*, 355–66. New York: Plenum Press.

Shrieves, Linda. 1990. "Midlife Babies: Pregnancy Risks after 35 Decrease as Medical Knowledge Matures." *Chicago Tribune* (October 21): Sec. 6, p. 8.

Shurtleff, Nathaniel Bradstreet, ed. 1853/1854. *Records of the Governor and Company of Massachusetts Bay in New England.* 5 vols. Vol. l, Dec. 13, 1636. Boston: W. White, Printer to the Common-wealth.

Sigler, Robert T. 1989. *Domestic Violence in Context.* Lexington, MA: Heath.

Silverman, Phyllis. 1988. "Research as a Process: Exploring the Meaning of Widowhood." In S. Reinharz and G. Rowles, eds., *Qualitative Gerontology*, 217–40. New York: Springer.

Silverstein, Brett, Laureen Perdue, Barbara Peterson, and Eileen Kelly. 1986. "The Role of the Mass Media in Promoting a Thin Standard of Bodily Attractiveness for Women." *Sex Roles* 14:519–32.

Simenauer, Jacqueline, and David Carroll. 1982. *Singles: The New Americans.* New York: Simon and Schuster.

Simon, Barbara L. 1987. *Never-Married Women.* Philadelphia: Temple University Press.

Simpson, Jeffrey, Bruce Campbell, and Ellen Berscheid. 1986. "The Association between Romantic Love and Marriage: Kephart (1967) Twice Revisited." *Personality and Social Psychology Bulletin* 12,3 (September): 363–72.

Simpson, Victor. 1991. "Europe's Liberal Laws Debated." *Milwaukee Journal* (May 12): J3.

Sims, Sheri. 1989. "Violent." *Chicago Tribune* (June 11): Sec. 6, pp. 1,6.

Skelton, G. 1989. "Many in Survey Who Had Abortions Cite Guilt Feelings." *Los Angeles Times* (March 19): 28.

Skipper, James K. Jr., and Gilbert Nass. 1966. "Dating Behavior: A Framework for Analysis and an Illustration." *Journal of Marriage and the Family* 28:412–20.

Skolnick, Arlene S., and Jerome H. Skolnick, eds. 1987. *The Family in Transition*, 6th ed. Glenview, IL: Scott, Foresman.

Slavin, Edward A. 1991. "What Makes a Marriage Legal?" *Human Rights* 18,1 (Spring):16–19.

Smith, Audrey D., and William J. Reid. 1986. *Role-Sharing Marriage.* New York: Columbia University Press.

Smith, Caroline, and Barbara Lloyd. 1978. "Maternal Behavior and Sex of Infant: Revisited." *Child Development* 49:1263–65.

Smith, Daniel, and Michael Hindus. 1975. "Premarital Pregnancy in America: 1640–1971." *Journal of Interdisciplinary History* 4 (Spring): 537–70.

Smith, Donna. 1990. *Stepmothering.* New York: St. Martin's Press.

Smith, Edward A., J. Richard Udry, and Naomi M. Morris. 1985. "Pubertal Development and Friends: A Biosocial Explanation of Adolescent Sexual Behavior." *Journal of Health and Social Behavior* 26:183–92.

Smith, Herman W. 1981. *Strategies of Social Research: The Methodological Imagination.* Englewood Cliffs, NJ: Prentice Hall.

Smith, J., J. Mercy, and J. Conn. 1988. "Marital Status and the Risk of Suicide." *American Journal of Public Health* 78,1:78–80.

Smith, J. A., and Robert G. Adler. 1991. "Children Hospitalized with Child Abuse and Neglect: A Case-Control Study." *International Journal* 5,4:437–45.

Smith, Lynn G., and Gordon Clanton. 1977. *Jealousy.* Englewood Cliffs, NJ: Prentice Hall.

Smith, Tom. 1990. "The Polls—a Report: The Sexual Revolution?" *Public Opinion Quarterly* 54 (Fall): 415–35.

"Smoking and Sperm." 1981. Science News (April 18): 247.

Snipp, C. Matthew. 1991. *American Indians: The First of This Land.* New York: Russell Sage Foundation.

Soldo, Beth J., and Emily M. Agree. 1988. *American's Elderly.* Washington, DC: Population Reference Bureau.

Solomon, Robert C. 1981. *Love, Emotion, Myth, and Metaphor.* Garden City, NY: Anchor Doubleday.

Sonestein, Freya, Joseph Pleck, and Leighton Ku. 1989. "Sexual Activity, Condom Use and AIDS Awareness among Adolescent Males." *Family Planning Perspective* 21,4:152–58.

Song, I. Young. 1991. "Single Asian American Women as a Result of Divorce: Depressive Affect and Changes in Social Support." In Sandra S. Volgy, ed., *Women, Men, and Divorce: Gender Differences in Separation, Divorce, and Remarriage,* 219–30. New York: Haworth Press.

South, Scott. 1985. "Economic Conditions and the Divorce Rate: A Time-Series Analysis of the Postwar United States." *Journal of Marriage and the Family* 47:31–41.

Southworth, Suzanne, and J. Conrad Schwarz. 1987. "Postdivorce Contact, Relationship with Father, and Heterosexual Trust in Female College Students." *American Journal of Orthopsychiatry* 57:371–82.

Spade, Joan. 1989. "Bringing Home the Bacon: A Sex-Integrated Approach to the Impact of Work on the Family." In Barbara Risman and Pepper Schwartz, eds., *Gender in Intimate Relationships,* 184–92. Belmont, CA: Wadsworth.

Spanier, Graham B. and Paul C. Glick. 1980. "Mate Selection Differentials between Whites and Blacks in the United States." *Social Forces* 53,3:707–25.

———. 1981. "Marital Instability in the United States: Some Correlates and Recent Changes." *Family Relations* 31 (July): 329–38.

Spanier, Graham B., Robert A. Lewis, and Charles L. Cole. 1975. "Marital Adjustment over the Family Life Cycle: The Issue of Curvilinearity." *Journal of Marriage and the Family* 37 (May): 263–75.

Spanier, Graham B., and Linda Thompson. 1988. "Moving toward Separation." In Norval D. Glenn and Marian T. Coleman, eds., *Family Relations: A Reader,* 326–41. Belmont, CA: Wadsworth.

Spitze, Glenna. 1988. "Women's Employment and Family Relations: A Review." *Journal of Marriage and the Family* 50:585–618.

Sprecher, Susan. 1989. "Pre-marital Sexual Standards for Different Categories of Individuals." *Journal of Sex Research* 26,2 (May): 232–48.

———, and Sandra Metts. 1989. "Development of the 'Romantic Beliefs Scale' and Examination of the Effects of Gender and Gender-Role Orientation." *Journal of Social and Personal Relationships* 6:387–411.

Sprey, Jetse. 1979. "Conflict Theory and the Study of Marriage and the Family." In Wesley Burr, R. Hill, F. I. Nye, and Ira L. Reiss, eds., *Contemporary Theories About the Family,* 20–22.

Springs, H. H. 1989. *New Age Community Guidebook.* Available from Community Bookshelf, Rte. l, Box 155-F, Rutledge, MO 63563.

Spruill, Julia C. 1938. *Women's Life and Work in the Southern Colonies.* New York: Russell and Russell.

Staines, Graham L., and Pam L. Libby. 1986. "Men and Women in Role Relationships." In Richard D. Ashmore and Frances K. DelBoca, eds., *The Social Psychology of Female–Male Relations: A Critical Analysis of Central Concepts,* 211–58. New York: Academic Press.

Stainton, M. C. 1985. "The Fetus: A Growing Member of the Family." *Family Relations* 34:321–26.

Stanford, E. Percil, K. Michael Peddecord, and Shirley A. Lockery. 1990. "Variations among the Elderly in Black, Hispanic, and White Families." In Timothy H. Brubaker, ed., *Family Relationships in Later Life,* 229–41. Newbury Park, CA: Sage.

Staples, Robert, ed. 1971. *The Black Family: Essays and Studies.* Belmont, CA: Wadsworth.

———. 1981a. "Black Singles in America." In Peter J. Stein, ed., *Single Life: Unmarried Adults in Social Context,* 40–51. New York: St. Martin's Press.

———. 1981b. *The World of Black Singles: Changing Patterns of Male/Female Relations.* Westport, CT: Greenwood Press.

———. 1988. "The Black American Family." In Charles H. Mindel, Robert Habenstein, and Roosevelt Wright, Jr. eds., *Ethnic Families in America: Patterns and Variations,* 303–24. New York: Elsevier.

———, ed. 1991. *The Black Family: Essays and Studies,* 4th ed. Belmont, CA: Wadsworth.

———, and Terry Jones. 1985. "Culture, Ideology, and Black Television Images." *Black Scholar* 16:10–20.

Stark, Evan, and Anne Flitcraft. 1988. "Violence among Intimates: An Epidemiological Review." In Vincent Van Hasselt, Randall Morrison, Alan Bellack, and Michael Hersen, eds. *Handbook of Family Violence*, 293–318. New York: Plenum.

Starr, Bernard D., and Marcella Bakur Weiner. 1981. *Sex and Sexuality in the Mature Years.* New York: Stein and Day.

Stayton, William R. 1984. "Lifestyle Spectrum 1984." *Sex Information and Educational Council of the U.S. Reports (SIECUS)* 12,3:1–4.

Steck, Loren, Diane Levitan, David McLane, and Harold H. Kelley. 1982. "Care, Need, and Conceptions of Love." *Journal of Personality and Social Psychology* 43,481–91.

Stein, Peter. 1976. *Single.* Englewood Cliffs, NJ: Prentice Hall.

———, ed. 1981. *Single Life: Unmarried Adults in Social Context.* New York: St. Martin's Press.

———, and Meryl Fingrutd. 1985. "The Single Life Has More Potential for Happiness Than Marriage and Parenthood for Both Men and Women." In Harold Feldman and Margaret Feldman, eds., *Current Controversies in Marriage and the Family*, 81–89. Beverly Hills, CA: Sage.

Steinfirst, Susan, and Barbara B. Moran. 1989. "The New Mating Game: Matchmaking via the Personal Columns in the 1980's." *Journal of Popular Culture* 22,4:129–40.

Steinmetz, Suzanne. 1977. "The Battered Husband Syndrome." *Victimology: An International Journal* 2,3–4:499–509.

———, and Murray Straus. 1974. *Violence in the Family.* New York: Harper and Row.

Stephan, Cookie W. and Walter G. Stephan. 1990. *Two Social Psychologies.* Belmont, CA: Wadsworth.

Sternberg, Robert J. 1986. "A Triangular Theory of Love." *Psychological Review* 93,2:119–35.

Stinnet, Nick, and Craig Birdsong. 1978. *The Family and Alternate Life Styles.* Chicago: Nelson-Hall.

Stockard, Jean, and Miriam M. Johnson. 1992. *Sex and Gender in Society*, 2d ed. Englewood Cliffs, NJ: Prentice Hall.

Stokes, Joseph P., and Judith S. Peyton. 1986. "Attitudinal Differences between Full-Time Homemakers and Women Who Work Outside the Home." *Sex Roles* 15:299–310.

Stoller, Eleanor P. 1983. "Parental Caregiving by Adult Children." *Journal of Marriage and the Family* 45:851–58.

Stone, Robyn, Gail L. Cafferata, and Judith Sangl. 1987. "Caregivers of the Frail Elderly: A National Profile." *Gerontologist* 27:616–26.

Straus, Murray. 1979. "Measuring Intra-Family Conflict and Violence: The Conflict Tactics Scale." *Journal of Marriage and the Family* 41:75–88.

———, and Richard Gelles. 1986. "Societal Change and Change in Family Violence from 1975 to 1985 as Revealed in Two National Surveys." *Journal of Marriage and the Family* 48:465–79.

———, and Suzanne Steinmetz. 1980. *Behind Closed Doors.* Garden City, NY: Anchor Books.

Stroebe, Wolfgang, C. A. Insko, V. D. Thompson, and B. D. Layton. 1971. "Effects of Physical Attractiveness, Attitude Similarity, and Sex on Various Aspects of Interpersonal Attraction." *Journal of Personality and Social Psychology* 18:79–91.

Strong, Brian, and Rebecca Reynolds. 1982. *Understanding Our Sexuality.* St. Paul, MN: West.

Strong, Bryan, Sam Wilson, Leah Miller Clarke, and Thomas Johns. 1978. *Human Sexuality.* New York: West.

"Study Reports Sex Bias in News Organizations." 1989. *New York Times* (April 11):C22.

Sulik, Kathleen, Malcolm Johnston, and Mary A. Webb. 1981. "Fetal Alcohol Syndrome: Ambriogenesis in a Mouse Model." *Science* 214 (November 20): 936–38.

Sullivan, Andrew. 1989. "Here Comes the Groom." *New Republic* (28 August): 20–2.

Sunshine, Linda. 1990. "Last Word." *Omni* 12,4 (January): 104.

Sussman, Marvin. 1985. "The Family Life of Old People." In Robert Binstock and Ethel Shanas, eds., *Handbook of Aging and the Social Sciences*, 415–49. New York: Van Nostrand Reinhold.

Sutton-Smith, Brian. 1971. "The Expressive Profile." In Americo Paredes and Richard Bauman, eds., *Toward New Perspectives in Folklore*, 80–92. Austin: University of Texas Press.

Swanbrow, Diane. 1989. "The Paradox of Happiness." *Psychology Today* (July/August): 37–39.

Sweet, James A., and Larry L. Bumpass. 1987. *American Families and Households.* New York: Russell Sage Foundation.

Szapocznik, Jose, and Roberto Hernandez. 1988. "The Cuban American Family." In Charles H. Mindel, Robert W. Habenstein, and Roosevelt H. Wright, Jr., eds., *Ethnic Families in America: Patterns and Variations*, 160–72. New York: Elsevier.

Tanfer, Koray. 1987. "Patterns of Premarital Cohabitation among Never-Married Women in the United States." *Journal of Marriage and the Family* 49:483–97.

Tannen, Deborah. 1990. *You Just Don't Understand: Women and Men in Conversation.* New York: Ballantine Books.

Tanner, D. 1978. *The Lesbian Couple.* Lexington, MA: Heath.

Tate, Nellie. 1983. "The Black Aging Experience." In R. L. McNeely and J. N. Colen, eds., *Aging in Minority Groups*, 93–120. Beverly Hills, CA: Sage.

Taylor, Robert J., and Linda M. Chatters. 1986. "Patterns of Informal Support to Elderly Black Adults: Family, Friends and Church Members." *Social Work* 31:432–38.

Teachman, Jay D., and Karen A. Polonko. 1990. "Cohabitation and Marital Stability in the United States." *Social Forces* 69,1 (September): 207–20.

Tennov, Dorothy. 1979. *Love and Limerence: The Experience of Being in Love*. Briarcliff Manor, NY: Stein and Day.

Thomas, Jeanne L. 1986. "Gender Differences in Satisfaction with Grandparenting." *Psychology and Aging* 1:215–19.

Thornton, Arland. 1990. "The Courtship Process and Adolescent Sexuality." *Journal of Family Issues* 11,3:239–73.

Tilly, Louise, and Joan W. Scott. 1978. *Women, Work and Family*. New York: Holt.

Totenberg, Nina. 1985. "How to Write a Marriage Contract." In Ollie Pocs and Robert Walsh, eds., *Marriage and Family: Annual Editions*, 46–47. Sluice Dock, Guilford, CT: Dushkin.

Tower, Cynthia Crosson. 1989. *Understanding Child Abuse and Neglect*. Boston: Allyn and Bacon.

Townsend, Bickley, and Kathleen O'Neil. 1990. "American Women Get Mad." *American Demographics* (August): 26–29, 32.

Tracy, L. 1990. "The Television Image in Children's Lives." *New York Times* (May 13): Sec. M.

Trent, Katherine, and Eve Powell-Griner. 1991. "Differences in Race, Marital Status, and Education among Women Obtaining Abortions." *Social Forces* 69,4:1121–41.

Tribe, Laurence H. 1990. *Abortion: The Clash of Absolutes*. New York: Norton.

Troll, Lillian. 1988. "New Thoughts on Old Families." *Gerontologist* 28,5:586–91.

Trovato, Frank, and Gloria Lauris. 1989. "Marital Status and Mortality in Canada: 1951–1981." *Journal of Marriage and the Family* 51:907–22.

Turner, Jonathan, and Alexandra Z. Maranski. 1979. *Functionalism*. Menlo Park, CA: Benjamin/Cummings.

Uhlenberg, Peter. 1980. "Death and the Family." *Journal of Family History* (Fall): 313–21.

———, and Kenneth Chew. 1986. "The Changing Place of Remarriage in the Life Course." *Current Perspectives of Aging and the Life Cycle* 2:23–52.

United Press International. 1990. "Men Love Looks, Women Love Money: U. M. Study." *Chicago Tribune*.

U.S. Bureau of the Census. 1971. "Marital Status and Living Arrangements: March 1971." *Current Population Reports*, Series P-20, No. 225. Washington, DC: U.S. Government Printing Office.

———. 1975. "Historical Statistics of the United States, Colonial Times to 1970." Bicentennial ed., Pt. 1. Washington, DC: U.S. Government Printing Office.

———. 1987. "Money Income and Poverty Status of Families and Persons in the United States: 1986 (Advance Data from the March 1987 Current Population Survey)." *Current Population Reports*, Series P-60, No. 157. Washington, DC: U.S. Government Printing Office.

———. 1989a. *Statistical Abstract of the United States*, 109th ed. Washington, DC: U.S. Government Printing Office.

———. 1989b. "Projections of the Population of the United States, by Age, Sex, and Race: 1988 to 2080." *Current Population Reports*, Series P-25, No. 1018. Washington, DC: U.S. Government Printing Office.

———. 1990a. "Marital Status and Living Arrangements." *Current Population Reports*, Series P-20, No. 445, Washington, DC: U.S. Government Printing Office.

———. 1990b. "Household and Family Characteristics: March 1990 and 1989." *Current Population Reports*, Series P-20, No. 447. Washington, DC: U.S. Government Printing Office.

———. 1990c. "Child Support and Alimony, 1987." *Current Population Reports*, Special Studies, Series P-23, No. 167. Washington, DC: U.S. Government Printing Office.

———. 1990d. "Money Income and Poverty Status in the United States, 1989. (Advance Data from the March 1990 Current Population Survey)." *Current Population Reports*, Series P-60, No. 168. Washington, DC: U.S. Government Printing Office.

———. 1990e. *Statistical Abstract of the United States: 1990*, 110th ed. Washington, DC: U.S. Government Printing Office.

———. 1991a. "Marital Status and Living Arrangements: March 1990." *Current Population Reports*. Series P-20, No. 450. Washington, DC: U.S. Government Printing Office.

———. 1991b. "Money Income and Poverty Status in the U.S., 1990." *Current Population Reports*, Series P-60, No. 174. Washington, DC: U.S. Government Printing Office.

———. 1991c. "Fertility of American Women: June, 1990." *Current Population Reports*, Series P-20, No. 454. Washington, DC: U.S. Government Printing Office.

———. 1991d. "Poverty in the United States: 1990." *Current Population Reports*, Series P-60, No. 175. Washington, DC: U.S. Government Printing Office.

———. 1991e. *Statistical Abstract of the United States*, 111th ed. Washington, DC: U.S. Government Printing Office.

———. 1991f. "Money Income of Households, Families, and Persons in the United States: 1990." *Current Population Reports*, Series P-60, No. 174. Washington, DC: U.S. Government Printing Office.

———. 1992a. "Marital Status and Living Arrangements: March 1991." *Current Population Reports*, Series P-20, No. 461. Washington, DC: U.S. Government Printing Office.

———. 1992b. "Who's Minding the Kids?" *Current Population Reports*, Series P-70, No. 30. Washington, DC: U.S. Government Printing Office.

———. 1992c. *Statistical Abstract of the United States*, 112th ed. Washington, DC: U.S. Government Printing Office.

———, 1993. "Marital Status and Living Arrangements: March 1992." *Current Population Reports*, Series P-20. Washington, DC: U.S. Government Printing Office.

U.S. Bureau of Labor Statistics. 1991a. *Employment and Earnings*. Washington, DC: U.S. Government Printing Office.

———. 1991b. *Working Women: A Chartbook*. Bulletin 2385 (August). Washington, DC: U.S. Government Printing Office.

———. 1992. *Employment and Earnings*. Washington, DC: U.S. Government Printing Office.

U.S. National Center for Health Statistics. 1988. "Weddings Performed in Religious Ceremonies." *Vital Statistics of the United States*, Annual. Washington, DC: U.S. Government Printing Office.

U.S. Senate Special Committee on Aging. 1991. *Aging America: Trends and Projections*. Washington, DC: U.S. Department of Health and Human Services.

U.S. Surgeon General's Report on Health Risks of Smoking. 1985 (January). Washington, DC: U.S. Government Printing Office.

Vazquez-Nuttall, Ena, Ivonne Romero-Garcia, and Brunilda DeLeon. 1987. "Sex Roles and Perceptions of Femininity and Masculinity of Hispanic Women: A Review of the Literature." *Psychology of Women Quarterly* 11:409–25.

Veevers, Jean E. 1980. *Childless by Choice*. Scarborough, Ontario: Butterworth.

Ventura, Stephanie J. 1988. "Births of Hispanic Parentage, 1985." *Monthly Vital Statistics Report* 36,11 (suppl.) (February 26).

Visher, Emily, and John Visher. 1982. *How to Win as a Stepfamily*. New York: Dembner Books.

Voydanoff, Patricia. 1987. *Work and Family*. Beverly Hills, CA: Sage Publications.

———. 1983. "Unemployment and Family Stress." In Helena Z. Lopata and Joseph H. Pleck, eds., *Research in the Interweave of Social Roles: Families and Jobs*, 239–50. Greenwich, CT: Jai Press.

Vuchinich, Samuel, E. Mavis Hetherington, Regina Vuchinich, and W. Glenn Clingempeel. 1991. "Parent–Child Interaction and Gender Differences in Early Adolescents' Adaptation to Stepfamilies." *Developmental Psychology* 27,4:618–26.

Wade-Lewis, M. 1989. "The Strengths of African-American Stepfamilies." In N. B. Maglin and N. Schiedewind, eds., *Women and Stepfamilies: Voices of Anger and Love*, 225–33. Philadelphia, PA: Temple University Press.

Wald, Esther. 1981. *The Remarried Family: Challenge and Promise*. New York: Family Service Association of America.

Walker, Kathryn E., and Margaret Woods. 1976. *Time Use: A Measure of Household Production of Goods and Services*. Washington, DC: American Home Economics Association.

Walker, Lenore. 1978. "Treatment Alternatives for Battered Women." In J. R. Chapman and M. Gates, eds., *The Victimization of Women*, 143–74. Beverly Hills, CA: Sage.

———. 1979. *The Battered Woman*. New York: Harper and Row.

———. 1984. *The Battered Woman Syndrome*. New York: Springer.

Wallace, Ruth A., and Alison Wolf. 1991. *Contemporary Sociological Theory*. Englewood Cliffs, NJ: Prentice Hall.

Waller, Douglas. 1992. "'Women Can't Fly Jets' and Other Myths." *Newsweek* (August 10): 36.

Waller, Willard. 1937. "The Rating and Dating Complex." *American Sociological Review* 2:727–35.

———, and Reuben Hill. 1951. *The Family: A Dynamic Interpretation*. New York: Dryden Press.

Wallerstein, Judith S. 1986. "Women after Divorce: Preliminary Report from a Ten-Year Follow-up." *American Journal of Orthopsychiatry* 56:65–77.

———. 1987. "Children of Divorce: Report of a Ten-Year Follow-up of Early Latency-Age Children." *American Journal of Orthopsychiatry* 57:199–211.

———, and Joan Kelly. 1980. *Surviving the Break-up: How Children Actually Cope with Divorce*. New York: Basic Books.

———, and Sandra Blakeslee. 1989. *Second Chances: Men, Women, and Children a Decade after Divorce*. New York: Ticknor and Fields.

Walsh, F. 1980. "The Family in Later Life." In E. A. Carter and M. McGoldrick, eds., *The Family Life Cycle: A Framework for Family Therapy*. New York: Gardner Press.

Walster, E., W. Walster, and J. Traupmann. 1978. "Equity and Premarital Sex." *Journal of Personality and Social Psychology* 36:82–92.

Watkins, S. J., J. A. Menken, and J. Bongaarts. 1987. "Demographic Foundations of Family Change." *American Sociological Review* 52:346–58.

Watson, Roy, and Peter DeMeo. 1987. "Premarital Cohabitation vs. Traditional Courtship: Their Effects on Subsequent Marital Adjustment: A Replication and Follow up." *Family Relations* 36:193–97.

Weeks, John R. 1989. *Population: An Introduction to Concepts and Issues*, 4th ed. Belmont, CA: Wadsworth.

Weibel-Orlando, Joan. 1990. "Grandparenting Styles: Native American Perspectives." In Jay Sokolovsky, ed., *The Cultural Context of Aging*, 109–25. New York: Bergin and Garvey.

Weiss, Robert. 1979. *Going It Alone: The Family Life And Social Situation of the Single Parent*. New York: Basic Books.

Weitzman, Lenore. 1977. "To Love, Honor, and Obey: Traditional Legal Marriage and Alternative Family Forms." In Arlene S. Skolnick and Jerome H. Skolnick, eds., *Family in Transition*, 2d ed., 288–313. Boston: Little, Brown.

———. 1981. *The Marriage Contract*. New York: Free Press.

———. 1985. *The Divorce Revolution: The Unexpected Social and Economic Consequences for Women and Children in America*. New York: Free Press.

Weitzman, Nancy, Beverly Birns, and Ronald Friend. 1985.

"Traditional and Nontraditional Mothers' Communication with Their Daughters and Sons." *Child Development* 56:894–96.

Wells, Robert. 1978. "Family History and Demographic Transition." In Michael Gordon, ed., *The American Family in Social-Historical Perspective*, 516–32. New York: St. Martin's Press.

Welter, Barbara. 1978. "The Cult of True Womanhood: 1820–1860." In Michael Gordon, ed., *The American Family in Social-Historical Perspective*, 313–33. New York: St. Martin's Press.

Westhoff, Charles F., and Noreen Goldman. 1988. "Figuring the Odds in the Marriage Market." In J. Gipson Wells, ed., *Current Issues in Marriage and the Family*, 39–46. New York: Macmillan.

Whisman, Mark A., and Neil S. Jacobson. 1988. "Depression, Marital Satisfaction, and Marital and Personality Measures of Sex Roles." *Journal of Marital and Family Therapy* 15:177–86.

White, Gary L. 1980. "Including Jealousy: A Power Perspective." *Personality and Social Psychology Bulletin* 6:222–27.

White, James. 1987. "Premarital Cohabitation and Marital Stability in Canada." *Journal of Marriage and the Family* 49:641–47.

White, Lynn K. 1979. "Sex Differentials in the Effects of Remarriage on Global Happiness." *Journal of Marriage and the Family* 41:869–76.

———. 1981. "A Note on Racial Differences in the Effect of Female Opportunity on Marriage Rates." *Demography* 18:349–54.

———. 1990. "Determinants of Divorce: A Review of Research in the Eighties." *Journal of Marriage and Family* 52:904–12.

———, and A. Booth. 1985. "The Quality and Stability of Remarriages: The Role of Stepchildren." *American Sociological Review* 50:689–98.

White, Lynn K., and Agnes Riedman. 1992. "When the Brady Brunch Grows Up: Step/Half and Fullsibling Relationships in Adulthood." *Journal of Marriage and the Family* 54:197–208.

Whiting, Beatrice, and Carolyn Pope Edwards. 1988. *Children of Different Worlds: The Formation of Social Behavior.* Cambridge, MA: Harvard University Press.

Whitsett, Doni, and Helen Land. 1992. "The Development of a Role Strain Index for Stepparents." *Families in Society: The Journal of Contemporary Human Services* 73,1:14–22.

"Who Has the Upper Hand?" 1988. *Ebony* 44,1 (November): 46–50.

Williams, John E., and Deborah L. Best. 1990. *Measuring Sex Stereotypes: A Multinational Study*, rev. ed. Newbury Park, CA: Sage.

Willie, Charles V. 1981. *A New Look at the Black Family.* Bayside, NY: General Hall.

Wilson, E. D. 1975. *Sociology: The New Synthesis.* Cambridge, MA: Harvard University Press.

Wilson, Elizabeth, and Sik Hung Ng. 1988. "Sex Bias in Visual Images Evoked by Generics: A New Zealand Study." *Sex Roles* 18:159–68.

Winch, Robert R., Thomas Ktsanes, and Virginia Ktsanes. 1954. "The Theory of Complementary Needs in Mate Selection: An Analytic and Descriptive Study." *American Sociological Review* 19:241–49.

Wineberg, Howard. 1988. "Duration between Marriage and First Birth and Marital Stability." *Social Biology* 35:91–102.

———. 1990. "Childbearing in Remarriage." *Journal of Marriage and the Family* 52:31–38.

"Women in Media Say Careers Hit 'Glass Ceiling'." 1988. *Eastern Express* (March 2): A9.

Women's Institute for Freedom of the Press. 1986. "1955 to 1985: Women in Prime Time TV Still Traditional, but New Treatment of Women's Rights Themes." *Media Report to Women* (November/December): 7.

Wong, Morrison G. 1988. "The Chinese American Family." In Charles Mindel, Robert W. Habenstein, and Roosevelt Wright, Jr., eds., *Ethnic Families in America: Patterns and Variations*, 230–57. New York: Elsevier.

Worden, J. William. 1982. *Grief Counseling and Grief Therapy: A Handbook for the Mental Health Practitioner.* New York: Springer-Verlag.

World Almanac Book of Facts, 1991. 1990. New York: Pharos Books.

Wright, James D. 1989. *Address Unknown: The Homeless in America.* New York: Aldine de Gruyter.

Wyman, Anne. 1989. "Area Child-Care Activists Say Dodd Proposal Has the Answers." *Boston Sunday Globe* (February 26): 12, 26.

Yankelovich, Daniel. 1981. "New Rules in American Life: Searching for Self-fulfillment in a World Turned Upside Down." *Psychology Today* (April): 37–39ff.

Yllo, Kersti, and Murray A. Straus. 1981. "Patriarchy and Violence Against Wives: The Impact of Structural and Normative Factors." Paper presented at the National Conference for Family Violence Researchers, Durham, N.H.

Young, N. F. 1972. "Socialization of Patterns among the Chinese in Hawaii." *Amerasia Journal* 1:31–51.

Zabin, Laurie S., and Samuel Clark, Jr. 1981. "Why They Delay: A Study of Teenage Family Planning Clinic Patients." *Family Planning Perspectives* 13:205–17.

Zablocki, Benjamin 1980. *Alienation and Charisma: A Study of Contemporary Communes.* New York: Free Press.

Zavella, Patricia. 1987. *Women's Work and Chicago Families: Cannery Workers of the Santa Clara Valley.* Ithaca, NY: Cornell University Press.

Zedeck, Sheldon, and Kathleen Mosier. 1990. "Work in the Family and Employing Organizations." *American Psychologist* 45,2:240–51.

Zube, Margaret. 1982. "Changing Behavior and Outlook of Aging Men and Women: Implications for Marriage in the Middle and Later Years." *Family Relations* 31:147–56.

Zuckerman, Diana M., and Donald H. Sayre. 1982. "Cultural Sex-Role Expectations and Children's Sex-Role Concepts." *Sex Roles* 8:853–62.

PHOTO CREDITS

CHAPTER 1
Gabe Palmer/Stock Market, 1; AP/Wide World Photos, 7; Culver Pictures, 12 (left); Photofest, 12 (right); T.H. O'Sullivan/Library of Congress, 17; Lionel Delevingne/Stock Boston, 20; Bettmann, 24; Dorothea Lange/Library of Congress, 26; AP/Wide World Photos, 27.

CHAPTER 2
Birthways Childbirth Resource Center, Inc., Redmond, WA, 31; David Young-Wolff/Photoedit, 35; Photofest, 40; Elizabeth Crews/The Image Works, 42; New York Public Library, 44; Pinderhughes, 51; (no credit), 52.

CHAPTER 3
Gordon E. Smith/Photo Researchers, 59; Bettmann, 65; Ken Karp, 69; Bob Daemmrich/The Image Works, 73; R. Lord/The Image Works, 81 (top left); Alan Carey/The Image Works, 81 (top right); AP/Wide World Photos, 81 (bottom).

CHAPTER 4
Will & Deni McIntyre/Photo Researchers, 85; Spencer Grant/Photo Researchers, 90; Photofest, 91; Art Resource, 93; Tony Freeman/Photoedit, 97; Photofest, 102; Michael Newman/Photoedit, 105; Laimute E. Druskis/Photo Researchers, 106.

CHAPTER 5
Curtis Willocks/Brooklyn Image Group, 115; Alpha Photo Associates/FPG International, 119; Jeff Isaac Greenberg/Photo Researchers, 121; Ira Kerschenbaum/Stock Boston, 124; Spencer Grant/Monkmeyer Press, 137; Photofest, 138.

CHAPTER 6
David Young-Wolff/Photoedit, 145; Bettmann, 150; Freeman/Grishaber/Photoedit, 155 (left); Fay Torresyap/Stock Boston, 155 (right); S. Gazin/The Image Works, 157; UPI/Bettmann, 161; Barbara Alper/Stock Boston, 165; The Photo Works/Monkmeyer Press, 172 (bottom); Rhoda Sidney/Monkmeyer Press, 177.

CHAPTER 7
Bob Daemmrich/The Image Works, 181; Charles Wilson Peale/Historical Society of Pennsylvania, 183; Bettmann, 184; Frank Siteman/Monkmeyer Press, 195; Bettmann, 198; Laima Druskis, 202; Jim Harrison/Stock Boston, 204.

CHAPTER 8
Photoedit, 207; Laima Druskis, 211; Randy Matusow, 212; Randy Matusow, 217; T. Shumsky/The Image Works, 223; Bobbie Kingsley/Photo Researchers, 228; Bob Daemmrich/The Image Works, 230.

CHAPTER 9
Sybil Shackman/Monkmeyer Press, 233; Mark Antman/The Image Works, 239; Elizabeth Crews/The Image Works, 242; UPI/Bettmann, 243; Rick Bowmer/AP/Wide World Photos, 252 (left); Laima Druskis, 252 (right); Ron Frehm/AP/Wide World Photos, 255; J. Scott Applewhite/AP/Wide World Photos, 257; Jim Mone/AP/Wide World Photos, 260.

CHAPTER 10
Merritt Vincent/Photoedit, 265; D.W. Fawcett/Science Source/Photo Researchers, 267 (top); Mary Kate Denny/Photoedit, 268 (left); Myrleen Ferguson/Photoedit, 268 (right); Bettmann, 278; Mike Greenlar/The Image Works, 283; David Young-Wolff/Photoedit, 286; Elizabeth Crews/The Image Works, 287; Jon Burbank/The Image Works, 288; Bettye Lane/Photo Researchers, 289.

CHAPTER 11
Mimi Forsyth/Monkmeyer Press, 295; Library of Congress, 298; Reuters/Bettmann, 299; Bob Daemmrich/The Image Works, 305; Rick Browne/Stock Boston, 315.

CHAPTER 12

Robert Brenner/Photoedit, 321; Photofest, 325; Mimi Forsyth/ Monkmeyer Press, 327; Michael Newman/Photoedit, 330; Photofest, 338; Robert Brenner/Photoedit, 340.

CHAPTER 13

Willie L. Hill, Jr./Stock Boston, 347; Rhoda Sidney/Stock Boston, 350; Gale Zucker/Stock Boston, 354; George Goodwin/Monkmeyer Press, 355; Ken Karp, 359; Joan Liftin/Actuality, Inc., 371.

CHAPTER 14

Louisa Preston/Photo Researchers, 375; Culver Pictures, 379; Bettmann, 380; Bill Bachmann/The Image Works, 381; J. Gerard Smith/Monkmeyer Press, 390; Mimi Forsyth/Monkmeyer Press, 391; Topham/OB/The Image Works, 394; Reprinted courtesy of Hallmark Cards, Inc., and Dorothy R. Colgan, 399 (top); Photofest, 399 (bottom).

CHAPTER 15

Bill Bachmann/The Image Works, 403; NBC/Photofest, 406; Carolyn Wendt/Actuality, 408; (no credit), 412; Barbara Alper/Stock Boston, 413; Elizabeth Crews/The Image Works, 418; John Eastcott/ Yva Momatiuk/The Image Works, 421; John Liftin/Actuality, 423; Ken Karp, 426.

CHAPTER 16

Robert Brenner/Photoedit, 431; Jon Chase/Stock Boston, 434; Joseph Nettis/Photo Researchers, 435; Bob Daemmrich/The Image Works, 440; Bob Daemmrich/The Image Works, 443; Dratch/The Image Works, 445.

APPENDIX E

Teri Stratford/Materials courtesy Planned Parenthood, NYC, 467; Wisconsin Pharmacal Company, 469.

NAME INDEX

Biden, J., 336
Billingsley, A., 11, 16
Bird, G., 212, 214
Birdsong, C., 192, 196, 204
Birns, B., 71
Black, D., 416
Blackwell, E., 164
Blackwell, H., 221
Blackwell, J.E., 291
Blakeslee, S., 365, 367, 368, 370
Blank, R., 268
Blassingame, J., 17
Blau, P., 39, 47
Block, J., 229–30
Blood, R.O., Jr., 414
Bluestone, B., 312
Blumstein, P., 36, 106, 154, 160, 168, 196, 200, 201
Bock, E.W., 133
Bohannan, P., 358, 384, 393
Bolig, R., 138
Bologh, R.W., 91
Boneparth, E., 365
Bongaarts, J., 405
Bonker, 305
Booth, A., 197, 354–55, 389, 397
Borden, L., 322
Borland, D.M., 101
Bossard, J., 133–34
Boswell, T.D., 302
Bound, J., 427
Bovee, T., 132, 225, 227
Bowman, M.E., 369
Bradsher, K., 189
Brand, E., 394–95
Brantley, J.N., 50
Bray, L., 80, 81
Brazelton, T.B., 277
Brecher, E., 163
Brehm, S.S., 103, 110, 168
Brewerton, T.D., 76
Brickman, A., 368
Brod, H., 66
Brodbar-Nemzer, J.Y., 357
Brody, E., 421, 422
Brody, G., 367
Bronstein, P., 71

Brotman, B., 204, 252
Brotman, H.B., 412, 419
Broverman, D.M., 79
Broverman, I., 79
Brown, B.W., 37
Brown, L., 258
Browne, A., 329
Browning, R., 413
Brubaker, T.H., 404, 413, 414, 415
Bryson, J., 111
Buehler, C., 362, 383
Bueler, J., 276
Bulcroft, K., 191
Bumpass, L.L., 3, 193, 197, 198, 354–57, 376, 382, 391, 412, 426
Bunch, C., 156
Bunin, S., 256
Burger, C., 424
Burger, J.M., 246
Burgess, E.W., 46
Burman, P., 312
Burns, L., 246
Burton, L., 416
Bush, G., 243, 318
Bushwall, S., 368
Bussey, K., 70
Butler, R., 405
Buunk, B.B., 198
Byers, J., 76

C

Cafferata, G.L., 412
Cahn, S., 396
Calhoun, A.W., 183, 378
Calhoun, C., 44
Calvert, C., 261
Calvert, M., 261
Calvin, J., 149
Campbell, B., 90
Campbell, M., 76
Cancian, F.M., 89, 103–4
Cantor, M.H., 420
Carballo-Diequez, A., 199
Cardell, M., 201
Cargan, L., 190

Carlier, A., 137
Carlsmith, J.M., 368
Carlson, C., 234
Carlson, J., 230
Carney, L., 219
Carr, L.G., 378
Carrigan, T., 56
Carroll, D., 190
Carroll, L., 177
Carson, J., 363
Carter, B., 75
Carter, H., 354
Castro-Martin, T., 376
Casuso, J., 201, 203
Catalono, D.J., 419
Cate, R.M., 140, 358
Catton, P., 305
Caulfield, M.D., 152
Cavanaugh, J., 418
Chafetz, J.S., 50
Chai, L., 227
Chambers-Schiller, L.V., 184
Chan, C.S., 199
Chan, F., 415
Chandra, A., 120
Chapman, D.G., 330
Chappell, N., 420, 421
Chatters, L.M., 416
Cheal, D., 41, 53
Chen, J.W., 368
Cherlin, A., 118, 194, 210, 353, 356, 364, 366, 370, 382, 383, 388, 396, 397, 417, 433
Cherukuri, R., 279
Chesley, L., 273
Chew, K., 378
Childress, A.C., 76
Chiriboga, D.A., 367
Chodorow, N., 51, 69
Christopher, F.S., 140
Chun, S.-H., 199
Clanton, G., 111
Clark, A.L., 414
Clark, S., Jr., 167
Clarke, L.M., 149, 164, 166
Clarke, S., 433
Clarkson, F.E., 79
Clayton, R.R., 226

Cleary, P.D., 78
Cleminshaw, H., 367
Clingempeel, W.G., 388, 393, 394–95
Clinton, B., 202, 243, 248, 318
Clinton, H.R., 77, 299
Close, G., 102
Coates, J., 81
Cochran, S.D., 125, 199, 200
Cockerham, W.C., 410, 411
Cockrum, J., 190
Coker, D.R., 70
Cole, C.L., 357
Cole, P., 415
Coleman, D., 139
Coleman, M., 79, 317, 378, 380, 381, 382, 388, 395
Coles, R., 153
Collins, P.H., 4, 286
Colosanto, D., 64, 67, 77
Compton, J., 140
Condran, G., 358
Condry, J., 76
Conn, C.P., 407
Conn, J., 427
Connel, J.P., 77–78
Connell, B., 56
Conner, K., 428
Constantine, J., 205
Constantine, L., 205
Cook, E.P., 254
Cook, K.V., 71
Cooke, D.J., 338
Cooney, T., 356, 366
Coontz, S., 3, 9, 12, 15, 21, 22
Copeland, M., 301
Cornell, C.P., 140, 326, 327, 341, 342, 344, 345
Cornfield, N., 204
Costa, F., 167
Cote, R.M., 121
Counts, D.A., 338
Couric, E., 309
Cowan, P.A., 393
Coward, R.T., 421
Cowley, G., 274
Cox, H., 424

Cox, M., 368
Cox, R., 368
Crispell, D., 238
Crosbie-Burnett, M., 388, 393, 396, 398
Crouter, A.C., 304
Cuber, J.F., 223–25
Cunningham-Burley, S., 418
Curran, D.J., 61, 62, 140, 216, 254, 277, 279, 298, 309, 323, 332, 334, 342, 344
Curry, G.E., 260
Curtis, J.R., 302
Curtis, R., Jr., 24
Cutler, B., 189

D

Dainton, M., 380
Daly, M., 323
Daniel, J.H., 328
Daniels, R., 22, 227, 237
Dannefer, D., 420
Daphne, J., 196
Darling, C., 151, 152
Darrett, B., 16
Davidson, K.B., 103
Davidson, W., 73
Davis, A., 246
Davis, J., 258
Davis, K., 91, 96, 97, 98, 102, 110
Davis, L.G., 451
Davis, M.S., 258
DeBartolo, A., 80
DeFrain, J., 238
DeGiulio, R.C., 425–26, 427
Degler, C., 16, 235
DeLamaster, J., 153
DeLeon, B., 66
Delora, J.S., 165
DeMeo, P., 197
D'Emilio, J., 151, 165, 166
Demo, D.H., 367, 368
Demos, J., 15, 20
Dermer, M., 99
De Spelder, L.A., 422

DeStefano, L., 64, 67, 77
Devall, E., 367
DeVall, W., 200
DeVault, M.L., 38
De Vita, C.J., 8, 27, 310, 383, 434
Devor, H., 63
Dickens, C., 362
Dickenson, R., 256
DiMattina, M., 259
Dinkmeyer, D., 230
Dion, K.K., 123
Dion, K.L., 123
Dobash, R., 330, 331
Dobson, C., 413
Dodge, S., 139
Doherty, W.J., 388
Doka, K., 419
Donatelle, R.J., 451
Donovan, J., 167
Dornbusch, S.M., 368
Dorning, M., 201
Douglas, M., 102
Downs, A.C., 70
Downs, E.A., 367
Draughon, M., 392
Dressel, P.L., 204–5
Droegemueller, W., 340
Duberman, L., 391
Duncan, G., 363, 427
Duncan, O., 39
Dunn, 326
Durkheim, E., 357
Dutton, D.G., 334, 337, 338
Duvall, E.M., 54–55, 404
Dweck, C.S., 73
Dworkin, A., 260
Dwyer, J., 421

E

Earle, A.M., 183
Eastwood, C., 325
Eckland, B., 228
Edelson, J.L., 330
Edmondson, B., 199
Edwards, A., 164
Edwards, C.P., 72

Edwards, J.N., 126, 262, 354–55
Eells, L.W., 381
Ehrenreich, B., 168
Ehrhardt, A., 63, 64, 70
Einstein, E., 393
Ellis, M.J., 124
Elmer-Dewitt, P., 246
Enna, B., 73
Erikson, E., 69, 240
Espin, O.M., 199
Etaugh, C., 187
Ettelbrick, P., 214
Evans, E., 428

F

Facteau, L., 418
Faderman, L., 106
Fausto-Sterling, A., 61, 62
Faux, M., 240
Feagin, J.R., 325–26, 332
Feldman, J., 279
Felt, J.C., 185, 237, 354–55
Fendrich, M., 304
Fengler, A., 421
Ferber, M.A., 41
Fernea, E., 219
Fernea, R., 219
Ferrante, J., 46
Ferraro, K.J., 360
Field, 285
Fillenbaum, G.G., 415
Fine, D., 386, 398
Fine, M., 386, 398
Fingrutd, M., 187
Finkbine, S., 248
Finkelhor, D., 328, 333, 341, 343, 344
Finkelman, P., 17
Finlay, B., 357
Finley, N.J., 416
Finn, S., 201
Fischman, J., 388
Fisher, T.D., 167
Fishman, B., 386, 389
Fitzgerald, L.F., 79
Flaherty, S.M.J., 418

Flitcraft, A., 337, 338
Foreit, K.G., 76
Forrest, J., 167
Foster, C.D., 314, 315
Fowler, S., 176
Fox, V.C., 378
Franklin, B., 183
Franklin, C.W., 55
Frazier, E.F., 353
Frederick, L., 303
Freedman, E.B., 107, 151, 165, 166
Freeman, R., 184, 185
Freud, S., 67–68, 152, 240
Fricke, K., 76
Friede, A., 276
Friend, R., 71
Frieze, I.H., 329
Fromm, E., 91, 92
Fuchs, V.R., 45
Furstenberg, F.F., Jr., 132, 356, 364, 365, 366, 370, 376, 381, 388, 395, 417, 433

G

Gagnon, J.H., 153, 159, 164
Gallo, F., 383
Ganong, L.H., 79, 378, 380, 381, 382, 388, 395
Garfinkel, I., 359
Garver, P., 418
Gebhard, P.H., 160, 163
Gecas, V., 365
Geiss, S.K., 360
Gelfand, D.E., 426
Gelles, R.J., 140, 326–30, 334, 340, 341, 342, 344, 345
Genovese, E.D., 17
George, L.K., 415
Gerrard, M., 177
Gerstel, N., 362
Giarrusso, R., 140
Gibson, R., 416
Giles-Sims, J., 391, 395
Gill, R.T., 166, 167, 234, 235

Keith, P., 191
Keith, V.M., 357
Keller, S., 44
Kelley, H.H., 99
Kellogg, 13, 14, 15, 16, 18, 19, 25, 26, 27
Kelly, E., 75
Kelly, J., 203, 367, 388, 393
Kempe, C.H., 340
Kemper, T., 91
Kennedy, J.B., 220
Kennedy, J.F., 141
Kennedy, R., Jr., 445
Kephart, W.M., 205
Kerckhoff, A.C., 133, 228
Kessler-Harris, A., 22, 297
Kevorkian, J., 424
Kidder, R.M., 208, 209
Kiernan, K., 193
Kim, P., 164
Kimbrell, A., 56
Kimmel, M.S., 158, 174, 176
Kinard, E.M., 368
Kinglsey, G., 370
Kingston, P.W., 303, 318
Kinsey, A., 151, 152, 159, 160, 163, 168, 363
Kiplinger, K.A., 444
Kirk, T., 370
Kirkpatrick, J.T., 341
Kitagawa, E.M., 237
Kitano, H.H.L., 227, 237
Kivett, V.R., 418
Kiyak, H.A., 408, 417, 420, 424
Klaus, E., 416
Klaus, P., 184, 185
Kleiman, C., 306, 310
Klein, D., 416
Klerman, G.L., 78
Klimek, D., 127
Knaub, P., 394–95
Knopf, M.F., 367
Kohlberg, L., 70
Kohn, M., 290
Kolbert, K., 262
Kolodny, 170, 171, 466
Koonin, L.M., 250

Kosberg, J.I., 344
Koss, M.P., 140
Kotelchuck, M., 328
Kotulak, R., 259
Koval, J., 140
Kretchner, A., 163
Ktsanes, T., 100
Ktsanes, V., 100
Ku, L., 166, 167
Kübler-Ross, E., 423–24

L

Lai, T., 66
Lakoff, R., 80
Land, H., 381, 392
Landers, S., 250
Landrine, H., 66
Langenbrunner, M., 362
Larche, D., 74
Laren, D., 427
LaRossa, M.M., 287
LaRossa, R., 287
Larson, D.C., 426
Larson, J., 199
LaRue, J., 76
Lasch, C., 7, 21, 322
Laslett, 14
Laswell, M.E., 95
Lauer, J., 210, 300, 367
Lauer, R., 210, 300, 367
Lauris, G., 362
Lavin, C., 187
Lawson, A., 154
Layton, B.D., 135
Lee, A., 204
Lee, G.R., 133, 414
Lee, J., 56
Lee, J.A., 92–95
LeMasters, E., 118, 238
Lengermann, P.M., 50
Leonard, K.E., 140
Less, L., 415
LeVay, S., 158
Lever, J., 72, 163
Levine, M.P., 174, 176
Levinger, G., 358
Levinson, D., 322

Levitan, D., 99
Levitan, S.A., 383
Levy, B., 139–40, 329
Levy, R.S., 383
Lewis, R.A., 357
Libby, P.L., 304
Lieberman, B., 151
Liem, R., 312
Light, D., 44
Lin, S., 384
Lindsey, L., 123, 130, 163, 286
Lipman, A., 427
Lips, H., 82
Liss, M.B., 71
Little, V., 420
Litwak, E., 53
Liu, K., 420
Lloyd, B., 60
Lloyd, P.C., 351
Lloyd, S., 140
Lloyd, S.A., 121
Lobenz, N., 95
Locin, M., 318
Lockery, S.A., 416, 421
Loeseke, D., 339
Loewenstein, 104
Logue, B.J., 427
Loiacano, D.K., 199
Lokey, H., 76
London, J., 299
London, K.A., 254, 256
Long, B.C., 79
Longino, C.F., Jr., 408, 427
Lopata, H.Z., 425
Lott, B., 332, 333
Loving, M., 226
Loving, R., 226
Lowery, C.R., 368
Lubin, B., 271
Luborsky, M., 419–20
Luker, K., 251
Luria, Z., 71
Lusky, A., 420
Luther, Martin., 149
Lye, D., 358
Lynch, J.J., 91
Lynn, D., 69
Lyon, J., 159

M

McAdoo, J.L., 291
McCarthy, L., 363
McCary, J.L., 147, 162
Maccoby, E., 72
McCormick, T., 37
MacDonald, K., 71
McGhee, J.L., 420
McGrath, E., 78
McHenry, P.C., 138
McIlwee, J.S., 310
Macionis, J., 436
Macklin, E.D., 195, 196
McLanahan, S., 357
McLane, D., 99
McLaren, A., 243
McLeod, B., 187
McMullan, L., 316
McNair, N., 455
McRoy, R.G., 256
McTaggart, L., 254–55
Madsen, W., 24
Maglin, N.B., 385
Maier, R., 156
Malinowski, B., 209
Malstrom, J., 187
Manton, K.G., 420
Maranski, A.Z., 43
Marciano, T.D., 237
Marcum, J., 24
Marecek, J., 201
Margolis, J., 376
Marion, R., 277
Markides, K.S., 414, 415
Martin, C.E., 151, 152, 159, 160, 163, 168, 363
Martin, C.L., 69, 72
Martin, L.L., 269, 277
Martin, S.E., 309
Martin, T.C., 3, 356
Martini, F., 460, 462
Marvin, L., 198
Marvin, M.T., 198
Marx, K., 43–44
Mason, B., 76
Masters, W., 151, 159, 160–62, 163, 169, 170, 171, 450, 452, 456, 466

Matthaei, J.A., 349
Matthews, S., 418
Maugh, T.H.H., 156, 160
Mauldin, T.A., 72, 367
Max, E., 369
Mays, V.M., 125, 199
Maza, P., 314, 315
Mead, M., 121, 203
Meeks, C.B., 72, 367
Melko, M., 190
Melton, W., 123
Menken, J.A., 405
Mercy, J., 427
Meredith, D., 365
Mertz, M.E., 419
Messinger, L., 377, 398
Messner, M., 158
Metress, E., 426
Metress, S., 426
Metts, S., 103
Middlebrook, P.N., 91
Miller, D.M., 330
Mills, C.W., 29, 314
Min, P.G., 227, 302
Mindel, C.H., 414, 415, 416
Minkoff, H.L., 279
Mintz, 13, 14, 15, 16, 18, 19, 25, 26, 27
Mirande, A., 24
Mirchandi, V.K., 105
Mirowsky, J., 304
Mitchell, J., 415
Moghissi, K.S., 256
Money, J., 63, 64, 70
Moore, J., 227
Moore, K.A., 356, 357
Moore, P., 407
Moore, W.E., 43
Moran, B.B., 137, 138
Morey, G., 366
Morgan, L., 362
Morgan, S.P., 358, 365
Morris, M., 242
Morris, N.M., 154
Mortimer, J.T., 299
Mosher, W.D., 245, 246, 253
Mosier, K., 316, 317
Mowery, J., 204

Moynihan, D.P., 40
Murphy, M., 342
Murstein, B.I., 88, 100, 103, 119, 126
Mutran, E., 416

N

Nass, G., 122
Nastasi, B.K., 368
Neal, A.G., 239
Needle, R.H., 388
Nellis, B., 163
Nelson, S., 73
Neugarten, B., 406, 417
Neugarten, D., 406
Newberger, E.H., 328
Newcomb, P.R., 196
Newcomer, S., 167
Nezu, A.M., 79
Nezu, C.M., 79
Ng, S.H., 72
Nock, S.L., 303, 357
Norton, A., 356
Novak, M.A., 62, 149, 150, 169, 274, 452
Noyes, J., 205
Nussbaum, H., 327

Oakley, A., 299
O'Connor-Roden, M., 191
O'Flaherty, K.M., 381
Ogintz, E., 187, 190
Ogletree, S., 76
O'Hare, W.P., 185, 237, 354–55
O'Kelly, C.G., 219
Olday, 196
Olds, S., 269, 274, 277
O'Leary, K.D., 360
Oleinick, L., 427
Olson, D.H., 210
Onassis, A., 220
O'Neil, J.M., 154
O'Neil, K., 304
Oppenheimer, V.K., 186
Oros, C.J., 140
Owen, R., 350

P

Pabst, M.S., 369
Pace, L., 229
Pachon, H., 227
Pagelow, M.D., 140, 328, 330, 333, 342
Painter, K., 175
Palazzini, M., 76
Palmore, E.B., 408, 415
Panter, G.G., 280
Papalia, D., 269, 274, 277
Papanek, H., 299, 300
Parke, R., 54
Parke, R.D., 71
Parkeh, A., 279
Parker, G., 235
Parnes, H., 415
Parron, E.M., 413
Parrot, A., 124
Parrot, W.G., 108
Parsons, T., 52–53, 302, 303
Pasley, K., 378, 388, 392, 397
Patterson, J., 164
Patterson, M., 76
Patzer, G.L., 135
Paul, St., 149
Pauly, B., 187
Peddecord, K.M., 416, 421
Peplau, L.A., 103, 140, 166, 200
Perdue, L., 75
Perry, J.D., 368, 450
Perry-Jenkins, M., 304
Peterman, D.J., 195
Peters, J., 203
Petersen, J., 163
Peterson, B., 75
Peterson, C., 415
Peterson, J., 415
Peterson, J.L., 367, 368, 388, 433
Peyton, J.S., 303
Phillips, R., 351
Pill, C.J., 396
Pillemer, K.A., 344
Pines, A., 109, 110, 111
Pitcher, B.L., 426

Pizzey, E., 328
Pleck, E., 322
Pleck, J., 166, 167, 318
Polonko, K.A., 197
Pomerleau, A., 71
Pomeroy, W.B., 151, 152, 159, 160, 163, 168, 363
Ponzetti, J., Jr., 358
Powell-Griner, E., 250
Powers, E., 16
Pratt, E.L., 229
Price-Bonham, S., 229
Priest, D., 301
Provenzano, F.J., 71
Punke, H.H., 184
Purcell, P., 73–74
Purnan, L., 349
Pyszczynski, T.A., 99

Q

Quadagno, J.S., 5, 351
Quayle, D., 7
Queen, S.A., 5, 351
Quitt, M.H., 378

R

Radbill, S., 324
Raffeld, P., 76
Rahe, R., 425
Ramu, G.N., 117, 118, 119, 120, 121, 133, 135, 226
Rank, M.R., 35
Rasmussen, P.K., 360
Rauma, D., 339
Rawlings, S., 133
Reagan, R., 351
Reed, R.B., 328
Reeder, S.J., 269, 277
Reeve, C., 300
Register, J.C., 415
Reid, W.J., 304
Reik, T.A., 111
Reinherz, H., 368
Reiss, I.L., 99, 100, 101, 117
Remondet, J.H., 367, 426

Rempel, J., 107, 109
Renzetti, C.M., 61, 62, 140, 216, 254, 277, 279, 298, 309, 323, 332, 334, 342, 344
Reskin, B.F., 309
Reynolds, R., 450
Rheingold, H.L., 71
Rhodes, P.H., 276
Rice, C., 428
Rich, A., 51, 157
Richmond-Abbott, M., 223
Ridley, C., 195
Riedman, A., 391
Riemer, B., 368
Rier, D., 23
Riessman, C.K., 365, 382
Riley, G., 16, 349, 350
Risman, B.J., 48, 49, 287
Rivers, C., 365
Roark, A.C., 277
Roberto, K.A., 417
Roberts, M.D., 416
Roberts, W.L., 413
Robertson, J., 79
Robinson, B., 317, 383
Robinson, J.G., 310
Robinson, J.P., 303
Rochlin, M., 158
Rodin, J., 110
Rollins, J., 186
Romero-Garcia, I., 66
Rosenkrantz, P.S., 79
Rosenthal, C.J., 416, 421
Rosenthal, E., 275
Ross, C.E., 304
Rossi, P.H., 314
Rothman, B.K., 254, 256
Rowland, B., 317
Roy, M., 326
Rubin, J.Z., 71
Rubin, L.B., 166, 167
Rubin, Z., 99, 103, 140
Rubinstein, R.L., 191, 419–20
Russell, C.S., 285, 413
Russell, D., 333
Russo, N.F., 78
Rutman, A.H., 16

S

Sabatelli, R.M., 433
Sadker, D., 73
Sadker, M., 73
Saenz, R., 303
Sager, C.J., 382
Saline, C., 328
Salovey, P., 110
Sambrano, S., 254, 256
Sanders, G.F., 370
Sandler, B.R., 74
Sandroff, R., 306
Sanger, M., 243
Sangl, J., 412
Santrock, J.W., 388
Sapiro, V., 160, 216, 218, 288
Sargent, A.G., 439
Saunders, D.G., 339
Sawhill, I.V., 356, 357
Sayre, 70
Scanzoni, J., 103, 302
Scheck, S.R., 103
Schiamberg, L.B., 272, 275, 276
Schmetzer, U., 199
Schneir, M., 23, 221
Schniedewind, N., 385
Schoen, R., 226
Schuldberg, D., 393
Schumm, W.A., 285, 413
Schwalbe, M.L., 365
Schwartz, F.N., 306
Schwartz, M.A., 183, 187, 188, 190
Schwartz, P., 36, 48, 49, 106, 154, 160, 168, 196, 200, 201
Schwarz, J.C., 357
Schweitzer, A., 260
Sciara, F.J., 368
Scott, B.M., 38, 123, 419
Scott, D.M., 23
Scott, J.P., 420
Scott, J.W., 15
Seagraves, K.B., 169
Sedlak, A., 339
Segal, S., 388

Seligmann, J., 200
Seltzer, J., 359
Serpe, R., 152
Settle, S.A., 368
Shanas, E., 404, 406, 415, 416, 420
Shapiro, J.L., 280–81
Shaw, D., 416
Shehan, C.L., 133, 414
Shelton, B.A., 196, 310
Shettel-Neuber, J., 111
Shinn, M., 368
Shneidman, E., 424
Shope, D.F., 164
Shorto, R., 289
Shostak, A., 187
Shrieves, L., 241
Shurtleff, N.B., 183
Siegel, M.A., 314, 315
Sigler, R.T., 324, 341
Silver, H.K., 340
Silverman, F.N., 340
Silverman, P., 428
Silverstein, B., 75
Simenauer, J., 190
Simon, B.L., 190
Simon, W., 153, 164
Simpson, J., 90
Simpson, L., 305
Simpson, V., 249
Sims, S., 339
Singh, S., 167
Sitterle, K.A., 388
Skelton, G., 251
Skipper, J.K.J., 122
Skolnick, A.S., 215
Skolnick, J.H., 215
Skoloff, G.N., 473, 474
Skyles, A., 388, 393, 398
Slavin, E.A., 199
Smith, A., 252
Smith, A.D., 304
Smith, C., 60
Smith, D., 34, 117, 169, 395, 397
Smith, E.A., 154
Smith, J., 427
Smith, J.A., 342, 343

Smith, J.C., 250
Smith, L., 76
Smith, L.G., 111
Smith, R., 424
Smith, R.H., 108
Smith, W.K., 141
Snipp, C.M., 226
Soldo, B.J., 416
Solomon, R.C., 88, 97
Sonestein, F., 166, 167, 177
Song, I.Y., 351
South, S., 356
Southworth, S., 357
Spade, J., 302
Spanier, G.B., 130, 194, 195, 356, 357, 358, 359, 381, 395
Spitze, G., 356
Sporakowski, M.J., 212, 214
Sprecher, S., 90, 103
Sprey, J., 230, 418
Springs, H.H., 203
Spruill, J.C., 184
Staines, G.L., 304
Stainton, M.C., 71
Stallone, S., 325
Stanford, E.P., 416, 421
Stanton, E.C., 235
Staples, R., 23, 120, 122, 130, 131, 378, 383
Stark, E., 337, 338
Starr, B.D., 170
Stayton, W.R., 168
Steck, L., 99
Steele, B., 340
Steele, J.B., 298, 434
Stein, P., 185–86, 187
Stein, P.J., 138
Steinberg, J., 327
Steinberg, L., 327
Steinfirst, S., 137, 138
Steinmetz, S., 326–27, 328, 329, 334, 339, 345
Stephan, C.W., 324
Stephan, W.G., 324
Stern, E., 261
Stern, W., 261
Sternberg, R.J., 92
Stewart, L., 73–74

Stinnet, N., 192, 196, 204
Stinnett, N., 394–95
Stockard, J., 103
Stokes, G., 153
Stokes, J.P., 303
Stoller, E.P., 422
Stone, G.W., 330
Stone, L., 221
Stone, R., 412
Stoneman, Z., 367
Stoper, E., 365
Straus, M.A., 276, 326–30, 334, 340, 341, 342, 345
Strickland, A.L., 422
Strickland, B.R., 78
Stroebe, W., 135
Strong, B., 149, 164, 166, 450
Su, S.S., 388
Sulik, K., 277
Sullivan, A., 214
Sullivan, T., 299
Sunshine, L., 139
Supancic, M., 354–55, 356, 357
Sussman, M., 416
Sutton-Smith, B., 380
Swanbrow, D., 91
Sweet, J., 197, 376, 382
Sweet, J.A., 193, 354–56, 412, 426
Szapocznik, J., 302

T

Tanfer, K., 194
Tannen, D., 80–81
Tanner, D., 124
Tate, N., 415
Taylor, R.J., 416
Teachman, J.D., 197
Tennov, D., 91, 97, 101, 102–3
Thernstrom, S.A., 166, 167, 234, 235
Thomas, C., 310
Thomas, J.L., 418
Thompson, L., 359
Thompson, V.D., 135
Thorne, B., 107

Thornton, A., 167
Thurnher, M., 367
Tiede, 345
Tilly, L., 15
Todd, M., 96, 97, 102
Totenberg, N., 220
Tower, C.C., 342, 343
Townsend, B., 304
Traupmann, J., 126
Trent, K., 250
Tribe, L.H., 247, 251
Troll, L., 416
Trovato, F., 362
Trump, D., 363
Truth, S., 23, 24
Trygstad, D.W., 370
Turner, J., 43
Tyson, M., 141

U

Udry, J.R., 154, 167
Uhlenberg, P., 356, 366, 378, 417
Ullman, J., 187

V

Valentino, R., 91
van Driel, B., 198
VanDusen, J.E., 151, 152
Van Heusen, J., 396
Vazquez-Nuttall, E., 66
Veevers, J.E., 241
Ventura, S.J., 237
Visher, E., 385, 390, 391, 393
Visher, J., 385, 390, 391, 393
Vogel, S.R., 79
Von Brook, P., 314, 315
Voydanoff, P., 296, 313
Vuchinich, R., 388, 393
Vuchinich, S., 388, 393

W

Wade-Lewis, M., 378
Wald, E., 376, 379, 380

Waldron, 193
Walker, K.E., 303
Walker, L., 329, 331, 339
Wallace, R.A., 44
Waller, W., 117, 118, 126
Wallerstein, J.S., 365, 367, 368, 370, 388, 393
Wallin, P., 414
Wallish, L., 394
Walls, B.F., 415
Wallstron, K., 424
Walsh, F., 427
Walsh, L.S., 378
Walster, E., 126
Walster, G.W., 99
Walster, W., 126
Warren, C., 165
Watkins, S.J., 405
Watson, R., 197
Wayne, J., 325
Weaver, C.N., 190
Webb, M.A., 277
Weeks, J.R., 237
Weibel-Orlando, J., 419
Weinberg, M., 125, 157, 200
Weiner, M.B., 170
Weinstein, K., 417
Weiss, R., 289
Weissman, M.M., 78
Weitzman, L., 215, 363, 364
Weitzman, N., 71
Wells, R., 235
Welter, B., 21
Westheimer, R., 155
Westhoff, C.F., 130, 131
Westoff, C., 240
Whipple, 450
Whisman, M.A., 79
White, G.L., 111
White, J., 197
White, L.K., 186, 354–55, 389, 391, 395, 397
White, P., 190
Whitehead, M.B., 260
Whiting, B., 72
Whitsett, D., 381, 392
Wicks, J.W., 239
Wilkerson, H., 209

Williams, J.E., 65
Williams, R.M., Jr., 354
Williams, S., 76
Willie, C.V., 291
Wilson, E., 72
Wilson, S., 149, 163, 164, 166
Winch, R.R., 100
Wineberg, H., 357, 391
Wishy, B., 23
Witzel, J., 190
Wolf, A., 44
Wolf, P., 183
Wolfe, D.M., 414
Wong, M.G., 22, 302
Woods, M., 303
Wooldridge, J., 226
Worden, J.W., 425
Wright, C.D., 350
Wright, J.D., 314, 316

X

Xue, L.R., 305

Y

Yankelovich, D., 193
Yeung, W., 227
Yllo, K., 328, 330
Young, A., 200
Young, I.E., 111
Young, N.F., 292

Z

Zabin, L.S., 167
Zablocki, B., 203, 204
Zavella, P., 302
Zedeck, S., 316, 317
Zellman, G., 140
Zill, N., 367, 368, 388
Zube, M., 414
Zukerman, D., 70
Zurcher, L.A., Jr., 256

SUBJECT INDEX

Age (*cont.*)
   marriage squeeze and, 130–31
   mate selection and, 133
   rape and, 332
   rate of remarriage and, 383
   self-esteem and, 78
   singlehood and, 185
   unemployment and, 313–14
Ageism, 405–6, 407
Age norms, 406
Age-order, step siblings and changes in, 390
Agglutination test, 270
Aging, sexuality and, 166, 170–71
Aging families, 54
Agreement, personal marriage, 220–22
Agriculture, fertility rate and, 234–35
AIDS, 146, 167, 172–77, 186, 423, 455
   children and, 176
   incidence of, 174–75
   as national and international issue, 176
   pregnancy and, 278–80
   sexual responsibility and prevention of, 176–77
   testing for, prior to marriage, 215
   transmission of, 173–74
   treatment of, 174
   women and, 175–76
Alcohol abuse, 9
   battering and, 338
Alcohol consumption during pregnancy, 277
Algonquin, 19
Alimony, 349, 350, 364
Alpha fetoprotein (AFP) screening, 275
Alternative birthing centers (ABCs), 282
Altruistic love, 92
Alyha, 62

Amae, 288–89
Ambivalents, 187
America: What Went Wrong? (Barlett & Steele), 434
American Association of Retired Persons (AARP), 411
American Medical Association, 247
American Psychiatric Association, 199
American Revolution, 184
Amniocentesis, 274–75
Amniotic sac, 271
Amour, 139
Anal stage, 67
Anatomy:
   reproductive, 459–62
      female, 459–60
      male, 461–62
   of sexuality, 449–52
      female, 449–51
      male, 451–52
Androgen-insensitive individuals, 63
Androgens, 61, 62
Androgynous individuals, 79
Androgynous love, 104
Androgynous norms, 33
Androgyny, 78
Anemia, sickle cell, 214–15, 274
Anger stage of dying, 423
Annulment, 372
Anorgasmia, 452
Anticipatory socialization, 121, 439
Antigen, 272
Antinatalist forces, 241, 242–43
Antisocial behavior of children of divorce, 368
Anus, 451
Apaches, 110
Areola, 269
Arousal, erotic, 160
Arranged marriages, 88, 89

Artificial insemination (AI), 256–57
Artificial insemination by a donor (AID), 257
Artificial insemination homologous (AIH), 257
Art of Loving, The (Fromm), 92
Ascribed statuses, 60
Asia, divorce in, 351
Asian-Americans. *See also* Race
   gender stereotypes of women, 66
   interracial marriage among, 226–27
   parenting styles of, 292
Assault:
   physical, 328–31, 340–42
   sexual:
      of children, 343–44
      defined, 329
      effects of, 336–38
      slavery and, 323
      of women, 331–33
Attraction, interpersonal:
   mate selection and, 134–35
   stimulus-value-role theory of, 126
Augmentation, 387
Austria, abortion in, 249
Authoritarian parenting style, 290
Authoritative parenting style, 290
Autoeroticism, 162–64
Automobile, mate selection and, 118
Autonomous and private family, myth of, 11
Awareness, fertility, 470
Azidothymidine (AZT), 174

B

Baby boom, 235
Baby Brokers, The (McTaggart), 255

Baby bust, 235–36
Bachelor party, 216
Bargaining stage of dying, 423
Bars, singles and gay, 136
Bartholin's glands, 450
Battered-child syndrome, 340–41
Battered men, 339–40
Battered-woman syndrome, 48, 329
Battered women, 328–31
   effects of abuse on, 336–39
   incidence of battery, 329–30
   reasons for staying in relationships, 330–31
   shelters for, 338–39
Beginning families, 54
Behaviorism, 69
Being love, 92
Belgium, abortion in, 249
Belly, empathy, 32
Berdache, 62
Bereavement, 422, 425
Best friend's love, 95
Beta subunit HCG radioimmunoassay test, 270
Bias(es). *See also* Discrimination; Racism
   in children's shows, 75
   in feminist theories, 50–51
   in functional analysis, 43
   in language, 72
   against singles in workplace, 189
   theoretical, 34–35
Bigamy, 213
"Binding out," 314
Binuclear families, 380
Birth centers, freestanding, 282–83
Birth control. *See* Contraception
Birth defects, 274

I

Idealization of women, 89
Identical twins, 268, 269
Identity, gender, 61, 70
Ideologies, 38, 87
Illness in elderly, 420–22
Illusion of unique invulnerability, 246
Imagination. *See* Sociological imagination
Immigration, 19th-century, 21–22
Imperatives, functional, 43
Impotence, 453
Incest, 332, 343
Incest taboo, 5, 130, 213
Income. *See also* Economic well-being; Finances
   distribution of, 434
   divorce and, 356
   power in family decision making and, 302
   after retirement, 415
   singlehood and, 189
Independent variable, 37
Individualistic singles, 188
Infancy, 7
Infanticide, 243, 324
Infatuated love, 92
Infatuation, love vs., 97–99
Infertility, 253–56
   adoption as solution to, 254–56
   causes of, 253
   consequences of, 253–54
Inhibited male orgasm, 453–54
Inhibited sexual excitement, 452
Insemination, artificial (AI), 256–57
Institution, defined, 2
Institutionalization of love in marriage, 90–91
Institutional racism, 11
Instrumental (male) roles, 53, 64

Insurance:
   cohabitation and, 198
   disability, 318
Intercourse, sexual:
   age at first, 166
   Christian tradition and, 149
   contemporary attitudes toward, 151
   among elderly, 414
   extramarital, 213
   Jewish tradition and, 148
   outside legal marriage, 213
   missionary position, 165
   painful, 454
   premarital, 90–91, 166
   unmarried, 152
   Victorian tradition and, 150
Interethnic marriage, 227–28
Interfaith marriage, 228–29
Intergenerational relationships, 415–16
Interracial adoptions, 255–56
Interracial dating, 123
Interracial marriage, 123, 225–27, 433
Interviews, 35–36, 38
Intimacy, 92
   as family function, 7
Intimate relationships, violence in, 139–41
Intrauterine devices (IUDs), 245, 271–72, 468
In vitro fertilization (IVF), 257–59
Involuntary part-time employment, 314
Involuntary stable singles, 187
Involuntary temporary singles, 187
Involved grandparenting, 417
Invulnerability, illusion of unique, 246
Iraq, marriage customs in, 219

Ireland, abortion in, 249
Iroquois, 19
Isolation, childlessness and, 419
Issues of social structure, public, 29, 314
Italy, abortion in, 249

J

Japanese Americans:
   interracial marriage among, 226–27
   relocation of, 26
Japanese model of child rearing, 288–89
Jealousy, 107–12
   destructive, 111–12
   envy vs., 108
   gender differences in, 110–11
   nature and pattern of, 109–10
Jewish tradition:
   of marriage, 211
   sexuality and, 148–49
Jews, interfaith marriage among, 228, 229
Job sharing, 317
Joint custody, 369

K

Kaposi's sarcoma (KS), 173
Key status, 61
Killing:
   of abuser, 338
   mercy (euthanasia), 423, 424
   of wives or partners, 334
Kin, fictive, 255
Kinship, 14
   Chicano, 23–24
   elderly and, 428
   extended, 18
Kinship terms for remarried families, 377

Korean Americans, interracial marriage among, 227

L

Labeling, 70
Labia majora, 449
Labia minora, 449
Labor, division of. *See* Division of labor
Labor (childbirth), 283–85
Laborers, Chinese, 22
Labor force, women in. *See* Working women
Labor-force participation rate, 296–97
Language, 46
   gender-role socialization through, 72
Laparoscope, 258
Laparoscopy, 465
Last-Chance Children: Growing Up with Older Parents (Morris), 242
Latchkey children, 27, 286, 317
Latent functions, 43
Later-life families, 403–30. *See also* Elderly
   age norms and, 406
   diversity in family life cycle, 405–6
   grandparenthood, 416–19
   great-grandparenthood, 419
   intergenerational relationships, 415–16
   marriages, 413–15
   sandwich generation, 404–5
   siblings in, 420
   social policy implications, 428
Latinas. *See also* Ethnicity
   child support and, 366
   fertility rates among, 237
   gender stereotypes of, 66

gender-role socialization
    by, 71–72
mate selection and, 134
remarriage by, 385
    consequences for chil-
      dren, 388–89
Parental consent to marriage,
    213
Parental divorce, children's
    divorce and, 357
Parental leaves, 49
Parent–child bond, 190,
    239
Parenthood, 237–41
    benefits of, 238–40
    costs of, 237–38
    delayed, 240–41
    gender differences in expe-
      rience of, 288–90
    lesbian and gay, 292
    parental roles, 285–87
    qualifications for, 242
Parenting. *See also* Child rear-
    ing
    in later life, 242
    made-in-Japan, 288–89
    roles of, 69
    split-shift employment
      and, 305–6
    styles of, 290–92
    unplanned, 419
Parents in Contemporary
    America (LeMasters
    & DeFrain), 238
Participant observation, 36,
    38
Partner, knowing one's, 441
Part-time employment, invol-
    untary, 314
Party, bachelor, 216
Passion, 92
Passionate love, 92
Passion cluster, 97, 98
Passive-congenial relation-
    ship, 224
Passive singles, 188
Patriarchal family, 4
Patriarchy, 50–51
    love and, 106–7

Patrilineality, 19
Patrilocality, 5
Peer(s):
    contraceptive behavior
      and, 246–47
    gender-role socialization
      by, 72–73
    learning sexuality and,
      154–55
    mate selection and, 132,
      134
Pelvic exam, 270
Penis, 161, 451
Penis envy, 68–69
Perineum, 449
Permanent-alternative-to-
    marriage type of
    cohabitation, 196
Permissive parenting style,
    290
Personal ads, 136–38
Personal contracts, 220–22
Personal fulfillment, child-free
    option and, 242
Personality needs, fulfillment
    of, 101
Personality stabilization, 53
Personal marriage agreement,
    220
Personal qualities, mate selec-
    tion and, 134–35
Personal troubles of milieu,
    29, 314
Perspective, defined, 41
Petting, 165
Phallic stage, 67
Phallocentric orientation, 156
Phencyclidine (PCP), 277
Philos, 88
Physical abuse during dates,
    139–40. *See also*
    Violence and abuse
Physical appearance, mate
    selection and, 134
Physical assault. *See also*
    Violence and abuse
    of children, 340–42
    of women (battering),
      328–31

Physiology of sexuality,
    160–62
Pill, the (oral contraceptives),
    244, 245, 467
Placement, social, 6
Placenta, 271
Plateau phase, 161
Platonic love, 88
Play:
    gender-role socialization
      through, 72–73
    parent–child, 71
    sexual, 153
Pleasuring, 164–65
Plymouth Colony, 378
Pneumocystis pneumonia, 173
Poland, abortion in, 249
Police officers, attitudes
    toward rape vic-
    tims, 333–34
Polish immigrants, 22
Politics of masculinity, 55–57
Polyandry, 3
    fraternal, 5
Polygamy, 3
Polygyny, 3
Pool of eligibles, 128–30
Poor, cohabitation by the,
    192, 194
Population control, 6
Portugal, abortion in, 249
Positive reinforcement
    (rewards), 69
Possessive love, 96
POSSLQS, 192
Postmarital sexuality, 169–70
Postpartum depression, 283
Postpartum period, 284
Poverty, 310–11
    among elderly, 410–11
    feminization of, 311
Power, 40
    economic, 44
    marital, 79
    motherhood as symbol of,
      287
Pragma, 92, 93
Predictability, trust and, 107
Preeclampsia, 273

Preejaculatory fluid, 161
Preembryos, 258
Pregnancy, 32, 166–68,
    269–70, 462
    accidental, 246
    AIDS and, 278–80
    ectopic, 271–72
    experience of, 292
    gender differences during,
      49
    sexuality during, 280
    sympathetic (couvade),
      281
    testing for, 270
Pregnancy Discrimination
    Act of 1978, 318
Pregnancy loss, 271–72
Premarital agreements,
    386
Premarital sexuality, 90–91,
    166
Premature births, 274
Premature ejaculation, 453
Prenatal development and
    care. *See*
    Childbearing
Prenuptial agreements, 220,
    222
Preschool children, 54
Priapism, 454
Primary anorgasmia, 452
Prime-time television, 75–77
Principle of legitimacy, 209
Prioritizing, conflict resolu-
    tion through, 307
Private and autonomous fam-
    ily, myth of, 11
Problems, family-related,
    434–36
Process theories of mate selec-
    tion, 127
Procreation, family of, 3
Professional singles, 188
Progestin, 466
Proletariat, 44
Pronatalist attitude, 240
Property rights, marriage and,
    217–18
Propinquity, 133–34

Social readjustment after divorce, 363
Social singles, 188
Social structure, 6
    public issues of, 29, 314
Sociological imagination, 29, 33
    in developing minitheory, 56
    feminist theory and, 50
Sociological Imagination, The (Mills), 29
Sociology:
    mainstream, 42
    of marriages and families, 32–33
Sole custody, 369
Sonogram, 275
Sororate, 19
Spain, abortion in, 249
Sperm, 266–67
Spermatozoa, 461
Spermicides, 469–70
Spina bifida, 274
"Spirit wedding," 219
Split custody, 350
Split-household family system, 22
Split-shift employment, 305–6
Sponge, contraceptive, 469
Spontaneity, friendship and, 97
Spontaneous abortion (miscarriage), 247, 271
Spouse as caregiver, 421
Squeeze, marriage, 130–31
Stabilization, personality, 53
Stalking laws, 335
Stations of divorce, 358–60
Status(es), 6
    dating and, 121
    defined, 60
    master (key), 61
    parenthood as means of achieving adult, 239
Stepchild–stepparent relationships, legal ambiguity of, 386

Stepfamilies, 4. *See also* Remarried families
    culture and, 379–80
    education and, 399–400
Stepfamily Association of America (SAA), 398
Stepfathers, 393
Stepmothers, 392–93
    negative image of, 380
Stepsibling relationships, 389–92
Stereotypes, 60–61
    gender, 65–66, 77–81. *See also* Gender differences; Gender-role socialization
    of singles, 183–84
Sterilization, 244–45, 465–66
    involuntary, 246
Stimulus-value-role theory, 126
Stitch rule, 334
Storge, 92, 93
Stress(es):
    of caregiving, 421–22
    stepmothers and, 392
    on 20th-century family, 25
Structural determinism, 49
Structural functionalism, 42–43
    on marriage, 209–10
Structure, defined, 42
"STUDS" (TV program), 138
Substance abuse during pregnancy, 277
Substitution, 387
Subsystems, 42
Suicide attempts, battering and, 337–38
Support in intergenerational relationships, 416
Supportive singles, 188
Support networks for singles, 190
Surname, 218, 445
Surrogate motherhood, 259–61

Surrogate-parent grandparenting, 417
Surveys, 35–36, 38
Survival strategies against sexual assault, 337
Sweat, night, 170
Sweden:
    abortion in, 249
    child care in, 307
    cohabitation in, 194
    parental-leave policy of, 318
"Swinging single" stereotype, 187
Switzerland, abortion in, 249
Symbolic interactionism, 42, 46
Symbolism of sexual activity, 246
Symbols, 46
Sympathetic pregnancy (couvade), 281
Synchronized retirement, 414
Syphilis, 456
System, defined, 42

T

Taboo, incest, 5, 130, 213
Task overload, 289–90
Tasks of the dying, 424
Tax code, stapfamilies and, 398–99
Tax laws, reproduction and, 6
Tay-Sachs disease, 274
T-cell (CD4 cell) monitoring, 174
Teachers, gender-role socialization by, 73–74
Teenaged mothers, 289
Teenage pregnancy, 167–68
Teenagers, families with, 54
Television, 74–75
    matchmaker programs in, 138
    prime-time, 75–77
    sexual scripts and, 155

Temporary-alternative-to-marriage type of cohabitation, 196
Tenting, 161
Teratogenic effects of drugs, 277
Testes (testicles), 452, 461
Testing type of cohabiting couples, 196
Testosterone, 170
Thalidomide, 248
Theoretical perspectives, 41–52
    conflict theory, 42, 43–45
    feminist theory, 49–52, 210
    microstructuralism, 48–49
    social-exchange theory, 42, 46–48
    structural functionalism, 42–43, 209–10
    symbolic interactionism, 42, 46
Theory:
    defined, 33
    -research linkage, 33–34
Theory models, 52–55
    defined, 41
    developmental family life-cycle, 54–55
    modified-extended-family, 53–54
    nuclear-family, 52–53
Tiwi of Australia, 219
Todas, 5, 110
Total fertility rate, 234
Total relationship, 224–25
Toxemia, 273
Toxic effects of drugs, 277
Toys, gender role socialization and, 71–72
Traditional family, myth of self-reliant, 10
Traditional or single retirement, 414
Traditional parenting style, 290
Transformation stage of widowhood, 425

violence against, 323
  battered women,
    328–31, 336–39
  criminal justice system
    and, 333–36
  effects of, 336–39
  sexual assault, 331–33
  on welfare, 35
Women-centered networks,
  286
Women-of-color feminist
  theory, 51
Woodland groups, 19
Work, 295–320. *See also*
  Working women
  child abuse and, 342
  child care and, 304–6
  commuter marriages,
    300–301
  dual-earner families, 300,
    302, 303–7, 432
  income and power in fam-
    ily decision mak-
    ing, 302
  marital happiness and, 303

mate selection in, 136
relationship contract on,
  442–43
role conflict resolution
  and, 306–8
spillover effects of, 296,
  303
traditional nuclear families
  and, 298–99
two-person career,
  299–300
Work ethic, Protestant, 90
Working class, 21
  children of, 22
  unmarried, elderly
    women, 191
Working poor, 314
Working women:
  African-American, 22–23
  child care and, 304–7
  divorce and, 356–57
  extramarital relationships
    and, 169
  gender gap in earnings,
    310, 364

husbands in division of
  household labor,
  303–4
increase in number of,
  33
labor-force participation
  rate, 297
marital happiness of,
  303
marriage rates of, 186
occupational distribution
  and, 308–9
power in household deci-
  sion making, 302
reasons women work,
  297–98
sexual harassment of,
  309–10
sexual permissiveness and,
  151
wages of, 310, 311
during World War II,
  26
Workplace, restructuring of,
  316–18

Work schedules, flexible, 49
World War II and its after-
  math, 26–27
Worth, comparable, 310

X

X-rated movies, 155
X-rays during pregnancy, 277
XY females, 63

Y

Yeast infection, 457
Yoruba, 351
Young-old, 408

Z

Zygote, 266
Zygote intrafallopian transfer
  (ZIFT), 252